ENVIRONMENTAL LAW

CASES AND MATERIALS

First Edition

by

Meinhard Doelle
BSc, LLB, LLM, JSD
Associate Professor, Associate Director,
Marine & Environmental Law Institute
Dalhousie Law School

Chris Tollefson
BA (Hon.), LLB, LLM
Professor of Law and Executive Director
Environmental Law Centre, Faculty of Law,
University of Victoria

CARSWELL®

© 2009 Thomson Reuters Canada Limited

NOTICE AND DISCLAIMER: All rights reserved. No part of this publication may be reproduced, stored in a retrieval system, or transmitted, in any form or by any means, electronic, mechanical, photocopying, recording or otherwise, without the prior written consent of the publisher (Carswell).

Carswell and all persons involved in the preparation and sale of this publication disclaim any warranty as to accuracy or currency of the publication. This publication is provided on the understanding and basis that none of Carswell, the author/s or other persons involved in the creation of this publication shall be responsible for the accuracy or currency of the contents, or for the results of any action taken on the basis of the information contained in this publication, or for any errors or omissions contained herein.

∞ The paper used in this publication meets the minimum requirements of American National Standard for Information Sciences — Permanence of Paper for Printed Library Materials, ANSI Z39.48-1984.

A cataloguing record for this publication is available from Library and Archives Canada.
ISBN 978-0-7798-2161-7

CARSWELL, A DIVISION OF THOMSON REUTERS CANADA LIMITED

One Corporate Plaza
2075 Kennedy Road
Toronto, Ontario
M1T 3V4

Customer Relations
Toronto 1-416-609-3800
Elsewhere in Canada/U.S. 1-800-387-5164
Fax 1-416-298-5082
www.carswell.com
E-mail www.carswell.com/email

Dedication

To Klara, Alida and Nikola
— Meinhard Doelle

To Nadine, Rory, Caius and Hannah
— Chris Tollefson

PREFACE

Environmental law can be a dauntingly challenging subject-matter for students, instructors and practitioners alike. In part, this is due to what are arguably generic features of this area of law, among them its wide-ranging scope, its interdisciplinary reach, and its fluid and amorphous character. Moreover, particularly in the Canadian context, the study of environmental law is complicated by constitutional and jurisdictional considerations, and by emerging Aboriginal rights and title jurisprudence.

Given these characteristics, in our view, foundational courses in Canadian environmental law should aspire to provide students both with an understanding of the breadth and nuance of the key themes and issues that animate this field of study and with theoretical and practical tools necessary to engage with these themes and issues as environmental law evolves in the years ahead.

In large measure, this book focuses on federal environmental law and practice. To provide comparative context, however, we have integrated statutory and jurisprudential illustrations from provincial law and from various other common law jurisdictions. We have also tried to ensure that the book exposes students to the interdisciplinary nature of environmental law (particularly its political, economic and scientific dimensions); to the leading theoretical debates featured within environmental law; and to the complex ways environmental law intersects with international law, Aboriginal law and natural resource law.

This book considers in depth the current state of and future prospects for Canadian environmental law in nine key areas: the interplay between international and domestic law; constitutional and jurisdictional issues; the common law; environmental regulatory models; compliance and enforcement issues; judicial review; environmental assessment; parks and wilderness protection; and endangered species. It then reprises the themes and issues covered in these chapters by means of an in-depth capstone chapter that addresses emerging developments in the rapidly evolving realm of climate change law and policy.

In each chapter we have included excerpts from leading Canadian environmental law cases and from decisions that are indicative of where future jurisprudence may develop. We have also incorporated academic commentary and critique, comparative materials from the United States and the Commonwealth, and provided notes and questions throughout with a view to focussing and distilling emerging themes and issues.

This project owes much to the extraordinary efforts of student researchers at the University of Victoria Faculty of Law and Dalhousie Law School. In this regard, we are grateful to Jameel Madhany (UVic Law 2009), whose contribution was made possible through a summer research fellowship sponsored by the law firm of Fraser, Milner, Casgrain; to Megan Shaw (UVic Law 2010), who played a major role in guiding the manuscript to completion, and to Sarah Sharp (UVic Law 2009), for her skillful assistance on the instructors' manual that accompanies this publication. We are also greatly indebted to Tim Thielmann, Jennifer Smith and Marianne Hopp who lent significant assistance to this project during their tenure as articling students at the UVic Environmental Law Centre, and to the Tula Foundation and the Law Foundation of British Columbia for their generous support of these articling positions. At Dalhousie, we are grateful to the able research assistance of students Matthew Jodrey (Dal Law 2006) and Jeff Naylor (Dal Law 2007) for their early research assistance with this project. We also acknowledge the invaluable feedback received from the 2008 environmental law class at Dalhousie, who tested and commented on a number of draft chapters.

Professor Tollefson would also like to thank his Faculty secretary, Mrs. Rosemary Garton, the staff of the Hippo Boutique Hotel in Cape Town for their hospitality during the final editing process, and especially his Environmental Law Centre colleagues — Deborah Curran, Mark Haddock, Holly Pattison and Calvin Sandborn — for their advice on and generous support throughout this endeavour.

We are grateful to the many authors of articles featured in this book for allowing us to use excerpts from their work, to those who we enlisted to offer comments on early drafts, and to colleagues and friends who have lent encouragement to us along the way. Deserving of special recognition in this regard are David Boyd, Alison Hall, Shi-Ling Hsu, Peter Mushkat, Devon Page, Krista Robertson, Kate Smallwood, O'Neil Smith and Stepan Wood.

Finally, we want to express our gratitude to our families for their unflagging support during the writing and editing process, and to our students — past, present and future — who inspired us to undertake this project.

CT & MD

June 25, 2009

TABLE OF CONTENTS

Chapter 8 Parks and Protected Areas

TABLE OF CASES

A case name accompanied by an asterisked page number appearing in bold face indicates a case that is reproduced in some material part.

1

INTERNATIONAL ENVIRONMENTAL LAW

Introduction

This chapter explores the role of international environmental law in the development of Canadian environmental law. This is a complex relationship that has evolved significantly over time. Historically, developments in international law tended to follow developments in the domestic realm. Countries generally tried to deal with environmental matters on their own, and pursued international cooperation only when domestic measures proved insufficient to address a problem. Over time, this has changed. In Canada, more and more of our domestic environmental measures have their origin in international commitments. Indeed, arguably, domestic action in the absence of some form of international commitment is becoming the exception rather than the rule.

The role of international law in our domestic legal system has also evolved. International law was historically seen as quite separate from domestic law in Canada. Some questioned whether international law was law at all. To the extent that international obligations were implemented, lawyers and courts focussed on the interpretation of the domestic instrument of implementation; generally, without resorting to the international law instrument that represented the source of the obligation or commitment. Gradually, with the shift to more contextual interpretation of domestic law (certainly the interpretation of legislation), lawyers have more frequently relied on international instruments to advance interpretations of domestic law in the interests of their clients. Courts have thereby been challenged to consider whether and how international law influences domestic environmental law.

In Part I, we provide a brief overview of some of the key sources of international law. The three primary stages of development of international environmental law are also introduced and summarized. Part II considers the principles Canadian courts have used when applying international law in the interpretation of domestic law, particularly in the environmental context. Building on these principles, Part III explores how the precautionary principle, which emerged as a soft law principle in the international law realm, is filtering into domestic law in Canada and elsewhere. Finally, in Part IV we provide an overview of some key international legal regimes — including the *Convention on Biological Diversity*, the *Basel Convention*, World Trade Organization agreements, and international investment agreements — that provide important context for, and in some cases may constrain, domestic initiatives to protect the environment.

Part I — Sources of International Law

Adapted from Meinhard Doelle, *From Hot Air to Action? Climate Change, Compliance and the Future of International Environmental Law*
(Toronto: Carswell, 2005)

International law consists of binding and non-binding principles, declarations, commitments, obligations and customs. Binding international law is generally referred to as hard law. The term used for non-binding components of international law is soft law. Hard law takes the form of either customary international law, or obligations set out in treaties. Customary law is generally binding on all States, whereas the treaty obligations are binding only on States who ratify the treaty. Some soft law principles are included in otherwise binding treaties, while others stem from declarations and other forms of international agreements that are non-binding. Agreements with binding obligations are generally subject to ratification, whereas those without binding commitments are generally not subject to ratification. Ratification is the process by which states agree to be bound by a treaty or other agreement. Ratification is achieved through execution of a formal document/instrument that states that the country will be and intends to be bound by the terms of the treaty.

Examples of obligations of customary international law include the principles of state sovereignty and the avoidance of trans-boundary harm. Soft law agreements dealing with environmental matters include the 1972 Stockholm Declaration and the 1992 Rio Declaration. Treaties have become the instrument of choice in the environmental law field, certainly for pressing global environmental challenges. Environmental issues that are addressed internationally through binding treaties include climate change, biodiversity, desertification, the management of toxic substances, and ozone layer depletion.

As discussed in more detail in Part II, these sources of international law can influence domestic environmental law in Canada in a variety of ways. Some hard and soft law will be implemented by Parliament or provincial legislatures through legislation. Some may be implemented by courts, especially through their role as the guardians of the development of the common law. International law, however, can also influence law enforcement, the exercise of discretion by administrative tribunals, and the actions of government officials. In short, international law can and does affect the full range of legal institutions and actors responsible for the development, interpretation and implementation of environmental law in Canada. Before we consider some of these influences in more detail, the following section offers some insights into the substance of international environmental law.

Evolving Substance of International Environmental Law

The birth of environmental law in North America is frequently traced back to the publication of Silent Spring by Rachel Carson in 1963. Its release led to the creation of environmental agencies and departments and the enactment of environmental legislation in Canada and the United States. Concerns about the environmental impact of human activity were raised in Europe around the same time and similarly led to development of domestic environmental laws in Western European countries. While both the quantity and the nature of legal activity with respect to environmental issues has evolved significantly, domestically and internationally, since the publication of Silent Spring, the roots of international environmental law go back much further. The following is a brief overview of its evolution at the international level in three stages, international environmental law before the Stockholm Conference on the Human Environment in 1972, from Stockholm to Rio in 1992, and developments since the Rio Conference.

Pre-Stockholm

Before the beginning of the 20th century, there were relatively few international agreements on environmental issues in place, and those that dealt with the environment in some form were concerned with very specific and short term human benefits to be preserved or protected through limited international cooperation. These agreements, negotiated in most cases on a bilateral, sometimes regional basis, were entered into in the context of an acceptance of unrestrained national sovereignty over natural resources. Substantively, they tended to deal with shared waterways and other instances where Parties identified a need to protect national interests in certain natural resources of commercial importance. Examples include agreements dealing with the Rhine River, and bilateral resource management agreements. These agreements tended to address access to resources rather than concern about the protection of the resources from pollution or other human interference.

The 1930's and 1940's brought a gradual consideration of broader conservation issues in the context of the negotiation of international environmental agreements. This period saw the negotiation of agreements on the preservation of fauna and flora in their natural state, on nature and wildlife preservation, and more specific agreements such as the International Whaling Convention and other agreements on fisheries and land based species.

The creation of the United Nations (UN) in 1945 marked a turning point in international law. The full impact of the United Nations on international environmental law, however, would not be felt for some time to come. The environment was not a focus of the United Nations during this period from 1945 until the late 1960s. At the same time, a number of organizations created under the UN umbrella did have some limited mandate to address environmental issues. They include the Food and Agriculture Organization (FAO), the United Nations Educational, Scientific and Cultural Organization (UNESCO), the World Health Organization (WHO), the International Maritime Organization (IMO) and the General Agreement on Tariffs and Trade (GATT).

The UN did hold its initial conference on the environment as early as 1949, even if only in the limited context of conservation and utilization of resources. This was followed by a conference, initiated by the UN General Assembly in 1954, on the Conservation of the Living Resources of the Sea leading to the 1958 Geneva Conventions. Other issues with environmental implications addressed through international treaties during this period included atomic energy, nuclear arms, and agreements on oil pollution, high seas fishing and wetlands.

The trend during this period of international environmental law was to react to specific issues of concern to individual (or groups of) nations. Efforts tended to be isolated, reactive, and lacking consistent structure and approach. There is little indication that the environmental issues addressed were considered in any broader context, be they linkages among environmental issues, trends that might suggest underlying problems in the direction taken by human kind, questions about overall limits to the ability of nature to absorb the impact of human activity, north-south equity issues, or intergenerational equity considerations.

From Stockholm to Rio

The year 1972 is generally recognized as the starting point for contemporary international environmental law. Not only was it the year of the United Nations Stockholm Conference on the Human Environment, but a number of issue-specific treaties were negotiated around the same time. More importantly, Stockholm marked the beginning of an explosion of international treaty making to address specific environmental issues for which international cooperation was deemed essential. Inspired by the birth of environmental movements in North America and Europe in the 1960s, and facilitated through the United Nations, the

1972 Conference on the Human Environment was the first global conference to consider environmental issues from a broader perspective.

The conference produced a number of non-binding instruments, and led to the creation of the United Nations Environment Programme (UNEP). It also provided the context for the negotiation of a number of binding multilateral treaties, such as the Convention on International Trade in Endangered Species (CITES), the London Ocean Dumping Convention, the World Heritage Convention, and the first regional seas convention. Most of the treaties between 1972 and 1992 were still stand alone treaties. This period, however, did mark the beginning of the framework convention-protocol approach which has become dominant in international environmental law in the last two decades. The first such agreement was the Barcelona Convention for the Protection of the Mediterranean Sea Against Pollution, signed in 1976.

In addition to the sheer volume of international agreements dealing with environmental matters inspired by the Stockholm Conference, the 1972 conference is considered a turning point in the development of international environmental law in two other respects: the creation of an international structure to champion environmental issues in the form of UNEP, and the first attempt at an overall (non-binding) substantive context for the development of international environmental law. The substantive context was provided through the Stockholm Declaration in the form of 26 guiding principles and supplemented by an action plan with over 100 recommendations for international action on a range of environmental issues.

The focus of the 26 guiding principles is anthropocentric, and very much based on the concept of state sovereignty over the use of nature within its borders, assuming that areas of incompatibility of state sovereignty and the obligation not to adversely affect other nations in the process will be limited and manageable through specific agreements on an issue by issue basis. Of particular note in this regard is Principle 21, perhaps the most commonly referenced part of the Stockholm Declaration, which provides as follows:

> States have, in accordance with the Charter of the United Nations and the principles of international law, the sovereign right to exploit their own resources pursuant to their own environmental policies, and the responsibility to ensure that activities within their jurisdiction or control do not cause damage to the environment of other states or of areas beyond the limits of national jurisdiction.

Principle 22 actually takes the issue of responsibility to other States one step further by recognizing, in general terms, the concept of liability and compensation for damage caused outside a State's border. The development of international law to deal with liability and compensation issues is identified for future negotiation. In hindsight, it seems that these two principles were negotiated with an expectation that human activities with extraterritorial environmental impact would be the exception rather than the rule, and an assumption that specific incidents of extra-territorial impact of human activity within the borders of a State could be dealt with either on a case-by-case basis through the development of issue-specific treaties, or through the development of general principles of liability and compensation. Clearly, these expectations have proven to be overly optimistic, and as a result neither of the two options for dealing with environmental challenges internationally has proven to be realistic, or effective, to date.

At the same time, the declaration contains perhaps less well-known language that suggests in hindsight a surprisingly enlightened and visionary understanding of our relationship to nature. Paragraph 1 of the preamble, for example, reads as follows:

> Man is both creature and moulder of his environment, which gives him physical sustenance and affords him the opportunity for intellectual, moral, social and spiritual growth. In the long and tortuous evolution of the human race on this planet a stage has been reached when, through the rapid acceleration of science and technology, man has acquired the power to transform his environment in countless ways and on an unprecedented scale. Both aspects of man's environment, the natural and the man-made, are essential to his well being and the enjoyment of basic human rights — even the right to life itself.

Other provisions of the Stockholm Declaration suggest a recognition that a healthy natural environment is a precondition for human well-being, a recognition that quality of life and other goals of humanity depend upon cooperation with nature rather than a domination of nature. The declaration made repeated reference to the need to address the challenges ahead in a spirit of cooperation between developed and developing countries by addressing the inequities suffered by much of the human population living in developing countries. The concept of intergenerational equity was also introduced.

Another principle of particular note that was introduced in the Stockholm Declaration is the principle of integration. Principle 13 states: "In order to achieve a more rational management of resources and thus to improve the environment, States should adopt an integrated and co-ordinated approach to their development planning so as to ensure that development is compatible with the need to protect and improve the environment for the benefit of their population". The principle of integration was so new, and foreign to States, that it took 20 years for this principle to re-emerge in Rio and be taken seriously by the global community.

In fact, States are still struggling to implement the concept of integration in an effective manner. Domestically, one of the contributing factors to the failure to integrate effectively is, arguably, the creation of Environment Departments in many States. Ironically, the creation of these departments also goes back to the Stockholm Declaration, which urges States to institutionalize environmental protection. It was this reference to the need for domestic institutions that resulted in the establishment of Departments of the Environment in many States. The creation of those Departments has in turn made domestic integration more difficult by isolating environmental concerns from more mainstream concerns such as health, education, and economic development.

As mentioned, another development in 1972 that qualifies as a turning point in the evolution of international environmental law is the creation of the United Nations Environment Programme (UNEP). The establishment of UNEP by the General Assembly of the United Nations was in direct response to the recommendations contained in the action plan that accompanied the Stockholm Declaration. The initial mandate of UNEP was to oversee and guide the implementation of the action plan agreed to in Stockholm. UNEP was to do this by serving as a catalyst for international coordination of national action, but without any formal authority to implement the action plan in the absence of international consensus. This has been followed up with more specific mandates assigned to UNEP by the General Assembly from time to time. Structurally, UNEP is run by a governing council and an executive director, as well as a secretariat to carry out the instructions of the executive director. UNEP is funded mainly through direct voluntary payments from member States rather than through the UN general budget.

UNEP has played a key role in raising awareness about environmental issues in the international community since 1972, and was a driving force behind many of the multilateral environmental agreements entered into since 1972. While the influence of UNEP over the substance of these agreements is very much open to debate, it seems clear that UNEP was a catalyst for many of the agreements negotiated, and was instrumental in ensuring that the principles of the Stockholm Declaration were at least considered in the negotiation process.

In addition, this period from 1972 to 1992 saw the emergence of the international environmental community as an influential player in the development of international environmental law. In particular, international environmental non-governmental organizations (ENGO's) such as the IUCN, Greenpeace, the World Wildlife Fund, Friends of the Earth and others became active participants in international negotiations, both as observers and as advisors to State negotiators. Their influence can be traced through to Rio as well as individual Multi-Lateral Environmental Agreements (MEAs) such as the UNFCCC.

Substantively, the period from Stockholm in 1972 to Rio in 1992 saw an explosion in the number of international instruments dealing with environmental issues. Examples include the 1979 Convention on Long-Range Transboundary Air Pollution, the Law of the Sea Convention of 1982, the Vienna Convention on the Protection of the Ozone Layer, the Basel Convention on the Transboundary Movements of Hazardous Wastes and their Disposal, and the Protocol on Environmental Protection under the Antarctic Treaty, to name a few. These agreements demonstrated the complexity of the environmental issues facing the global community, the increasing number of environmental issues reaching a crisis level, and the unpreparedness of the international community to address these issues in a timely, effective, and coordinated manner in the absence of specific agreements on each environmental challenge discovered.

Almost without exception, the problems tackled in these agreements are still with us today. Furthermore, in the process of trying to address some of these problems, others have been created or exacerbated. Finally, most have been addressed without making any real progress on the fundamental issues raised, but not resolved, through the Stockholm Declaration, such as the conflict between state sovereignty and extraterritorial responsibility, the connection between environmental protection and equity, and the implication of the connections among economic development, quality of life, and protection of nature for the development and implementation of international environmental law.

At least some of these failures seem to have been recognized by UNEP and the world community in the years leading up to the 20th anniversary of Stockholm, resulting in the establishment of the Brundtland Commission, the publication of Our Common Future, and the follow-up negotiations leading up to the 1992 United Nations Conference on Environment and Development (UNCED) in Rio. In the next Section, the impact of the Rio Conference on international efforts to deal with these challenges will be briefly considered.

From Rio to the Present

The time leading up to UNCED in 1992 was marked on the one hand by another flurry of multilateral environmental agreements, particularly on a number of global environmental challenges. Ozone Layer Depletion, Climate Change and Biodiversity are perhaps the most notable global environmental issues for which agreements were negotiated during this period. On the other hand, the time leading up to UNCED was also marked by efforts to reflect on the evolution of environmental law since Stockholm. The Brundtland Commission, with its publication of Our Common Future in 1987, is generally recognized as the most influential initiative in this regard. Brundtland provided the context for negotiations leading up to Rio, particularly with respect to the negotiations leading to the Rio Declaration and Agenda 21.

Given this, the similarities between the Stockholm and Rio Declarations are surprising, suggesting limited progress over the 20 years in our collective understanding of the problems and possible solutions. A number of key principles from Stockholm, such as principles 21, 22 are repeated, with minor changes, in Rio. The main change in the Rio Declaration is its attempt, following the approach advocated by the Brundtland Commission, to integrate environmental, equity, and economic issues. In the process, Rio arguably advocates, at least in developing countries, for development as a precondition to addressing environmental issues. In the process, the concept of sustainable development has all too often become an excuse for the environmental impact of development, rather than a measuring stick to separate sustainable from unsustainable human activity.

Two additions to the Rio Declaration that possess the potential for positive contributions to the evolution of environmental law are the precautionary principle and the polluter pays principle. Both have been widely applied and their status under customary international law is being openly debated. Both have influenced the negotiation of specific instruments and the evolution of regimes since 1992, as has the concept of sustainable development and the concept of integrating economic, environmental and equity issues in tackling environmental challenges.

After a flurry of activity leading up to and following UNCED in 1992, developments in international environmental law have been modest in the past decade. While issues such as Ozone Layer Depletion, for example, caught the attention of the international community during this dynamic period leading up to UNCED, issues such as biodiversity and climate change seem to be progressing at a much slower pace since the signing of the respective framework conventions in 1992. The World Summit on Sustainable Development, held in 2002 in Johannesburg, was by most accounts a minute step forward at best.

There are a number of principles that have emerged from the evolution of international environmental law to date. First in time, but still very much a factor today in the development and implementation of international environmental law is the concept of state sovereignty over natural resources, modified by state responsibility for environmental impact outside its territory as set out in Principle 21 of the Stockholm Declaration. More recently, this principle has been supplemented with the concept of sustainable development, perhaps the driving force behind the development of international environmental law since 1992. Still emerging to varying degrees, in terms of influence over the evolution of international environmental law, are: the precautionary principle, the polluter pays principle, and the concept of common but differentiated responsibility.

Other changes in international environmental law include the changing role of non-governmental actors in the development and implementation of international law, and the emergence of environmental impact assessment, economic instruments, monitoring, reporting, and verification as favoured implementation tools. As the stakes have become higher and the sheer number of obligations has increased, there has also been a renewed interest in the question of compliance. One crucial area identified in Stockholm, in which progress has been slow, is with respect to the development of international environmental law on liability and compensation for extraterritorial environmental damage. While some specific instruments may provide opportunities to establish liability and seek compensation, there is no overall framework for the establishment of liability and compensation as contemplated in Principle 22 of the Stockholm Declaration. In fact, Principle 13 of the Rio Declaration, at best, mirrors the expressed need to develop international law in this area, without demonstrating any tangible progress.

Notes and Questions

Progress with respect to liability for trans-boundary harm in violation of customary law has been slow. In some rare cases, such as the Trail Smelter arbitration between Canada and the US, compensation for air pollution that moved from a Canadian smelter into the US, liability is settled through a mutually agreed upon process (See *Trail Smelter Arbitration United States v. Canada* (1931–1941), 3 R.I.A.A. 1905). More often, the issue is dealt with at a diplomatic level on a state by state basis, or left unresolved. One of the consequences has been that those affected have sought other recourse. An ongoing disagreement between the US and Canada over pollution of the Columbia river, resulting from the still operating Trail Smelter, recently resulted in enforcement action by the US Environmental Protection Agency directly against the Canadian company on the basis that it is polluting US territory. For a more detailed discussion of this case and its implications, see Neil Craik, "Trail Smelter Redux: Transboundary Pollution and Extraterritorial Jurisdiction" (2004) 14 J.E.L.P. 139 and Michael Robinson-Dorn, "The Tail Smelter: Is What's Past Prologue? EPA Blazes a New Trail for CERCLA" (2006) 14 N.Y.U. Envtl. L. J. 233.

Part II — Relevance and Application of International Law in the Canadian Environmental Law Context

In this Part, we consider how, and to what extent, international norms, principles, commitments and obligations translate into Canadian domestic law. A key focus is the use of international law by Canadian courts. In the process, however, you will be challenged to think about the different ways international law has shaped, and has the potential to shape, the substance and implementation of domestic environmental law. As a starting point, consider the following survey of case law dealing with the role of international law in interpreting domestic law.

The following article considers three main issues: (1) the means by which international treaty obligations are translated into domestic law; (2) the use of international law as an aid in the interpretation of domestic legislation; and (3) the extent to which customary international law forms part of Canadian domestic law.

Elizabeth Brandon, "Does International Law Mean Anything in Canadian Courts?"
(2001) 11 J. Env. L. & Prac. 399

Introduction

The number of international agreements related to the environment has grown rapidly in the past few decades, and the trend is set to continue. Canada is a party to many of these agreements, and promotes an 'environmentally friendly' image of itself abroad. However, international agreements are of little consequence unless they are implemented and enforced at the national level. Numerous international courts and legal mechanisms exist to resolve disputes between States and to monitor their implementation of certain agreements. However, these facilities generally do not provide a forum for individuals to take issue with their governments for a failure to enforce international obligations that have been implemented through national legislation, except in the area of human rights.

Although international monitoring agencies may apply political pressure to governments that are not conforming to their international legal obligations, these influences may not be sufficient to ensure enforcement. There is even less pressure on a government to conform where it is not involved in a dispute with another government, and therefore not subject to the jurisdiction of a court or dispute settlement body. Thus the responsibility of ensuring compliance with international law is often left to the government itself, or to individuals and pressure groups within the State. The enforcement of international law has become the most critical issue facing those who oversee its operation at the international level, and those who seek to rely upon it at the domestic level.

Implementation of international law may be achieved through legislative, regulatory and policy measures by governments, depending on the type of action required by each international agreement or legal principle. National courts also have a role in implementation, by interpreting and applying the laws enacted by governments to meet their international obligations. Courts may also play a more indirect part in implementation, by relying upon international legal principles and materials, and foreign judicial decisions, as a basis for their decisions. The various methods used by Canadian courts to apply international law will be discussed in this article. In addition, avenues that are often neglected in legal argument will be explored.

Until more recently, Canadian judges and litigators have made only limited use of international law in legal argument, particularly in the area of environmental litigation. [. . .] The slowness of the Canadian legal community to make use of international law, and particularly environmental treaties and principles, could derive partly from its lack of familiarity with them. It may also be attributed to the breadth of issues often covered by environmental treaties, and the general objectives that tend to be used in them instead of specific measures. However, the traditional legal stance — which viewed international law as existing outside of domestic law — may also, in a general sense, have discouraged litigators and judges from using international law. These factors mean that international law tends to be neglected in legal dialogue because it is often seen as irrelevant, imprecise or non-binding and therefore of little consequence. As a result, the judiciary is given few opportunities to develop skills in utilizing international law in decision-making.

Political and constitutional factors shape the way in which international law is accepted as part of domestic law. Until recently, the Canadian approach to treaties has been understood as firmly dualist, viewing them as distinct from domestic law until they have been implemented through government action. The approach to customary international law is less clear-cut. Although there is a belief that Canada is monist, in that customary legal principles apply directly to domestic law without needing specific implementation, the issue is far from settled. Some judicial decisions have required, expressly or implicitly, the transformation of customary law into domestic law. However, the recent decision of *Suresh v. Canada (Minister of Citizenship & Immigration)*, suggests that such 'transformation' is unnecessary and that customary law may be invoked at least indirectly. The *Suresh* decision arguably has the same significance for the status of treaties in domestic law.

International law is also treated with caution where it is perceived to jeopardize the distribution of powers between the federal and provincial governments. Moreover, the concept of parliamentary sovereignty may dissuade the courts from readily accepting the authority of international law. It is conceded that the Canadian constitutional framework poses a challenge to the widespread use of many types of international law. However, these factors need not, and should not, be obstacles to drawing from international environmental law in domestic courts . . .

Implementation of Treaty Obligations

According to the view traditionally taken by Canadian courts and lawmakers, a treaty becomes legally binding within Canada only when the federal Executive has signed and ratified the treaty, and it has been implemented by the appropriate legislature through specific legislation. The dualist position holds that a treaty cannot be in any way relevant to Canadian law unless all of these steps have been taken. Therefore, without domestic action, the international commitments entered into by the Canadian government would be of no consequence within Canada and unenforceable in Canadian courts.

However, the traditional view conflicts with the long-standing rule of statutory interpretation that a legislature is presumed not to legislate in violation of international law. As a result of this presumption, it could be said that 'unimplemented' or 'unincorporated' treaties have also influenced Canadian law, even if they have not been recognized as directly applicable. This conclusion is supported by recent developments in Canadian judicial reasoning, marked by the important decisions of *Baker v. Canada (Minister of Citizenship & Immigration)*, [1999] 2 S.C.R. 817, *Suresh v. Canada (Minister of Citizenship & Immigration)*, [2002] 1 S.C.R. 3 and *Ahani v. Canada (Minister of Citizenship & Immigration)*, [2002] 1 S.C.R. 72.

Treaties Implemented Through Domestic Legislation

As noted above, the traditional approach to implementation of international law insists that specific implementing legislation is required for a treaty to have domestic effect. However, as van Ert observes, judicial thinking has now evolved to the point where an implementing statute need not make any mention at all of the treaty it implements. He contends that "the task of determining whether an act seeks to implement a treaty is no different than that of discerning the legislature's intent more generally". Thus a statute that does not rely directly on the text of the treaty but simply effects legal changes adequate to fulfill Canada's treaty obligations, would be acceptable.

Express incorporation by reference

Where there is legislation which sets out a treaty text in full or expressly refers to its implementation, and which has the specific purpose of implementing that treaty, the parliamentary intention seems sufficiently clear. While a treaty that has been set out in the schedule to a statute need not be accompanied by an express intention to implement, such intention should be discernable from the statutory provisions. The normal tools of statutory interpretation would be employed to assess the legislative intention, including presumptions of conformity with international law.

For a handful of environment-related treaties, the Canadian Parliament has enacted specific legislation which not only indicates an implementing purpose in its short title, but also gives an express approval of the treaty and even includes the full text of the treaty as a schedule (the *Convention on Salvage, Convention for Safe Containers, Comprehensive Nuclear Test Ban Treaty, Convention on Chemical Weapons*, and *Migratory Birds Convention*). [. . .]

Partial incorporation

For domestic legislation which only partially incorporates a treaty, a similar argument to the above may be constructed on a smaller scale. The courts should view this method of implementation as importing at least some provisions of a treaty directly into Canadian law. In addition, the context of the treaty as a whole should inform the application of those provisions as part of the legislative regime. [. . .]

Limited references to a treaty in the statute

Where a statute contains only limited references to a particular treaty — for example, in its preamble, or in the definitions section — there may be sufficient grounds for establishing that Parliament in fact intended to implement the treaty as a whole. This approach was successful in *R. v. Crown Zellerbach Canada Ltd.*, in which the Supreme Court of Canada recognized the *Ocean Dumping Control Act* as directed to the implementation of Canada's obligations under the *London Convention on the Prevention of Marine Pollution by Dumping*. It reached this conclusion in the absence of an express legislative statement as to this purpose, relying instead upon several references to the Convention in the Act, provisions modeled closely on the Convention's annexes, and the Act's schedules which incorporated amendments to the Convention. While the majority did not directly apply the Convention text, it could arguably have done so on the basis that an intention to implement was established. [. . .]

Legislation containing a general power to implement treaties

Reliance by the government on a general implementation power contained in a statute to give effect to a particular treaty is evidence of an intention to implement that treaty. A general implementation power is commonly phrased as a power "to implement relevant international agreements," or a power to implement a particular treaty or type of treaty. While this type of legislation does not actually incorporate the treaty text, it provides a general power to implement the treaty and may also mirror its provisions. The implementing clause is usually located at the beginning of the statute.

An example of this practice is the legislative framework that has been put in place to meet Canada's obligations under the *Convention on International Trade in Endangered Species of Wild Fauna and Flora (CITES)*. The *Wild Animal and Plant Protection and Regulation of International and Interprovincial Trade Act (WAPPRIITA)* allows the Governor in Council to make regulations for carrying out the purposes of the Act, including regulations "generally to implement [CITES]". The purpose of the Act is "to protect certain species of animals and plants, particularly by implementing the Convention and regulating international and interprovincial trade in animals and plants". The text of the statute incorporates the permit requirements of the Convention. [. . .]

Patent Treaty Implementation by Legislation and/or Policy

A strong contention may be made that a treaty should be considered implemented because a combination of factors — the legislative and policy framework, together with representations from the Government — patently show that it is implemented. Where the legislative and regulatory measures taken by Government accord with the requirements of the treaty, and Government has expressed a belief that the treaty is 'implemented' or 'applicable,' there is a sufficient basis for this contention. An international legal perspective strongly supports taking a broad, flexible view of what constitutes implementation.

This contextual approach to determining whether implementation has occurred may be used for three scenarios. The first is where the Government has assessed its existing laws prior to ratification of a treaty, and deemed them adequate to meet the treaty commitments. This practice may be called 'passive incorporation'. The second scenario is where the Government takes positive steps to legislate and regulate in response to its treaty obligations, but stops short of expressly incorporating the treaty. Implementation is particularly patent in this situation, as an intention to implement is often easily discernable.

The third scenario would arise where the Government has only taken policy measures to comply with a treaty, but that treaty can nevertheless be considered implemented because its requirements have been met. In each of the above situations, evidence of implementation relies on the provisions of the individual treaty, the actions taken by the Government to comply with those provisions, and any expressions by the Government as to the status of the treaty in relation to Canada. If all three of these factors correlate, it must be assumed that the treaty is indeed implemented and therefore directly applicable to domestic law. [. . .]

Passive incorporation

'Passive incorporation' may be said to occur when the government or legislature concludes that domestic law is already in line with the treaty and, therefore, no further measures are needed. This conclusion is generally reached prior to either signature or ratification of the treaty. It enables the Government to claim, before both its citizens and international treaty bodies, that Canada is bound by norms that are already implemented. This practice is common in relation to human rights treaties, which tend to be ratified on the basis that no new legislation is required. It is also becoming apparent for environmental treaties, particularly where federal Parliament may lack a solid jurisdictional basis for implementing the treaty through specific environmental legislation.

The phenomenon of passive incorporation is of particular relevance to Canada because it seems to be the preferred implementing technique of the Canadian Government for a number of environmental treaties. Canada has ratified a great number of international treaties, which are often ratified on the basis of existing conformity with the new treaty provisions. But ratification on this basis is problematic, as it inevitably leaves the courts with the difficult task of assessing Canada's compliance with international obligations in the absence of express implementing legislation.

Thus the courts need to look to other sources to confirm that the obligations are implemented — the existing legislative and policy framework, expressions of the government's intention to be bound by the relevant treaty, and the terms of the treaty itself. When a treaty to which Canada is a party enters into force, the Canadian Parliament (or, if appropriate, the provincial legislatures) must enact any legislation that may be necessary for the performance of the treaty obligations. Therefore, it is a common practice, although not a constitutional requirement, for the government to determine whether new legislation is necessary to fulfill Canada's treaty obligations.

In Canada, it is apparent that legislative action is generally not required for agreements concerning administrative or political matters, but is required for treaties which would impose financial burdens on the government, or "alter the law of the land". Although environment-related treaties tend to involve the taking of policy measures rather than the imposition of specific financial commitments, some treaties employ a range of tools to achieve their goals. They may involve large public expenditure together with changes to laws to prohibit certain activities or regulate resource use.

Given the common government practice of assessing Canada's legislative framework prior to signing a treaty, significance can be attached to legislative inaction by the government following signature. This inaction signals that the existing legislative or policy framework has been deemed adequate to fulfill the treaty obligations. The strong presumption that the Canadian government intends to comply with its international legal obligations should lead the courts' approach to a treaty in this situation. Absent any clear indications to the contrary, one must presume that the government intended to implement the treaty, thus making it relevant to the interpretation of domestic law.

One example of passive incorporation is the *Ramsar Convention on Wetlands of International Importance especially as Waterfowl Habitat*. Canada has ratified the Convention but, according to the Canadian Wildlife Service, it has not specifically incorporated it into domestic law. Although many federal and provincial policies exist for wetland preservation, they do not expressly address Canada's obligations under the Convention. However, according to the Federal Government, the Convention was deemed "self-implementing" and is used as a facilitating mechanism for domestic laws.

By early 2002, 36 sites within Canada had been designated for protection under the *Ramsar Convention*. Federal and provincial governments cooperate on site nominations and a procedure manual is used to interpret the *Ramsar Convention* guidelines for site designation. It appears that the federal and provincial governments already view the Convention as implemented without the need for legislation. Accordingly, the provisions of the *Ramsar Convention* may be considered relevant to the Canadian wetland management framework and to domestic law in general. [. . .]

Implementation by positive action

It may be evident from positive measures taken by the government that those measures were intended to fulfil Canada's treaty commitments. To determine whether a particular treaty has been implemented in this way, and where the relevant legislation does not have an express implementing purpose, a close examination of the legislative and regulatory framework is required. The specific requirements of the relevant treaty must be kept in mind during this analysis for comparative purposes.

Guidance for looking beyond the confines of a statute to ascertain parliamentary intention is found in the landmark English case of *Salomon v. Commissioners of Customs & Excise*. Diplock L.J. stated that if it is plain from extrinsic evidence that the enactment was intended to fulfil obligations under a particular treaty, no express reference to the treaty in the statute is needed. [. . .] A court may also be entitled to look at parliamentary reading speeches to identify the scope and purpose of a statute. [. . .]

The *Montreal Protocol on Substances that Deplete the Ozone Layer* provides a useful example of a treaty that has patently been implemented through positive measures taken by the Canadian Government. Canada has signed and ratified the *Montreal Protocol* and its amendments, committing itself to deadlines for the phasing-out of several substances. The position taken by the federal government is that, since signing the *Montreal Protocol* in 1987, "Canada has adopted adequate regulations to meet its *Montreal Protocol* commitments".

The clear targets and timelines set out by the Protocol make it easier to determine whether Canada's laws do in fact match up with its obligations. The legislative framework comprises the federal *Ozone-Depleting Substances Regulations* and the *Federal Halocarbon Regulations*, both made under the *Canadian Environmental Protection Act, 1999*. The regulations are supplemented by non-statutory initiatives such as national action plans and mandatory codes of practice. All of the provinces and one territory have pollution prevention regulations, and municipalities are also taking action. In addition, the regulatory impact analysis statement in support of the *ODS Regulations* clearly identified Canada's obligations under the *Montreal Protocol* as the central justification for the regulations. Evidently, the combination of regulations and policy addresses Canada's ozone protection commitments and future phase-out targets.

The close correlation between Canada's regulations and policies for phasing out ozone-depleting substances, and the provisions of the *Montreal Protocol*, provide sufficient evidence of Parliament's intention to implement those provisions. If further proof is needed, one need only look to the relevant regulatory impact analysis statements and government press releases. Domestically, Canada has kept up with the continual revisions of the *Montreal Protocol* timelines and, at least on paper, there are no regulatory gaps. Thus it should be possible to contend that the *Montreal Protocol* is in fact implemented into domestic law and should be taken into account by decision-makers where relevant.

Policy measures

Environmental treaties are often distinctive for their lack of hard rules and their preference for policy measures and general principles, instead of legislation, to achieve the desired goals. Indeed, non-legislative measures may be the only feasible way of achieving certain treaty goals. 'Policy measures' could encompass measures for voluntary compliance, economic incentives, 'action plans', educational programs, allocation of financial resources, and environmental management plans.

A government may respond to its treaty obligations simply by assessing its policy framework and making any necessary changes. If a government takes policy measures in order to comply with its treaty obligations, thereby achieving the treaty goals, that treaty should be viewed as implemented. At the international level, and in the eyes of the government, these efforts are sufficient to carry out the treaty obligations. Thus the precise tools a government uses for implementation are irrelevant — the importance lies in the end result and the requisite government intention. From an international law viewpoint, the treaty is already deemed 'implemented' once its requirements are met, and it would be difficult for individual governments to refute this.

Thus a domestic policy that reflects or refers to the provisions of a treaty can be used as an implementing vehicle for that treaty. Conversely, a treaty can be of indirect legal effect if it is relevant to domestic policy and the exercise of statutory authority — regardless of whether Canada has signed the treaty. [. . .]

A prominent example of the notion that some provisions of a treaty can be implemented through non-legislative means is the *Convention on Biological Diversity*. The Canadian Government has ratified the Convention but has not specifically implemented it through legislation. However, an intention to implement the *Convention on Biological Diversity* through domestic policy and other measures is evident from government practice. The Government has used a range of non-statutory instruments to meet most of its obligations under the Convention, such as the Canadian Biodiversity Strategy and eight sectoral policies, and has repeatedly expressed its firm commitment to it. Such policy measures conform to the provisions of the Convention, which contain broad principles and focus on policy-making rather than legislation. Therefore it appears from an international and domestic perspective that the Convention is at least partially implemented, and thus relevant in Canada with respect to those implemented provisions.

At a minimum, courts should interpret domestic laws to conform as far as possible with Canada's commitments to the *Convention on Biological Diversity* even if it is deemed unimplemented as a whole. Some of the central principles in the Convention have been acknowledged in the preambles to federal and provincial legislation. Moreover, five provinces currently have specific endangered species legislation and the Federal Government is attempting to enact the same legislation. These legislative provisions provide sufficient grounds for the courts to refer to the *Convention on Biological Diversity* for elucidation when they engage in statutory interpretation.

The *Convention on Biological Diversity* is relevant not only as an interpretative aid, but to the exercise of statutory authority by government decision-makers. In particular, where policies exist that reflect the values and principles of the Convention, the responsible statutory authorities should ensure that these objectives are safeguarded. It is clear from *Baker* that the relevance of treaties does not begin and end with statutory interpretation, but reaches more widely to all areas in which government authority is exercised.

International Law as an Interpretative Aid for Domestic Legislation

International law, including treaties, also becomes relevant to Canadian law in the interpretation of domestic statutes. Recognition of this source of law has grown rapidly in recent years. The role of international law is already evident where the statute involved is considered to implement the international principle or treaty. However, as mentioned above, it is now emerging that international law may be applied indirectly even where it cannot be considered already implemented through legislation or policy.

The interpretation of a statute is guided by the need for a contextual approach, which requires that domestic legislation be read in light of the conditions in which it was created, its purpose and object, any other relevant legal developments, and the social values of the present day. The ordinary rules of statutory interpretation dictate that the words of a statute must be interpreted in accordance with their 'total context'. Thus it is contended that the contextual approach should take into account relevant legal principles and materials — regardless of whether they originate within or outside of Canada — if they reflect Canadian values and aspirations. [. . .]

Despite recent judicial developments, there are no clear boundaries defining the use that may be made of international law as an aid to statutory interpretation. Even unratified and unsigned treaties have been considered by Canadian courts to be a useful interpretative aid. Likewise, courts have drawn freely from customary law, international tribunal decisions, and international declarations. This trend suggests that the courts will turn to international legal materials for clarification when the need arises, regardless of their binding status. Thus international law can be used as an interpretative aid wherever it is relevant and persuasive, because it expresses important principles and values. Arguably, Canadian laws must be presumed to comply with these international principles and values unless it has been made clear in each instance that Canada will be acting otherwise.

Implemented treaties

As noted above, Canadian courts already use international law to interpret a treaty that has been implemented through domestic legislation. Based on the assumption that the statute is intended to implement the treaty, the latter may subsequently be used as a proper aid to interpretation. The courts have been prepared to refer to an underlying treaty (the subject of the implementing legislation) not only when the statute contains an ambiguity (either patent or latent), but before such an ambiguity is identified. [. . .]

Unimplemented treaties

Until relatively recently, it was not clear whether unimplemented treaties could be considered as part of the 'total context' of domestic legislation. According to the prevailing view of international law, treaties would not become legally relevant unless specifically implemented. This view insists that the international and domestic legal spheres are separate and that international law must be 'transformed' or 'translated' into domestic law to have any effect.

It is submitted that the argument for 'transformation' ignores the influence already wielded by international law within Canada. This influence is recognized by Toope:

> The process of relating international law to domestic law is not a translation of norms from outside. Rather, Canadian voices join with foreign voices, weaving an increasingly rich and multi-textured narrative of international law.

The traditional insistence on implementing legislation has enabled Canada to "shield the executive from the consequences of its voluntary decision to enter into and therefore be bound by the [treaty]". There are signs that this ability to avoid the legal effects of ratifying a treaty is now being eroded. As Toope argues, recent cases such as *Baker* and other foreign jurisprudence pose "salutary challenges to governmental hypocrisy (or perhaps incompetence) in ratifying international treaties and failing to address the domestic law implications of those treaties".

The trend represented by the cases of *Baker*, *Suresh*, and *Ahani* demonstrates that an unimplemented treaty may indeed be highly relevant — albeit not directly applicable — to domestic legislation and decision-making. The Supreme Court of Canada in *Baker* widened the purview of the contextual approach to statutory interpretation. It concluded that the legal context should include any relevant values and principles expressed by the international community and reflected in Canadian legislation or policy. An unimplemented treaty could provide valuable guidance for the Court in seeking to clarify the provisions of the statute. [. . .]

The implication from *Baker* and *Suresh*, supported by other Canadian and foreign case law, is that the provisions of any treaty ratified by the government can be relevant in many ways to domestic laws and decision-making. As a result, arguably international principles and treaties need not be specifically implemented into domestic law to be relevant, and even instrumental, to the process of statutory interpretation. This development represents a sharp divergence from the traditional judicial approach, which asserts that treaties are of no domestic effect unless implemented through legislation.

Treaties not ratified by Canada

The notion of a 'total' legal context may be further extended to encompass treaties that have not been ratified or even signed by Canada. This extension would be consistent with the need expressed in *Baker*, *Suresh* and *Ahani* to take relevant international values and principles into account when engaging in statutory interpretation. Other cases add support because they specifically refer to the relevance of unratified and unsigned treaties to domestic law. [. . .]

Where Canada has signed a treaty but has not yet ratified it, it may nevertheless be obliged to act in accordance with the general purpose of that treaty. Article 18 of the *Vienna Convention on the Law of Treaties* imposes an obligation on signatory states not to defeat the object and purpose of a treaty prior to its entry into force. Thus a signatory state should refrain from acting to frustrate the objectives of a treaty until it has made clear its intention whether to ratify the treaty. For this reason, it should not be assumed that the act of signature is devoid of any effect. The act of signature has particular importance for states that engage in a rigorous constitutional check of domestic laws prior to signature. In Canada, the general government practice for some, but not all, treaties is to examine closely the draft treaty text, to consult the provinces if appropriate, and then to take any necessary legislative action to implement the treaty.

It has already been seen that the courts are prepared to look to ratified but unimplemented treaties when interpreting domestic legislation. There does not appear to be any reason why treaties signed but not ratified by the Canadian Government should be accorded less importance by the courts. The focus of the Supreme Court of Canada in *Baker* was not on the implemented status of the treaty, but the relevance of its values to Canadian society. Arguably, the values expressed in a treaty become relevant to Canadian law as soon as that treaty has been finalized by the signatories. This contention carries even more weight if the treaty is actually in force, and if Canada participated actively in its negotiation. The unratified treaty is no less an expression of international values and principles, and thus it must be taken into account by government decision-makers in their exercise of authority, and the courts when interpreting a statute.

Customary International Law as Part of Domestic Law

Customary international law provides a useful vehicle for a closer analysis of the relationship between international law and domestic law. Customary rules are clearly recognized as a source of international law by the *Statute of the International Court of Justice*. The precise legal relationship between customary international law — which is built upon these rules — and domestic Canadian law is a subject of some contention. Canadian case law to date has not produced a clear statement as to whether customary law may automatically be considered part of domestic law and thus directly applied. [. . .]

Arguably . . . foreign jurisprudence and recent Canadian case law support the direct application of norms of customary international law in the domestic sphere, in much the same manner domestic legislation is applied. Even where the precise status of a customary norm is unclear [. . .] an emerging or established norm may be highly relevant to domestic law. In fact, any attempt by a government to derogate from such a norm without reasonable justification should be actively discouraged by the courts.

A controversial and relatively recent development in international environmental law is the 'precautionary principle', also called the precautionary 'approach' or 'concept.' The principle has been described in many different ways, but generally it states that in cases where there are threats to human health and the environment the fact that there is no scientific uncertainty over those threats should not be used as the reason for not taking action to prevent harm.

The growth in popularity of the precautionary principle has led to extensive references to it in the texts of treaties and declarations. Thus it is arguable that, at a minimum, states have widely acknowledged its existence as a principle of international law. Sands ventures further in suggesting that evidence of state practice is now sufficient to demonstrate that the precautionary principle has customary law status. Foreign jurisprudence appears to support this conclusion, and Canadian courts are beginning to acknowledge its existence, as in the Supreme Court of Canada decision of *114957 Canada Ltée (Spray-Tech, Société d'arrosage) v. Hudson (Ville)*.

Even if customary international law is not directly applicable . . . the courts are entitled to use it as an aid to statutory interpretation. In *Baker*, the Supreme Court of Canada cited with approval the following passage from Driedger on the Construction of Statutes:

> [T]he legislature is presumed to respect the values and principles enshrined in international law, both customary and conventional. These constitute a part of the legal context in which legislation is enacted and read. In so far as possible, therefore, interpretations that reflect these values and principles are preferred. [. . .]

The endorsement in the *Baker* and *Spray-Tech* decisions of the use of international law as an interpretative aid means that the precautionary principle remains relevant even if it has not yet reached customary legal status. Given the presumption of conformity with international law, Canada's domestic laws must be interpreted in a broader legal context that takes into account both binding and non-binding international principles. Canada has ratified several treaties in which the precautionary approach or principle is mentioned. Many references to the principle have also been made in non-binding international documents. Based on the rationale in *Baker* and *Suresh*, these international legal principles may be considered relevant to domestic law because they reflect the values of the international community.

Conclusions

A gradual narrowing of the gap between the international and domestic legal spheres has led to a change in the concept of treaty implementation. This change is apparent in Canada, among other states, from an examination of developments in judicial reasoning. From an international legal viewpoint, a treaty may be considered implemented if the actions taken by individual states correspond with their treaty obligations. In Canada, from a domestic legal perspective, the focus has shifted from the question of whether a treaty has been specifically implemented through legislation, to whether government had an intention to implement the treaty.

It is contended that the method of implementation is less important than are indications of an intention to implement. An implementing intention that evidences a strong compliance with treaty requirements will clearly be the most persuasive indication that the treaty is of domestic effect. An intention to implement alone may be insufficient, and it should either be accompanied by positive measures by government or follow from an assessment of the existing regulatory framework. It must be possible to pinpoint a decision by the government to take implementing action or to accept the current framework as adequate. The more closely this positive action, or existing framework, corresponds to the terms of the treaty, the more accurately it may be viewed as actually implementing that treaty. [. . .]

The future direction of international law in Canada presents a challenge to all participants in the judicial process. In particular, the relationship between international and domestic law will inevitably be put to the test in environment-related litigation, as Canada ratifies growing numbers of environmental treaties. In the interval, and until the relationship between international and Canadian law is clarified, the legal community should draw widely from the international legal sources available to it. The large body of international law, encompassing treaties, declarations, international legal principles, and customary law, is a fertile source of legal argument to be used in domestic litigation. International environmental law offers a promising opportunity to bridge the gap between international obligations undertaken by Canada, and its domestic actions.

Notes and Questions

1. Governments may choose to implement their treaty obligations expressly, through direct incorporation in domestic legislation. According to Brandon, treaty obligations can also be deemed to be incorporated into domestic law in a number of ways. What are they?

2. It is well settled that Canadian courts may look to treaties that Canada has ratified and implemented as an aid to interpreting domestic legislation. Can they also rely on unimplemented or unratified treaties to this end? Is their use more limited? How?

3. What is customary international law? What determines whether a legal principle has achieved this status? According to Brandon, what domestic legal implications flow from a principle being recognized as customary international law? Can international norms that are yet to be recognized as customary international law still be used by courts as an interpretive aid?

4. Since the Brandon article was first published in 2001, the federal government has enacted new legislation dealing with endangered species (the *Species at Risk Act*) and national parks (the *Canada National Parks Act*): see Chapters 8 and 9. When you review the materials on these federal statutes, consider whether they can be seen to be implementing the Convention on Biodiversity, in part or in whole, and what role various articles of the Convention could play in interpreting the provisions of these two statutes.

Since the Brandon article, there have been a number of cases decided by the Supreme Court of Canada that invoke or rely on international law. Below we include excerpts from three examples: *114957 Canada Ltée (Spray-Tech, Société d'arrosage) v. Hudson (Ville)*, [2001] 2 S.C.R. 241; *Gosselin v. Quebec (Attorney General)*, [2002] 4 S.C.R. 429; and *Canadian Foundation for Children v. Canada*, [2004] 1 S.C.R. 76, 2004 SCC 4. In reviewing these cases, consider carefully whether they shed any further light on the domestic relevance of the various sources of international law (treaties, customary international law and international soft law), and on the principles relating to implementation of international treaty obligations.

. . . . .

114957 Canada Ltée (Spray-Tech, Société d'arrosage) v. Hudson (Ville)
[2001] 2 S.C.R. 241

[The majority reasons in *Spraytech* are notable in that they represent a particularly robust illustration of the use of international law in interpreting and, in the end, in upholding the validity of domestic legislation in the environmental context. Portions of this decision are reproduced elsewhere in this book (see Chapter 3). Here we excerpt extracts from the majority reasons of L'Heureux-Dubé J. bearing directly on the role of international law. The case arose as a result of a challenge to validity of by-laws enacted by the Town of Hudson that restricted the use of pesticides. The challenge was brought by a group of landscaping companies.]

L'HEUREUX-DUBÉ J.:

The context of this appeal includes the realization that our common future, that of every Canadian community, depends on a healthy environment. [. . .]

Regardless of whether pesticides are in fact an environmental threat, the Court is asked to decide the legal question of whether the Town of Hudson, Quebec, acted within its authority in enacting a by-law regulating and restricting pesticide use.

The case arises in an era in which matters of governance are often examined through the lens of the principle of subsidiarity. This is the proposition that law-making and implementation are often best achieved at a level of government that is not only effective, but also closest to the citizens affected and thus most responsive to their needs, to local distinctiveness, and to population diversity. La Forest J. wrote for the majority in *R. v. Hydro-Québec*, [1997] 3 S.C.R. 213 at p. 296, that the protection of the environment is a major challenge of our time. It is an international problem, one that requires action by governments at all levels (emphasis added). His reasons in that case also quoted with approval a passage from *Our Common Future*, the report produced in 1987 by the United Nations World Commission on the Environment and Development. The so-called Brundtland Commission recommended that local governments [should be] empowered to exceed, but not to lower, national norms" [. . .]

The appellants are landscaping and lawn care companies operating mostly in the region of greater Montreal, with both commercial and residential clients. They make regular use of pesticides approved by the federal *Pest Control Products Act*, R.S.C. 1985, c. P-9, in the course of their business activities and hold the requisite licences under Quebec's *Pesticides Act*, R.S.Q. c. P-9.3.

The respondent, the Town of Hudson, is a municipal corporation governed by the *Cities and Towns Act*, R.S.Q., c. C-19 (*AC.T.A.*). It is located about 40 kilometres west of Montreal and has a population of approximately 5,400 people, some of whom are clients of the appellants. In 1991, the Town adopted By-law 270, restricting the use of pesticides within its perimeter to specified locations and for enumerated activities. The by-law responded to residents' concerns, repeatedly expressed since 1985. The residents submitted numerous letters and comments to the Towns Council. The definition of pesticides in By-law 270 replicates that of the *Pesticides Act*. [. . .]

[*Ed note*: After analyzing the statutory scheme to determine whether the Town had authority to enact the impugned by-law, the majority offered the following views on the relevance of the precautionary principle and international law]

To conclude this section on statutory authority, I note that reading s. 410(1) to permit the Town to regulate pesticide use is consistent with principles of international law and policy. My reasons for the Court in *Baker v. Canada (Minister of Citizenship and Immigration)*, [1999] 2 S.C.R. 817 at p. 861, observed that the values reflected in international human rights law may help inform the contextual approach to statutory interpretation and judicial review. As stated in *Driedger on the Construction of Statutes*, *supra*, at p. 330:

> [T]he legislature is presumed to respect the values and principles enshrined in international law, both customary and conventional. These constitute a part of the legal context in which legislation is enacted and read. *In so far as possible, therefore, interpretations that reflect these values and principles are preferred*. [Emphasis added.]

The interpretation of By-law 270 contained in these reasons respects international law's precautionary principle, which is defined as follows at para. 7 of the *Bergen Ministerial Declaration on Sustainable Development* (1990): "In order to achieve sustainable development, policies must be based on the precautionary principle. Environmental measures must anticipate, prevent and attack the causes of environmental degradation. Where there are threats of serious or irreversible damage, lack of full scientific certainty should not be used as a reason for postponing measures to prevent environmental degradation".

Canada advocated inclusion of the precautionary principle during the Bergen Conference negotiations (D. VanderZwaag, CEPA Issue Elaboration Paper No. 18, *CEPA and the Precautionary Principle/Approach* (1995), at p. 8). The principle is codified in several items of domestic legislation: see for example the *Oceans Act*, S.C. 1996, c. 31, Preamble (para. 6); *Canadian Environmental Protection Act, 1999*, S.C. 1999, c. 33 (*ACEPA*), s. 2(1)(a); *Endangered Species Act*, S.N.S. 1998, c. 11, ss. 2(1)(h) and 11(1).

Scholars have documented the precautionary principle's inclusion in virtually every recently adopted treaty and policy document related to the protection and preservation of the environment (D. Freestone and E. Hey, Origins and Development of the Precautionary Principle, in D. Freestone and E. Hey, eds., *The Precautionary Principle and International Law* (1996), at p. 41. As a result, there may be currently sufficient state practice to allow a good argument that the precautionary principle is a principle of customary international law (J. Cameron and J. Abouchar, The Status of the Precautionary Principle in International Law, in *ibid.*, at p. 52). See also O. McIntyre and T. Mosedale, The Precautionary Principle as a Norm of Customary International Law (1997), 9 *J. Env. L.* 221, at p. 241 (the precautionary principle has indeed crystallized into a norm of customary international law). The Supreme Court of India considers the precautionary principle to be part of the Customary International Law (*A.P. Pollution Control Board v. Nayudu*, 1999 S.O.L. Case No. 53 at p. 8). See also *Vellore Citizens Welfare Forum v. Union of India*, [1996] Supp. 5 S.C.R. 241. In the context of the precautionary principle's tenets, the Town's concerns about pesticides fit well under their rubric of preventive action. [. . .]

Disposition

I have found that By-law 270 was validly enacted . . . For these reasons, I would dismiss the appeal with costs.

Notes and Questions

1. What sources of international law are invoked by L'Heureux-Dubé J. in the reasons above? How do these sources inform her conclusions with respect to the precautionary principle?

2. What does the case suggest is the appropriate role of international law in the interpretation of domestic legislation?

3. Did it matter in this case that the legislation was provincial, dealing with powers delegated to municipalities?

4. What difference did it make that the provision in question was a discretionary provision? What if a municipality refused to exercise its discretion in a precautionary manner?

5. Does the case tell us anything about the role of international law with respect to the common law? Could the precautionary principle be used to reverse the onus of proof in some torts dealing with environmental and human health risks? We return to consider this and other issues relating to the precautionary principle in the Part III.

. . . . .

Gosselin v. Quebec (Attorney General)
[2002] 4 S.C.R. 429, 2002 SCC 84

[This case concerned the validity of a social assistance program in Quebec. Under the program, individuals entitled to social assistance were broken into two groups, those under and those over 30 years of age. For individuals under 30, the program established a base amount payable that was lower than the base amount for individuals over 30. In order to qualify for the higher base amount, individuals under 30 had to enrol in designated work activities or education programs. A key legal issue was whether the program violated section

45 of the *Quebec Charter* which provides that every person in need has a right to "measures of financial assistance and to social measures provided for by law, susceptible of ensuring such person an acceptable standard of living". In addressing this question, the SCC was split over the relevance of the *International Covenant on Economic, Social and Cultural Rights*, an international treaty which Canada has signed and ratified.]

McLACHLIN C.J:

Was s. 45 intended to make the adequacy of a social assistance regime's specific provisions subject to judicial review . . .? Had the legislature intended such an exceptional result, it seems to me that it would have given effect to this intention unequivocally, using precise language. There are examples of legal documents purporting to do just that. For example, Article 11(1) of the *International Covenant on Economic, Social and Cultural Rights*, 993 U.N.T.S. 3, recognizes "the right of everyone to an adequate standard of living for himself and his family, including adequate food, clothing and housing, and to the continuous improvement of living conditions". Article 22 of the *Universal Declaration of Human Rights*, G.A. Res. 217 A (III), U.N. Doc. A/810, at 71 (1948), provides that "[e]veryone, as a member of society, has the right to social security" and is "entitled to realization . . . of the economic, social and cultural rights indispensable for his dignity and the free development of his personality". Article 25(1) provides that:

> Everyone has the right to a standard of living adequate for the health and well-being of himself and of his family, including food, clothing, housing and medical care and necessary social services, and the right to security in the event of unemployment, sickness, disability, widowhood, old age or other lack of livelihood in circumstances beyond his control.

In contrast to these provisions, which unambiguously and directly define the rights to which individuals are entitled (even though they may not be actionable), s. 45 of the *Quebec Charter* is highly equivocal. Indeed, s. 45 features two layers of equivocation. Rather than speaking of a right to an acceptable standard of living, s. 45 refers to a right to measures. Moreover, the right is not to measures that ensure an acceptable standard of living, but to measures that are susceptible of ensuring an acceptable standard of living. In my view, the choice of the term "susceptible" underscores the idea that the measures adopted must be oriented toward the goal of ensuring an acceptable standard of living, but are not required to achieve success. In other words, s. 45 requires only that the government be able to point to measures of the appropriate *kind*, without having to defend the wisdom of its enactments. This interpretation is also consistent with the respective institutional competence of courts and legislatures when it comes to enacting and fine-tuning basic social policy.

For these reasons, I am unable to accept the view that s. 45 invites courts to review the adequacy of Quebec's social assistance regime. The *Social Aid Act* provides the *kind* of "measures provided for by law" that satisfy s. 45. I conclude that there was no breach of s. 45 of the *Quebec Charter* in this case.

L'HEUREUX-DUBÉ J. (dissenting):

I subscribe entirely to the exhaustive analysis of s. 45 of the *Quebec Charter* undertaken by Robert J.A. in his dissenting opinion in the Quebec Court of Appeal. For the reasons he expresses, I conclude as he does as to a violation of s. 45 of the *Quebec Charter* in the present case.

As Robert J.A. states (at p. 1092): [TRANSLATION] Section 45 of the *Quebec Charter* thus bears a very close resemblance to article 11 of the *International Covenant on Economic, Social and Cultural Rights*, which, as the Court of Appeal notes, para. 10 of the *Report on the Fifth Session* of the United Nations Committee on Economic, Social and Cultural Rights further specifies as containing: "a minimum core obligation to ensure the satisfaction of, at the very least, minimum essential levels [of subsistence needs and the provision of basic services]" (*ibid.*, at p. 1093).

I am also in agreement that the *Quebec Charter* [TRANSLATION] "was intended to establish a domestic law regime that reflects Canada's international commitments" and that

> [TRANSLATION] the quasi-constitutional right guaranteed by section 45 to social and economic measures susceptible of ensuring an acceptable standard of living includes, at the very least, the right of every person in need to receive what Canadian society objectively considers sufficient means to provide the basic necessities of life.

Notes and Questions

As seen above, both the majority and the dissent considered Canada's international human rights obligations in order to provide context for the interpretation of section 45 of the *Quebec Charter*. Where they disagreed was whether the *Quebec Charter* was intended to implement specific international human rights obligations. Thus if the majority had agreed with L'Heureux-Dubé J. that section 45 was intended to implement international human rights obligations, it seems likely that it would have been prepared to read these international obligations into section 45. What difference does it make to the role of international law in interpreting section 45, whether the section was intended to implement the international treaty or not?

. . . . .

Canadian Foundation for Children v. Canada
[2004] 1 S.C.R. 76, 2004 SCC 4

[The last of our three illustrative cases arose as a *Charter* challenge to section 43 of the *Criminal Code*, which permits school teachers and parents to use minor corrective force in some circumstances without facing criminal sanction. It provides:

> Every schoolteacher, parent or person standing in the place of a parent is justified in using force by way of correction toward a pupil or child, as the case may be, who is under his care, if the force does not exceed what is *reasonable under the circumstances* (emphasis added).

The Foundation sought a declaration that section 43 violated sections 7, 12, and 15 of the *Charter of Rights and Freedoms*. A key issue in the case was the meaning of the phrase, "reasonable under the circumstances" under section 43. The Foundation contended that this phrase was unconstitutionally vague. In considering this argument, the SCC makes reference to various sources of international law.]

McLACHLIN C.J.

The first limitation arises from the behaviour for which s. 43 provides an exemption, simple non-consensual application of force. Section 43 does not exempt from criminal sanction conduct that causes harm or raises a reasonable prospect of harm. It can be invoked only in cases of non-consensual application of force that results neither in harm nor in the prospect of bodily harm. This limits its operation to the mildest forms of assault. People must know that if their conduct raises an apprehension of bodily harm they cannot rely on s. 43. Similarly, police officers and judges must know that the defence cannot be raised in such circumstances.

Within this limited area of application, further precision on what is reasonable under the circumstances may be derived from international treaty obligations. Statutes should be construed to comply with Canada's international obligations: *Ordon Estate v. Grail*, [1998] 3 S.C.R. 437, ¶137. Canada's international commitments confirm that physical correction that either harms or degrades a child is unreasonable.

Canada is a party to the United Nations *Convention on the Rights of the Child*. Article 5 of the Convention requires state parties to

> respect the responsibilities, rights and duties of parents or . . . other persons legally responsible for the child, to provide, in a manner consistent with the evolving capacities of the child, appropriate direction and guidance in the exercise by the child of the rights recognized in the present Convention.

Article 19(1) requires the state party to

> protect the child from all forms of physical or mental violence, injury or abuse, neglect or negligent treatment, maltreatment or exploitation, including sexual abuse, while in the care of parent(s), legal guardian(s) or any other person who has the care of the child. [Emphasis added.]

Finally, Article 37(a) requires state parties to ensure that "[n]o child shall be subjected to torture or other cruel, inhuman or degrading treatment or punishment" (emphasis added). This language is also found in the *International Covenant on Civil and Political Rights*, Can. T.S. 1976 No. 47, to which Canada is a party. Article 7 of the Covenant states that "[n]o one shall be subjected to torture or to cruel, inhuman or degrading treatment or punishment". The preamble to the *International Covenant on Civil and Political Rights* makes it clear that its provisions apply to "all members of the human family". From these international obligations, it follows that what is "reasonable under the circumstances" will seek to avoid harm to the child and will never include cruel, inhuman or degrading treatment.

Neither the *Convention on the Rights of the Child* nor the *International Covenant on Civil and Political Rights* explicitly require state parties to ban all corporal punishment of children. In the process of monitoring compliance with the *International Covenant on Civil and Political Rights*, however, the Human Rights Committee of the United Nations has expressed the view that corporal punishment of children in schools engages Article 7's prohibition of degrading treatment or punishment: see for example, *Report of the Human Rights Committee*, vol. I, UN GAOR, Fiftieth Session, Supp. No. 40 (A/50/40) (1995), at paras. 426 and 434; *Report of the Human Rights Committee*, vol. I, UN GAOR, Fifty-fourth Session, Supp. No. 40 (A/54/40) (1999), at para. 358; *Report of the Human Rights Committee*, vol. I, UN GAOR, Fifty-fifth Session, Supp. No. 40 (A/55/40) (2000), at paras. 306 and 429. The Committee has not expressed a similar opinion regarding parental use of mild corporal punishment.

Section 43's ambit is further defined by the direction to consider the circumstances under which corrective force is used. National and international precedents have set out factors to be considered. Article 3 of the *European Convention on Human Rights*, 213 U.N.T.S. 221, forbids inhuman and degrading treatment. The European Court of Human Rights, in determining whether parental treatment of a child was severe enough to fall within the scope of Article 3, held that assessment must take account of "all the circumstances of the case, such as the nature and context of the treatment, its duration, its physical and mental effects and, in some instances, the sex, age and state of health of the victim": Eur. Court H.R., *A. v. United Kingdom*, judgment of 23 September 1998, *Reports of Judgments and Decisions* 1998-VI, p. 2699. These factors properly focus on the prospective effect of the corrective force upon the child, as required by s. 43.

By contrast, it is improper to retrospectively focus on the gravity of a child's wrongdoing, which invites a punitive rather than corrective focus. "[T]he nature of the offence calling for correction", an additional factor suggested in *R. v. Dupperon* (1984), 16 C.C.C. (3d) 453 (Sask. C.A.), at p. 460, is thus not a relevant contextual consideration. The focus under s. 43 is on the correction of the child, not on the gravity of the precipitating event. Obviously, force employed in the absence of any behaviour requiring correction by definition cannot be corrective.

Determining what is "reasonable under the circumstances" in the case of child discipline is also assisted by social consensus and expert evidence on what constitutes reasonable corrective discipline. The criminal law often uses the concept of reasonableness to accommodate evolving mores and avoid successive "fine-tuning" amendments. It is implicit in this technique that current social consensus on what is reasonable may be considered. It is wrong for caregivers or judges to apply their own subjective notions of what is reasonable; s. 43 demands an objective appraisal based on current learning and consensus. Substantial consensus, particularly when supported by expert evidence, can provide guidance and reduce the danger of arbitrary, subjective decision making.

Based on the evidence currently before the Court, there are significant areas of agreement among the experts on both sides of the issue [. . .] Corporal punishment of children under two years is harmful to them, and has no corrective value given the cognitive limitations of children under two years of age. Corporal punishment of teenagers is harmful, because it can induce aggressive or antisocial behaviour. Corporal punishment using objects, such as rulers or belts, is physically and emotionally harmful. Corporal punishment which involves slaps or blows to the head is harmful. These types of punishment, we may conclude, will not be reasonable.

Contemporary social consensus is that, while teachers may sometimes use corrective force to remove children from classrooms or secure compliance with instructions, the use of corporal punishment by teachers is not acceptable. Many school boards forbid the use of corporal punishment, and some provinces and territories have legislatively prohibited its use by teachers: see, e.g., *Schools Act, 1997*, S.N.L. 1997, c. S-12.2, s. 42; *School Act*, R.S.B.C. 1996, c. 412, s. 76(3); *Education Act*, S.N.B. 1997, c. E-1.12, s. 23; *School Act*, R.S.P.E.I. 1988, c. S-2.1, s. 73; *Education Act*, S.N.W.T. 1995, c. 28, s. 34(3); *Education Act*, S.Y. 1989-90, c. 25, s. 36. This consensus is consistent with Canada's international obligations, given the findings of the Human Rights Committee of the United Nations noted above. Section 43 will protect a teacher who uses reasonable, corrective force to restrain or remove a child in appropriate circumstances. Substantial societal consensus, supported by expert evidence and Canada's treaty obligations, indicates that corporal punishment by teachers is unreasonable.

Notes and Questions

1. Unlike *Gosselin*, whether the legislative provision at issue was an attempt to implement treaty obligations was not an issue in this case. In fact, it seems clear that section 43 of the *Criminal Code* is not intended to implement Canada's international obligations. Rather, the issue was whether the provision being challenged was consistent with Canada's international human rights obligations. Is the SCC's use of binding international human rights obligations in this case in keeping with the analysis in the Brandon article? Is the approach in this case consistent with the majority in *Gosselin*, which took the view that the provision at issue was not an attempt to implement treaty obligations?

2. The most recent SCC case dealing with the relationship between international and domestic law is *R. v. Hape*, 2007 SCC 26. In this case, the court approves an "adoptionist" approach to the reception of customary international law. In the words of Lebel J.:

> In my view, following the common law tradition, it appears that the doctrine of adoption operates in Canada such that prohibitive rules of customary international law should be incorporated into domestic law in the absence of conflicting legislation. The automatic incorporation of such rules is justified on the basis that international custom, as the law of nations, is also the law of Canada unless, in a valid exercise of its sovereignty, Canada declares that its law is to the contrary. Parliamentary sovereignty dictates that a legislature may violate international law, but that it must do so expressly. Absent an express derogation, the courts may look to prohibitive rules of customary international law to aid in the interpretation of Canadian law and the development of the common law.

Is the approach in *Hape* consistent with the analysis offered in the Brandon article? Can you think of a good reason not to apply the same approach to ratified treaties?

Part III — Domestic Application of the Precautionary Principle: A Case Study

In the previous Part, we examined the general principles that govern the application of international law in the domestic realm, particularly environmental law. To take this inquiry further, we now turn to a case study that focusses on the growing incorporation and influence of the precautionary principle in domestic law, of which the decision in *Spraytech* is but one illustration. The precautionary principle provides a useful vehicle for this case study for several reasons. First of all, it is a highly influential soft law principle in international law. Secondly, it been incorporated into a number of binding international treaties, making it binding on member states in the context of those treaties. As well, as alluded to in *Spraytech*, there has been an ongoing debate about the status of the principle under customary international law. Thirdly, the principle has been incorporated into a variety of environmental statutes in Canada. And finally, the principle has been at the centre of ongoing debates about the adequacy of the common law in dealing with environmental cases, especially in response to scientific uncertainty and the burden of proof in tort cases involving risk of harm resulting from contamination.

As you review the excerpts from the following article, consider the opportunities to use international law to advance the application of the precautionary principle in Canada.

Chris Tollefson & Jamie Thornback, "Litigating the Precautionary Principle in Domestic Courts"
(2008) 19 J. Env. L. & Prac. 33

Divining the Meaning and Implications of the Precautionary Principle

The origins and implications of the precautionary principle are the subject of a considerable and growing scholarly literature. Derivative of the maxim "better safe than sorry", at its core the principle seeks to formalize precaution as a regulatory obligation in the face of environmental threats and scientific uncertainty. In the domain of international law, the principle began to emerge in the early 1980s most notably in the World Charter for Nature (1982). Since that time, it has become a central feature of close to one hundred international agreements and been incorporated into scores of domestic environmental and public health laws worldwide.

Differing formulations of the precautionary principle abound. The most widely-cited version of the precautionary principle is found in Principle 15 of the Rio Declaration (*1992*):

> Where there are threats of serious or irreversible damage, lack of full scientific certainty shall not be used as a reason for postponing cost-effective measures to prevent environmental degradation.

This relatively permissive or "weak" version of the principle is frequently contrasted with a more rigourous version famously approved by environmental activists and scholars at the 1998 Wingspread Conference:

> When an activity raises threats to the environment or human health, precautionary measures should be taken, even if some cause-and-effect relationships are not fully established scientifically.

The chameleon-like nature of the principle has tended to undermine reasoned consideration and debate of its precise meaning and implications. In an effort to provide an operational taxonomy of the principle, Sandin argues that its various formulations can be usefully analyzed along four key dimensions: *threat*, *uncertainty*, *action* and *command*. Under Sandin's approach, *threat* refers to the nature of the imminent harm to the "state of the world" (particularly its seriousness and (ir)reversibility), while *uncertainty* connotes "our (lack of) knowledge as [to] whether and how this threat might materialize". Under most formulations of the principle, where both the threat and uncertainty meet defined thresholds, an *action* obligation is triggered (e.g., to consider "cost effective measures to prevent environmental degradation", "preventative measures" or "regulatory steps"). Finally, the *command* dimension prescribes the legal status of the action to be taken (which may be framed in either mandatory or permissive language, "shall" or "may".)

According to Sandin, a key challenge to operationalizing the precautionary principle lies in the imprecision with which the dimensions of "threat", "uncertainty", "action" and, to a lesser extent, "command" are typically framed. This imprecision problem may be difficult to remedy due to what is, in effect, a "lowest common denominator" phenomenon: namely, that the overall precision of particular formulation of the principle is directly correlated to its least precise dimension. This, he argues, is also true of what he terms the "strength" of the principle (the degree of precaution required by the principle). Thus, the robustness of any particular formulation of the precautionary principle is a function of its weakest element.

Sandin's analysis provides an instructive counterpoint to what appears to be a growing backlash against the principle in academic circles particularly amongst American scholars. While some of these critiques raise compelling questions about the coherence and viability of precaution as a legal principle, others seem motivated by a desire to discredit the principle by portraying it, and its proponents, in alarmist and provocative terms.

One of the more vocal critics of the precautionary principle in its various formulations is Cass Sunstein. Dismissing weak versions of the principle as "unobjectionable, even banal", he attacks stronger versions with surprising ferocity:

> The real problem with the Precautionary Principle in its strongest forms is that it is incoherent; it purports to give guidance, but it fails to do so, because it condemns the very steps that it requires. The regulation that the principle requires always gives rise to risks of its own — and hence the principle bans what it simultaneously mandates. I therefore aim to challenge the Precautionary Principle not because it leads in bad directions, but because read for all its worth, it leads in no direction at all. The principle threatens to be paralyzing, forbidding regulation, inaction, and every step in between.

While critiques such as this are usually targeted at more robust formulations of the principle, Sunstein and others nonetheless advocate for a highly restrictive application of the precautionary principle to "catastrophic risks" so as to avoid its misapplication to lesser risks as a result of irrational fear.

Other academics, however, contend that a proper understanding of the precautionary principle can reduce, not amplify, the effects of irrational fear. Important groundwork on this front has been laid by Professor Applegate. Applegate argues that a "tamed" understanding of the precautionary principle is beginning to emerge. Under this emerging conception, the precautionary principle can provide a procedural vehicle for decision-making in the face of uncertainty. Traditionally, where the principle has not been considered as part of a decision-making process, regulators have only taken a risk into account when it rises to a relatively high standard of certainty. In contrast, where the principle is part of the regulatory equation, a decision-maker is empowered to (and, in some instances, obliged) to take it into account. However, this response must be proportional to the risk, and must adapt as knowledge of the risk becomes more certain. [. . .]

Bringing the Precautionary Principle into Domestic Litigation

There are two distinct avenues for the precautionary principle to enter domestic litigation: through the domestic application of international law, or through its application as a principle of domestic law. Each of these categories may be further subdivided. International law may be applied directly, as binding in its own right; or it may apply indirectly, as an interpretive aid. Likewise, stand-alone principles of domestic law may be derived either from common law or statutory sources.

Direct Application of International Law

Domestic legal systems are broadly classified as either monist or dualist. In monist jurisdictions, both international and domestic law tend to be conceived as elements of a unitary system of law administered by the judiciary. As a result, in these jurisdictions, international law is directly binding on courts, without any further action by the legislature or executive. In contrast, dualist jurisdictions treat international and domestic law as two discrete systems. Before international law can be applied by a court, steps must be taken to render it part of domestic law according to ordinary constitutional principles. For example, a treaty provision is not binding on domestic courts until the legislature has enacted a statute that implements its terms.

Of course, theory rarely maps directly to reality. Some states which are typically thought to be dualist may require treaties to be implemented by legislatures, but may apply customary international law directly. Other states, though considered to be monist, place limits on the direct application of international law, such as requirements that treaties be "self-executing" before they can have domestic effect. Canada is an example of the former; while the United States exemplifies the latter. Thus, in many situations, whether a particular rule of international law can be applied directly by the courts will be a contentious issue.

To date, few courts have accepted that the precautionary principle, as a rule of international law, can be directly applied in domestic litigation. One prominent exception is the Supreme Court of India. In *Vellore Citizens Welfare Forum v. Union of India*, it held that the principle should be deemed to be incorporated into domestic law:

> Even otherwise once [the precautionary principle and polluter pays principle] are accepted as part of the Customary International Law there would be no difficulty in accepting them as part of the domestic law. It is almost an accepted proposition of law that the rules of Customary International Law which are not contrary to the municipal law shall be deemed to have been incorporated in the domestic law and shall be followed by the courts of law.

The significance of this statement must be tempered by the fact that the court had already held that, by operation of applicable constitutional and statutory provisions, the precautionary principle was part of domestic Indian environmental law. This leaves open the question of whether the court would have so readily applied the principle had this not been the case. Also unanswered by the *Vellore* decision are the nature and the weight of the evidence necessary to conclude that the precautionary principle has become a binding norm of customary international law. There are certainly good arguments to be made that, by virtue of state practice, the precautionary principle has now achieved this status, though this conclusion remains controversial.

Indirect Application of International Law

An alternative way for international law to affect domestic litigation is for it to be applied indirectly as an interpretive aid. Generally, courts will be reluctant to apply the precautionary principle in this way if it is inconsistent with applicable domestic law. However, if domestic law is capable of being interpreted in a manner consistent with the precautionary principle, it may play a persuasive interpretive role. This opens the door to the principle being considered in domestic litigation by courts that would otherwise shy away from direct application of the principle as a norm of international law.

The Supreme Court of Canada's decision in *Spraytech* is a good example of the indirect application of international law. While the status of the principle in international law was not fully argued before the Court, the majority reasons cite scholarly opinion to the effect that "a good argument" could be made that it had become "a principle of customary international law". The majority went on to employ the principle as a relevant consideration in upholding the validity of a municipal ban on pesticide use. As such, the decision makes it clear that principles of international law — even those that are not binding on Canada — may be taken into account when interpreting domestic law.

Proponents of the precautionary principle would no doubt have preferred the Supreme Court to have found that, where possible, domestic law must be interpreted in accordance with the precautionary principle. Arguably, this would have been the result if the principle had been shown to be a binding norm of international law. However, until Canadian courts have accepted the precautionary principle as binding, *Spraytech* allows the principle to be invoked in a persuasive manner. If an advantage in this result can be found, it is that parties will not be required to convince a court that Canada would be in breach of its international obligations if the court did not apply the principle. [. . .]

The Common Law

The precautionary principle may also emerge within the common law of a domestic legal system. Where international law is applied, directly or indirectly, the development of a common law precautionary principle may be accelerated. Of course, it is also possible for the principle to emerge completely independently of international law. The common law of Australia, perhaps more than that of any other jurisdiction, has been receptive to arguments about the precautionary principle. In 1998, Charmian Barton explored the use of the principle by Australian courts and argued that, "The acceptance of the principle as a necessary consideration in environmental cases is evidence of its emergence as a common law doctrine".

One of the best known and earliest Australian decisions is *Leatch v. National Parks and Wildlife Service*. In this case, a municipal council planned to build a road through an area that may have contained several endangered species. Although alternative routes could have been chosen, the Director-General of the National Parks and Wildlife Service issued the city a permit to allow it to take or kill endangered fauna in the area they had selected. The decision to issue the permit was appealed to the Land and Environment Court of New South Wales. The relevant legislation did not require the precautionary principle to be applied. Thus, the plaintiffs argued that the principle should be incorporated from international law. Stein J. stated:

> It seems to me unnecessary to enter into this debate. In my opinion the precautionary principle is a statement of common sense and has already been applied by decision-makers in appropriate circumstances prior to the principle being spelt out. It is directed towards the prevention of serious or irreversible harm to the environment in situations of scientific uncertainty. Its premise is that where uncertainty or ignorance exists concerning the nature or scope of environmental harm (whether this follows from policies, decisions or activities), decision makers should be cautious.

As a principle of "common sense" that was not excluded by the relevant legislation, Stein J. held that the precautionary principle was a relevant factor to take into account when deciding whether the permit to take or kill should be issued. In applying the principle, he concluded that the permit should not be granted. In his view, there was insufficient information about the impact that the road would have on a giant burrowing frog population which was believed to be in the area. Alternative routes which had been deemed to be more expensive had to be reconsidered, taking into account the environmental costs of each proposal. It is important to note, however, that Stein J. did not hold that the precautionary principle prohibited road-building of the road through frog habitat but rather that, prior to authorizing construction, regulators were required to secure reliable information about habitat impacts and to properly weigh the advantages and disadvantages of alternative routes. [. . .]

Statutory Law

The precautionary principle may also become domestic law through implicit or explicit adoption in domestic statutes. A growing number of jurisdictions have enacted legislation that explicitly incorporates the precautionary principle either as a substantive decisional criterion or in preambular language. These include the European Union, Australia, Canada, Kenya, and Brazil. In Canada, for example, the principle finds expression a variety of federal statutes including the *Species at Risk Act*, the *Oceans Act*, the *Canadian Environmental Protection Act*, the *Canadian Environmental Assessment Act*, and recently tabled amendments to the *Fisheries Act*.

The principle is also beginning to play an important role in domestic law through what is often termed "implicit incorporation". This commonly occurs in the context of statutory regimes governing pharmaceuticals, food, and pesticides. Often, these regimes will shift the burden of proof to the proponent of a new product. Thus, rather than being allowed to manufacture and distribute products until they have been shown to cause harm to humans or the environment, proponents are required to demonstrate that their products have undergone testing that ensures designated safety standards. For example, U.S. federal law prohibits the introduction of new drugs into interstate commerce until the Federal Drug Administration is satisfied that the results of "adequate tests by all methods reasonably applicable" show that the drugs are safe for their intended use.

At first blush, these illustrations of implicit legislative incorporation of the principle may not seem particularly relevant in litigation that does not bear on the validity of the applicable legislation. Nonetheless, we would argue that that these illustrations can be of indirect assistance in various ways. These include reassuring the judiciary that the precautionary principle can and does operate as a norm of state practice; and bolstering arguments that the principle forms part of an emerging domestic common law and or is evolving toward achieving the status of customary international law.

These arguments will be made even stronger when the principle is explicitly adopted. The European Community ("EC") added the precautionary principle to the EC Treaty with the Maastricht Treaty of 1992. Article 174(2) of the EC Treaty now reads:

> Community policy on the environment shall aim at a high level of protection taking into account the diversity of situations in the various regions of the Community. It shall be based on the precautionary principle and on the principles that preventive action should be taken, that environmental damage should as a priority be rectified at source and that the polluter should pay.

This Article is both explicitly referred to and implicitly implemented in Directives and Regulations. For example, the *Habitats Directive* provides that a plan or project "likely to have a significant effect" may proceed only after national authorities have "ascertained that it will not adversely affect the integrity of the site". The European Court of Justice has referred to Article 174(2) when interpreting subsidiary legislation: see *ARCO Chemie Nederland Ltd and Vereniging Dorpsbeland Hees*. [. . .] The inclusion of the precautionary principle in EC treaties and subsidiary legislation has also had an impact on the domestic law of member states.

Australia has codified the precautionary principle, and other principles of environmental law, in the *Environment Protection and Biodiversity Conservation Act, 1999*. Section 3A sets out "principles of ecologically sustainable development", including the precautionary principle:

> (b) if there are threats of serious or irreversible environmental damage, lack of full scientific certainty should not be used as a reason for postponing measures to prevent environmental degradation;

The principle has also been incorporated into the 1992 *Intergovernmental Agreement on the Environment* and the legislation of some territorial governments. Inclusion of the principle in domestic legislation has led to much greater consideration of the principle by courts and administrative tribunals.

Notes and Questions

1. What difference does it make to its implementation in Canada whether the precautionary principle is customary international law?

2. Reflecting on the principles and cases covered in earlier parts of the chapter, do you agree with the authors' assessment of the range of avenues available for the incorporation and application of the precautionary principle into environmental law in Canada?

3. Under what conditions do you think the principle should be applied in Canada?

4. One of the most common applications that has been advocated for the principle is to reverse the onus of proving harm. What are the implications of such an approach in case of tort law? What about regulatory decisions about the use and release of substances?

Part IV — Key International Environmental Regimes to Watch

We conclude this chapter with a brief overview of four key international regimes with implications for domestic environmental law, to which we return in other chapters. The first of these regimes is the 1992 *Convention on Biological Diversity*. We discuss the implementation of aspects of this Convention in Chapter 8 (parks and wilderness protection) and Chapter 9 (species at risk). The second regime is the 1989 *Basel Convention* on the movement of hazardous waste. Implementation issues for this Convention are addressed in Chapter 4 (environmental regulation). We also consider the environmental implications of the General Agreement on Tariffs and Trade (GATT) and other environmental implications of World Trade Organization; likewise we consider the environmental implications of the North American Free Trade Agreement (NAFTA) and other international agreements governing foreign investment. Linkages between these international regimes and domestic environmental law are revisited in Chapter 4.

Convention on Biological Diversity (CBD)

Elli Louka, *International Environmental Law, Fairness, Effectiveness and World Order*
(Cambridge: Cambridge University Press, 2006) at 299–303

The Biodiversity Convention is the first attempt to deal globally with biodiversity protection. The convention is a framework convention. It does not establish biodiversity protection standards but attempts to create the outline of a regime for biodiversity protection by focusing on *in situ* conservation and, marginally, on the restoration of deteriorated ecosystems and gene bank, management. Declaration of national sovereignty over natural resources, intellectual property rights, and technology transfers become the vehicles for the establishment of such a regime.

The convention emphasizes that states must preserve biodiversity "as far as possible and as appropriate" by undertaking measures that would protect biodiversity in nature or in gene banks. The convention clearly places biodiversity resources under national sovereignty. The convention places emphasis on national and bilateral action based on the presumption that biodiversity can be protected more effectively at the national/bilateral level.

Gene bank development is a supplemental goal in the overall scheme of biodiversity protection. The convention explicitly provides that states must adopt measures of gene bank development "for the purpose of complementing *in situ* measures". *Ex situ* conservation measures should preferably take place in the country of origin. Because most genetic resources are located in developing countries and gene banks are located in developed countries, the convention calls for an increase in the number of gene banks in the developing world. The convention also proposes that it is best for each country to have its own gene banks, an approach that is too limited and not very practicable. Given the possibilities presented by developing regional and even international gene banks, it is not cost-efficient for many developing countries to keep their own gene banks. In the area of gene bank development, self-sufficiency is costly, and collaboration is certainly a more cost-effective means to conserve germplasm.

The article on *in situ* conservation presents this type of conservation as the most fundamental method of protecting biodiversity. States must "as far as possible and as appropriate" establish a system of protected areas; develop guidelines for the selection and management of protected areas; regulate and manage biological resources both within and outside protected areas; promote "environmentally sound and sustainable development" in areas adjacent to protected areas; and adopt the necessary regulatory measures for the protection of endangered species. States must manage and control the risks associated with the release of bioengineered organisms and prevent the introduction of exotic species that may have adverse impacts on endemic species and habitats.

Overall, the article on *in situ* conservation seems intentionally vague so as to give states some latitude in designing their conservation programs. Because in practice *in situ* conservation often has meant total preservation of protected areas based on evictions of the people who inhabit those areas, it would have been desirable if the provisions on *in situ* conservation included a clause that ensured that *in situ* conservation will not be pursued by violating human dignity and human rights.

It must be acknowledged, however, that the Biodiversity Convention is one of the first international treaties to recognize the rights of indigenous peoples and local communities to their "knowledge", "innovations", and "practices". The Biodiversity Convention provides that the consent of indigenous peoples is needed to utilize their knowledge and that there should be equitable sharing of the benefits derived from such knowledge. The specifics of equitable sharing, however, still resist practical application. Parties must submit to the Conference of the Parties (COP) the measures taken to implement the convention. Parties must also submit an evaluation of the effectiveness of these measures in accomplishing the convention's objectives. Reporting on the effectiveness of measures to preserve biodiversity must be based on an accurate assessment of the existing biodiversity. Many attempts have been made to assess the world's biodiversity resources and to value these resources so that the goals of biodiversity protection become more concrete.

More than ten years have elapsed from the signing of the Biodiversity Convention, but not much has happened in terms of making the convention a functional instrument for the protection of biodiversity. Most of the debate on implementation focuses on the issue of access to genetic resources and equitable sharing of benefits derived from biotechnology that is based on such resources. Other issues that have preoccupied the Conference of the Parties include:

- the protection of coral reefs;
- the protection of agricultural biological diversity;
- conducting EIAs and SEAs;
- the global taxonomy initiative;
- the implementation of article 8(j) regarding the rights of indigenous peoples to their knowledge.

- the development of an ecosystem approach;
- the establishment of incentive measures for the protection of diversity by taking into account the distributional impacts of such measures;
- the integration of biodiversity protection into sectors of the economy;
- the protection of forest biodiversity; and
- the protection of coastal areas and integrated coastal zone management.

The Biodiversity Convention has [. . .] three objectives:

- the conservation of biological diversity;
- the sustainable use of its components; and
- and the fair and equitable sharing of benefits arising out of the utilization of genetic resources.

The convention affirms national sovereignty over biodiversity resources. The convention sidelines prior regimes that generated perceptions that biodiversity resources located under the Jurisdiction of a state can be freely accessed.

The convention provides that access to genetic resources must be subject to the prior informed consent of the country of origin. The convention requires state parties to develop legislative and administrative measures in order to share "in a fair and equitable way . . . the benefits arising from the commercial and other utilization of genetic resources" with state parties that provide genetic resources. Although the convention does not give the specifics of fair and equitable sharing, it provides that such sharing must occur on mutually agreed terms. The convention provides for access to and transfer of technology, such as biotechnology, to developing countries "under fair and most favourable terms". Article 19 provides that each party must take measures to provide for the participation in technological research activities by parties, especially developing countries, which provided the genetic resources for such research. State parties must take measures to advance priority access, on a fair and equitable basis, by developing countries, to benefits coming from technology. Such access is provided, however, if the technology is based on the genetic resources found in these developing countries.

The convention clarifies that new and additional financial resources are needed to enable developing countries to meet "the agreed full incremental costs" of implementing the convention. The extent to which developing countries are to implement the convention depends on developed countries executing their commitments with regard to the provision of financial resources and transfer of technology. In this context, the convention elucidates — in a spirit echoing concerns vocalized during the WSSD summit — that the implementation of the convention by developing countries "will take fully into account the fact that . . . development and eradication of poverty are the first and overriding priorities of the developing country Parties". A financial mechanism is to be established that would provide resources to developing countries.

The convention recognizes the rights of indigenous peoples in their knowledge and innovations. The convention provides that states must encourage the equitable sharing of benefits arising from the utilization of knowledge, innovations, and practices of indigenous peoples.

Notes and Questions

1. The Convention is intended both to protect biodiversity and ensure an equitable sharing of the benefits arising from the use of genetic resources. How well does the CBD appear to balance these goals?

2. The major threats to biodiversity are generally recognized to be habitat loss, climate change, invasive species and pollution. How effectively are these threats recognized in the mandate of the CBD to protect biodiversity?

3. Canada has ratified the CBD. What legislation do you think is needed to comply with Canada's commitments under the convention? Compare your answer with what steps Canada has actually taken on the biodiversity front as discussed in Chapters 8 and 9.

The Basel Convention

Ifeoma Onyerikam, *Achieving Compliance with the Basel Convention on Transboundary Movement of Hazardous Wastes*
(University of Alberta Faculty of Law, 2007) [unpublished]

Prior to 1989, transboundary movements of hazardous wastes were governed by the international law principle of "good neighborliness" or *sic utere tuo, ut alienum non laedas.* This simply means that States have an obligation to control activities within their jurisdiction and ensure that activities within their jurisdiction do not harm the resources of other States. As a general principle, the scope of its application was narrow and there was no enforcement mechanism to ensure compliance. Though this principle over time had developed into a rule of customary international law, the problems associated with the application of customary international law made it difficult for States to rely solely on this rule to regulate transboundary movement of hazardous waste. That was why, in 1981, the Governing Council of the United Nations Environmental Programme (UNEP) mandated a group of officials expert in environmental law to determine subject areas for increased global and regional co-operation for expansion of environmental law.

Toxic waste transport, handling and disposal were identified as one of the major subject areas for increased international co-operation. One reason for the identification of hazardous wastes as an area deserving international co-operation could be linked to the growing demand by industrialized nations for disposal sites in the developing States, especially in Africa, and the number of accidents from hazardous wastes transportation and disposal that occurred within that decade. The disappearance of landfill sites in the industrialized nations, the escalating disposal costs between the industrialized nations and the converse cheap disposal costs in the developing world and the difficulty of obtaining approval for incineration facilities contributed to the demand for waste disposal in developing States. [. . .]

The Conference of the Plenipotentiaries on the Global Convention on the Control of Transboundary Movements of Hazardous Wastes was thus convened in Basel from March 20–22, 1989 (hereinafter the Basel Conference). [. . .] 116 States were represented. The draft convention was considered and adopted by the parties on March 22, 1989. [. . .] 36 States signed the Convention on March 22, 1989.

The *Basel Convention* finally entered into force on May 5, 1992 upon the deposit of the 20th instrument of accession. The delay in the ratification by States could be attributed to several controversies raised during the negotiations. For instance, the African nations (supported by some non-governmental organizations like Greenpeace) were in favour of a complete ban of all transboundary waste shipment, whereas some of the developed nations advocated for regulation rather than a complete ban. Failing to meet their main objectives, the

African nations nevertheless insisted on stringent measures, which were accepted by some of the industrialized nations, while others refused and deferred their signature.

The refusal by States to adopt a complete ban of transboundary movements of hazardous wastes did not deter the African nations from pursuing, and insisting on, a complete ban. Their efforts yielded fruits in March 1994 when the parties by Decision II/12 adopted the Basel Ban. The Basel Ban aims at banning the transport of hazardous wastes from OECD States to non-OECD States, whether for recycling or disposal. [. . .]

Although the Ban Amendment has been incorporated into the *Basel Convention* as Article 4A, it has not entered into force having not received the required number of ratifications. The delay in ratification may be attributed to the possible loss of economic gains from the transactions by the developing world, such as China, India, and the Philippines, that depend economically on the recyclable wastes. The developing countries are attracted by the foreign exchange to be earned from hazardous wastes transactions even though they often do not have the appropriate disposal or recycling facilities. [. . .]

The *Basel Convention* has undergone further amendments. The absence of provisions on liability and compensation in the Convention, coupled with the concerns expressed by developing countries of lack of funds and technology to combat accidental spills and illegal dumping, led to negotiations on a liability protocol. The necessity for such a liability protocol was based on the provisions of Article 13 of the *Rio Declaration* and the need to provide for third party liability. Negotiations were concluded and parties adopted the *Basel Protocol* on December 10, 1999 at the 5th Conference of the parties. The *Protocol* aims at providing a comprehensive regime of liability and compensation for damage resulting from transboundary movement of hazardous wastes and other wastes.

The *Basel Protocol* is not yet in force having not received the required number of ratifications to bring it into force. The delay in ratification could be linked to issues of implementation and costs.

Scope and Objectives

The Convention only applies to wastes that are "hazardous" and are subject to transboundary movement. A waste is hazardous if: it is listed in Annex I; it exhibits any of the characteristics in Annex III, such as flammability, explosivity, toxicity, and ecotoxicity; or it is defined as hazardous by the national laws of any State. Transboundary movement has been defined as "movement of hazardous wastes or other wastes from an area under the national jurisdiction of a State to or through an area under the national jurisdiction of another State provided two States are involved". This means that wastes not subject to transfrontier movement are not covered under the Convention. This definition is significant in that it covers not only obvious cases of transfrontier movement, for example, movement from the generating State to the disposing State, but also situations where the disposer and the generator are in the same State but during the course of the shipment the waste passes through another State. Radioactive wastes and wastes arising from the normal operations of a ship are excluded from the scope of the Convention. These types of wastes are excluded because other treaties or international instruments already cover them.

The key objectives of the *Basel Convention* are to minimize the generation of hazardous wastes in terms of quantity and dangerousness, dispose of hazardous wastes as close to the source of generation as possible, ensure an environmentally sound disposal of wastes, and as far as possible reduce the movement of hazardous wastes and the risks of accidents associated with such transportation.

Relevant Provisions of the Basel Convention

Generally, State parties are required *inter alia* to reduce the generation of hazardous wastes by adopting clean production methods, ensure that wastes generated are disposed of in an environmentally sound manner, refrain from exporting hazardous wastes to States that have banned the importation of the hazardous wastes, obtain the prior consent of the importing and transit States before exporting any waste from its territory, and comply with provisions of the Convention in the transboundary movement of the hazardous wastes and the international rules on packaging and labeling of products for shipment. [. . .]

The obligations imposed on the parties can be grouped into two: transportation obligations and disposal obligations. The Convention requires that exportation of hazardous wastes should only take place where the exporting State lacks the technical capacity and expertise to dispose of the wastes in an environmentally sound manner, or the waste is required as a raw material for recycling or recovery in the State of import. This requirement imposes two conditions that must be simultaneously satisfied before exportation can take place. Firstly, the exporting State must demonstrate lack of technical capacity and expertise to dispose of the wastes. Secondly, the importing State must have the technical expertise and appropriate disposal or recycling facilities to manage the hazardous wastes in an environmentally sound manner. Where both conditions are not satisfied, an exporting State is prohibited from exporting the hazardous wastes.

Environmentally sound management of wastes requires that there exist appropriate disposal facilities and precautionary measures for the management of hazardous wastes. It also involves addressing the issue of hazardous wastes through an "integrated life cycle approach" that involves strong controls from the generation of hazardous wastes to storage, transport, treatment, re-use, recycling, recovery and final disposal. The obligation to ensure that exported wastes are managed in an environmentally sound manner in the country of import has been imposed on the exporting State. There is evidence to show that States have on some occasions violated or ignored this obligation. For instance, the constant movement of hazardous wastes to developing States such as China, India and African States, where the wastes are disposed of in an unsound manner, is evidence of such non-compliance by States. A Greenpeace news report indicates that tones of hazardous wastes from computer and other metal scraps were continually dumped in China in 2005 and that the hazardous wastes were recycled manually. The Basel Action Network, a non-governmental organization, reports that about 500 containers filled with used electronic equipment are exported to Lagos, Nigeria every month where they are resold and the remainder dumped in landfills and later burnt, releasing dangerous substances into the environment.

Notes and Questions

1. The *Basel Convention* has been implemented in Canada through regulations under the *Canadian Environmental Protection Act*. Canadian government efforts ostensibly aimed at implementing the Convention gave rise to a lawsuit brought by SD Myers (a US-based hazardous waste disposal company) under the investor claim provisions of NAFTA chapter 11: see further discussion Chapter 4 (environmental regulation).

2. Based on the article above, can you assess the effectiveness of this Convention in preventing the shipment of hazardous material to developing countries that lack the capacity to ensure proper disposal?

3. What, if any, improvement would you make to the Convention? Can you think of reasons why these improvements were not included?

World Trade Institutions

Elli Louka, *International Environmental Law, Fairness, Effectiveness and World Order*
(Cambridge: Cambridge University Press, 2006) at 383–394

The free movement of goods and services among states has been the exception rather than the norm in international trade. Countries have regulated international trade through a number of tariff and nontariff barriers. Every country has enacted its share of tariff and nontariff rules that put restrictions on foreign imports, thereby making foreign products more expensive than domestic products. These rules have acted as a barrier to international trade and have limited the choices available to the ultimate consumer.

Ideas of liberalism that free trade should be pursued for the benefit of the ultimate consumer, through the gradual elimination of tariff and nontariff barriers, launched the negotiations in 1946 for the development of an International Trade Organization. Eventually, countries agreed to adopt a milder version of a General Agreement on Tariffs and Trade (GATT). GATT acted as a legal agreement/quasi-legal institution for the regulation of international trade with the ultimate goal of bringing down the barriers to trade.

Since its inception in 1946, GATT has gone through several rounds of tariff reductions. In 1994, after seven years of negotiations, the World Trade Organization (WTO) emerged. The WTO manages a legal apparatus that includes the provisions of GATT as well as a General Agreement on Trade in Services (GATS), an Agreement on Trade-Related Aspects of Intellectual Property Rights (TRIPs), an Agreement on Sanitary and Phytosanitary Measures (SPS), and an Understanding on Rules and Procedures Governing the Settlement of Disputes (DSU). These agreements were opened for signature at Marrakesh in 1994 and entered into force in 1995.

The WTO has become the institution through which all important trade matters are discussed, including conflicts between national policies and trade. As an international institution, the WTO presents a much-needed institutional framework alongside the International Monetary Fund (IMF) and the World Bank. The WTO has had already the opportunity to examine many matters that were previously reserved for national policy making. Such is the intrusion of the WTO into national and international policy making that some argue that the WTO is becoming a central lawmaking and adjudicative institution in international affairs. [. . .]

The Treaties

From its beginnings, GATT included provisions that were designed to reduce tariff and nontariff barriers. What has been called the "national treatment rule" included in article III of GATT provides that once goods have been imported from another member country they must be treated, by the laws of the importing country, no less favorably than goods produced domestically. Another rule that has been invoked frequently in international transactions is the "most favored nation" rule that provides that member states of the GATT must treat equally their trading partners by providing the same conditions to all of them for imports and exports of "like goods".

Article XX constitutes one of the most discussed articles of GATT because it provides general exceptions to the rules of GATT. Article XX allows for exceptions to free trade for the protection of natural resources and the environment. Article XX provides that:

> Subject to the requirement that such measures are not applied in a manner which would constitute a means of arbitrary or unjustifiable discrimination between countries where the same conditions pre-

> vail, or disguised restriction on international trade nothing in this Agreement shall be construed to prevent the adoption or enforcement by any contracting party of measures:
>
> > . . . (b) necessary to protect human, animal or plant life or health;
> >
> > . . . (g) relating to the conservation of exhaustible natural resources if such measures are made effective in conjunction with restrictions on domestic production or consumption.

GATS contains a general exceptions clause in article XIV, which is similar to that included in article XX of GATT. One of the purposes of the new Committee on Trade and Environment (CTE), created under the auspices of WTO, is to examine the interconnection among trade, services, and the environment to determine whether article XIV requires any modification.

Another WTO agreement that goes to the heart of consumer protection involves the Sanitary and Phytosanitary Measures (SPS) Agreement. The SPS agreement provides that member states may adopt sanitary and phytosanitary measures for the purposes of food safety, human, animal, and plant health and safety. But it provides simultaneously that SPS measures must be based on science, should not create unnecessary obstacles to trade, should not arbitrarily discriminate between countries where the same conditions apply. Furthermore, SPS measures must be based on a risk assessment and must be transparent.

The TRIPs agreement provides that countries can recognize patents on most products and processes including pharmaceuticals, modified microorganisms, and rrucrobiological processes (namely, blotechnology devices). Countries can protect plant varieties under patents or other *sui generis* systems, for instance, various versions of plant breeders' rights. The agreement gives countries some sort of discretion in deciding whether patents can be granted to "essentially biological processes for the production of plants and animals" (art. 27.3(b)). There also are exceptions to the provision of intellectual property rights if the refusal to grant such rights is done to protect public order, morality, human, animal, and plant life or health or to avoid adverse environmental effects (art. 27.2). However, the refusal to grant a patent cannot be based on an explanation that the national laws and regulations of a country have yet to approve the product or process. Thus, although this exception could be used occasionally to avert the assertion of intellectual property rights for environmental reasons, it is likely to be strictly interpreted and unlikely to be used lightly for granting derogations from the spirit of the agreement.

Dispute Settlement

The 1994 WTO agreement includes an Annex on "Understanding on Rules and Procedures Governing the Settlement of Disputes" (DSU). The DSU establishes the Dispute Settlement Body (DSB), ad hoc panels and the Appellate Body. The purpose of the DSB is to administer the dispute settlement proceedings. It is comprised of all members of the WTO and it is a political rather than a Judicial body. If members of the WTO face a dispute, they may refer the dispute to the DSB, which, in turn, would try to mediate the issue. If mediation or conciliation fails, the parties may ask the DSB to convene a panel. Unlike the recommendations of GATT panels, the recommendations of the WTO panels become binding when they are adopted by the DSB, an adoption that is deemed automatic within sixty days, unless a consensus is formed in the DSB against a panel's recommendation. Furthermore, unlike GATT proceedings, panel decisions can be appealed before the Appellate Body on legal grounds. Again, the report of the Appellate Body is deemed to be automatically adopted by the DSB unless there *is* a consensus against its adoption.

The DSU has increased the power of panels significantly. [As such] the decisions of the panels are not . . . vulnerable to the capriciousness of a member state. This dispute settlement procedure makes possible, for the first time, in the GATT/WTO system third-party adjudication. The general discontent with GATT dispute settlement arrangement, which led to the adoption of the DSU, is indicative of the quest in the international system for effective dispute resolution mechanisms.

Traditional public international law acts as a sort of constitutional law that provides a set of basic norms, and guidelines for their interpretation. The lack of a dispute resolution tribunal with mandatory jurisdiction in international law sets the DSU of the WTO as an enviable exception. *[. . .]*

1998 Shrimp-Turtle Case

The *Shrimp-Turtle* case involved the extraterritorial application of the U.S. endangered species legislation. According to this legislation, the United States required those who capture shrimp to use approved Turtle Excluder Devices (TEDS) at all times and in all areas (with certain exceptions) where there was the likelihood that shrimp harvesting would affect sea turtles.

Section 609(a) of the Act 31 required the Secretary of Commerce to initiate bilateral or multilateral agreements with foreign governments with regard to the adoption of similar conservation measures by other countries. Section 609(b)(1) imposed an import ban on shrimp harvested with technology that would adversely affect turtles. For shrimp to be imported, they would have to be certified. There are two types of certification that are required annually. The first certification would be issued to countries that have a fishing environment that does not pose a threat to the taking of turtles in the course of shrimp harvesting. The second certification would be granted to countries that provide documentation that they maintain a regulatory program similar to that of the United States. In addition, these countries would have to prove that the incidental taking of sea turtles is comparable to that of the United States. The program put in place by a foreign government had to be comparable to the U.S. program in terms of effectiveness and had to provide for credible enforcement. Countries in the Caribbean/western Atlantic region were exempted from certification for three years, during which time they had to phase in a regulatory program. [. . .]

Because the United States regulations were in accord with article XX(g), the question was whether they fulfilled the requirements of the chapeau of article XX. Legitimate measures adopted in accordance with article XX(g) must not be used

> in a manner which would constitute a means of arbitrary or unjustifiable discrimination between countries where the same conditions prevail, or a disguised restriction on international trade.

The Appellate Body elaborated further on the level of review required by the chapeau of article XX.

> 1. the measures adopted must not constitute arbitrary discrimination between countries where the same conditions prevail;
>
> 2. the measures adopted must not constitute *unjustifiable* discrimination between countries where the same conditions prevail;
>
> 3. the measures adopted must not constitute a *disguised* restriction on international trade.

According to the Appellate Body, the chapeau of article XX is an expression of the principle of good faith. The principle of good faith is a principle of general law and an international rule and it controls the exercise of rights of states.

The Appellate Body concluded that the U.S. measures were an "unjustifiable discrimination" because they imposed on an exporting WTO member the adoption of identical regulatory requirements to those applied by the United States. The Appellate Body claimed, thus, that the United States established "a rigid and unbending standard. The U.S. measures failed to take into account "different conditions" that may occur in the territory of other state members of WTO. The failure of the United States to use diplomacy, before engaging in the imposition of unilateral measures, and the failure to enter into negotiations with the affected states constituted the basis of discriminatory behavior". The Appellate Body mentioned the decision taken by the Ministers at Marrakesh to establish a Permanent Committee on Trade and Environment (CTE). In that decision, the ministers referred to the Rio Declaration and Agenda 21 that established the terms of reference of the CTE. The Appellate Body also referred to a number of international instruments and the importance of reaching consensus on the adoption of measures that deal with the global environment (e.g., article 5 of the Biodiversity Convention and the Convention on the Conservation of Migratory Species of Wild Animals). [. . .]

Because the Appellate Body therefore found that the U.S. regulations constituted an arbitrary and unjustifiable discrimination, it did not proceed further to examine the third standard provided for by the chapeau of article XX — that of "disguised restriction on international trade".

In making this final determination, the Appellate Body took pains to emphasize that its decision does not constitute an intrusion into the public policy matters of states:

> We have *not* decided that the protection and preservation of the environment is of no significance to the Members of the WTO. Clearly, it is. We have *not* decided that the sovereign nations that are Members of the WTO cannot adopt effective measures to protect endangered species, such as sea turtles. Clearly they can and should. And we have *not* decided that sovereign states should not act together bilaterally, plurilaterally or multilaterally, either within the WTO or in other international fora, to protect endangered species or to otherwise protect the environment. Clearly, they should and do [emphasis in the original].

2001 Shrimp-Turtle Case

After the conclusion of the 1998 *Shrimp-Turtle* case, the United States modified its regulations. According to the new regulations, a country may apply for certification even if it does not use TEDS. In such a case, the country has to prove that it is implementing and enforcing a "comparably effective" regulatory program. The United States also entered into multilateral negotiations with the states concerned, including Malaysia, so as to proceed with a multilateral agreement for protection of sea turtles in the course of shrimp harvesting. The negotiations were not fruitful; as a result, the United States resolved to ban the imports of shrimp from Malaysia. Malaysia claimed that the United States had an obligation, according to the 1998 decision of the Appellate Body, not only to enter into negotiations but also to conclude an agreement.

The panel viewed the obligation of the United States, as imposed by the 1998 *Shrimp-Turtle* decision, as an obligation to negotiate in good faith an international agreement rather than as an obligation to conclude an agreement, and ruled against Malaysia.

The Appellate Body agreed with the panel. The Appellate Body argued additionally that requiring the United States to conclude an agreement with Malaysia in order to avoid a characterization of the turtle protective measure as arbitrary or discriminatory — would amount to giving Malaysia in effect a veto power over whether the United States can fulfill its obligations under the WTO. The Appellate Body concurred with the panel that the efforts of the United States regarding the negotiation of an agreement with Malaysia were serious and good faith efforts on the basis of "active participation and financial support to the negotiations". Thus, the Appellate Body concluded that a commitment to an, in principle, multilateral method would give ground to unilateral action when the multilateral approach fails to produce desirable results.

Asbestos Case

Another article of the GATT that has come under scrutiny is Article III(4), which includes the national treatment requirement. Article III(4) states:

> The products of the territory of any Member imported into the territory of any other Member shall be accorded treatment no less favorable than that accorded to *like products* of national origin in respect of all laws, regulations and requirements affecting their internal sale, offering for sale, purchase, transportation, distribution or use . . . [emphasis added].

The question that came before the panel was whether Canadian imports into France, such as asbestos fibers, are like certain other kinds of fibers. According to the French authorities, supported by the EU, asbestos fibers were not "like" other fibers because of the health risks associated with asbestos. Canada, by contrast, argued that health risks should not be taken into account when deciding on the likeness of products. The panel agreed with Canada by applying four criteria that had been applied unfailingly in prior cases when deciding the "likeness as below" of products:

1. the properties, nature, and quality of products;
2. the end-uses of products;
3. consumer's tastes and habits; and
4. the tariff classification of products.

The EU sought to reverse the panel's decision, claiming, *inter alia*, that the panel erred in its application of the concept of like products because it excluded from its consideration the health risks associated with asbestos fibers. The Appellate Body" agreed with the EU and specified that the inquiry into the first criterion of physical properties of a product should include an analysis of the risks posed by the product on human health. The Appellate Body ruled that the carcinogenicity and toxicity of asbestos fibers are an aspect of their physical properties that separates them from other fibers. The Appellate Body ruled that the panel erred when it failed to take into account evidence relating to the consumers' tastes and habits in relation to asbestos fibers and other fibers.

Notes and Questions

1. What opportunities do you see for WTO/GATT trade rules to play a constructive role in addressing environmental issues internationally?

2. What threats do the WTO/GATT rules pose for the development of international environmental law?

3. How do you expect these international trade rules to affect environmental law and policy in Canada? Do you see them as a net positive or negative influence? Explain.

International Investment Agreements

Chris Tollefson & W.A.W. Neilson, "Investor Rights and Sustainable Development" in Kevin Gallagher, ed., *Handbook and Trade and Environment* (Edward Elgar, 2009)

Controversy surrounding the protection of investor rights through international investment agreements (IIAs) is of longstanding. This has been particularly so in the context of the relationship between developed countries (DCs) and their least developed country (LDC) counterparts. From a LDC perspective, such protections have traditionally been seen as a substantial derogation from state sovereignty; fettering not only the ability of a host state to determine domestic policy priorities (most notably with respect to resource management and development) but also, more generally, its ability to regulate the activities of transnational corporate (TNC) investors.

The constraining impact of IIAs on domestic policy space has also been a thorny issue within the more developed economies. Here the overriding concern has been the impact of IIAs on the ability of governments to enact measures to protect the environment and public health. Given these various concerns, it is perhaps not surprising that, over the last twenty years, three successive initiatives to broker broad-based multilateral investment treaties (under the auspices of the United Nations, the OECD and most recently the WTO) have ended in failure.

Yet despite this pervasive skepticism about and resistance to IIAs, the last two decades has nonetheless seen a dramatic consolidation of investor rights in the realm of international law that has been accompanied by an unprecedented expansion in global foreign direct investment (FDI). During this period, both FDI flows and FDI stock have expanded over fifteen-fold (UNCTD, 2006). In keeping with historical patterns, the predominant share (approximately 60%) of FDI has flowed from North to South. This dramatic growth in FDI has been paralleled by the emergence of highly complex and burgeoning international investment governance regime. This regime is comprised of a complex global network of well over 2500 IIAs over 1500 of which have been concluded within the last fifteen years. The vast majority of these IIAS are bilateral investment treaties (BITs) between DCs and LDCs although there are also a handful of regional investment treaties, most notably those contained in the 1994 North American Free Trade Agreement (NAFTA). The volume and magnitude of investor claims being submitted to arbitration has also risen sharply. As of June 2006, the total number of known investment-related arbitrations was 248, two-thirds of which were filed after 2001 the majority of which seek damages in the tens or hundreds of million dollars.

[Below we consider] the implications of this emerging IIA network for the ability (and indeed the appetite) of states to pursue domestic sustainable development policies. In framing our topic in this way, we have been mindful of the need to consider the relationship between IIAs and the capacity of governments to protect the environment and public health and likewise the relationship between IIAs and resource management and development. As it has evolved in international law scholarship, the concept of sustainable development not only embraces these concerns but emerging public participation, good governance and human rights norms. In what follows we reflect on the nature and extent of the tension between domestic sustainable development policy in this broad sense and investor rights under the emerging IIA regime.

The tension between investor rights and sustainable development

In the years following the watershed 1999 protests at the WTO trade meetings in Seattle, few issues have stirred more controversy within the broader globalization debate than investor rights. During this period, investor rights and their implications for domestic sustainable development initiatives have become front page news in jurisdictions around the world. Many of the most recent suits have targeted LDCs. Argentina has been particularly hard-hit facing close to thirty such suits, many arising out of its financial restructuring of 2002. Within the last two years alone, arbitral tribunals have ruled against it on four occasions. Other Latin American countries (including Ecuador, Bolivia, Peru and Mexico) have also faced or are facing investor suits as are several former Soviet Republics and African states.

Ongoing high profile claims include a suit brought by UK-based water TNC Biwater seeking damages from Tanzania for canceling a water and sewerage privatization deal; a suit by EU investors against South Africa seeking compensation for legislation aimed at bolstering black participation in the mining sector; a suit by the oil giant Occidental Petroleum against Ecuador in connection with the cancellation of oil leases due to allegations of environmental degradation and human rights abuses; and a suit by Texas farming interests claiming that the Mexico has infringed on their water rights. Frequently the damages sought, and in several recent cases awarded, have been in excess of a $100 million.

Developed states have also been increasingly been forced to defend themselves from analogous investor claims. Canada and the United States have each been sued close to a dozen times under NAFTA's investor rights provisions (Chapter 11) for various government measures in the realms of environmental protection, public health and resource management. In two of these cases, Canada has ended up paying compensation (one an out-of-court settlement of a claim arising out of ban on import of the fuel additive MMT; a second involving an arbitral ruling that a federal ban on the export of PCB waste violated NAFTA). To date, the United States has enjoyed more success most notably in its successful defence of a claim arising from a fuel additive ban in the *Methanex* litigation. However, several environmental protection-based claims are pending against both countries including a suit against Canada for banning the pesticide Lindane, and another against the United States targeting environmental measures imposed by the state of California on an open pit gold mining operation licenced to a Canadian mining company.

Environmental and social justice NGOs and scholars critical of the emerging IIA regime have voiced a variety of concerns with respect to both the substantive rules embedded in the regime and process by which these rules are enforced. They contend that the IIA regime represents a neo-liberal inspired Economic Bill of Rights for TNCs that undermines the sovereignty of host countries (often LDCs desperate to attract FDI) to determine and implement key environmental and sustainable development priorities. It is also contended that IIAs are asymmetrical: conferring rights but imposing no correlative responsibilities on investors. Moreover, critics claim that the legal uncertainty surrounding the scope and ambit of investor rights combined with the economic risks and costs associated with defending potential claims has a chilling effect on governments' willingness to regulate in the public interest. Finally, it is argued that the arbitral processes and fora currently in place to adjudicate these cases (ICSID, UNCITRAL and other bodies originally constituted to deal with private international commercial disputes) are ill-suited to deal with what are fundamentally public policy matters.

Defenders of the current IIA regime typically reject the 'sovereignty critique' described above out of hand. While it is generally conceded that such agreements significantly strengthen the hand of TNCs when dealing with host states, most would strongly contend that entry into the regime is itself an exercise of sovereign will, reflecting a reasoned political judgment that the supposed costs of entry are outweighed by the benefits in terms of increased FDI. They also point out that accession into the IIA regime is not an all-or-nothing proposition since governments are allowed to reserve (exempt) from such agreements certain economic sectors or non-conforming measures. Further, although some regime defenders will concede that the IIA jurisprudence is inconsistent and unpredictable, and that many early investment treaties failed adequately to recognize the right of host states to regulate in the public interest, most strongly assert that it is premature to draw conclusions about what remains an embryonic regime. Indeed, it is claimed that tribunals 'get it right' most of the time, even in cases frequently cited by opponents as illustrations of where they have erred. Likewise, arguments about "regulatory chill" are characteristically dismissed as unproven and premature. And while there is some acceptance in these quarters of the need for procedural reform, most argue that the necessary changes can be incrementally accommodated within existing arbitral institutions.

Investor protection architecture and procedures

Given the limitations of early treaties of 'Friendship, Commerce and Navigation' and the difficulties of securing multilateral investment treaty agreements, countries in recent decades have turned to IIAs to promote and protect foreign direct investment. It is estimated that by 2006 over 2500 IIAs will have been negotiated, convincing evidence of their primacy as the principal public international law instruments governing foreign investment. IIAs impose binding obligations on partner states with respect to their treatment of foreign investment as a major beneficial force for economic development. Enforcement of these protection and facilitation standards occurs through direct investor-state arbitration. Successful claims result in an award of damages in favour of the investor that are largely immune from meaningful appeal or review.

The great majority of the IIAs follow a standard pattern in detailing the obligations of the host state's treatment of an investment. The investor rights provisions found in NAFTA's Chapter 11 are illustrative. Under NAFTA, these rights (also known as disciplines) which when breached entitle an investor to sue a directly host state for damages, include: the right to national treatment and most favoured nation treatment (Articles 1102 and 1103); the right to international minimum standards of treatment (Article 1105); the right to be free from certain performance requirements (Article 1106); and the right to be compensated for expropriation of their investment (Article 1110).

Neither under the NAFTA nor in most other IIAs is the legal relationship between these private rights of action by aggrieved investors and the right of states to pursue sustainable development policies directly addressed. At the same time, such agreements typically provide a remarkably broad berth for investor rights. For example, under the NAFTA the range of governmental 'measures' that can trigger an investor claim includes 'any law, regulation, procedure, requirement or practice' emanating from any level of government (municipal, provincial or federal) or other arms of the state including the judiciary. Indeed, there is no requirement that the complained of "measure" have legal force or effect. Likewise, "investments" eligible for protection include not only direct investments but also debt security or loans to an enterprise or equity securities in an enterprise. A NAFTA tribunal has even held that a company's "market share" is a protected "investment".

Conferring upon investors a broad right to sue host states directly for damages in a legally binding, international adjudicative forum represents a seismic shift in international law. Prior to the emergence of IIAs, investors were forced to seek redress either by persuading their home state to champion their claim or to pursue litigation in the not always hospitable venue of the host state's domestic courts. Under provisions of modern day BITs, investors are transformed into 'private attorney generals' empowered to press their claims before arbitral tribunals organized under the auspices of variety of fora including: ICSID (International Centre for the Settlement of Investment Disputes), the ICC (International Chamber of

Commerce), the SCC (Stockholm Chamber of Commerce) and UNCITRAL (UN Commission on International Trade Law).

Most IIAs set out a relatively standard set of procedures, including a notice of dispute to the host government, the selection of the particular tribunal, followed by the appointment of the panel of arbitrators and the conduct of the arguments by memorials, the exchange of evidence and the oral hearing itself in a non-public forum. Arbitrators tend to be trade law scholars, retired judges or members of the commercial arbitration bar. Each party to an arbitration proposes a list of acceptable arbitrators from which its counterpart must select. The two arbitrators selected in this fashion then confer with a view to selecting a Chair. Increasingly, critics have questioned whether this method of appointment adequately ensures arbitral independence.

(In)consistency between the IIA Regime and sustainable development goals

As a result of tribunal rulings under NAFTA's Chapter 11 as well as the growing torrent of litigation under various BITs, the emerging IIA regime has increasingly been characterized by critics as a serious impediment to sustainable development. A frequent point of departure for this critique is the asymmetric nature of the obligations IIAs respectively impose on host states, home states and foreign investors. While such agreements invariably impose on host states a broad range of legal responsibilities to investors, typically they contain no correlative obligations on investors. Moreover, they are generally silent with respect to obligations of the investor's home jurisdiction 'to ensure its nationals comply with standards of conduct in their operations abroad'.

It is also contended that the content and uncertainty surrounding the investor rights that IIAs enshrine is inconsistent with sustainable development norms. The controversy surrounding the content of these new rights is considered in more detail below. Regardless of the ostensible intent underlying these provisions, however, few would dispute that the ascendancy of the IIA regime has created considerable uncertainty with respect to the ability of host states to address serious health, consumer and environmental concerns without incurring liability to investors. This is underscored by the experience under NAFTA where tribunals have enunciated interpretations of its national treatment, international minimum standard of treatment, and expropriation provisions that are much broader (and hence more favourable to investors) that is generally accepted in international law. Whether and to what extent this uncertainty has created 'regulatory chill' — causing governments to resile from enacting measures aimed at promoting sustainable development — is a matter of considerable debate.

This uncertainty is compounded by the failure of most IIAs to address or define how investor rights are to be balanced against sustainable development considerations. A recent analysis of over seventy-one BITs confirms that references to sustainable development principles are the exception rather than the rule, even in non-binding, preambular language. Moreover, most IIAs, including NAFTA's Chapter 11, are silent with respect to the 'traditionally accepted prerogative of governments to protect public health and the environment', resulting in considerable controversy over how and whether competing private and public interests are to be balanced. This is in sharp contrast to the GATT where Article XX explicitly provides a justificatory basis for measures of this kind. A related source of uncertainty is whether host governments can invoke the precautionary principle to uphold legal measures against investors which it claims to have taken to protect legitimate public interests in health, consumer safety or environmental protection.

A third area of concern relates to the arbitral process itself. Here the critique is two-fold: that the tribunals that have jurisdiction over such disputes are poorly equipped and ill-disposed to address the complex 'public' nature of issues raised; and that the prevailing arbitral processes lack transparency and openness in terms of access to documents, hearings and public participation. While some steps have recently been taken to alleviate this perceived 'democratic deficit', particularly in the NAFTA context, the tribunal competence and public participation remain key issues for many critics of the emerging IIA regime.

Notes and Questions

1. A key issue of contention in this area is what the authors refer to as the "asymmetric" nature of obligations under IIAs. While such agreements spell out in detail the obligations of host states to foreign investors, they typically impose no correlative responsibilities on foreign investors with respect to the management or operation of their investments nor do they normally impose any obligations on signatory states "to ensure its nationals comply with standards of conduct in their operations abroad". Are these issues that future IIAs should remedy? What steps could be taken to address these concerns, particularly as they relate to promoting sustainable development norms?

2. Should IIAs include a justificatory provision that would allow a host government to rely upon the precautionary principle to defend against claims made by investors? In light of the discussion of the principle earlier in this chapter, what challenges might present themselves in crafting a justificatory provision (akin to Article XX in the GATT) of this kind?

3. For an instructive illustration of the how IIA-based rights can collide with domestic regulatory initiatives, consider the claim brought by SD Myers against the Canadian government in connection with the latter's decision to ban the export of PCB waste: see Chapter 4.

References

We thank the copyright holders for their permission to reproduce their materials.

S. Barrett, *Environment and Statecraft: the Strategy of Environmental Treaty-Making* (New York: Oxford University Press, 1993)

P. Birnie *et al.*, *International Law & the Environment*, 2d ed. (Oxford: Oxford University Press, 2002)

D. Bodansky, J. Brunnee & E. Hey, eds., *The Oxford Handbook of International Environmental Law* (Oxford: Oxford University Press, 2007)

M. Doelle, *From Hot Air to Action? Climate Change, Compliance and the Future of International Environmental Law* (Toronto: Thomson Carswell, 2005)

K. Gallagher, ed., *Handbook and Trade and Environment* (Edward Elgar, 2009)

D. Hunter, J. Salzman & D. Zaelke, *International Environmental Law and Policy* (New York: Foundation Press, 2002)

H.M. Kindred, "The Use and Abuse of International Legal Sources by Canadian Courts: Searching for a Principled Approach" in Oonagh E. Fitsgerald, ed., *The Globalized Rule of Law: Relationships between International and Domestic Law* (Toronto: Irwin Law Inc., 2006)

H.M. Kindred, *et al.*, eds., *International Law: Chiefly as Interpreted and Applied in Canada*, 7th ed. (Toronto: Emond Montgomery, 2006)

E. Louka, *International Environmental Law: Fairness, Effectiveness and World Order* (Cambridge: Cambridge University Press, 2006). © Elli Louka 2006. Reprinted with the permission of Cambridge University Press.

A. Newcombe, "Sustainable Development and International Treaty Law" (2007) 8 Journal of World Investment & Trade 357

B.J. Richardson & S. Wood, *Environmental Law for Sustainability: A Reader* (Portland, OR: Hart Publishing, 2006)

C. Tollefson, "Games without Frontiers: Investor Claims and Citizen Submissions under the NAFTA Regime" (2002) 27 Y.J. Int'l L. 141

C. Tollefson, "*Metalclad v. United Mexican States* Revisited: Judicial Oversight of NAFTA's Chapter Eleven Investor-State Claim Process" (2002) 11 Minn. J. Global Trade 183

G. Van Harten, *Investment Treaty Arbitration and Public Law* (Oxford: Oxford University Press, 2007)

2

THE COMMON LAW

Introduction

The common law has been defined as "the system of jurisprudence, which originated in England and was later applied in Canada, that is based on judicial precedent rather than legislative enactments" (Canadian Law Dictionary, 1983). Elsewhere it has been described as "a few broad and comprehensive principles, founded on reason, natural justice, and enlightened public policy, modified and adapted to the circumstances of all of the particular cases which fall within it". (Shaw J., Mass S.C.). Among its defining features are its adaptability, its solicitude for individual rights (especially property rights) and the unique interpretive and law-making role that it assigns to the courts.

The three branches of the common law are property, contract and tort, which together comprise what is often referred to as the realm of private law. All three branches tend to involve the interpretation of individual rights in the context of bilateral relationships, with each playing a (somewhat) distinct role. Thus, property law addresses issues arising out of rights (including ownership and lesser interests) in personal and real property; contract law deals with bargained for (and sometimes un-bargained for) rights and obligations arising in the context of contractual relations; while tort law provides principles for adjudicating claims arising from harms caused beyond the realm of contract.

Historically, what we would refer to today as "environmental harms" were addressed, if at all, within one or more of these three branches of the common law. Thus if an individual leased another's land and caused it to become contaminated, the landlord could potentially, depending on the relevant facts, rely on property, contract or tort law (or some combination of all three) to seek a remedy. Starting in the 1970s, in part as a reaction to perceived inadequacies of the common law, environmental legislation of various kinds began to be enacted. Over time, indeed, these new environmental laws came to be seen by many as superceding the common law as a means of responding to environmental harms. The nature and implications of these legislative initiatives are addressed in many of the other chapters. Here, however, we focus on the present and future of the common law — most notably tort law — as a means of recognizing both private and public interests and rights to a clean and safe environment.

The structure of this chapter is as follows. Part I is an introduction to the application of tort law in environmental cases that focusses on two illustrative cases: *Palmer v. Nova Scotia Forest Industries* (1983), 60 N.S.R. (2d) 271 and *Cambridge Water Co. v. Eastern Counties Leather Plc* (1993), [1994] 2 A.C. 264 (U.K. H.L.). Part II considers one of the key legal challenges for plaintiffs in cases of environmental harm: proof of causation. Part III considers the role of class action legislation in promoting access to justice in cases involving environmental harms. Part IV considers how, in some cases, the common law has been relied on as a means of deterring or discouraging public engagement in environmental decision making by means of Strategic Lawsuits against Public Participation (also known as

SLAPP suits). Finally, in Part V, we consider emerging developments in environmental tort law, including the potential recognition of the public trust doctrine and a new role for what might be termed public environmental rights, developments which have been given significant impetus by the Supreme Court of Canada's decision in *British Columbia v. Canadian Forest Products Ltd.*, [2004] 2 S.C.R. 74.

Part I — Applying Traditional Tort Law in Environmental Cases

Tort law affords plaintiffs the means of seeking a remedy for environmental harms by relying on several different causes of action. These include negligence, nuisance, the tort in *Rylands v. Fletcher* (1868), L.R. 3 H.L. 330 (U.K. H.L.), trespass, and battery. Plaintiffs will often plead multiple causes of action in a single case, as shown in the *Palmer* and *Cambridge Water Co.* cases. At the outset, it is worth reprising the requisite elements of these various torts.

Negligence has, over time, assumed a dominant role in litigation around environmental harms. To establish such a claim a plaintiff must show that they were owed a duty of care, that the defendant breached the required standard of care, that they suffered damage, and that this damage was caused (factually and legally) by the defendant: see *Mustapha v. Culligan of Canada Ltd.*, 2008 SCC 27. The vexing nature of proving factual and legal causation (also known as remoteness) in negligence actions for personal injury is canvassed in depth in Part II.

The tort of nuisance takes two forms: private nuisance and public nuisance. A private nuisance claim alleges that the defendant unreasonably interfered with the plaintiff's use and enjoyment of an interest in land, causing foreseeable harm to the plaintiff. Private nuisance protects the quality of possession of land. Private nuisance, therefore, requires the plaintiff to have a sufficient property interest to be able to bring the claim. Other key factors, considered in determining whether an interference with possession of land is unreasonable, include: whether there is damage to the land; the gravity and duration of the interference; the nature of the neighbourhood; the utility of the defendant's activities; and the sensitivity of the plaintiff. Private nuisance was pleaded by the plaintiffs in both the *Palmer* and *Cambridge Water* cases.

The tort of public nuisance, in contrast, arises where there is an infringement of public as opposed to private rights. The ambit of what qualifies as "public" rights, as discussed in Part V, is the subject of some debate. Traditionally, such rights have been considered to include rights to access and use public waterways and highways as well as certain other public amenities. Because the Crown is considered to be the guardian of public rights, private citizens do not ordinarily have standing to sue for public nuisance; except with the consent of the Attorney General (in a relator action) or where, as a result of the nuisance, they have suffered special damage that is distinct from that suffered by members of the general public.

The tort of "strict liability" is commonly seen as originating in the case of *Rylands v. Fletcher*. It arises where the defendant brings a dangerous substance onto their land, which then escapes and causes injury to another. In this tort, liability is said to be strict in that whether the defendant acted negligently is legally irrelevant. A limiting requirement, however, in such cases is that the plaintiff must show that the defendant's activity constituted a non-natural use of the land in question. A key issue in the *Cambridge Water* case concerned whether the damage suffered by the plaintiff in such an action must be reasonably foreseeable. This tort, as we shall see, was also pleaded in *Palmer*.

Trespass to land involves the intentional and unjustifiable interference with another's possession of land. There is no need for physical damage or knowledge of ownership, as trespass protects the right of possession. Direct entry is a key element of trespass to land.

This raises interesting legal issues with respect to activities that involve spraying, vibration and smells. As we shall see, trespass to land was a central issue in the *Palmer* case. Trespass to the person, in the form of assault or battery, has, in rare circumstances, been used in cases of environmental harm causing personal injury.

In considering how these principles have been applied, the balance of this chapter will explore several themes, including the role of the burden of proof, causation, and quantification of damage. It is also important to bear in mind the importance of remedial issues.

The standard remedy in tort law is monetary compensation, designed to make the plaintiff "whole". In other words, the focus of tort law is to award a successful plaintiff an amount of monetary damages that will restore him or her, as much as money can permit, to the position he or she would have been in had the tort not occurred. This approach means, in many cases, that environmental harm that cannot be assigned a market value will go uncompensated, that polluters will not be required to pay the full cost of the harm they have caused, and that the environment will not be restored to its prior condition.

A key area of environmental litigation is assessing damages in cases involving contaminated sites. The typical case involves historical contamination of a property from a neighbouring property that was engaged in a high risk activity, such as the operation of a gas station. Most provinces have laws that require the current owner of the site to undertake remediation. Usually, however, such laws only require remediation that eliminates ongoing risks to human health and the environment, rather than restoring the environment to its original condition. The common law is thus often the only resort for the innocent neighbour. Courts have struggled in these cases to agree on the appropriate basis for compensation. Some have favoured awarding damages on the basis of the cost of remediating the property to pre-contamination conditions. Others have focussed on the effect of the residual contamination on the value of the property in combination with clean up to the satisfaction of government officials. For two cases involving very different approaches, see *Tridan Developments Ltd. v. Shell Canada Products Ltd.*, 2002 CarswellOnt 1, 154 O.A.C. 1, 57 O.R. (3d) 503 (Ont. C.A.) and *Cousins v. McColl-Frontenac Inc.*, 2007 CarswellNB 549, 2007 CarswellNB 550, 2007 NBCA 83 (N.B. C.A.). The recent Supreme Court of Canada decision in *British Columbia v. Canadian Forest Products Ltd.* (see *infra* Part V) also addresses this important question.

The main alternative to monetary damages in tort law is injunctive relief. Injunctive relief can take the form of interim relief pending a final resolution of a legal dispute. It can also take the form of permanent injunctive relief as part of the final resolution of the dispute. As we will see in the *Palmer* case below, the availability of injunctive relief is discretionary and unpredictable. More often than not, courts are faced with balancing environmental harm against economic benefits.

The first of the two cases we consider in this Part arose as a result of concerns, shared by residents of Cape Breton, Nova Scotia, about the use of herbicides by a forest company on adjacent forest lands pursuant to a provincially-issued permit. The legal basis for their claim is set out in the judgment extracted below. In this judgment, the court considers the residents' claim for permanent, *quia timet* injunction, a permanent order seeking to prevent anticipated damage before it occurs.

The case was brought at a time when there was an active debate about the health and environmental risks of some of the chemicals present in the herbicides to be sprayed; today, the harmful effects of these chemicals are well documented and undisputed. The case is, therefore, just as much about the ability of the common law to act in a preventative and precautionary manner as it is about the legal requirements of nuisance, trespass, and strict liability. Finally, it is worth pointing out that while the case involves a number of plaintiffs who stood to be adversely affected by the spraying program in very similar ways, the action was brought by way of a representative action and not a class action since class action legislation had not been enacted at that time. The most notable impact of this was that the issue of costs played a major role in the case, both in the way the plaintiffs were able to present their case, and the way that the costs award against the plaintiffs essentially precluded an appeal. We will return to this issue in Part III.

Palmer v. Nova Scotia Forest Industries
(1983), 60 N.S.R. (2d) 271

NUNN, J.: — This is an application by the named plaintiffs in their individual capacities and as representatives of others for an injunction restraining the defendant, a company engaged in the forest industry in Nova Scotia, from spraying certain areas in the Province of Nova Scotia with phenoxy herbicides.

The action was originally brought in the late summer of 1982 when the plaintiffs obtained from this court per Burchell, J., an interim injunction restraining any spraying by the defendant pursuant to a license to spray during 1982 issued by the Nova Scotia Department of the Environment. The injunction was subsequently lifted by the Nova Scotia Court of Appeal in December, 1982 on the ground that no spraying could take place until the summer of 1983 and that there could be a full trial and hearing of the issues by that time.

The matter was then brought to trial in Sydney commencing May 2, 1983, with the relief claimed, in the statement of claim, to be a permanent injunction restraining the spraying of 2,4-D (Esteron 600), 2,4,5-T with its contaminant TCDD, and Esteron 3-3E, which is a mixture of 2,4-D and 2,4,5-T.

The trial commenced, by agreement of the parties, on the basis that although the defendant's license to spray was only for 1982, it was the defendant's intention, if spraying were permitted or not contested, to apply for a new license for 1983. It appeared that such a license would be granted if applied for in the absence of any restriction by this court. This was a troublesome matter, which I pointed out to the parties before and during the trial, as the court does not issue a useless injunction. Without a license there is nothing to enjoin. However, as I stated, it was in the interests of the parties, and the public generally, that this matter be heard and disposed of. It was on this basis, and by agreement, that the matter continued.

The trial consumed 21 days of taking evidence, 2 days of oral argument and further written briefs. The plaintiffs tendered 35 witnesses and the defendant 14. Aside from most of the named plaintiffs, all the rest of the witnesses with but a few exceptions were experts — highly educated in their various fields to which they gave evidence. There were approximately 150 filed exhibits which included 12 volumes of reports of the plaintiff's experts and 5 volumes of reports of the defendant's experts. Attached to the expert reports were literally hundreds of scientific articles and excerpts from scientific articles.

The subject of dioxins and chlorophenols has been widely disputed in many countries of the world both politically and before regulatory agencies. To my knowledge this is the first occasion where the dispute has reached the courts in Canada. [. . .]

John Dan MacIntyre, retired, of West Bay Road, plaintiff and a representative of others at or near site D — MacIntyre Mountain, owns a 100 acre farm which adjoins the site. His residence is two miles below the site. He uses the farm for growing vegetables and potatoes and for pasture for a horse and some cows, and his family pick blueberries and hunt in the area. . . . His family and some other neighbours live on the opposite side of the Trans Canada Highway from the site. He, his family and neighbours get their water from Rough Brook which adjoins his farm. He testified that this brook gets muddy after a rain storm which is indicative of some silting in this area. Rough Brook is actually on the site. His garden is located approximately one-half mile from the site. His concern was the possible harm the spray would create to his water and health. [. . .]

Brian GooGoo, a full-blooded MicMac Indian, lives on the Whycocomagh Reserve which is 1 1/2 miles from Site E — Skye Mountain and located at the base of the mountain. He was formerly a chief and has been delegated by the Whycocomagh Indian Band to represent the Band in a representative capacity in this action.

As part of life on the Reserve, the Indians hunt, fish, pick berries, medicinal bark, roots and herbs on the Reserve and on Crown lands. They fish eels, trout, salmon, flatfish, oysters and lobsters in the Bras D'Or Lakes into which a number of streams flow from Skye Mountain.

The concern here is that their way of life is being threatened by the effect the spray program will have on the area and to their health through their water and food supply. This witness asserted such effects are an interference with his people's aboriginal rights to carry out their life-style activities as they have done for centuries. He suggested a greater interference with those aboriginal rights by the very fact that the defendant has come upon some of those Crown lands, by virtue of leases, cut the timber and destroyed wild life without any consultation with the Indians. This latter aspect may very well be beyond the scope of the matters involved in this action. [. . .]

Gerard MacLellan, a research assistant with the Nova Scotia Department of Environment, testified that he processed the applications for spray permits made by the defendant. In so doing he followed the usual procedure of sending copies of the application to four governmental bodies, namely, the Nova Scotia Departments of Health, Fisheries, Lands and Forests and Environment Canada. He flew over the sites by helicopter, wrote up the technical report which is attached to the permit and forwarded the information to his Minister who approved them and issued the licenses or permits to spray. His visitation to the sites was cursory, perhaps five minutes at each to oversee the area and checks for homes and water in or near the proposed spray area. His was not an environmental assessment. [. . .]

Finally, I now turn to . . . the main issue, whether or not the plaintiffs are entitled to injunctive relief. The relief claimed is set forth in the statement of claim as follows:

- a permanent injunction enjoining the defendant from spraying the phenoxy herbicides 2,4-D and 2,4,5-T at the sites,
- a declaration that the plaintiffs have the right to be free of exposure to the phenoxy herbicides 2,4-D and 2,4,5-T.
- the costs of this action,
- such other relief as this Honourable Court thinks just.

The legal causes of action on which the relief is claimed are alleged to arise from the proposed spraying by the defendant and fall within the following categories:

- private nuisance;
- trespass to land;
- the rule in *Rylands v. Fletcher*;
- the right of riparian owners to water undiminished in quality;
- the right of landowners to groundwater free of chemical contamination;

- breach of the *Fisheries Act*, R.S.C. 1970, c. F-14 and particularly ss. 30, 31(1) and 32(2). [. . .]

The essence of private nuisance is explained by Salmond and Heuston on The Law of Torts (18th Ed.), at p. 48:

> The generic conception involved in private nuisance may really be found in the fact that liability in nuisance flows from an act or omission whereby a person is annoyed, prejudiced or disturbed in the enjoyment of land, whether by physical damage to the land or by interference with the enjoyment of the land or with his exercise of an easement, profit or other similar right or with his health, comfort or convenience as occupier of such land. [. . .]

The law is clear, however, that only some substantial interference with a person's enjoyment of property gives rise to an action in nuisance. Equally clear is the requirement that there must be proof of damage. In Halsbury's Laws of England (4th Ed.), vol. 34, p. 105 this proposition is put as follows:

> The damage need not consist of pecuniary loss but it must be material or substantial, that is, it must not be merely sentimental, speculative or trifling, or damage that is merely temporary, fleeting or evanescent . . .

In the present case the allegation is that these offending chemicals, if they get to the plaintiffs' land, will interfere with the health of the plaintiffs thereby interfering with their enjoyment of their lands. Clearly such an interference, if proved, would fall within the essence of nuisance. As a serious risk of health, if proved, there is no doubt that such an interference would be substantial. In other words, the grounds for the cause of action in nuisance exist here provided that the plaintiffs prove the defendant will actually cause it, i.e., that the chemicals will come to the plaintiffs' lands and that it will actually create a risk to their health.

Trespass to land, on the other hand, does not require proof of damage and is actionable per se. As stated in Salmond and Heuston on The Law of Torts, supra:

> It is a trespass [to land] to place anything upon the plaintiff's land, or to cause any physical object or noxious substance to cross the boundary of the plaintiff's land, or even simply to come into physical contact with the land . . .

Again there is no doubt in my mind that, if it is proved that the defendant permits any of these substances on the plaintiffs' lands, it would constitute a trespass and be actionable [. . .] Again, entitlement to a remedy, will be based upon proof as to whether such substances will be deposited on the lands of the plaintiff [. . .]

The rule in *Rylands v. Fletcher* (1868), L.R. 3 H.R. 330, is a simple one, of long standing in English jurisprudence. The rule is stated in Salmond and Heuston on The Law of Torts (18th Ed.), supra, at p. 297:

> This principle is one of the most important examples of absolute or strict liability recognized by our law — one of the chief instances in which a man acts at his peril and is responsible for accidental harm, independently of the existence of either wrongful intent or negligence. The rule may be formulated thus: The occupier of land who brings and keeps upon it anything likely to do damage if it escapes is bound at his peril to prevent its escape, and is liable for all the direct consequences of its escape, even if he has been guilty of no negligence.

No elaboration of the rule or applications of it are necessary. It is for the plaintiffs to prove the constituent elements — its likelihood to do damage, its escape and the direct consequences.

The complete burden of proof, of course, rests upon the plaintiffs throughout for all issues asserted by them. If the spraying had actually occurred, they would have to prove by a preponderance of probabilities the essential elements of either or all of the alleged causes of action as I have set them out. However, the spraying has not occurred and this application is for a "quia timet" injunction. This can be translated as "which he fears". In other words, a plaintiff does not have to wait until actual damage occurs. Where such damage is apprehended, an application for a "quia timet" injunction is an appropriate avenue to obtain a remedy which will prevent the occurrence of the harm. That remedy also, however, is not without its limitations.

In *Attorney General v. Corporation of Manchester*, [1893] 2 Ch. 87, Chitty, J., states at p. 92:

> The principle which I think may be properly and safely extracted from the quia timet authorities is, that the plaintiff must show a strong case of probability that the apprehended mischief will, in fact, arise.

This passage was approved by Anglin, J., in the Supreme Court of Canada in *Matthew v. Guardian Insurance Company* (1918), 58 S.C.R. 47, at p. 61 and is still the proper principle to consider in an application of this kind.

It was argued by the plaintiffs that the principle as expressed in Salmond and Heuston on The Law of Torts, *supra*, is more appropriate. At p. 555 they state as follows:

> In all cases, however, it seems necessary that there shall be a sufficient degree of probability that the injury will be substantial and will be continued, repeated, or committed at no remote period, and damages will not be a sufficient or adequate remedy.

It was suggested that this demonstrates that there is no set standard of proof that has to be met — simply that the risk that the plaintiff's right will be breached be significantly great in all the circumstances.

I fail to see the difference suggested. A "strong case of probability" and "a sufficient degree of probability" create only a semantic difference and not a difference in substance. I prefer the former as more clearly setting forth the proper principle. This does not impose an impossible burden nor does it deprive the court of its ability to consider the balance of convenience or inconvenience or hardship between the parties nor the size or amount of the injury or distress which might occur. All of these are factors which are woven into the fabric of "a strong probability" and are considered in determining whether the burden or proof has been met.

The plaintiffs must, however, prove the essential elements of a regular injunction, namely irreparable harm and that damages are not an adequate remedy as they are also essential elements of the "quia timet" injunction.

Finally, any injunction is a discretionary remedy and sufficient grounds must be established to warrant the exercise by the court of its discretion.

I am satisfied that a serious risk to health, if proved, would constitute irreparable harm and that damages would not be an adequate remedy. Further, recognizing the great width and elasticity of equitable principles, I would have no hesitation in deciding that such a situation would be one of the strongest which would warrant the exercise of the Court's discretion to restrain the activity which would create the risk.

This matter thus reduces itself now to the single question. Have the plaintiffs offered sufficient proof that there is a serious risk of health and that such serious risk of health will occur if the spraying of the substances here is permitted to take place? [. . .]

By way of background, the phenoxy herbicides are a group of herbicides which have been widely used in many parts of the world since the late 1940's and early 1950's. They are selective in that they affect only certain types of vegetation, namely broad-leaved plants, and have no, or little effect on conifers. They are a family of compounds having similar chemical and biological properties but each member compound differs in effect on individual plants. The two family members concerned here are 2,4-D (2,4-dichlorophenoxyacetic acid) and 2,4,5-T (2,4,5-trichlorophenoxyacetic acid).

2,4,5-T and all of its derivative herbicides contain a chemical contaminant formed in the manufacturing process, unavoidably to the present time and of no value, known as 2,3,7,8-tetrachlorodibenzo-p-dioxin and referred to as TCDD. Originally the quantity of TCDD in the manufactured product was in the range of 80 parts per billion but, over the years, improvements in manufacturing techniques have reduced this amount to less than 0.1 parts per million. In fact the present supply of 2,4,5-T held by the defendant has been formulated with a TCDD content indicated as "non-detectible" at 0.01 parts per million. The herbicide 2,4-D is free of any TCDD contamination.

Both herbicides have been widely used in Canada, and elsewhere, upon agricultural crops, forests, roadside and railroad rights-of-way in vast quantities and, only until recently, without too much precaution. In comparison to other uses, forestry has used only a small percentage of the total used.

Phenoxy herbicides are used to discriminate between the unwanted plants and those desired to be retained or encouraged. In a forestry site they are used to release the young conifers from competition. In Nova Scotia those competitors are the hardwoods, such as aspen, birch and maple, and raspberry. Their use is not designed to kill all competition but to permit light to reach the young conifers and decrease competition for soil nutrients and moisture. After a few years the young conifers will outgrow the competition and be permanently released. In Nova Scotia the evidence is, and I accept it, that the situation requires one treatment, and perhaps a second after 3 to 5 years, over a forty-year period. Treatment is usually applied in early summer when susceptibility is greatest but it can be applied in late summer or early fall. The benefits, of course, are a greater yield over a shorter period of time of the conifer forest.

The contaminant TCDD is one of the most toxic chemicals known to man. One witness described it as "exquisitely toxic". Much has been written on TCDD and its effects. It has been indicated that there are upwards of 40,000 different articles on the subject. A great number of those were submitted to the Court. It is not my intention to summarize those, nor is it necessary, as almost every scientific witness as well as the regulatory agencies have already done that. While there are opposing views, and the whole field is not without some uncertainty, there is no dearth of writings. So there can be no doubt that everything submitted was considered by me, I have read every article submitted to me, a formidable task in itself, and I now join the group who has reviewed all the relevant literature, although I am far from convinced that this volume of documents was necessary for this case.

Having mentioned regulatory agencies, it is appropriate to indicate that most countries, including Canada, have regulatory agencies, whose function it is to regulate and control the use of new chemical compounds before they are exposed to the environment. [. . .]

As to Canada and the United Kingdom, both have registered 2,4-D and 2,4,5-T for forestry use with a maximum TCDD level of 0.1 parts per million. Registration for use in Canada for 2,4-D was in 1947 and 2,4,5-T in 1952. In both jurisdictions reviews are made periodically after reviews of the literature and independent study by highly trained and competent scientists. The evidence indicates this to be an ongoing process. In both countries registration for use is still in effect and neither jurisdiction has accepted that there are valid studies which would cause them to cancel the registration. The provincial Department of Environment is also involved in this ongoing process as it relates to Nova Scotia and that department has not registered the use of these herbicides.

To some extent this case takes on the nature of an appeal from the decision of the regulatory agency and any such approach through the courts ought to be discouraged in its infancy. Opponents to a particular chemical ought to direct their activities towards the regulatory agencies or, indeed, to government itself where broad areas of social policy are involved. It is not for the courts to become a regulatory agency of this type. It has neither the training nor the staff to perform this function. Suffice it to say that this decision will relate to, and be limited to, the dispute between these parties [. . .] Having accepted Mr. Ross' testimony and accepting the evidence of Donald Freer and Exhibit D-70 that the defendant's supply of 2,4,5-T is formulated with a TCDD content of "non detectible" at 0.01 parts per million, it is obvious that the amount of TCDD to be sprayed in Nova Scotia by the defendant is infinitesimally small. After hearing Lt. Col. Thalken I do not accept Dr. Wulfman's suggestion that storage may affect the product in any way.

It is, therefore, in the light of this concentration of TCDD that I must consider whether the plaintiffs have met the burden of proof. [. . .]

A great deal of the evidence submitted related to animal studies where TCDD were reported to have caused various effects indicating it to be, among other things, fetotoxic, teratagenic, carcinogenic and to cause immunological deficiencies, enzymatic changes, liver problems and the like. Also it is alleged to bioaccumulate and be persistent both in soil and in tissue. I do not pretend to have included all of its effects, but those are the most major. I was asked to make findings of fact in all of these areas, but I decline to do so. Nothing would be added to the body of scientific fact by any such determination by this court. That TCDD has had all of these effects is undoubtedly true in the experiments described, but, in every case, the effect must be related to dose. In the animal studies the doses are extremely high and, in all cases, many, many thousands of times greater than any dose which could be received in Nova Scotia.

Human studies are a different matter because actual testing is not an acceptable process in our society. I do note that Dr. Newton, another of the defence witnesses, participated in some actual testing on himself and several others, without any apparent harmful result. The human information comes from a number of studies made in various countries of the world. Some resulted from industrial accidents, some from the Vietnam experiences and some from massive industrial exposure. It was in this area that a great deal of the evidence was directed. I am satisfied that in all these cases the exposure was massive, either through accident or industrial exposure or the Vietnam War.

. . . The evidence discloses that where particular health effects alleged to be caused by exposure were investigated, they were found not to be attributable to exposure. I refer particularly here to the evidence of Dr. Kilpatrick and the experience in the United Kingdom.

While I am on this point, I must indicate something that has troubled me throughout this case. In the past 35 years these chemicals have had extremely high world-wide use and for most of those the TCDD content was many hundreds of times higher than that used today. It has been used in agriculture (widely used in the growth of rice), forestry, roadside and railway rights-of-way, etc., yet there is no evidence in the countries of use, except the Hardell results, already referred to, of proven injury to health from these uses with a few exceptions related to those actually spraying, i.e., massive personal occupationally-related exposure situations. Apparently those workers were unaware of possible harm with a corresponding lack of concern for care. 2,4-D itself has had extremely high use in agriculture throughout this time, again with no obvious ill effects. I find this dearth of evidence to be astonishing in view of the health effects alleged.

This brings me to the next suggestion by the plaintiffs which is that cancer, as a disease, has a long incubation period and the effects of dioxin cannot be known until time passes, approximately 40 years, so that it can be determined whether dioxin is indeed carcinogenic in humans. This again is not my function. I am to determine only if there is a probability of risk to health. To this point in time there is not sufficient acceptable evidence despite 35 years of use. One of the plaintiffs' witnesses, Dr. Daum, suggested that the only approach is to wait that period without permitting any further use. I cannot accept that. She is working from the premise that any substance should be proved absolutely safe before use but, as commendable as that may be, it is not practical nor is it in conformity with currently accepted determinations for use of many substances. I doubt very much if any substance can be proved absolutely safe.

If all substances which are carcinogenic or otherwise toxic were removed from use, we would have no air to breathe or potable water and many common everyday products, necessary to our life, would be removed. The key to the use of all these is dosage. Where it can be determined that there is a safe dosage, according to acceptable scientific standards, then a substance can be used. Our regulatory agencies and scientists around the world are daily involved in this very area.

As well, virtually all chemicals are toxic, but those in use generally are safe if used below the toxic levels, i.e., if the dose received is below the safety levels. Scientists also determine a "no observable effect level". That is a level of intake of any particular substance where no effect is observed. It is, in most cases, far below the safe level, at least several orders of magnitude (each order being a multiple of 10) lower. [. . .]

I am satisfied that the overwhelming currently accepted view of responsible scientists is that there is little evidence that, for humans either 2,4-D or 2, 4,5-T is mutagenic or carcinogenic and that TCDD is not an effective carcinogen, and further, that there are no-effect levels and safe levels for humans and wildlife for each of these substances [. . .]

Having reached this point it is appropriate to add that the evidence of risk assessments clearly indicates that any risk here in Nova Scotia, if, indeed, there is a risk at all, is infinitesimally small and many, many times less than one in a million which level, apparently, is regarded as a safe and acceptable risk by most of the world's regulatory agencies. Putting this in perspective, as indicated by Dr. Wilson in his evidence, the risk of cancer to a smoker is 1 in 800 and for a non-smoker continuously in the same room with smokers it is 1 in 100,000, while the risk to a person drinking two litres of water per day from a stream immediately after being sprayed (which will not happen with buffer zones) is 1 in 100,000 million or 100,000 times less than 1 in a million, which itself is regarded as a *de minimus* risk.

To my mind, after hearing all the evidence and reading all the exhibits, there is no doubt that the weight of current responsible scientific opinion does not support the allegations of the plaintiffs. I feel it is my responsibility, in view of the nature of this matter, to add that, while I do not doubt the zeal of many of the plaintiffs' scientific witnesses or their ability, some seemed at many times to be protagonists defending a position, thereby losing some of their objectivity. There was a noticeable selection of studies which supported their view and a refusal to accept any criticism of them or contrary studies. Where the study was by anyone remotely connected with industry there was a tendency to leap to the "fox in the chicken coop" philosophy, thereby ruling out the value of the study as biased. In my view a true scientific approach does not permit such self-serving selectivity, nor does it so readily decry a study on the basis of bias.

I had the opposite impression of the scientific witnesses offered by the defendant. I did not detect any sense of partisanship. They related their work, their involvement with the substances, the results of their studies and their considerations of other studies in a professional, scientific manner and I therefore found their opinions to be reliable and, indeed, I accepted them as such. [. . .]

Having made this finding, it is unnecessary for me to consider the matter of riparian rights or groundwater rights. Since I have accepted that no risk to health has been proved, I need not consider these areas. Were I required to do so, and perhaps to allay public fears, I will add that the strongest evidence indicates that these substances sprayed in the Nova Scotia environment will not get into or travel through the rivers or streams, nor will they travel via groundwater to any lands of the plaintiffs who are adjacent to or near the sites to be sprayed.

Further, if any did the amount would be so insignificant that there would be no risk.

I need not consider whether any particular area need be sprayed, whether other substances should be used, or whether manual release is a better approach. While considerable evidence was adduced in this regard, it is not the court's function to direct how the defendant should manage its affairs or carry out its activities. My only concern is whether or not the defendant should be restrained from the proposed activity. While those factors may have been considered in the wide discretionary area if an injunction were to be granted, they do not arise when the plaintiffs have not proved the grounds for an injunction.

There is, accordingly, no nuisance, real or probable. As to trespass, none has been proved as probable to occur. Possibilities do not constitute proof. Similarly, there has been no basis established for the application of the rule in *Rylands v. Fletcher*, as neither the danger of the substance nor the likelihood of its escape to the plaintiffs' lands has been proved.

Therefore, the answer to the single remaining question I posed earlier which has two parts — have the plaintiffs offered sufficient proof that there is a serious risk of health and that such serious risk of health will occur if the spraying of the substances here is permitted to take place — is, for each part, in the negative. [. . .]

The plaintiffs, therefore, fail in this action and the defendant is entitled to its costs . . .

Notes and Questions

1. Consider carefully the "single question" identified by Justice Nunn. How does the question relate to the legal test for granting injunctive relief? What does it tell us about the court's approach to nuisance, strict liability and trespass?

2. Can you differentiate, in Justice Nunn's reasoning, between the tests for the torts of nuisance, strict liability and trespass on the one hand, and the test for granting injunctive relief on the other?

3. In your view, based on his findings of fact, were the tests for the torts of nuisance, trespass or strict liability made out?

4. What about negligence? Could a case in negligence have been made out based on the facts before the court?

5. Justice Nunn comments in the decision that this case almost takes the form of an appeal of the regulatory decisions to approve the use of herbicides in Canada, and to permit the spraying in the area in question. What role does this suggest for the common law with respect to the compensation of harm caused by pollution permitted by an approval?

6. Nunn J. awarded costs against the plaintiffs despite the fact that the case had many hallmarks of "public interest" litigation. For many of the plaintiffs, this adverse costs award presented dire financial consequences. Ultimately, the plaintiffs agreed to abandon his appeal in return for the defendant agreeing to forego its entitlement to costs. In your view, had the case been appealed, what would have been the plaintiffs' strongest legal arguments for overturning Nunn J.'s judgment at trial? For further discussion of costs-related issues in public interest cases, see Chapter 6.

The next case is a landmark 1994 decision of the House of Lords concerning the ambit and nature of the rule in *Rylands v. Fletcher*. The *Cambridge Water Co. v. Eastern Counties Leather Plc* case has been criticized by some as restricting the ambit of recovery in cases of historic pollution, particularly where the impugned conduct was consistent with prevailing industrial practices and scientific knowledge when the pollution occurred. It has been applauded by others for the same reason.

At trial, the plaintiff pleaded negligence, private nuisance and *Rylands v. Fletcher*. By the time the matter reached the House of Lords, the only live issue was whether the defendant should be liable under the third of these torts. In addressing this issue, two legal questions were central to the court's decision: (1) whether the reasonable foreseeability of damage was an element of the tort; and (2) whether the defendant's storage and use of the chemical solvents constituted a "non-natural use of land" under the rule in *Rylands v. Fletcher*.

Cambridge Water Co. v. Eastern Counties Leather Plc
(1993), [1994] 2 A.C. 264 (U.K. H.L.)

LORD GOFF OF CHIEVELEY: My Lords, this appeal is concerned with the question whether the appellant company, Eastern Counties Leather plc (ECL), is liable to the respondent company, Cambridge Water Co (CWC), in damages in respect of damage suffered by reason of the contamination of water available for abstraction at CWC's borehole at Sawston Mill near Cambridge. The contamination was caused by a solvent known as perchloroethene (PCE), used by ECL in the process of degreasing pelts at its tanning works in Sawston, about 1¾ miles away from CWC's borehole, the PCE having seeped into the ground beneath ECL's works and thence having been conveyed in percolating water in the direction of the borehole. CWC's claim against ECL was based on three alternative grounds, viz negligence, nuisance and the rule in *Rylands v Fletcher* (1868), LR 3 HL 330.

The judge, Ian Kennedy J, dismissed CWC's claim on all three grounds — on the first two grounds, because (as I will explain hereafter) he held that ECL could not reasonably have foreseen that such damage would occur, and on the third ground because he held that the use of a solvent such as PCE in ECL's tanning business constituted, in the circumstances, a natural use of ECL's land. The Court of Appeal, however, allowed CWC's appeal from the decision of the judge, on the ground that ECL was strictly liable for the contamination of the water percolating under CWC's land, on the authority of *Ballard v Tomlinson* (1885), 29 Ch D 115, and awarded damages against ECL in the sum assessed by the judge, viz £1,064,886 together with interest totalling £642,885, and costs. It is against that decision that ECL now appeals to your Lordships' House, with leave of this House. [. . .]

ECL was incorporated in 1879, and since that date has continued in uninterrupted business as a manufacturer of fine leather at Sawston. ECL employs about 100 people, all of whom live locally. Its present works are, as the judge found, in general modern and spacious, and admit of a good standard of housekeeping.

The tanning process requires that pelts shall be degreased; and ECL, in common with all other tanneries, has used solvents in that process since the early 1950s. It has used two types of chlorinated solvents — organochlorines known as TCE (trichloroethene) and PCE. Both solvents are cleaning and degreasing agents; and since 1950 PCE has increasingly been in common, widespread and everyday use in dry-cleaning, in general industrial use (e.g., as a machine cleaner or paint-thinner), domestically (e.g., in 'Dab-it-off') and in tanneries. PCE is highly volatile, and so evaporates rapidly in air; but it is not readily soluble in water.

ECL began using TCE in the early 1950s and then changed over to PCE, probably sometime in the 1960s, and continued to use PCE until 1991. The amount so used varied between 50,000 and 100,000 litres per year. The solvent was introduced into what were (in effect) dry-cleaning machines. This was done in two different ways. First, from the commencement of use until 1976, the solvent was delivered in 40 gallon drums; as and when the solvent was needed, a drum was taken by forklift truck to the machine and tipped into a tank at the base of the machine. Second, from 1976 to 1991, the solvent was delivered in bulk and kept in a storage tank, from which it was piped directly to the machine.

There was no direct evidence of the actual manner in which PCE was spilled at ECL's premises. However, the judge found that the spillage took place during the period up to 1976, principally during the topping up process described above, during which there were regular spillages of relatively small amounts of PCE onto the concrete floor of the tannery. It is known that, over that period, the minimum amount which must have been spilled (or otherwise have entered the chalk aquifer below) was some 3,200 litres (1,000 gallons); it is not possible even to guess at the maximum. However, as the judge found, a reasonable supervisor at ECL would not have foreseen, in or before 1976, that such repeated spillages of small quantities of solvent would lead to any environmental hazard or damage — i.e., that the solvent would enter the aquifer or that, having done so, detectable quantities would be found down-catchment. Even if he had foreseen that solvent might enter the aquifer, he would not have foreseen that such quantities would produce any sensible effect upon water taken down-catchment, or would otherwise be material or deserve the description of pollution. I understand the position to have been that any spillage would have been expected to evaporate rapidly in the air, and would not have been expected to seep through the floor of the building into the soil below. The only harm that could have been foreseen from a spillage was that somebody might have been overcome by fumes from a spillage of a significant quantity.

I turn to CWC. CWC was created under its own Act of Parliament in 1853 (the Cambridge University and *Town Waterworks Act 1853* (16 & 17 Vict c xxiii), and is a licensed supplier of water following implementation of the *Water Act 1989*. Its function is to supply water to some 275,000 people in the Cambridge area. It takes all its water by borehole extraction from underground strata, mainly the middle and lower chalk prevalent in the area. Since 1945 public demand for water has multiplied many times, and new sources of supply have had to be found. In 1975 CWC identified the borehole at Sawston Mill as having the potential to meet a need for supply required to avert a prospective shortfall, and to form part of its long term provision for future demand. It purchased the borehole in September 1976. Before purchase, tests were carried out on the water from the borehole; these tests indicated that, from the aspect of chemical analysis, the water was a wholesome water suitable for public supply purposes. Similar results were obtained from tests carried out during the period 1979–83. At all events CWC, having obtained the requisite statutory authority to use the borehole for public sector supply, proceeded to build a new pumping station at a cost of £184,000; and Sawston Mill water entered the main supply system in June 1979.

Meanwhile, in the later 1970s concern began to be expressed in scientific circles about the presence of organic chemicals in drinking water, and their possible effects. Furthermore, the development of, inter alia, high resolution gas chromatography during the 1970s enabled scientists to detect and measure organochlorine compounds (such as PCE) in water to the value of micrograms per litre (or parts per billion) expressed as 5g/litre.

In 1984 the World Health Organisation (WHO) published a Report on Guidelines for Drinking Water Quality (vol 1: recommendations). Although not published until 1984, the Report was the product of discussion and consultation during several years previously, and its recommendations appear to have formed the basis of an earlier EEC Directive, as well as of later UK Regulations. Chapter 4 of the Report is concerned with 'Chemical and Physical Aspects', and Ch 4.3 deals with organic contaminants, three of which (including TCE and PCE) were assigned a 'Tentative Guideline Value'. The value so recommended for TCE was 305g/litre, and for PCE 105g/litre.

The EEC Directive relating to the Quality of Water intended for Human Consumption (80/778/EEC) was issued on 15 September 1980. Member states were required to bring in laws within two years of notification, and to achieve full compliance within five years. The Directive distinguished between 'Maximum Admissible Concentration' (MAC) values and 'Guide Level' (GL) values, the former being minimum standards which had to be achieved, and the latter being more stringent standards which it was desirable to achieve. TCE and PCE were assigned a GL value of only 15g/litre, i.e., 30 times and 10 times respectively lower than the WHO Tentative Guideline Values.

The United Kingdom responded to the Directive by Department of the Environment circular 20/82 dated 15 August 1982. The effect was that, as from 18 July 1985, drinking water containing more than 15g/litre of TCE or PCE would not be regarded as 'wholesome' water for the purpose of compliance by water authorities with their statutory obligations under the *Water Act 1973*. However, following a regulation made in 1989 (SI 1989/1147) the prescribed maximum concentration values for TCE and PCE have been respectively 305g/litre and 105g/litre, so that since 1 September 1989 the United Kingdom values have been brought back into harmony with the WHO Tentative Guideline Values. [. . .]

The conclusions reached by British Geological Society, and by the expert witnesses instructed by CWC and ECL in the present litigation, were as follows. Neat PCE had travelled down through the drift directly beneath ECL's premises, and then vertically downwards through the chalk aquifer until arrested by a relatively impermeable layer of chalk marl at a depth of about 50 metres. Thus arrested, the neat PCE had formed pools which were dissolving slowly in the groundwater and being carried down aquifer in the direction of Sawston Mill at the rate of about 8 metres per day, the travel time between pool and Sawston Mill being about 9 months, and the migration of the dissolved phase PCE being along a deep, comparatively narrow, pathway or 'plume'. On the balance of probabilities, this narrow plume had reached Sawston Mill and been at least materially responsible for the PCE concentrations found there. [. . .]

From the foregoing history, the following relevant facts may be selected as being of particular relevance:

> (1) The spillage of PCE, and its seepage into the ground beneath the floor of the tannery at ECL's works, occurred during the period which ended in 1976, as a result of regular spillages of small quantities of PCE onto the floor of ECL's tannery.
>
> (2) The escape of dissolved phase PCE, from the pools of neat PCE which collected at or towards the base of the chalk aquifers beneath ECL's works, into the chalk aquifers under the adjoining land and thence in the direction of Sawston Mill, must have begun at some unspecified date well before 1976 and be still continuing to the present day.
>
> (3) As held by the judge, the seepage of the PCE beneath the floor of ECL's works down into the chalk aquifers below was not foreseeable by a reasonable supervisor employed by ECL, nor was it foreseeable by him that detectable quantities of PCE would be found down-catchment, so that he could not have foreseen, in or before 1976, that the repeated spillages would lead to any environmental hazard or damage. The only foreseeable damage from a spillage of PCE was that somebody might be overcome by fumes from a substantial spillage of PCE on the surface of the ground.
>
> (4) The water so contaminated at Sawston Mill has never been held to be dangerous to health. But under criteria laid down in the UK Regulations, issued in response to the EEC Directive, the water so contaminated was not 'wholesome' and, since 1985, could not lawfully be supplied in this country as drinking water. [. . .]

Foreseeability of damage in nuisance

It is against this background that it is necessary to consider the question whether foreseeability of harm of the relevant type is an essential element of liability either in nuisance or under the rule in *Rylands v Fletcher*. I shall take first the case of nuisance. In the present case, as I have said, this is not strictly speaking a live issue. Even so, I propose briefly to address it, as part of the analysis of the background to the present case.

. . . We are concerned with the liability of a person where a nuisance has been created by one for whose actions he is responsible. Here, as I have said, it is still the law that the fact that the defendant has taken all reasonable care will not of itself exonerate him from liability, the relevant control mechanism being found within the principle of reasonable user. But it by no means follows that the defendant should be held liable for damage of a type which he could not reasonably foresee; and the development of the law of negligence in the past sixty years points strongly towards a requirement that such foreseeability should be a prerequisite of liability in damages for nuisance, as it is of liability in negligence. For if a plaintiff is in ordinary circumstances only able to claim damages in respect of personal injuries where he can prove such foreseeability on the part of the defendant, it is difficult to see why, in common justice, he should be in a stronger position to claim damages for interference with the enjoyment of his land where the defendant was unable to foresee such damage. Moreover, this appears to have been the conclusion of the Privy Council in *The Wagon Mound (No 2), Overseas Tankship (UK) Ltd v Miller Steamship Co Pty Ltd*, [1966] 2 All ER 709, [1967] 1 AC 617. The facts of the case [arise] from a public nuisance caused by a spillage of oil in Sydney Harbour. [In concluding that in cases of this kind] foreseeability is an essential element, Lord Reid [stated]:

> It could not be right to discriminate between different cases of nuisance so as to make foreseeability a necessary element in determining damages in those cases where it is a necessary element in determining liability, but not in others. So the choice is between it being a necessary element in all cases of nuisance or in none. In their Lordships' judgment the similarities between nuisance and other forms of tort to which *The Wagon Mound (No. 1)*, [1961] 1 All ER 404, [1961] AC 388 applies far outweigh any differences, and they must therefore hold that the judgment appealed from is wrong on this branch of the case. It is not sufficient that the injury suffered by the respondents' vessels was the direct result of the nuisance if that injury was in the relevant sense unforeseeable.

It is widely accepted that this conclusion, although not essential to the decision of the particular case, has nevertheless settled the law to the effect that foreseeability of harm is indeed a prerequisite of the recovery of damages in private nuisance, as in the case of public nuisance. I refer in particular to the opinion expressed by Professor Fleming in his book on Torts (8th edn, 1992) pp 443-444. It is unnecessary in the present case to consider the precise nature of this principle; but it appears from Lord Reid's statement of the law that he regarded it essentially as one relating to remoteness of damage.

Foreseeability of damage under the rule in *Rylands v Fletcher*

It is against this background that I turn to the submission advanced by ECL before your Lordships that there is a similar prerequisite of recovery of damages under the rule in *Rylands v Fletcher* (1866), LR 1 Exch 265.

I start with the judgment of Blackburn J in *Fletcher v Rylands* itself. His celebrated statement of the law is to be found where he said (at 279-280):

> We think that the true rule of law is, that the person who for his own purposes brings on his lands and collects and keeps there anything likely to do mischief if it escapes, must keep it in at his peril, and, if he does not do so, is prima facie answerable for all the damage which is the natural consequence of its escape. He can excuse himself by showing that the escape was owing to the plaintiff's default; or perhaps that the escape was the consequence of vis major, or the act of God; but as nothing of this sort exists here, it is unnecessary to inquire what excuse would be sufficient. The general rule, as above stated, seems on principle just. The person whose grass or corn is eaten down by the escaping cattle of his neighbour, or whose mine is flooded by the water from his neighbour's reservoir, or whose cellar is invaded by the filth of his neighbour's privy, or whose habitation is made unhealthy by the fumes and noisome vapours of his neighbour's alkali works, is damnified without any fault of his own; and it seems but reasonable and just that the neighbour, who has brought something on his own property which was not naturally there, harmless to others so long as it is confined to his own property, but which he knows to be mischievous if it gets on his neighbour's, should be obliged to make good the damage which ensues if he does not succeed in confining it to his own property. But for his act in bringing it there no mischief could have accrued, and it seems but just that he should at his peril keep it there so that no mischief may accrue, or answer for the natural and anticipated consequences. And upon authority, this we think is established to be the law whether the things so brought be beasts, or water, or filth, or stenches.

In that passage Blackburn J spoke of 'anything likely to do mischief if it escapes'; and later he spoke of something 'which he knows to be mischievous if it gets on to his neighbour's [property]', and the liability to 'answer for the natural and anticipated consequences'. Furthermore, time and again he spoke of the strict liability imposed upon the defendant as being that he must keep the thing in at his peril; and, when referring to liability in actions for damage occasioned by animals, he referred (at 282) to the established principle 'that it is quite immaterial whether the escape is by negligence or not'. The general tenor of his statement of principle is therefore that knowledge, or at least foreseeability of the risk, is a prerequisite of the recovery of damages under the principle; but that the principle is one of strict liability in the sense that the defendant may be held liable notwithstanding that he has exercised all due care to prevent the escape from occurring. [. . .]

The point is one on which academic opinion appears to be divided: cf Salmond and Heuston on Torts (20th edn, 1992) pp 324-325, which favours the prerequisite of foreseeability, and Clerk and Lindsell on Torts (16th edn, 1989) para 25.09, which takes a different view. However, quite apart from the indications to be derived from the judgment of Blackburn J in *Fletcher v Rylands*, LR 1 Exch 265 itself, the historical connection with the law of nuisance must now be regarded as pointing towards the conclusion that foreseeability of damage is a prerequisite of the recovery of damages under the rule. I have already referred to the fact that Blackburn J himself did not regard his statement of principle as having broken new ground; furthermore, Professor Newark has convincingly shown that the rule in *Rylands v Fletcher* was essentially concerned with an extension of the law of nuisance to cases of isolated escape. Accordingly since, following the observations of Lord Reid when delivering the advice of the Privy Council in *The Wagon Mound (No 2)*, [1966] 2 All ER 709 at 717, [1967] 1 AC 617 at 640, the recovery of damages in private nuisance depends on foreseeability by the defendant of the relevant type of damage, it would appear logical to extend the same requirement to liability under the rule in *Rylands v Fletcher*.

Even so, the question cannot be considered solely as a matter of history. It can be argued that the rule in *Rylands v Fletcher* should not be regarded simply as an extension of the law of nuisance, but should rather be treated as a developing principle of strict liability from which can be derived a general rule of strict liability for damage caused by ultra-hazardous operations, on the basis of which persons conducting such operations may properly be held strictly liable for the extraordinary risk to others involved in such operations. As is pointed out in Fleming on Torts (8th edn, 1992) pp. 327-328, this would lead to the practical result that the cost of damage resulting from such operations would have to be absorbed as part of the overheads of the relevant business rather than be borne (where there is no negligence) by the injured person or his insurers, or even by the community at large. Such a development appears to have been taking place in the United States, as can be seen from the Restatement of Torts (2d) vol 3 (1977). The extent to which it has done so is not altogether clear; and I infer from para 519, and the comment on that paragraph, that the abnormally dangerous activities there referred to are such that their ability to cause harm would be obvious to any reasonable person who carried them on. [. . .]

Like the judge in the present case, I incline to the opinion that, as a general rule, it is more appropriate for strict liability in respect of operations of high risk to be imposed by Parliament, than by the courts. If such liability is imposed by statute, the relevant activities can be identified, and those concerned can know where they stand. Furthermore, statute can where appropriate lay down precise criteria establishing the incidence and scope of such liability.

It is of particular relevance that the present case is concerned with environmental pollution. The protection and preservation of the environment is now perceived as being of crucial importance to the future of mankind; and public bodies, both national and international, are taking significant steps towards the establishment of legislation which will promote the protection of the environment, and make the polluter pay for damage to the environment for which he is responsible — as can be seen from the WHO, EEC and national regulations to which I have previously referred. But it does not follow from these developments that a common law principle, such as the rule in *Rylands v Fletcher*, should be developed or rendered more strict to provide for liability in respect of such pollution. On the contrary, given that so much well-informed and carefully structured legislation is now being put in place for this purpose, there is less need for the courts to develop a common law principle to achieve the same end, and indeed it may well be undesirable that they should do so.

. . . it appears to me to be appropriate now to take the view that foreseeability of damage of the relevant type should be regarded as a prerequisite of liability in damages under the rule. Such a conclusion can, as I have already stated, be derived from Blackburn J's original statement of the law; and I can see no good reason why this prerequisite should not be recognised under the rule, as it has been in the case of private nuisance. [. . .] It would moreover lead to a more coherent body of common law principles if the rule were to be regarded essentially as an extension of the law of nuisance to cases of isolated escapes from land, even though the rule as established is not limited to escapes which are in fact isolated. I wish to point out, however, that in truth the escape of the PCE from ECL's land, in the form of trace elements carried in percolating water, has not been an isolated escape, but a continuing escape resulting from a state of affairs which has come into existence at the base of the chalk aquifer underneath ECL's premises. Classically, this would have been regarded as a case of nuisance; and it would seem strange if, by characterising the case as one falling under the rule in *Rylands v Fletcher*, the liability should thereby be rendered more strict in the circumstances of the present case.

The facts of the present case

Turning to the facts of the present case, it is plain that, at the time when the PCE was brought onto ECL's land, and indeed when it was used in the tanning process there, nobody at ECL could reasonably have foreseen the resultant damage which occurred at CWC's borehole at Sawston.

However, there remains for consideration a point adumbrated in the course of argument, which is relevant to liability in nuisance as well as under the rule in *Rylands v Fletcher*. It appears that, in the present case, pools of neat PCE are still in existence at the base of the chalk aquifer beneath ECL's premises, and the escape of dissolved phase PCE from ECL's land is continuing to the present day. On this basis it can be argued that, since it has become known that PCE, if it escapes, is capable of causing damage by rendering water available at boreholes unsaleable for domestic purposes, ECL could be held liable, in nuisance or under the rule in *Rylands v Fletcher*, in respect of damage caused by the continuing escape of PCE from its land occurring at any time after such damage had become foreseeable by ECL.

For my part, I do not consider that such an argument is well founded. Here we are faced with a situation where the substance in question, PCE, has so travelled down through the drift and the chalk aquifer beneath ECL's premises that it has passed beyond the control of ECL. To impose strict liability on ECL in these circumstances, either as the creator of a nuisance or under the rule in *Rylands v Fletcher*, on the ground that it has subsequently become reasonably foreseeable that the PCE may, if it escapes, cause damage, appears to me to go beyond the scope of the regimes imposed under either of these two related heads of liability. This is because when ECL created the conditions which have ultimately led to the present state of affairs — whether by bringing the PCE in question onto its land, or by retaining it there, or by using it in its tanning process — it could not possibly have foreseen that damage of the type now complained of might be caused thereby. Indeed, long before the relevant legislation came into force, the PCE had become irretrievably lost in the ground below. In such circumstances, I do not consider that ECL should be under any greater liability than that imposed for negligence. [. . .]

I wish to add that the present case may be regarded as one of what is nowadays called historic pollution, in the sense that the relevant occurrence (the seepage of PCE through the floor of ECL's premises) took place before the relevant legislation came into force; and it appears that, under the current philosophy, it is not envisaged that statutory liability should be imposed for historic pollution (see e.g. the Council of Europe's Draft Convention on Civil Liability for Damages Resulting from Activities Dangerous to the Environment (Strasbourg, 29 January 1993) art 5.1, and para 48 of the Explanatory Report). If so, it would be strange if liability for such pollution were to arise under a principle of common law.

In the result, since those responsible at ECL could not at the relevant time reasonably have foreseen that the damage in question might occur, the claim of CWC for damages under the rule in *Rylands v Fletcher* must fail.

Natural use of land

I turn to the question whether the use by ECL of its land in the present case constituted a natural use, with the result that ECL cannot be held liable under the rule in *Rylands v Fletcher*. In view of my conclusion on the issue of foreseeability, I can deal with this point shortly.

The judge held that it was a natural use. He said:

> In my judgment, in considering whether the storage of organochlorines as an adjunct to a manufacturing process is a non-natural use of land, I must consider whether that storage created special risks for adjacent occupiers and whether the activity was for the general benefit of the community. It seems to me inevitable that I must consider the magnitude of the storage and the geographical area in which it takes place in answering the question. Sawston is properly described as an industrial village, and the creation of employment is clearly for the benefit of that community. I do not believe that I can enter upon an assessment of the point on a scale of desirability that the manufacture of wash leathers comes, and I content myself with holding that this storage in this place is a natural use of land.

It is a commonplace that this particular exception to liability under the rule has developed and changed over the years. It seems clear that in *Fletcher v Rylands* (1866), LR 1 Ex 265 itself Blackburn J's statement of the law was limited to things which are brought by the defendant onto his land, and so did not apply to things that were naturally upon the land. Furthermore, it is doubtful whether in the House of Lords in the same case Lord Cairns, to whom we owe the expression 'non-natural use' of the land, was intending to expand the concept of natural use beyond that envisaged by Blackburn J. Even so, the law has long since departed from any such simple idea, redolent of a different age; and, at least since the advice of the Privy Council delivered by Lord Moulton in *Rickards v Lothian*, [1913] AC 263 at 280, [1911-13] All ER Rep 71 at 80, natural use has been extended to embrace the ordinary use of land. [. . .]

Rickards v Lothian itself was concerned with a use of a domestic kind, viz the overflow of water from a basin whose runaway had become blocked. But over the years the concept of natural use, in the sense of ordinary use, has been extended to embrace a wide variety of uses, including not only domestic uses but also recreational uses and even some industrial uses.

It is obvious that the expression 'ordinary use of the land' in Lord Moulton's statement of the law is one which is lacking in precision. There are some writers who welcome the flexibility which has thus been introduced into this branch of the law, on the ground that it enables judges to mould and adapt the principle of strict liability to the changing needs of society; whereas others regret the perceived absence of principle in so vague a concept, and fear that the whole idea of strict liability may as a result be undermined. A particular doubt is introduced by Lord Moulton's alternative criterion 'or such a use as is proper for the general benefit of the community'. If these words are understood to refer to a local community, they can be given some content as intended to refer to such matters as, for example, the provision of services; indeed the same idea can, without too much difficulty, be extended to, for example, the provision of services to industrial premises, as in a business park or an industrial estate. But if the words are extended to embrace the wider interests of the local community or the general benefit of the community at large, it is difficult to see how the exception can be kept within reasonable bounds. [. . .]

Fortunately, I do not think it is necessary for the purposes of the present case to attempt any redefinition of the concept of natural or ordinary use. This is because I am satisfied that the storage of chemicals in substantial quantities, and their use in the manner employed at ECL's premises, cannot fall within the exception. For the purpose of testing the point, let it be assumed that ECL was well aware of the possibility that PCE, if it escaped, could indeed cause damage, for example by contaminating any water with which it became mixed so as to render that water undrinkable by human beings. I cannot think that it would be right in such circumstances to exempt ECL from liability under the rule in *Rylands v Fletcher* on the ground that the use was natural or ordinary. The mere fact that the use is common in the tanning industry cannot, in my opinion, be enough to bring the use within the exception, nor the fact that Sawston contains a small industrial community which is worthy of encouragement or support. Indeed I feel bound to say that the storage of substantial quantities of chemicals on industrial premises should be regarded as an almost classic case of non-natural use; and I find it very difficult to think that it should be thought objectionable to impose strict liability for damage caused in the event of their escape. It may well be that, now that it is recognised that foreseeability of harm of the relevant type is a prerequisite of liability in damages under the rule, the courts may feel less pressure to extend the concept of natural use to circumstances such as those in the present case; and in due course it may become easier to control this exception, and to ensure that it has a more recognisable basis of principle. For these reasons, I would not hold that ECL should be exempt from liability on the basis of the exception of natural use.

However, for the reasons I have already given, I would allow ECL's appeal with costs before your Lordships' House and in the courts below.

Notes and Questions

1. How do the trial judge and the House of Lords differ in their view of what constitutes a "non-natural use of land"? Which approach do you prefer? Explain.

2. Do you agree with the House of Lords that foreseeability should be a pre-condition to recovery under *Rylands v. Fletcher*? Under this ruling, who is liable for unforeseeable harm resulting from an unnatural use of land?

3. What role does the House of Lords see for government in addressing the issue of harm resulting from environmental pollution?

4. Compare the House of Lords' comments on the role of government through legislation to Justice Nunn's comments on the federal and provincial regulatory process in place for the approval and application of herbicides.

5. Legislators have taken various steps to address the shortcomings of the common law with respect to historic pollution. In the context of contaminated sites, this has taken the form of site remediation requirements that facilitate recovery of remediation costs from historic polluters (often defined in broad terms as "persons responsible" deemed statutorily liable for historic on-site activities) A variety of issues have proven controversial including the definition of "persons responsible", retrospective/retroactive application of the legislation, and apportionment of liability: see *Workshop Holdings Ltd. v. CAE Machinery Ltd.* (2003), 50 C.E.L.R. (N.S.) 11, 177 B.C.A.C. 70. Is historic pollution a problem that should primarily be left to legislators? To what extent should the common law be relied upon in this setting?

6. The mix of common law and legislation dealing with many aspects of environmental harm raises many legal issues. One such issue is whether and under what circumstances a statutory authority or duty to act should exempt a public official from liability for engaging in conduct that would ordinarily constitute a tort under the common law. See *Mandrake Management Consultants Ltd. v. Toronto Transit Commission* (1993), 11 C.E.L.R. (N.S.) 100 (Ont. C.A.) for a discussion of this issue in the context of noise and vibration from the Toronto subway system. Leading cases from the SCC include *Tock v. St. John's (City) Metropolitan Area Board* (1989), 64 D.L.R. (4th) 620, and *Ryan v. Victoria (City)*, [1999] 1 S.C.R. 201.

7. Another key issue in understanding the relationship between the common law and legislation in the environmental field is the effect of legislative efforts to regulate human activity on the common law. The court in *Palmer* was clearly influenced by regulatory decisions to allow the spraying of the herbicides in question. This issue is perhaps most apparent in the context of the duty of care under negligence. What if any effect should, for example, a regulatory approval for a certain concentration of a pollutant in effluent have on the duty of care imposed on the operator?

8. Finally, it is important to be aware that special principles apply to the liability in negligence of public authorities. In this setting, courts draw a distinction between acts/omissions that are "operational" in nature as opposed to those that have occurred as the result of a deliberate "policy" decision: see *Just v. British Columbia* (1989), 64 D.L.R. (4th) 689 (S.C.C.). Where the alleged tort arises out of a policy decision, courts will often conclude the government should be exempted from owing a duty of care to the plaintiff. On the other hand, where the harm arises out of an operational decision or activity, courts are more inclined to impose liability: see, for example, *Gauvin v. Ontario (Ministry of the Environment)* (1995), 22 C.E.L.R. (N.S.) 277; aff'd (1997), 26 C.E.L.R. (N.S.) 325 (Ont. Div. Ct.), and *Holland v. Saskatchewan (Minister of Agriculture, Food & Rural Revitalization)*, 2008 SCC 42.

Part II — Understanding the Limits of Traditional Torts

In Part I, we have seen some of the challenges involved in using the tort system to prevent or compensate harm to the environment. Both *Palmer* and *Cambridge Water* illustrate vividly the difficulties faced by plaintiffs when seeking to establish liability in tort for environmental harms. Some of these are a direct function of scientific uncertainty, some are a function of legal rules, systemic barriers, and judicial attitudes; and some are a function of the complex interplay between law and science. A compelling illustration of the lattermost phenomenon is the law of causation, which is the topic explored in this Part.

Lynda Collins, "Material Contribution to Risk and Causation in Toxic Torts"
(2001) 11 J. Env. L. & Prac. 105

In traditional tort scenarios, "causal indeterminacy arises randomly and always signifies a substantial chance that the defendant in fact harmed no-one". In contrast, causal uncertainty in toxic torts results from the inherent nature of the substances and injuries at issue. Frequently, although it is certain that a defendant has negligently caused harm to someone, all that an individual plaintiff can show is that the defendant materially contributed to her risk of developing the type of injury which she ultimately sustained. Where there is insufficient scientific evidence for the plaintiff to demonstrate on a balance of probabilities that a toxic defendant's negligence constituted a preponderance of the global risk factors (i.e., 51%), the plaintiff will fail on a traditional causation analysis. This holds true even where the defendant's negligence caused a significant increase in risk (for example, a 30% increase). Thus, traditional principles may deny recovery even where a defendant has fallen below minimum societal standards of conduct in its handling of toxic substances, this culpable behaviour has created a risk of harm to an innocent plaintiff, and a plaintiff has suffered injury within the area of risk. In this context, "[t]he all-or-nothing outcome of the but-for test all too often results in a 'nothing', inconsistent with modern expectations". As a result, the hegemony of the but-for test is being challenged in Canada, the U.S., and Australia.

The Scientific and Legal Nature of Toxic Torts

Toxic torts involve injuries caused by the negligence or other legally culpable conduct of persons having control over toxic substances. The scientific nature of toxics and toxic injury contributes to the legal difficulties inherent in toxic torts. For example, many of the injuries in toxic torts have long latency periods, during which evidence may be lost and subsequent supervening causal events may have occurred. A second and related difficulty is the existence of multiple potential causes of the injuries, such as cancer, that are at issue in toxic torts.

Further, the injurious encounter in toxic torts takes place partially on a microscopic level (molecules of a toxic substance entering the plaintiff's body), making the causation inquiry complex and difficult. The nature of the dispersal of injurious agents by toxic defendants renders the project of causal tracing difficult if not impossible in many cases. This is in contrast to the conventional tort claim. [. . .] Indeed, in toxic torts, all evidence material to the issue of causation must necessarily be [circumstantial] as no eye witness exists who can directly observe a chemical (molecule) leaving the defendant's plant and follow it until it enters the plaintiff's body where they can further observe it as a disease process is initiated.

Traditional principles of causation were not designed to deal with this kind of inherent causal uncertainty and may operate unfairly to place the burden of scientific uncertainty on innocent plaintiffs rather than negligent defendants.

The Traditional Test For Causation

At common law, causation is generally regarded as having two components. Legal or proximate causation ("remoteness"), which will not be examined here, involves a policy assessment of the degree of proximity between factual cause and injury which is necessary in order to justify the imposition of legal liability. In contrast, factual causation, the subject of the present discussion, is a quasi-scientific inquiry into the mechanistic relationship between the plaintiff's injury and the defendant's conduct. The factual causation analysis is generally seen as an inquiry into "the simple question of what happened, of whether the defendant's conduct produced the injury". However, as discussed below, the choice of one or another approach to factual causation rests squarely on a policy decision as to which party should bear the burden of uncertainty.

According to the traditional test for factual causation, a plaintiff must demonstrate, on a balance of probabilities that but for the defendant's negligence, she would not have sustained her loss. In other words, the defendant's negligence must constitute a *sine qua non* of the plaintiff's losses. In cases where a plaintiff suffers damage as a result of multiple causes, the but-for test is supplemented by a test of material contribution; i.e., causation will be established if it can be shown that the defendant materially contributed to the loss. In other words, it is not necessary for the plaintiff to show that the defendant's negligence was the sole cause of her loss. Courts recognize that there will frequently be a myriad of other background events which are necessary preconditions to the injury occurring . . . As long as a defendant is part of the cause of an injury, the defendant is liable, even though his act alone was not enough to create the injury. There is no basis for a reduction of liability because of the existence of other preconditions: defendants remain liable for all injuries caused or materially contributed to by their negligence.

The standard of proof in a traditional causation analysis action is the balance of probabilities and the burden of proof rests on the plaintiff. Thus, if a plaintiff can prove based on a probability of 51% or greater that the defendant's negligence caused or materially contributed to her loss, then factual causation is treated as a certainty and the plaintiff will be able to recover 100% of her past losses from the defendant (subject to a possible discount for the plaintiff's contributory negligence). If the evidence falls short of a 51% probability of causation, the plaintiff will have failed to discharge her burden of proof and will recover nothing. However, causation need not be proved to a level of scientific precision and may be inferred from very little affirmative evidence when the facts lie peculiarly within the knowledge of the defendant.

Finally, in contrast to the treatment of past losses, future losses flowing from an injury that has already been proved are not subject to the all-or-nothing causation analysis. Rather, once the underlying injury is proven on a balance of probabilities, future or hypothetical damages arising therefrom may be recoverable even when the likelihood of their occurring is less than 51%. However, damages for future or hypothetical losses are discounted by the probability that the loss will not occur, or that the loss would have occurred without the defendant's wrongdoing.

Generic v. Specific Causation and Probabilistic Evidence

In applying the but-for test to the factual causation inquiry, courts must explicitly or implicitly analyze two inter-related conceptual components of factual causation: generic causation and specific causation. In order to succeed a plaintiff must show both that the defendant's conduct was capable of causing the kind of injury sustained by the plaintiff (generic causation) and that it actually caused the plaintiff's injury (specific causation). A finding of specific causation necessarily entails a finding of generic causation (but not vice versa) and for this reason, the two are often collapsed in conventional tort cases. In contrast, "the analysis is attenuated and bifurcated in the toxic tort action". Toxic tort victims face serious obstacles under both headings.

Under the rubric of generic causation, toxic tort plaintiffs bear the burden of scientific uncertainty which surrounds many of the substances and illnesses at issue in toxic torts. Frequently, evidence sufficient to establish generic causation on a balance of probabilities simply does not exist.

Often there is insufficient medical knowledge about the illness, including which factors can initiate the disease process and the length of the latency period before it becomes expressed as a clinical symptom. Due to obvious ethical considerations, it is not possible to conduct controlled experiments on humans to shed light on these unanswered questions.

As a result of the impossibility of experimental research into these questions, scientific certainty may be unattainable. Thus, to establish generic causation, or material contribution to risk, plaintiffs must rely on statistical or "probabilistic" evidence emanating primarily from the field of epidemiology. [. . .] Epidemiology is "the study of the distribution of a disease or a physiological condition in human populations and of the factors that influence the distribution". Epidemiological research produces evidence of "causal associations" between particular illnesses and potential pathogens by studying disease incidence in identified populations, (e.g., those that have been exposed to asbestos in the workplace and those that have not).

There has been considerable academic controversy regarding the admissibility and sufficiency of epidemiologic and other probabilistic evidence on the issue of causation in toxic torts. Courts in the U.S. have generally responded to probabilistic evidence with "continuing discomfort and suspicion but such data have not been ruled out at least in the absence of other evidence". [. . .] However, epidemiological evidence has been admitted and relied upon for a finding of factual causation in a number of high profile cases. For example, in *Allen v. United States* (1984), 588 F. Supp. 247 the plaintiffs brought an action against the

Atomic Energy Commission alleging that they got cancer from exposure to radiation resulting from nuclear testing. In finding for the plaintiffs the court held:

> Where the injuries are causally indistinguishable, and where experts cannot determine whether an individual injury arises from culpable human cause or non-culpable natural causes, evidence that there is an increased incidence of injury in a population following exposure to the defendant's risk-creating conduct may justify an inference of "causal linkage" between the defendant's conduct and the plaintiff's injuries. In Canada, plaintiffs have generally been permitted to adduce probabilistic epidemiological evidence in tort litigation. [. . .] Epidemiological evidence was admitted and given substantial consideration in *Buchan v. Ortho Pharmaceutical (Can.) Ltd.* (1984), 46 O.R. (2d) 113 and *Snell v. Farrell*, [1990] 2 S.C.R. 311. These cases demonstrate that probabilistic proof that a defendant's negligence constituted a preponderance of global risk factors does meet the but-for or material contribution to injury test.

However, even where courts admit and give appropriate weight to probabilistic scientific evidence, and adopt the appropriate legal standard of proof, application of the traditional approach to causation (under which the plaintiff bears the burden of scientific uncertainty) may still prevent the plaintiff from recovering. Referring to epidemiological evidence, Fleming writes, "In some of the cases, such evidence implicates the defendant as well as other causes without reaching a magical 51% probability". In these cases, the traditional approach may prevent recovery even where the plaintiff can demonstrate a material contribution to risk, unless evidence of that risk is considered sufficient to give rise to an inference of causation under the flexible approach articulated in *Snell.*

The problem of establishing causation on a balance of probabilities in toxic torts is exacerbated by the inherent difficulties involved in the importation of scientific notions of proof into the legal arena. While proof in a civil case is defined as a probability of 51% or greater, the scientific community does not consider a proposition to have been proven until it has been established to a degree of certainty of 95% or more. Thus, even where a causal relationship sufficient to meet legal standards exists, it may be difficult or impossible for a toxic tort plaintiff to produce a scientist willing to testify that the causal connection has been proven. Theoretically, courts should simply apply the legal standard to the scientific evidence, but experience has shown that judges sometimes implicitly adopt the scientific standard. Where this occurs, it is virtually impossible for the toxic tort plaintiff to establish causation in the presence of scientific uncertainty.

Specific Causation: Indeterminate Defendants, Indeterminate Plaintiffs, and Indeterminate Harm

As noted above, once a plaintiff in a toxic tort action has proven that the defendant's conduct was capable of causing the type of injury she sustained, she must then demonstrate, on a balance of probabilities, that the defendant actually caused her particular injuries. In this regard, causal uncertainty manifests in a number of scenarios.

The Indeterminate Defendant

In one scenario, the plaintiff may be able to establish that she has been injured as a result of one or more of a group of negligent defendants but may not be able to identify which one was the cause-in-fact of her injury. This scenario is known as an indeterminate defendant case and is exemplified in the diethylstilbestrol (DES) cases of which *Sindell v. Abbott Laboratories* (1980), 607 P. 2d 924 is probably the most famous. In that case, the plaintiff, who suffered vulvic cancer as a result of her mother's ingestion of DES during pregnancy was unable to identify the specific manufacturer who made the drug taken by her mother. On the traditional approach the plaintiff would have failed because she could not make out causation against any specific defendant. As discussed below, the court in *Sindell* adopted a controversial theory of market share liability to permit recovery.

The Indeterminate Plaintiff

Unlike the vulvic cancer at issue in *Sindell*, many of the injuries suffered by plaintiffs in toxic torts are not so closely related to specific substances as to be considered "signature illnesses". Where plaintiffs suffer non-signature illnesses present at background levels in the general population, it may be difficult or impossible to prove that the plaintiff would not have contracted the illness but for exposure to the defendant's toxin(s), due to the multiplicity of risk factors. All that can be shown is that the plaintiff belongs to a class of people whose risk of illness was materially increased as a result of the defendant's negligence and that the plaintiff's injury is consistent with the negligently created risk. Waddams illustrates this dilemma, known as plaintiff indeterminacy, with the following example.

> The defendant pollutes the air and increases the risk to the whole population of Australia of contracting skin cancer, raising the risk, let us say, from 10 per 100 000 to 19 per 100 000. On these figures, no particular plaintiff with cancer can show that the defendant probably caused the disease: more probably than not the plaintiff would have contracted it in any case. Should the defendant be liable? If so, should the plaintiff recover full compensation, or only 9/19ths of it?

Indeterminate Harm and the Future Claimant

A third kind of indeterminacy, which is sometimes viewed as a subset of the indeterminate plaintiff, is the scenario of the future claimant, or indeterminate harm. In this case, a plaintiff may be able to show that a particular defendant has increased her risk of contracting a specific illness or group of illnesses. However, she has not yet developed any injury and has no way of ascertaining whether illness will in fact manifest. This scenario raises the prospect of recovery on a number of bases; in such circumstances plaintiffs could claim for the cost of medical monitoring, for mental distress caused by exposure to the risk (e.g. cancerphobia), and for the intangible loss of value to the plaintiff caused by exposure to risk.

The Flexible Application of the Traditional Approach: *Snell v. Farrell*

Before examining the alternative risk-based theories in greater detail, it is useful to question the necessity of resorting to these alternative approaches. In *Snell v. Farrell*, the Supreme Court of Canada had an opportunity to reconsider the traditional approach to causation in negligence. In that case the plaintiff suffered atrophy in her optic nerve following surgery to remove a cataract. The trial judge found that the doctor was negligent in continuing the surgery after the appearance of a retrobulbar bleed, but the medical experts who testified were uncertain as to whether this negligence was the cause of the optic nerve atrophy. There were a number of plausible non-culpable explanations for the injury and no way of ascertaining directly which scenario had actually occurred.

Despite this factual uncertainty, the trial judge in *Snell*, relying on the English case of *McGhee*, [1973] 1.W.L.R. 1 (H.L.) discussed further below, found that the case fell "within an emerging branch of the law of causation" which imposes on the defendant the burden of disproving causation where material contribution to risk is made out. The Court of Appeal upheld this approach despite the fact that in the interim the House of Lords had reinterpreted *McGhee* in *Wilsher v. Essex Area Health Authority*, [1988] 1 All E.R. 871 firmly re-entrenching the but-for test and the traditional allocation of the burden of proof, and rejecting material contribution to risk as proof of causation.

In *Snell* the Supreme Court of Canada considered the criticisms that have been leveled against the traditional but-for approach to causation. Sopinka J. prefaced the causation analysis as follows:

> The traditional approach to causation has come under attack in a number of cases in which there is concern that due to the complexities of proof, the probable victim of tortious conduct will be deprived of relief . . . The challenge to the traditional approach has manifested itself in cases dealing with non-

> traumatic injuries such as man-made disease resulting from the widespread diffusion of chemical products, including product liability cases in which a product which can cause injury is widely manufactured and marketed by a large number of corporations. . . . The question that this Court must decide is whether the traditional approach to causation is no longer satisfactory in that plaintiffs in malpractice suits are being deprived of compensation because they cannot prove causation where it in fact exists.

Sopinka, J. went on to express some willingness to consider the adoption of burden-shifting alternatives to the traditional approach, if these could be shown to be necessary. In an oft-quoted *obiter* he stated:

> If I were convinced that defendants who have a substantial connection to the injury were escaping liability because plaintiffs cannot prove causation under currently applied principles, I would not hesitate to adopt one of these alternatives.

He concluded, however, that the traditional test was capable of dealing with causal indeterminacy and the adoption of alternatives was therefore unnecessary.

This holding in itself may not have foreclosed the possibility of causation reform in tort law but for Sopinka J.'s further finding that adoption of the alternatives was undesirable based on principle and policy. He made an implicit finding that adoption of the burden-shifting alternatives would be unjust, stating that it would "have the effect of compensating plaintiffs where a substantial connection between the injury and the defendant's conduct is absent". He also intimated that adoption of alternative standards of causation could lead to a liability crisis such as the U.S. malpractice crisis of the 1970's. Sopinka J. did preserve the reversal of the burden of proof where two defendants negligently fire in the direction of a plaintiff, tortiously destroying the means of proof at the plaintiff's disposal but he rejected the extension of this principle to a situation in which the plaintiff's injury may have resulted from non-culpable causes or behaviour.

Despite this rejection of radical reform, the Supreme Court's judgment in *Snell* did leave room for recovery in cases of causal indeterminacy (i.e., where material contribution to risk is all that can be established). Indeed, Sopinka J. asserted that the traditional approach is inherently capable of permitting recovery in such circumstances and that dissatisfaction with the traditional test results from its "too-rigid application by the courts in many cases". He then went on to clarify the flexibility inherent in the traditional approach. Sopinka J. reiterated the principle that "the allocation of the burden of proof is not immutable. Both the burden and the standard of proof are flexible concepts". He held that in circumstances in which the facts lie peculiarly within the knowledge of the defendant, "very little affirmative evidence on the part of the plaintiff will justify the drawing of an inference of causation in the absence of evidence to the contrary".

While Sopinka J. rejected the characterization of such inferential reasoning as a shift in the evidentiary burden to the defendant, it likely operates to the same effect. Indeed the Court noted that Canadian decisions after *Wilsher*, while accepting its interpretation of *McGhee* (rejecting the reversal of the burden of proof on causation) appeared to reach the same result as they would have under the principles articulated in *McGhee*. [. . .]

In *Snell* Sopinka J. affirmed that causation need not be determined to a level of scientific precision, adopting the statement of Lord Salmon in *Alphacell Ltd. v. Woodward* that "[c]ausation is essentially a practical question of fact which can best be answered by ordinary common sense rather than abstract metaphysical theory". The so-called "common sense" approach to causation has received considerable support in the common law world and appears to offer a real possibility of success for victims of toxic torts without discarding the traditional principles of causation. [. . .]

Taken together with a liberal treatment of epidemiological and other probabilistic evidence, this approach could substantially mitigate the unfair disadvantage to toxic tort plaintiffs resulting from scientific uncertainty. Indeed, one commentator writes that the Court's articulation of causation in *Snell*

> . . . leads one to suggest that the dissatisfaction which has arisen in environmental litigation because of the seeming inability of the law of torts to redress incidents of environmental harm is misplaced. The cure for it may lie with litigants to recognize and exploit the flexible nature of the burden of proof, which Sopinka J. has affirmed with clarity.

While the case law since *Snell* does leave room for some cautious optimism with respect to toxic tort plaintiffs' ability to recover under traditional principles, the relative paucity of toxic tort litigation in Canada must reflect significant ongoing barriers. In addition to the extraordinary costs associated with toxic tort litigation (due primarily to the need for extensive scientific evidence), it may be that the uncertainty caused by *Snell* has discouraged many plaintiffs from going forward. [. . .]

However, the Supreme Court of Canada's decision in *Hollis v. Dow Corning Corp*, indicates that the substantive information gap that typically exists as between plaintiffs and defendants in toxic torts may suffice to justify a flexible application of traditional standards. In that case, involving personal injury resulting from breast implants, the court relaxed the but-for standard by relieving the plaintiff of proving that her doctor would have warned her of the pertinent risks had the manufacturer provided the doctor with the necessary information. In justifying this relief, the Court treated the situation as analogous to *Cook v. Lewis*, relying on the fact that the plaintiff "was in a position of great informational inequality" with respect to both the doctor and the manufacturer. If this is the standard for measuring the *Snell* criterion that the facts lie particularly within the knowledge of the defendant, it should not be difficult for most toxic tort plaintiffs to qualify. It is self-evident that corporations producing toxic substances will generally have far superior access to knowledge pertaining to these chemicals than would an ordinary citizen. If substantial informational inequality is a sufficient justification for a flexible application of the but-for test in the context of multiple negligent defendants in a products liability case, it may also be seen as an adequate basis for the drawing of causal inferences in the presence of uncertainty in other kinds of toxic torts.

Thus, the flexible application of the traditional test articulated in *Snell* has proven sufficient to permit many toxic tort plaintiffs to recover. The practical effect of *Snell* is to permit a finding of causation of a plaintiff's injury based on proof of material contribution to risk in many cases. However, *Snell* maintains proof of causation of actual injury as the theoretical basis for the imposition of liability. For policy reasons discussed below, I would advocate for the displacement of this traditional approach in toxic torts in favour of the treatment of material contribution to risk as rebuttable proof of causation and the creation of a new tort of negligent creation of risk.

Alternative Approaches and Risk-Based Liability

While there has been substantial controversy regarding the ability of toxic tort plaintiffs to recover under traditional approaches to causation, many scholars have proposed, and some courts have adopted, alternative approaches which explicitly address the causation difficulties inherent in these cases. These approaches exist along a continuum ranging from relatively modest modifications of the traditional injury-based approach to pure risk-based liability.

In a meta-analysis of case law and scholarship dealing with factual causation, Robertson discerns five alternatives to the traditional but-for test. These are: the material contribution/substantial factor test (already a part of Canadian law); altering the burden of proof; concerted action theory; market share liability; and the redefinition of 'injury' (i.e., the creation of a new tort of wrongful risk creation). Gerecke argues that the alternatives are unified in their imposition of liability on the basis of causation of risk rather than injury. In fact, the so-called 'risk-based' alternatives differ significantly in their treatment of risk versus injury within the causation analysis.

A strong risk-based approach dispenses with the need to prove causation of the plaintiff's injury on a balance of probabilities, and imposes liability based on the negligent creation of non-trivial risk. A less radical form of risk-based liability treats proof of causation of risk as a proxy for proof of causation of injury; this may take the form of the imposition of a legal or evidentiary burden on the defendant, or the imposition on a group of risk-producers of liability for a plaintiff's full loss based on concerted action theory. The two major theories that will be discussed here are i) the reversal of the onus of proof of causation in a standard negligence action (a weaker risk-based approach) and ii) dispensing with the requirement of proof of causation of injury in favour of the imposition of liability for the negligent creation of risk itself (a stronger risk-based approach). The latter may be accomplished through the explicit creation of a new tort or as a radical judicial innovation within a traditional negligence action.

Reversing the Onus of Proof

An early attempt at devising an alternative approach to causation in the presence of scientific uncertainty is the English case of *McGhee*. In that case, the plaintiff developed dermatitis as a result of exposure to brick dust in his workplace. The employer was found to be negligent in failing to provide showers to workers, but scientific uncertainty regarding the causes of dermatitis precluded a positive conclusion as to whether the failure to shower caused the condition or whether it would have developed even with the benefit of showers. Lord Wilberforce articulated a version of risk-based liability in which proof of risk is allowed to stand in for proof of injury. He held that:

> . . . where a person has, by breach of duty of care, created a risk, and injury occurs within the area of that risk, the loss should be borne by him unless he shows that it had some other cause.

This burden could be imposed on a defendant as a legal burden of disproving causation on a balance of probabilities or as an evidentiary burden requiring the defendant to adduce some evidence to disprove causation after which point the original allocation of burdens of proof would be reactivated and the plaintiff would have to go on to prove causation on a balance of probabilities. [. . .] a number of Canadian cases after *McGhee* followed Lord Wilberforce's approach, imposing liability in the absence of a showing by the plaintiff of but-for causation of actual injury. However, in *Snell*, the Supreme Court of Canada followed the *Wilsher* interpretation of *McGhee* and rejected the shifting of any burden of proof to the defendant. Nevertheless, Lord Wilberforce's approach remains a cogent model, worthy of consideration by legislative reformers.

Liability for Risk

Since *McGhee* a number of American courts have treated proof of risk as a sufficient basis for recovery, allowing for recovery (to differing degrees) from the defendant when the plaintiff makes a showing of risk alone. In *Collins v. Eli Lilly Co.*, the Wisconsin Supreme Court adopted a "radical version of the risk contribution theory" allowing a plaintiff to sue any one of a group of negligent manufacturers of DES and recover 100% of her damages on proof of "possible causation" of her injury. The plaintiff was not required to bring any evidence with respect to the chronological or geographical distribution of DES by the chosen defendant linking that defendant with the DES that caused her injury. The court explicitly based the imposition of *de facto* joint liability on the fact that "each defendant contributed to the risk of injury to the public and, consequently, the risk of injury to the individual plaintiffs".

Similarly, in *Martin v. Abbot Laboratories*, the Washington Supreme Court allowed a plaintiff to recover from one possible defendant among a group of negligent DES manufacturers but permitted each individual manufacturer to limit its liability to its market share. In *Hymowitz v. Eli Lilly and Co*, the New York court took risk-based liability to its extreme, holding a DES manufacturer liable even though it demonstrated that it did not produce the drug taken by the plaintiff's mother. The Court explained:

> Because liability here is based on the over-all risk produced, and not causation in a single case, there should be no exculpation of a defendant who, although a member of the market producing DES for pregnancy use, appears not to have caused a particular plaintiff's injury.

In this case, the court did not treat proof of risk as a proxy for proof of injury. Rather, it effectively elevated the negligent creation of risk to a tort in itself, and then imposed the cost of the plaintiff's full losses as the measure of damages and liability. Another version of the creation of a new tort of negligent risk creation is to collapse the causation inquiry with the assessment of damages, awarding plaintiffs a percentage of their full losses based on the probability that the loss was caused by the defendant's negligence. Gerecke explains: Liability for risk exposure will permit the plaintiff to recover in some circumstances when he or she previously would have been barred; however, the award will be discounted to the extent that it is likely that the plaintiff's injury was caused by risk factors other than the defendant's negligence. Thus, it is also referred to as "proportional liability".

Gerecke proposes this "risk as injury" thesis as a "unified approach" to the indeterminate defendant, the indeterminate plaintiff, and the indeterminate harm/future claimant scenarios. In the indeterminate defendant situation, a plaintiff who can prove that her injury resulted from the negligent conduct of one or more of an identifiable group of defendants may achieve full or close to full recovery for her losses. The most famous example of this approach is the California case of *Sindell* referred to above. In that case, the court imposed liability on the defendant manufacturers of DES based on their share of the DES market at the time when the plaintiff's mother would have bought the drug. In effect, the court allowed recovery against each defendant based on the probability that it produced the drug that caused the plaintiff's harm, if the plaintiff could join a substantial proportion of the producers of DES. Since this inevitably results in imposing liability on manufacturers who did not in fact cause the plaintiff's harm, the imposition of liability must be based on the negligent creation of risk rather than injury to a particular plaintiff. [. . .]

In the case of the indeterminate plaintiff, the application of the "risk as injury" thesis operates differently. Returning to the example provided by Waddams, in a case where a defendant increased the risk of skin cancer from 10 out of 100 000 to 19 out of 100 000, each potential plaintiff in the class of people with skin cancer would recover 9/19ths of her losses.

Some advocates of the risk-as-injury thesis would require indeterminate plaintiffs to proceed against the defendant through a class action. In this way, the defendant would be compelled to compensate the entire class of people who were negligently exposed to the unreasonable risk. This collectivist approach to recovery by plaintiffs as a class seems highly attractive when measured against the objective of deterrence as it results in a defendant ultimately paying for the total amount of injury it created. However, it is seriously inadequate when viewed from the perspective of compensation; those plaintiffs whose injury was not caused by the defendant's conduct receive an undeserved windfall while those whose losses were caused by the defendant may be seriously under-compensated.

With respect to indeterminate harm/future claimants, a risk-as-injury approach (i.e., the creation of a new tort) would permit recovery in claims which are completely barred by the traditional approach. Again, indeterminate harm arises where a plaintiff can demonstrate that a defendant has increased her chances of developing a particular disease by a specified amount, but the plaintiff has not yet, and may never develop that illness. [. . .]

The adoption of proportional recovery in the causation analysis would impose liability on a defendant upon proof of causation of risk alone. In contrast, the imposition of probabilistically discounted liability for future losses in the damages analysis maintains actual injury as the fundamental basis for liability since the issue does not arise until after causation of an underlying injury has been proven on a balance of probabilities. Thus, the Court's insistence on the distinction between past and future events may be seen as a rejection of pure risk-based liability. While *Snell* has had the effect of allowing recovery where material contribution to risk is all that can be established, the Court's explicit rejection of even the weaker form of risk-based liability embodied in *McGhee* suggests that Canadian courts are at least doctrinally committed to the injury-based approach.

Despite the poor prospects of Canadian courts adopting a purely risk-based alternative approach to causation in toxic torts, there remains a strong argument that such an initiative should be taken by legislatures.

Conclusion

The scientific uncertainty surrounding toxic injury requires the adoption of alternative approaches to causation in order to permit recovery in many cases. The argument for adopting a risk-based approach to causation in toxic torts is sound in theory and in substance. More importantly, it responds to a compelling need in modern society which the current traditional injury-based approach is unable to adequately address [. . .]

If tort law is to remain relevant in the twenty-first century, it must find a way to redress these modern wrongs. Just as the development of mass manufacture and mass transportation in the early part of the 20th century required the revolutionary extension of liability effected by *McAlister (Donoghue) v. Stevenson*, the "chemicalization of society" requires the further extension of tort law into risk-based liability in order to deter and compensate victims for the bodily harm caused by toxic torts. While *Snell v. Farrell* constituted a step in this direction, it maintained injury as the theoretical basis for liability and failed to provide plaintiffs with the certainty necessary to justify the expense of commencing an action.

The imposition of a reverse onus on causation where material contribution to risk has been made out coupled with the more radical creation of a new tort of negligent creation of risk constitutes a clear and just response to the problem of toxic torts. As one commentator wrote . . . two decades ago, "[t]he need for these or related proposals is clear; the time for our legislatures to act is past due".

Notes and Questions

1. Based on the above article, identify the key deficiencies in current Canadian tort law with respect to causation in the toxic tort context.

2. Do you agree with the reforms advocated by the author with respect to reversing the onus of proof in material contribution situations? Do you support what she describes as the "more radical" step of creating a new tort of negligent creation of risk?

3. To what extent do you share her pessimism about the potential for these reforms to evolve through the common law as opposed to through legislative action?

4. Some commentators have suggested that the basic objectives of tort law are undermined by the causation issue in combination with the latency of harm in many environmental cases. Assuming that the three objectives of tort law are compensation, deterrence, and corrective justice, do you agree? See Albert C. Lin, "Beyond Tort: Compensating Victims of Environmental Toxic Injury" (2004-2005) 78 S. Cal. L. Rev. 1439 at 1444–1453.

Part III — Class Action Suits and Environmental Tort Claims

While a longstanding part of American law, class actions are a relatively new phenomenon in Canada, yet one that is of growing importance. Class action legislation is now in force in eight provinces, with only Nova Scotia and PEI having yet to enact such a law. While there are some important differences amongst these various laws, all require a representative of the class to obtain certification before commencing a class action. This can be costly; lawyers specializing in the field report that securing in complex cases certification can cost more than $1 million in legal and expert fees and disbursements. On the other hand, once an action is certified, under most class action regimes the plaintiffs are either immune from the spectre of being liable for adverse costs awards or qualify to have such costs paid out of a dedicated fund set aside for this purpose. As well, in many cases, certification will create powerful incentives for the defendant to agree to an out of court settlement of the claim.

When class actions first came to Canada, many commentators were optimistic about their potential to redress access to justice barriers in the environmental law context. For instance, Justice Rothman (formerly of the Quebec Court of Appeal) observed that "[t]he class action recourse seems to me a particularly useful remedy in appropriate cases of environmental damage", particularly where the numerous potential plaintiffs were similarly affected by air and water pollution, and would otherwise be deterred from seeking legal recourse by the cost and complexity of litigation.

It would appear, however, that with respect to environmental harms, class actions have yet to make a substantial difference in terms of promoting access to justice. According to Professor Heather McLeod-Kilmurray:

> Although class actions are designed to empower group litigation, environmental class actions are rarely permitted. This is partly because their claims for private law actions seeking monetary compensation cause courts to focus on individual aspects of the problem, and the collective harm caused by widespread environmental effects is overlooked. Because most environmental lawsuits are prohibitively complex and expensive for individuals to litigate, this results in a denial of justice. It also prevents courts from playing their institutional role in the struggle to craft appropriate legal responses . . . Greater focus on the role of groups and the collective nature of environmental harms would lead to different approaches to interpreting class action procedure: [see Heather McLeod-Kilmurray, "*Hoffman v. Monsanto*: Courts, Class Actions, and Perceptions of the Problem of GM Drift" (2007) 27 Bul. Sci., Tech & Soc. 188)

Consider the following critical commentary that focusses on two leading appellate level decisions in the environmental class action context: *Hollick v. Metropolitan Toronto (Municipality)*, 2001 SCC 68 and *Pearson v. Inco Ltd.* (2005), 261 D.L.R. (4th) 629 (Ont. C.A.). This commentary focusses on the Ontario *Class Proceedings Act*, which in most relevant respects is akin to those in force in most other Canadian provinces that have class action laws.

Grant Boyle, "Can class actions be used to secure environmental rights in Ontario?" *Ecobulletin*

(CBA National Environmental, Energy and Resources Section Law Newsletter: November 2007)

Introduction

How can class actions be used to secure environmental justice? To the extent that class actions are intended to foster access to justice, and modification in important policy areas, one would think that health and environmental impacts of industrial pollution would make the cut. Environmental pollution continues as a major threat to societal well-being in Canada and around the world, and polls have recently shown that Canadians rate the environment as a primary public concern. In December 2006, the UK Treasury described climate change as the "greatest and widest ranging externality ever seen".

One might also expect that an environmental class action would be particularly accessible to claimants in a jurisdiction like Ontario, which passed the *Class Proceedings Act* in 1992. Further, the Supreme Court of Canada has said that class actions are important in modern market economies for addressing such problems as "environmental wrongs".

This paper suggests, however, that despite this conceptual compatibility, environmental class actions (and particularly those that claim health damages from pollution) are unlikely to be certified under current legislation. The problem lies primarily with the incompatibility, or at least the perception of incompatibility, between the need for judicial economy in such proceedings and the inherently individual nature of health-related damages from pollution.

Background

In *Western Canada Shopping Centres v. Dutton*, [2001] 2 S.C.R. 534, [*Dutton*], the Supreme Court traced the origins of class actions back to the English courts of equity in the 17th and 18th centuries, which developed class actions when joinder became too cumbersome to deal with pre-limited liability, commercial litigation against business co-operatives. The courts of equity aimed to balance fairness and efficiency in the interest of "complete justice". With the fusion of law and equity at the end of the 19th century, class actions were given a more restrictive approach, but were revived at the end of the 20th century with the rise of mass consumption and increased incidence of "many suitors with the same grievance". [. . .]

[The court in *Dutton* also underscored] the importance of class actions for addressing environmental pollution:

> The class action plays an important role in today's world. The rise of mass production, the diversification of corporate ownership, the advent of the mega-corporation, and the recognition of environmental wrongs have contributed to its growth . . . environmental pollution may have consequences for citizens all over the country. . . . The class action offers a means of efficiently resolving such disputes in a manner that is fair to all parties.

Class action certification under s. 5(1) of the Ontario *Class Proceedings Act*

A key provision in the Act is s. 5(1), which sets out the requirements for certifying a class action . . . a person wishing to proceed with a class action must make a motion for certification and meet the following tests:

(a) the pleadings or the notice of application discloses a cause of action;

(b) there is an identifiable class of two or more persons that would be represented by the representative plaintiff or defendant;

(c) the claims or defences of the class members raise common issues;

(d) a class proceeding would be the *preferable procedure* for the resolution of the common issues;

(e) there is a representative plaintiff or defendant who,

(i) would fairly and adequately represent the interests of the class,

(ii) has produced a plan for the proceeding that sets out a workable method of advancing the proceeding on behalf of the class and of notifying class members of the proceeding, and

(iii) does not have, on the common issues for the class, an interest in conflict with the interests of other class members. (emphasis added)

It would appear that s. 5(1)(d) — the requirement that the class proceeding is the preferable procedure — has emerged as the key criterion in assessing whether to certify an environmental class proceeding. This section was the stumbling block for the appellant in *Hollick v. Metropolitan Toronto* in which the Supreme Court refused to certify a class that claimed damages relating to pollution emanating from a landfill managed by the City of Toronto. In that case, the court found there was a cause of action, identifiable class, and common issues, but found the class action not to be the preferable procedure because there was no access to justice issue (the class members could have taken other action like small claims). Behaviour modification was not an issue (the court cited other means to deter polluters through the *Ontario Environmental Bill of Rights* or *Environmental Protection Act*) and there was insufficient judicial economy (the common issues were considered negligible in relation to the individual issues).

The judicial economy section of the preferable procedure analysis in *Hollick* is particularly noteworthy. The chief justice said: "There is no reason to think that any pollution was distributed evenly across the geographic area or time period specified in the class definition. On the contrary it is likely that some areas were affected more seriously than others and some areas were affected at one time while other areas were affected at other times". The Ontario Court of Appeal in *Hollick* said:

> No common issue other than liability was suggested and I cannot devise one that would advance the litigation. An issue such as "Did the defendant emit pollutants into the atmosphere over a six-year period, and if so, when, and to what extent?" would result in a virtual Royal Commission into the operation of this landfill site without any measurable advance in the litigation.

In *Pearson v. Inco Ltd.*, the Supreme Court refused leave for appeal a decision by the Ontario Court of Appeal to certify a class of residents who suffered from nickel oxide pollution from a smelter run by Inco. In that case the lower courts refused to certify the class because of its broad claims for health-related damages, which were viewed by the court as inherently individualistic. However, the class subsequently reduced its claim to property losses alone and the court of appeal granted certification, satisfied that a Ministry of Environment announcement concerning the pollution led to a *general* fall in property prices. The court remarked:

> As the claim was originally framed in this case, a class proceeding would also not have the advantage of judicial economy. The individual claims of injury to health and related claims would dwarf the resolution of the common issues. With the narrowing of the claim that is no longer the case. The claim now concerns the single issue of reduction in property values.

The good and bad news for environmental class actions

On the one hand, the *Pearson* case represents a positive development for environmental class actions related to property damages. In this regard, the case could open the way for a range of class proceedings where the individual assessments required are limited to property damage rather than health effects damages. The challenge for future class actions like *Pearson* will be to show that a loss in property values resulted from the pollution in question, a test which would need to be met under the common issues requirement: s. 5(1)(c).

On the other hand, the combined effects of *Hollick* and *Pearson* are quite damaging for environmental class actions where claims are for effects on individual health. As noted above, the health claims in *Pearson* were held in the lower court to preclude certification, even though the risks posed to health were serious. And given the fact that most forms of pollution have divergent effects on people, depending on physical geography and human physiology, successful class actions for health claims from pollution are not likely to arise any time soon under Ontario law.

The judicial economy requirement behind class action certification that arises in the 5(1)(d) analysis could overwhelm environmental class actions claiming health damages in Ontario. On one hand this seems to makes sense, since judicial economy has been a cornerstone of the rationale supporting class actions in general — apparently since they were first used in the 17th century. Moreover, Parliament may be in a better position to address widespread environmental impacts than the courts are. However, where judicial economy emerges as paramount, one must inquire into the resultant trade-offs in access to justice and, in the case of class proceedings in Ontario, the trade-off in behaviour modification goals. It seems an odd result that environmental class actions related to health damages, among all others, are not accessible to Ontarians.

Some potential solutions

Certainly, the Act contains a number of provisions that would allow the proponent of an environmental class action to urge a given court to take a flexible approach. Section 6(1) says that a class cannot be barred because individual assessment of damages would be required. Section 5(2) allows the court to identify subclasses where appropriate. Conceivably, this could allow several environmental classes to emerge, where one turned out to be too broad. [*Ed note*: Analogous provisions are likewise found in other provincial class action laws.]

Also, s. 25 appears to offer an efficient way to compile outstanding divergent issues in an environmental class action claim. Section 25(1) allows the court to certify the class, while at the same time assessing individual issues. Section 25(1)(b) in particular allows for the appointment of "one or more persons to conduct a reference" to assess individual issues. Section 25(1)(c) goes on to allow "any other manner" to be employed for this end. Finally, a proponent could wage a strong and compelling argument under the access to justice and behaviour modification aspects of the preferable procedure test in s. 5(1)(d).

Still, the combined effects of the judicial economy imperative and the inherently individual and divergent nature of pollution impacts on people's health makes certification seem challenging in such cases based on the jurisprudence addressed above. In the face of such a dilemma, proponents of environmental class actions could develop new arguments. One possible route forward could be to allege some form of generalized liability akin to the liability tobacco companies now face for the public healthcare costs of smokers as measured by a general standard.

The Supreme Court has shown that it is open to innovations in class certifications. In *Rumley v. British Colombia*, which involved alleged sexual, physical and emotional abuse at a residential school for children with disabilities, the Supreme Court sanctioned the concept of "systemic liability" in order to certify a class whose claims in negligence against one institution spanned a 40-year period. Although environmental class action claims certainly differ from *Rumley* in a number of ways, the case does show that the court can be flexible in finding a sufficient range of common issues, where it seems as if individual issues prevail. On this point, the fact that the Ontario Court of Appeal in *Pearson* was willing to certify, while acknowledging the need for individual property assessments, suggests similar treatment could be argued for health effects.

Conclusion

At present, while environmental pollution appears amenable to a class action proceeding in theory, an Ontario court would be unlikely to certify a class proceeding where individual health damages from pollution are claimed. From the perspective of future environmental class action proponents, the certification of a class in *Pearson* for property damages from pollution opens a door. However, health impacts (perhaps the impacts that are most closely associated with the policy concerns which make environmental class actions compelling opportunities) are not yet on the table as manifest in cases like *Pearson* and *Hollick*. Barring a very innovative or flexible reading of the Act that alters the individual treatment of health damages or minimizes the importance of judicial economy in relation to access to justice and behaviour modification, the class proceeding in Ontario is best described as incapable of securing such rights.

Notes and Questions

1. Should rules for class action suits be different for environmental cases than in other tort claims? Explain.

2. What difference would it have made to the *Palmer* case if it had proceeded by way of a class action suit?

3. What, if any, changes would you make to the rules for certifying class action suits? How would these changes improve the effectiveness of tort law in the environmental field?

4. The Supreme Court of Canada has recently rendered judgment in another environmental class action case: *Barrette v. St. Lawrence Cement Inc.*, 2008 SCC 64. In this case, residents of a suburb of Québec City brought a class action against St. Lawrence Cement Inc. for neighbourhood disturbances related to the operation of a cement plant in that city. In the result, the SCC affirmed the right of the neighbours to bring actions for environmental harm under article 976 of the Quebec *Civil Code*. It also distinguished its earlier holding in *Hollick*, a case where it affirmed a decision to deny certification due to the diversity of harms experienced by class members. In *Barrette*, the Court concluded that members of the class experienced similar injuries, and that the trial judge had discretion to assess damages on an "averaged" basis so as to facilitate the litigation.

5. In early February 2009, a BC coastal First Nation filed the first-ever class action based on Aboriginal rights alleging that the BC Government should be held liable for damages as a result of licencing the operation of open-cage fish farms that it alleges has contributed to a steep decline in wild salmon stocks that its members have traditionally relied on for food and ceremonial purposes: see *Chief Robert Chamberlin (on his own behalf and behalf of the Kwicksutaineuk/Ah-Kwa-Mish First Nation) v. the Queen in the Right of the Province of British Columbia*. As of the date of publication, the action is awaiting a certification decision.

Part IV — Tort Litigation Aimed at Deterring Public Participation

Tort litigation can also be harnessed to discourage public participation in environmental decision making and, more generally, in public debate surrounding environmental issues. The activities targeted in such suits include what many would consider to be at the core of a robust democracy: reporting health or environmental violations; filing complaints with government agencies; circulating petitions; information picketing; writing letters to government or the media; speaking at community, environmental or land use planning meetings; providing information to the media; and engaging in public information campaigns. Strategic lawsuits against public participation (SLAPP) suits characterize these ostensibly lawful activities as tortious: alleging defamation, inducing breach of contract, conspiracy and interference with contractual relations, and various other economic torts.

In the United States, SLAPP suits have reached epidemic proportions prompting over twenty states to enact anti-SLAPP legislation. In addition to these statutory protections, defendants targeted in SLAPP suits filed in US courts can invoke the protection of the "right to petition" government as guaranteed by the First Amendment to the US Constitution. SLAPP targets in Canada, at this point, enjoy neither legislative nor constitutional protection. While the province of British Columbia became to the first province to pass anti-SLAPP legislation (*Protection of Public Participation Act*, S.B.C. 2001, c. 19) in 2001, this law was later repealed following a change in government. No other province has of yet enacted similar legislation (although, as we discuss *infra*, this will likely occur soon in the province of Quebec). Moreover, since the *Charter* has been interpreted as not applying in "private litigation" (see *Dolphin Delivery Ltd. v. R.W.D.S.U., Local 580*, [1986] 2 S.C.R. 573) unlike their American counterparts, Canadian SLAPP targets are precluded from defending themselves by relying on *Charter* protections such as freedom of expression and association.

In Canada, SLAPP suits have been particularly prominent in the realm of environmental and land use decision making. According to one Canadian commentator, "SLAPPs directly threaten the core values of modern environmental law and policy: the right of citizens to participate in decision-making . . . [moreover] as public participation is enhanced both quantitatively and qualitatively so too will the incentive increase for powerful interests to respond by bringing [SLAPP suits]."

Chris Tollefson, "Strategic Lawsuits Against Public Participation: Developing A Canadian Response"
(1994) 73 Can. Bar Rev. 200

> . . . The conceptual thread that binds [SLAPPs] is that they are suits without substantial merit that are brought by private interests to stop citizens from exercising their political rights or to punish them for having done so. SLAPP suits function by forcing the target into the judicial arena where the SLAPP filer foists upon the target the expenses of a defense. The longer the litigation can be stretched out, the more litigation can be churned, the greater the expense that is inflicted, the closer the SLAPP filer moves to success . . . The ripple effect of such suits in our society is enormous. Persons who have been outspoken on issues of public importance targeted in such suits or who have witnessed such suits will often choose in the future to stay silent. (*Gordon v. Marrone*, 590 N.Y.S. 2d 649 (1992) at 656)

Measuring and Defining the SLAPP Phenomenon

The magnitude of the SLAPP phenomenon is difficult to assess. [SLAPP experts] Canan and Pring estimate that every year in the United States "hundreds, perhaps thousands" of SLAPPs are filed. A number of factors complicate the task of quantifying the phenomenon more precisely. On their face, SLAPPs closely resemble ordinary tort lawsuits; indeed their success depends upon maintaining this external appearance. Even more problematic, for obvious reasons, is determining with what frequency and results the mere threat of a SLAPP is being deployed. Finally, while there is some agreement as to the basic hallmarks of a SLAPP there remains considerable uncertainty as to how SLAPPs should be defined in legal terms.

One of the key reasons for this lack of definitional consensus is that, in the American context, there is a broad agreement that SLAPPs should be subjected to special common law and statutory procedures to minimize their detrimental effects. Consequently, much hinges on whether or not a suit is deemed to be a SLAPP. Canan and Pring advocate a fourfold SLAPP identification test. To qualify as a SLAPP, a law suit must be:

(1) a civil complaint or counterclaim for damages or injunctive relief;

(2) filed against a non-governmental individual or group;

(3) because of their communications to a government body, official or the electorate;

(4) on an issue of public interest or concern.

The third requirement of this definition implicitly incorporates First Amendment jurisprudence dealing with the right to petition clause; a provision which American courts have interpreted to immunize from civil liability a wide variety of communications to government. Only those forms of communication which this jurisprudence recognizes as being protected, according to Canan and Pring, constitute "communications" for the purposes of this requirement. [. . .] this term has been judicially construed to embrace abroad range of lawful, non-violent communicative activities including lobbying, letter writing, demonstrations, economic boycotts and litigation.

Some commentators have criticized Canan and Pring's definition as being too open-ended. Others have contended it is too narrow. Waldman has recently argued that the third "public interest or concern" arm of the definition is unworkably vague. Moreover, he claims that the definition fails to exclude certain types of petitioning activity which in his view should not be shielded from civil liability: namely, petitioning which is pursued for purely self interested or malicious reasons.

The "public interest or concern" arm of the Canan and Pring definition has also been criticized by Cosentino, but for reasons diametrically opposed to those of Waldman. Cosentino contends that this terminology implies that the defendant's motives in petitioning the government are relevant in determining whether a lawsuit is a SLAPP. This, in his view, is dangerous in that it is capable of being interpreted as requiring a defendant to show that she was acting out of an altruistic concern for the public good. He fears that a requirement of this type would exclude from anti-SLAPP protection many deserving cases involving what might be characterized as "self-interested" petitioning, such as NIMBY based opposition to land development proposals.

These criticisms of Canan and Pring's definition highlight one of the most daunting challenges for anti-SLAPP law reform: deciding how far it is necessary to go to protect public participation in government from litigation chill. The Canan and Pring definition contemplates that not all public participation will qualify for special anti-SLAPP protection; only participation with respect to issues of "public interest or concern". Leaving aside the obvious indeterminacy of this principle (about which Waldman is rightly concerned), there remains the question of whether petitioning activity is any less deserving of protection merely because of the public profile of the issue or the motives of the petitioner.

However, here are also problems with taking a more expansive approach which protects, in a more absolute way, the right to participate in government. This latter approach is controversial in that it ultimately leads to the proposition that all forms of participation in government — even acts which harm or defame others — should be immunized from civil law consequences.

Why Winning isn't enough for the SLAPP Target

While a SLAPP target cannot afford to lose the suit, rarely is that a real prospect. Nor is it enough for a SLAPP target ultimately to win the suit on the merits. Unless the target can have the suit dismissed summarily, there is a strong possibility it will win a legal battle only to lose the political war. In these respects, the situation confronted by SLAPP defendants differs qualitatively from that faced by defendants in ordinary litigation.

Unfortunately, existing rules of civil procedure do little to assist SLAPP targets to secure speedy dismissal of SLAPP claims. Under the civil rules in most jurisdictions, unless a defendant can establish that the claim is "frivolous or vexatious", courts will ordinarily allow the claim to proceed to trial, particularly if the parties disagree on any material factual issues. This is a very difficult burden for a defendant to meet, especially prior to discoveries having taken place. A further obstacle to obtaining summary dismissal is the absence of an affirmative obligation requiring a plaintiff to detail the particulars of the allegations upon which it intends to rely in support of its claim. Even where a plaintiff is ordered to provide particulars, the defendant is typically left speculating as to the precise nature of the case it must defend.

The civil rules are equally ineffectual when it comes to deterring SLAPPs from being filed in the first place. This is attributable, in large measure, to the rules governing "costs". Ordinarily at the conclusion of a lawsuit, the successful party recovers "party and party" costs from its opponent. Usually this award represents approximately one-third of the actual expenses incurred by the prevailing party in the course of the lawsuit. In cases involving particularly egregious conduct on the part of the losing party, courts will award "solicitor and client costs" which will come close to covering the full expenses of the victorious party. But awards of this kind are rare. Consequently, since in ordinary litigation the victor is left with out-of-pocket legal expenses even after being awarded "costs", for many litigants the costs award has come to be regarded as something of an afterthought. The "main event" is the outcome on the merits.

Because SLAPP filers are almost invariably better financed than their opponents and characteristically pursue litigation for reasons other than prevailing on the merits, adverse cost awards — even if awarded on a more generous solicitor and client basis — represent, in economic terms, a relatively minor cost of doing business. For a SLAPP target, on the other hand, these cost rules can be extremely onerous. Not only is it likely that a target, regardless of the outcome of the suit, will never be fully compensated for litigation expenses but, to the extent that these expenses are recovered, this takes place only after all litigation is finally concluded.

Notes and Questions

1. In *Daishowa Inc. v. Friends of the Lubicon* (1998), 158 D.L.R. (4th) 699 (Ont. Gen. Div.), the plaintiff, one of the world's largest pulp and paper companies, was targeted in a boycott campaign mounted by a small Toronto-based advocacy group known as the Friends of the Lubicon (FOL). The goal of the campaign was to secure Daishowa's agreement not to log on un-treatied lands in northern Alberta, claimed by the Lubicon Cree, until the Lubicon's title claim had been resolved. The campaign consisted of various activities including information picketing at various retail locations where the company's paper products were in use, and efforts to persuade Daishowa wholesale purchasers not to renew their supply contracts. Daishowa alleged these actions constituted a tortious conspiracy to injure its business, an interference with its contractual relations, and an inducement to its clients to breach their contracts. Daishowa also alleged the FOL's use of the term "genocide" in its campaign literature was defamatory.

At the end of a 28-day trial, the trial judge dismissed the case against the defendants with the exception of the defamation claim, in respect of which it awarded damages of $1. Daishowa filed but later abandoned an appeal. Consider whether, in your view, the *Daishowa* case can, in all the circumstances, be considered as a SLAPP suit.

2. One of the first judicial considerations of SLAPPs in Canada was *Fraser v. Saanich (District)*, 32 C.E.L.R. (N.S.) 143 (B.C. S.C.). In this case, a developer sued a group of residents who had campaigned against her attempt to rezone a property for development purposes. The lawsuit alleged conspiracy and a variety of other economic torts. The trial judge dismissed the action summarily, finding that it "not only contains an unreasonable claim, is meritless and devoid of any factual foundation, but also has been used as an attempt to stifle the democratic activities of the defendants, the neighbourhood residents. I find the plaintiffs' conduct reprehensible and deserving of censure by an award of special costs".

3. As noted above, British Columbia is the only Canadian province to enact anti-SLAPP legislation. Commentators have argued that effective anti-SLAPP legislation must contain three key elements: (1) procedural reforms that expedite early identification and dismissal of SLAPP suits; (2) measures to mitigate the costs and burden of defending such suits; and (3) provisions aimed at discouraging the filing of such suits. A related drafting challenge is to balance the right of plaintiffs to have access to the court system against the right of defendants to be protected from legal intimidation in connection with lawful democratic activities. Below is draft legislation that many predict will soon be enacted into law in the province of Quebec. Consider to what extent, and how effectively, these amendments respond to the drafting priorities noted above.

Proposed Quebec SLAPP Legislation

The Code of Civil Procedure (R.S.Q., chapter C-25) is amended by inserting the following after article 54 in Chapter III of Title II of Book I concerning the powers of courts and judges:

Power To Impose Sanctions For Abuse of Procedure in First Instance

54.1. A court of first instance may, at any time, on request or even on its own initiative, declare an action or pleading abusive and impose a sanction on the party concerned. The abuse of procedure may consist in a claim or pleading that is clearly unfounded, frivolous or dilatory or in a conduct that is vexatious or quarrelsome. It may also consist in bad faith, in a use of procedure that is excessive or unreasonable or causes prejudice to another person, or in a perversion of the ends of justice, in particular if it operates to restrict freedom of expression in public debate.

54.2. If a party establishes that an action or pleading is *prima facie* an abuse of procedure, the onus is on the party who instituted the action or filed the pleading to show that the action or pleading is not an excessive or unreasonable use of procedure and is justified in law.

54.3. If there is an abuse of procedure, the court may dismiss the action, strike out a submission or require that it be amended, reject a pleading or terminate or refuse to allow an examination.

54.4. The court may, if it considers it appropriate,

(1) subject the furtherance of the action or the pleading to certain conditions;

(2) require undertakings from the party concerned with regard to the orderly conduct of the proceeding;

(3) suspend the case for the period it determines;

(4) recommend to the chief judge or chief justice that special case management be ordered; or

(5) for serious reasons, if justified by the circumstances, and if the court notes that the financial situation of a party would prevent the party from properly arguing the party's case, order that a provision for costs in a specified amount be paid to that party.

54.5. In ruling on the abusive character of an action or pleading, the court may order that a provision for costs be reimbursed, condemn a party to pay, in addition to the costs, damages in reparation for the prejudice suffered by another party, including the fees and extrajudicial costs incurred by that party and, if justified by the circumstances, award punitive damages. If the amount of the damages is not admitted or may not be established easily at the time the action or pleading is declared abusive, the court may summarily rule on the amount, or reserve the right of a party to have the amount determined by the competent court within the time and under the conditions determined by the court.

54.6. If the abuse of procedure is committed by a legal person or a person who acts as the administrator of the property of another, the directors and officers of the legal person who took part in the decision or the administrator of the property of another may be personally condemned to pay damages. If the abuse of procedure results from a party's quarrelsomeness, the court may also prohibit the party from instituting legal proceedings without the authorization of the chief judge or chief justice.

Part V — Towards a Recognition of Common Law Public Rights in the Environmental Context

In the final Part, we reflect on what is both a newly-emerging as well as in some ways an ancient feature of the common law: namely, the notion of public rights. While the common law is typically seen as being oriented towards protecting private/individual rights, especially those relating to property, closer scrutiny suggests that the common law has also recognized and loaned protection to collective/public rights. Likely the clearest illustration of this dimension is the tort of public nuisance. Another illustration, albeit one that remains inchoate in Canadian law, is the public trust doctrine. This doctrine, which is rooted in Roman law, has come to play a significant role in US environmental law as we will discuss in this Part and in Chapter 9. As a result of the recent Supreme Court of Canada decision in *British Columbia v. Canadian Forest Products Ltd.*, [2004] 2 S.C.R. 74, 2004 SCC 38, some commentators are predicting that in coming years the doctrine could have a similarly transformative impact on Canadian environmental law.

To consider the current and future role of common law-based public rights in Canadian environmental law, we offer first an article that provides a brief introduction to the public trust doctrine authored by Preston C.J., of the New South Wales Land and Environment Court. We then provide an excerpt from the SCC's much-discussed decision in *Canfor*, which offers some instructive observations both on the topic of the public trust doctrine and the tort of public nuisance. Finally, we include extracts from two commentaries on *Canfor* that chart its implications for Canadian environmental law.

Justice B. J. Preston, *The Role of the Judiciary in Promoting Sustainable Development: The Experience of Asia and the Pacific*
(University of Sydney Research Paper No. 08/46, 2008)

The concept of the "public trust" has its roots in Roman law, and was based on the idea that certain common resources such as the air, waterways and forests were held in trust by the State for the benefit and use of the general public. A broader conception of the public trust holds that the earth's natural resources are held in trust by the present generation for future generations. In this way, public trust law may be "the strongest contemporary expression of the idea that the legal rights of nature and of future generations are enforceable against contemporary users".

The essence of the public trust is that the State, as trustee, is under a fiduciary duty to deal with the trust property, being the common natural resources, in a manner that is in the interests of the general public. Hence, the State cannot alienate the trust property unless the public benefit that would result outweighs the loss of the public use or "social wealth" derived from the area. Although it was not until the early 1970s that the doctrine was explicitly applied as a mechanism for protecting the environment and managing resources, elements of it can be seen in much earlier cases.

In the Scottish case of *Lord Advocate v. Clyde Navigation Trustees*, the Lord Advocate, on behalf of the Crown, sought an order preventing a statutory body from dumping dredge waste in Loch Long. His claim was based on the idea that Loch Long was part of the kingdom, the Crown was the proprietor of the Loch, and thus the Crown had title to prevent interference with its rights unless they had been assigned to someone else. Referring to the existence of a trust and "trust subjects", the Court of Session granted the remedy sought by the Crown, stating clearly that "the Crown must use the property in the public interest".

In Australia, the concept of the doctrine of public trust can be traced back to an early dispute over a proposed coalmine in Sydney Harbour in the 1890s. A government authority granted a lease to a private company over an area of the northern foreshore. At issue was the effect this would have on the natural beauty of the area and "whether the people of Sydney and especially of St Leonards were to have the right to go over these water frontages". A young barrister objecting to the mine wrote to a newspaper declaring, "We in Sydney are the trustees for all Australia and of all time of that national heritage of beauty which gives to us our pride of place amongst the capitals of this continent and endows us with a reflected glory amongst the people of all nations who visit us".

When the case was heard in 1895, the New South Wales Land Appeal Court adopted public trust reasoning, holding that the Crown was under an obligation to use public land for the "health recreation, and enjoyment" of the people, and occupied "a position in relation to public lands something in the nature of a trustee under an obligation to dispose of, or alienate those lands, whether permanently or temporarily, only in the interest and for the benefit of the people of this Colony".

Professor Joseph Sax resurrected and expanded the concept of a public trust many decades later. In a famous article published in the *Michigan Law Review*, Sax explored the extent to which the public trusteeship constrains the State, and concluded that three types of restrictions on government authority are imposed by a public trust. First, "the property subject to the trust must not only be used for a public purpose, but it must be held available for use by the general public". Secondly, the trust property may not be sold. And thirdly, "the property must be maintained for particular types of uses, such as navigation, recreation, or fishery". While realising that some elements of the public trust will inevitably be transferred into private ownership and control, Sax argued that the doctrine had "the breadth and substantive content which might make it useful as a tool of general application for citizens seeking to develop a comprehensive legal approach to resource management problems".

The public trust doctrine has, to differing extents, become part of the law of all countries with a common law heritage, and many maintain that it should play a principal part in sustainable resource allocation and decision-making. While traditionally applied primarily to waterways and rivers, the doctrine has now been extended to protect other natural resources from private use and harm as a tool of environmental conservation.

British Columbia v. Canadian Forest Products Ltd.
[2004] 2 S.C.R. 74, 2004 SCC 38

BINNIE J. — In the summer of 1992, a forest fire swept through the Stone Creek area of the Interior of British Columbia about 35 kilometres south of Prince George. Approximately 1,491 hectares were burned over, including areas where the appellant Canadian Forest Products Ltd. ("Canfor") and other tenure holders were licensed to log, areas of steep slopes where it was uneconomic to log, still other areas where the trees were too immature to log, and areas along watercourses subsequently declared by the Crown to have too much environmental value to permit logging at all. It is the assessment of compensation for the Crown's claim for environmental damage in these last-identified areas, called Environmentally Sensitive Areas ("ESAs"), that has created particular difficulty.

There is no longer any dispute about responsibility for the blaze. In the previous year, Canfor had carried out a controlled burn of its slashing and other logging waste, which failed to extinguish itself over the winter as expected. This fact went undetected because of the negligence of Canfor. The fire flared up again at the end of June 1992. The trial judge found that, while Canfor's negligence contributed to the failure to suppress the resurrection of the fire, the Crown's inadequate firefighting efforts also contributed to the loss ([1999] B.C.J. No. 1945 (QL)). He considered it impossible to apportion degrees of fault or blameworthiness and thus divided responsibility evenly The Court of Appeal varied his decision by allocating 70 percent of the responsibility to Canfor and 30 percent to the Crown ((2002), 100 B.C.L.R. (3d) 114, 2002 BCCA 217). These findings are no longer in issue.

At trial, the Crown claimed damages for three categories of loss:

(1) Expenditures for suppression of the fire and restoration of the burned-over areas;

(2) Loss of stumpage revenue from trees that would have been harvested in the ordinary course (harvestable trees); and,

(3)Loss of trees set aside for various environmental reasons (non-harvestable or protected trees).

The trial judge awarded the Crown $3,575,000 under the first heading (which was an agreed figure), but otherwise dismissed the claim on the basis the Crown had failed to prove a compensable loss with respect either to harvestable or non-harvestable trees. [. . .]

The Court of Appeal dismissed the Crown's appeal on damages with respect to the harvestable trees, but awarded compensation for "diminution of the value" of the non-harvestable trees at a figure equivalent to one third of their commercial value. The task of assessing the commercial value of the non-harvestable trees, if the parties could not agree to it, was referred back to the trial court. This award is the subject matter of Canfor's appeal.

The Crown considers the award of compensation to be inadequate and in its cross-appeal claims the "auction value" of the standing timber in both harvestable and non-harvestable areas as of the date of the fire plus a premium over and above auction value for the degradation of the environment caused by destruction of the non-harvestable trees. In the alternative, it seeks an award of stumpage fees, plus the environmental premium on the non-harvestable trees. Canfor attacks the Crown's methodology and says that, on the evidence, the Crown has been overcompensated, not undercompensated, by the courts in British Columbia.

The question of compensation for environmental damage is of great importance. As the Court observed in *R. v. Hydro-Québec*, [1997] 3 S.C.R. 213, ¶85, legal measures to protect the environment "relate to a public purpose of superordinate importance" In *Friends of the Oldman River Society v. Canada (Minister of Transport)*, [1992] 1 S.C.R. 3, the Court declared, at p. 16, that "[t]he protection of the environment has become one of the major challenges of our time". In *Ontario v. Canadian Pacific Ltd.*, [1995] 2 S.C.R. 1031, "stewardship of the natural environment" was described as a fundamental value. Still more recently, in *114957 Canada Ltée (Spraytech, Société d'arrosage) v. Hudson (Town)*, [2001] 2 S.C.R. 241, 2001 SCC 40, the Court reiterated, at para.1:

> . . . our common future, that of every Canadian community, depends on a healthy environment. . . . This Court has recognized that "(e)veryone is aware that individually and collectively, we are responsible for preserving the natural environment . . . environmental protection [has] emerged as a fundamental value in Canadian society" . . .

If justice is to be done to the environment, it will often fall to the Attorney General, invoking both statutory and common law remedies, to protect the public interest. In this case, the Attorney General has not resorted to statutory remedies (as under s. 161(1) of the *Forest Act*, R.S.B.C. 1979, c.140 (now R.S.B.C. 1996, c. 157), for payment where timber is damaged or destroyed) but has sought damages at common law. The present appeal raises, therefore, the Attorney General's ability to recover damages for environmental loss, the requirement of proof of such loss and a principled approach to the assessment of environmental compensation at common law.

The Crown in right of British Columbia says it sues not only in its capacity as property owner but as the representative of the people of British Columbia, for whom the Crown seeks to maintain an unspoiled environment. Thus the claim for an environmental premium is made "in recognition of the fact that it [the Crown], and the public on whose behalf it owned the Protected Trees, valued them more highly as part of a protected ecosystem". The Crown frames the issue on appeal as the valuation of tort damages for a "publicly owned resource", and makes reference to the "worth to society" of the trees in their protected state. The Crown states that "[f]air compensation also requires that wrongdoers pay the public for damaging their ecosystems". In thus framing its claims, the Crown invokes its role as *parens patriae*.

The relationship between the Crown's status as property owner and the Crown as *parens patriae* is one of the issues presented for consideration, as is the Crown's hybrid role as regulator of the forest industry and at the same time recipient of a revenue stream established and limited by its own regulatory system. [. . .]

A claim for environmental loss, as in the case of any loss, must be put forward based on a coherent theory of damages, a methodology suitable for their assessment, and supporting evidence. No one doubts the need for environmental protection but, in this case, apart from the cost of reforestation, which was agreed to, the Crown claims only stumpage and "diminution of the value of the timber" within the burned-over area. The environment includes more than timber, but no allegations of loss were made in that regard. The pleadings, in other words, suggested a fairly narrow commercial focus and that is how the claim was defended.

The evidentiary record is also singularly thin on what precise environmental loss occurred, apart from damage to trees, and what value should be placed on it. The evidence of the Crown's own valuation experts, Deloitte & Touche, offered no support for the Crown's present expanded posture on environmental loss.

We cannot treat the Crown's argument as evidence; nor can we read into the record a theory of valuation that, rightly or wrongly, was supported by none of the experts. The Crown may have a more substantial environmental claim than is before us but she didn't prove it. Thus, while I would not interfere with the Court of Appeal's disposition of the claim in respect of the harvestable timber, in my opinion, with respect, the Crown did not establish its claim for compensation for environmental damage. I would therefore allow Canfor's appeal in that respect. The Crown's cross-appeal should be dismissed. [. . .]

Can the Crown also sue as a representative of the public to enforce the public interest in an unspoiled environment? If the Crown cannot do so, who (if anyone) can? Reference was made to *Prince Rupert (City) v. Pederson* (1994), 98 B.C.L.R. (2d) 84 (C.A.), where the court held that a municipal corporation cannot recover for the loss of "amenities" on behalf of its inhabitants arising from the destruction of trees.

In this Court, the Crown suggested that it was entitled to collect damages in negligence, "to effectively deter environmental harm and compensate the public for environmental damage". Canfor took the position that any such claim amounted to a "public law" remedy available only under special legislation such as the United States' *Comprehensive Environmental Responses, Compensation, and Liability Act of 1980*, 42 U.S.C. §§9601–9675 (1982 Supp. V 1987) ("*CERCLA*"), often called the "Superfund" law. Such losses are not, Canfor says, recoverable by a landowner in tort. The Crown's argument, Canfor implies, confuses distributive justice with corrective justice. Canfor was supported in this regard by the industry intervener, the Council of Forest Industries ("COFI") and others. Canfor and COFI took the view that when the Crown sues in tort, it is limited to the rights of a private party. It was conceded that there is an accepted role for the Attorney General as defender of the public interest in the law of public nuisance, but the remedy available in such cases is injunctive, not compensatory.

Historically, of course, the Attorney General, representing the Crown, has been the appropriate party to sue for abatement of a public nuisance. Recently, the Court adopted as correct the proposition that "any activity which unreasonably interferes with the public's interest in questions of health, safety, morality, comfort or convenience" is capable of constituting a public nuisance: *Ryan v. Victoria (City)*, [1999] 1 S.C.R. 201 at para. 52. It seems to me that the act of Canfor in burning down a public forest is capable of constituting a public nuisance. It was also negligence.

While a public nuisance may also be a crime (see *Criminal Code*, R.S.C. 1985, c. C-46, s. 180(1)), it is more often the subject of injunction proceedings brought by the Attorney General on behalf of the public. The usual objective is abatement. As put by McLachlin J. (as she then was) in *Stein v. Gonzales* (1984), 14 D.L.R. (4th) 263 (B.C. S.C.), "[p]ublic rights, including claims for public nuisance, can only be asserted in a civil action by the Attorney-General as the Crown officer representing the public" (p. 265). McLachlin J. went on to say that it is the "Attorney-General who is entrusted and charged with the duty of enforcing public rights" (p. 268). [. . .].

It is true that the role of the Attorney General has traditionally been to seek a stop to the activity that is interfering with the public's rights. This has led to a view that the only remedy available to the Attorney General is injunctive relief. Some commentators regard the injunction as the "public remedy" obtained by the Attorney General, while damages are a "private remedy" available to those private citizens who have suffered a special loss such as personal injury or damage to private property: see, e.g., P. H. Osborne, *The Law of Torts* (2nd ed. 2003), at p. 364. The reality, of course, is that it would be impractical in most of these environmental cases for individual members of the public to show sufficient "special damages" to mount a tort action having enough financial clout to serve the twin policy objectives of deterrence to wrongdoers and adequate compensation of their victims: *Bazley v. Curry*, [1999] 2 S.C.R. 534. Class actions will have a role to play but, as Professor Klar notes, "[w]hat has made public nuisance a particularly ineffective private law remedy is the special damages requirement" (L.N. Klar, *Tort Law* (3rd ed. 2003), at p. 647).

Canadian courts have not universally adhered to a narrow view of the Crown's available remedies in civil proceedings for public nuisance. In *The Queen v. The Ship Sun Diamond*, [1984] 1 F.C. 3 (T.D.), the federal Crown sought damages in relation to cleanup costs it had incurred to mitigate damage from an oil spill in the waters off Vancouver. Damages were awarded for the cost of the water cleanup activities, in addition to costs to clean Crown-owned beach and foreshore property. Walsh J. commented, "what was done was reasonable *and appears to be a good example of the parens patriae principle with the Crown . . . acting as what is referred to in civil law as 'bon père de famille'*" (pp. 31-32 emphasis added)).

In *Attorney General for Ontario v. Fatehi*, [1984] 2 S.C.R. 536, the Province sought damages in relation to the cost of cleaning up a public highway following an accident. This Court held that Ontario was entitled to claim damages for harm to its property, like any other private property owner, and needed no statutory authority to bring such an action. [. . .]

The British Columbia Law Reform Commission in its *Report on Civil Litigation in the Public Interest*, *supra*, suggested that the reluctance of the courts to award damages against those who commit a public nuisance should be relaxed somewhat to provide an effective remedy (pp. 70-71). See also Ontario Law Reform Commission, *Report on Damages for Environmental Harm* (1990) ("*OLRC Report*"), at pp. 11–13.

In my view, Canfor takes too narrow a view of the entitlement of the Crown, represented by the Attorney General, to pursue compensation for environmental damage in a proper case.

Canadian courts have suggested that even municipalities have a role to play in defence of public rights. In *Scarborough v. R.E.F. Homes Ltd.* (1979), 9 M.P.L.R. 255 (Ont. C.A.), Lacourcière J.A., in an oral decision, said at p. 257 that:

> In our judgment, the municipality is, *in a broad general sense, a trustee of the environment* for the benefit of the residents in the area of the road allowance and, indeed, for the citizens of the community at large. [Emphasis added.]

This expression was referred to, without elaboration, by L'Heureux-Dubé J. in *114957 Canada, supra,* at para. 27.

The notion that there are public rights in the environment that reside in the Crown has deep roots in the common law: see, e.g., J.C. Maguire, "Fashioning an Equitable Vision for Public Resource Protection and Development in Canada: The Public Trust Doctrine Revisited and Reconceptualized" (1997), 7 J. Env. L. & Prac. 1. [. . .]

A similar notion persisted in European legal systems. According to the French *Civil Code*, art. 538, there was common property in navigable rivers and streams, beaches, ports, and harbours. A similar set of ideas was put forward by H. de Bracton in his treatise on English law in the mid-13th century (*Bracton on the Laws and Customs of England* (1968), vol. 2, at pp. 39-40):

> By natural law these are common to all: running water, air, the sea and the shores of the sea . . . No one therefore is forbidden access to the seashore . . .
>
> All rivers and ports are public, so that the right to fish therein is common to all persons. The use of river banks, as of the river itself, is also public by the *jus gentium* . . .

By legal convention, ownership of such public rights was vested in the Crown, as too did authority to enforce public rights of use. According to de Bracton, *supra*, at pp. 166-67:

> (It is the lord king) himself who has ordinary jurisdiction and power over all who are within his realm. . . . He also has, in preference to all others in his realm, privileges by virtue of the *jus gentium*. (By the *jus gentium*) things are his . . . which by natural law ought to be common to all . . . Those concerned with jurisdiction and the peace . . . belong to no one save the crown alone and the royal dignity, nor can they be separated from the crown, since they constitute the crown.

Since the time of de Bracton it has been the case that public rights and jurisdiction over these cannot be separated from the Crown. This notion of the Crown as holder of inalienable "public rights" in the environment and certain common resources was accompanied by the procedural right of the Attorney General to sue for their protection representing the Crown as *parens patriae*. This is an important jurisdiction that should not be attenuated by a narrow judicial construction.

As stated, in the United States the *CERCLA* statute provides legislative authority for government actions in relation to the "public interest", including environmental damage, but this is not the only basis upon which claims in relation to the environment can be advanced by governments at the state and federal levels.

Under the common law in that country, it has long been accepted that the state has a common law *parens patriae* jurisdiction to represent the collective interests of the public. This jurisdiction has historically been successfully exercised in relation to environmental claims involving injunctive relief against interstate public nuisances: see, e.g., *North Dakota v. Minnesota*, 263 U.S. 365 at p. 374 (1923); *Missouri v. Illinois*, 180 U.S. 208 (1901); *Kansas v. Colorado*, 206 U.S. 46 (1907); *Georgia v. Tennessee Copper Co.*, 206 U.S. 230 (1907); and *New York v. New Jersey*, 256 U.S. 296 (1921). In *Tennessee Copper*, Holmes J. held for the Supreme Court of the United States, at p. 237, that, "the State has an *interest independent* of and behind the titles of its citizens, in all the earth and air within its domain" (emphasis added).

The American law has also developed the notion that the states hold a "public trust". Thus, in *Illinois Central Railroad Co. v. Illinois*, 146 U.S. 387 (1892), the Supreme Court of the United States upheld Illinois' claim to have a land grant declared invalid. The State had granted to the railroad in fee simple all land extending out one mile from Lake Michigan's shoreline, including one mile of shoreline through Chicago's central business district. It was held that this land was impressed with a public trust. The State's title to this land was

> different in character from that which the State holds in lands intended for sale. . . . It is a title held in trust for the people of the State that they may enjoy the navigation of the waters, carry on commerce over them, and have liberty of fishing therein freed from the obstruction or interference of private parties. [p. 452]

The deed to the railway was therefore set aside.

The *parens patriae* and "public trust" doctrines have led in the United States to successful claims for monetary compensation. Thus in *New Jersey, Department of Environmental Protection v. Jersey Central Power and Light Co.*, 336 A.2d 750 (N.J. Super. Ct. App. Div. 1975), the State sued a power plant operator for a fish kill in tidal waters caused by negligent pumping that caused a temperature variation in the fish habitat. The State sought compensatory damages for the harm to public resources. The court concluded that the State had the "right and the fiduciary duty to seek damages for the destruction of wildlife which are part of the public trust" in "compensation for any diminution in that [public] trust corpus" [. . .]

It seems to me there is no legal barrier to the Crown suing for compensation as well as injunctive relief in a proper case on account of public nuisance, or negligence causing environmental damage to public lands, and perhaps other torts such as trespass, but there are clearly important and novel policy questions raised by such actions. These include the Crown's potential liability for *inactivity* in the face of threats to the environment, the existence or non-existence of enforceable fiduciary duties owed to the public by the Crown in that regard, the limits to the role and function and remedies available to governments taking action on account of activity harmful to public enjoyment of public resources, and the spectre of imposing on private interests an indeterminate liability for an indeterminate amount of money for ecological or environmental damage.

This is not a proper appeal for the Court to embark on a consideration of these difficult issues. The Crown's own expert evidence treated the Crown as owner of Crown forests seeking compensation on the same basis as any other landowner for stumpage and "diminution of the value of the timber". Reliance was placed on s. 11(1) of the *Crown Proceeding Act*, R.S.B.C. 1996, c. 89, which provides that "the rights of the parties must, subject to this Act, be as nearly as possible the same as in a proceeding between persons". Of course it is perfectly open to the Crown to assert its private law rights as a property owner: *Fatehi, supra*, and *Toronto Transportation Commission v. The King*, [1949] S.C.R. 510. The groundwork for a claim on some broader "public" basis was not fully argued in the courts below. The Crown now suggests that it claimed "commercial value as a proxy" for environmental damage but, with respect, the pleadings suggest otherwise. It would be unfair to the other parties to inject such far-reaching issues into the proceedings at this late date.

I therefore proceed on the basis that the Crown's entitlement in this particular case is limited to entitlement in the role the Crown adopted in its statement of claim, namely that of the landowner of a tract of forest.

Notes and Questions

1. To what extent does *Canfor* open the door to the emergence of the public trust doctrine in Canada? What fact situations are most likely to provide a basis for expanding on and consolidating the status of the doctrine in Canadian law?

2. In a case involving the province of Prince Edward Island and the federal Crown in 2006, PEI alleged that the federal government had violated its public trust obligations in its allocation of fishing licences. A motion to strike

the statement of claim for failing to disclose a cause of action failed. The court essentially accepted that a claim based on the public trust doctrine can in principle succeed. See *Prince Edward Island v. Canada (Minister of Fisheries & Oceans)*, 2006 PESCAD 27 (P.E.I. C.A.).

The following commentary suggests a range of potential implications of the *Canfor* decision.

Jerry V. DeMarco, Marcia Valiante & Marie-Ann Bowden, "Opening the Door for Common Law Environmental Protection in Canada: The Decision in *British Columbia v. Canadian Forest Products Ltd.*"
(2005) 15 J. Env. L. & Prac. 233

The decision in *Canfor* is the latest in a series of Supreme Court of Canada cases to chart a positive future for environmental law in Canada. Most evident with the legacy of Mr. Justice LaForest, we have seen a Supreme Court with a heightened sense of environmental responsibility that has manifested itself in progressive decision-making. Be it an expanded role of municipalities in environmental protection, adoption of the polluter pays rule, or acceptance of the precautionary principle, the Court has actively engaged in the promotion of environmental protection as "a fundamental value in Canadian society."

Public Nuisance and Public Trust

. . . When commencing the action, British Columbia based its claim in negligence and identified the nature of the harm as damage to the Crown's property interest in the trees, which included harvestable and non-harvestable trees set aside for ecological purposes, plus the costs of fighting the fire and restoring the forest. In the B.C. courts, Canfor was held liable in negligence, contributing 70% to the fire that destroyed the trees. Because of the difficulty of valuing trees with no market value B.C.'s recovery was limited, as discussed above.

In the Supreme Court of Canada, British Columbia tried to recast its argument in support of recovery of damages for ecological harm. Supported by the interveners Sierra Club of Canada, David Suzuki Foundation, and the federal Attorney General, the provincial Crown argued that its interest in the trees goes beyond that of an ordinary property owner, that the Crown also holds public lands and resources on behalf of the people of the Province, as a guardian, and can therefore also recover damages to compensate the public for harm to their ecological interest in the forest. The implication of accepting this argument would be to entitle B.C. to recover damages to which a private landowner would not be entitled, and presumably, result in a larger award if proper evidence were to be provided.

Conceptually, then, the argument goes, this was not just the Crown's loss but also the public's. As representative of the public's rights in the forest, the Attorney General would be entitled to seek compensation on their behalf. The interveners argued that this compensation would then have to be put toward restoration and protection of the forest and not into general revenues.

Canfor and the forestry industry interveners argued that any claim on behalf of the public must be founded on a statutory scheme because such "public" damages are not recoverable in tort. In their view because there was no statutory scheme, there could be no recovery on this basis. Canfor did concede that the Crown is entitled to defend the public interest in the case of a public nuisance, but that injunction, not damages, is the only recognized remedy in such an action.

Binnie J. rejected Canfor's position as "too narrow a view of the entitlement of the Crown, represented by the Attorney General, to pursue compensation for environmental damage in a proper case". That this was not a proper case quickly became clear but Binnie J. went on to discuss his interpretation of this type of claim. He concluded that "there is no legal barrier to the Crown suing for compensation as well as injunctive relief in a proper case on account of public nuisance, or negligence causing environmental damage to public lands, and perhaps other torts such as trespass . . .". There are three elements to this conclusion with respect to public nuisance. First, the Attorney General representing the Crown is the proper party to sue to stop a public nuisance. "The notion that there are public rights in the environment that reside in the Crown has deep roots in the common law" and in civil law systems. These rights are vested in the Crown on behalf of the public and the Attorney General has the procedural right to sue for their protection under the Crown's parens patriae jurisdiction.

Second, the court should take a broad view of what constitutes a public nuisance. Quoting from the Supreme Court's decision in *Ryan v. Victoria (City)*, a public nuisance is "any activity which unreasonably interferes with the public's interest in questions of health, safety, morality, comfort or convenience". Here, Binnie J. concludes that "the act of Canfor in burning down a public forest is capable of constituting a public nuisance. It was also negligence".

Third, while the usual objective of a public nuisance action is abatement, injunction is not the only remedy available. The traditional view is that injunction is the only remedy because of its nature as a "public remedy" compared with the "private remedy" of damages. However, some Canadian courts have awarded damages in public nuisance actions, and this is supported by provincial law reform commissions. Binnie J.'s conclusion is that damages are not precluded. The key is to find an effective remedy in each case. In this case, injunction would not have been an effective remedy.

Given the conclusions on these three elements, why then did the majority hold that this was not a proper case for awarding damages on the grounds of public nuisance? On this point, the dissenting judgment of LeBel J. described Binnie J.'s inconsistency thus: "My colleague speaks of the importance of the Crown's *parens patriae* jurisdiction, and argues that it should not be attenuated by a narrow judicial construction. Unfortunately, he then goes on to adopt just such a narrow judicial construction by limiting the Crown's entitlement" to that of a private landowner.

Binnie J. discussed two reasons for his hesitation to use this as the basis for the Crown's entitlement. One reason was that the "groundwork for a claim on some broader 'public' basis was not fully argued in the courts below" so it "would be unfair to the other parties to inject such far-reaching issues into the proceedings at this late date". The pleadings were narrowly drawn and the majority was not willing to stray beyond them, though Binnie J. did accept that the facts as pleaded and found below did support a finding of public nuisance, even if that cause of action was not initially pleaded.

Binnie J.'s second reason was that a claim for compensation for environmental harm on the basis of public nuisance would raise "clearly important and novel policy questions" that should not be addressed for the first time in the higher courts. The novel policy questions include:

> the Crown's potential liability for inactivity in the face of threats to the environment, the existence or non-existence of enforceable fiduciary duties owed to the public by the Crown in that regard, the limits to the role and function and remedies available to governments taking action on account of activity harmful to public enjoyment of public resources, and the spectre of imposing on private interests an indeterminate liability for an indeterminate amount of money for ecological or environmental damage.

This passage overestimates the novelty of these lingering questions with respect to public nuisance. Public nuisance is a well-established cause of action in Canadian law used in a wide range of circumstances and does not raise policy concerns about Crown duties and liability for inaction. There is no question that the Attorney General is the guardian of public rights protected by this cause of action even though others may also have standing. The only significant uncertainty previously unaddressed by the Supreme Court was whether damages are a proper remedy for public nuisance, and Binnie J. had little trouble accepting that notion, so that alone does not explain his hesitation. It is really the final issue regarding indeterminate liability that likely posed the greatest barrier for the majority [especially] . . . given the lack of evidence in valuing the environmental harm in this case [. . .].

On the substantive question of the basis of liability, Binnie J. referred to both the concepts of public nuisance and "public trust". Public trust came up because, in the Supreme Court in support of the Crown's entitlement to compensation for ecological harm, it was argued that the Crown is not simply the guardian of the public interest, but is a trustee, holding Crown resources on behalf of the public as beneficiaries. The argument built on statements made in previous cases that governments are, in a broad sense, trustees for the environment. This argument led Binnie J. into a discussion of the public trust doctrine, well-developed in the U.S., but so far not accepted in Canadian law despite its origins in common legal traditions.

In the U.S., the doctrine was originally based on a recognition of public rights of access, navigation, commerce and fishing in tidal and navigable waters and the duty on the state to ensure that those rights continued even if land was alienated to private parties. This developed into a cause of action by members of the public against a state that had substantially impaired the public's interest. As the environmental movement gained momentum in the early 1970s, the public trust doctrine was asserted as a way of protecting the environment. State courts in the U.S. began to accept a broader range of public resources as subject to public trust protection and used the concept in different ways, as a rule of statutory construction, as a limitation on the exercise of discretion and in some cases as requiring positive action by a state. Because this developed at the state level, there is a great deal of variation between states, but in some, trust protection extends beyond navigable waters to tributaries, adjacent lands, wildlife, and parkland. Many states have enhanced the use of the doctrine by adopting legislation or constitutional amendments explicitly recognizing that public resources are held in trust.

In Canada, despite common legal foundations, the public trust doctrine has not developed. It appears that "there is no reported Canadian case wherein a common law public trust argument has been advanced". And, in the first case to argue a statutory trust, the concept was rejected. In *Green v. Ontario*, a researcher at Pollution Probe brought an action for breach of trust against the Crown for allowing a private company to excavate and remove sand dunes on public lands near Sandbanks Provincial Park. On preliminary motions, the Ontario High Court rejected the establishment of a trust arising under the *Provincial Parks Act* using traditional trust analysis. As well, the court held that the plaintiff had no standing to bring the action, having suffered no particular damage to himself. This decision apparently deterred further test cases in this area, though public trust has from time to time been argued. [*Ed note:* The *Green* decision is excerpted in Chapter 9.]

While the majority does not accept that public trust is the basis for the Crown's entitlement to compensation in this case, by raising it, the Supreme Court has left it open for the Crown or public interest litigants to come forward in appropriate circumstances and argue a case on the basis of the public trust doctrine. It is not necessary, as was argued by Canfor, to look only to statutory compensation schemes, but the common law remains open. It is hard to reach firm conclusions based on the majority's comments on the public trust doctrine. However, given that the court made the effort to discuss the issue in some depth despite the fact that no party or intervener had canvassed U.S. public trust law in their arguments, it suggests a positive or sympathetic attitude that may manifest itself more fully in a future case (if pleaded properly and supported by evidence at trial). This will provide a spark of hope to those who have long "cast an envious eye south of the border" at the ability of U.S. groups to use the courts to hold state decision-makers accountable on this basis.

But should Canadians pursue an American-style public trust doctrine through the courts? In the U.S., it has taken more than 30 years to move the doctrine from protection of public water rights toward environmental and resource protection more generally. Even now, the results are quite variable between states and there are still many debates about the fundamentals. Some question whether far-reaching societal change is possible through reliance on the doctrine and argue that its use has impeded environmental protection. Attempting to recreate the U.S. model here should only be seen as one plank of a larger strategy, and not necessarily a panacea. The essential goal of such a strategy would be to develop a flexible environmental cause of action that can be brought by public interest plaintiffs that captures the idea that the Crown holds public lands and resources on behalf of present and future generations of Canadians and must therefore be held accountable for how it deals with those lands and resources, and the environment more generally. Its dealings should be guided by the criteria of ecosystem protection and sustainability. Bolstered by comments in *Canfor* and of developments in Canadian law since *Green*, other avenues may help to achieve this result.

Certainly the courts are more open to public interest standing than was the case in 1972. The cases allowing for public interest standing in constitutional and administrative litigation all came after that time. The courts are also much more supportive of environmental protection objectives. The Supreme Court in particular has repeatedly upheld the efforts of all levels of government to protect the environment and has reaffirmed the importance of environmental values to Canadian society. In some jurisdictions, legislation would also provide a short cut to an environmental trust obligation.

Perhaps the most important developments have been those in fiduciary law and the application of equitable principles to relationships between the Crown and certain classes of citizens. The *Guerin* case is a landmark in the development of fiduciary law in the context of Crown-Aboriginal relations and, despite its sui generis nature based on their historical relationship and the nature of the Aboriginal interest in land, some commentators see the case as providing the seeds for a recognition of parallel obligations to the public with respect to Crown resources. Beyond *Guerin*, a new species of civil claim has emerged, which seeks to hold government decision makers accountable for breaching fiduciary obligations to certain citizens where the requirements for a true trust have not been met, but where a statutory provision authorizes government to act in the interests of a particular group. Recognition of such public fiduciary obligations has the potential to expand significantly the role of civil actions as a means of reviewing government decision making, and may result in a fusion of public law and private law remedies for the misuse of discretion.

Pulling these disparate strands together into a claim will be challenging, but the positive attitude of the Supreme Court in Canfor and other cases suggests it may at last bear fruit.

In summary, the majority of the Supreme Court could have dealt with the Crown's claim as a public nuisance and likely would have if the case had been pleaded differently. If it had done so, the only open issue would have been whether damages can be an appropriate remedy. Binnie J. makes it clear that he thinks so in this type of case, if there are proper pleadings and evidence. This likely resolves a key issue respecting the availability of damages in public nuisance claims. Binnie J. went on to discuss public trust concepts as well, thus opening the door to the further development of that area of the law in Canada. In doing so, Binnie J. signaled that the court might be sympathetic to future arguments based on a public trust analysis or similar approach. In particular, Binnie J.'s reference to novel questions relating to the "Crown's potential liability for inactivity in the face of threats to the environment" and "the existence or non-existence of enforceable fiduciary duties owed to the public by the Crown in that regard" seems to be an invitation for test cases in these areas. This leaves the issue of standing for the public as one of the only remaining hurdles to the development of a more environmentally beneficial common law jurisprudence in Canada. This should provide encouragement to prospective public interest litigants who seek to demonstrate that government trustees not only have the option to protect public natural resources but the obligation to do so. This would be a welcome development.

Conclusion

Perhaps more than any other Supreme Court of Canada environmental law decision, the Canfor judgment raises more questions than it answers. Not surprisingly then, its ultimate significance will largely rest on how it is used and applied. Will the Court's recognition of oft-externalized values evolve into eventual compensation for them? If so, this could cause Canadian common law to yield an important societal benefit (as well as a more direct benefit to litigants seeking compensation in such cases). Will the Court's conclusion on remedies available in public nuisance cases encourage Attorneys-General to utilize this important tool? Will options for public interest litigants continue to expand in Canada such that they may have standing in public nuisance, public trust, or other cases that affect broad public interests? Will government entities be subject to further legal obligations (e.g. trusts, fiduciary obligations, and others) to protect the environment? By raising these important questions against a backdrop that emphasized the importance of environmental protection measures, Canfor has the potential to be a watershed in Canadian environmental law.

Notes and Questions

1. What are the implications of applying *Canfor*, which involved an action brought by the provincial Crown, to a tort claim between private litigants? Can the goal of compensating for environmental harms be achieved without a dramatic liberalization of the rules of standing (e.g. to non-human interests and future generations)?

2. As we move from considering the common law to legislative efforts to deal with the environmental impacts of human activities, keep in mind the question whether the common law or legislation is better suited to deal with specific aspects of the problem. What issues are better left to judges to decide; and what issues are better left to elected officials and administrative tribunals?

The following article adopts a more ambitious and speculative approach to the significance of *Canfor* and the challenges ahead for public interest environmental law. In this article, Andrew Gage argues the *Canfor* should be seen as part of a broader paradigm shift in how we imagine and advocate for environmental rights.

Andrew Gage, "Asserting the Public's Environmental Rights"
(BC Continuing Legal Education Society, 2008)

Public interest environmental lawyers have taken heart from statements of the Supreme Court of Canada about the fundamental importance of environmental protection to Canadians. However, despite such pronouncements and increased judicial sympathy, the law's approach to environmental protection remains largely unchanged from 30 years ago . . . I believe that environmental lawyers have failed to articulate a compelling story about the legal nature of environmental problems . . .

We need to think outside the box in coming up with story-shifting arguments . . .. . . in my view one of the most compelling and flexible arguments that we can use to shift the story involves turning to the very old idea of public rights. If the public has legal rights in respect of natural features this fact completely changes the relationship between the public and both industry and government.

The Nature of Public Environmental Rights

A public right is a legally enforceable right held not by an individual, or a community, but by the public at large. La Forest J., in his classic text on water law, explained:

> By public rights is not meant rights owned by government, whether federal, provincial or municipal. These bodies may own land and water rights . . . in the same way as private individuals, in which case they are, in a manner of speaking, public rights. But what is here called public rights are those vested in the public generally, rights that any member of the public may enjoy.

. . . The Supreme Court of Canada, in *Canfor*, adopted the phrase "public environmental rights" in relation to such rights, noting that: "The notion that there are public rights in the environment that reside in the Crown has deep roots in the common law". In particular, the court quoted several early authorities that spoke of public rights in respect of "running water, air, the sea and the shores of the sea".

Public environmental rights can play an important role in environmental law.

1. Public rights represent a direct counter-point to private rights that otherwise dominate legal analysis; in particular, they emphasizes public access to resources that are often privatized;

2. Public rights reflect how the environmental community often talks about air, water and land use issues.

3. Unlike *Charter* rights, the public's rights are not limited to claims involving human health, but apply to most issues where the public has an historic use of, or interest in, environmental features;

What public environmental rights exist?

Despite the Supreme Court's comments about the long roots of the idea of public environmental rights in the common law, the idea has not had a lot of recent attention, and lawyers, and judges, may be skeptical that they exist in Canadian law — other than the well established public rights to fish and to use waterways for navigation.

In fact, however, there is judicial and statutory authority in support of the existence of a wide range of public rights in respect of natural features and lands. These include rights to use air; air; fish and continued existence of fish habitat; use water for navigation, and likely for domestic purposes; use parkland and other lands dedicated for a public purpose; hunt wildlife in accordance with the law.

Jerry De Marco has recently suggested that the Supreme Court of Canada has recently indicated that a more general right to a safe environment exists. In addition to the court's statements in *Canfor*, he summarizes these authorities as follows:

> Taken together, the judgments in *Canadian Pacific, Hydro-Quebec* and *Imperial Oil*, as well as several provincial and territorial statutes, clearly recognize the existence of environmental rights. [These cases] provide further recognition of duties and entitlements that are similar to environmental rights.
>
> . . .

The relationship between these concepts need to be explored — but there is ample support for the view that public environmental rights do exist at common law. There is every reason to suppose that the Supreme Court was correct in suggesting that Public Environmental Rights exist in Canada, and they can form the basis for new developments in environmental law in Canada.

Relationship of Public Nuisance to Public Rights

To the extent that law schools and text books discuss public rights at all it is primarily in relation to the law of public nuisance, which has frequently been expressed as an action to enforce public rights.

This is not to say that there is no debate about that definition. Some academic definitions of public nuisance appear to point to a more nebulous "public interest" that may not have the status of full rights, but which is nonetheless enforceable through the courts: "A public nuisance has been defined as any activity which unreasonably interferes with the public's interest in questions of health, safety, morality, comfort or convenience".

However, other academics and much of the case law emphasizes the public rights aspect of the tort: "the conduct complained of must amount to . . . an attack upon the rights of the public to live their lives unaffected by inconvenience, discomfort or other forms of interference". The tort of public nuisance has also been described as an "injury to the 'property of mankind'".

No matter which definition is used, the tort of public nuisance has features which are attractive to public interest environmental litigants who see themselves as asserting the public's interest in respect the environment . . .

Public rights and conservation

Traditionally, public rights have been understood in terms of the public's right to make use of land or a resource. As such, they are a mixed blessing from an environmental point of view, since they are a consumptive right. Indeed, in the case of the public right to use water, the courts began emphasizing the unique private rights of riparian owners in part because of concerns about water conservation.

Although public rights have traditionally been conceived of as rights to use resources or land, there are several reasons to believe that they may also have a more general environmental protection or conservation aspect.

First, the Supreme Court in *Canfor* suggested as much. In that case Canadian Forest Products was held to be potentially liable for environmental harm for a negligently set forest fire in respect of non-harvestable timber. However, there was no suggestion that the public was likely to directly use that timber; nor was there evidence that the river, fish or wildlife likely to be impacted by the forest fire were used by the public. Rather, the public rights in question gave rise, in the court's view, to a general public interest in the ecological services provided by the forest.

Canfor suggests that the public may have a right to the conservation of environmental features, independently of any actual use of the resource. In some ways this may be one of the most significant aspects of *Canfor*.

Second, the public includes not just the user but also the community at large and even future generations. It is for this reason that Jerry DeMarco has suggested that the concept of environmental rights can help the law move away from a focus on the individual:

> Embracing environmental rights might, for example, put a priority on collective public rights, rather than just individual rights. Broader environmental rights may even allow us to question the human-centred ends that dominate human discourse and law making. . . . And the interrelated concepts of intergenerational equity, sustainability and public trust may help serve to end the discounting of the future.

Third, the case law concerning aboriginal rights of aboriginal people have emphasized the importance of conservation in respect of these resources. Thus the aboriginal rights cases have held that conservation is a valid legislative objective that can justify interference with the aboriginal rights. Similarly, aboriginal title cases emphasize the need to manage these commonly held lands in a way that recognizes the community's ongoing relationship with the land: see *Delgamuukw* (SCC, 1997).

Adopting the concept of "continuity of relationship" in relation to public rights, which, like aboriginal rights, are collectively held, could be an important step in reconciling aboriginal law with the wider common law.

Fourth, when legislation regulates the use of public environmental rights, it is natural for the courts to assume that it is ensuring conservation of the public right. Consequently, the use-focus of public rights is not so problematic when environmental rights are used to interpret environmental legislation.

Given modern concern for the environment, it makes sense that the courts should allow public rights law to evolve in a way that recognizes the principle of intergenerational equity and the importance of managing resources that the public has rights in respect of in a sustainable manner.

How can we use Public Environmental Rights?

In general, the conversation of how to assert public rights has begun and ended with the tort of public nuisance. This tort is both the most obvious way to raise public rights and one of the most difficult — due to the limitations of standing associated with the tort. However, there are other ways that public rights can be raised in environmental litigation. These include: as a means of interpreting environmental legislation; and as a basis for asserting a fiduciary duty owed by the Crown to protect such rights;

Standing in public nuisance claims

The primary obstacle to asserting public rights through the tort of public nuisance has been the restrictive rules about who can bring such a claim. In general, only the Attorney General — or his or her designate — can bring a claim. In a modern era of environmental legislation, the government generally pursues environmental protection through statutory means, meaning that public nuisance claims as an environmental protection tool has at first glance been largely emasculated.

There is, of course, an exception to this rule of standing: an individual who has suffered "special harm" as a result of the public nuisance will have standing to bring a claim. Unfortunately, uncertainty about what this term means, and a small number of environmental cases which adopted an extremely restrictive definition of the term, has meant that few public nuisance cases are initiated by public interest litigants.

The most frequently cited case on the issue of public nuisance standing in an environmental context is *Hickey v. Electric Reduction Co.* Furlong, C. J., in *Hickey*, held that fishermen did not have standing to bring a claim in public nuisance for an oil spill because they had merely suffered a greater amount of harm from the impact of the spill on the public's right to fish and not a harm "peculiar" to themselves . . .

If public nuisance is to be used by public interest environmental lawyers to advance public environmental rights, this approach to public nuisance must be challenged. Fortunately there are multiple grounds for doing so.

First, *Hickey*, while often cited, is a trial court decision which has rarely been applied; the vast majority of public nuisance cases have held that individuals suffering direct financial loss as a result of interference with a public right do suffer "special harm". This principle has been applied to individuals who suffered a disproportionate degree of harm as a result of the obstruction of a public highway or a navigable river, or the contamination of a river.

. . . there are also a series of cases, primarily related to highways and other public spaces, in which community organizations or municipalities with a special interest in the nuisance complained of were granted such standing. These cases, which further emphasize a broad approach to standing, are difficult to reconcile with the "special harm" rule.

The apparent contradiction between these approaches has been noted by the courts and remains a live issue.

Second, the courts might consider abandoning the public nuisance standing rule altogether. The courts, since *Hickey*, have replaced this standing test with a new public interest standing test in constitutional and administrative law challenges. Academic criticism of the restrictions on standing in public nuisance cases, combined with over thirty rules of experience with the more progressive public interest standing test, provide compelling reasons to modernize the public nuisance standing rule.

There may be other arguments that can be developed to widen the ability of a public interest litigant, or an affected member of the public, to sue in public nuisance. However, public interest lawyers have not tried to bring such cases. While there are important barriers to such a case (expense, and the risk of adverse costs, fear of expanding the bad precedent in *Hickey*), it seems to me there is still potential to develop public nuisance torts as an important tool in the public interest environmental lawyer's toolbox.

Interpreting Environmental Laws

However, even without resorting to public nuisance claims, the argument that the public has rights in respect of the environment has the potential to transform how we understand environmental legislation. . . . This transformation begins with the well established principle that legislation should be interpreted, where possible, as not infringing existing legal rights. The principle is routinely applied in relation to private property rights and aboriginal rights, but few lawyers are aware of the body of case law applying the same principle to public rights . . .

This presumption of interpretation started with cases concerning the Crown's prerogative powers and the question of whether the Crown can interfere with public rights absent authority from Parliament. Thus, a public right "can only be modified or extinguished by an authorizing statute, and as such a Crown grant of land of itself does not and cannot confer a right to interfere with navigation".

According to this principle, grants or licenses made by the Crown will not be interpreted, absent a clear intention to do so, as authorizing interference with public rights . . .

This principle is also applicable to the interpretation of legislation . . .. [and] . . . it can even constrain the apparently unlimited discretion of a statutory decision-maker, on the basis that if the legislature had intended the discretion to be used in a way inconsistent with the public right, it would have said so explicitly . . .

Emphasizing public environmental rights as an important source of the interpretation of environmental legislation is particularly important in that it turns the mainstream legal story about the role of environmental legislation on its head. According to the mainstream view environmental law is a modern innovation. Prior to the modern era environmental concerns were minor or non-existent, and new laws were required after the industrial revolution to restrain the worst excesses of the market place and of private property rights. Environmental legislation is viewed as representing a departure from a previous era where private property owners were allowed to do whatever they wanted, provided there was no direct interference with other property owners.

By interpreting an environmental statute with reference to environmental rights and responsibilities that exist at common law, instead of ignoring that common law context, a very different understanding of environmental legislation emerges. According to this view, the common law has, since its inception, recognized public rights in respect of the environment. Environmental concerns may now have an unprecedented importance, but they have always been an important concern of the legal system. As a result, private property owners have acquired their property subject to a pre-existing common law duty not to negatively affect the rights of their neighbours, including public environmental rights; government regulation develops and expands upon the existing public rights in respect of a clean environment, adding additional remedies and powers to protect those rights.

Consider the differences in perspective:

The public's environmental interests are protected by statute alone	The Public has common law rights in respect of Environment
Government's job is to balance private rights and environmental interests; where there is a conflict, the private rights, as the earlier of the two, should be favoured.	Government's job is to protect both public and private rights; where there is a conflict, the public rights, as the earlier of the two, should be favoured.
Until environmental legislation is enacted, the environment has no legal protection. New environmental laws, therefore, can be viewed as restricting or infringing on private rights.	At common law a violation of the public's environmental rights amounts to a public nuisance. Environmental legislation expands on the protections available to these public rights. Private land owners were already obliged to avoid infringing public rights, so environmental legislation generally will not create new liability or infringe on existing private rights.
Government has discretion to allow interference with the environment. If the Legislator intends to restrict that discretion it would do so in clear language.	If the Legislator intended to give government discretion to interfere with public environmental rights, it would do so in clear and unambiguous language.
The government owes procedural fairness to people directly affected by government decision, but not to the general public.	Public rights are as significant to government decisions as private ones; the government has a duty to consult the public, as holders of environmental rights, as well as people more directly affected by government decisions.

One major advantage to this paradigm shift is that it reflects the way, in the author's experience, that the public tends to understand their relationship to environmental values. While there is no single monolithic entity known as the public, many, probably most, members of the public believe that they have a right to clean air, and to clean water. They believe that the government will protect these rights. Consequently, the public environmental rights framework represents both a way to translate concerns of members of the public into legal language and, conversely, a way to explain environmental law in a way that may understandable to members of the public.

Public Trust Doctrine

A concept that is closely related to the idea of public environmental rights, is the "Public Trust Doctrine". This doctrine holds that there are certain public rights that are so important that the Crown holds them in trust for the public at large.

It has occasionally been argued that if the public trust doctrine were imported from U.S. jurisprudence into Canadian law this would result in the public gaining rights in respect of the environment. It is my feeling that public rights do not depend upon the existence of a trust for their legal effect; as I have pointed out above, public rights have a direct impact on how environmental legislation should be interpreted, as well as forming a compelling story about the legal role of environmental legislation. Indeed, I have argued that a particularly strong presumption that legislation will be interpreted in light of common law public environmental rights will have effects that look very much like some versions of the public trust doctrine, but without any reference to trust law.

Nonetheless, the existence of a trust in respect of public environmental rights could only strengthen the legal effect of such rights, and may expand their impact beyond the walls of statutory authority. In addition, there is some recent academic and judicial comment on the subject, and it remains quite possible that the Canadian courts will eventually adopt some version of the public trust doctrine in respect of some or all of the public environmental rights. This development, if it occurs, would further strengthen the new paradigm, adding the idea of a fiduciary obligation to an already compelling story.

Conclusion

Public environmental rights are one of several story-changing arguments that have the potential to alter how public interest environmental lawyers argue cases. It allows us to better represent the views of public interest litigants, as well as presenting new arguments and legal tools. The Supreme Court of Canada has signaled that the common law can evolve to address fundamental values of environmental protection. However, we need to articulate a new — or perhaps an updated version of an old — vision of where and how the law can evolve. We cannot expect judges to supply a vision that we do not ourselves have. Public environmental rights are a critical piece of that vision.

References

We thank the copyright holders for their permission to reproduce their materials.

W. Branch, *Class Actions in Canada* (Aurora: Canada Law Book, 2005)

L. M. Collins, "Material Contribution to Risk and Causation in Toxic Torts" (2001) 11 J. Env. L. & Prac. 105. Reprinted by permission of Lynda M. Collins, Assistant Professor, Environmental Law Group, University of Ottawa, Common Law Section.

J. DeMarco, M. Valiante & M. Bowden, "Opening the Door for Common Law Environmental Protection in Canada: The Decision in *British Columbia v. Canadian Forest Products Ltd*". (2005) 15 J. Env. L. & Prac. 233

E.S. Knutsen, "Ambiguous Cause-In-Fact And Structured Causation: A Multi-Jurisdictional Approach" (2003) 38 Tex. Int'l L.J. 249

P.B. Kutner, "The End of *Rylands v. Fletcher? Cambridge Water Co. v. Eastern Counties Leather Plc*". (1995-1996) 31 Tort & Ins. L. J. 73

A.C. Lin, "Beyond Tort: Compensating Victims of Environmental Toxic Injury" (2004-2005) 78 S. Cal. L. Rev. 1439

H. McLeod-Kilmurray, "*Hollick* and Environmental Class Actions: Putting Substance into Class Action Procedures" (2002-2003) 34 Ottawa L.R. 263

B. Pardy, "Risk, Cause, and Toxic Torts: A Theory for a Standard of Proof" (1988-1989) 10 Advocates' Q. 277

B.H. Powell, "Cause for Concern: An Overview of Approaches to the Causation Problem in Toxic Tort Litigation" (1999) 9 J. Env. L. & Prac. 227

C. Tollefson, "Strategic Lawsuits Against Public Participation: Developing A Canadian Response" (1994) 73 Can. Bar Rev. 200

B.H. Wildsmith, "Of Herbicides and Human Kind: Palmer's Common Law Lessons" (1986) 24 Osgoode Hall L. J. 161

3

Jurisdiction over the Environment

Introduction

This chapter considers the broad topic of jurisdiction over the environment. Often this topic is addressed solely in terms of the constitutional division of powers as it relates to matters of environmental law and policy. How the Canadian Constitution allocates jurisdiction over the environment and what the Supreme Court of Canada has said on this subject are clearly important. But in this chapter we also propose to explore some other important questions and issues.

One question is the relationship between legal jurisdiction over the environment, and the actual dynamics and nature of Canadian environmental law and policy in practice. A critical question in this regard is whether, and to what extent, the jurisdictional uncertainty and conflict, reflected in much of the caselaw we will review, presents a serious and enduring obstacle to grappling with the pressing environmental challenges we collectively confront.

We also believe it is important to explore the interplay between the division of powers and related constitutional issues including the jurisdiction of local government over environmental matters, and intersection between jurisdiction over the environment and Aboriginal rights as guaranteed by section 35 of the Constitution.

In Part I we provide a basic overview of constitutional jurisdiction and interpretive doctrine. Part II considers a selection of leading Supreme Court of Canada decisions, arising in the division of powers context, that address jurisdiction over environmental law. Part III considers the extent to which these legal decisions have influenced the nature and dynamics of Canadian environmental law and policy, both in terms of policy and legal outcomes and the manner in which federal and provincial governments have interacted around environmental issues. And, in Part IV, we introduce some emerging environment-related jurisdictional issues — including Aboriginal rights and local government — to which we return later in this book.

Part I — An Overview of the Division of Powers and the Environment[1]

At the time of Confederation, neither level of government was assigned exclusive responsibility over environmental matters; indeed the concept of "environment" as a constitutional subject matter would not emerge until about a century later. Instead, both levels of government were granted responsibilities that have since been recognized to have implications for the protection and preservation of our natural environment. Analysis of the Cana-

1 This section is based, in part, on Chapter 4 in M. Doelle, *The Federal Environmental Assessment Process: A Guide and Critique* (Markham: LexisNexis Butterworths, 2008) at 51.

dian Constitution from the perspective of how it allocates responsibility for environmental protection began in earnest in the 1970s. In particular, articles written by Dale Gibson ("Constitutional Jurisdiction over Environmental Management in Canada" (1973) 23 U. Toronto L. J. 54) and Paul Emond ("The Case for a Greater Federal Role in the Environmental Protection Field: An Examination of the Pollution Problem and the Constitution" (1972) 10 Osgoode Hall L.J. 647) at this time started to consider the extent of federal jurisdiction before there were any serious efforts at the federal level to fully exercise these responsibilities.

The Supreme Court of Canada began to confront the tension between the division of powers and environmental protection in the early 1980s, in cases dealing with fisheries and marine pollution issues. The most important landmarks in its environmental law jurisprudence in the division of powers setting, that we shall be examining shortly in some detail, are *R. v. Crown Zellerbach Canada Ltd.*, [1988] 1 S.C.R. 401; *Friends of the Oldman River Society v. Canada (Minister of Transport)*, [1992] 1 S.C.R. 3 and *R. v. Hydro-Québec*, [1997] 3 S.C.R. 213.

Jurisdictional issues in the area of natural resources and the environment have been a source of considerable friction between federal and provincial governments for some time. In particular, battles between the federal government and Alberta over the control of energy production and consumption have featured prominently, especially in the period following the energy crisis of the 1970s. More recently, similar issues have been raised in the context Canada's ability to implement the Kyoto Protocol.

Relevant provisions of the Canadian Constitution include those in the original 1867 *British North America Act* and the 1982 *Constitution Act*. Identifying provincial jurisdiction over the environment is generally a straightforward matter. Of particular note is that since public lands in Canada (and, by extension the resources associated with these lands) are predominantly vested in the provincial Crown, the provinces wield significant proprietary rights as putative landowner. This state of affairs is subject to an important caveat, to which we will return in Part III. Emerging judicial authority suggests that provincial Crown title is subject to section 35 of the Constitution which, in turn, guarantees underlying existing aboriginal rights, including aboriginal title: see *Tsilhqot'in Nation v. British Columbia*, 2007 BCSC 1700. This, of course, has significant implications for provinces, such as British Columbia, where title to much of the landbase has yet to be resolved through treaty negotiations.

Courts have also traditionally conferred broad legislative authority upon the provinces, which is relevant in the environmental context. The primary constitutional basis for this jurisdiction is *property and civil rights* (subsection 92(13)). Provincial legislative authority also flows from other enumerated heads of power including: *matters of a merely local or private nature* (subsection 92(16)), and jurisdiction over *mines and minerals* (section 109), *non-renewable natural resources, forestry and electrical energy* (section 92A), *municipal institutions* (subsection 92(8)), and *local works and undertakings* (subsection 92(10)), except those under federal control. It is important to note that provincial heads of power are frequently subject to some limitations in light of either exclusive or concurrent federal jurisdiction over subject matters that overlap with these provincial heads of power. This will be canvassed in Part II. Furthermore, provincial jurisdiction is restricted to the territory of the province, the limits of which are an ongoing area of uncertainty in many coastal areas.

The territorial reach of federal jurisdiction extends to all of Canada, including all provinces and territories as well as Canada's territorial waters. However, since federal Crown land is relatively limited in nature (except in the northern territories) federal jurisdiction depends primarily on legislative heads of power specifically enumerated in the Constitution. The list of relevant heads of power is therefore much longer. The result is a patchwork of federal powers superimposed on a carpet of provincial powers. In some cases, the federal powers restrict provincial powers; in other areas, both levels of government have concurrent jurisdiction. In many cases, the scope of the federal power with respect to environmental issues is still evolving, making it difficult to get a clear picture of the respective constitutional boundaries within which these two levels of government operate.

The key federal heads of power can be organized into two categories, *conceptual* powers and *functional* powers. This categorization goes back to the early 1970s, and has been broadly adopted by academics and courts alike, particularly in the environmental context. The conceptual/functional distinction is described by Prof. Emond as follows:

> The heads of power under the BNA Act that may support federal involvement in the environmental control field fall neatly into two distinct categories — conceptual powers and functional powers. The first provides general federal competence to legislate over a broad range of important activities, which by analogy include environmental quality; the second specifically gives Parliament control over certain activities that are closely related to pollution in the sense that they may be adversely affected by, or may in fact contribute to the pollution problem.

Conceptual Powers

On the conceptual side, there are a number of federal powers that have the potential to be relevant in the environmental field. These include: the criminal law power (subsection 91(27)), the federal spending power, the federal taxation power (subsection 91(3)), the trade and commerce power (subsection 91(2)) and the residual power with respect to Peace, Order and Good Government (POGG) (section 91). With each of these conceptual powers, there are some applications in the environmental context that are relatively uncontroversial and others that are more controversial and uncertain.

Federal use of the *criminal law power* to implement prohibitions with stiff penalties to prevent harm to human health is well established. However, as the legislative scheme in question becomes more complex, and is more regulatory in nature, deployment of the criminal law power becomes more controversial. The 1997 SCC case of *R. v. Hydro-Québec* has resolved at least some of these issues, by confirming environmental protection as a legitimate purpose of the exercise of the criminal law power, and approving of the embedding of criminal law measures within a broader regulatory scheme. Limits and uncertainties, however, remain. For example, the more precautionary the regulatory approach and the less clear the evidence of harm, the greater the debate over the use of this head of power is likely to be. Most importantly, perhaps, the criminal law power is limited in the tools available to protect the environment to some form of prohibition or restriction with a penalty for non-compliance. As was pointed out by Emond in the 1970s, while the criminal law power may be broad insofar as allowing the federal government to weigh in on many environmental issues, it does not necessarily empower it to mount the most effective "multi-level attack on the problem that employs various regulatory and remedial tools".

The federal *spending power* complements the command and control approach authorized under the criminal law power. It can either be used directly to influence those engaged in activities, or support provincial environmental protection initiatives. It can be used to provide incentives to those engaged in harmful activities to reduce their environmental impact, and reward environmental innovation and superior performance. The potential of this power was described as far back as 1972 as allowing for the implementation of national environmental policies akin to the implementation of universal health care. The precise breadth of the spending power remains somewhat uncertain. However, its exercise does not involve compulsion of resistant or disinterested provinces; it is unlikely that the *bona fide* exercise of this power would be interpreted as being in conflict with provincial jurisdiction.

The federal *taxation power* similarly has the potential to supplement the command and control approach authorized under the criminal law power. This power can be used in two different ways to support federal efforts in the environmental field. One would be a non-targeted revenue generating approach, essentially to support the use of the federal spending power or to fund command and control efforts. The other lies in influencing behaviour by taxing undesirable behaviour and providing tax relief to more desirable alternatives. In many cases, both purposes can work in combination to help achieve an environmental objective. As with all federal powers, the spending power cannot be used as a colourable device to invade provincial jurisdiction.

The *trade and commerce power* has generally been interpreted narrowly. This is due to judicial concerns about the potential for conflict between this power and the broad provincial jurisdiction over property and civil rights. In *Parsons v. Citizens' Insurance Co.* (1880), 4 S.C.R. 215, the trade and commerce power was limited to trade and commerce that crosses a provincial or international border. The case left open the possibility of general trade and commerce affecting the whole country also coming within this head of power. Given recent comments from the SCC, it is questionable whether the trade and commerce power significantly adds to the powers of the federal government to take measures to protect the natural environment from the effects of human activity. There may be circumstances, however, such as Canadian participation in an international emissions trading system, where the trade and commerce power will be applicable.

Federal jurisdiction to legislate with respect to *Peace, Order, and Good Government* (POGG), is a residual power, one that applies to subject matters not already assigned to the exclusive jurisdiction of either level of government. Two branches have emerged over time, an "emergency" branch, and a "national concern" branch. The emergency power has been relatively uncontroversial. It has allowed Parliament to step in and legislate in areas otherwise beyond federal jurisdiction at times of war or during a similar national crisis. As certain environmental issues reach the status of a national crisis, this branch of POGG may very well be utilized by Parliament on a temporary basis. The national concern branch has extended the reach of POGG beyond emergencies to subject matters that either did not exist at Confederation, such as air or space travel, or to matters that have evolved from local issues to issues of national concern.

It is the national concern branch that has been the most relevant and controversial in the environmental context. Key environmental cases dealing with the application of the national concern branch of POGG include SCC rulings in *R. v. Crown Zellerbach Canada Ltd.*, [1988] 1 S.C.R. 401, *Ontario Hydro v. Ontario (Labour Relations Board)*, [1993] 3 S.C.R. 327 and *R. v. Hydro-Québec*, [1997] 3 S.C.R. 213. In addition to the general concept that a subject matter has become of national concern, the key elements of the test that have evolved for the national concern branch include the "singleness", "distinctiveness", and "indivisibility" of the subject matter. Finally, the court has to consider the extra-provincial impact of the failure of a province to adequately deal with the subject matter.

Functional Powers

For conceptual powers, the jurisdictional connection is generally between a given environmental issue and the response measure, be that taxation, spending, or a command and control response. The exception to this is the POGG power, which essentially provides a means for adding new functional heads of power. On the functional side, the jurisdictional connection is generally between the environment and a head of power that assigns jurisdiction over all, or some aspect, of a natural resource to the federal government.

Some functional heads of power grant federal jurisdiction directly over a component of the environment potentially threatened by human activities. Other functional heads of power grant federal jurisdiction over activities that pose a threat to the environment. Key functional heads of federal power include sea coast and inland fisheries, navigation and shipping, federal works and undertakings, and canals, harbours, rivers, and lake improvements.

Federal jurisdiction over *sea coast and inland fisheries* under subsection 91(12) is perhaps the functional power with the most obvious connection to environmental protection. On the surface, it may appear that this head of power grants exclusive right over the fishing industry and the protection of fish and its habitat to the federal government. It is important to note, however, the reference to fisheries as opposed to fish. In practice, provinces have retained considerable jurisdiction under general heads of power such as property and civil rights, particularly with respect to privately owned fisheries, and fish processing.

Navigation and shipping, under subsection 91(10), have been treated as separate heads of power by the courts. With respect to navigation, the federal government has exclusive control over matters concerning navigation in all navigable waters, regardless of whether the title in a particular watercourse rests with a province or is in private hands. While provinces therefore cannot control navigation, they may still have other areas of jurisdiction with respect to the same watercourses. Examples of areas of overlapping jurisdiction and potential for conflict include dams for purposes of power production, flood control, or water resource control. While federal power over navigation has been interpreted broadly, jurisdiction over shipping has historically been interpreted more narrowly to be limited to interprovincial and international shipping.

Subsections 92(10) and 91(29) combine to grant federal jurisdiction over *certain works and undertakings*. Subsection 92(10) lists a number of specific works and undertakings dealing with a variety of modes of communication and transportation of an interprovincial nature. In addition, it provides authority for Parliament to declare other works to be for the advantage of two or more provinces and thereby declared to be federal works. As with other federal powers, the power to make a statutory declaration is limited in that it cannot be used as a colourable device to intrude into provincial jurisdiction. The power has been exercised with respect to works such as grain elevators, warehouses, an international bridge, and a local railway.

Jurisdiction over canals, harbours, rivers, and lake improvements complements other functional powers over fisheries, navigation and shipping and federal works and undertakings. Federal jurisdiction over watercourses and a range of human activities associated with them is thereby solidified. The subsequent acceptance by the SCC of marine pollution as a new head of federal power under POGG in *Crown Zellerbach* further complements this jurisdiction.

As the foregoing illustrates, the task of identifying the boundaries between federal and provincial jurisdiction over environmental issues can be daunting. A comprehensive review of the interpretive tools and legal principles applied by the courts to resolve these issues in the context of a particular case are neither possible nor necessary, as they have been covered well elsewhere. A brief discussion of the following issues is nevertheless useful:

1. Exclusive versus concurrent jurisdiction
2. Limited power to delegate
3. Interjurisdictional immunity
4. Functional and conceptual powers
5. Role of territory and ownership
6. Treaty implementation

One of the critical issues in determining the jurisdictional boundaries between the federal and provincial levels of government in Canada is whether the jurisdiction granted to one level is concurrent or exclusive. In cases where one level of government has exclusive jurisdiction over a certain aspect of an activity, the other level of government cannot legislate the same aspect of that activity. However, there may be another aspect of the same activity that is within the jurisdiction of the other level of government. In case of concurrent or overlapping jurisdiction, both levels of government can legislate. If both legislate, federal legislation prevails in case of any inconsistencies.

The ability of one level of government to delegate (directly or impliedly) to another is limited. This means, among other things, that the failure of one level of government to exercise its exclusive jurisdiction does not empower the other level of government generally to step into the void. While legislative delegation is not permitted, administrative arrangements that have had the effect of delegating responsibility have been upheld.

A third issue worth noting is the concept of interjurisdictional immunity, which deals with the extent to which one level of government is bound to follow laws passed by another level of government. The general proposition is that there are constitutional limits on the ability of a province to bind the federal government to its environmental laws. The reverse (i.e. the ability of the federal government to bind the provincial crown to its environmental laws) is not a constitutional principle but remains an issue of legislative construction. Federal environmental laws, if validly enacted, and clear in their application to the provincial Crown, have generally been upheld.

For practical purposes, it is useful to distinguish between jurisdiction over a substantive issue and the jurisdiction to implement a particular response. This distinction is implicit in the functional/conceptual distinction between federal powers discussed above. Functional powers tend to limit the range of environmental issues to which the federal government can respond, whereas the conceptual powers tend to limit the availability of federal response measures. From a federal perspective, therefore, attention to this interaction between functional and conceptual powers becomes important when contemplating potential action on environmental issues.

Territory and ownership play a central role in any jurisdictional analysis. Territory is an important constraint on provincial jurisdiction in that provinces do not have jurisdiction to legislate in pith and substance outside the boundaries of their respective provinces. For example, a province cannot regulate activities in marine waters surrounding the province unless those waters form part of the territory of that province. Provincial legislation is permitted, however, to have incidental effects outside provincial borders. Ownership, on the other hand, is sometimes critical on the federal side, in that federal ownership of land or other property within the territory of a province allocates federal jurisdiction over matters that would otherwise be within the exclusive jurisdiction of the province.

A central issue in the environmental field has been the extent to which the federal government has the jurisdiction to implement international treaty obligations it accepts on Canada's behalf. With respect to some issues, such as marine pollution and migratory birds, there is unequivocal federal jurisdiction over the subject matter of the treaty. The federal government's role in negotiating environmental protection treaties is however not limited to environmental issues within a federal jurisdiction. When the federal government negotiates treaties and undertakes obligations to protect or enhance aspects of the environment that are within provincial jurisdiction (such as treaties designed to conserve non-renewable resources) this raises difficult implementation issues. We consider this question in relation to the Kyoto Protocol in Chapter 10.

Part II — Federalism and the Environment in the Supreme Court of Canada

It was not until well over 100 years after Confederation that the Supreme Court began to grapple with the federalism implications of growing concern over the environment. Three cases, all decided in the 1980s, are often regarded as the Court's initial forays into this new jurisprudential realm. The first two, *R. v. Fowler*, [1980] 2 S.C.R. 213 and *R. v. Northwest Falling Contractors Ltd.*, [1980] 2 S.C.R. 292, were decided based on existing functional powers. The third, *R. v. Crown Zellerbach Canada Ltd.*, [1988] 1 S.C.R. 401, considered the application of a number of conceptual powers to the environment.

All three cases dealt with federal legislation that was seeking to control the impact of private operations on marine ecosystems. In *Fowler*, the accused had deposited wood debris into a stream during forestry operations in violation of a provision of the *Fisheries Act* specifically dealing with the deposit of wood debris into a watercourse. This provision made it an offence to deposit waste *per se* without proof that the deposit adversely affected fish or fish habitat. Because of the lack of nexus between the prohibited action and harm to fish and fish habitat, the Supreme Court held that the relevant provision was *ultra vires* federal jurisdiction under subsection 91(12).

In *Northwest Falling*, the accused was charged under what is now subsection 36(3) of the *Fisheries Act* for depositing a deleterious substance into waters frequented by fish. In this case, the challenge to the legislation failed. For the court, what was critical was that subsection 36(3), unlike the provision struck down in *Fowler*, contemplated a clear nexus between the prohibited act and federal jurisdiction to protect fish and fish habitat.

Of these three early cases, by far the most important to an understanding of the relationship between the division of powers and the environment is *Crown Zellerbach*.

R. v. Crown Zellerbach Canada Ltd.
[1988] 1 S.C.R. 401

[The facts in *Crown Zellerbach* are somewhat akin to those in *Fowler* and *Northwest Falling* in that all three involved charges arising out of forestry operations in British Columbia. In this case, however, the prosecution was pursued under the federal *Ocean Dumping Control Act* (OCDA). As there was no clear nexus between the charging provisions of the OCDA and the protection of fish and fish habitat, *Fowler* precluded the Crown from relying on s. 91(12). As such, it sought to defend the impugned provisions on other grounds. To this end, it invoked the federal peace, order and good government power (POGG).

The majority, per Le Dain J., concluded that marine pollution had become a matter of national concern, and had a sufficient singleness, distinctiveness and indivisibility to come under the national concern branch of the POGG test. It also concluded that the impact on provincial jurisdiction of recognizing marine pollution as a new head of exclusive federal power could be justified in the circumstances. Justice La Forest, for the dissent, disagreed on a number of grounds. As we shall see, his reasons evince a deep concern about the implications of assigning to the federal government such a broad exclusive jurisdiction, a theme to which he returns in his reasons in *Oldman River* four years later.]

Consider the following excerpts from the decision:

LE DAIN J.: The question raised by this appeal is whether federal legislative jurisdiction to regulate the dumping of substances at sea, as a measure for the prevention of marine pollution, extends to the regulation of dumping in provincial marine waters. In issue is the validity of s. 4(1) of the *Ocean Dumping Control Act*, S.C. 1974-75-76, c. 55, which prohibits the dumping of any substance at sea except in accordance with the terms and conditions of a permit, the sea being defined for the purposes of the Act as including the internal waters of Canada other than fresh waters. [. . .]

The general purpose of the *Ocean Dumping Control Act* is to regulate the dumping of substances at sea in order to prevent various kinds of harm to the marine environment. The Act would appear to have been enacted in fulfilment of Canada's obligations under the *Convention on the Prevention of Marine Pollution by Dumping of Wastes and other Matter*, which was signed by Canada on December 29, 1972. [. . .]

The concerns of the Act are reflected in the nature of the prohibited and restricted substances in Schedules I and II and in the factors to be taken into account by the Minister of the Environment in granting permits to dump, which are set out in ss. 9 and 10 of the Act and in Schedule III. What these provisions indicate is that the Act is concerned with marine pollution and its effect on marine life, human health and the amenities of the marine environment. There is also reference to the effect of dumping on navigation and shipping and other legitimate uses of the sea.

Section 4(1) of the Act, with the contravention of which the respondent was charged, reads as follows:

> 4. (1) No person shall dump except in accordance with the terms and conditions of a permit.

The respondent carries on logging operations on Vancouver Island in connection with its forest products business in British Columbia and maintains a log dump on a water lot leased from the provincial Crown for the purpose of log booming and storage in Beaver Cove, off Johnstone Strait, on the northeast side of Vancouver Island. [. . .] At the relevant time the only permit held by the respondent under the Act was one issued on or about July 28, 1980, effective until July 25, 1981, to dump at a site in Johnstone Strait some 2.2 nautical miles from the place where the woodwaste was dumped. [. . .]

On the appeal to this Court the constitutional question was framed as follows: Is section 4(1) of the *Ocean Dumping Control Act*, S.C. 1974-75-76, c. 55, *ultra vires* of the Parliament of Canada, and, in particular, is it *ultra vires* of the Parliament of Canada in its application to the dumping of waste in the waters of Beaver Cove, an area within the province of British Columbia? [. . .]

Before considering the application of the federal peace, order and good government power it is necessary to express an opinion as to the effect of the judgments of this Court in *Fowler* and *Northwest Falling*, because of the particular reliance that was placed on them in the judgments below and in the argument of the respondent and the provincial Attorneys General in this Court. [. . .]

I agree with Schmidt Prov. Ct. J. and the British Columbia Court of Appeal that federal legislative jurisdiction with respect to seacoast and inland fisheries is not sufficient by itself to support the constitutional validity of s. 4(1) of the Act because that section, viewed in the context of the Act as a whole, fails to meet the test laid down in *Fowler* and *Northwest Falling*. While the effect on fisheries of marine pollution caused by the dumping of waste is clearly one of the concerns of the Act it is not the only effect of such pollution with which the Act is concerned. A basis for federal legislative jurisdiction to control marine pollution generally in provincial waters cannot be found in any of the specified heads of federal jurisdiction in s. 91 of the *Constitution Act, 1867*, whether taken individually or collectively.

It is necessary then to consider the national dimensions or national concern doctrine (as it is now generally referred to) of the federal peace, order and good government power as a possible basis for the constitutional validity of s. 4(1) of the Act, as applied to the control of dumping in provincial marine waters. [. . .]

From this survey of the opinion expressed in this Court concerning the national concern doctrine of the federal peace, order and good government power I draw the following conclusions as to what now appears to be firmly established:

1. The national concern doctrine is separate and distinct from the national emergency doctrine of the peace, order and good government power, which is chiefly distinguishable by the fact that it provides a constitutional basis for what is necessarily legislation of a temporary nature;

2. The national concern doctrine applies to both new matters which did not exist at Confederation and to matters which, although originally matters of a local or private nature in a province, have since, in the absence of national emergency, become matters of national concern;

3. For a matter to qualify as a matter of national concern in either sense it must have a singleness, distinctiveness and indivisibility that clearly distinguishes it from matters of provincial concern and a scale of impact on provincial jurisdiction that is reconcilable with the fundamental distribution of legislative power under the Constitution;

4. In determining whether a matter has attained the required degree of singleness, distinctiveness and indivisibility that clearly distinguishes it from matters of provincial concern it is relevant to consider what would be the effect on extra-provincial interests of a provincial failure to deal effectively with the control or regulation of the intra-provincial aspects of the matter.

This last factor, generally referred to as the "provincial inability" test and noted with apparent approval in this Court in *Labatt, Schneider* and *Wetmore*, was suggested, as Professor Hogg acknowledges, by Professor Gibson in his article, "Measuring 'National Dimensions'" (1976), 7 *Man.* L.J. 15, as the most satisfactory rationale of the cases in which the national concern doctrine of the peace, order and good government power has been applied as a basis of federal jurisdiction. As expounded by Professor Gibson, the test would appear to involve a limited or qualified application of federal jurisdiction. As put by Professor Gibson at pp. 34-35:

> By this approach, a national dimension would exist whenever a significant aspect of a problem is beyond provincial reach because it falls within the jurisdiction of another province or of the federal Parliament. It is important to emphasize however that the *entire* problem would not fall within federal competence in such circumstances. Only that aspect of the problem that is beyond provincial control would do so. Since the "P.O. & G.G." clause bestows only residual powers, the existence of a national dimension justifies no more federal legislation than is necessary to fill the gap in provincial powers. For example, federal jurisdiction to legislate for pollution of interprovincial waterways or to control "pollution price-wars" would (in the absence of other independent sources of federal competence) extend only to measures to reduce the risk that citizens of one province would be harmed by the non-co-operation of another province or provinces. [. . .]

This would appear to contemplate a concurrent or overlapping federal jurisdiction which, I must observe, is in conflict with what was emphasized by Beetz J. in the *Anti-Inflation Act* reference-that where a matter falls within the national concern doctrine of the peace, order and good government power, as distinct from the emergency doctrine, Parliament has an exclusive jurisdiction of a plenary nature to legislate in relation to that matter, including its intra-provincial aspects. [. . .]

Marine pollution, because of its predominantly extra-provincial as well as international character and implications, is clearly a matter of concern to Canada as a whole. The question is whether the control of pollution by the dumping of substances in marine waters, including provincial marine waters, is a single, indivisible matter, distinct from the control of pollution by the dumping of substances in other provincial waters. The *Ocean Dumping Control Act* reflects a distinction between the pollution of salt water and the pollution of fresh water. The question, as I conceive it, is whether that distinction is sufficient to make the control of marine pollution by the dumping of substances a single, indivisible matter falling within the national concern doctrine of the peace, order and good government power.

Marine pollution by the dumping of substances is clearly treated by the *Convention on the Prevention of Marine Pollution by Dumping of Wastes and other Matter* as a distinct and separate form of water pollution having its own characteristics and scientific considerations. [. . .]

There remains the question whether the pollution of marine waters by the dumping of substances is sufficiently distinguishable from the pollution of fresh waters by such dumping to meet the requirement of singleness or indivisibility. In many cases the pollution of fresh waters will have a pollutant effect in the marine waters into which they flow, and this is noted by the U.N. Report, but that report, as I have suggested, emphasizes that marine pollution, because of the differences in the composition and action of marine waters and fresh waters, has its own characteristics and scientific considerations that distinguish it from fresh water pollution. Moreover, the distinction between salt water and fresh water as limiting the application of the *Ocean Dumping Control Act* meets the consideration emphasized by a majority of this Court in the *Anti-Inflation Act* reference — that in order for a matter to qualify as one of national concern falling within the federal peace, order and good government power it must have ascertainable and reasonable limits, in so far as its impact on provincial jurisdiction is concerned.

For these reasons I am of the opinion that s. 4(1) of the *Ocean Dumping Control Act* is constitutionally valid as enacted in relation to a matter falling within the national concern doctrine of the peace, order and good government power of the Parliament of Canada, and, in particular, that it is constitutional in its application to the dumping of waste in the waters of Beaver Cove. I would accordingly allow the appeal, set aside the judgments of the Court of Appeal and Schmidt Prov. Ct. J. and refer the matter back to the Provincial Court judge. The constitutional question should be answered as follows:

> Is section 4(1) of the *Ocean Dumping Control Act*, S.C. 1974-75-76, c. 55, *ultra vires* of the Parliament of Canada, and, in particular, is it *ultra vires* of the Parliament of Canada in its application to the dumping of waste in the waters of Beaver Cove, an area within the province of British Columbia?
>
> Answer: No.

LA FOREST J. (dissenting) — The issue raised in this appeal involves the extent to which the federal Parliament may constitutionally prohibit the disposal of substances not shown to have a pollutant effect in marine waters beyond the coast but within the limits of a province. [. . .]

I see no more merit in the submission, which appeared in the appellant's written submission, that the prohibition in s. 4(1) is justifiable as criminal law, and it is significant that counsel rather ignored this submission in his oral argument. It may be true that some of the items listed in the schedules to the Act could be harmful to human health if dumped in water, and it is also true that a prohibition properly directed at the protection of health might be justifiable as an exercise of the criminal law power; see *Reference re Validity of Section 5(a) of the Dairy Industry Act*, [1949] S.C.R. 1 at pp. 49-50. But it is difficult to see how the impugned provision preventing the dumping into marine waters of any substance, however innocuous, can be said to be aimed at the protection of health. [. . .]

There remains, then, the appellant's argument that s. 4(1) is valid as legislation respecting ocean pollution under the peace, order and good government clause. [. . .]

I start with the proposition that what is sought to be regulated in the present case is an activity wholly within the province, taking place on provincially owned land. Only local works and undertakings are involved, and there is no evidence that the substance made subject to the prohibition in s. 4(1) is either deleterious in any way or has any impact beyond the limits of the province. It is not difficult, on this basis, to conclude that the matter is one that falls within provincial legislative power unless it can somehow be established that it falls within Parliament's general power to legislate for the peace, order and good government of Canada.

Peace, Order and Good Government

There are several applications of the peace, order and good government power that may have relevance to the control of ocean pollution. One is its application in times of emergency. The federal Parliament clearly has power to deal with a grave emergency without regard to the ordinary division of legislative power under the Constitution. The most obvious manifestation of this power is in times of war or civil insurrection, but it has in recent years also been applied in peacetime to justify the control of rampant inflation; see *Re: Anti-Inflation Act, supra.* But while there can be no doubt that the control of ocean pollution poses a serious problem, no one has argued that it has reached such grave proportions as to require the displacement of the ordinary division of legislative power under the Constitution.

A second manner in which the power to legislate respecting peace, order and good government may be invoked in the present context is to control that area of the sea lying beyond the limits of the provinces. The federal government may not only regulate the territorial sea and other areas over which Canada exercises sovereignty, either under its power to legislate respecting its public property, or under the general power respecting peace, order and good government under s. 91 (*Reference re Offshore Mineral Rights of British Columbia*, [1967] S.C.R. 792) or under s. 4 of the *Constitution Act, 1871* (U.K.), 34 & 35 Vict., c. 28. I have no doubt that it may also, as an aspect of its international sovereignty, exercise legislative jurisdiction for the control of pollution beyond its borders; see *Reference re Newfoundland Continental Shelf*, [1984] 1 S.C.R. 86.

In legislating under its general power for the control of pollution in areas of the ocean falling outside provincial jurisdiction, the federal Parliament is not confined to regulating activities taking place within those areas. It may take steps to prevent activities in a province, such as dumping substances in provincial waters that pollute or have the potential to pollute the sea outside the province. Indeed, the exercise of such jurisdiction, it would seem to me, is not limited to coastal and internal waters but extends to the control of deposits in fresh water that have the effect of polluting outside a province. Reference may be made here to *Interprovincial Co-operatives Ltd. v. The Queen*, [1976] 1 S.C.R. 477, where a majority of this Court upheld the view that the federal Parliament had exclusive legislative jurisdiction to deal with a problem that resulted from the depositing of a pollutant in a river in one province that had injurious effects in another province. This is but an application of the doctrine of national dimensions triggering the operation of the peace, order and good government clause.

It should require no demonstration that water moves in hydrologic cycles and that effective pollution control requires regulating pollution at its source. That source may, in fact, be situated outside the waters themselves. It is significant that the provision of the *Fisheries Act* upheld by this Court in *Northwest Falling Contractors Ltd. v. The Queen, supra*, as a valid means of protecting the fisheries not only prohibited the depositing of a deleterious substance in water, but *in any place* where it might enter waters frequented by fish. Given the way substances seep into the ground and the movement of surface and ground waters into rivers and ultimately into the sea, this can potentially cover a very large area. Indeed, since the pollution of the ocean in an important measure results from aerial pollution rather than from substances deposited in waters, similar regulations could be made in respect of substances that so pollute the air as to cause damage to the ocean or generally outside the provinces. [. . .]

The power above described can be complemented by provisions made pursuant to the criminal law power. Thus specific provisions prohibiting the deposit of particular substances could be devised in a manner similar to the prohibitions in the *Food and Drugs Act*, R.S.C. 1970, c. F-27. The combination of the criminal law power with its power to control pollution that has extra-provincial dimensions gives the federal Parliament very wide scope to control ocean pollution. While it would not be proper for me to enter into the validity of the provisions of the *Clean Air Act*, S.C. 1970-71-72, c. 47, which were upheld in *Re Canada Metal Co. and The Queen* (1982), 144 D.L.R. (3d) 124 (Man. Q.B.), those provisions do indicate that a combination of the general federal legislative power and the criminal power could go a long way towards prohibiting the pollution of internal waters as well as those in territorial waters and the high seas.

In fact, as I see it, the potential breadth of federal power to control pollution by use of its general power is so great that, even without resort to the specific argument made by the appellant, the constitutional challenge in the end may be the development of judicial strategies to confine its ambit. It must be remembered that the peace, order and good government clause may comprise not only prohibitions, like criminal law, but regulation. Regulation to control pollution, which is incidentally only part of the even larger global problem of managing the environment, could arguably include not only emission standards but the control of the substances used in manufacture, as well as the techniques of production generally, in so far as these may have an impact on pollution. This has profound implications for the federal-provincial balance mandated by the Constitution. The challenge for the courts, as in the past, will be to allow the federal Parliament sufficient scope to acquit itself of its duties to deal with national and international problems while respecting the scheme of federalism provided by the Constitution.

However widely one interprets the federal power to control ocean pollution along the preceding line of analysis, it will not serve to support the provision impugned here, one that, as in the *Fowler* case, *supra*, is a blanket prohibition against depositing *any* substance in waters without regard to its nature or amount, and one moreover where there is, in Martland J.'s words, at p. 226 of that case, "no attempt to link the proscribed conduct to actual or potential harm" to what is sought to be protected; in *Fowler*, the fisheries, here, the ocean. As in *Fowler*, too, there is no evidence to indicate that the full range of activities caught by the provision cause the harm sought to be prevented. [. . .]

Why Parliament should have chosen to enact a prohibition in such broad terms is a matter upon which one is left to speculate. It may be that, in view of the lack of knowledge about the effects of various substances deposited in water, it may be necessary to monitor all such deposits. We have no evidence on the extent to which it is necessary to monitor all deposits into the sea to develop an effective regime for the prevention of ocean pollution. A system of monitoring that was necessarily incidental to an effective legislative scheme for the control of ocean pollution could constitutionally be justified. But here not only was no material advanced to establish the need for such a system, the Act goes much further and prohibits the deposit of any substance in the sea, including provincial internal waters. If such a provision were held valid, why would a federal provision prohibiting the emission of any substance in any quantity into the air, except as permitted by federal authorities, not be constitutionally justifiable as a measure for the control of ocean pollution, it now being known that deposits from the air are a serious source of ocean pollution? [. . .]

To allocate environmental pollution exclusively to the federal Parliament would, it seems to me, involve sacrificing the principles of federalism enshrined in the Constitution. As Professor William R. Lederman has indicated in his article, "Unity and Diversity in Canadian Federalism: Ideals and Methods of Moderation" (1975), 53 Can. Bar Rev. 597, at p.

610, environmental pollution "is no limited subject or theme, [it] is a sweeping subject or theme virtually all-pervasive in its legislative implications". If, he adds, it "were to be enfranchised as a new subject of federal power by virtue of the federal general power, then provincial power and autonomy would be on the way out over the whole range of local business, industry and commerce as established to date under the existing heads of provincial powers". And I would add to the legislative subjects that would be substantially eviscerated the control of the public domain and municipal government. Indeed as Beetz J. in *Re: Anti-Inflation Act, supra*, at p. 458, stated of the proposed power over inflation, there would not be much left of the distribution of power if Parliament had exclusive jurisdiction over this subject. For similar views that the protection of environmental pollution cannot be attributed to a single head of legislative power, see P. W. Hogg, *Constitutional Law of Canada* (2nd ed. 1985), at pp. 392 and 598; Gérald A. Beaudoin, "La protection de l'environnement et ses implications en droit constitutionnel" (1977), 23 McGill L.J. 207.

It is true, of course, that we are not invited to create a general environmental pollution power but one restricted to ocean pollution. But it seems to me that the same considerations apply. I shall, however, attempt to look at it in terms of the qualities or attributes that are said to mark the subjects that have been held to fall within the peace, order and good government clause as being matters of national concern. Such a subject, it has been said, must be marked by a singleness, distinctiveness and indivisibility that clearly distinguishes it from matters of provincial concern. In my view, ocean pollution fails to meet this test for a variety of reasons. In addition to those applicable to environmental pollution generally, the following specific difficulties may be noted. First of all, marine waters are not wholly bounded by the coast; in many areas, they extend upstream into rivers for many miles. The application of the Act appears to be restricted to waters beyond the mouths of rivers (and so intrude less on provincial powers), but this is not entirely clear, and if it is so restricted, it is not clear whether this distinction is based on convenience or constitutional imperative. Apart from this, the line between salt and fresh water cannot be demarcated clearly; it is different at different depths of water, changes with the season and shifts constantly; see U.N. Report, op. cit., at p. 12. In any event, it is not so much the waters, whether fresh or salt, with which we are concerned, but their pollution. And the pollution of marine water is contributed to by the vast amounts of effluents that are poured or seep into fresh waters everywhere (id., at p. 13). There is a constant intermixture of waters; fresh waters flow into the sea and marine waters penetrate deeply inland at high tide only to return to the sea laden with pollutants collected during their incursion inland. Nor is the pollution of the ocean confined to pollution emanating from substances deposited in water. In important respects, the pollution of the sea results from emissions into the air, which are then transported over many miles and deposited into the sea; see id., at p. 15; I.J.C. Report, op. cit., at p. 22. I cannot, therefore, see ocean pollution as a sufficiently discrete subject upon which to found the kind of legislative power sought here. It is an attempt to create a federal pollution control power on unclear geographical grounds and limited to part only of the causes of ocean pollution. Such a power then simply amounts to a truncated federal pollution control power only partially effective to meet its supposed necessary purpose, unless of course one is willing to extend it to pollution emanating from fresh water and the air, when for reasons already given such an extension could completely swallow up provincial power, no link being necessary to establish the federal purpose.

This leads me to another factor considered in identifying a subject as falling within the general federal power as a matter of national domain: its impact on provincial legislative power. Here, it must be remembered that in its supposed application within the province the provision virtually prevents a province from dealing with certain of its own public property without federal consent. A wide variety of activities along the coast or in the adjoining sea involves the deposit of some substances in the sea. In fact, where large cities like Vancouver are situated by the sea, this has substantial relevance to recreational, industrial and municipal concerns of all kinds. As a matter of fact, the most polluted areas of the sea adjoin the coast; see U.N. Report, op. cit., at pp. 3-4. Among the major causes of this are various types of construction, such as hotels and harbours, the development of mineral resources and recreational activities (id., at p. 3). These are matters of immediate concern to the province. They necessarily affect activities over which the provinces have exercised some kind of jurisdiction over the years. Whether or not the "newness" of the subject is a necessary criterion for inventing new areas of jurisdiction under the peace, order and good government clause, it is certainly a relevant consideration if it means removing from the provinces areas of jurisdiction which they previously exercised. As I mentioned, pollution, including coastal pollution, is no new phenomenon, and neither are many of the kinds of activities that result in pollution.

A further relevant matter, it is said, is the effect on extra-provincial interests of a provincial failure to deal effectively with the control of intra-provincial aspects of the matter. I have some difficulty following all the implications of this, but taking it at face value, we are dealing here with a situation where, as we saw earlier, Parliament has extensive powers to deal with conditions that lead to ocean pollution wherever they occur. The difficulty with the impugned provision is that it seeks to deal with activities that cannot be demonstrated either to pollute or to have a reasonable potential of polluting the ocean. The prohibition applies to an inert substance regarding which there is no proof that it either moves or pollutes. The prohibition in fact would apply to the moving of rock from one area of provincial property to another. I cannot accept that the federal Parliament has such wide legislative power over local matters having local import taking place on provincially owned property. The prohibition in essence constitutes an impermissible attempt to control activities on property held to be provincial in *Reference re Ownership of the Bed of the Strait of Georgia and Related Areas*, *supra*. It may well be that the motive for enacting the provision is to prevent ocean pollution, but as Beetz J. underlines in *Re: Anti-Inflation Act*, *supra*, Parliament cannot do this by attempting to regulate a local industry, although it can, of course, regulate the activities of such an industry that fall within federal power, whether such activities are expressly encompassed within a specific head of power, e.g., navigation, or affect areas of federal concern, e.g., health under the criminal law power, or cause pollution to those parts of the sea under federal jurisdiction. But here the provision simply overreaches. In its terms, it encompasses activities — depositing innocuous substances into provincial waters by local undertakings on provincial lands — that fall within the exclusive legislative jurisdiction of the province.

Finally, it was argued that the provision might be read down to apply to federal waters only, but I do not think this is possible. One need only look at the broad definition of "the sea" in s. 2(2) and (3) to appreciate the comprehensive reach of the Act. Besides, it is well known that many bays and other internal bodies of waters in Canada fall within the limits of the provinces. Many of the federal internal waters are located in the Arctic and have been expressly dealt with by the federal government.

Disposition

I would dismiss the appeal with costs and reply to the constitutional question in the affirmative.

Notes and Questions

1. What would have been the outcome in *Fowler* and *Northwest Falling* if the court had applied the POGG test as set out by the majority in *Crown Zellerbach*? Conversely, what would have been the outcome in *Crown Zellerbach* if the case had been decided purely on the basis of the federal government's functional powers over fisheries and navigation?

2. What is your sense of the importance placed on the role of the federal government in the field of environmental protection by the majority and the dissent?

3. What is at the heart of the disagreement between majority and dissent on the application of the POGG test to the *Ocean Dumping Control Act*?

4. What impact does the use of POGG have on the role of the provinces? What would happen if these provisions were upheld based on the criminal law power instead of POGG?

5. What role does La Forest J.'s dissent suggest for the use of the criminal law power as the basis for establishing a federal role in the environmental protection field?

6. Do you find the functional/conceptual distinction to be a useful way to understand federal jurisdiction over the environment? Can you think of other ways to categorize the powers allocated?

Friends of the Oldman River Society v. Canada (Minister of Transport) [1992] 1 S.C.R. 3

[Some four years after *Crown Zellerbach*, the Supreme Court of Canada was o consider the scope of federal environmental jurisdiction. In *Oldman River*, the central issue was the basis and breadth of federal jurisdiction over environmental assessment.

This is a complex question with several dimensions. A threshold question is the nature of federal jurisdiction to engage in environmental assessment in the first place. However, this question cannot be answered fully in the abstract. To some extent, the answer will depend on the nature of the proposed activity to be assessed, and the scope of the assessment that is being contemplated: see Chapter 7 for further discussion of EA-related issues. *Oldman River* does not resolve all these issues; however, it remains the seminal case on federal jurisdiction over environmental assessment.

The case arises out of a broader controversy with a rich history: see Chapter 6 where related litigation mounted by opponents of the dam is recounted. The current case arose as an application for *certiorari* and *mandamus* respectively against the Ministers of Transport and Fishereis with respect to federal approval of a proposed dam along the Oldman River in Alberta. It was brought by Friends of the Oldman River Society in order to force both Ministers to seek an environmental assessment process under the EARP Guidelines Order before making a decision on whether to allow the proposed dam to proceed. The Minister of Transport had issued a permit under the NWPA without applying EARP, and the Minister of Fisheries had refused to apply either the *Fisheries Act* or the EARP process. At the Supreme Court, a number of intervenors were granted standing to address the critical issue in the case, whether the environmentalassessment process established through the EARP Guidelines Order was a valid exercise of federal jurisdiction.]

Consider the following excerpts from the decision:

> LA FOREST J.: — The protection of the environment has become one of the major challenges of our time. To respond to this challenge, governments and international organizations have been engaged in the creation of a wide variety of legislative schemes and administrative structures. In Canada, both the federal and provincial governments have established Departments of the Environment, which

> have been in place for about twenty years. More recently, however, it was realized that a department of the environment was one among many other departments, many of which pursued policies that came into conflict with its goals. Accordingly at the federal level steps were taken to give a central role to that department, and to expand the role of other government departments and agencies so as to ensure that they took account of environmental concerns in taking decisions that could have an environmental impact.

To that end, s. 6 of the *Department of the Environment Act*, R.S.C., 1985, c. E-10, empowered the Minister for the purposes of carrying out his duties relating to environmental quality, by order, with the approval of the Governor in Council, to establish guidelines for use by federal departments, agencies and regulatory bodies in carrying out their duties, functions and powers. Pursuant to this provision the *Environmental Assessment and Review Process Guidelines Order* ("*Guidelines Order*") was established and approved in June 1984, SOR/84-467. In general terms, these guidelines require all federal departments and agencies that have a decision-making authority for any proposal, i.e., any initiative, undertaking or activity that may have an environmental effect on an area of federal responsibility, to initially screen such proposal to determine whether it may give rise to any potentially adverse environmental effects. If a proposal could have a significant adverse effect on the environment, provision is made for public review by an environmental assessment panel whose members must be unbiased, free of political influence and possessed of special knowledge and experience relevant to the technical, environmental and social effects of the proposal.

The present case raises the constitutional and statutory validity of the *Guidelines Order* as well as its nature and applicability. These issues arise in a context where the respondent Society, an environmental group from Alberta, by applications for *certiorari* and mandamus, seeks to compel two federal departments, the Department of Transport and the Department of Fisheries and Oceans, to conduct a public environmental assessment pursuant to the *Guidelines Order* in respect of a dam constructed on the Oldman River by the Government of Alberta. That government had itself conducted extensive environmental studies which took into account public views. However, since the project affects navigable waters, fisheries, Indians and Indian lands, federal interests are involved. Specifically, the Society argues that the Minister of Transport must approve the project under the *Navigable Waters Protection Act*, R.S.C., 1985, c. N-22, and in doing so is required to provide for public assessment of the project pursuant to the *Guidelines Order*. It also argues that the Minister of Fisheries and Oceans has a similar duty in the performance of his functions under the *Fisheries Act*, R.S.C., 1985, c. F-14 [. . .]

I come now to a step of prime importance in this action. On March 10, 1986 the Alberta Department of the Environment applied to the federal Minister of Transport for approval of the work under s. 5 of the *Navigable Waters Protection Act*. That provision provides that no work is to be built in navigable waters without the prior approval of the Minister. In assessing the application, the Minister considered the project's effect on marine navigation and approved the application on September 18, 1987 subject to certain conditions relating to marine navigation. I underline, however, that he did not subject the application to an assessment under the *Guidelines Order*. As we shall see, whether he should have done so raises several of the major issues in this appeal. [. . .]

The constitutional question asks whether the *Guidelines Order* is so broad as to offend ss. 92 and 92A of the *Constitution Act, 1867*. However, no argument was made with respect to s. 92A for the apparent reason that the Oldman River Dam project does not, in the appellants' view, fall within the ambit of that provision. At all events, the matter is of no moment. The process of judicial review of legislation which is impugned as *ultra vires* Parliament was recently elaborated on in *Whitbread v. Walley*, *supra*, and does not bear repetition here, save to remark that if the *Guidelines Order* is found to be legislation that is in pith and substance in relation to matters within Parliament's exclusive jurisdiction, that is the end of the matter. It would be immaterial that it also affects matters of property and civil rights

(*Whitbread*, at p. 1286). The analysis proceeds first by identifying whether in pith and substance the legislation falls within a matter assigned to one or more of the heads of legislative power.

While various expressions have been used to describe what is meant by the "pith and substance" of a legislative provision, in *Whitbread v. Walley* I expressed a preference for the description "the dominant or most important characteristic of the challenged law". Naturally, the parties have advanced quite different features of the *Guidelines Order* as representing its most important characteristic. For Alberta, it is the manner in which it is said to encroach on provincial rights, although no specific matter has been identified other than general references to the environment. Alberta argues that Parliament has no plenary jurisdiction over the environment, it being a matter of legislative jurisdiction shared by both levels of government, and that the *Guidelines Order* has crossed the line which circumscribes Parliament's authority over the environment. The appellant Ministers argue that in pith and substance the *Guidelines Order* is merely a process to facilitate federal decision-making on matters that fall within Parliament's jurisdiction — a proposition with which the respondent substantially agrees.

The substance of Alberta's argument is that the *Guidelines Order* purports to give the Government of Canada general authority over the environment in such a way as to trench on the province's exclusive legislative domain. Alberta argues that the *Guidelines Order* attempts to regulate the environmental effects of matters largely within the control of the province and, consequently, cannot constitutionally be a concern of Parliament. In particular, it is said that Parliament is incompetent to deal with the environmental effects of provincial works such as the Oldman River Dam.

I agree that the *Constitution Act, 1867* has not assigned the matter of "environment" *sui generis* to either the provinces or Parliament. The environment, as understood in its generic sense, encompasses the physical, economic and social environment touching several of the heads of power assigned to the respective levels of government. Professor Gibson put it succinctly several years ago in his article "Constitutional Jurisdiction over Environmental Management in Canada" (1973), 23 *U.T.L.J.* 54, at p. 85:

> . . . "environmental management" does not, under the existing situation, constitute a homogeneous constitutional unit. Instead, it cuts across many different areas of constitutional responsibility, some federal and some provincial. And it is no less obvious that "environmental management" could never be treated as a constitutional unit under one order of government in any constitution that claimed to be federal, because no system in which one government was so powerful would be federal.

I earlier referred to the environment as a diffuse subject, echoing what I said in *R. v. Crown Zellerbach Canada Ltd.*, *supra*, to the effect that environmental control, as a subject matter, does not have the requisite distinctiveness to meet the test under the "national concern" doctrine as articulated by Beetz J. in *Reference re Anti-Inflation Act*, *supra*. Although I was writing for the minority in *Crown Zellerbach*, this opinion was not contested by the majority. The majority simply decided that marine pollution was a matter of national concern because it was predominately extra-provincial and international in character and implications, and possessed sufficiently distinct and separate characteristics as to make it subject to Parliament's residual power.

It must be recognized that the environment is not an independent matter of legislation under the *Constitution Act, 1867* and that it is a constitutionally abstruse matter which does not comfortably fit within the existing division of powers without considerable overlap and uncertainty. A variety of analytical constructs have been developed to grapple with the problem, although no single method will be suitable in every instance. Some have taken a functional approach by describing specific environmental concerns and then allocating responsibility by reference to the different heads of power; see, for example, Gibson, *supra*. Others have looked at the problem from the perspective of testing the ambit of federal powers according to their general description as "conceptual" or "global" (e.g., criminal law, taxation, trade and commerce, spending and the general residuary power) as opposed to "functional" (e.g., navigation and fisheries), see P. Emond, "The Case for a Greater Federal Role in the Environmental Protection Field: An Examination of the Pollution Problem and the Constitution" (1972), 10 Osgoode Hall L.J. 647, and M. E. Hatherly, *Constitutional Jurisdiction in Relation to Environmental Law*, background paper prepared for the Protection of Life Project, Law Reform Commission of Canada (1984).

In my view the solution to this case can more readily be found by looking first at the catalogue of powers in the *Constitution Act, 1867* and considering how they may be employed to meet or avoid environmental concerns. When viewed in this manner it will be seen that in exercising their respective legislative powers, both levels of government may affect the environment, either by acting or not acting. [. . .]

It must be noted that the exercise of legislative power, as it affects concerns relating to the environment, must, as with other concerns, be linked to the appropriate head of power, and since the nature of the various heads of power under the *Constitution Act, 1867* differ, the extent to which environmental concerns may be taken into account in the exercise of a power may vary from one power to another. For example, a somewhat different environmental role can be played by Parliament in the exercise of its jurisdiction over fisheries than under its powers concerning railways or navigation since the former involves the management of a resource, the others activities. The foregoing observations may be demonstrated by reference to two cases involving fisheries. In *Fowler v. The Queen*, [1980] 2 S.C.R. 213, the Court found that s. 33(3) of the *Fisheries Act* was *ultra vires* Parliament because its broad prohibition enjoining the deposit of "slash, stumps or other debris" into water frequented by fish was not sufficiently linked to any actual or potential harm to fisheries. However, s. 33(2), prohibiting the deposit of deleterious substances *in any place* where they might enter waters frequented by fish, was found *intra vires* Parliament under s. 91(12) in *Northwest Falling Contractors Ltd. v. The Queen*, [1980] 2 S.C.R. 292.

The provinces may similarly act in relation to the environment under any legislative power in s. 92. Legislation in relation to local works or undertakings, for example, will often take into account environmental concerns. What is not particularly helpful in sorting out the respective levels of constitutional authority over a work such as the Oldman River dam, however, is the characterization of it as a "provincial project" or an undertaking "primarily subject to provincial regulation" as the appellant Alberta sought to do. That begs the question and posits an erroneous principle that seems to hold that there exists a general doctrine of interjurisdictional immunity to shield provincial works or undertakings from otherwise valid federal legislation. [. . .]

What is important is to determine whether either level of government may legislate. One may legislate in regard to provincial aspects, the other federal aspects. Although local projects will generally fall within provincial responsibility, federal participation will be required if the project impinges on an area of federal jurisdiction as is the case here.

There is, however, an even more fundamental fallacy in Alberta's argument, and that concerns the manner in which constitutional powers may be exercised. In legislating regarding a subject, it is sufficient that the legislative body legislate on that subject. The practical purpose that inspires the legislation and the implications that body must consider in making its decision are another thing. Absent a colourable purpose or a lack of *bona fides*, these considerations will not detract from the fundamental nature of the legislation. A railway line may be required to locate so as to avoid a nuisance resulting from smoke or noise in a municipality, but it is nonetheless railway regulation.

An Australian case, *Murphyores Incorporated Pty. Ltd. v. Commonwealth of Australia* (1976), 136 C.L.R. 1 (H.C.), illustrates the point well in a context similar to the present. There the plaintiffs carried on the business of mining for mineral sands from which they produced zircon and rutile concentrates. The export of those substances was regulated by the *Customs (Prohibited Exports) Regulations* (passed pursuant to the Commonwealth's trade and commerce power) and approval from the Minister of Minerals and Energy was required for their export. The issue in the case arose when an inquiry was directed to be made under the *Environment Protection (Impact of Proposals) Act* 1974-1975 (Cth), into the environmental impact of mineral extraction from the area in which the plaintiffs had their mining leases. The Minister responsible informed the plaintiffs that the report of that inquiry would have to be considered before allowing any further export of concentrates.

The plaintiffs contended that the Minister could only consider matters relevant to "trading policy" within the scope of the Commonwealth's trade and commerce power, rather than the environmental concerns arising from the anterior mining activity which was predominantly a state interest. That argument was unanimously rejected, Stephen J. putting it as follows, at p. 12:

> The administrative decision whether or not to relax a prohibition against the export of goods will necessarily be made in the light of considerations affecting the mind of the administrator; but whatever their nature the consequence will necessarily be expressed in terms of trade and commerce, consisting of the approval or rejection of an application to relax the prohibition on exports. It will therefore fall within constitutional power. The considerations in the light of which the decision is made may not themselves relate to matters of trade and commerce but that will not deprive the decision which they induce of its inherent constitutionality for the decision will be directly on the subject matter of exportation and the considerations actuating that decision will not detract from the character which its subject matter confers upon it.

I hasten to add that I do not mean to draw any parallels between the Commonwealth's trade and commerce power as framed in the Australian Constitution and that found in the Canadian Constitution. Obviously there are important differences in the two documents, but the general point made in *Murphyores* is nonetheless valid in the present case. The case points out the danger of falling into the conceptual trap of thinking of the environment as an extraneous matter in making legislative choices or administrative decisions. Clearly, this cannot be the case. Quite simply, the environment is comprised of all that is around us and as such must be a part of what actuates many decisions of any moment.

Environmental impact assessment is, in its simplest form, a planning tool that is now generally regarded as an integral component of sound decision-making. Its fundamental purpose is summarized by R. Cotton and D. P. Emond in "Environmental Impact Assessment", in J. Swaigen, ed., *Environmental Rights in Canada* (1981), 245, at p. 247:

> The basic concepts behind environmental assessment are simply stated: (1) early identification and evaluation of all potential environmental consequences of a proposed undertaking; (2) decision making that both guarantees the adequacy of this process and reconciles, to the greatest extent possible, the proponent's development desires with environmental protection and preservation.

As a planning tool it has both an information-gathering and a decision-making component which provide the decision maker with an objective basis for granting or denying approval for a proposed development; see M. I. Jeffery, *Environmental Approvals in Canada* (1989), at p. 1.2, {SS} 1.4; D. P. Emond, *Environmental Assessment Law in Canada* (1978), at p. 5. In short, environmental impact assessment is simply descriptive of a process of decision-making.

The *Guidelines Order* has merely added to the matters that federal decision makers should consider. If the Minister of Transport was specifically assigned the task of weighing concerns regarding fisheries in weighing applications to construct works in navigable waters, could there be any complaint that this was *ultra vires*? All that it would mean is that a decision maker charged with making one decision must also consider other matters that fall within federal power. I am not unmindful of what was said by counsel for the Attorney General for Saskatchewan who sought to characterize the *Guidelines Order* as a constitutional Trojan horse enabling the federal government, on the pretext of some narrow ground of federal jurisdiction, to conduct a far ranging inquiry into matters that are exclusively within provincial jurisdiction. However, on my reading of the *Guidelines Order* the "initiating department" assigned responsibility for conducting an initial assessment, and if required, the environmental review panel, are only given a mandate to examine matters directly related to the areas of federal responsibility affected. Thus, an initiating department or panel cannot use the *Guidelines Order* as a colourable device to invade areas of provincial jurisdiction which are unconnected to the relevant heads of federal power.

Because of its auxiliary nature, environmental impact assessment can only affect matters that are "truly in relation to an institution or activity that is otherwise within [federal] legislative jurisdiction"; see *Devine v. Quebec (Attorney General)*, [1988] 2 S.C.R. 790 at p. 808. Given the necessary element of proximity that must exist between the impact assessment process and the subject matter of federal jurisdiction involved, this legislation can, in my view, be supported by the particular head of federal power invoked in each instance. In particular, the *Guidelines Order* prescribes a close nexus between the social effects that may be examined and the environmental effects generally. [. . .]

I should make it clear, however, that the scope of assessment is not confined to the particular head of power under which the Government of Canada has a decision-making responsibility within the meaning of the term "proposal". Such a responsibility, as I stated earlier, is a necessary condition to engage the process, but once the initiating department has thus been given authority to embark on an assessment, that review must consider the environmental effect on all areas of federal jurisdiction. There is no constitutional obstacle preventing Parliament from enacting legislation under several heads of power at the same time; see *Jones v. Attorney General of New Brunswick*, [1975] 2 S.C.R. 182, and *Knox Contracting Ltd. v. Canada*, [1990] 2 S.C.R. 338 at p. 350. In the case of the *Guidelines Order*, Parliament has conferred upon one institution (the "initiating department") the responsibility, in the exercise of its decision-making authority, for assessing the environmental implications on all areas of federal jurisdiction potentially affected. Here, the Minister of Transport, in his capacity of decision maker under the *Navigable Waters Protection Act*, is directed to consider the environmental impact of the dam on such areas of federal responsibility as navigable waters, fisheries, Indians and Indian lands, to name those most obviously relevant in the circumstances here.

In essence, then, the *Guidelines Order* has two fundamental aspects. First, there is the substance of the *Guidelines Order* dealing with environmental impact assessment to facilitate decision-making under the federal head of power through which a proposal is regulated. As I mentioned earlier, this aspect of the *Guidelines Order* can be sustained on the basis that it is legislation in relation to the relevant subject matters enumerated in s. 91 of the *Constitution Act, 1867*. The second aspect of the legislation is its procedural or organizational element that coordinates the process of assessment, which can in any given case touch upon several areas of federal responsibility, under the auspices of a designated decision maker, or in the vernacular of the *Guidelines Order*, the "initiating department". This facet of the legislation has as its object the regulation of the institutions and agencies of the Government of Canada as to the manner in which they perform their administrative functions and duties. This, in my view, is unquestionably *intra vires* Parliament. It may be viewed either as an adjunct of the particular legislative powers involved, or, in any event, be justifiable under the residuary power in s. 91. [. . .]

The Court adopted a similar approach in the related situation that arose in *Jones v. Attorney General of New Brunswick, supra.* There this Court dealt with the constitutional validity, on a division of powers basis, of certain provisions of the *Official Languages Act*, R.S.C. 1970, c. O-2, the *Evidence Act* of New Brunswick, R.S.N.B. 1952, c. 74, and the *Official Languages of New Brunswick Act*, S.N.B. 1969, c. 14. The federal legislation made English and French the official languages of Canada, and the impugned provisions recognized both languages in the federal courts and in criminal proceedings. Laskin C.J. held, at p. 189:

> I am in no doubt that it was open to the Parliament of Canada to enact the *Official Languages Act* (limited as it is to the purposes of the Parliament and Government of Canada and to the institutions of that Parliament and Government) as being a law "for the peace, order and good government of Canada in relation to [a matter] not coming within the classes of subjects . . . assigned exclusively to the Legislatures of the Provinces". The quoted words are in the opening paragraph of s. 91 of the *British North America Act*; and, in relying on them as constitutional support for the *Official Languages Act*, I do so on the basis of the purely residuary character of the legislative power thereby conferred. *No authority need be cited for the exclusive power of the Parliament of Canada to legislate in relation to the operation and administration of the institutions and agencies of the Parliament and Government of Canada.* Those institutions and agencies are clearly beyond provincial reach. [Emphasis added.]

The Court went on to uphold the federal legislation on the additional grounds that it was valid under Parliament's criminal jurisdiction (s. 91(27)) and federal power over federal courts (s. 101). Laskin C.J. also remarked that there was no constitutional impediment preventing Parliament from adding to the range of privileged or obligatory use of English and French in institutions or activities that are subject to federal control. For similar reasons, the provincial legislation providing for the use of both official languages in the courts of New Brunswick was upheld on the basis of its power over the administration of justice in the province (s. 92(14)).

In the end, I am satisfied that the *Guidelines Order* is in pith and substance nothing more than an instrument that regulates the manner in which federal institutions must administer their multifarious duties and functions. Consequently, it is nothing more than an adjunct of the federal legislative powers affected. In any event, it falls within the purely residuary aspect of the "Peace, Order, and Good Government" power under s. 91 of the *Constitution Act, 1867*. Any intrusion into provincial matters is merely incidental to the pith and substance of the legislation. It must also be remembered that what is involved is essentially an information gathering process in furtherance of a decision-making function within federal jurisdiction, and the recommendations made at the conclusion of the information gathering stage are not binding on the decision maker. Neither the initiating department nor the panel are given power to subpoena witnesses, as was the case in *Canadian National Railway Co. v. Courtois*, [1988] 1 S.C.R. 868, where the Court held that certain provisions of the *Act respecting occupational health and safety*, S.Q. 1979, c. 63, which, *inter alia*, allowed the province to investigate accidents and issue remedial orders, were inapplicable to an interprovincial railway undertaking. I should add that Alberta's extensive reliance on that decision is misplaced. It is wholly distinguishable from the present case on several grounds, most importantly that the impugned provincial legislation there was made compulsory against a federal undertaking and was interpreted by the Court as regulating the undertaking.

For the foregoing reasons I find that the *Guidelines Order* is *intra vires* Parliament and would thus answer the constitutional question in the negative. [. . .]

On the matter of costs, it is my view that this is a proper case for awarding costs on a solicitor-client basis to the respondent Society, given the Society's circumstances and the fact that the federal Ministers were joined as appellants even though they did not earlier seek leave to appeal to this Court.

Notes and Questions

1. With respect to environmental assessment, how does *Oldman River* affect the ability of either level of government to make integrated decisions about a project's contribution to long term sustainability?

2. Justice La Forest, now writing for a majority of eight to one, starts his judgment with a number of very broad statements on the importance of environmental issues and the implications this has for the court's approach to

the division of powers between the federal and provincial governments. What developments in the realm of international environmental law, emerging at the time of the decision, may have played a role in the Court's analysis?

3. The starting point for La Forest J.'s constitutional analysis is the recognition that both federal and provincial decision makers affect the environment, "either by acting or not acting". He illustrates the implications of this using a hypothetical interprovincial railway project, which would be subject to the exclusive jurisdiction of the federal government. What is the significance of this example?

4. In reviewing the decision, it is important to consider carefully whether a particular comment relates to the jurisdiction granted under the EARP Guidelines Order, or the limits imposed by the Constitution. Second, it is important to separate constitutional limits from practical limits. In other words, as there may be sound, practical reasons in many cases for the federal decision maker not to exercise its power to the limits of its jurisdiction.

5. There are several questions to be considered in a comprehensive analysis of federal constitutional jurisdiction regarding an EA of a proposed activity. The first is whether there is jurisdiction to conduct a federal assessment of a proposal. Related to this is a consideration of constitutional limits on the scope of the proposal assessed. Next, are there constitutional limits on the scope of the assessment to be carried out? Finally, are there constitutional limits on the final decision, either in terms of whether the proposal can be rejected or in terms of conditions imposed? What does *Oldman River* say about each of these discrete questions?

6. Carefully consider the court's comments to the effect that an assessment can consider environmental effects on all areas of federal jurisdiction. Can you reconcile the court's focus on the need for integrated assessments and decision making with this statement? In light of the railway example, and the reference to *Murphyores Incorporated Pty. Ltd. v. Commonwealth of Australia*, is the court here indicating that environmental effects that are outside federal jurisdiction cannot be considered?

7. Assume that the Oldman River dam project has a significant adverse effect on forests. Can the Minister refuse to issue an approval under the *Navigable Waters Protection Act* because of concerns over the impact on forests? Does it make a difference whether the impact on an area of provincial jurisdiction is considered in combination with an impact on federal jurisdiction? In other words, does it matter whether there are impacts on navigation in addition to the impacts on forests? What if there are impacts on fish and impacts on forests? What if the only impacts are on forests?

R. v. Hydro-Québec
[1997] 3 S.C.R. 213

[Chronologically, the next important Supreme Court of Canada case to address division of powers issues in the environmental context arose out of charges laid in the mid-1990s against Hydro Quebec under the newly-proclaimed *Canadian Environmental Protection Act* (CEPA). The charges related to an accidental discharge of PCB waste into a Quebec river. Hydro-Québec argued that the relevant CEPA provisions, upon which the charges were based, were unconstitutional. The Quebec courts called upon to hear this challenge all agreed that CEPA was *ultra vires* the federal government, setting the stage for what has become a landmark Supreme Court of Canada decision.]

Consider the following excerpts from the decision:

The CHIEF JUSTICE and IACOBUCCI J. (dissenting):

The Pith and Substance of the Legislation

The manner of analysing matters involving division of powers is well established: see Hogg, *supra*, at p. 15-6. The law in question must first be characterized in relation to its "pith and substance", that is, its dominant or most important characteristic. One must then see if the law, seen in this light, can be successfully assigned to one of the government's heads of legislative power.

In this case, the Quebec Court of Appeal held that, although one of the effects of Part II of the Act is to protect human life and health, its pith and substance lies in the protection of the environment (at p. 405):

> [TRANSLATION] It can be seen from a careful examination of the provisions at issue that Parliament has chosen to regulate the release of toxic substances into the environment for the stated purpose of protecting human life and health. There is of course no question that one of the effects of the adopted measures is to promote the protection of human life and health. However, it is my view that the pith and substance of both the *Chlorobiphenyls Interim Order* and the enabling provisions pursuant to which it was made is the protection of the environment.

The respondent Hydro-Québec and the *mis en cause* the Attorney General of Quebec agree with this characterization and suggest that the true goal of the legislation is the regulation of environmental protection, writ large. The appellant, on the other hand, argues that the true object of Part II of the Act is simply the control of pollution caused by toxic substances (like PCBs), which are capable of being dispersed into the environment and whose level of toxicity is such as to pose a serious risk of harm to the environment and to human health and life. Several interveners support this claim, submitting that the impugned provisions seek simply to create national standards for the control of toxic substances. [. . .]

The Act is not, as was suggested by the appellant, aimed specifically at chemical substances; rather, it purports to cover "any distinguishable kind of organic or inorganic matter, whether animate or inanimate". Section 11 determines when a substance will be "toxic", and therefore subject to federal regulation:

> 11. For the purposes of this Part, a substance is toxic if it is entering or may enter the environment in a quantity or concentration or under conditions
>
> (a) having or that may have an immediate or long-term harmful effect on the environment;
>
> (b) constituting or that may constitute a danger to the environment on which human life depends; or
>
> (c) constituting or that may constitute a danger in Canada to human life or health.

Paragraphs 11(a) through (c) are not cumulative. It will suffice to bring a substance under federal regulatory control that it pose a risk to human life or health, part of the environment upon which human life depends, *or* the environment itself.

In this regard, we note that we cannot, with respect, agree with our colleague, La Forest J., that the criteria found in s. 11 are simply a "drafting tool" or that to speak of s. 11 as a definition is "misleading". The purpose of this section is to delineate from the category of "substances" (as defined by s. 3) those particular substances which qualify for regulation under ss. 34 and 35. It does so by specifying that "toxic" substances are, for the purposes of Part II, those which are capable of posing one of the threats listed above. This seems to us a clear statement of Parliament's intentions in this area. [. . .]

Nothing in the Act suggests that "toxic" is to be defined by any criteria other than those given in s. 11. Moreover, no special definition is given to the terms "harmful effect" and "danger". It is, in our view, accordingly clear from the wording of the legislation that "toxicity" is intended to be conditional upon meeting the criteria set out in ss. 3 and 11(a) to (c). If a substance (which can be essentially anything) poses or may pose a risk to human life or health, or to the environment upon which human life depends, or to any aspect of the environment itself, it qualifies as toxic according to the Act and may be made the subject of comprehensive federal regulation. [. . .]

In light of these factors, we believe the pith and substance of Part II of the Act lies in the wholesale regulation by federal agents of any and all substances which may harm any aspect of the environment or which may present a danger to human life or health. That is, the impugned provisions are in pith and substance aimed at protecting the environment and human life and health from any and all harmful substances by regulating these substances. It remains to be seen whether this can be justified under any of the heads of power listed in s. 91 of the *Constitution Act, 1867*. In that connection, we will begin by considering s. 91(27), the criminal law power.

The Criminal Law Power

Parliament has been given broad and exclusive power to legislate in relation to criminal law by virtue of s. 91(27): *RJR-MacDonald Inc. v. Canada (Attorney General)*, [1995] 3 S.C.R. 199; *Scowby v. Glendinning*, [1986] 2 S.C.R. 226. This power has traditionally been construed generously. As La Forest J. noted in *RJR-MacDonald*, at p. 240, "[i]n developing a definition of the criminal law, this Court has been careful not to freeze the definition in time or confine it to a fixed domain of activity".

Nevertheless, the criminal law power has always been made subject to two requirements: laws purporting to be upheld under s. 91(27) must contain prohibitions backed by penalties; and they must be directed at a "legitimate public purpose" (*Scowby*, at p. 237). As Rand J. stated in the *Margarine Reference*, *supra*, at pp. 49-50:

> A crime is an act which the law, with appropriate penal sanctions, forbids; but as prohibitions are not enacted in a vacuum, we can properly look for some evil or injurious or undesirable effect upon the public against which the law is directed. That effect may be in relation to social, economic or political interests; and the legislature has had in mind to suppress the evil or to safeguard the interest threatened. . . . Is the prohibition then enacted with a view to a public purpose which can support it as being in relation to criminal law? Public peace, order, security, health, morality: these are the ordinary though not exclusive ends served by that law [. . .]

Criminal law under s. 91(27) must attempt to achieve a criminal public purpose through the imposition of prohibitions and penalties. Colourable attempts to invade areas of provincial jurisdiction under the guise of criminal legislation will be declared *ultra vires*. As La Forest J. wrote in *RJR-MacDonald*, at p. 246:

> The scope of the federal power to create criminal legislation with respect to health matters is broad, and is circumscribed only by the requirements that the legislation must contain a prohibition accompanied by a penal sanction and must be directed at a legitimate public health evil. *If a given piece of federal legislation contains these features, and if that legislation is not otherwise a "colourable" intrusion upon provincial jurisdiction, then it is valid as criminal law.* . . . [Emphasis added.] [. . .]

The next step is therefore to examine the impugned provisions and determine whether they meet these criteria. In our view, they fall short. While the protection of the environment is a legitimate public purpose which could support the enactment of criminal legislation, we believe the impugned provisions of the Act are more an attempt to regulate environmental pollution than to prohibit or proscribe it. As such, they extend beyond the purview of criminal law and cannot be justified under s. 91(27).

(i) — A Legitimate Public Purpose

The appellant and several interveners urged us to uphold the provisions as related to health, one of the criminal public purposes recognized in the *Margarine Reference*, *supra*. In this regard, they cited numerous studies outlining the hazardous effects of PCBs, which were the subject of the Interim Order that gave rise to this litigation. [. . .] With respect, the toxicity of PCBs, while clearly important to the environment itself, is not directly relevant to this appeal, since what is at issue is not simply the Interim Order, but the enabling provisions under which that order was enacted. That is, the question is not whether PCBs pose a danger to human health, which it appears they clearly do, but whether the Act purports to grant federal regulatory power over substances which may *not* pose such a danger.

In our view, there is no question but that the Act does so. [. . .] It is not necessary that a substance constitute a danger to human life or health for it to be labelled "toxic" and brought under federal control; under s. 11(a), it is enough that it may have a harmful effect on the environment. It is not even necessary to show that the aspect of the environment threatened be one upon which human life depends; this is made a separate category under s. 11(b), and should not, therefore, be read into s. 11(a). A substance which affected groundhogs, for example, but which had no effect on people could be labelled "toxic" under s. 11(a) and made subject to wholesale federal regulation.

By defining "toxic" in this way, Parliament has taken explicit steps to ensure that no risk to human life or health, direct or indirect, would have to be proven before regulatory control could be assumed over a given substance. As such, we cannot see how the provisions can be upheld as legislation relating to health. Their scope extends well beyond matters relating to human health into the realm of general ecological protection. Parliament's clear intention was to allow for federal intervention where the environment itself was at risk, whether or not the substances concerned posed a threat to human health and whether or not the aspect of the environment affected was one on which human life depended. Having specifically excluded both direct and indirect danger to human health as preconditions for the application of these provisions, Parliament cannot now say that they were enacted in order to guard against such dangers.

To the extent that La Forest J. suggests that this legislation is supportable as relating to health, therefore, we must respectfully disagree. We agree with him, however, that the protection of the environment is itself a legitimate criminal public purpose, analogous to those cited in the *Margarine Reference, supra.* We would not add to his lucid reasoning on this point, save to state explicitly that this purpose does not rely on any of the other traditional purposes of criminal law (health, security, public order, etc.). To the extent that Parliament wishes to deter environmental pollution specifically by punishing it with appropriate penal sanctions, it is free to do so, without having to show that these sanctions are ultimately aimed at achieving one of the "traditional" aims of criminal law. The protection of the environment is itself a legitimate basis for criminal legislation.

However, we still do not feel that the impugned provisions qualify as criminal law under s. 91(27). While they have a legitimate criminal purpose, they fail to meet the other half of the *Maragarine Reference* test. The structure of Part II of the Act indicates that they are not intended to prohibit environmental pollution, but simply to regulate it. As we will now explain in further detail, they are not, therefore, criminal law: see *Hauser, supra*, at p. 999.

(ii) — Prohibitions Backed by Penalties

Ascertaining whether a particular statute is prohibitive or regulatory in nature is often more of an art than a science. As Cory J. acknowledged in *Knox Contracting, supra*, what constitutes criminal law is often "easier to recognize than define" (p. 347). Some guidelines have, however, emerged from previous jurisprudence.

The fact that a statute contains a prohibition and a penalty does not necessarily mean that statute is criminal in nature. Regulatory statutes commonly prohibit violations of their provisions or regulations promulgated under them and provide penal sanctions to be applied if violations do, in fact, occur. Any regulatory statute that lacked such prohibitions and penalties would be meaningless. However, as La Forest J. himself recognized in *Thomson Newspapers Ltd. v. Canada (Director of Investigation and Research, Restrictive Trade Practices Commission)*, [1990] 1 S.C.R. 425 at pp. 508–17, and in *R. v. McKinlay Transport Ltd.*, [1990] 1 S.C.R. 627 at p. 650, the penalties that are provided in a regulatory context serve a "pragmatic" or "instrumental" purpose and do not transform the legislation into criminal law. (Also see *Wetmore, supra, Scowby, supra*, and *Knox Contracting, supra.*) In environmental law, as in competition law or income tax law, compliance cannot always be ensured by the usual regulatory enforcement techniques, such as periodic or unannounced inspections. Hence, in order to ensure that legal standards are being met, a strong deterrent, the threat of penal sanctions, is necessary. [. . .]

At the same time, however, a criminal law does not have to consist solely of blanket prohibitions. It may, as La Forest J. noted in *RJR-MacDonald*, *supra*, at pp. 263-64, "validly contain exemptions for certain conduct without losing its status as criminal law". See also *Lord's Day Alliance of Canada v. Attorney General of British Columbia*, [1959] S.C.R. 497; *Morgentaler*, *supra*; *R. v. Furtney*, [1991] 3 S.C.R. 89. These exemptions may have the effect of establishing "regulatory" schemes which confer a measure of discretionary authority without changing the character of the law, as was the case in *RJR-MacDonald.*

Determining when a piece of legislation has crossed the line from criminal to regulatory involves, in our view, considering the nature and extent of the regulation it creates, as well as the context within which it purports to apply. A scheme which is fundamentally regulatory, for example, will not be saved by calling it an "exemption". As Professor Hogg suggests, *supra*, at p. 18–26, "the more elaborate [a] regulatory scheme, the more likely it is that the Court will classify the dispensation or exemption as being regulatory rather than criminal". At the same time, the subject matter of the impugned law may indicate the appropriate approach to take in characterizing the law as criminal or regulatory.

Having examined the legislation at issue in this case, we have no doubt that it is essentially regulatory in nature, and therefore outside the scope of s. 91(27). In order to have an "exemption", there must first be a prohibition in the legislation from which that exemption is derived. Thus, the *Tobacco Products Control Act*, S.C. 1988, c. 20, at issue in *RJR-MacDonald*, *supra*, contained broad prohibitions against the advertising and promotion of tobacco products in Canada. Section 4 of that Act provided that "[n]o person shall advertise any tobacco product offered for sale in Canada". It also provided a labelling requirement in the form of a prohibition, stating in s. 9 that it was illegal to sell tobacco products without printed health warnings. Any exemptions from these general prohibitions were just that — exceptions to a general rule.

In the legislation at issue in this appeal, on the other hand, no such prohibitions appear. [. . .] In fact, the only time the word "prohibition" appears in s. 34(1) [of CEPA] is in s. 34(1)(l), which provides that the Governor in Council *may*, at his or her discretion, prohibit the manufacture, import, use or sale of a given substance. Clearly, this is not analogous to the broad general prohibitions found in the statutes cited above.

The only other mentions of prohibition in relation to the impugned provisions are in ss. 113(f) and 113(i) of the Act, which provide that failure to comply with a regulation made under ss. 34 or 35 is an offence. The prohibitions, such as they are, are ancillary to the regulatory scheme, not the other way around. This strongly suggests that the focus of the legislation is regulation rather than prohibition. [. . .]

In this case, there *is* no offence until an administrative agency "intervenes". Sections 34 and 35 do not define an offence at all: which, if any, substances will be placed on the List of Toxic Substances, as well as the norms of conduct regarding these substances, are to be defined on an on-going basis by the Ministers of Health and the Environment. It would be an odd crime whose definition was made entirely dependent on the discretion of the Executive. This further suggests that the Act's true nature is regulatory, not criminal, and that the offences created by s. 113 are regulatory offences, not "true crimes": see *R. v. Wholesale Travel Group Inc.*, [1991] 3 S.C.R. 154, *per* Cory J. Our colleague, La Forest J., would hold that the scheme of the impugned Act is an effective means of avoiding unnecessarily broad prohibitions and carefully targeting specific toxic substances. The regulatory mechanism allows the schemes to be changed flexibly, as the need arises. Of course, simply because a scheme is effective and flexible does not mean it is *intra vires* the federal Parliament.

This is particularly true in light of the striking breadth of the impugned provisions. The 24 listed heads of authority in s. 34 allow for the regulation of every conceivable aspect of toxic substances; in fact, in case anything was left out, s. 34(1)(x) provides for regulations concerning "any other matter necessary to carry out the purposes of this Part". It is highly unlikely, in our opinion, that Parliament intended to leave the criminalization of such a sweeping area of behaviour to the discretion of the Ministers of Health and the Environment. [. . .]

The appellant relies on this Court's decision in *RJR-MacDonald, supra*, arguing that the statutory regime in this case is analogous to that upheld (on division of powers grounds) in *RJR-MacDonald*. We believe this reliance is, with respect, misplaced. As noted above, the legislation at issue in *RJR-MacDonald* contained broad prohibitions, tempered by certain exemptions. The impugned provisions in this case, on the other hand, involve no such general prohibition. In our view, they can only be characterized as a broad delegation of regulatory authority to the Governor in Council. The aim of these provisions is not to prohibit toxic substances or any aspect of their use, but simply to control the manner in which these substances will be allowed to interact with the environment.

RJR-MacDonald, may be further distinguished, in our view. The *Tobacco Products Control Act* addressed a narrow field of activity: the advertising and promotion of tobacco products. The impugned provisions here deal with a much broader area of concern: the release of substances into the environment. This Court has unanimously held that the environment is a subject matter of shared jurisdiction, that is, that the Constitution does not assign it exclusively to either the provinces or Parliament: *Oldman River, supra*, at p. 63; see also *Crown Zellerbach, supra*, at pp. 455-56, *per* La Forest J. A decision by the framers of the Constitution not to give one level of government exclusive control over a subject matter should, in our opinion, act as a signal that the two levels of government are meant to operate in tandem with regard to that subject matter. One level should not be allowed to take over the field so as to completely dwarf the presence of the other. This does not mean that *no* regulation will be permissible, but wholesale regulatory authority of the type envisaged by the Act is, in our view, inconsistent with the shared nature of jurisdiction over the environment. As La Forest J. noted in his dissenting reasons in *Crown Zellerbach*, at p. 455, "environmental pollution alone [i.e. as a subject matter of legislative authority] is itself all-pervasive. It is a by-product of everything we do. In man's relationship with his environment, waste is unavoidable".

We agree completely with this statement. Almost everything we do involves "polluting" the environment in some way. The impugned provisions purport to grant regulatory authority over all aspects of any substance whose release into the environment "ha[s] or . . . may have an immediate or long-term harmful effect on the environment" (s. 11(a)). One wonders just what, if any, role will be left for the provinces in dealing with environmental pollution if the federal government is given such total control over the release of these substances. Moreover, the countless spheres of human activity, both collective and individual, which could potentially fall under the ambit of the Act are apparent. Many of them fall within areas of jurisdiction granted to the provinces under s. 92. Granting Parliament the authority to regulate so completely the release of substances into the environment by determining whether or not they are "toxic" would not only inescapably preclude the possibility of shared environmental jurisdiction; it would also infringe severely on other heads of power assigned to the provinces.[. . .].

For all of the above reasons, we are unable to uphold the impugned provisions of the Act under the federal criminal law power. That being said, we wish to add that none of this should be read as foredooming future attempts by Parliament to create an effective national — or, indeed, international — strategy for the protection of the environment. We agree with La Forest J. that achieving such a strategy is a public purpose of extreme importance and one of the major challenges of our time. There are, in this regard, many measures open to Parliament which will not offend the division of powers set out by the Constitution, notably the creation of environmental crimes. Nothing, in our view, prevents Parliament from outlawing certain kinds of behaviour on the basis that they are harmful to the environment. But such legislation must actually seek to *outlaw* this behaviour, not merely regulate it.

Other potential avenues include the power to address interprovincial or international environmental concerns under the peace, order and good government power, which is discussed below. Parliament is not without power to act in pursuit of national policies on environmental protection. But it must do so pursuant to the balance of powers assigned by ss. 91 and 92. Environmental protection must be achieved in accordance with the Constitution, not in spite of it. As Professor Bowden concludes in her case comment on *Oldman River*, *supra*, (1992), 56 Sask. L. Rev. 209, at pp. 219-20, "it is only through legislative and policy initiatives at and between both levels of government that satisfactory solutions may be attainable".

The impugned provisions are not justified under s. 91(27) of the *Constitution Act, 1867*. We will now consider the appellant's second argument, namely that the provisions may be upheld under the peace, order and good government power.

Peace, Order and Good Government

The appellant argues that ss. 34 and 35 of the Act fall within the residual jurisdiction of Parliament under the peace, order and good government (POGG) power to legislate respecting matters of national concern, as provided for in the introductory paragraph of s. 91 of the *Constitution Act, 1867*. No argument is made with respect to the national emergency branch of POGG, and therefore only the national concern doctrine is at issue.

The jurisprudence of this Court with respect to the peace, order and good government provision of the Constitution was thoroughly reviewed by Le Dain J. for the majority in *Crown Zellerbach* [. . .]

Assuming that the protection of the environment and of human life and health against any and all potentially harmful substances could be a "new matter" which would fall under the POGG power, we must then determine whether that matter has the required "singleness, distinctiveness and indivisibility that clearly distinguishes it from matters of provincial concern" and whether its "impact on provincial jurisdiction . . . is reconcilable with the fundamental distribution of legislative power under the Constitution". Only if these criteria are satisfied will the matter be one of national concern. [. . .]

The test for singleness, distinctiveness and indivisibility is a demanding one. Because of the high potential risk to the Constitution's division of powers presented by the broad notion of "national concern", it is crucial that one be able to specify precisely what it is over which the law purports to claim jurisdiction. Otherwise, "national concern" could rapidly expand to absorb all areas of provincial authority. As Le Dain J. noted in *Crown Zellerbach*, *supra*, at p. 433, once a subject matter is qualified of national concern, "Parliament has an exclusive jurisdiction of a plenary nature to legislate in relation to that matter, including its intra-provincial aspects". [. . .]

Having concluded that the requirement of singleness, distinctiveness and indivisibility was not satisfied, it is unnecessary to examine the second criterion of the national concern test. The subject matter at issue does not qualify as a national concern matter and, since it was not suggested that it could be upheld as a matter of national emergency, it is therefore not justified by the peace, order and good government power. [. . .]

The Trade and Commerce Power

The interveners Pollution Probe et al. submit, in the alternative, that ss. 34 and 35 of the Act as well as the Interim Order can be sustained as an exercise of the federal trade and commerce power under s. 91(2) of the *Constitution Act, 1867*. More specifically, they argue that the "general trade and commerce power" recognized in *General Motors of Canada Ltd. v. City National Leasing*, [1989] 1 S.C.R. 641, can justify the federal regulations, which are aimed at controlling the use and release of toxic substances in the course of commercial activities.

Pollution Probe et al. refer to Laskin C.J.'s comments in *Wetmore*, *supra*, at p. 288, that the part of the *Food and Drugs Act* that regulated the labelling, packaging and manufacture of food and drug products "invites the application of the trade and commerce power". These comments, they argue, should similarly apply to those parts of the Interim Order and s. 34(1) that address the manufacture, sale and commercial use of PCBs and other toxic substances.

We reject these submissions for two main reasons. First, it is clear that the "pith and substance" of the impugned legislation does not concern trade and commerce, even if trade and commerce *may* be affected by the application of these provisions. The interveners Pollution Probe et al. seem to recognize this insofar as they submit that the trade and commerce power merely provides "supplemental authority" for upholding the Interim Order and the enabling provisions.

Secondly, even if it could be assumed that certain parts of s. 34(1) of the Act were aimed at the regulation of trade and commerce (e.g. those paragraphs dealing with importing and exporting), the remainder of s. 34(1) would, based on the arguments adduced above, be *ultra vires* Parliament and would have to be struck down. Assuming that the "trade and commerce" elements could be saved, therefore, they would have to be "severed" from the paragraphs of s. 34(1) that would be struck down. It is not altogether clear that this could be done, particularly since the portion of the statute remaining after severance must be capable of standing independently of the severed portion. In this case, the paragraphs are too "inextricably bound" to be able to survive independently (see Hogg, *supra*, at p. 15-21). For these reasons, we cannot agree with the interveners' submission that the impugned legislation can be justified as an exercise of the federal trade and commerce power.

LA FOREST J. — This Court has in recent years been increasingly called upon to consider the interplay between federal and provincial legislative powers as they relate to environmental protection. Whether viewed positively as strategies for maintaining a clean environment, or negatively as measures to combat the evils of pollution, there can be no doubt that these measures relate to a public purpose of superordinate importance, and one in which all levels of government and numerous organs of the international community have become increasingly engaged. In the opening passage of this Court's reasons in what is perhaps the leading case, *Friends of the Oldman River Society v. Canada (Minister of Transport)*, [1992] 1 S.C.R. 3 at pp. 16-17, the matter is succinctly put this way:

> The protection of the environment has become one of the major challenges of our time. To respond to this challenge, governments and international organizations have been engaged in the creation of a wide variety of legislative schemes and administrative structures.

The all-important duty of Parliament and the provincial legislatures to make full use of the legislative powers respectively assigned to them in protecting the environment has inevitably placed upon the courts the burden of progressively defining the extent to which these powers may be used to that end. In performing this task, it is incumbent on the courts to secure the basic balance between the two levels of government envisioned by the Constitution. However, in doing so, they must be mindful that the Constitution must be interpreted in a manner that is fully responsive to emerging realities and to the nature of the subject matter sought to be regulated. Given the pervasive and diffuse nature of the environment, this reality poses particular difficulties in this context.

This latest case in which this Court is required to define the nature of legislative powers over the environment is of major significance. The narrow issue raised is the extent to and manner in which the federal Parliament may control the amount of and conditions under which Chlorobiphenyls (PCBs) — substances well known to pose great dangers to humans and the environment generally — may enter into the environment. However, the attack on the federal power to secure this end is not really aimed at the specific provisions respecting PCBs. Rather, it puts into question the constitutional validity of its enabling statutory provisions. What is really at stake is whether Part II ("Toxic Substances") of the *Canadian Environmental Protection Act*, R.S.C., 1985, c. 16 (4th Supp.), which empowers the federal Ministers of Health and of the Environment to determine what substances are toxic and to prohibit the introduction of such substances into the environment except in accordance with specified terms and conditions, falls within the constitutional power of Parliament. [. . .]

In considering how the question of the constitutional validity of a legislative enactment relating to the environment should be approached, this Court in *Oldman River, supra*, made it clear that the environment is not, as such, a subject matter of legislation under the *Constitution Act, 1867*. As it was put there, "the *Constitution Act, 1867* has not assigned the matter of 'environment' *sui generis* to either the provinces or Parliament" (p. 63). Rather, it is a diffuse subject that cuts across many different areas of constitutional responsibility, some federal, some provincial (pp. 63-64). Thus Parliament or a provincial legislature can, in advancing the scheme or purpose of a statute, enact provisions minimizing or preventing the detrimental impact that statute may have on the environment, prohibit pollution, and the like. In assessing the constitutional validity of a provision relating to the environment, therefore, what must first be done is to look at the catalogue of legislative powers listed in the *Constitution Act, 1867* to see if the provision falls within one or more of the powers assigned to the body (whether Parliament or a provincial legislature) that enacted the legislation (*ibid.* at p. 65). If the provision in essence, in pith and substance, falls within the parameters of any such power, then it is constitutionally valid.

Though pith and substance may be described in different ways, the expressions "dominant purpose" or "true character" used in *R. v. Morgentaler*, [1993] 3 S.C.R. 463 at pp. 481-82, or "the dominant or most important characteristic of the challenged law" used in *Whitbread v. Walley*, [1990] 3 S.C.R. 1273 at p. 1286, and in *Oldman River, supra*, at p. 62, appropriately convey the meaning to be attached to the term. If a provision dealing with the environment is really aimed at promoting the dominant purpose of the statute or at addressing the impact of a statutory scheme, and the scheme itself is valid, then so is the provision.

In examining the validity of legislation in this way, it must be underlined that the nature of the relevant legislative powers must be examined. Different types of legislative powers may support different types of environmental provisions. The manner in which such provisions must be related to a legislative scheme was, by way of example, discussed in *Oldman River* in respect of railways, navigable waters and fisheries. An environmental provision may be validly aimed at curbing environmental damage, but in some cases the environmental damage may be directly related to the power itself. There is a considerable difference between regulating works and activities, like railways, and a resource like fisheries, and consequently the environmental provisions relating to each of these. Environmental provisions must be tied to the appropriate constitutional source.

Some heads of legislation may support a wholly different type of environmental provision than others. Notably under the general power to legislate for the peace, order and good government, Parliament may enact a wide variety of environmental legislation in dealing with an emergency of sufficient magnitude to warrant resort to the power. But the emergency would, of course, have to be established. So too with the "national concern" doctrine, which formed the major focus of the present case. A discrete area of environmental legislative power can fall within that doctrine, provided it meets the criteria first developed in

Reference re Anti-Inflation Act, [1976] 2 S.C.R. 373, and thus set forth in *Crown Zellerbach*, *supra*, at p. 432:

> For a matter to qualify as a matter of national concern in either sense it must have a singleness, distinctiveness and indivisibility that clearly distinguishes it from matters of provincial concern and a scale of impact on provincial jurisdiction that is reconcilable with the fundamental distribution of legislative power under the Constitution;

Thus in the latter case, this Court held that marine pollution met those criteria and so fell within the exclusive legislative power of Parliament under the peace, order and good government clause. While the constitutional necessity of characterizing certain activities as beyond the scope of provincial legislation and falling within the national domain was accepted by all the members of the Court, the danger of too readily adopting this course was not lost on the minority. Determining that a particular subject matter is a matter of national concern involves the consequence that the matter falls within the exclusive and paramount power of Parliament and has obvious impact on the balance of Canadian federalism. In *Crown Zellerbach*, the minority (at p. 453) expressed the view that the subject of environmental protection was all-pervasive, and if accepted as falling within the general legislative domain of Parliament under the national concern doctrine, could radically alter the division of legislative power in Canada.

The minority position on this point (which was not addressed by the majority) was subsequently accepted by the whole Court in *Oldman River*, *supra*, at p. 64. The general thrust of that case is that the Constitution should be so interpreted as to afford both levels of government ample means to protect the environment while maintaining the general structure of the Constitution. This is hardly consistent with an enthusiastic adoption of the "national dimensions" doctrine. That doctrine can, it is true, be adopted where the criteria set forth in *Crown Zellerbach* are met so that the subject can appropriately be separated from areas of provincial competence.

I have gone on at this length to demonstrate the simple proposition that the validity of a legislative provision (including one relating to environmental protection) must be tested against the specific characteristics of the head of power under which it is proposed to justify it. For each constitutional head of power has its own particular characteristics and raises concerns peculiar to itself in assessing it in the balance of Canadian federalism. This may seem obvious, perhaps even trite, but it is all too easy (see *Fowler v. The Queen*, [1980] 2 S.C.R. 213) to overlook the characteristics of a particular power and overshoot the mark or, again, in assessing the applicability of one head of power to give effect to concerns appropriate to another head of power when this is neither appropriate nor consistent with the law laid down by this Court respecting the ambit and contours of that other power. In the present case, it seems to me, this was the case of certain propositions placed before us regarding the breadth and application of the criminal law power. There was a marked attempt to raise concerns appropriate to the national concern doctrine under the peace, order and good government clause to the criminal law power in a manner that, in my view, is wholly inconsistent with the nature and ambit of that power as set down by this Court from a very early period and continually reiterated since, notably in specific pronouncements in the most recent cases on the subject.

The Criminal Law Power

Section 91(27) of the *Constitution Act, 1867* confers the exclusive power to legislate in relation to criminal law on Parliament. The nature and ambit of this power has recently been the subject of a detailed analytical and historical examination in *RJR-MacDonald*, *supra*, where it was again described (p. 240), as it has for many years, as being "*plenary in nature*" (emphasis added). [. . .]

What appears from the analysis in *RJR-MacDonald* is that as early as 1903, the Privy Council, in *Attorney-General for Ontario v. Hamilton Street Railway Co.*, [1903] A.C. 524 at pp. 528-29, had made it clear that the power conferred on Parliament by s. 91(27) is "the criminal law in its *widest sense*" (emphasis added). Consistently with this approach, the Privy Council in *Proprietary Articles Trade Association v. Attorney-General for Canada*, [1931] A.C. 310 (hereafter *PATA*), at p. 324, defined the criminal law power as including any prohibited act with penal consequences. As it put it, at p. 324: "The criminal quality of an act cannot be discerned . . . by reference to any standard but one: Is the act prohibited with penal consequences?" This approach has been consistently followed ever since and, as *RJR-MacDonald* relates, it has been applied by the courts in a wide variety of settings. Accordingly, it is entirely within the discretion of Parliament to determine what evil it wishes by penal prohibition to suppress and what threatened interest it thereby wishes to safeguard, to adopt the terminology of Rand J. in the *Margarine Reference*, *supra*, at p. 49, cited *infra*.

Contrary to the respondent's submission, under s. 91(27) of the *Constitution Act, 1867*, it is also within the discretion of Parliament to determine the extent of blameworthiness that it wishes to attach to a criminal prohibition. So it may determine the nature of the mental element pertaining to different crimes, such as a defence of due diligence like that which appears in s. 125(1) of the Act in issue. This flows from the fact that Parliament has been accorded plenary power to make criminal law in the widest sense. This power is, of course, subject to the "fundamental justice" requirements of s. 7 of the *Canadian Charter of Rights and Freedoms*, which may dictate a higher level of *mens rea* for serious or "true" crimes; cf. *R. v. Wholesale Travel Group Inc.*, [1991] 3 S.C.R. 154, and *R. v. Rube*, [1992] 3 S.C.R. 159, but that is not an issue here.

The *Charter* apart, only one qualification has been attached to Parliament's plenary power over criminal law. The power cannot be employed colourably. Like other legislative powers, it cannot, as Estey J. put it in *Scowby v. Glendinning*, [1986] 2 S.C.R. 226 at p. 237, "permit Parliament, simply by legislating in the proper form, to colourably invade areas of exclusively provincial legislative competence". To determine whether such an attempt is being made, it is, of course, appropriate to enquire into Parliament's purpose in enacting the legislation. As Estey J. noted in *Scowby*, at p. 237, since the *Margarine Reference*, it has been "accepted that some legitimate public purpose must underlie the prohibition". Estey J. then cited Rand J.'s words in the *Margarine Reference* (at p. 49) as follows:

> A crime is an act which the law, with appropriate penal sanctions, forbids; but as prohibitions are not enacted in a vacuum, we can properly look for some evil or injurious or undesirable effect upon the public against which the law is directed. That effect may be in relation to social, economic or political interests; and the legislature has had in mind to suppress the evil or to safeguard the interest threatened.

I simply add that the analysis in *Scowby* and the *Margarine Reference* was most recently applied by this Court in *RJR-MacDonald*, *supra*, at pp. 240-41.

In the *Margarine Reference*, *supra*, at p. 50, Rand J. helpfully set forth the more usual purposes of a criminal prohibition in the following passage:

> Is the prohibition . . . enacted with a view to a public purpose which can support it as being in relation to criminal law? Public peace, order, security, health, morality: these are the ordinary though not exclusive ends served by that law. . . . [Emphasis added.]

See also *Morgentaler*, *supra*, at p. 489; *RJR-MacDonald*, at p. 241. As the final clause in the passage just cited indicates, the listed purposes by no means exhaust the purposes that may legitimately support valid criminal legislation. Not only is this clear from this passage, but subsequent to the *Margarine Reference*, it is obvious from Rand J.'s remarks in *Lord's Day Alliance of Canada v. Attorney General of British Columbia*, [1959] S.C.R. 497 at pp. 508-9, that he was in no way departing from Lord Atkin's statement in the *PATA* case, *supra* (he cited the relevant passage with approval). His concern in the *Margarine Reference*, as he indicates in the *Lord's Day* case (at p. 509), was that "in a federal system distinctions must be made arising from the true object, purpose, nature or character of each particular enactment". In short, in a case like the present, all one is concerned with is colourability. Otherwise, one would, in effect, be reviving the discarded notion that there is a "domain" of criminal law, something Rand J., like Lord Atkin before him, was not prepared to do. All of this is, of course, consistent with the view, most recently reiterated in *RJR-MacDonald*, at pp. 259–61, that criminal law is not frozen in time.

During the argument in the present case, however, one sensed, at times, a tendency, even by the appellant and the supporting interveners, to seek justification solely for the purpose of the protection of health specifically identified by Rand J. Now I have no doubt that that purpose obviously will support a considerable measure of environmental legislation, as perhaps also the ground of security. But I entertain no doubt that the protection of a clean environment is a public purpose within Rand J.'s formulation in the *Margarine Reference*, cited *supra*, sufficient to support a criminal prohibition. It is surely an "interest threatened" which Parliament can legitimately "safeguard", or to put it another way, pollution is an "evil" that Parliament can legitimately seek to suppress. Indeed, as I indicated at the outset of these reasons, it is a public purpose of superordinate importance; it constitutes one of the major challenges of our time. It would be surprising indeed if Parliament could not exercise its plenary power over criminal law to protect this interest and to suppress the evils associated with it by appropriate penal prohibitions.

This approach is entirely consistent with the recent pronouncement of this Court in *Ontario v. Canadian Pacific Ltd.*, [1995] 2 S.C.R. 1031, where Gonthier J., speaking for the majority, had this to say, at para. 55:

> It is clear that over the past two decades, citizens have become acutely aware of the importance of environmental protection, and of the fact that penal consequences may flow from conduct which harms the environment. . . . [. . .]

This is, of course, in line with the thinking of various international organisms. The World Commission on Environment and Development (the Brundtland Commission) in its report *Our Common Future* (1987) (see at pp. 219-20, and pp. 224-25) long ago recommended the adoption of appropriate legislation to protect the environment against toxic and chemical substances, including the creation of national standards that could be supplemented by local legislation. [. . .]

What the foregoing underlines is what I referred to at the outset, that the protection of the environment is a major challenge of our time. It is an international problem, one that requires action by governments at all levels. And, as is stated in the preamble to the Act under review, "Canada must be able to fulfil its international obligations in respect of the environment". I am confident that Canada can fulfil its international obligations, in so far as the toxic substances sought to be prohibited from entering into the environment under the Act are concerned, by use of the criminal law power. The purpose of the criminal law is to underline and protect our fundamental values. While many environmental issues could be criminally sanctioned in terms of protection of human life or health, I cannot accept that the criminal law is limited to that because "certain forms and degrees of environmental pollution can directly or indirectly, sooner or later, seriously harm or endanger human life and human health", as the paper approvingly cited by Gonthier J. in *Ontario v. Canadian Pacific*, *supra*, observes. But the stage at which this may be discovered is not easy to discern, and I agree with that paper that the stewardship of the environment is a fundamental value of our society and that Parliament may use its criminal law power to underline that value. The criminal law must be able to keep pace with and protect our emerging values.

In saying that Parliament may use its criminal law power in the interest of protecting the environment or preventing pollution, there again appears to have been confusion during the argument between the approach to the national concern doctrine and the criminal law power.

The national concern doctrine operates by assigning full power to regulate an area to Parliament. Criminal law does not work that way. Rather it seeks by discrete prohibitions to prevent evils falling within a broad purpose, such as, for example, the protection of health. In the criminal law area, reference to such broad policy objectives is simply a means of ensuring that the prohibition is legitimately aimed at some public evil Parliament wishes to suppress and so is not a colourable attempt to deal with a matter falling exclusively within an area of provincial legislative jurisdiction.

The legitimate use of the criminal law I have just described in no way constitutes an encroachment on provincial legislative power, though it may affect matters falling within the latter's ambit. [. . .]

I conclude that Parliament may validly enact prohibitions under its criminal law power against specific acts for the purpose of preventing pollution or, to put it in other terms, causing the entry into the environment of certain toxic substances. I quite understand that a particular prohibition could be so broad or all-encompassing as to be found to be, in pith and substance, really aimed at regulating an area falling within the provincial domain and not exclusively at protecting the environment. A sweeping prohibition like this (and this would be equally true of one aimed generally at the protection of health) would, in any case, probably be unworkable. But the attack here ultimately is that the impugned provisions grant such a broad discretion to the Governor in Council as to permit orders that go beyond federal power. I can imagine very nice issues being raised concerning this matter under certain types of legislation, though in such a case one would tend to interpret the legislation narrowly if only to keep it within constitutional bounds. But one need not go so far here. For, it seems to me, as we shall see, when one carefully peruses the legislation, it becomes clear enough that Parliament has stayed well within its power.

Though I shall deal with this issue in more detail once I come to consider the legislation, it is well at this point to recall that the use of the federal criminal law power in no way precludes the provinces from exercising their extensive powers under s. 92 to regulate and control the pollution of the environment either independently or to supplement federal action. The situation is really no different from the situation regarding the protection of health where Parliament has for long exercised extensive control over such matters as food and drugs by prohibitions grounded in the criminal law power. This has not prevented the provinces from extensively regulating and prohibiting many activities relating to health. The two levels of government frequently work together to meet common concerns. The cooperative measures relating to the use of tobacco are fully related in *RJR-MacDonald*, *supra*. Nor, though it arises under a different technical basis, is the situation, in substance, different as regards federal prohibitions against polluting water for the purposes of protecting the fisheries. Here again there is a wide measure of cooperation between the federal and provincial authorities to effect common or complementary ends. It is also the case in many other areas. The fear that the legislation impugned here would distort the federal-provincial balance seems to me to be overstated.

One last matter requires comment. The specific provision impugned in this case, the Interim Order, would seem to me to be justified as a criminal prohibition for the protection of human life and health alone (a purpose upheld most recently in *RJR-MacDonald*). That would also at first sight appear to be true of many of the prohibited uses of the substances in the List of Toxic Substances in Schedule I. So if the protection of the environment does not amount to a valid public purpose to justify criminal sanctions, it would be simply a question of severing those portions of s. 11 of the Act that deal solely with the environment to ensure the validity of the Interim Order and the rest of the enabling provisions. After all, the protection of the environment, as we earlier saw, is closely integrated, directly or indirectly, with the protection of health. But for my part, I find this exercise wholly unnecessary. The protection of the environment, through prohibitions against toxic substances, seems to me to constitute a wholly legitimate public objective in the exercise of the criminal law power. Humanity's interest in the environment surely extends beyond its own life and health.

The Provisions Respecting Toxic Substances

The respondent, the *mis en cause* and their supporting interveners primarily attack ss. 34 and 35 of the Act as constituting an infringement on provincial regulatory powers conferred by the Constitution. This they do by submitting that the power to regulate a substance is so broad as to encroach upon provincial legislative jurisdiction. That is because of what they call the broad "definition" given to toxic substances under s. 11, and particularly para. (a), thereof which, it will be remembered, provides that:

> 11. For the purposes of this Part, a substance is toxic if it is entering or may enter the environment in a quantity or concentration or under conditions
>
> (a) having or that may have an immediate or long-term harmful effect on the environment;

This, along with the expansive definitions of "substance" and "environment" in s. 3(1), makes it possible, they say, in effect to regulate any substance that can in any way prove harmful to the environment.

I cannot agree with this submission. As I see it, the argument focusses too narrowly on a specific provision of the Act and for that matter only on certain aspects of it, and then applies that provision in a manner that I do not think is warranted by a consideration of the provisions of the Act as a whole and in light of its background and purpose. I shall deal with the latter first. Before doing so, however, I shall comment briefly on the concern expressed about the breadth of the phraseology of the Act. As Gonthier J. observed in *Ontario v. Canadian Pacific*, *supra*, this broad wording is unavoidable in environmental protection legislation because of the breadth and complexity of the subject and has to be kept in mind in interpreting the relevant legislation [. . .]. In light of this, he went on to hold that environmental protection legislation should not be approached with the same rigour as statutes dealing with less complex issues in applying the doctrine of vagueness developed under s. 7 of the *Charter*. The effect of requiring greater precision would be to frustrate the legislature in its attempt to protect the public against the dangers flowing from pollution. He thus summarized his view, at para. 58:

> In the environmental context, each one of us is vulnerable to the health and property damage caused by pollution. Where the legislature provides protection through regulatory statutes such as the EPA, it is appropriate for courts to take a more deferential approach to the *Charter* review of the offences contained in such statutes. [. . .]

I turn then to the background and purpose of the provisions under review. Part II does not deal with the protection of the environment generally. It deals simply with the control of toxic substances that may be released into the environment under certain restricted circumstances, and does so through a series of prohibitions to which penal sanctions are attached. It replaces the *Environmental Contaminants Act*, first enacted in 1975 (S.C. 1974-75-76, c. 72), which was intended to control substances entering or capable of entering into the environment in a quantity or concentration sufficient to constitute *a danger* to health or the environment; see s. 4. The continuity of policy is evident from the fact that the toxic substances controlled under the earlier legislation including PCBs were automatically included as Schedule I of the present legislation, entitled "List of Toxic Substances".

The underlying purpose for the enactment of the present Act, so far as toxic substances are concerned, is evident from a series of reports of studies made in the mid-1980s; see Environment Canada, *From Cradle to Grave: A Management Approach to Chemicals* (1986); Environment Canada and Health and Welfare Canada, *Final Report of the Environmental Contaminants Act Amendments Consultative Committee* (1986). What these reveal is that the earlier Act was clearly deficient in identifying substances that could be toxic and that what was really needed was a regime whereby the government could assess material that could be harmful to health and the environment before the substance was already in use. [. . .]

There was no intention that the Act should bar the use, importation or manufacture of all chemical products, but rather that it should affect only those substances that are dangerous to the environment, and then only if they are not regulated by law. The report recognized that "[a] great deal of our industrial strength and economic progress is based upon the use of chemicals" (p. 2), and that only a fraction of these were "believed to be hazardous but few have been assessed to make sure" (p. 2).

The manner of assessment traditionally employed — related as it was to the concern for "pollution that could be seen, touched, smelled or tasted" and "cleaning up a mess after it occurred" (p. 3) — was no longer adequate. As the report put it (at p. 3):

> Toxic chemical contamination cannot be handled in this way. Ordinary sense perception cannot identify chemical contamination because it is usually invisible until the damage, sometimes irreparable damage, has been done. *Since chemical pollution exists at the molecular level, it cannot usually be treated, contained or recovered from the environment. And since its effects are pervasive and long term, rather than local or immediate, quick-fix measures are not practical.* [Emphasis added.]

Not surprisingly, the report emphasized the need to improve the procedures for assessing whether chemical substances were hazardous; see e.g. pp. 10-11. The Act would operate through the listing of chemicals, including "a schedule of dangerous chemicals which are subject to regulation under the [Act]" (p. 15).

The impugned Act appears to me to respond closely to these objectives. The subject of toxic substances is dealt with principally in Part II of the Act. It begins, we saw, with s. 11, which has been described as a "definition" in argument. While the provision has some properties of a definition, to speak of it in this way is misleading and does not do full justice to its purpose and function. It should be observed that it does not purport to define a "toxic substance" in the manner in which s. 3 defines various concepts, e.g. "air contaminant", "air pollution", etc. which describes with finality what the defined concept means. Rather, it sets forth that a substance can only be toxic, for the purposes of Part II, if it is entering or may enter the environment in a quantity or concentration or under conditions that result in the detrimental effects on the environment, human life and human health described in paras. (a) to (c). [. . .]

I add that the determination of whether the various components of s. 11 are satisfied in respect of particular substances is by no means an easy task. Whether substances enter or may enter the environment in a quantity, concentration or conditions sufficient to have the effects set forth in that provision are not matters that are generally known. Rather these are matters that must be ascertained by assessments or tests set forth in s. 15, and in accordance with a procedure that requires consultation with the provinces, the informed community and the general public with a view to determining whether certain substances "are toxic or capable of becoming toxic", to use the expression employed in the provisions of Part II dealing with testing, beginning with the Ministers' weeding out most substances by establishing a priority list of substances to be tested. [. . .] In light of this, it is difficult to believe "toxic" is not given its ordinary meaning in the Act, and that s. 11 is, therefore, simply a drafting tool for the demarcation of those aspects of toxicity that are to be considered in the tests required in the sections that follow.

What the assessments described in Part II are aimed at is the selection of new items to add to the List of Toxic Substances set forth in Schedule I. Thus s. 11 is the first of a series of provisions respecting testing or assessment for toxicity. The first step in the process of assessment is s. 12, which requires the Ministers to compile a Priority Substances List in respect of substances to which the Ministers are satisfied priority should be given in assessing whether they are toxic or capable of becoming toxic; this list and any amendments to it are published in the *Canada Gazette*, and the provinces and other interested parties are informed (s. 12(2) and (3)). The process of testing is a detailed one and includes informing the provinces and other interested groups and the public at all stages; see, for example, s. 13. In performing their duties, the Ministers are given broad powers to collect data, conduct investigations and correlate and evaluate any data so obtained (see, for example, s. 15). The testing process culminates in a decision of the Ministers to recommend or not to recommend that a substance be added to the List of Toxic Substances in Schedule I of the Act, and, if a recommendation is made, what regulations should be made in respect of the substance under s. 34 [. . .].

In summary, as I see it, the broad purpose and effect of Part II is to provide a procedure for assessing whether out of the many substances that may conceivably fall within the ambit of s. 11, some should be added to the List of Toxic Substances in Schedule I and, when an order to this effect is made, whether to prohibit the use of the substance so added in the manner provided in the regulations made under s. 34(1) subject to a penalty. These listed substances, toxic in the ordinary sense, are those whose use in a manner contrary to the regulations the Act ultimately prohibits. This is a limited prohibition applicable to a restricted number of substances. The prohibition is enforced by a penal sanction and is undergirded by a valid criminal objective, and so is valid criminal legislation.

This, in my mind, is consistent with the terms of the statute, its purpose, and indeed common sense. It is precisely what one would expect of an environmental statute — a procedure to weed out from the vast number of substances potentially harmful to the environment or human life those only that pose significant risks of that type of harm. Specific targeting of toxic substances based on individual assessment avoids resort to unnecessarily broad prohibitions and their impact on the exercise of provincial powers. [. . .]

I turn now to a more detailed examination of the provisions of the Act impugned in the present case [. . .] s. 34 authorizes the Governor in Council to make regulations setting forth the restrictions imposed on those using or dealing with such substances. Failure to comply with any such restriction constitutes an offence and is punishable on summary conviction by a fine not exceeding three hundred thousand dollars or a term of imprisonment not exceeding six months, or both; or, on indictment, by a fine not exceeding one million dollars or a term of imprisonment not exceeding three years, or both (s. 113(f), (o) and (p)).

Without attempting to regurgitate the whole of s. 34, I shall simply give some flavour of the nature of the prohibitions created by the regulations made thereunder. Generally, s. 34 includes regulations providing for or imposing requirements respecting the quantity or concentration of a substance listed in Schedule I that may be released into the environment either alone or in combination with others from any source, the places where such substances may be released, the manufacturing or processing activities in the course of which the substance may be released, the manner and conditions of release, and so on. In short, s. 34 precisely defines situations where the use of a substance in the List of Toxic Substances in Schedule I is prohibited, and these prohibitions are made subject to penal consequences. [. . .]

What Parliament is doing in s. 34 is making provision for carefully tailoring the prohibited action to specified substances used or dealt with in specific circumstances. This type of tailoring is obviously necessary in defining the scope of a criminal prohibition, and is, of course, within Parliament's power. As Laskin C.J. noted in *Morgentaler v. The Queen*, [1976] 1 S.C.R. 616 at p. 627: "I need cite no authority for the proposition that Parliament may determine what is not criminal as well as what is". [. . .]

In truth, there is a broad area of concurrency between federal and provincial powers in areas subjected to criminal prohibitions, and the courts have been alert to the need to permit adequate breathing room for the exercise of jurisdiction by both levels of government. [. . .]

This type of approach is essential in dealing with amorphous subjects like health and the environment. In my reasons for the minority in *Crown Zellerbach*, *supra*, (addressing an issue which the majority did not discuss), I had this to say about the matter as it relates to environmental pollution (at p. 455):

> . . . environmental pollution . . . is . . . all-pervasive. It is a by-product of everything we do. In man's relationship with his environment, waste is unavoidable. The problem is thus not new, although it is only recently that the vast amount of waste products emitted into the atmosphere or dumped in water has begun to exceed the ability of the atmosphere and water to absorb and assimilate it on a global scale. There is thus cause for concern and governments at every level have begun to deal with the many activities giving rise to problems of pollution. [. . .]

I observe that in enacting the legislation in issue here, Parliament was alive to the need for cooperation and coordination between the federal and provincial authorities. This is evident throughout the Act. In particular, under s. 34(2), (5) and (6), Parliament has made it clear that the provisions of this Part are not to apply where a matter is otherwise regulated under other equivalent federal or provincial legislation.

In *Crown Zellerbach*, I expressed concern with the possibility of allocating legislative power respecting environmental pollution exclusively to Parliament. I would be equally concerned with an interpretation of the Constitution that effectively allocated to the provinces, under general powers such as property and civil rights, control over the environment in a manner that prevented Parliament from exercising the leadership role expected of it by the international community and its role in protecting the basic values of Canadians regarding the environment through the instrumentality of the criminal law power. Great sensitivity is required in this area since, as Professor Lederman has rightly observed, environmental pollution "is no limited subject or theme, [it] is a sweeping subject or theme virtually all-pervasive in its legislative implications"; see W. R. Lederman, "Unity and Diversity in Canadian Federalism: Ideals and Methods of Moderation" (1975), 53 *Can. Bar Rev.* 597, at p. 610.

Turning then to s. 35, I mentioned that it is ancillary to s. 34. It deals with emergency situations. The provision, it seems to me, indicates even more clearly a criminal purpose, and throws further light on the intention of s. 34 and of the Act generally. It can only be brought into play when the Ministers believe a substance is not specified in the List in Schedule I or is listed but is not subjected to control under s. 34. In such a case, they may make an interim order in respect of the substance if they believe "immediate action is required to deal with a significant danger to the environment or to human life or health".

In sum, then, I am of the view that Part II of the Act, properly construed, simply provides a means to assess substances with a view to determining whether the substances are sufficiently toxic to be added to Schedule I of the Act (which contains a list of dangerous substances carried over from pre-existing legislation), and provides by regulations under s. 34 the terms and conditions under which they can be used, with provisions under s. 35 for by-passing the ordinary provisions for testing and regulation under Part II in cases where immediate action is required. I have reached this position independently of the legal presumption that a legislature intends to confine itself to matters within its competence; see *Reference re Farm Products Marketing Act*, [1957] S.C.R. 198 at p. 255; *Nova Scotia Board of Censors v. McNeil*, [1978] 2 S.C.R. 662 at p. 688. However, it follows that the position I have taken would by virtue of the presumption displace a possible reading of the Act that would render it unconstitutional.

Since I have found the empowering provisions, ss. 34 and 35, to be *intra vires*, the only attack that could be brought against any action taken under them would be that such action went beyond the authority granted by those provisions; in the present case, for example, such an attack might consist in the allegation that PCBs did not pose "a significant danger to the environment or to human life or health" justifying the making of the Interim Order. This would seem to me to be a tall order. The fact that PCBs are highly toxic substances should require no demonstration. This has become well known to the general public and is supported by an impressive array of scientific studies at both the national and international levels. [. . .]

From what appears in these studies, one can conclude that PCBs are not only highly toxic but long lasting and very slow to break down in water, air or soil. They do dissolve readily in fat tissues and other organic compounds, however, with the result that they move up the food chain through birds and other animals and eventually to humans. They pose significant risks of serious harm to both animals and humans. As well they are extremely mobile. They evaporate from soil and water and are transported great distances through the atmosphere. High levels of PCBs have been found in a variety of arctic animals living thousands of kilometres from any major source of PCBs. The extent of the dangers they pose is reflected in the fact that they were the first substance sought to be controlled in Canada under the *Environmental Contaminants Act*, the predecessor of the present legislation. They were also the first substance regulated in the United States under the *Toxic Substances Control Act*, 15 U.S.C. §2605(c). [. . .]

I conclude, therefore, that the Interim Order is also valid under s. 91(27) of the *Constitution Act, 1867*.

Appeal allowed with costs, LAMER C.J. *and* SOPINKA, IACOBUCCI *and* MAJOR JJ. *dissenting*.

Notes and Questions

1. What are the key differences in the approach to the criminal law power test taken by La Forest J. for the majority and by Lamer C.J. for the dissent?

2. What is the purpose of CEPA according to the majority and the dissent? Do you agree with the majority that it is appropriate to determine the purpose by relying on the implementation of the process and the regulations passed to date, or was the dissent correct in emphasizing the broad definition of "toxic"?

3. The majority seems confident that recognizing broad federal jurisdiction under the criminal law power will not adversely affect the ability of the provinces to regulate toxic substances. The dissent is of the view that by upholding CEPA under the criminal law power, the regulatory authority of the provinces will be undermined. Who is right?

4. Could CEPA have been upheld under other conceptual powers, such as POGG or trade and commerce? In light of the cases in this chapter, how likely do you think it is that the court would have upheld CEPA under these heads of power, had the majority not found that the criminal law power was sufficient? What would have been the implication of such an approach? What potential do you see for the use of the emergency branch of POGG in the environmental field? The application of the emergency branch of POGG is discussed in Chapter 10 in the context of climate change.

Part III — The Politics and Practicalities of Jurisdiction over the Environment

You have now considered in detail some of the Supreme Court of Canada's leading constitutional cases in the environmental area. As you will discern, collectively they underscore the need for coordinated action on environmental issues and affirm the constitutional basis for federal leadership in this area. Yet, an ongoing theme to which we will return throughout this book — and which figures centrally in scholarly writing on Canadian environmental law and policy — is a sense that overall effective intergovernmental coordination and federal leadership around environmental issues has been lacking.

In the Introduction, one of the questions we posed was whether, and to what extent, the jurisdictional uncertainty and conflict, as reflected in many of the cases you have now read, is a serious and enduring obstacle to grappling with the pressing environmental challenges we collectively confront? Put it another way, to what extent can we ascribe to the division of powers, as interpreted in these cases, responsibility for some of the shortcomings we observe in environmental law and policy outcomes? Your views on these questions may evolve as you read on in this book. Bearing this in mind, consider a recent article that considers what Canadian academics from several disciplines have to say about this and related topics. A key thesis of this article is that to understand jurisdiction over the environment in the Canadian context, requires more than simply a familiarity with the leading cases and sections 91 and 92 of the *Constitution Act.*

William R. MacKay, "Canadian Federalism and the Environment: The Literature"

(2004) 17 Geo. Int'l Envtl. L. Rev. 25

[. . .] Although political negotiation has been the dominant force in shaping environmental policy in Canada, the jurisprudence remains important. Historically, the courts have recognized the concurrent jurisdiction of the two levels of government and have discouraged federal unilateralism. Nevertheless, two court decisions have increased the potential scope of federal legislative power.

[*Ed Note:* Discussion of *R. v. Crown Zellerbach* and *R. v. Hydro-Québec* omitted.]

Despite the importance of these decisions, a purely legalistic description of federal-provincial jurisdictions over environmental policy is misleading. Theories of intergovernmental relations tend to reveal more about environmental policy than a strict analysis of the constitutional powers. . . . recent [intergovernmental relations] literature on environmental policy-making . . . addresses three themes:

- Factors affecting the federal role in Canadian environmental policy
- The dominant pattern of intergovernmental relations in Canadian environmental policy
- The preferred model of intergovernmental relations with respect to environmental policy

Factors Affecting the Federal Role in Canadian Environmental Policy

. . . Overall, the literature in this field concludes that the federal government has been historically restrained in exercising authority in the environmental field. However, there were times when the federal government took a more active role in environmental policy. Initially, scholars explained federal involvement in the environmental field as reflective of the constitutional restraints placed on the federal government by the constitution. Gradually, however, as federal powers in this area were expanded by constitutional decisions, academics observed a shift in the basis of federal timidity from fear of constitutional toe stepping to a fear of provincial resistance. More recently, scholars have noted that the lack of federal action is based on the waxing and waning of external pressure on the federal government to take action. These three distinct explanations provide reasons for the historically weak federal role interspersed by periods of federal intervention. The three reasons, constitutional constraint, provincial resistance, and external pressure on the federal government will now be examined in more detail.

Constitutional Constraints

Many authors suggest that the federal government has been constrained by limited constitutional authority. These authors, writing primarily before the Supreme Court decision of *R. v. Crown Zellerbach*, generally agreed that the provinces had strong claims to jurisdiction over the environment within their borders. However, as its constitutional authority to intervene in the environment became wider as a result of Supreme Court decisions expanding the Criminal Law power and the "peace order and good government" (POGG) power, the federal government became more involved in environmental management. Many academics see the expansion of its constitutional mandate as the primary impetus for the federal government's eventual involvement in environmental management.

The federal government, following the expansion of its constitutional jurisdiction under the *Crown Zellerbach* decision, undertook several important legislative initiatives. Most importantly, the *Canadian Environmental Protection Act* (CEPA) was passed in 1988. CEPA consolidated a number of federal environmental acts, including the *Clean Air Act*, the *Environmental Contaminants Act*, and the *Ocean Dumping Control Act* (the impugned legislation of the *Crown Zellerbach* decision). More important, CEPA provided for federal authorities to regulate and control toxic substances, a domain until then predominantly controlled by the provinces. The federal *Pulp and Paper Effluent Regulations* were amended in 1990 to allow the federal Department of the Environment to issue separate pollution control permits rather than having federal control requirements incorporated into provincially issued permits. Federal officials therefore had more direct access to enforcement proceedings. The *Canadian Environment Assessment Act* (CEAA) was passed in 1992. The CEAA creates a statutory obligation for a compulsory federal environmental impact assessment for development projects that are financed by the federal government, sited on federal lands, or subject to federal legal authority. Finally, the federal "Green Plan" was initiated in 1990. The Green Plan is designed to promote and fund environmentally sustainable projects and programs across several government departments and in co-ordination with the private sector and the provinces. Starting with an initial federal commitment of three billion dollars Canadian in new spending, the Green Plan committed the government of Canada to reducing waste generation by fifty percent by the year 2000; developing new processes to ensure all federal policies are subject to prior environmental assessment, promoting the practice of applied sustainable development in the forestry, agricultural, and fisheries industries; and regulating up to forty-four priority toxic substances in five years.

Initially, therefore, the literature addressing federalism and the environment focused on the constitutional powers of the federal government as an explanation for the historically weak federal role in the field. Scholars point out that the court took action when the Supreme Court recognized the federal government's expanded environmental powers. However, scholars are also quick to point out that in the years following the Court's recognition of possible federal activism, the federal government was reluctant to use its newly granted power to effect environmental change. Literature in the field then sought new explanations for federal inactivity.

Legal scholars argue that the federal government has taken a surprisingly limited view of its own environmental powers despite its increased presence in the environmental field. Scholars note that even when the federal government was given a broader constitutional mandate from the *Crown Zellerbach* decision, it was reluctant to press for greater control over environmental policy-making due to provincial resistance. Robert Franson and Alastair Lucas suggest that "the excuse of constitutional difficulties is used as a smokescreen to hide a basic unwillingness on the part of those involved to take the actions that are necessary". Professor Lucas attributes the federal timidity to an unwillingness to confront the provinces, which were highly protective of their jurisdiction over natural resources. Lucas states that much of the federal leadership is coloured by the implicit restraints in the "political constitution", which Lucas defines as the understood role of the federal and provincial governments in environmental policy-making, notwithstanding clear federal constitutional authority. These underlying restraints help to explain federal reluctance to "push its legal regulatory mandate . . . in the face of provincial opposition". [. . .]

Given the provincial Crowns' ownership of virtually all natural resources, these scholars believe a preferential role was given to locally dominant economic interests. The result is that provincial environmental policy often reflects the close links between provincial governments and industry. [. . .]

According to many scholars, the federal government has avoided unilateral action because of the conflict with the provinces it engenders. Indeed, the provinces continue to exercise the greater share of environmental authority. The federal government has asserted its authority in matters with extra-provincial or international implications but it is generally unwilling to press for a greater role. Instead, the federal government favoured a collaborative approach to interprovincial relations with respect to the environment. The main reason for this, according to many academics, is the fear that if the federal government were to take a leading, visible role in the environment, this strengthened presence would be perceived as federal interference provoking separatist sentiment in Québec and objections from provinces highly dependent on natural resource revenue.

External Pressures

Constitutional constraints and provincial opposition to federal control offer a limited explanation of the restricted role often taken by the federal government in environmental policy. Recently, academics have taken a broader approach to explaining intergovernmental relations with respect to environmental policy-making. Kathryn Harrison and others increasingly argue that the explanation for federal and provincial roles in environmental protection is not complete without considering governments' electoral incentives to extend or defend their jurisdiction over the environment in the first place. Other scholars point to international pressure as an important factor in the expansion of government jurisdiction (particularly federal) in the environmental area.

Harrison notes that environmental protection usually involves diffuse benefits and concentrated costs, and thus it offers few political benefits but significant political costs. According to Harrison, one can expect the opponents of environmental regulation to be better organized, informed, and funded than the supporters. Additionally, since environmental protection typically involves imposing costs on business, stronger environmental standards will often run counter to voters' concerns about the economy. Where environmental concerns in the general public are high, however, (for example, after a major environmental disaster) or when the economy is doing well and voters are less concerned about loss of jobs or deleterious economic effects, the benefits become less diffuse and the price imposed on industry less costly to the politicians. Governments will then respond with more environmental protection. Harrison concludes that this is a better explanation for infrequent federal action on the environment than the federal government's concerns about provincial resistance or constitutional restraints.

Instead, Kathryn Harrison argues, the real impetus to a larger federal role [in the years following *Crown Zellerbach*] was the greater importance of environmental protection to the electorate by the mid 1980s. The mid 1980s constitute an appropriate dividing line in analyzing Canadian environmental policy . . .. air and water pollution control and depletion of natural resources dominated the first generation of environmental policy. The second generation of environmental policy (after the mid 1980s) is marked by more diverse global and local issues. . . . Harrison [and others contend] that the federal government entered the field of environmental policymaking because it was faced with the interdependencies and externalities represented by pressure from both international coalitions and local environmental groups for higher and more consistent environmental standards. Grace Skogstad similarly notes:

> [S]trong international pressures for governments to formulate environmentally sustainable policies have created new incentives for governments at both levels to become actively involved in protecting the environment. [. . .]

Locally, environmentalists have played a role in pressuring the federal government to take on a greater role in the environment. Environmentalists have also challenged the appropriateness of the relatively closed process of policymaking. According to Neil Hawke, these activist positions were validated by legal decisions that legitimized a voice for citizen groups in resource development projects: see *Friends of the Oldman River v. Canada (Minister of Transport)* [. . .]

When scholars began discussing reasons for the lack of a strong federal role in the environmental field, the general consensus was that the federal government lacked the constitutional power to intervene and that it feared igniting provincial opposition. More recently most scholars point to public environmental concern, both domestic and international, as the impetus for federal involvement. The consensus among many academics today is that the close relationship between industry and government that determined environmental policy in the past has shifted to a broader consultative process with greater public involvement, especially from environmental groups (although industry, of course, is still an important player). As a result, the federal government has played a larger role in what was once an area of provincial constitutional jurisdiction with little federal involvement. Most scholars now view the principal explanation for this to be external pressure on the federal government, both domestic and international, rather than expanded federal constitutional power or provincial acquiescence to federal involvement. These conclusions provide a useful lesson to federal policy-makers. The development of environmentalism as a national political cause provides a powerful antidote to constitutional restraint and provincial resistance to national environmental standards.

The Dominant Pattern of Intergovernmental Relations in Canadian Environmental Policy

. . . Most academics conclude that [over time] the collaborative model [of Canadian environmental policy] has prevailed. Moreover, the ascendancy of the collaborative model came at the same time many warned of federal domination of the field in the wake of the *Crown Zellerbach* and *Hydro-Québec* decisions. Scholars see evidence of the pre-eminent role of the collaborative model in the use of equivalency agreements in federal legislation. Under an equivalency agreement the province's local laws apply if its environmental standards are equivalent to federal standards.

According to Steven Kennett, in most cases governments will favour a competitive model. Indeed, Kennett notes that unilateralism (competitive federalism) is the normal (or as Kennett says, the baseline) condition under which governments operate. According to Kennett, incentives to co-operate exist when unilateralism leads to direct costs or foregone benefits. Governments are therefore most likely to co operate in two circumstances. The first is where co-operation gives a government greater control over domestic policy agendas than does unilateralism. Therefore, where there are significant interdependencies or externalities beyond the government's control, co-operation becomes necessary for effective policy. Co-operation may also allow for the best policy instruments to be used in light of expertise, constitutional powers, or regional (or national) concerns and to avoid duplication. Second, intergovernmental conflict may also impose political costs, and to reduce these costs governments will try to induce co-operation. Therefore, for Kennett, the collaborative approach is the natural one in an area such as the environment where the shared policy fields and many mobilized interests constitute externalities beyond either government's control, making collaboration necessary for effective policy.

Kennett's observations seem prophetic, as many scholars note (many with resignation) that the collaborative approach was largely institutionalized in the time between 1998 and 2000. Mark Winfield describes this period as being marked by "the most important developments in federalism and environmental policy in Canada of the past 30 years". This period was preceded by the *Statement on Interjurisdictional Co-operation*, signed by the provinces and the federal government in 1990. The statement committed the provinces and federal government to co-operate on environmental policy to avoid duplication and work toward harmonization of environmental standards. The immediate result was the establishment of the Canadian Council of Ministers of the Environment (CCME) in 1993. In 1995, after much consultation with stakeholders and provincial and federal officials, the *Environment Management Framework Agreement* (EMFA) was released. The document committed the provincial governments to conclude sub-agreements in different areas of environmental regulation that harmonize standards and reduce duplication. However, the provinces eventually rejected the EMFA.

The EMFA was in large part revived by the *Canada-Wide Accord on Environmental Harmonization*, signed by the Federal Environment Minister and her provincial counterparts (except Québec) on January 29, 1998. The *Accord* sets out the goals of the harmonization initiative and includes a framework for the contents of the substantive sub-agreements. Decisions pursuant to the *Accord* are to be "consensus based" and "driven by the commitment to achieve the highest level of environmental quality within the context of sustainable development". Three sub-agreements have been signed under the Accord's auspices — including the *Sub-Agreement on Inspections*, the *Sub-Agreement on Canada-Wide Standards*, and the *Sub-Agreement on Environmental Assessment*. All of these sub-agreements, like the Accord itself, emphasize the delivery of environmental protection by the government best situated to deliver the service. Indeed, there is an absolute bar on action by the level of government not charged with service delivery. In most cases this will be the provincial government.

There are several other federal-provincial agreements regarding environmental governance. Scholars point to such federal-provincial agreements as evidence of the importance of the political regime in environmental governance in Canada. F.L. Morton, specifically points to such bilateral agreements as proof that:

> The real centre of action in determining jurisdictional responsibilities has not been in the courts but at the administrative level of federal-provincial negotiation. To forget this is to misunderstand the Canadian reality. As a result of these developments, academics by and large conclude that the collaborative approach that has dominated intergovernmental relations towards the environment has become part of the core of the Canadian environmental policy regime.

[*Ed note:* A similar dynamic and approach was seen more recently in the federal-provincial discussions surrounding development and drafting of *Species at Risk Act*: See Chapter 9.]

The Preferred Model of Intergovernmental Relations with Respect to Environmental Policy

Much of the literature in the environment and federalism field focuses on the preferred model of intergovernmental relations. [This final] section of the paper will examine the arguments advanced by academics regarding intergovernmental relations models and environmental policy. First, [it]notes that the literature by and large concludes that although not the ideal pattern to facilitate effective national environmental policy, the collaborative model dominates in Canada. Second, despite the predominance of the collaborative model, it is also important to examine how choosing a particular model will determine whether environmental policy is based on enforceable legal obligations or non-enforceable guidelines. Third, the choice of model will promote either provincial or federal control of the environment.

Collaboration vs. Competition

Advocates of collaboration stress the advantages of joint action. With joint action, unnecessary duplication is avoided. Moreover, potential obstruction by provincial governments in implementing unilaterally imposed federal standards is reduced and intergovernmental conflict is reduced. Using environmental assessment as an example, Kennett notes that industry pressure on both levels of government for "one project, one assessment" has led to a demand for federal-provincial collaboration to avoid duplicate assessment requirements. Nevertheless, on the whole, academic opinion on intergovernmental relations and environmental policy generally disfavours the current model of collaborative federalism.

A major criticism of collaborative federalism, as it is practiced in the environmental field, is the "race to the bottom" that the current model engenders. Collaboration virtually precludes federal intervention absent provincial support. The result of the provinces' power under the collaborative regime and the corollary impotence of the federal government is weak environmental standards and the creation of pollution havens. Advocates of competition, on the other hand, say unilateralism promotes healthy federal-provincial competition to satisfy voters. Moreover, competition facilitates oversight of each level of government by the other. [. . .] Winfield notes that the period of competitive federalism was characterized by upward competition between the federal government and the provinces to increase visibility and solidify their reputations as champions of the environment.

[But] the fact remains that the collaborative model is entrenched in the federal-provincial environmental regime and is generally favoured by the federal government in all fields where jurisdiction is shared. In that light, scholars generally take the view that the best means of maintaining the federalist peace achieved by collaboration is to ensure that the decision-making process is one that supports collaboration yet has significant legal force to prevent neglect of environmental issues. Of course, the same criticism could be made of the international institutional arrangements designed to address environmental concerns, which lack any formal dispute resolution agreements and are marked by collaborative relations among states zealously guarding their sovereignty.

Therefore, the choice of the intergovernmental relations model has important repercussions for scholars. Collaboration or competition lead to different legal instruments with different degrees of enforceability. Further, the choice of intergovernmental relations will affect which government is dominant in the environmental policy-making field.

Legal Enforceability

In many ways, however, the above criticisms are not of collaborative federalism generally but rather of the institutional structure established to implement environmental policy. Central to the dissatisfaction expressed by many academics of collaborative federalism as practiced in Canadian environmental policy is a condemnation of intergovernmental agreements and their lack of legal enforceability. Debora VanNijnatten notes that the elaborate intergovernmental policy-making system created in Germany is a collaborative model but is effective in reaching agreements on national standards, ensuring those standards are high, and supporting implementation and enforcement of the high standards. VanNijnatten points out that the chief reasons for this are the strict enforcement provisions the Länder (provincial government) are subject to under the German intergovernmental regime. In contrast, under the CCME regime, a government found to have fallen below the standards set by the process must undergo six months of consultation with the other governments. If these consultations prove fruitless, the government may withdraw from the sub-agreement. VanNijnatten points out that all the agreements produced by the CCME process are outlines of what governments should do rather than uniform binding standards.

Alastair Lucas and Cheryl Sharvit address the legal force of the *Canada-Wide Accord on Environmental Harmonization*. The authors note that the Accord exemplifies the collaborative model of intergovernmental relations but the price paid for the federal peace is non-binding legal commitments. Lucas and Sharvit conclude that the intergovernmental agreements entered into with respect to environmental protection are generally unenforceable. The agreements, according to Lucas and Sharvit, do not meet the legal requirements of a binding contract and are merely ministerial decisions that cannot bind the governments in any substantial way. [. . .]

On the other hand, Steven Kennett is less pessimistic about the enforceability of intergovernmental agreements on the environment. Kennett applies the concepts of "hard" and "soft" law, which are central to the international law paradigm. [. . .] According to Kennett, diplomacy is used to advance from the formulation of general principles to the adoption of legally binding rules and formal intergovernmental arrangements. This is readily applicable to the federal structure in Canada. Kennett notes that although intergovernmental environmental agreements are soft law, soft law has been used as a means of encouraging the evolution of law in broad areas of environmental management. This is particularly true in situations that require global solutions. Kennett adds that the domestic adoption of soft law does not in itself portend a new division of environmental powers between national and sub-national governments. However, Kennett maintains that, at least in a Canadian context, the growing use of framework agreements and accords in federal-provincial co-operation on natural resources and environmental management bears some similarity to framework conventions in the context of international law. [. . .]

The disagreement over enforceability reflects the overall disagreement over which model of intergovernmental relations should prevail in environmental policy-making in Canada. Where collaboration generally produces federal-provincial agreements whose enforceability is unclear, the federal unilateralism made possible by competitive federalism produces legislation binding on Canadians in all provinces. The debate over enforceability thus mirrors the main disagreement among scholars over what level of government should have primary legislative power over the environment.

Federal vs. Provincial Control

Most of the literature criticizes the collaborative model because it seems to result in the devolution of legislative power to the provinces. Provincial control is considered to inevitably lead to deleterious effects on the environment.

As a result, many academics feel that the federal government should use its substantial powers to act unilaterally to impose national standards in the environment, as condoned by the Supreme Court in both *Hydro-Québec* and *Crown Zellerbach*. Environmentalists have even charged in the federal court that the federal government has fettered its authority by entering into the *Accord on Environmental Harmonization*. Ultimately, the court did not accept this argument.

Advocates of federal responsibility emphasize economies of scale in studying environmental problems and developing technically complex standards. The scholars note that the federal government is better able to respond to interprovincial spillovers of environmental problems. They further note that the federal government can provide greater resistance to regionally dominant interests. Finally, the scholars note the importance of strong national standards to overcome a potential race to the bottom. [. . .]

Anthony Scott sees devolution of environmental powers as the inevitable abandonment of environmental management by both levels of government. Scott maintains that provincial governments receive even more advice and demands than the federal government, where the environment is a less important ministry. As a result, provinces lack both the resources and the political will to screen information from both environmentalists and client resource users in the same way that the federal government can. Consequently, many provinces download environmental management to crown corporations, local governments, and even private corporations that favour economic development over environmental protection.

At the same time, there are others that see benefits to significant provincial roles. Diverse provincial policies may be able to better satisfy geographically diverse citizen preferences concerning environmental protection. [. . .]

Experimentation could also be a benefit of an increased a provincial role. Both Steven Kennett and Grace Skogstad note that devolution may encourage policy experimentation. Different policies may be tested in different provinces and their effectiveness gauged without engaging the nation as a whole. [. . .]

Proponents of provincial control note that provincial governments have a more intimate knowledge of local environmental problems and can tailor solutions to local circumstances. . . . regional governments may have more detailed and first-hand knowledge of environmental problems and a greater attachment to the specific ecosystems. Steven Kennett summarizes the potential problems with uniform environmental standards as:

> The problem with process standardization is that it runs counter to the federal principle that regional diversity is to be respected. In fact, one would expect inter-provincial variation in EA (Environmental Assessment) regimes within a federal system where significant authority regarding resource use, industrial development and environmental protection is in provincial hands. These differences reflect variations in circumstances and political preferences across the country.

In the end, the environment is such a large and diverse field of legislative competence that most authors doubt either level of government could be completely divested of its respective power to manage the environment. As Dale Gibson notes:

> . . . environmental management could never be treated as a constitutional unit under one order of government in any constitution that claimed to be federal, because no system in which one government was so powerful would be federal.

Conclusion

Scholars generally conclude that collaborative federalism has in large part eclipsed the other models of intergovernmental relations in environmental policy-making in Canada. Scholars point to a general assumption that changes to the federal bargain cannot be achieved through formal constitutional change without great difficulty. Instead, the literature notes that governments now favour intergovernmental agreements. This is evident in a wide range of policy fields. It is especially true with the environment where collaborative federalism has become "the hallmark of environmental policy in Canada". The literature points to a number of explanations for this trend. First, collaborative federalism is now generally preferred in all shared policy fields, and this preference has naturally been extended to the environment. Second, the federal government has recently used its long dormant legislative power to enter the environmental arena in response to international and local pressure. Third, the federal government has consistently favoured a collaborative model in order to avoid offending the provinces, which have traditionally guarded their legislative powers in this area to protect vital natural resource industries.

Although many academics favour a strong federal role and less collaboration in policy-making, most conclude that no model of intergovernmental relations alone will likely be effective in advancing effective environmental policies. Different problems will inevitably call for different approaches. However, the federal government has in recent times been reluctant to act unilaterally or to compete with the provinces in delivering environmental services. Moreover, the collaborative model has been institutionalized . . . As a result of the institutionalization, the literature now questions the appropriateness of using the collaborative model to the exclusion of any other model in environmental policy and laments that the institutionalization of the process means it will likely be the rule in environmental policy-making for some time.

Notes and Questions

1. In this article, it is argued that the historical record reveals a general lack of federal leadership on environmental issues "interspersed by periods of federal intervention". What explanations does the author offer for this pattern? How compelling do you find these explanations?

2. Compare and contrast the competitive and collaborative models of environmental policy outlined in this article. What are the most salient distinctions between these models? Why has the collaborative model enjoyed such dominance?

Part IV — Emerging Issues in Jurisdiction over the Environment

In this concluding Part, we turn our attention to two themes that will undoubtedly figure prominently in environmental law and policy in the years ahead. The first concerns the relationship between environmental protection (and, more broadly the sustainable management of natural resources) and the constitutionally guaranteed rights of Canadian Aboriginal peoples. We return to this theme in many of the ensuing chapters in this book. For now our goal is to provide an introduction to the complex and fluid nature of this relationship, flagging some of the key questions and challenges that it presents for practitioners, policy and decision-makers and courts. A second theme canvassed in this Part is the increasingly significant role played by local governments in environmental protection in both hard law and soft law settings.

Aboriginal Rights and Jurisdiction over the Environment

Enacted in 1982, section 35 of the Constitution plays a central and defining role in any consideration of the relationship between jurisdiction over the environment and Aboriginal rights. It reads as follows:

> (1) The existing aboriginal and treaty rights of the aboriginal peoples of Canada are hereby recognized and affirmed.
>
> (2) In this Act, "aboriginal peoples of Canada" includes the Indian, Inuit and Métis peoples of Canada.
>
> (3) For greater certainty, in subsection (1) "treaty rights" includes rights that now exist by way of land claims agreements or may be so acquired [. . .]

This section provides constitutional protection to aboriginal rights existing as of 1982. These rights include those secured by past and future treaties as well as unextinguished customary rights that are found to exist by the courts. Where the aboriginal right in question is one secured by treaty, the language of the treaty is scrutinized to give definition to the right in question: see *Mikisew Cree First Nation v. Canada (Minister of Canadian Heritage)*, [2005] 3 S.C.R. 388 (discussed in Chapter 8). Aboriginal rights may, however, also exist independent of treaty entitlements. Subsequent case law has established that there are two varieties of rights protected under section 35 that fall into this latter category. The first are rights that protect activities that comprise an "element of a practice, custom or tradition integral to the distinctive culture of the aboriginal group claiming that right": see *R. v. Van der Peet*, [1996] 2 S.C.R. 507. This, for example, would include rights to hunt, gather, fish and use timber. The second form is Aboriginal title. Aboriginal title is a much broader entitlement that encompasses the right to exclusive use and occupation of land for a variety of purposes, which need not be aspects of those Aboriginal practices, customs and traditions which are integral to distinctive Aboriginal cultures: see *Delgamuukw v. British Columbia*, [1997] 3 S.C.R 1010. Both of these forms of Aboriginal rights are unique (or *sui generis*) in that they are inalienable (i.e. they cannot be transferred, sold or surrendered to anyone other than the Crown). They are also distinct from other types of property rights in that they are held communally.

Canadian governments, whether acting in their regulatory or legislative capacities, are precluded by virtue of section 35 from infringing existing Aboriginal rights unless such action meets a justification test. The nature of this test differs depending on whether the affected right relates to a protected traditional activity, or to Aboriginal title.

Since 1982, a considerable body of jurisprudence has developed that elaborates the nature and scope of the rights guaranteed under section 35. In many of the early cases, section 35 was relied upon to provide a defence from regulatory prosecutions, often under federal fisheries laws: see *R. v. Sparrow*, [1990] 1 S.C.R 1075; *R. v. Van der Peet*, [1996] 2 S.C.R. 507; and *R. v. Gladstone*, [1996] 2 S.C.R. 723. In cases such as these, the Aboriginal defendants challenged the legislative authority under which charges were mounted as being inconsistent with section 35 aboriginal rights. In many of these cases, courts have concluded that the impugned provision interferes with a constitutionally protected aboriginal right. In this situation, courts must then determine whether the infringement can be justified on the basis that the impugned provision "minimally impairs" the asserted right and that it advances a legitimate overarching governmental concern for resource conservation. Where the Crown fails to meet this test, the case law underscores that priority must be given to aboriginal food and ceremonial requirements.

More recently, section 35 has been deployed as a basis for seeking judicial review for resource development licensing and permitting decisions made by provincial authorities: see *Haida Nation v. British Columbia (Minister of Forests)*, [2004] 3 S.C.R. 511; *Taku River Tlingit First Nation v. British Columbia (Project Assessment Director)*, [2004] 3 S.C.R. 550; *Mikisew Cree First Nation v. Canada (Minister of Canadian Heritage)*, *supra* and *Dene Tha' First Nation v. Canada (Minister of Environment)*, 2006 FC 265 (see Chapter 6). Here the courts have developed an ever-burgeoning jurisprudence that seeks to define the Crown's duty to consult and accommodate Aboriginal rights prior to making decisions or taking actions that might undermine or impair Aboriginal rights. A key issue in this case law concerns the nature and extent of the duty to consult and accommodate with respect to unproven (non-Treaty based) Aboriginal rights and title claims.

Jurisdictional issues have also arisen, albeit much more rarely, in the context of legal actions seeking to establish Aboriginal title. To date, only two such cases have gone to trial: see *Delgamuukw v. British Columbia*, *supra*, and *Tsilhqot'in Nation v. British Columbia*, 2007 BCSC 1700. Both have arisen in British Columbia where, unlike much of the rest of Canada, treaties between the Crown and First Nations have yet to be concluded over much of the landbase. The *Tsilhqot'in* case has particularly significant implications in terms of provincial Crown jurisdiction over resource management. In this case, following a lengthy trial, the trial judge concluded that the plaintiff First Nation had led evidence sufficient to establish Aboriginal title over a large territory in the north-central part of the province. Ultimately, he declined on technical grounds to make the declaration of Aboriginal title being sought. Nonetheless, in *obiter*, he offered the view that had such a declaration been made this would render provincial resource management laws, including laws authorizing forestry activities on the lands in question, *ultra vires*. The case is currently under appeal.

First Nations have also sought to rely on constitutional division of powers arguments as a means of ousting or constraining provincial regulation in the resource management context: see *Kitkatla Band v. British Columbia (Minister of Small Business, Tourism & Culture)*, [2002] 2 S.C.R. 146, 2002 SCC 31 and *Paul v. British Columbia (Forest Appeals Commission)*, [2003] 2 S.C.R. 585, 2003 SCC 55. In cases such as these, it has been argued that the impugned provincial laws trench on exclusive federal jurisdiction over "Indians and lands reserved for Indians" under subsection 91(24) of the Constitution. The *Paul* case is of special interest for our purposes. Had the challenge in this case been successful, it would have precluded provincially constituted tribunals, including those with statutory jurisdiction over resource management and environmental protection, from considering questions of section 35 Aboriginal rights.

What follows are extracts from two Supreme Court of Canada decisions that offer some instructive reflections on some of the questions just discussed.

. . . . .

Taku River Tlingit First Nation v. British Columbia (Project Assessment Director)

[2004] 3 S.C.R. 550

McLACHLIN C.J. (for the Court):

This case raises the issue of the limits of the Crown's duty to consult with and accommodate Aboriginal peoples when making decisions that may adversely affect as yet unproven Aboriginal rights and title claims. The Taku River Tlingit First Nation ("TRTFN") participated in a three-and-a-half-year environmental assessment process related to the efforts of Redfern Resources Ltd. ("Redfern") to reopen an old mine. Ultimately, the TRTFN found itself disappointed in the process and in the result.

I conclude that the Province was required to consult meaningfully with the TRTFN in the decision-making process surrounding Redfern's project approval application. The TRTFN's role in the environmental assessment was, however, sufficient to uphold the Province's honour and meet the requirements of its duty. Where consultation is meaningful, there is no ultimate duty to reach agreement. Rather, accommodation requires that Aboriginal concerns be balanced reasonably with the potential impact of the particular decision on those concerns and with competing societal concerns. Compromise is inherent to the reconciliation process. In this case, the Province accommodated TRTFN concerns by adapting the environmental assessment process and the requirements made of Redfern in order to gain project approval. I find, therefore, that the Province met the requirements of its duty toward the TRTFN.

The Tulsequah Chief Mine, operated in the 1950s by Cominco Ltd., lies in a remote and pristine area of northwestern British Columbia, at the confluence of the Taku and Tulsequah Rivers. Since 1994, Redfern has sought permission from the British Columbia government to reopen the mine, first under the *Mine Development Assessment Act*, S.B.C. 1990, c. 55, and then, following its enactment in 1995, under the *Environmental Assessment Act*, R.S.B.C. 1996, c. 119. During the environmental assessment process, access to the mine emerged as a point of contention. The members of the TRTFN, who participated in the assessment as Project Committee members, objected to Redfern's plan to build a 160-km road from the mine to the town of Atlin through a portion of their traditional territory. However, after a lengthy process, project approval was granted on March 19, 1998 by the Minister of Environment, Lands and Parks and the Minister of Energy and Mines ("Ministers").

The Redfern proposal was assessed in accordance with British Columbia's *Environmental Assessment Act*. The environmental assessment process is distinct from both the land use planning process and the treaty negotiation process, although these latter processes may necessarily have an impact on the assessment of individual proposals. [. . .]

Through the environmental assessment process, the TRTFN's concerns with the road proposal became apparent. Its concerns crystallized around the potential effect on wildlife and traditional land use, as well as the lack of adequate baseline information by which to measure subsequent effects. It was the TRTFN's position that the road ought not to be approved in the absence of a land use planning strategy and away from the treaty negotiation table. The environmental assessment process was unable to address these broader concerns directly, but the project assessment director facilitated the TRTFN's access to other provincial agencies and decision makers. For example, the Province approved funding for wildlife monitoring programs as desired by the TRTFN (the Grizzly Bear Long-term Cumulative Effects Assessment and Ungulate Monitoring Program). The TRTFN also expressed interest in TRTFN jurisdiction to approve permits for the project, revenue sharing, and TRTFN control of the use of the access road by third parties. It was informed that these issues were outside the ambit of the certification process and could only be the subject of later negotiation with the government. [. . .]

The TRTFN brought a petition in February 1999 under the *Judicial Review Procedure Act*, R.S.B.C. 1996, c. 241, to quash the Ministers' decision to issue the Project Approval Certificate on administrative law grounds and on grounds based on its Aboriginal rights and title [set out here history below . . .]

In *Haida Nation v. British Columbia (Minister of Forests)*, [2004] 3 S.C.R. 511, 2004 SCC 73, heard concurrently with this case, this Court has confirmed the existence of the Crown's duty to consult and, where indicated, to accommodate Aboriginal peoples prior to proof of rights or title claims. The Crown's obligation to consult the TRTFN was engaged in this case. The Province was aware of the TRTFN's claims through its involvement in the treaty negotiation process, and knew that the decision to reopen the Tulsequah Chief Mine had the potential to adversely affect the substance of the TRTFN's claims.

On the principles discussed in Haida, these facts mean that the honour of the Crown placed the Province under a duty to consult with the TRTFN in making the decision to reopen the Tulsequah Chief Mine. In this case, the process engaged in by the Province under the *Environmental Assessment Act* fulfilled the requirements of its duty. The TRTFN was part of the Project Committee, participating fully in the environmental review process. It was disappointed when, after three and a half years, the review was concluded at the direction of the Environmental Assessment Office. However, its views were put before the Ministers, and the final project approval contained measures designed to address both its immediate and long-term concerns. The Province was under a duty to consult. It did so, and proceeded to make accommodations. The Province was not under a duty to reach agreement with the TRTFN, and its failure to do so did not breach the obligations of good faith that it owed the TRTFN.

Did the Province Have a Duty to Consult and if Indicated Accommodate the TRTFN?

The Province argues that, before the determination of rights through litigation or conclusion of a treaty, it owes only a common law "duty of fair dealing" to Aboriginal peoples whose claims may be affected by government decisions. It argues that a duty to consult could arise after rights have been determined, through what it terms a "justificatory fiduciary duty". Alternatively, it submits, a fiduciary duty may arise where the Crown has undertaken to act only in the best interests of an Aboriginal people. The Province submits that it owes the TRTFN no duty outside of these specific situations.

The Province's submissions present an impoverished vision of the honour of the Crown and all that it implies. As discussed in the companion case of *Haida*, supra, the principle of the honour of the Crown grounds the Crown's duty to consult and if indicated accommodate Aboriginal peoples, even prior to proof of asserted Aboriginal rights and title. The duty of honour derives from the Crown's assertion of sovereignty in the face of prior Aboriginal occupation. It has been enshrined in s. 35(1) of the *Constitution Act, 1982*, which recognizes and affirms existing Aboriginal rights and titles. Section 35(1) has, as one of its purposes, negotiation of just settlement of Aboriginal claims. In all its dealings with Aboriginal peoples, the Crown must act honourably, in accordance with its historical and future relationship with the Aboriginal peoples in question. The Crown's honour cannot be interpreted narrowly or technically, but must be given full effect in order to promote the process of reconciliation mandated by s. 35(1).

As discussed in *Haida*, what the honour of the Crown requires varies with the circumstances. It may require the Crown to consult with and accommodate Aboriginal peoples prior to taking decisions: *R. v. Sparrow*, [1990] 1 S.C.R. 1075 at p. 1119; *R. v. Nikal*, [1996] 1 S.C.R. 1013; *R. v. Gladstone*, [1996] 2 S.C.R. 723; *Delgamuukw v. British Columbia*, [1997] 3 S.C.R. 1010, ¶168. The obligation to consult does not arise only upon proof of an Aboriginal claim, in order to justify infringement. That understanding of consultation would deny the significance of the historical roots of the honour of the Crown, and deprive it of its role in the reconciliation process. Although determining the required extent of consultation and accommodation before a final settlement is challenging, it is essential to the process mandated by s. 35(1). The duty to consult arises when a Crown actor has knowledge, real or constructive, of the potential existence of Aboriginal rights or title and contemplates conduct that might adversely affect them. This in turn may lead to a duty to change government plans or policy to accommodate Aboriginal concerns. Responsiveness is a key requirement of both consultation and accommodation.

The federal government announced a comprehensive land claims policy in 1981, under which Aboriginal land claims were to be negotiated. The TRTFN submitted its land claim to the Minister of Indian Affairs in 1983. The claim was accepted for negotiation in 1984, based on the TRTFN's traditional use and occupancy of the land. No negotiation ever took place under the federal policy; however, the TRTFN later began negotiation of its land claim under the treaty process established by the B.C. Treaty Commission in 1993. As of 1999, the TRTFN had signed a Protocol Agreement and a Framework Agreement, and was working towards an Agreement in Principle. The Province clearly had knowledge of the TRTFN's title and rights claims.

When Redfern applied for project approval, in its efforts to reopen the Tulsequah Chief Mine, it was apparent that the decision could adversely affect the TRTFN's asserted rights and title. The TRTFN claim Aboriginal title over a large portion of northwestern British Columbia, including the territory covered by the access road considered during the approval process. It also claims Aboriginal hunting, fishing, gathering, and other traditional land use activity rights which stood to be affected by a road through an area in which these rights are exercised. The contemplated decision thus had the potential to impact adversely the rights and title asserted by the TRTFN.

The Province was aware of the claims, and contemplated a decision with the potential to affect the TRTFN's asserted rights and title negatively. It follows that the honour of the Crown required it to consult and if indicated accommodate the TRTFN in making the decision whether to grant project approval to Redfern, and on what terms.

What Was the Scope and Extent of the Province's Duty to Consult and Accommodate the TRTFN?

The scope of the duty to consult is "proportionate to a preliminary assessment of the strength of the case supporting the existence of the right or title, and to the seriousness of the potentially adverse effect upon the right or title claimed" (*Haida*, supra, at para. 39). It will vary with the circumstances, but always requires meaningful, good faith consultation and willingness on the part of the Crown to make changes based on information that emerges during the process.

There is sufficient evidence to conclude that the TRTFN have prima facie Aboriginal rights and title over at least some of the area that they claim. Their land claim underwent an extensive validation process in order to be accepted into the federal land claims policy in 1984. The Department of Indian Affairs hired a researcher to report on the claim, and her report was reviewed at several stages before the Minister validated the claim based on the TRTFN's traditional use and occupancy of the land and resources in question. In order to participate in treaty negotiations under the B.C. Treaty Commission, the TRTFN were required to file a statement of intent setting out their asserted territory and the basis for their claim. An Aboriginal group need not be accepted into the treaty process for the Crown's duty to consult to apply to them. Nonetheless, the TRTFN's claim was accepted for negotiation on the basis of a preliminary decision as to its validity. In contrast to the Haida case, the courts below did not engage in a detailed preliminary assessment of the various aspects of the TRTFN's claims, which are broad in scope. However, acceptance of its title claim for negotiation establishes a prima facie case in support of its Aboriginal rights and title.

The potentially adverse effect of the Ministers' decision on the TRTFN's claims appears to be relatively serious. The chambers judge found that all of the experts who prepared reports for the review recognized the TRTFN's reliance on its system of land use to support its domestic economy and its social and cultural life (para. 70). The proposed access road was only 160 km long, a geographically small intrusion on the 32,000-km2 area claimed by the TRTFN. However, experts reported that the proposed road would pass through an area critical to the TRTFN's domestic economy [. . .] The TRTFN was also concerned that the road could act as a magnet for future development. The proposed road could therefore have an impact on the TRTFN's continued ability to exercise its Aboriginal rights and alter the landscape to which it laid claim.

In summary, the TRTFN's claim is relatively strong, supported by a prima facie case, as attested to by its acceptance into the treaty negotiation process. The proposed road is to occupy only a small portion of the territory over which the TRTFN asserts title; however, the potential for negative derivative impacts on the TRTFN's claims is high. On the spectrum of consultation required by the honour of the Crown, the TRTFN was entitled to more than the minimum receipt of notice, disclosure of information, and ensuing discussion. While it is impossible to provide a prospective checklist of the level of consultation required, it is apparent that the TRTFN was entitled to something significantly deeper than minimum consultation under the circumstances, and to a level of responsiveness to its concerns that can be characterized as accommodation.

Did the Crown Fulfill its Duty to Consult and Accommodate the TRTFN?

The process of granting project approval to Redfern took three and a half years, and was conducted largely under the *Environmental Assessment Act*. As discussed above, the Act sets out a process of information gathering and consultation. The Act requires that Aboriginal peoples whose traditional territory includes the site of a reviewable project be invited to participate on a project committee.

The question is whether this duty was fulfilled in this case. A useful framework of events up to August 1st, 2000 is provided by Southin J.A. at para. 28 of her dissent in this case at the Court of Appeal. Members of the TRTFN were invited to participate in the Project Committee to coordinate review of the project proposal in November 1994 and were given the original two-volume submission for review and comment: Southin J.A., at para. 39. They participated fully as Project Committee members, with the exception of a period of time from February to August of 1995, when they opted out of the process, wishing instead to address the issue through treaty talks and development of a land use policy.

The Final Project Report Specifications ("Specifications") detail a number of meetings between the TRTFN, review agency staff and company representatives in TRTFN communities prior to February 1996 [. . .] Redfern also contracted an independent consultant to conduct archaeological and ethnographic studies with input from the TRTFN to identify possible effects of the proposed project on the TRTFN's traditional way of life [. . .]. The Specifications document TRTFN's written and oral requirements for information from Redfern concerning effects on wildlife, fisheries, terrain sensitivity, and the impact of the proposed access road, of barging and of mine development activities. [. . .]

The TRTFN declined to participate in the Road Access Subcommittee until January 26, 1998. The Environmental Assessment Office appreciated the dilemma faced by the TRTFN, which wished to have its concerns addressed on a broader scale than that which is provided for under the Act. The TRTFN was informed that not all of its concerns could be dealt with at the certification stage or through the environmental assessment process, and assistance was provided to it in liaising with relevant decision makers and politicians.

With financial assistance the TRTFN participated in many Project Committee meetings. Its concerns with the level of information provided by Redfern about impacts on Aboriginal land use led the Environmental Assessment Office to commission a study on traditional land use by an expert approved by the TRTFN, under the auspices of an Aboriginal study steering group. [. . .]

While acknowledging its participation in the consultation process, the TRTFN argues that the rapid conclusion to the assessment deprived it of meaningful consultation. After more than three years, numerous studies and meetings, and extensions of statutory time periods, the assessment process was brought to a close in early 1998. [. . .] Shortly thereafter, the project approval certification was issued.

It is clear that the process of project approval ended more hastily than it began. But was the consultation provided by the Province nonetheless adequate? On the findings of the courts below, I conclude that it was.

The chambers judge was satisfied that any duty to consult was satisfied until December 1997, because the members of the TRTFN were full participants in the assessment process (para. 132). I would agree. The Province was not required to develop special consultation measures to address TRTFN's concerns, outside of the process provided for by the *Environmental Assessment Act*, which specifically set out a scheme that required consultation with affected Aboriginal peoples.

The Act permitted the Committee to set its own procedure, which in this case involved the formation of working groups and subcommittees, the commissioning of studies, and the preparation of a written recommendations report. The TRTFN was at the heart of decisions to set up a steering group to deal with Aboriginal issues and a subcommittee on the road access proposal. The information and analysis required of Redfern were clearly shaped by TRTFN's concerns. By the time that the assessment was concluded, more than one extension of statutory time limits had been granted, and in the opinion of the project assessment director, "the positions of all of the Project Committee members, including the TRTFN had crystallized" (Affidavit of Norman Ringstad, at para. 82 (quoted at para. 57 of the Court of Appeal's judgment)). The concerns of the TRTFN were well understood as reflected in the

Recommendations Report and Project Report, and had been meaningfully discussed. The Province had thoroughly fulfilled its duty to consult.

As discussed in *Haida*, the process of consultation may lead to a duty to accommodate Aboriginal concerns by adapting decisions or policies in response. The purpose of s. 35(1) of the *Constitution Act, 1982* is to facilitate the ultimate reconciliation of prior Aboriginal occupation with de facto Crown sovereignty. Pending settlement, the Crown is bound by its honour to balance societal and Aboriginal interests in making decisions that may affect Aboriginal claims. The Crown may be required to make decisions in the face of disagreement as to the adequacy of its response to Aboriginal concerns. Balance and compromise will then be necessary.

The TRTFN in this case disputes the adequacy of the accommodation ultimately provided by the terms of the Project Approval Certificate. It argues that the Certificate should not have been issued until its concerns were addressed to its satisfaction, particularly with regard to the establishment of baseline information.

With respect, I disagree. Within the terms of the process provided for project approval certification under the Act, TRTFN concerns were adequately accommodated. In addition to the discussion in the minority report, the majority report thoroughly identified the TRTFN's concerns and recommended mitigation strategies, which were adopted into the terms and conditions of certification. These mitigation strategies included further directions to Redfern to develop baseline information, and recommendations regarding future management and closure of the road.

Project approval certification is simply one stage in the process by which a development moves forward. In *Haida*, the Province argued that although no consultation occurred at all at the disputed, "strategic" stage, opportunities existed for *Haida* input at a future "operational" level. That can be distinguished from the situation in this case, in which the TRTFN was consulted throughout the certification process and its concerns accommodated.

The Project Committee concluded that some outstanding TRTFN concerns could be more effectively considered at the permit stage or at the broader stage of treaty negotiations or land use strategy planning. The majority report and terms and conditions of the Certificate make it clear that the subsequent permitting process will require further information and analysis of Redfern, and that consultation and negotiation with the TRTFN may continue to yield accommodation in response. [. . .] It is expected that, throughout the permitting, approval and licensing process, as well as in the development of a land use strategy, the Crown will continue to fulfill its honourable duty to consult and, if indicated, accommodate the TRTFN.

Conclusion

In summary, I conclude that the consultation and accommodation engaged in by the Province prior to issuing the Project Approval Certificate for the Tulsequah Chief Mine were adequate to satisfy the honour of the Crown. The appeal is allowed.

Notes and Questions

1. In *Taku*, citing *Haida Nation*, the Court suggests that the content of the duty to consult and accommodate should be "proportionate to a preliminary assessment of the strength of the case supporting the existence of the right or title, and to the seriousness of the potentially adverse effect upon the right or title claimed". Do you agree with how the Court applied this test on the facts in *Taku*? What are the implications of this approach for the future of test set out *Haida Nation*?

2. What is the apparent basis for the Court's conclusion in this case that the TRTFN has been accommodated? Do you agree with this conclusion?

3. It would appear that the Court was swayed by the Project Committee's conclusion that some of the TRTFN's concerns were better addressed at a later stage in the regulatory process. Do you agree with the Court's approach in this regard? What considerations may have influenced it in reaching this conclusion?

The next case presents a distinct jurisdictional issue with significant implications in terms of the relationship between Aboriginal rights and jurisdiction over the environment. In this case, it was argued that provincial regulatory tribunals are constitutionally constrained from adjudicating section 35 rights in the discharge of their statutory mandates.

Paul v. British Columbia (Forest Appeals Commission)
[2003] S.C.J. No. 34

[This appeal arose out of proceedings commenced against Paul under the *BC Forest Practices Code* (the Code) for felling Crown timber without permission. Paul argued that, in taking the timber to build a deck on his residence, he was exercising a constitutionally protected aboriginal right. Further, he contended that the Forest Appeals Commission, which pursuant to the Code was empowered to hear appeals in such cases, lacked constitutional jurisdiction to adjudicate the defence upon which he relied.]

BASTARACHE J (for the Court):

. . . the parties conceded that the Code is in its entirety valid provincial legislation. In any case, it is clear to me that the Code is legislation in relation to development, conservation and management of forestry resources in the province, under s. 92A(1)(b) of the *Constitution Act, 1867*. There was no argument made that the entire Code, or that portion treating appeals before the Commission, has as its true meaning, essential character, or core matters relating to Indians and lands reserved for the Indians (s. 91(24)) or to any other federal head of power. More specifically, there was no suggestion that, in operation, the law's effects on Indians are so significant as to reveal a pith and substance that is a matter under exclusive federal competence: *Kitkatla Band v. British Columbia (Minister of Small Business, Tourism and Culture)*, [2002] 2 S.C.R. 146; *Reference re Firearms Act (Can.)*, [2000] 1 S.C.R. 783, ¶18.

As a law of general application, the Code applies ex proprio vigore to Indians, to the extent that it does not touch on the "core of Indianness" and is not unjustifiably inconsistent with s. 35 of the *Constitution Act, 1982*. There is no need to consider whether s. 88 of the *Indian Act* would revive the statute and render it applicable.

In the classic federalism cases, the vires of legislation is challenged: *Reference re Firearms Act (Can.)*, supra; *Global Securities Corp. v. British Columbia (Securities Commission)*, [2000] 1 S.C.R. 494. Here the question is the relationship between valid provincial legislation and matters under the federal competence to legislate under s. 91(24).

Incidental Effects

The doctrine of incidental effects holds that where there is a valid provincial law of general application, the provincial law applies if its effects upon matters within federal legislative competence are "merely incidental, irrelevant for constitutional purposes" [. . .] In other words, as Iacobucci and Major JJ. put it in *Ordon Estate v. Grail*, [1998] 3 S.C.R. 437,

¶81, "it is constitutionally permissible for a validly enacted provincial statute of general application to affect matters coming within the exclusive jurisdiction of Parliament". Since all relevant provisions of the Code are valid provincial legislation, it follows that by virtue of the doctrine of incidental effects, any impact of the Code upon aboriginals is irrelevant for classification purposes. It remains to be seen, however, whether the law's application to specific factual contexts can be put in issue.

Interjurisdictional Immunity

The doctrine of interjurisdictional immunity is engaged when a provincial statute trenches, either in its entirety or in its application to specific factual contexts, upon a head of exclusive federal power. The doctrine provides that, where the general language of a provincial statute can be read to trench upon exclusive federal power in its application to specific factual contexts, the statute must be read down so as not to apply to those situations [. . .] In *Bell Canada v. Quebec (Commission de la santé et de la sécurité du travail)*, [1988] 1 S.C.R. 749, this Court held that a provincial occupational health and safety statute was inapplicable to a federal undertaking. More relevant, for present purposes, in *Delgamuukw*, supra, at para. 181, Lamer C.J. held that s. 91(24) protects a "core" of Indianness from provincial laws of general application, through operation of the doctrine of interjurisdictional immunity. See also *Kitkatla Band*, supra, at para. 75: in that case it was not established that the impugned provisions affected "the essential and distinctive core values of Indianness", and thus they did not "engage the federal power over native affairs and First Nations in Canada".

The question, then, is whether, in a valid law of general application, provisions that empower a provincially constituted administrative tribunal to hear and rule upon arguments relating to aboriginal rights as they arise in execution of its provincial mandate trench upon the core of Indianness. If so, those provisions will be inapplicable to Indians.

Application: Adjudication Versus Legislation

Lambert J.A., in the British Columbia Court of Appeal, concluded that such provisions would touch the core of Indianness. The doctrine of interjurisdictional immunity would, accordingly, render those enabling provisions inapplicable to questions of aboriginal law. It is helpful to review the heart of his reasoning on this point, at para. 72:

> The existence and extent of aboriginal title and aboriginal rights has been held in *Delgamuukw* to come within the essential core of Indianness. That being so, I cannot imagine that a law granting quasi-judicial jurisdiction to determine matters of aboriginal title and aboriginal rights could be anything other than equally and co-extensively within the core of Indianness. As such it fulfils the conditions for application of the principle of interjurisdictional immunity. . . .

This short passage reveals the fundamental error in the analysis of the majority of the Court of Appeal. It equates legislation respecting the "existence and extent of aboriginal title and aboriginal rights" (a legislative or regulatory function) with legislation enabling a board "to determine matters of aboriginal title and aboriginal rights" (an adjudicative function) (emphasis added). The respondent made the same error, stating in his factum that "the province's power to enact the jurisdiction-granting sections of the Code cannot extend to matters that are not within the province's legislative competence" (respondent's factum, at para. 105).

Legislation that triggers the doctrine of interjurisdictional immunity purports to regulate indirectly matters within exclusive federal competence, that is, to alter rights and obligations. [. . .] To my knowledge, none of the authorities applying the doctrine of interjurisdictional immunity has done so in respect of an adjudicative function. The function at issue in this appeal is one of identifying where existing aboriginal rights affirmed by s. 35 of the

Constitution Act, 1982 prevail over provisions in the Code. The Commission's enabling provisions do not attempt to supplement or amend the constitutional and federal rules respecting aboriginal rights. Indeed, the question is whether the legislature may empower the Commission to take cognizance of existing constitutional rights and rights under federal rules, not to alter or supplant them. In my view, as I shall explain, there is no reason under the Constitution that the legislature may not so empower the Commission. [. . .]

The conclusion that a provincial board may adjudicate matters within federal legislative competence fits comfortably within the general constitutional and judicial architecture of Canada. In determining, incidentally, a question of aboriginal rights, a provincially constituted board would be applying constitutional or federal law in the same way as a provincial court, which of course is also a creature of provincial legislation. At the hearing all parties agreed that a provincial court may determine s. 35 issues. [. . .]

The conclusion sought by the respondent would pose intractable difficulties for administrative tribunals in the execution of their tasks. A provincially constituted board cannot respect the division of powers under the *Constitution Act, 1867* if it is unable to take into account the boundary between provincial and federal powers. [. . .] Indeed, a multitude of administrative tribunals, both provincial and federal, routinely make determinations respecting matters within the competence of the other legislator. [. . .] In short, in applying their enabling legislation, boards must take into account all applicable legal rules, both federal and provincial. I therefore decline to accept the respondent's argument and its logical extension that the practices just described are constitutionally impermissible.

Further reasons persuade me to reject the respondent's general position that questions relating to aboriginal rights are untouchable by a provincially created tribunal by virtue of their falling within federal legislative competence. It is necessary to examine side by side two provisions in the Constitution. The one on which the respondent relies heavily is s. 91(24), which empowers Parliament to legislate in relation to "Indians, and Land reserved for the Indians". The other is s. 35 of the *Constitution Act, 1982*. Unless otherwise specified, such as official language rights in the *Charter* particular to New Brunswick, every right in the *Constitution Act, 1982* applies to every province as well as to the federal government. Section 35 therefore applies to both provinces and the federal government. [. . .] By virtue of s. 35, then, laws of the province of British Columbia that conflict with protected aboriginal rights do not apply so as to limit those rights, unless the limitation is justifiable according to the test in Sparrow, supra. I find it difficult to think that the Province cannot, when administering a provincial regulatory scheme, attempt to respect its constitutional obligation by empowering an administrative tribunal to hear a defence of aboriginal rights.

Sparrow stands for the proposition that government regulation, including provincial regulation, may, by legislation, infringe an aboriginal right if that infringement is justified. Though this is not the basis of the Commission's jurisdiction, where legislation justifiably infringing rights is possible, surely adjudication by the Commission, which simply takes existing rights into account, must be permissible. This conclusion follows from the distinction between legislation and adjudication and the nature of their impact upon rights. [. . .]

I wish to reiterate a point acknowledged by the respondent himself, namely that a province lacks the constitutional capacity to extinguish aboriginal rights and aboriginal title. This is because the clear and plain intent necessary to extinguish an aboriginal right would make a law one in relation to Indians and Indian lands and thus ultra vires the province: *Delgamuukw*, supra, at para. 180. I will now explain why, in two important respects, a determination by an administrative tribunal, such as the Commission, is very different from both the extinguishment of a right and legislation in relation to Indians or aboriginal rights.

First, and most important, any adjudicator, whether a judge or a tribunal, does not create, amend or extinguish aboriginal rights. Rather, on the basis of the evidence, a judicial or administrative decision maker may recognize the continued existence of an aboriginal right, including its content and scope, or observe that the right has been properly extinguished by a competent legislative authority. Of course the decision maker may also conclude on the evidence that the aboriginal right simply has not been proven at all.

Admittedly, within the administrative state, the line between adjudication and legislation is sometimes blurred. Administrative tribunals that develop and implement policy while adjudicating disputes, such as the Competition Tribunal and a provincial Securities Commission, come to mind. Indeed, this Court's standard of review jurisprudence is sensitive to the deference that may be appropriate where an expert tribunal is simultaneously adjudicating and developing policy, which may sometimes be viewed as a legislative function: *Canada (Deputy Minister of National Revenue) v. Mattel Canada Inc.*, [2001] 2 S.C.R. 100; *Pushpanathan v. Canada (Minister of Citizenship and Immigration)*, [1998] 1 S.C.R. 982. There is, however, a crucial distinction between a board that has been empowered by valid legislation to make policy within an area that is intra vires the enabling legislator, and a provincial board that is called upon, in executing its mandate, to answer incidentally a legal question relating to the Constitution or to federal law. No one has suggested that the Legislature has the constitutional power to enable a board to determine questions of aboriginal law on the basis of policy considerations favourable to the Province.

Second, while both provincially constituted courts and provincially constituted tribunals may consider the Constitution and federal laws, there is nevertheless one important distinction between them that the respondent overlooked. Unlike the judgments of a court, the Commission's decisions do not constitute legally binding precedents, nor will their collective weight over time amount to an authoritative body of common law. They could not be declaratory of the validity of any law. Moreover, as constitutional determinations respecting s. 91(24) or s. 35, the Commission's rulings would be reviewable, on a correctness basis, in a superior court on judicial review: *Westcoast Energy Inc. v. Canada (National Energy Board)*, [1998] 1 S.C.R. 322, ¶40; *Canadian Pacific Ltd. v. Matsqui Indian Band*, [1995] 1 S.C.R. 3, ¶23; *Douglas/Kwantlen Faculty Assn. v. Douglas College*, [1990] 3 S.C.R. 570. To avoid judicial review, the Commission would have to identify, interpret, and apply correctly the relevant constitutional and federal rules and judicial precedents. As a result of the contrast between the general application of a provincial law by a court and the specific, non-binding effect of a board's particular decision, there is a substantial difference

The Present Role of the Commission and the Core of Indianness

The preceding point brings me to consider the role of the Commission in this case. Recall that the general prohibition against cutting Crown timber appears in s. 96(1) of the Code, and is not attacked in this appeal. The question, then, is not whether that prohibition unjustifiably infringes an aboriginal right. The question is whether provisions that would enable the Commission to hear a defence of aboriginal right are unconstitutional. I have already noted that the determinations of the Commission respecting aboriginal rights would be reviewable on a correctness standard. Provincial officials cannot initiate any inquiry into aboriginal rights before the Commission. Instead, a question of aboriginal law will arise only when a respondent raises an aboriginal right before the Commission in seeking relief from a general prohibition or other regulatory provision in the Code. I do not see how, by raising a defence of aboriginal right, a respondent should be able to alter the primary jurisdiction of the Commission or halt its proceedings. The nature of a particular defence should be seen as secondary to the Commission's primary jurisdiction. A person accused of violating the Code should not be able to oust the Commission's jurisdiction relating to forestry simply by raising a particular defence and thereby highlighting a constitutional dimension of the main issue. In any event, constitutional law doctrines aside, I think it would be most convenient for aboriginal persons to seek the relief afforded by their constitutionally protected rights as early as possible within the mechanisms of the administrative and judicial apparatus.

The respondent has failed to grasp the distinction between adjudication by a provincially created tribunal, on the one hand, and limits on regulation by a province of a matter under federal competence, on the other. Taking this distinction into account, I cannot see how the ability to hear a defence based on s. 35 would constitute an indirect intrusion on the defining elements of "Indianness". The "core" of Indianness has not been exhaustively defined. It encompasses the whole range of aboriginal rights that are protected by s. 35(1): *Delgamuukw*, supra, at para. 178. For present purposes, it is perhaps more easily defined negatively than positively. The core has been held not to include labour relations (*Four B Manufacturing Ltd. v. United Garment Workers of America*, [1980] 1 S.C.R. 1031) and highway traffic regulation on reserves (*R. v. Francis*, [1988] 1 S.C.R. 1025). On the evidence adduced in *Kitkatla Band*, supra, at para. 70, the status or capacity of Indians was found not to be impaired by the impugned *Heritage Conservation Act*, R.S.B.C. 1996, c. 187. Given that these substantive matters were held not to go to the core of Indianness, I cannot see how the procedural question in this appeal can. The respondent has failed to demonstrate that the procedural right to raise at first instance a defence of aboriginal rights in a superior court, as opposed to before a provincially constituted tribunal, such as the Commission, goes to the core of Indianness.

I conclude, therefore, primarily on the basis that adjudication is distinct from legislation, that the Legislature of British Columbia has the constitutional power to enable the Commission to determine questions relative to aboriginal rights as they arise in the execution of its valid provincial mandate respecting forestry.

Notes and Questions

1. To what extent was the Supreme Court's decision affected by practical, as opposed to purely legal, considerations? Had the Court accepted Paul's argument how would his aboriginal rights defence ultimately have been adjudicated?

2. Based on *Paul*, it is now settled law that provincial environmental and resource management tribunals can be vested with authority to consider and decide legal questions relating to rights protected under section 35 of the *Constitution*. For a recent illustration of the complexities and challenges associated with this newly affirmed jurisdiction see *Xats'ull First Nation v. Director (Environmental Management Act)* (May 9, 2008), Decision No. 2006 EMA-006(a) (B.C. Environmental Appeal Board). In this case, in a split decision, the Board dismissed an appeal alleging that the Ministry had failed to discharge its duty to consult (as required by *Taku* and *Haida Nation*) prior to approving an amendment to a permit allowing for the discharge of mine tailings.

Municipal Jurisdiction

The role of municipalities is only indirectly guided by constitutional considerations. Municipalities derive their powers from the provinces. Provinces are constitutionally empowered to pass on aspects of their own jurisdiction to municipalities. Most provinces have consolidated their legislative delegation of power in some form of *Municipal Government Act*. Such legislation tends to give municipalities power and responsibility over a range of local matters, many of which have environmental implications and connections.

A critical function of a municipality is to make land use decisions within its boundaries. Available tools include zoning powers, development permits, and subdivision approval requirements. Through zoning by-laws, municipalities can control what range of activities are possible. Through zoning, a municipality can promote public and active transportation, restrict, control high risk industrial activities, encourage redevelopment of contaminated sites, and otherwise influence the environmental impact of human activities within its boundaries.

In many municipalities, development permits are required for major new developments. This provides a municipality with the ability to influence whether, and how, major developments within its boundaries are implemented. A subset of such developments is proposals for new subdivisions. Many municipalities have separate processes in place for the approval of subdivisions. The implications of new subdivisions for transportation, municipal services, and the loss of habitat are influencing how municipalities are exercising these powers. As with all municipal powers, the provinces also retain the ability to direct municipalities on how to make land use decisions through provincial land use policies or similar measures.

Examples of other powers often delegated by provinces to municipalities include: the power to pass by-laws dealing with noise and odour; the control of cosmetic pesticide use; the collection and disposal of solid waste; and litter within the boundaries of the municipality. Most legislation also includes some general provisions that allow municipalities to pass by-laws for the general health and welfare of its residents. In some cases, a subject matter may be completely delegated. Often, however, provinces set general rules on a subject matter through separate provincial legislation and then allow municipalities to decide on how to best implement them within their boundaries.

Many provinces have passed provincial laws dealing with solid waste management. Such laws may also establish what materials have to be re-processed, re-used or recycled. They may also set general rules for the handling and processing of various waste streams. Provincial regulations may also establish design criteria for landfills, composting facilities, tire storage facilities and facilities that incinerate medical waste. Municipalities, in turn, tend to be responsible for collection of material and for ensuring that the material is properly sorted and taken to approved facilities.

A key emerging jurisdictional concern is the relationship between a growing appetite on the part of local governments to use their regulatory powers to promote environmentally sustainable practices within their boundaries and analogous and potentially competing powers that are constitutionally vested provincially and federally. In *Friends of the Oldman River Society v. Canada (Minister of Transport)*, La Forest J. offered observations on the need for the courts to respect and promote the ability of both levels of government to tackle the mounting environmental challenges of the day. As citizens and community organizations increasingly turn to local governments as a readily accessible and available vehicle for translating their environmental values and preferences into regulation, should by extension the courts construe generously powers vested by provinces in their elected local officials and tribunals?

Earlier, in Chapter 1, we considered the 2001 decision of the Supreme Court of Canada in *114957 Canada Ltée (Spraytech, Société d'arrosage) v. Hudson (Town)* in the context of the majority's invocation of the precautionary principle. As we saw, the majority's invoked this principle to bolster its conclusion that a bylaw restricting the use of pesticides enacted by the Town of Hudson was constitutional. We now return to this decision to explore more fully the Supreme Court's approach to the interesting and timely jurisdictional issues raised in the case.

114957 Canada Ltée (Spray-Tech, Société d'arrosage) v. Hudson (Town) [2001] 2 S.C.R. 241

L'HEUREUX-DUBÉ J.:

The context of this appeal includes the realization that our common future, that of every Canadian community, depends on a healthy environment. In the words of the Superior Court judge: "Twenty years ago there was very little concern over the effect of chemicals such as pesticides on the population. Today, we are more conscious of what type of an environment we wish to live in and what quality of life we wish to expose our children [to]". This Court has recognized that "[e]veryone is aware that individually and collectively, we are responsible for preserving the natural environment . . . environmental protection [has] emerged as a fundamental value in Canadian society": *R. v. Canadian Pacific Ltd.*, [1995] 2 S.C.R. 1031, ¶55 (S.C.C.). See also *Friends of the Oldman River Society v. Canada (Minister of Transport)*, [1992] 1 S.C.R. 3 at pp. 16-17 (S.C.C.).

Regardless of whether pesticides are in fact an environmental threat, the Court is asked to decide the legal question of whether the Town of Hudson, Quebec, acted within its authority in enacting a by-law regulating and restricting pesticide use.

The case arises in an era in which matters of governance are often examined through the lens of the principle of subsidiarity. This is the proposition that law-making and implementation are often best achieved at a level of government that is not only effective, but also closest to the citizens affected and thus most responsive to their needs, to local distinctiveness, and to population diversity. La Forest J. wrote for the majority in *Canada (Procureure générale) c. Hydro-Québec*, [1997] 3 S.C.R. 213 (S.C.C.), at p. 296, that "the protection of the environment is a major challenge of our time. It is an international problem, one that requires action by *governments at all levels*" (emphasis added). His reasons in that case also quoted with approval a passage from *Our Common Future*, the report produced in 1987 by the United Nations' World Commission on the Environment and Development. The so-called "Brundtland Commission" recommended that "local governments [should be] empowered to exceed, but not to lower, national norms" (p. 220).

There are now at least 37 Quebec municipalities with by-laws restricting pesticides: John Swaigen, "The Hudson Case: Municipal Powers to Regulate Pesticides Confirmed by Quebec Courts" (2000), 34 C.E.L.R. (N.S.) 162, at p. 174. Nevertheless, each level of government must be respectful of the division of powers that is the hallmark of our federal system; there is a fine line between laws that legitimately complement each other and those that invade another government's protected legislative sphere. Ours is a legal inquiry informed by the environmental policy context, not the reverse.

Facts

The appellants are landscaping and lawn care companies operating mostly in the region of greater Montreal, with both commercial and residential clients. They make regular use of pesticides approved by the federal *Pest Control Products Act*, R.S.C. 1985, c. P-9, in the course of their business activities and hold the requisite licences under Quebec's *Pesticides Act*, R.S.Q., c. P-9.3.

The respondent, the Town of Hudson ("the Town"), is a municipal corporation governed by the *Cities and Towns Act*, R.S.Q., c. C-19 ("*C.T.A.*"). It is located about 40 kilometres west of Montreal and has a population of approximately 5,400 people, some of whom are clients of the appellants. In 1991, the Town adopted By-law 270, restricting the use of pesticides within its perimeter to specified locations and for enumerated activities. The by-law responded to residents' concerns, repeatedly expressed since 1985. The residents submitted numerous letters and comments to the Town's Council. The definition of pesticides in By-law 270 replicates that of the *Pesticides Act*.]

In November 1992, the appellants were served with a summons by the Town to appear before the Municipal Court and respond to charges of having used pesticides in violation of By-law 270. The appellants pled not guilty and obtained a suspension of proceedings in order to bring a motion for declaratory judgment before the Superior Court (under art. 453 of Quebec's *Code of Civil Procedure*). They asked that the court declare By-law 270 (as well as By-law 248, which is not part of this appeal) to be inoperative and *ultra vires* the Town's authority.

The Superior Court denied the motion for declaratory judgment, finding that the by-laws fell within the scope of the Town's powers under the *C.T.A.* This ruling was affirmed by a unanimous Quebec Court of Appeal. [. . .]

Issues

There are two issues raised by this appeal:

(1) Did the Town have the statutory authority to enact By-law 270?

(2) Even if the Town had authority to enact it, was By-law 270 rendered inoperative because of a conflict with federal or provincial legislation?

Did the Town have the statutory authority to enact By-law 270?

In *R. v. Sharma*, [1993] 1 S.C.R. 650 (S.C.C.), at p. 668, this Court recognized "the principle that, as statutory bodies, municipalities 'may exercise only those powers expressly conferred by statute, those powers necessarily or fairly implied by the expressed power in the statute, and those indispensable powers essential and not merely convenient to the effectuation of the purposes of the corporation' [. . .] Included in this authority are "general welfare" powers, conferred by provisions in provincial enabling legislation, on which municipalities can draw. As I.M. Rogers points out, "the legislature cannot possibly foresee all the powers that are necessary to the statutory equipment of its creatures . . . Undoubtedly the inclusion of 'general welfare' provisions was intended to circumvent, to some extent, the effect of the doctrine of *ultra vires* which puts the municipalities in the position of having to point to an express grant of authority to justify each corporate act" (Ian MacFee Rogers, *The Law of Canadian Municipal Corporations*, 2nd ed. (looseleaf, updated 2001, release 1), cum. supp. to vol. 1 (Toronto: Carswell: 1971), at p. 367).

Section 410 *C.T.A.* is an example of such a general welfare provision and supplements the specific grants of power in s. 412. More open-ended or "omnibus" provisions such as s. 410 allow municipalities to respond expeditiously to new challenges facing local communities, without requiring amendment of the provincial enabling legislation. There are analogous provisions in other provinces' and territories' municipal enabling legislation: see *Municipal Government Act*, S.A. 1994, c. M-26.1, ss. 3(c) and 7; *Local Government Act*, R.S.B.C. 1996, c. 323, s. 249; *Municipal Act*, S.M. 1996, c. 58, C.C.S.M., c. M225, ss. 232 and 233; *Municipalities Act*, R.S.N.B. 1973, c. M-22, s. 190(2), First Sched.; *Municipal Government Act*, S.N.S. 1998, c. 18, s. 172; *Cities, Towns and Villages Act*, R.S.N.W.T. 1988, c. C-8, ss. 54 and 102; *Municipal Act*, R.S.O. 1990, c. M.45, s. 102; *Municipal Act*, R.S.Y. 1986, c. 119, s. 271.

While enabling provisions that allow municipalities to regulate for the "general welfare" within their territory authorize the enactment of by-laws genuinely aimed at furthering goals, such as public health and safety, it is important to keep in mind that such open-ended provisions do not confer an unlimited power. Rather, courts faced with an impugned by-law enacted under an "omnibus" provision such as s. 410 *C.T.A.* must be vigilant in scrutinizing the true purpose of the by-law. In this way, a municipality will not be permitted to invoke the implicit power granted under a "general welfare" provision as a basis for enacting by-laws that are in fact related to ulterior objectives, whether mischievous or not. [. . .]

Within this framework, I turn now to the specifics of the appeal. As a preliminary matter, I agree with the courts below that By-law 270 was not enacted under s. 412(32) *C.T.A.* [. . .] As a result, since there is no specific provision in the provincial enabling legislation referring to pesticides, the by-law must fall within the purview of s. 410(1) *C.T.A.* The party challenging a by-law's validity bears the burden of proving that it is *ultra vires*: see *Kuchma v. Tache (Rural Municipality)*, [1945] S.C.R. 234 at p. 239 (S.C.C.), and *Fountainhead Fun Centre Ltd. v. Montréal (Ville)*, [1985] 1 S.C.R. 368 at p. 395 (S.C.C.).

Section 410(1) *C.T.A.* provides that councils may "make by-laws:

> (1) To secure peace, order, good government, health and general welfare in the territory of the municipality, provided such by-laws are not contrary to the laws of Canada, or of Québec, nor inconsistent with any special provision of this Act or of the *Charter*.

In *Nanaimo (City) v. Rascal Trucking Ltd.*, [2000] 1 S.C.R. 342, 2000 SCC 13 (S.C.C.), at para. 36, this Court quoted with approval the following statement by McLachlin J. (now Chief Justice) in *Shell Canada Products Ltd. v. Vancouver (City)*, [1994] 1 S.C.R. 231 (S.C.C.), at p. 244:

> Recent commentary suggests an emerging consensus that courts must respect the responsibility of elected municipal bodies to serve the people who elected them and exercise caution to avoid substituting their views of what is best for the citizens for those of municipal councils. *Barring clear demonstration that a municipal decision was beyond its powers, courts should not so hold.* In cases where powers are not expressly conferred but may be implied, courts must be prepared to adopt the "benevolent construction" which this Court referred to in *Greenbaum*, and confer the powers by reasonable implication. Whatever rules of construction are applied, they must not be used to usurp the legitimate role of municipal bodies as community representatives. [Emphasis added.]

The appellants argue that By-law 270 imposes an impermissible absolute ban on pesticide use. They focus on s. 2 of the by-law, which states that: "The spreading and use of a pesticide is prohibited throughout the territory of the Town". In my view, the by-law read as a whole does not impose such a prohibition. By-law 270's ss. 3 to 6 state locations and situations for pesticide use. As one commentary notes, "by-laws like Hudson's typically target non-essential uses of pesticides. That is, it is not a total prohibition, but rather permits the use of pesticides in certain situations where the use of pesticides is not purely an aesthetic pursuit (e.g. for the production of crops)": Swaigen, *supra*, at p. 178. [. . .]

In *Shell*, *supra*, at pp. 276-277, Sopinka J. for the majority quoted the following with approval from Rogers, *supra*, §64.1, at p. 387:

> In approaching a problem of construing a municipal enactment a court should endeavour firstly to interpret it so that the powers sought to be exercised are in consonance with the purposes of the corporation. The provision at hand should be construed with reference to the object of the municipality: to render services to a group of persons in a locality with a view to advancing their health, welfare, safety and good government.

In that case, Sopinka J. enunciated the test of whether the municipal enactment was "passed for a municipal purpose". Provisions such as s. 410(1) *C.T.A.*, while benefiting from the generosity of interpretation discussed in *Nanaimo*, *supra*, must have a reasonable connection to the municipality's permissible objectives. As stated in *Greenbaum*, *supra*, at p. 689: "municipal by-laws are to be read to fit within the parameters of the empowering provincial statute where the by-laws are susceptible to more than one interpretation. However, courts must be vigilant in ensuring that municipalities do not impinge upon the civil or common law rights of citizens in passing *ultra vires* by-laws".

Whereas in *Shell*, the enactments' purpose was found to be "to affect matters beyond the boundaries of the City without any identifiable benefit to its inhabitants" (p. 280), that is not the case here. The Town's By-law 270 responded to concerns of its residents about alleged health risks caused by non-essential uses of pesticides within Town limits. Unlike *Shell*, in which the Court felt bound by the municipal enactments' "detailed recital of . . . purposes", the by-law at issue requires what Sopinka J. called the reading in of an implicit purpose. Based on the distinction between essential and non-essential uses of pesticides, it is reasonable to conclude that the Town by-law's purpose is to minimize the use of allegedly harmful pesticides in order to promote the health of its inhabitants. This purpose falls squarely within the "health" component of s. 410(1). As Ruth Sullivan appositely explains in a hypothetical example illustrating the purposive approach to statutory interpretation:

> Suppose, for example, that a municipality passed a by-law prohibiting the use of chemical pesticides on residential lawns. With no additional information, one might well conclude that the purpose of the by-law was to protect persons from health hazards contained in the chemical spray. This inference would be based on empirical beliefs about the harms chemical pesticides can cause and the risks of exposure created by their use on residential lawns. It would also be based on assumptions about the relative value of grass, insects and persons in society and the desirability of possible consequences of the by-law, such as putting people out of work, restricting the free use of property, interfering with the conduct of businesses and the like. These assumptions make it implausible to suppose that the municipal council was trying to promote the spread of plant-destroying insects or to put chemical workers out of work, but plausible to suppose that it was trying to suppress a health hazard. (*Driedger on the Construction of Statutes*, 3rd ed. (Toronto: Butterworths, 1994), at p. 53)

Kennedy J. correctly found that the Town Council, "faced with a situation involving health and the environment", "was addressing a need of their community". In this manner, the municipality is attempting to fulfil its role as what the Ontario Court of Appeal has called the "trustee of the environment" *Scarborough (Borough) v. R.E.F. Homes Ltd.* (1979), 9 M.P.L.R. 255 at p. 257 (Ont. C.A.).

The appellants claim that By-law 270 is discriminatory and therefore *ultra vires* because of what they identify as impermissible distinctions that affect their commercial activities. There is no specific authority in the *C.T.A.* for these distinctions. Writing for the Court in *Sharma*, *supra*, at p. 668, Iacobucci J. stated the principle that:

> . . . in *Fountainhead Fun Centre Ltd. v. Montréal (Ville)*, *supra*, this Court recognized that discrimination in the municipal law sense was no more permissible between than within classes (at pp. 405-6). Further, the general reasonableness or rationality of the distinction is not at issue: discrimination can only occur where the enabling legislation specifically so provides *or where the discrimination is a necessary incident to exercising the power delegated by the province* (*Fountainhead Fun Centre Ltd. v. Montréal (Ville)*, *supra*, at pp. 404-6). [Emphasis added.] [. . .]

Without drawing distinctions, By-law 270 could not achieve its permissible goal of aiming to improve the health of the Town's inhabitants by banning non-essential pesticide use. If all pesticide uses and users were treated alike, the protection of health and welfare would be sub-optimal. For example, withdrawing the special status given to farmers under the by-law's s. 4 would work at cross-purposes with its salubrious intent. Section 4 thus justifiably furthers the objective of By-law 270. Having held that the Town can regulate the use of pesticides, I conclude that the distinctions impugned by the appellants for restricting their businesses are necessary incidents to the power delegated by the province under s. 410(1) *C.T.A.* They are "so absolutely necessary to the exercise of those powers that [authorization has] to be found in the enabling provisions, by necessary inference or implicit delegation". *Arcade Amusements*, *supra*, at p. 414, quoted in *Greenbaum*, *supra*, at p. 695.

To conclude this section on statutory authority, I note that reading s. 410(1) to permit the Town to regulate pesticide use is consistent with principles of international law and policy. My reasons for the Court in *Baker v. Canada (Minister of Citizenship & Immigration)*, [1999] 2 S.C.R. 817 (S.C.C.), at p. 861, observed that "the values reflected in international human rights law may help inform the contextual approach to statutory interpretation and judicial review. As stated in *Driedger on the Construction of Statutes*, *supra*, at p. 330:

> [T]he legislature is presumed to respect the values and principles enshrined in international law, both customary and conventional. These constitute a part of the legal context in which legislation is enacted and read. *In so far as possible, therefore, interpretations that reflect these values and principles are preferred.* [Emphasis added.]

The interpretation of By-law 270 contained in these reasons respects international law's "precautionary principle", which is defined as follows at para. 7 of the *Bergen Ministerial Declaration on Sustainable Development* (1990):

> In order to achieve sustainable development, policies must be based on the precautionary principle. Environmental measures must anticipate, prevent and attack the causes of environmental degradation. Where there are threats of serious or irreversible damage, lack of full scientific certainty should not be used as a reason for postponing measures to prevent environmental degradation.

Canada "advocated inclusion of the precautionary principle" during the Bergen Conference negotiations (David VanderZwaag, *CEPA Issue Elaboration Paper No. 18, CEPA and the Precautionary Principle/Approach* (Ottawa: Environment Canada, 1995), at p. 8). The principle is codified in several items of domestic legislation: see, for example, the *Oceans Act*, S.C. 1996, c. 31, Preamble (para. 6); *Canadian Environmental Protection Act, 1999*, S.C. 1999, c. 33 ("*CEPA*"), s. 2(1)(a); *Endangered Species Act*, S.N.S. 1998, c. 11, ss. 2(1)(h) and 11(1).

Scholars have documented the precautionary principle's inclusion "in virtually every recently adopted treaty and policy document related to the protection and preservation of the environment" (D. Freestone and E. Hey, "Origins and Development of the Precautionary Principle", in David Freestone and Ellen Hey, eds., *The Precautionary Principle and International Law* (The Hague: Kluwer Law International, 1996), at p. 41. As a result, there may be "currently sufficient state practice to allow a good argument that the precautionary principle is a principle of customary international law" (James Cameron and Juli Abouchar, "The Status of the Precautionary Principle in International Law", in *ibid.*, at p. 52). See also Owen McIntyre and Thomas Mosedale, "The Precautionary Principle as a Norm of Customary International Law" (1997), 9 *J. Env. L.* 221, at p. 241 ("the precautionary principle has indeed crystallized into a norm of customary international law"). The Supreme Court of India considers the precautionary principle to be "part of the Customary International Law" (*A.P. Pollution Control Board v. Nayudu*, 1999 S.O.L. Case No. 53 at p. 8). See also *Vellore Citizens Welfare Forum v. Union of India*, [1996] Supp. 5 S.C.R. 241. In the context of the precautionary principle's tenets, the Town's concerns about pesticides fit well under their rubric of preventive action.

Even if the Town had authority to enact it, was By-law 270 rendered inoperative because of a conflict with federal or provincial legislation?

This Court stated in *Hydro-Québec*, *supra*, at p. 286, that *Oldman River*, *supra*, "made it clear that the environment is not, as such, a subject matter of legislation under the *Constitution Act, 1867*. As it was put there, 'the *Constitution Act, 1867* has not assigned the matter of "environment" *sui generis* to either the provinces or Parliament' (p. 63). Rather, it is a diffuse subject that cuts across many different areas of constitutional responsibility, some federal, some provincial (pp. 63-64)". As there is bijurisdictional responsibility for pesticide regulation, the appellants allege conflicts between By-law 270 and both federal and provincial legislation. These contentions will be examined in turn.

Federal Legislation

The appellants argue that ss. 4(1), 4(3) and 6(1)(j) of the *Pest Control Products Act* ("*PCPA*"), and s. 45 of the *Pest Control Products Regulations* allowed them to make use of the particular pesticide products they employed in their business practices. They allege a conflict between these legislative provisions and By-law 270. In *Multiple Access Ltd. v. McCutcheon*, [1982] 2 S.C.R. 161 (S.C.C.), at p. 187, Dickson J. (later Chief Justice) for the majority of the Court reviewed the "express contradiction test" of conflict between federal and provincial legislation. At p. 191, he explained that "there would seem to be no good reasons to speak of paramountcy and preclusion except where there is actual conflict in operation as where one enactment says 'yes' and the other says 'no'; 'the same citizens are being told to do inconsistent things'; compliance with one is defiance of the other". [. . .] Bylaw 270, as a product of provincial enabling legislation, is subject to this test.

Federal legislation relating to pesticides extends to the regulation and authorization of their import, export, sale, manufacture, registration, packaging, and labelling. The *PCPA* regulates which pesticides can be registered for manufacture and/or use in Canada. This legislation is permissive, rather than exhaustive, and there is no operational conflict with By-law 270. No one is placed in an impossible situation by the legal imperative of complying with both regulatory regimes. Analogies to motor vehicles or cigarettes that have been approved federally, but the use of which can nevertheless be restricted municipally, well illustrate this conclusion. There is, moreover, no concern in this case that application of By-law 270 displaces or frustrates "the legislative purpose of Parliament". See *Multiple Access*, *supra*, at p. 190; *Bank of Montreal*, *supra*, at pp. 151 and 154.

Provincial Legislation

Multiple Access also applies to the inquiry into whether there is a conflict between the by-law and provincial legislation, except for cases (unlike this one) in which the relevant provincial legislation specifies a different test. The *Multiple Access* test, namely "impossibility of dual compliance", [. . .] was foreshadowed for provincial-municipal conflicts in *dicta* contained in this Court's decision in *Arcade Amusements*, *supra*, at p. 404. There, Beetz J. wrote that "otherwise valid provincial statutes which are *directly contrary* to federal statutes are rendered inoperative by that conflict. Only the same type of conflict with provincial statutes can make by-laws inoperative: Ian M. Rogers, *The Law of Canadian Municipal Corporations*, vol. 1, 2nd ed., 1971, No. 63.16" (emphasis added). [. . .]

Some courts have already made use of the *Multiple Access* test to examine alleged provincial-municipal conflicts. For example, [see] . . . *British Columbia Lottery Corp. v. Vancouver (City)* (1999), 169 D.L.R. (4th) 141 (B.C. C.A.), at pp. 147-148, the British Columbia Court of Appeal . . .. [in this case] the court summarized the applicable standard as follows: "A true and outright conflict can only be said to arise when one enactment compels what the other forbids".

As a general principle, the mere existence of provincial (or federal) legislation in a given field does not oust municipal prerogatives to regulate the subject matter: [see]. *St-Michel Archange (Municipalité) c. 2419-6388 Québec Inc.*, [1992] R.J.Q. 875 (Que. C.A.). [. . .]

In this case, there is no barrier to dual compliance with By-law 270 and the *Pesticides Act*, nor any plausible evidence that the legislature intended to preclude municipal regulation of pesticide use. The *Pesticides Act* establishes a permit and licensing system for vendors and commercial applicators of pesticides and thus complements the federal legislation's focus on the products themselves. Along with By-law 270, these laws establish a tri-level regulatory regime.

According to s. 102 of the *Pesticides Act*, as it was at the time By-law 270 was passed: "The provisions of the *Pesticide Management Code* and of the other regulations of this Act prevail over any inconsistent provision of any by-law passed by a municipality or an urban community". Evidently, the *Pesticides Act* envisions the existence of complementary municipal by-laws. As Duplessis and Hétu, *supra*, at p. 109, put it, [TRANSLATION] "the Quebec legislature gave the municipalities the right to regulate pesticides, provided that the by-law was not incompatible with the regulations and the *Management Code* enacted under the *Pesticides Act*". Since no *Pesticide Management Code* has been enacted by the province under s. 105, the lower courts in this case correctly found that the by-law and the *Pesticides Act* could co-exist. In the words of the Court of Appeal, at p. 16: [TRANSLATION] "The *Pesticides Act* thus itself contemplated the existence of municipal regulation of pesticides, since it took the trouble to impose restrictions". [. . .]

Disposition

I have found that By-law 270 was validly enacted under s. 410(1) *C.T.A.* Moreover, the by-law does not render dual compliance with its dictates and either federal or provincial legislation impossible. For these reasons, I would dismiss the appeal with costs.

Notes and Comments

LeBel J. (with Iacobucci and Major JJ. concurring) authored reasons that agreed with the majority's disposition but, likely in an attempt to signal his reluctance to endorse L'Heureux-Dubé J.'s observations about international law, noted that he viewed this case as posing "an administrative and local government law issue".

References

We thank the copyright holders for their permission to reproduce their materials.

J. Benidickson, *Environmental Law*, 3rd ed. (Irwin: 2009)

S. Blackman, *et al.*, "The Evolution of Federal/Provincial Relations in Natural Resource Management" (1994) 32 Alta. L. Rev. 511

S. Deimann, "*R. v. Hydro-Quebec*: Federal Environmental Regulation as Criminal Law" (1998) 43 McGill L. J. 923

M. Doelle, "CEAA, New Uncertainties, but a Step in the Right Direction" (1994) 4 J. Env. L. & Prac. 59.

P. Emond, "The Case for a Greater Federal Role in the Environmental Protection Field: An Examination of the Pollution Problem and the Constitution" (1972) 10 Osgoode Hall L. J. 647

D. Gibson, "Constitutional Jurisdiction over Environmental Management in Canada" (1973) 23 U. Toronto L. J. 54

J. Hanebury, "Environmental Impact Assessment and the Constitution: The Never-Ending Story" (1999) 9 J. Env. L. & Prac. 169

K. Harrison, *Passing the Buck: Federalism and Canadian Environmental Policy* (Vancouver: UBC Press, 1996)

B. Hobby, *et al.*, eds., *Canadian Environmental Assessment Act: An Annotated Guide* (Aurora: Canada Law Book, 1995)

S.A. Kennett, "Federal Environmental Jurisdiction after *Oldman*" (1993) 38 McGill L.J. 180

A.W. MacKay, "The Supreme Court of Canada and Federalism: Does/Should Anyone Care Anymore?" (2001) 80 Can. Bar Rev. 241

W.R. MacKay, "Canadian Federalism and the Environment: The Literature" (2004) 17 Geo. Int'l Envtl. L. Rev. 25. Reprinted with permission of the publisher, Georgetown International Environmental Law Review © 2004.

M. Warkentin, "*Friends of the Oldman River Society v. Canada (Minister of Transport)*" (1992) 26 U.B.C. L. Rev. 313

4

ENVIRONMENTAL REGULATION

Introduction

The goal of this chapter is to provide a conceptual and practical overview and analysis of the topic of environmental regulation. The breadth and diversity of this topic make it a daunting one for environmental law students and instructors alike. It is also an area in which, particularly in the realm of industrial pollution and climate change impacts, the public has strong appetite to see governments play a more rigourous and effective regulatory role than they have to date. Yet, while there appears to be a consensus that governments need to do more to protect the environment, there is also a broad sense that regulatory approaches employed in the past need to be rethought. Indeed, as we discuss shortly, many scholars and policy-makers claim that we need to radically reconfigure how we regulate the environment.

This chapter provides an overview of the emerging debate over the future of environmental regulation; at the same time, it seeks to put this debate in context by introducing the key concepts necessary to understand and critique current approaches. Part I offers some competing perspectives on the historical development and future trajectory of Canadian environmental law by reviewing two influential articles authored in the early 1990s during the peak of the last wave of public concern over environmental issues. Part II is devoted to providing an overview of environmental standard setting process and the key concepts and terminology that pervade the current debate over future of environmental regulation including the distinction and relative merits of management-, technology- and performance-based forms of standard. Part III considers the current state of the debate over the future of environmental regulation and related issues including the evolving role of government and the emergence of new regulatory tools and approaches. Finally, in Part IV we offer a closer look at the architecture and operation of two of Canada's most important federal environmental laws: the *Fisheries Act* and the *Canadian Environmental Protection Act*.

Part I — Evolving Perspectives on Environmental Regulation

McAllister Opinion Research, *Environmental Monitor 2007* (Vancouver: September 7, 2007)

A newly-released poll by the Environmental Monitor research program shows that seven in ten (70%) Canadians now call this country's pollution laws inadequate, up sharply from 11 years ago when just fewer than half (41%) felt this way.

The Environmental Monitor poll also found that when Canadians are asked to spontaneously name their top environmental concern, the most frequent mention is global warming (29%), up nine points nationally from July 2006. When asked to rate the seriousness of climate change, 66 percent of Canadians view climate change as a "very serious" problem, up from 57 percent in 2006 and 44 percent in 2000.

Comparing this data to other countries polled, Canadians rank among the top five countries I the world for their views on the seriousness of climate change — 84 percent of Brazilians rate climate change a very serious problem, followed by China (70%), India (68%) and Canada, tied with Mexico and France. Interestingly, a bare majority of Americans (50%) view climate change as a very serious problem.

The Environmental Monitor poll finds that while more Canadians than ever now favour stricter regulation of industrial pollution, sentiments vary according to industrial sector. Asked about stricter regulations for various industries to combat global warming, clear majorities strongly favour these for the chemical industry (67%), oil and gas industry (62%) and the automobile industry (58%). Just 43 percent strongly favour stricter regulations for the forestry, manufacturing and mining industries. . . .

"Canadians are growing increasingly concerned about the threat of climate change" says Angus McAllister, president of McAllister Opinion Research. "The public was initially open to less onerous alternatives to regulation like voluntary measures and tax incentives. But when the performance of a particular sector is perceived to be lagging, the public is quick to demand regulation, and are slow to back off".

Drawing on the firms' 20-nation polling over 15 years, GlobeScan President Doug Miller observes, "Canadians are among the mot concerned citizens in the world today about the seriousness of climate change — and that's saying a lot given the worldwide surge in concern over the past four years". . . .

Today Environmental Monitor research shows that air pollution comes in second to global warming, as a spontaneously mentioned environmental issue. However, the research shows when top air pollution concerns are probed, these are likely to be global warming, greenhouse gases, and fossil fuel emissions.

Concern about global warming is by far the highest in Canada's North, while lowest in Quebec. Global warming is the top concern in all other regions, including Alberta. University graduates and young adults under 25 are most likely to name global warming as a concern, while high school graduates and women aged 55+ are least likely to do so.

Asked how much can be done to reduce the amount of future climate change or global warming, nearly eight in ten (79%) Canadians express the view that a great deal or a good amount can be done. An identical question asked in a Washington Post/Stanford poll in April 2007 shows that just 63% of Americans say a great deal or a good amount can be done. McAllister says, "Canadians expect Canada to be a world leader when it comes to solving environmental problems". The pollster cautions that this means higher expectations to environmental performance and greater potential to disappoint when these expectations are not met.

D. Paul Emond, "The Greening of Environmental Law"

(1991) 36 McGill L.J. 742

Environmental law has changed dramatically over the last twenty years since modern environmental protection statutes were first enacted in Canada. While the word "greening" is perhaps somewhat over-used, it does, in my view, describe the stages through which environmental law has "progressed" over this period, and the levels of consciousness or frustration through which environmental counsel have moved. This paper organize[s] the development of environmental law into three stages of consciousness. The labels that best describe each stage are: symbolic regulation; preventive regulation; and mutual or co-operative problem-solving.

While there are a variety of ways in which one might trace evolving perceptions of pollution and legal responses to those changing perceptions, I believe that both fit nicely into the three distinct stages noted above. Each stage is characterized by a unique perception or definition of the problem and that in turn has prompted a particular response. Furthermore, each response has encouraged a unique form of participation from the principal actors — the regulatory departments, the corporations and the public interest groups. . . . The stages are not mutually exclusive. All three overlap as one set of perceptions and definitions fades into another. Not all jurisdictions have adopted similar approaches to solving environmental problems, although I believe that all are moving slowly or will be forced to move towards the third, "greener", more enlightened and more effective approach to the issues of pollution and environmental degradation.

Stage One: Symbolic Regulation

. . . The focus at this point in the regulatory cycle is on the obvious — smoke — stacks spewing black smoke into the sky, or outfall pipes discharging fibrous sludge into lakes and rivers. Without trying to belittle these early regulatory efforts, this form of regulation follows a predictable pattern. First, the regulation usually responds to either an environmental "catastrophe" such as an Exxon Valdez or to recent revelations about consumption practices and impending environmental doom. The Club of Rome painted an especially vivid picture in 1972 of the environmental nightmare that lay ahead unless governments intervened to curb growth and promote conservation. Notwithstanding the rhetorical outrage of the public and crusading legislators, the regulatory legislation that followed was flawed. It invariably vested enormous discretion in the regulator and thus laid the foundation for a process in which the enthusiasm and zeal of the optimistic regulator could be converted into the comfortable working relationship of the cynical environmental manager. Dependent on the regulated for information and legitimacy, both the regulator and the regulated had no real option other than to strike a symbiotic balance in which each contributed to the political well being of the other.

Failures of Symbolic Regulation

The structural problems with these early approaches to pollution control can be summarized in the following way. First, the process is reactive rather than anticipatory. Like the courts, the regulatory mechanisms do not "kick in" until a problem has been identified. By then, most regulation comes too late to solve all but the simplest of problems. Secondly, the process generally lacks legitimacy. By assuming that "the government" speaks for the public; by excluding public interest participation, the process is perceived as being little more than symbolic reassurance for an apprehensive and increasingly cynical public. Environmental regulation has become a convenient phrase to describe a cosy relationship in which industry makes relatively minor reductions in their pollution in return for government approval of their activities. A third problem is that as site specific and technical regulation increases, liability begins to shift from the regulated to the regulator. Ultimately, industry is able to demand that government set the regulatory standards and write the specifications for the pollution control equipment. If those standards are met, the fault then lies with the standard and hence with those who set the standard, not with the polluter. The fourth problem is that the definition of the problem — market and technological failures destines the regulators to define success in terms of technological fixes and market adjustments. Neither definition, however, addresses the underlying social problems that have lead to pollution. Finally, knowledge about the problem is growing in more or less direct proportion to the level of regulatory effort, with the result that the problem is continually being redefined in response to increased regulatory effort. Regulatory solutions — usually expressed in terms of maximum permissable levels of pollutants — are obsolete almost as soon as the standard is announced. Finding a solution is like shooting at a moving target; with the trigger attached to the target. Each new regulatory initiative changes society's perception of the problem and the solution. The result? A strategy focused on solving yesterday's problems that is just not working.

Stage Two: Preventive Regulation

Both the pollution problem and its perceived causes change as society moves into a second level of environmental consciousness. The problem is no longer described as "gross pollution" — blackened skies and sludge-filled northern lakes — it is now more subtle and insidious, and less obvious. Perhaps the most frightening aspect of this new order of pollution relates to what has come to be described as "exquisite toxics" — odourless, colourless, tasteless and deadly substances, such as dioxins, P.C.B.s and furans. The problem is often described as one of "environmental risk" and surfaces as the deadly toll that is documented in epidemiological studies exposing birth defects, allergies and mutations. Many pollutants are bio-accumulative. Others are relatively harmless on their own but when released into the environment combine with other toxins to create a deadly synergy.

Another dimension of the problem centres around what has traditionally been called land use planning or resource allocation decisions. At one level, these planning problems are described by the neighbourhood battle cry of "Not in My Backyard" (N.I.M.B.Y.). At another level they are described by the persistent and unrelenting opposition to cutting last stands of old growth forests, to committing last wild rivers to hydro-electric development, or to despoiling significant natural landscape with transmission facilities. Both types of decisions are irreversible, at least in the short to medium term, and both involve long term impacts, with relatively little opportunity to remediate.

. . . . .

Failures of Preventive Regulation

While preventive regulation is clearly an improvement over earlier regulatory efforts, this approach continues to suffer from many of the earlier problems. It continues to rely far too heavily on an adjudicative model of dispute resolution: adjudication is used to fashion environmental policy; adjudication is used to put policies, to the extent that they are ever expressed, into effect; and, of course, adjudication, in the form of prosecutions, is used to enforce policy. There is little opportunity for the parties to seek out creative, innovative solutions. In fact, given the uncertainty and unpredictability of the process, the incentives are all in the opposite direction. Proponents attempt to overwhelm opponents with enormous quantities of largely irrelevant information, and opponents cross-examine witnesses on every conceivable issue. One side hopes to win through exhaustion and attrition; the other, by stumbling across the "fatal flaw" in the proponent's case. The resources consumed in this "charade" are so great that environmental assessments are saved for the "mega project", leaving the vast majority of problems to be dealt with through the less comprehensive, and often ineffectual, approval process.

A further failure of the preventive approach is that because it loads up the approval process for new projects with elaborate assessment and hearing requirements, there is a built-in bias in favour of the status quo. In one sense, this is environmentally sound. Procedures that slow down the rush toward new activities by requiring a sober second thought cannot help but benefit the environment. On the other hand, to the extent that the process prefers old problems such as leaking toxic waste disposal sites, to new solutions, it imposes an enormous cost on the environment.

Finally, recent amendments to the traditional environmental protection statutes have done much to eliminate the last vestiges of the cozy relationship between the regulator and the regulated. While this is certainly to be applauded, there is now growing concern in corporate Canada that increased prosecutorial activity undermines any incentive to work cooperatively with government and the scientific community to solve environmental problems. Few still seek a "sweet deal" from governments. What responsible corporations now want is recognition that there are no simple solutions to pollution problems and that society's resources should be deployed to find solutions, not fight over alternatives.

Stage Three: Co-operative Problem-Solving

. . . Not much has worked very well in the environmental protection field up to this point. Granted there have been some notable successes, but the general consensus seems to be that we are slipping further and further behind. The problem is that the approach has generally been wrong. It has proceeded from an adversarial, competitive, rights-oriented model that was destined to siphon off creative energies in a contest of rights regulated only by the logic of justice and due process. The focus has been on defining rights and fine-tuning the dispute resolution process, rather than on solving environmental problems. What is needed is a new model that will redirect these energies toward practical solutions to real environmental problems. This model must be based on principles that emphasize interdependence, connectedness, respect, obligation, and co-operative approaches to problem-solving.

Problems and Prospects for Co-operative Problem-Solving

Any call for a new co-operative approach to solving environmental problems must address several problems or concerns. One concern relates to the danger that mediation, with its emphasis on accommodation and compromise, will deter large-scale structural changes in political and societal institutions, that only court adjudication can accomplish, and that it will thus serve the interests of the powerful against the disadvantaged?

A second concern might be expressed in terms of the relationship between process and result. Is it correct to assume, for example, that environmental disputes can be resolved through a focus on dispute resolution process(es)? Is the attempt to find a better process misplaced? At some point, one is bound to become sceptical about the ability of seemingly "fair" processes to sanction and legitimize "wrong" results. Related to the general question about the role of process in solving more specific environmental problems is the question about the role of negotiation and co-operative problem solving. Negotiation presupposes compromise. And yet, as environmental issues are increasingly defined in terms of values and ethics — neither of which may be susceptible to compromise — there is some doubt about just how far negotiation can respond to the value demands of environmentalists.

Third, as has already been noted above, this approach to dispute resolution presupposes a group of practitioners with a different orientation from those who practice in the judicial system. The result of the lawyer's orientation and the litigation paradigm on which it is based is that "lawyers tend not to recognize mediation as a viable means of reaching a solution; and worse, they regard the kinds of unique solutions that mediation can produce as threatening to the best interests of their clients". Until lawyers accept a legitimate role for a co-operative approach to problem-solving, environmental regulation will not move forward to generate the creative, innovative solutions we so urgently need.

Notwithstanding these challenges, the prospects for this co-operative approach to solving environmental problems are very exciting indeed. Government, however, must take a far more creative and pro-active role in terms of facilitating such an approach to resolving environmental disputes — perhaps to the point of legislatively mandating negotiation and mediation.

Conclusion

By and large, this paper has focused on process. It has attempted to describe the correlation between a problem — or more precisely the way in which a problem is defined — and the process or processes for resolving that problem. Thus, regulation — initially symbolic regulation — describes a process response to the problem of market and technological failure. Similarly, environmental assessments and environmental audits are processes for anticipating irreversible environmental problems. Finally, negotiation and co-operative problem-solving are ways of addressing and solving highly complex, interdependent, multi-party environmental problems. The first two processes are largely, but not exclusively, adversarial in nature and assume that solutions will emerge from a clash of rights — that is, the right to participate in economic activity versus the right to a clean environment. The third, however, follows from the apparently novel premise that we are all in this mess together — that we are all part of the problem and thus we must all be part of the solution.

What is the role of law in all of this? Clearly, the plethora of new statutes and regulations suggests a key role. Laws, however, do not solve problems. Indeed, it sometimes seems that environmental problems are growing at more or less the same rate as new laws are being passed. Laws create a complex of rights, obligations, liabilities, incentives and disincentives — a framework within which parties can or cannot solve problems. What environmental laws must now do is: (1) recognize the legitimacy of negotiation, mediation and other innovative means of problem-solving; (2) establish a regime of rights and obligations that ensures that all parties are able to participate effectively in the process; and (3) recognize the limits of co-operative problem-solving.

Notes and Questions

1. In this piece, authored almost twenty years ago, Emond envisages progress towards a model in which law facilitates co-operative problem solving to tackle then current and newly emerging environmental challenges. This chronological model progressively more sophisticated and effective forms of environmental regulation emerging over time.

2. Do you agree with main features and assumptions of his analysis? To what extent, has his vision been borne out? Has the context of the challenges confronting environmental regulation changed in key ways or has it remained essentially the same as when the article was first published?

3. In an article published only a few years later, M'Gonigle *et al.* offer a contrasting view of the nature of and challenges confronting environmental law, contending that existing environmental regulation in Canada for the most part is characterized by what they term "permissive regulation". Portraying this is a "paradigm in crisis", they argue the way ahead is to take uncertainty seriously by transitioning to a model of regulation that focuses on "preventative design". As you read extracts from this piece, consider whether and to what extent we have moved in this direction. Consider also, whether and to what extent Emond and M'Gonigle *et al.* can be said to concur in the either the diagnosis or prescription of what was ailing Canadian environmental law at the time these articles were written.

R. Michael M'Gonigle, T. Lynne Jamieson, Murdoch K. McAllister & Randall M. Peterman, "Taking Uncertainty Seriously: From Permissive Regulation to Preventative Design in Environmental Decision Making"

(1994) 32 Osgoode Hall L.J. 99

In the past decade, the growing scale and impact of the industrial use of hazardous substances have raised concerns in Canada and around the world. After decades of widespread usage, compounds once thought to be harmless, like polychlorinated biphenyls (PCBs), dioxins, and chloro-fluorocarbons (CFCs), have become household names because of increasing evidence of their serious and, in some cases, potentially catastrophic effects. Many industrial activities and by-products have followed a pattern of an initial judgement of safety, followed by uncertainty and circumstantial evidence of harm, acrimonious debate, and finally hard evidence of detrimental effects. With the dramatic increase in recent years in the use of artificial chemical substances, a regulatory approach that permits specific discharges of industrial by-products, subject to an "acceptable" limit that is based on uncertain scientific information, may no longer be adequate for assuring acceptable environmental quality.

. . . Of particular concern is the pattern of scientific inference and legal regulation that underlies our current control strategy for industrial pollution. This pattern has focused largely on what we know, rather than what we do not know; that is, it has emphasized cause-and-effect relationships that can be demonstrated between substances and the environment, and not relationships that may exist but which, despite extensive scientific testing, remain hidden. This pattern applies to more than just toxic substances. Failure to detect an effect when one exists is a common problem associated with the widely used, discharge-based regulatory approach in Canada, the approach that we call "permissive regulation". Although this problem also pervades other sectors, such as fisheries management and timber harvesting, it has been rarely acknowledged by scientists, legislators, environmental decision makers, or the judiciary in Canada. In contrast, a new regulatory approach oriented to the character of the whole industrial process, an approach that we call "preventative design", is being developed in other jurisdictions to deal with precisely this problem. . . .

Permissive Regulation: The Paradigm in Crisis

Underlying the legislation and common law described above is a way of thinking about the control of toxic pollution that is largely taken for granted. This is the "paradigm" of permissive regulation, which permits discharges into, or activities in, a receiving environment, some of which may occur only to a specified limit which purportedly reflects "safe" levels. The problems associated with the paradigm are evident in the common but ill-considered and incorrect assumptions about how the environment assimilates waste, how scientific research is done, how reliable the results of such research are, and how regulatory agencies operate. These problems undermine the paradigm on both theoretical and practical levels, and lead to growing criticism of permissive regulation worldwide.

The Assumption of Assimilative Capacity

The permissive regulation paradigm is based on the philosophy of what might be called the "assimilative capacity" theory of pollution control. Under this theory, "allowable" levels of polluting behaviours, or levels of discharge into the receiving environment, are permitted in accordance with the central assumption that the environment has an enduring capacity to assimilate these prescribed levels of pollutants without harm. With the increasing experience of the environmental "surprises" referred to above, this approach has, in recent years, come under mounting international criticism by governments, non-governmental organizations, and international regulatory bodies.

. . . Muldoon and Valiante have made a similar critique in the Canadian context and point to five structural changes needed in the regulatory framework. These changes require the shift from: (1) a medium-specific to cross-media approach, (2) a waste-management to a reduction-of- toxic-use-at-the-source approach, (3) a focus on allowable concentrations to one on absolute load reductions, (4) point-source to non-point-source pollution control, and (5) inter-jurisdictional regulation to an ecosystem approach.

The Assumption of Scientific Knowledge

Underlying the assumption of assimilative capacity is a corresponding assumption that we are, in some way, basing our regulations and allowable limits on firm scientific knowledge. It is not necessary to review in detail the statistical and research problems discussed above, but it is useful here to consider how these problems restrict our ability to actually protect environmental quality on a scientific basis. Indeed, the range of problems are so great that the very character of the regulatory process as "scientific" must be called into question.

First, is the sheer scale of the regulatory problem. There are presently some 30,000 to 45,000 industrial emissions and effluents that remain unassessed with regard to toxicity, and between 500 and 1,000 new chemicals that are introduced each year. When regulation occurs on a substance-by-substance basis (as is common with the current permissive approach), a huge diversity of chemicals necessarily escapes regulation, including a large number of new substances introduced annually. This is so, at least partly, because the amount of testing required to determine whether a chemical is dangerous enough to regulate is prohibitively expensive and time-consuming

In addition to the huge number of chemicals in use, it is difficult to set criteria for determining which of those substances require priority action. The generally accepted criteria are toxicity, persistence, and bioaccumulation. However, because of the concerns discussed earlier, these are rendered quite subjective as guides to identifying what to regulate and what thresholds of harm should be set. [*Ed note*: For further on the process, see discussion of CEPA *infra* this chapter.]

Testing has historically focused on acute toxicity, rather than on sub-lethal, chronic, or cumulative effects, so that the database of scientific knowledge in the latter areas is extremely limited. Yet, as one critic noted in relation to Canadian regulations under the CEPA, for many highly toxic substances, "it is their chronic effects and their potential to cause severe damage over the longer term at sub-lethal levels of exposure that is cause for concern and serious regulatory prohibitions". At the final stages of the regulatory process, without such data on regulated substances, prosecutors trying to establish environmental damage must rely on the testimony of toxicological and epidemiological expert witnesses, whose testimony is based on a variety of scientific studies. Unfortunately, these studies deal with "issues of causality in terms of statistical probabilities [and] [t]raditionally, the courts have been reluctant to accept probabilistic evidence as showing causation".

It is in this realm of hidden relationships that surprising results are so often experienced, given the temporal and spatial latencies associated with so many cause-effect relationships. For example, in the case of carcinogenesis, the latency period between exposure to a cancer-causing substance and the appearance of a tumour may range between five and forty years. . . . Chronic effects that result from long-term, low-level exposure to toxic or hazardous substances often go undetected until considerable damage has been done. Even when the potential harm is large but subject to some uncertainty, or when the proximate sources of the damage are not easily established, or when the delay between exposure and effect is large, regulation may be delayed pending the availability of more conclusive evidence.

In this light, it is not surprising that the courts have often cited intervening causes, remoteness, and foreseeability as reasons to deny liability in such cases. This is especially a problem in industrialized areas, where several point sources of the same or different pollutants may contribute to the causation of the same disease. The denial of a claim on such bases may occur "even though it is generally accepted that excessive exposure to the pollutant is unhealthy". Whatever the obstacle, the courts' denial of liability in these terms points to the inherent difficulties of demonstrating causation when spatial and temporal latencies exist. [*Ed note*: See further discussion in Chapter 2.]

The Assumption of Effective Regulation

The assumption of assimilative capacity when science is uncertain has led to serious practical problems for government agencies in the implementation of permissive regulatory strategies. For instance, the success of any regulatory system based on a substance-by-substance approach is dependent on access of the regulatory agency to high levels of funding, expert staffing, and sufficient research and enforcement facilities. The vast number of chemicals to be tested for toxicity and monitored in industrial effluents, in addition to the large number and types of individual industrial operations subject to regulation, create difficult practical problems for regulatory agencies. For example, in place of independent government testing and monitoring programmes, regulatory agencies often rely on industry research and even self-policing. This puts the government at a disadvantage because-the industry is then "uniquely well supplied with information on product and process characteristics, abatement technology and costs, production and effluent volumes, and numerous other variables". Even where industry testing is honestly undertaken, agencies may not have sufficient resources or access to the raw data to allow them to evaluate properly the experimental design and the statistical power of the results.

The combination of the above factors — the problematic assumption of assimilative capacity, the limited scientific understanding of environmental effects, and constrained agency resources — has created a situation in which the environment is effectively treated as a free good. This leads to externalization of the true costs of industrial production through the degradation of environmental quality and an increase in public health risks. Yet, in attempting to correct this after the fact, private citizens and public regulators may confront significant transaction costs, including the costs of litigation, negotiation, and regulation. Avoiding these costs leads to economically inefficient outcomes which may favour polluters. For example, where a Crown prosecutor weighs the costs of litigation against its potential benefits, pollution may not be penalized until the harm to individuals exceeds their transaction costs. In Canada, this situation has encouraged a strategy based on negotiated, rather than enforced, compliance between industry and government.

Negotiations between the stakeholders in environmental regulation (government, industry, and the public) as the basis for setting standards may be an effective approach, so long as all affected parties are involved in the process and the ability of government to force technological development is not compromised . . . Negotiation as the basis for ensuring compliance is, however, even more problematic, as it may politicize what should be a predictable enforcement process, ultimately making compliance voluntary. This tends to be the case where a continuous negotiating process costs less for the industry than actually complying with existing regulations. In British Columbia, this strategy led to the widespread granting of exceptions to compliance. . . .

In conclusion, the regulatory paradigm underlying Canadian pollution legislation is critically weakened by a number of problems: its assumption of the environment's assimilative capacity, its failure to acknowledge the implications of scientific uncertainty, and its unrealistic expectations of regulatory agencies. In short, such a system of regulation does not ensure long-term environmental quality as it was designed to do but, instead, inefficiently employs agency resources to facilitate the externalization of the environmental and social costs of industrial production.

Precedents for Incremental Reform

In response to the difficulties experienced with permissive regulation, many national governments and international regulatory bodies have begun to shift from the control of pollution to varying degrees of pollution reduction. In addition to alternative approaches, however, the potential exists for incremental reforms within the framework of permissive regulation itself.

Lowering the Standard of Proof

A number of precedents exist in common law tort actions where the standard of proof has been lowered to protect environmental values and public health. American courts have shown a particular willingness to accept uncertain scientific information as sufficient to establish a fact on "the preponderance of the evidence".

Creation of Risk as Evidence

Since many types of harm that have potentially severe consequences are also characterized as having a low probability of occurrence, application of the traditional standard of proof may lead to downplaying the likelihood and thus the potentially high costs of the defendant's actions on society. Lowering the standard of proof, by accepting evidence of "creation of risk", allows the courts to make decisions which minimize judicial subjectivity when confronted with uncertain proof of causation to avoid serious harm which may have only a small probability of occurrence; and, at the same time, to achieve broader societal values. [*Ed note*: See further discussion in Chapter 2.]

In effect, risk-benefit analysis alters what needs to be proven by relieving the plaintiff of demonstrating that the occurrence of harm is more probable than not. Instead, the plaintiff need only show both that there exists a mere risk of harm, and that the costs of that risk to the plaintiff outweigh the benefits to the defendant. Similarly, in enforcing regulatory standards, substituting a "risk-benefit analysis" approach for a damage-oriented, punitive approach could effectively lower the standard of proof by allowing the plaintiff to establish merely that the expected costs of potential environmental degradation that could be induced are greater than the expected benefits. A common approach to calculating the expected costs and benefits of proposed activities is to measure the possible cost of environmental degradation multiplied by the probability of occurrence, against the expected benefit of a new technology or development multiplied by the probability that there will be a benefit.

[Problems in implementing this approach include . . .] estimating costs and benefits as many of the variables in a risk assessment are unquantifiable, and the probabilities of occurrence of different outcomes, as well as the range of possible outcomes, may not be known with any degree of certainty. In addition, treatment of intangible costs, intergenerational effects, and synergistic and cumulative effects assessment are difficult, given the uncertainties involved.

Despite these limitations, the risk-benefit approach has important implications for the Canadian environmental regulatory framework, which have not allowed for the "creation of risk" as adequate proof of an offence. For instance, causing harm to the receiving environment is not directly prohibited under the B.C. *Waste Management Act* [now the *Environmental Management Act*], even though this may be the intent of the Act. The focus instead is on preventing unauthorized discharges which cause pollution. In this regard, the prosecution must establish that the discharge fits the statutory definition of pollution — "the presence in the environment of substances or contaminants that substantially alter or impair the usefulness of the environment" — rather than just demonstrating the creation of a risk as sufficient proof of this element of the offence.

Similarly, for offences under sections 35(1) and 36(3) of the *Fisheries Act* the standard of proof would be lowered if it were sufficient to establish that an accused's activity put a fish habitat at risk. Indeed, the standard and burden of proof required to establish elements of an offence under the *Fisheries Act* have been somewhat relaxed through the use of inferences. It is yet to be seen whether risk of harm will be sufficient to regulate substances under

CEPA, although the phrase "may have an immediate or long-term harmful effect on the environment" . . .

The Right to Environmental Quality

In the United States, a number of states have enacted legislation that specifically seeks to secure a right to environmental quality by lowering the standard of proof and, on some issues, by shifting the burden onto the defendant. Similar to the judicial acceptance of "creation of risk", acts like the *Michigan Environmental Protection Act* alter the standard and burden of proof rules. The plaintiff may establish a prima facie case by showing that the defendant's actions are merely likely to harm the environment. The burden of proof then shifts to the defendant, who must show that his or her conduct was reasonable "by way of an affirmative defence, that there is no feasible and prudent alternative . . . and that such conduct is consistent with the promotion of the public heath, safety and welfare in light of the state's paramount concern for the protection of its natural resources". The MEPA defines a violation as the "impairment" of a "natural resource", but the Act does not establish a threshold which must be met by the plaintiff, thus making it possible for the courts to apply the statute flexibly. The MEPA also allows the court to "determine the validity, applicability and reasonableness of the standard", and, if the court decides that a standard is deficient, it may "direct the adoption of a standard approved and specified by the court". *[Ed note*: See discussion of an analogous law reform proposal for Canada in Chapter 5.]

Establishing the affirmative defence may be onerous for the defendant. Abrams argues that "[i]f a low level of environmental harm satisfies the threshold, defendants will be forced to explore alternative courses of action in a greater range of cases". If so, this could be a significant step toward a more preventative and less legalistic approach to environmental protection. In assessing alternatives, economic criteria must not determine the outcome. Rather, it should be shown that there are unique non-economic problems which preclude the selection of other alternatives.

This single technique of emphasizing alternative processes encourages the courts to make innovative decisions in spite of scientific uncertainty about causal relationships, thus reducing the potential costs to society and to the environment . . . Such an approach has not yet made an appearance in Canadian legislation.

Shifting the Burden of Proof

A few common law precedents exist in which the traditional allocation of the burden of proof has been reversed so that the defendant had to prove that he was not the cause of the injury. The theory of "alternate liability" applies in situations in which there is more than one possible defendant or cause of harm. As discussed above, the negligence of the two defendants had been established, but the plaintiff could not prove which one was at fault and, therefore, caused the injury. The court reversed the burden so as to require each defendant to absolve himself by showing on a balance of probabilities that he was not to be held responsible for the injury. In other words, the defendants were given the task of proving that their actions were not harmful.

The applicability of the alternative liability rule to environmental regulatory issues is, however, limited since it requires that harm already have occurred, that there is a proven and limited number of possible causes of the harm, and that the negligence of the defendants has been established. The overall burden on the prosecution is thus still high, especially in quasi-criminal regulatory environmental offences where the higher standard of proof beyond a reasonable doubt is still applied. In such cases, each defendant would only need to raise a doubt that points to one of the others as the cause of harm to make it difficult to convict any of the defendants.

Going beyond the alternative liability rule is the common law tort standard of strict liability where "[a]nyone having care or control of a substance likely to do harm [is] to be held strictly liable for the consequences should it escape". Strict liability, which does not reverse the burden of proof but removes the burden of establishing the defendant's negligence, has been explicitly recognized in some environmental protection acts in Canada. For instance, under the "*Ontario Spills Act*" the costs of clean-up are subject to absolute liability rules, and strict liability is applied to loss or damage from spills. Plaintiffs are not required to show that the defendant was at fault or was negligent in allowing the spill, but the "due diligence defence" is open to the defendant once the offence has been shown: see *R. v. Sault Ste. Marie* . . .

While the strict liability offence does shift some of the legal burden onto the polluter, the extensive investigation and the use of expert witnesses required to rebut the due diligence defence add to the expense and difficulty of prosecuting a strict liability offence. [Also] strict liability offences [are vulnerable to be] challenged under section 11(d) of the *Canadian Charter of Rights and Freedoms*, which provides the right "to be presumed innocent until proven guilty", and under section 7 of the *Charter*, the "right to life, liberty and security of the person . . . in accordance with the principles of fundamental justice".: [*Ed note*: See further discussion in Chapter 5.]

Structural Reform Through Preventative Design

The lack of judicial innovation in Canada to overcome intractable problems of establishing causation is an example of the impediments to effective environmental protection within the existing regulatory and judicial framework. More important still are the technical and scientific problems that regulators who rely on "end-of-pipe" solutions face daily. . . . Thus, for example, the solution for improving local air quality, tall stacks, was a major source of acid rain. Similarly, technologies to remove heavy metals from effluent streams or particulate matter from tall stacks merely transferred the pollution to landfills in the form of sludges or fly-ash, which may then leach into the surrounding water table.

Overcoming both the inherent contradictions of permissive regulation and the escalating pollution problem requires a new regulatory approach which does not merely treat waste once it has been generated, but deals with it at its source through new production processes. A range of terms have been used to describe this new approach, such as waste minimization, waste reduction, toxics use reduction, best available technology, and clean production.

Several precedents exist for such structural reforms, and an examination of them provides us with a detailed model for a "preventative design" strategy. Such a strategy takes a "precautionary approach" . . . by creating a presumption of harm and translates this presumption into a comprehensive new procedure and administrative framework for regulation of the entire production process.

Precedents for Structural Reform

Historically, initial demands for a more precautionary approach arose from the deteriorating state of the shared rivers and enclosed seas of northern Europe. In the mid-1980s, new concepts such as "low waste/non-waste and low-emission/non-emission technologies" were being considered to deal with an emerging crisis. A number of national governments, notably those of Germany and the Netherlands, began to move toward a more preventative or "precautionary" approach with new legislation that sought to encourage waste prevention and clean technology. These goals have been promoted through licensing and siting requirements for waste management facilities, operational standards, and the wide use of economic incentives such as pollution charges and direct financial support for research, development, and implementation of so-called clean technologies.

... in the United States, early signs of a new approach were evident by the mid-1980s. The 1984 *Hazardous and Solid Waste Amendments to the Resource Conservation and Recovery Act* outlined a national policy on waste management, which stated that "wherever feasible, the generation of hazardous waste, is to be reduced or eliminated as expeditiously as possible". Included in the amendments were requirements that firms using or manufacturing toxics must report their efforts to reduce the volume and toxicity of waste prior to treatment ...

This cause has been taken up most aggressively at the state, rather than the federal, level, with the 1989 Massachusetts *Toxic Use Reduction Act* setting the U.S. national standard. In response to substantial public interest pressure from the National Toxics Campaign, the new legislation establishes a statewide goal of reducing toxic waste generation by 50 per cent by 1997.

In October 1990, the American federal government passed the *Pollution Prevention Act* which also sets out a national policy on pollution prevention and source reduction. The Act is intended to improve Environmental Protection Agency (EPA) data collection systems and the dissemination of information regarding the reduction of toxic emissions in all media, and to assist the government in providing information on, and technical assistance for, source reduction. Under the *Pollution Prevention Act*, the Administrator of the EPA will establish an office that will develop and implement a strategy to promote source reduction; investigate methods of coordinating, streamlining, and improving public access to data collected under existing environmental statutes; develop an inventory of existing data; and consider developing consistent report formats, nomenclature and data storage and retrieval systems ...

Both conceptually and in practice, Canadian legislative policy lags far behind these initiatives. Internationally, the International Joint Commission (of which Canada is a co-member with the United States) has, since 1978, articulated in its Great Lakes Water Quality Agreement the goal of "zero discharge" for persistent toxic pollutants. To help achieve this, in 1990, the Commission called for a reverse onus provision so that a chemical should be assumed to be harmful unless demonstrated otherwise. Nationally and provincially, however, despite the fact that 3.5 million tonnes of hazardous wastes are generated annually by Canadian industry, "there is neither an explicit national policy nor legislative provisions promoting source reduction". Meanwhile, many provincial governments remain within the old regulatory paradigm ...

Conclusion

In contrast to the piecemeal [Canadian] approach to reforming the present paradigm of permissive regulation, the revolution in regulatory strategies, evident in a diverse number of multilateral agencies, state and national governments, points to a new paradigm which has gained wide international acceptance. Canadian legislation, regulatory action, and environmental decision making have yet to recognize this dramatic shift. To facilitate this transition in Canada, a new approach is needed.

This new approach is that of preventative design. The permissive model is no longer viable because it cannot work well in the face of the large uncertainties presently found. Its failure demands a comprehensive rethinking and restructuring of existing legislation, as well as a basic reorientation of judicial decision making. Standards must no longer be set without the recognition of uncertainty. Instead, the inescapable presence of uncertainty should lead to a shift of the regulatory burden onto those seeking to utilize, and profit from, our common environment's questionable assimilative capacity ...

Rigorous science recognizes the need to account for uncertainty. The application of statistical power analysis to test design is a crucial step, and this formal recognition of uncertainty can become the foundation of the precautionary principle and the paradigm of preventative design. This model of regulation now has precedents to follow . . . These precedents point to the importance of new management techniques (economic penalties are an essential tool) and agencies oriented to technology-forcing and industrial design. As the review of American legislation concludes, "[g]overnment action is needed to provide incentives and information to fundamentally change industry's focus on pollution control towards toxics use reduction". Similarly, the judiciary must be more cognizant of the implications of scientific uncertainty in order to respond realistically and imaginatively to problems of causation. Reallocating the burden of proof from the environmental management agencies or public to the polluter, and setting appropriate standards of proof, are important ways to begin.

Notes and Questions

1. The preceding article has been excerpted at some length due to the wide range of relevant issues it canvasses. M'Gonigle *et al.* make the case both for incremental and structural reforms. Many of the incremental reforms for which they advocate are aimed at remedying perceived weaknesses or defects in common law approaches to environmental regulation. Ultimately, however, they contend that the cause of structural reform must be championed through the enactment of national legislation that takes "uncertainty seriously" through adoption of a precautionary approach to environmental protection. To what extent have we seen incremental or, indeed, structural reforms of the type they promoted? What factors (constitutional, institutional, ideological) account for the progress (or lack of it) that we have witnessed?

2. An important phenomenon that neither of the preceding articles anticipate or discuss that took centre-stage in environmental law debates during the mid-1990s and continues to hold considerable sway concerns the role of market forces and civil society organizations in "governing" the environment. A key feature of this trend was a growing sense that enhancing environment outcomes required new ways of thinking about the role of government.

Increasingly, it was argued that traditional *government*-centred prescriptions (often termed command and control approaches) were less likely to succeed than *governance*-based ones premised in the idea that businesses, consumers, and civil society organizations were often better positioned to leverage change. The merits of this emerging governance model of environmental stewardship, it is argued, are especially compelling in terms of ensuring that environmental leadership and best practices are recognized and rewarded: on this theme, see Gunningham and Sinclair *Leaders and Laggards* (2002). Later, in Part III we canvass the origins and nature of increasing influential approach to environmental protection. In the next Part, however, we lay the conceptual foundation for that discussion by introducing some key concepts and terminology relevant to environmental standard setting.

Part II — Environmental Standard-Setting and Forms of Standard

Environmental Standard Setting

Before attempting to assess the nature and relative merits of differing *forms* of standard, it is instructive to consider how standards are developed in general terms. To do this, we will consider how environmental protection standards, particularly those in the pollution-control context, are developed. Standard setting is typically conceived of as a four-stage chronological process that consists of (1) setting an objective, (2) developing criteria, (3) establishing an ambient quality standard, and (4) defining an individualized operational standard. Ordinarily, as part of this final stage of the process, the government regulator will issue as licence or permit to a firm that will specify its compliance obligations. [As we shall discuss shortly, the form of standard embedded in such licences or permits can vary.] In the "command and control" terminology, that is often employed in this area of law, this permit or licence supplies the legal "command" which the regulated party is bound to obey. In Chapter 5, we will consider in some detail the "control" measures upon which government can rely to monitor and secure compliance with these commands. Below, however, we turn first to a more detailed description of the process by which environmental standards are set.

C. Tollefson, F. Gale & D. Haley, *Setting the Standard*
(UBC Press, 2008)

All standard-setting processes, whether undertaken by governments or private entities, should, in theory, proceed from a clear definition of the overarching outcome(s) that the regime exists to achieve. Defining these objectives is a quintessentially political choice, a judgment about values (Franson, Franson, and Lucas 1982). Typically, the objective will be stated in broad, categorical terms (i.e., securing safe drinking-water; protecting biodiversity). However, this is not always true. A case in point is the statement of objectives set out in the regulations recently enacted by the BC government to implement its new results-based forest practices legislation. For each of the different forest values (soils, timber, wildlife, biodiversity, and so on), the discrete objective is stated as being to conserve the value in question "without unduly reducing the supply of timber from BC forests" see *Forest and Range Practices Act*, s. 510.

Where the standard takes the form of hard law, the articulation of these threshold objectives will sometimes occur in legislation or, more often, by means of a legally enforceable regulation (as is the case with recently passed regulations under British Columbia's new results-based *Forest and Range Practices Act*). Where the standard is being developed by a non-governmental entity, these outcomes will usually form part of an organizational mission statement or code of practice . . .

Having identified the objective that a standard exists to protect, the next task is to identify the criteria by which to gauge whether that objective is being achieved or compromised. This is typically a daunting scientific undertaking. Whether the objective is safeguarding potable water or protecting ungulate winter habitat, the range of potential threats, and the nature of the interaction amongst these threats, can be highly complex. Inevitably, therefore, there are knowledge gaps in the "dose-response" relationship . . . As a result, a pragmatic approach is frequently adopted and criteria are formulated on the basis of a limited number of parameters (i.e., threats, risks, etc.) of greatest and/or most obvious concern. . . .

The third generic step in the process is the formulation of ambient quality standards. This process has both a technical and a political dimension. It involves taking the data generated by the criteria-identification process and undertaking an evaluation that considers how, in light of this data, the objective(s) identified can best be achieved, taking account of the costs, benefits, and risk acceptability associated with setting the standard at different levels. Identification of the ambient standard is often thought of in terms of the receiving environment's carrying capacity. It can take various forms . . . It may be expressed in the form of an upper limit on the mass or concentration of harmful substances in the receiving environment, or it may, alternatively, prescribe the lower limit of desired substances. When governments engage in this type of analysis (many Canadian governments do not), ambient standards are typically established informally in the form of policy.

The final stage in a standard-setting process involves moving from a statement of the desired ambient outcome to creating standards that define the permissible behaviour of the individual party the standard is purporting to regulate. In the context of point-source air and water pollution, this is typically referred to as a "discharge standard". Once again, this process is both scientific/technical and political, requiring a complex assessment of both the incremental impact of the activity being regulated and the costs/benefits and compliance issues associated with different standard prescriptions. Governments frequently express standards of this kind in pollution permits adapted to suit the particular circumstances of the applicant and the airshed or watershed within which they are proposing to operate.

In Canada, the prevailing practice with respect to air- and water-pollution permits has been to express discharge standards in terms of an upper limit for the mass or concentration of specified substances that the permit holder is entitled to release into the environment over a designated period of time. In contrast, the United States has adopted a distinctly different approach to permitting. There, in recognition of the difficulties associated with individually calibrating discharge standards in a manner that does not compromise ambient standards, the dominant legislative approach has been to issue technology-based permits. Under this approach, the permissible level of discharge is defined with reference to the level of environmental protection the permit holder could achieve using the best available technology (BAT) — in this case, the best available pollution-control technology.

Forms of Standard

Regulators use three main forms of standard to influence behaviour. Before discussing their relative merits, it is worth offering some ideal-type definitions. *Performance-based standards* are intended to be a specific and measurable indicator of a desired objective to be achieved; they leave broad discretion as to how to achieve this objective to the regulated firm. In contrast, in their pure form, *technology-based standards* are silent about desired outcomes; instead, they specify a particular technology, input, or mode of operation that is thought to optimally promote the overall objective of the standard. Finally, *management-based standards* (also known as process-based standards) eschew specification of both outcomes and means, opting instead to promote achievement of identified policy objectives by obliging operators to undertake specified management-planning activities.

. . . in regulating air and water pollution, Canadian governments have tended to employ performance-based standards; their American counterparts have elected to use technology-based ones. Over the last two decades, considerable research has been carried out to examine the experience of using both forms of standard in these and other jurisdictions. In contrast, both the experience with, and the literature considering the efficacy of, management-based standards has been much sparser. A helpful way to conceive of the relationship between these three forms of standard has recently been offered by Coglianese and Lazar. They argue that, in developing standards, regulators can choose to intervene at various stages of a firm's production process: the planning stage, the acting stage, or the output stage. The goal of such intervention is to correct market failure by seeking to promote the production of social-good outputs (i.e., environmental protection) without unduly fettering the production of the private-good outputs (i.e., timber). As the Table below illustrates, management-based standards represent an intervention in a firm's planning processes; technology-based standards can be seen as an intervention in the operational or "acting" stage; and performance-based standards constitute an intervention at the output stage, specifying what social outputs must (or must not) be attained.

Stage of Production	**Planning**	**Acting**	**Outputs**
Form of Standard	Management-based	Technology-based	Performance-based

Source: adapted from Coglianese and Lazar (2003).

Prescriptiveness and Standard Form

A key feature of the debate over the relative merits of these three forms of standard is the often-asserted proposition that performance- and management-based approaches are superior to technology-based standards because they are less prescriptive. This "prescriptiveness" critique is seldom fully elaborated, but it appears to refer to the extent to which a particular form of regulation constrains firm actions and decisions while imposing additional (and potentially unnecessary) production costs. The above schemata helps demonstrate the fallacy of this critique. When they are seen as reflecting different "moments" for intervention in the production process, all three forms of standard are potentially prescriptive in the relevant sense. How prescriptive depends, in turn, more on the content as opposed to the form of the standard in question.

Although technology-based standards are clearly prescriptive in terms of production methods, they are notably non-prescriptive in terms of management planning and, more significantly, outcomes or outputs. Similarly, the prescriptiveness of management-based standards can vary widely, from a simple exhortation that operators implement a generic environmental management system, to a standard that tightly specifies the nature of planning to be undertaken and requires government signoff before production activity can proceed.

Performance-based standards also vary considerably in their prescriptiveness, Depending on whether the standard in question is loosely or tightly specified. The specificity of a standard in this regard is often closely related to whether the standard is qualitative or quantitative in nature. To illustrate, assume that the standard's objective is maintaining slope stability and preventing soil erosion. A qualitative performance standard could be framed so that it turns this desired outcome into a mandatory obligation by implicitly adding the words "thou shalt" (i.e., thou shalt maintain slope stability and prevent soil erosion). Conversely, the same outcome could be sought through the use of a quantitative performance standard framed as follows: "No tree felling shall take place on slopes that exceed 35 degrees". This latter formulation — clearly a performance-based standard — is, on its face, highly prescriptive in that it purports to override the manager's discretion as to where and when to log.

Arguably, by foreclosing the potential for a manager to seek to achieve the expressed objective (maintaining slope stability and preventing soil erosion), the quantitative standard is more prescriptive than management- or technology-based standards that could be crafted to secure the same goal. Under a management-based standard, where the slope in question was greater than thirty-five degrees, a requirement that the manager conduct slope stability tests or third-party assessments prior to logging might be triggered. Under such an approach, if the tests confirmed that logging could occur without compromising the slope stability or creating soil erosion, the manager would be at liberty to proceed. It is also possible to posit a technology-based standard that preserves a relatively broad scope of managerial autonomy. For example, such a standard could stipulate that logging can take place on slopes of over thirty-five degrees, but only if a specified mode of low-impact harvesting (i.e., helicopter logging) were employed.

Private Autonomy versus Certainty

The corollary of the prescriptiveness critique discussed above is the assertion that performance standards, relative to other forms of standard, are superior in terms of preserving private autonomy. The preceding hypothetical situation shows that this generalization is misleading. Performance standards can sometimes preserve private autonomy; however, the extent to which they do so will depend on the congruency between the objective that the standard exists to advance and the form of standard itself. The greater the congruency, the more discretion the regulated party will enjoy in determining how to meet the standard. Thus a performance standard that transforms the desired objective (stable slopes) into a generic mandatory obligation ("thou shalt protect slope stability") preserves much greater private autonomy than one that specifies a narrower or subsidiary goal (prohibiting or restricting logging on slopes of greater than a specified steepness). As a general proposition, therefore, qualitative performance standards rate much higher than quantitative ones in terms of private autonomy. Indeed, as we have argued, quantitative performance standards are often highly prescriptive.

It is important to recognize that preserving private autonomy comes at a price in terms of certainty that the promulgated standard will achieve the policy objective it exists to serve. In other words, all other things being equal, it can be argued that the more generic and imprecise the formulation of a performance standard, the higher the risk the objective of the standard will be compromised. Whether, and in what circumstances, the risks inherent in performance-based standards are worth the potential benefits in terms of promoting other values (such as reducing industry regulatory costs, promoting innovative practices, etc.) is a question that must be assessed on a case-specific basis. Relevant to this determination will be the nature and importance of the objective the standard exists to promote and the pervasiveness, severity, (ir)reversibility, and probability of the risk that the regulated activity will compromise this objective. Also relevant will be the circumstances, and particularly the compliance history, of the party being regulated. Different strategies may be advisable depending on whether the regulator's goal is to create incentives for industry leaders or, alternatively, to police the activities of their laggard counterparts: see Gunningham and Sinclair 2002.

Another set of issues relate to the "ownership of uncertainty" . . . Assuming we can assess who benefits and who loses from the uncertainty that some types of performance standard introduce, should the beneficiaries be called upon to bear a higher level of accountability in the event that an objective is compromised? In other words, should greater private accountability be the quid pro quo for greater private autonomy? Or should parties regulated under an open-ended performance standard be able to defend their failure to meet the standard by claiming "due diligence", as their counterparts regulated under more prescriptive regimes are able to do?

Protecting private autonomy by enacting a standard that confers broad managerial discretion to choose how compliance is to be achieved can also have a cost in terms of transparency and public participation. The move toward an approach under which managers are mandated to develop in-house strategies to meet the requirements of a pure performance standard inevitably leads to heavy reliance on complex, predictive models of performance. Even assuming members of the public are given access to this modelling information (which is by no means assured), their ability to effectively participate in regulatory decision making will decline as the complexity of the analysis increases. This professionalization of standard setting also has the potential to undermine the capacity for meaningful regulatory oversight by government or private standard-setting bodies, causing them to rely more heavily on third-party experts (e.g., academics, consultants, certifiers) or, alternatively, accepting on faith analyses provided by private managers.

Measuring, Evaluating, and Verifying Performance

It is broadly accepted that performance standards work best "when actual performance can be measured, evaluated and verified" . . . As we have noted, in standards where there is a close congruency between the objective to be achieved and the form of standard, uncertainty arises, with the result that measurement, evaluation, and verification of performance can be undermined.

To minimize this uncertainty (and enhance the potential for accurately measuring, evaluating, and verifying performance), one obvious option is to employ quantitative performance standards. This prospect raises its own questions. One set of questions concern what is being measured and to what extent it serves as a reliable indicator that the objective the standard exists to promote is being achieved. In theory, the most reliable quantitative indicator would be one that offers a direct measure of the condition of an ambient environmental value (i.e., ambient water or soil conditions; the continued viability of specified listed species in the area being logged). Because such ambient values are, by definition, affected by a variety of other natural and non-natural factors, however, quantitative performance standards are typically crafted so as to measure the incremental impact of the activity being regulated. They thus normally take the form of discharge or resource impact standards (i.e., they prescribe acceptable discharge limits or restrict logging to slopes of more than thirty-five degrees).

Even carefully crafted discharge standards do not, of course, eliminate uncertainty with respect to measuring whether the objective is being met. For instance, there will always be some uncertainty in what we referred to earlier as the dose-response relationship — in other words, the nature of the relationship between the behaviour the standard targets and the impact of that behaviour on the ambient environment. As well, because of the diversity of environments within which the activity being regulated occurs (of which forestry is a prime example), a generalized standard that may be consistent with the achievement of the objective in one context may not be appropriate in others. Indeed a one-size-fits-all quantitative performance standard can be under-protective of the desired objective in some contexts, and over-protective in others. Thus, under particularly sensitive soil conditions, logging on slopes of less than thirty-five degrees may well have significant environmental consequences. Conversely, where soil conditions are less sensitive, or if a low-impact logging method is used, it is plausible that harvesting could occur on slopes steeper than the standard prescribes without the objective of the standard being put in jeopardy.

There is also, in this context, the looming question of who is responsible for measuring, evaluating, and verifying performance. The logistical and resource challenges associated with these various tasks were a primary reason why, in first-generation environmental laws, the US government opted to employ a technology-based BAT approach. For similar reasons, many have been critical of the BC government's decision to replace the *Forest Practices Code* with results-based legislation, particularly given dramatic and ongoing budget cutbacks at the Ministry of Forests. The dilemma, of course, is that any potential gains in terms of the cost of regulatory oversight that might be achieved by moving toward a performance-based model are likely to be nullified if responsibility for measuring, evaluating, and verifying performance remains with the regulator. Indeed, many would argue that performance-based regulation, which offers the potential to reduce business costs, will actually lead to a significant increase in government administration costs if administered in a reasonably robust fashion. This is particularly so given the diversity of regulatory compliance arrangements that performance-based standards authorize.

Governments are, of course, not alone in expressing concerns on this front. To the extent that open-ended performance-based standards (as opposed to more easily auditable management- or technology-based standards) play a key role in voluntary codes, the task of certifiers is made more difficult. More importantly, however, unless there is broad confidence that the standards articulated are subject to rigorous and regular measurement, evaluation, and verification, their perceived legitimacy (and ultimately their viability) will be put in jeopardy.

Choosing the Optimal Form of Standard

A consensus appears to be emerging that choosing the best form of standard requires careful consideration of a variety of context-specific factors, including the logistics associated with measuring, evaluating, and verifying achievement of the objectives of the standard, as well as the nature of the "regulated community".

It is claimed, for example, that where it is a relatively straightforward matter to assess whether a standard's objective is being achieved (by means of measurable indicators or other well-correlated proxies, for example), and if it can be done at a relatively low cost, a preference should be given to performance-based standards. Alternatively, where it may be difficult or costly to monitor firm-level performance, and where the regulated sector is relatively homogenous, the best regulatory option may be one that is technology-based. This is especially likely to be true when the relationship between action and output is well understood and can be easily evaluated.

However, where the regulated community is composed of "heterogeneous enterprises facing heterogeneous conditions", there is emerging agreement that a strong theoretical justification exists for management-based standards, all other things being equal. Adopting this option, it is said, allows operators to deploy their informational resources and act on their private incentives insofar as they are not inconsistent with achieving the standard's broader public objectives. To make such a system work, however, two key considerations will be, first, whether to exhort or actively enforce management planning, implementation, or both; and, second, the degree of overlap between a firm's private interests and society's needs.

Notes and Questions

1. Do you agree with the authors', contention that the choice of what form of standard regulators should adopt should be entirely context-dependent? Should the default preference, as many in business would argue, be for performance-based standards?

2. In selecting a form of standard, what should be the most decisive factors? What form(s) of standard are most suitable for regulating the environmental impacts of the following sectors and/or industries: nuclear technology; computer component manufacturing; drycleaners; autoparts recyclers; mining; fisheries; forestry; airlines?

Part III — The Emerging Governance-based Approach to Environmental Regulation

Contemporary debate over the future of environmental regulation is influenced by a variety of factors. A common feature is an appetite for new approaches borne, certainly at least in part, out of a sense that traditional regulatory approaches (whether cast in M'Gonigle *et al.*'s terminology as "permissive regulation" or by business critics as prescriptive "command and control" regulation) has failed. Increasingly there is a consensus that governments cannot nor should be expected to "do it all"; as it is often expressed, governments "should steer not row". Thus, as several of the authors suggest below, while command and control should remained the preferred mode of regulation in some contexts, in others there are good reasons to contemplate new forms of regulation aimed at enlisting the market forces and civil society in promoting more sustainable environmental outcomes. In short, this emerging literature on "new" or "reconfigured" environmental regulation argues for a new conception of both how we "govern" the environment and who the "we" includes.

Kathryn Harrison, "Talking with the Donkey: Cooperative Approaches to Environmental Protection"

(1999) 2 Journal of Industrial Ecology 51

In the past decade, governments throughout the world have expressed growing interest in more flexible cooperative approaches to environmental protection. In the United States, this trend can be viewed as a reaction against the uniquely conflictual American approach to environmental regulation. This perspective is reflected in U.S. President Clinton's statement that

> The adversarial approach that has often characterized our environmental system precludes opportunities for creative solutions that a more collaborative system might encourage. When decision-making is shared, people can bridge differences, find common ground, and identify new solutions. To reinvent environmental protection, we must first build trust among traditional adversaries (Clinton and Gore 1995).

Interestingly, there is also renewed interest in cooperative policy instruments in countries such as the Netherlands, Canada, Australia, the United Kingdom, and Japan, where environmental regulation has traditionally been relatively cooperative. Thus, the European Union's Fifth Action Plan (EC 1996) states that

> Whereas previous environmental measures tended to be prescriptive in character with an emphasis on the "thou shalt not" approach, the new strategy leans more towards a "let's work together" approach. This reflects the growing realization in industry and in the business world that not only is industry a significant part of the (environmental) problem but it must also be part of the solution. The new approach implies, in particular, a reinforcement of the dialogue with industry and the encouragement, in appropriate circumstances, of voluntary agreements and other forms of self-regulation.

Cooperative approaches to environmental policy emphasize the valuable expertise residing in the business community and thus take seriously . . . the industrial firm as an "agent of change" rather than the "culprit" responsible for environmental degradation. Further, many policy instruments of particular interest to industrial ecology — covenants, extended producer responsibility, ecolabeling, and so on — rely to varying degrees on cooperation and voluntariness. Finally, some have speculated that voluntary approaches may be particularly amenable to forging collaborative networks across the product life cycle.

Clearly, the term "cooperative approaches" to environmental protection encompasses a wide variety of approaches, from more flexible enforcement of regulations to voluntary agreements, with much in-between. The first objective of this article is to provide a conceptual framework to distinguish among policy instruments predicated on cooperation between government and nongovernmental actors. The second is to focus on a subset of those approaches, voluntary agreements between government and business, and to examine theoretical arguments and empirical evidence concerning their effectiveness.

The article concludes that little empirical evidence exists concerning the environmental benefits of voluntary agreements. This is attributable, in part, to the recent nature of these policy reforms. However, the paucity of empirical evaluations also reflects more fundamental challenges in evaluating voluntary programs, which are characterized by self-selection and voluntary reporting and by an inadequate commitment to program evaluation by advocates of voluntary programs.

"Command and Control" versus Cooperation

As noted above, interest in cooperative approaches arises in large part from disenchantment with "command and control" regulation. The command and control model of uniform mandatory standards has been subject to a litany of criticisms. It has been argued that uniform standards are economically inefficient, that development and revision of formal regulations are unnecessarily slow, and that command and control regulation encourages end-of-pipe solutions rather than pollution prevention. Command and control regulation has also been criticized for specifying technologies rather than performance standards, thus stifling innovation and increasing costs to business; for failure to provide incentives for firms to go beyond compliance; and for a fragmented media-specific, pollutant-specific, and sector-specific approach. And finally, it is often argued that command and control regulation is unnecessarily adversarial and legalistic.

These are serious critiques indeed, although it should be noted that not all are uncontroversial. For instance, many argue that regulation is an important stimulus for, rather than impediment to, innovation. More importantly, analysts of environmental policy must be wary of the tendency to use the term "command and control" as a pejorative catchall for any and all criticisms of environmental regulation, because the term denies important differences among regulatory approaches and contexts. For instance, there is nothing inherent in the policy instrument of regulation (broadly defined as rules of behavior backed by sanctions legitimately available to government) that requires regulators to specify control techniques or to limit their focus to individual media, nor is the regulatory process in other countries as adversarial and litigious as in the United States. By the same token, one must resist the temptation to embrace equally diverse cooperative approaches as a panacea for all that ails regulation. As discussed below, many cooperative approaches that have been adopted in recent years are, in fact, regulatory. Moreover, cooperative approaches do not necessarily avoid media or technology specificity.

It is also important to acknowledge that to some degree interest in cooperative approaches may have little to do with the effectiveness of regulation in achieving environmental objectives. Governments routinely balance multiple policy objectives in choosing policy instruments. The choice of cooperative approaches thus may be driven more by concerns about the impacts of inflexible regulations on industrial competitiveness than by a desire to achieve a higher level of environmental protection. Alternatively, governments placing a high priority on deficit reduction may embrace voluntary cooperative approaches simply because they can no longer afford to pursue regulatory programs in the face of budgetary restraint. The evaluation of the effectiveness of voluntary approaches in the latter half of this article will thus consider multiple policy objectives of protecting the environment, cost effectiveness for both government and business, and democratic accountability and participation.

It is also noteworthy that the emphasis on cooperative approaches may in part reflect their political popularity rather than administrative effectiveness. Politicians may embrace cooperative nonregulatory approaches because they are unwilling to impose the costs of regulation on powerful business interests. The fact that cooperative approaches can be adopted for reasons that have little to do with environmental or other policy objectives (other than reelection) provides all the more reason to carefully evaluate the effectiveness of these new approaches to environmental protection.

Defining Cooperation

It is important to clarify at the outset just what is meant by "cooperation", because the term is likely to have different meaning from different perspectives. The Oxford Concise Dictionary defines cooperation as "working together to the same end". Several aspects of this definition warrant closer examination. First is the implicit question of just who is "working together". Many cooperative approaches that have emerged in recent years focus on partnerships between business and government, to the exclusion of other parties. Such approaches may enhance government cooperation with one group at the expense of conflict with others, such as environmentalists, who may resent exclusion or have substantive objections to agreements reached between government and business. One person's cooperation thus may be another's conflict. Consistent with recent policy developments, this article focuses on approaches that promote cooperation between business and government, although other parties may be involved as well.

A second element of the definition of cooperation concerns commonality of objectives. Cooperation is predicated on some measure of agreement or consent. However, when one is considering agreements between government and nongovernmental interests, the nature of that consent requires closer examination. This is because government, unlike private actors, has legitimate authority to coerce others (subject of course to constitutional limitations). This raises the question of whether business — government agreement with respect to environmental policy constitutes genuine cooperation, in the same way as one might question whether handing over one's wallet to an armed assailant constitutes cooperation. Bearing this in mind, one can envision various cooperative approaches situated along a continuum that varies in the extent of explicit or implied government coercion. From a practical perspective, the issue is that some approaches to public policy are *more cooperative* than others. The following section revisits this notion of a continuum in offering a simple typology of cooperative approaches.

The third element of the definition of cooperation is "working together". Government and business may collaborate in devising or implementing policies, or both. It is questionable, however, whether a government's choice not to intervene at all can be considered a form of business — government cooperation.

A Typology of Cooperative Approaches

One of the most straightforward typologies of policy instruments is that offered by Doern and Phidd (1992) who argue that governments choose among five broad classes of policy tools:

- Regulation (legal requirements backed by government sanctions);
- Government enterprise (direct provision of goods and services by either government agencies or government-owned enterprises);
- Expenditure;
- Exhortation;
- Inaction

In terms of the familiar analogy of how to get a donkey to pull a cart, these policy instruments correspond to using a stick to coerce the donkey (regulation), the driver pulling the cart herself (government enterprise), inducing the donkey to move with carrots (expenditure), encouraging the donkey through ear stroking and persuasion (exhortation), and leaving it up to whomever want the goods in the cart to work out their own arrangements with the donkey (government inaction).

These categories are, of course, not as simple as they seem. There is a broad range of tools within each category. Moreover, as noted above, there can also be a fine line between informal persuasion and formal regulation, because a donkey that has felt the stick in the past may respond to ear stroking less out of good will than fear. However, this typology nonetheless offers a useful starting point to distinguish among the variety of cooperative approaches to environmental protection that have emerged in recent years.

The vast majority of cooperative reforms fall into the three categories of regulation, exhortation, and government inaction. Assuming comparable policy objectives, these three classes of policy instruments can be placed along a continuum of coerciveness from regulation to exhortation to government inaction (Doern and Phidd 1992), although with considerable variation within each category. The following discussion reviews recent reforms in each of these categories, from most to least coercive.

Regulation: Kinder, Gentler Sticks

Compliance Support

Many cooperative reforms adopted in recent years are adaptations to traditional regulation. For instance, although mandatory compliance with regulations is still the norm, regulators in many jurisdictions are increasingly willing to assist regulated interests by clarifying requirements and providing technical advice on how to achieve compliance. Such programs are increasingly popular among the U.S. states, particularly as the reach of regulatory programs extends to increasingly small enterprises, which have fewer resources to devote to legal and environmental affairs.

Flexible Approaches to Compliance

A substantial body of literature argues that greater rates of compliance can be achieved by a cooperative and flexible approach to *enforcement* than an adversarial one. Proponents of cooperative enforcement argue that although frequent resort to the stick may compel greater compliance among firms inclined to evade the law, it risks destroying the good will of a much larger number of law-abiding firms, who resent being treated like criminals. Such firms may respond with perfunctory compliance with the narrow letter of the law rather than public-spirited efforts to comply with the intent of the law. At worst, a "culture of resistance" may emerge, in which firms help each other identify and exploit loopholes in regulations. Proponents of cooperative enforcement advocate a "tit for tat" strategy of initial forgiveness combined with increasingly stringent sanctions in the face of recalcitrant behavior.

A critical assumption underlying this argument is that there are more "good apples" than "bad apples". However, other scholars adopt an assumption consistent with public choice and neoclassical economic theory that virtually all firms are "bad apples" motivated exclusively by profits and thus inclined to comply with regulations only if anticipated sanctions outweigh the financial benefits of noncompliance. Quantitative comparisons of actual rates of compliance in response to different enforcement regimes are few and conflicting. Despite this, there has been growing attention to a variety of reforms to promote flexible and cooperative enforcement, including

- Reduced compliance monitoring for firms with certified environmental management systems;
- Guarantees of confidentiality for self-audits, with reduction or waiver of penalties in the event of voluntary disclosure and correction of noncompliance;
- Negotiated compliance agreements, which waive enforcement actions in exchange for a firm's commitment to a program to achieve compliance;
- Variances from regulatory requirements for firms pursuing innovative control strategies.

Cooperative Development of Regulatory Standards

The discussion thus far has concerned more cooperative ways to *implement* regulations. However, cooperation can also be extended to *development* of regulations in the first place. Cooperative standards development can take a variety of forms.

First, the number of participants in cooperative standard setting can vary. In Canada, Japan, and European countries with corporatist traditions of developing policies in concert with key interests, environmental standards have traditionally been set through bipartite negotiation with the regulated industry. Amid criticisms from excluded groups, some countries are now turning to multipartite processes. In Canada, "multistakeholder consultations" have become the norm in environmental standard setting at the federal level. The approach is similar to negotiated rulemaking in the United States. The U.S. Common Sense Initiative also attempted to achieve consensus among diverse interests on new approaches to environmental regulation. The number of participants in cooperative rulemaking thus can range from two to several dozen, with obvious implications for the speed, cost, and likelihood of agreement.

Mechanisms for public involvement in regulatory decision making also differ in the weight given to input from nongovernmental actors and the emphasis placed on consensus. When input is viewed as simply advisory to government decision makers, as in notice and comment rulemaking, there is no need for a single recommendation to emerge from nongovernmental participants. However, if there is a presumption that participants' recommendations will carry considerable weight, mechanisms to bring diverse societal interests together and to resolve their differences are more important. Regulatory negotiations often rely on a decision rule of consensus, although this has been criticized by some as overly resistant to change.[4]

Exhortation: Talking with the Donkey

Governments can seek to persuade individuals or firms to change their behavior in a variety of ways. Although such approaches are nominally voluntary, in that no formal legal requirement is applied, they vary in degree of coerciveness. Closest to regulation along the spectrum of coercion are "voluntary agreements" between business and industry and government-sponsored codes of conduct. Voluntary agreements, such as the Dutch covenants discused below, are characterized by strong expectations on the part of government that industry will comply. Such agreements are typically accompanied by an explicit or implied threat of regulation or other mandatory instruments should voluntary measures fail. Voluntary agreements or codes are usually negotiated by government and the private sector. Although many agreements take the form of nonbinding "gentlemen's agreements", others are legally binding contracts. Such contracts can still be considered voluntary, however, in the sense that the parties consent to assume certain obligations, in contrast to laws and regulations, which apply equally to all regardless of consent.

In contrast to voluntary agreements, governmental efforts to persuade target groups to change their behavior via "voluntary challenges" involve little or no arm-twisting in the form of threats of regulation or penalties for nonparticipation. Requirements of participation tend to be very flexible. Examples of these less coercive voluntary challenge programs include the U.S. Environmental Protection Agency's (EPA's) 33/50 program and Environment Canada's Accelerated Reduction/Elimination of Toxics program (ARET) . . . discussed below.

The least coercive approaches in this category are education and information dissemination programs, which may be directed at either the business community or consumers. Here, government does not explicitly encourage particular actions but does so implicitly by providing particular kinds of information to influence consumers' or firms' behavior. Examples of educational programs seeking to influence business include pollution prevention clearinghouses that provide information about pollution prevention techniques, while efforts to inform consumers include environmental awards for businesses and government-sponsored ecolabeling programs.

Government Inaction: Leaving the Donkey Alone

The final policy tool is for government to do nothing, leaving it to civil society to address a given environmental problem. Government coercion may still be a factor in this category, as when an implied threat of coercion causes actors to change their behavior in anticipation of government intervention, although in other cases the objectives of governmental and non governmental actors may fortuitously coincide. Approaches in this category, including the Forest Stewardship Council, the Coalition for Environmentally Responsible Economies (CERES) Principles, Responsible Care, and International Standards Organization (ISO) 14000, essentially parallel the exhortation programs discussed above but with some entity other than government doing the educating or persuading. Programs in this category tend to rely on cooperation among nongovernmental actors rather than between government and business, and thus are not examined in detail in this article.

. . . . .

Jody Freeman & Daniel Farber, "Modular Environmental Regulation"
(2005) 54 Duke L.J. 795–912.

Environmental law and natural resource management feature another important debate over the preferred tools of environmental regulation — a debate that pits traditional "command and control" regulation (referred to here as prescriptive regulation) against market mechanisms, which are thought to be more efficient. Emissions trading schemes are the most common form of market mechanism in environmental regulation thus far. The most familiar example is the acid rain program in the *Clean Air Act* (CAA). Emissions trading schemes allocate pollution rights within an industrial sector or geographic region based on the theory that firms that can reduce their emissions at a lower cost will be encouraged to do so by a market mechanism in which they can sell their excess allocation to firms for which such reductions would be more expensive. This presumably accomplishes the ultimate regulatory goal (which government still establishes) in the most efficient way.

In contrast, prescriptive regulation usually requires that all firms in a given industrial sector reduce emissions equally. Such an approach is too costly, the argument goes, because it fails to account for the marginal cost of compliance among differently situated firms. Uniform regulation is widely thought to be intrusive, interfering with the industrial process by mandating the adoption of particular technologies regardless of the peculiarities of different industrial processes. Another related criticism of prescriptive regulation, especially at the national level, is that it is too "centralized" and coarse grained to respond adequately to differences in local conditions, let alone to the diversity of local preferences regarding the degree of pollution control that is appropriate given its costs. Centralized top-down regulation is thought to inhibit the kind of policy and institutional innovations that come only from local knowledge and experience.

Prescriptive regulation is also widely believed to inhibit technological innovation because firms required to reduce emissions to the same level have no incentive to develop new technologies that could reduce emissions even further below the agency standard. Another more practical concern is that much of the information most relevant to prescriptive regulators is in the hands of industry, including information about the costs of controlling emissions, operational details about industrial processes, and rates of compliance. Unless ordered to do so, industry has little incentive to reveal this kind of information fully. Without this information, agencies will find implementation difficult. And prescriptive regulation requires procedures, such as rulemaking, that tend to be slow, cumbersome, conflict ridden, and, therefore, costly. The pace of rulemaking makes it difficult to respond to rapid changes in technology or new information.

In view of this critique, the standard advice of economists is to move toward a system of market-based incentives. Already, there are proposals to extend emissions trading to pollutants other than sulfur dioxide, as in the Bush administration's Clear Skies initiative, as well as to carbon, as recent legislation proposes. Other proposals go beyond the air context to address different settings and harms. Examples include watershed-based effluent trading and wetlands mitigation banking. Moving further in the direction of market approaches would also presumably require making greater use of a wider range of mechanisms, including effluent taxes, deposit-refund systems, and user fees such as those levied in "Pay-As-You-Throw" waste collection systems.

Advocates of prescriptive regulation argue two things in response to the critique just described: first, that many of the assumptions about the uniformity, inflexibility, and high cost of prescriptive regulation are either wrong or overstated; and second, that prescriptive regulation is still necessary as the backbone of the regulatory system because market mechanisms are risky and frequently do not deliver on their promise. Indeed, although some market experiments are reputed to be enormous successes (e.g., the *Clean Air Act*'s Acid Rain program), the empirical record on their performance is, in fact, mixed. Advocates of conventional prescriptive regulation argue that despite its imperfections, command and control has delivered significant environmental gains.

Even those favorably disposed to market mechanisms in theory will concede that significant problems of design and enforcement can in practice inhibit their ability to deliver environmental benefits. For example, political considerations tend to dominate the initial allocation of entitlements in market regimes (as was the case with allocation of units of sulfur dioxide pollution in the acid rain program), which can undermine their purported efficiency. Markets can be too narrowly or broadly drawn, and prices can be set inaccurately. To establish an effluent tax or design an emissions trading system, the government must establish a shadow price — a price that reflects the real costs of pollution — but the unavailability of a market benchmark makes this a difficult undertaking. This, of course, is the problem with public goods like the environment: the ostensible market justification for intervening in environmental regulation in the first place is that the market is unable to price environmental harms properly. In addition, the more the system is tailored to local conditions, whether by adjusting the effluent or emissions tax to account for variations in harm, or by establishing a system of "exchange rates" for permits, the more cumbersome the system becomes.

Trading schemes can falter because of difficulties both in valuing environmental commodities and ensuring that trades involve commensurate goods. It may be especially challenging to devise market approaches to natural resource management rather than pollution, because natural resources, like ecosystems, perform functions that may be enormously difficult to value and to trade Markets can also create "hotspots" of concentrated pollution, which can disproportionately affect subpopulations, leading to claims of distributional inequity. Again, to the extent that the market regime is tailored to address such distributional concerns, some efficiencies may be lost.

Finally, market mechanisms generally require some easily monitored indicator that can be subject to trading or tax. This may be feasible for some pollution problems (as with sulfur dioxide, which is emitted by a fairly small number of power plants) but it is more difficult to implement in other contexts in which there are large numbers of sources or in which the emissions rates are hard or expensive to monitor. This is the case with the pollutants that contribute to ground level ozone.

And so the debate goes. Framing the debate between prescriptive versus market based regulation in either-or terms echoes the dichotomous nature of the federalism debate. In reality, both environmental law and natural resource management rely on a mix of mechanisms. Moreover, neither kind of instrument is as "pure" as the two poles of the debate would suggest: virtually every market mechanism of environmental regulation depends on some prescribed government limit, such as setting a cap, in the emissions trading context, beneath which trades occur. And in all of these regimes, the government — either Congress through legislation or agencies through regulation — plays a crucial role in monitoring and adjusting the rules to respond to new events or information.

Similarly, prescriptive regulations, such as technology-based standards, are not as uniform and rigid as some would suggest. Most standards are performance standards that firms can achieve in any way they choose (although admittedly, the easiest assurance of compliance is to adopt whatever technology the relevant agency used to set the standard). Most importantly, prescriptive regulation always relies to some extent on adjustments in light of economic realities — both in the initial phase of level setting, when the regulatory agency takes account of industrial processes and capacities in choosing the standard, and later, when agencies negotiate particular permits. There is also considerable flexibility in the enforcement process, when agencies must determine whether firms are out of compliance and what must be done in response. The so-called "command and control" system is infused with negotiation and accommodation. To label it "uniform", "rigid", and "centralized", although rhetorically powerful, is somewhat misleading. In practice, levels established by regulation frequently operate more like targets than like strict requirements. There are market-driven limits, in other words, to the extent to which government both "commands" and "controls" firm behavior.

The point is this: twenty years of experience suggests that it is impossible to declare a clear winner in this debate. Whether an instrument works optimally depends on a variety of factors, some of which are easier to predict and control than others. These include: the sophistication of the market participants; the size and diversity of the market; the vulnerability of the environmental "good" or "service" to accurate valuation; the vulnerability of the regime to political rigging in the allocation process; and the potential for gaming, shirking, and cheating by the regulated entities, among other things. The challenge now is to mix and match instruments in a way that is sensitive to the contexts — political, economic, geographical — in which they are deployed, and to remember that no matter how well-designed regulatory or management tools might be in theory, for their success they each require effective implementation and monitoring.

. . . . .

Chris Tollefson, David Haley & Fred Gale, *Setting the Standard*
(UBC Press, 2008)

The critique of command-and-control-style regulation can, in many ways, be seen as the result of an ongoing, sometimes overtly ideological, battle over US environmental policy. Paradoxically, federal American environmental laws became a target for sustained critique not because they had failed, but in large measure because they had succeeded. Most of these laws — most notably the *Clean Air Act*, the *Clean Water Act*, and the *Resource Conservation and Recovery Act* — were enacted within a single decade, between 1970 and 1980. Unlike other federal jurisdictions, where national governments, for various constitutional and political reasons, have tended to eschew taking a leadership role in tackling environmental issues, in the United States these laws reflected a broad consensus that the federal government not only had the legal authority (founded on the powerful Commerce Clause) to take leadership on environmental issues, but that it was also politically obliged (and, arguably, best situated) to do so.

The American approach was anomalous in terms of the scope of the federal role; it was also unique in terms of its reliance on a particular mode of regulation. Virtually all the federal environmental laws enacted in this period employed best available technology (BAT) standards. Under these standards, regulated facilities were obliged to install the most stringent pollution-control technology available, up to the point that the costs of doing so would cause them to shut down. For the most part, BAT standards were sector specific and were typically applied uniformly on a national basis. These American laws were also unique insofar as they provided legal means (known as "citizen suits") by which citizens could challenge permit holders and governments for failing to comply with or effectively enforce legal obligations prescribed by these permitting arrangements [*Ed note*: See further discussion of citizen suits as an enforcement mechanism in Chapter 5.]

The decision to adopt the BAT approach was justified on various grounds: among other benefits, they minimized government monitoring and enforcement costs, enhanced public scrutiny and participation in compliance efforts, reduced the potential for "regulatory capture" and other forms of political manipulation, and minimized inter-state competition that might arise from the potential for pollution havens.

By most accounts, over the ensuing quarter-century these laws, and the programs that were funded to implement them at the federal and state levels, brought about significant improvements in environmental quality. These improvements were particularly notable in relation to discharges from single point sources. Before long, however, these first-generation environmental laws came under sustained criticism.

Although the critics usually conceded that these first-generation laws had been successful in "picking the low-hanging fruit", they argued that the BAT model was in many ways highly inefficient. They claimed, for example, that one-size-fits-all approaches (such as BAT) ignore basic cost-benefit analysis by failing to take into account the social benefits of reducing pollution in a given setting (relative to the costs of securing those benefits) or the differential ability of firms within a given sector to meet the BAT standard. Critics also railed at the costs to business of the culture of legal adversarialism that, they claimed, the laws promoted. Moreover, they contended that, although a case could be made that BAT was an effective means of regulating industry laggards, it provided no incentive for more responsible firms to make research and development investments in new pollution-control technologies. For these reformers, the policy prescription was clear. Having combated the first-generation challenges of curbing the most serious and pressing major sources of pollution, the time had come to enact a second generation of laws that were capable of leveraging further pollution reductions in circumstances where the marginal cost of achieving progress was typically high, and that could also address discharges from small, non-point sources, including those in the consumer, services, and agricultural sectors.

The reformers' critique did not go unchallenged. Defenders of the prevailing legal regime pointed to its record of achievement in enhancing air and water quality, to the additional regulatory costs associated with requiring federal agencies to undertake additional cost-benefit and risk analyses, to the dangers of leaving to the market (through pollution-trading regimes and other less state-centric instruments favoured by reformers) determinations with respect to risk exposure at the local level, and, perhaps above all, to the state's obligation to actively engage in safeguarding environmental values as public goods.

Through much of the late 1980s and early 1990s, this debate was cast as a classic showdown between proponents of free markets and defenders of a strong, interventionist state. By the mid-1990s, with the arrival of the Clinton administration, a shift in the tenor of the debate began to emerge. At this point, it was becoming clear that the ambitious legislative aspirations of the reformers were unlikely to be realized in the short term, if at all. At the same time, their critique was having an impact in a more interstitial fashion. Starting in the early 1990s, the US Environmental Protection Agency drew on the reformers' arguments to initiate a variety of programs aimed at combating the perceived rigidities and inflexibilities associated with first-generation laws. Among them were programs that facilitated pollution credit trading and provided new incentives, including regulatory relief, for superior environmental performers. Existing legislative arrangements were left largely intact.

By the mid-1990s, a debate that had focused on US environmental law and been dominated by American legal scholars and economists began to expand outward. There was a growing sense that the regulatory questions being mooted in relation to the future of US environmental law were of much wider significance. The most important of the new contributions to the debate is an approach to regulatory reform that its Australian originators termed "smart regulation" (Gunningham and Grabosky 1998; Gunningham and Sinclair 2002).

The thesis promoted by Gunningham and his colleagues is deceptively simple: a pluralistic, flexible, context-specific approach should be taken to instrument choice in the realm of environmental policy and beyond. Drawing on case studies of regulatory innovation in North America, Europe, and Australia, the authors contend that framing the choice of instrument in ideological terms — state versus market — was unhelpful. Moreover, it is important not to underestimate the successes of, nor the continuing need for, command-and-control-style regulation. However, they argued that, in many cases, better environmental outcomes can be leveraged by deploying a mix of policy instruments tailored to the particular goals and circumstances of the regulatory context. Governments can also achieve better results (given static or declining budgets) if they harness resources from outside the public sector by engaging directly with regulated parties, communities, and civil society organizations. In this regard, governments should "steer not row" and should, where possible, "govern from a distance". To this end, they should be ready to engage in continuing governance experiments aimed at identifying and testing new ways to share governance responsibilities by empowering business and civil society through information, networks, and partnerships.

The debate over "smart regulation" has produced a remarkable outpouring of scholarly work. Many governments have adopted the term to provide intellectual justification for a wide range of public-sector regulatory reform initiatives. In the United States, for example, federal agencies are now directed by executive order (originally issued by President Clinton and later affirmed by President Bush) to specify performance objectives, rather than behaviour, whenever this is feasible as they craft new regulations. Many federal agencies, including the Environmental Protection Agency, the Nuclear Regulatory Commission, and the federal Highway Administration, to name a few, are piloting performance-based regulatory programs. The influence of the smart-regulation critique has also resonated in potentially sweeping law and policy reforms taking place in many other Western liberal democracies, including Canada, the United Kingdom, and Australia.

N. Gunningham, "Reconfiguring Environmental Regulation: Next Generation Policy Instruments"[2]

The environmental impact of industry, especially pollution, has been subject to regulation for at least three decades, under an approach that is somewhat unfairly called "command and control" regulation. This approach typically specifies standards, and sometimes technologies, with which the regulated must comply (the "command") or be penalized (the "control"). It commonly requires polluters to apply the best feasible techniques to minimize the environmental harm caused by their activities. Command and control has achieved some considerable successes, especially in terms of reducing air and water pollution. However, this "first generation" of environmental regulation has been widely criticized by economists for inhibiting innovation and for its high costs, inflexibility and diminishing returns.

The problems of command and control can be overstated and its considerable achievements too easily dismissed. At the same time, its limitations have led policymakers and regulators to recognize that it provides only a part of the policy solution, particularly in a rapidly changing, increasingly complex and interdependent world. However, regulatory reform must take place in an environment of shrinking regulatory resources, making it neces-

2 Online: « http://www.crdi.ca/fr/ev-110171-201-1-DO_TOPIC.html » accessed May 18, 2008.

sary in some contexts to design strategies capable of achieving results even in the absence of a credible enforcement regime (as when dealing with small and medium-sized enterprises), and in almost all circumstances to extract the "biggest bang" from a much diminished "regulatory buck". . . .

The crucial question is: where should one go next in terms of regulatory policy? The challenge is to find ways to overcome the inefficiencies of traditional regulation, to devise better ways of encouraging innovation and of achieving environmental protection at an acceptable economic and social cost. This will involve the design of a "second phase" of regulation: one that still involves government intervention, but selectively and in combination with a range of market and non-market solutions, and of public and private regulatory orderings.

In designing innovative regulation, it is crucial to remember that "one size does not fit all". Different sized organizations experience different challenges in complying with regulations, and very different regulatory strategies will be needed to address them (contrast the issues in regulating transnational corporations with those of regulating small and medium-sized enterprises). So, too, it is necessary to design different strategies for different industry sectors: what is appropriate for the chemical industry may be entirely inappropriate for regulating agriculture . . .

Broadly speaking, policy instruments can be located on a continuum from the least to the most interventionist. For example, the paradigm case of the latter is command and control regulation in the American mould: highly prescriptive and enforced coercively. At the other extreme are instruments such as pure voluntarism, education and some information-based approaches. In between (in escalating degrees of intervention) lie mechanisms such as self-regulation and economic instruments.

Self-regulation

Self-regulation is not a precise concept, but for present purposes it may be defined as a process whereby an organized group regulates the behaviour of its members. Most commonly it involves an industry-level organization (as opposed to the government or individual firms) setting rules and standards (codes of practice) relating to the conduct of firms in the industry.

Because standard-setting and identification of breaches are the responsibility of practitioners, with detailed knowledge of the industry, this will arguably lead to more practicable standards, more effectively policed. There is also the potential for utilizing peer pressure and for successfully internalizing responsibility for compliance. Moreover, because self-regulation contemplates ethical standards of conduct that extend beyond the letter of the law, it may significantly raise standards of behaviour and lead to a greater integration of environmental issues into the management process. Finally, and crucially, in some circumstances and forms, self-regulation holds out the possibility of encouraging dissemination of information about new technologies and of thereby facilitating their more rapid introduction.

Yet in practice, self-regulation often fails to fulfil its theoretical promise. The evidence suggests that self-regulation is rarely effective in achieving compliance (i.e., obedience by the target population/s with regulation/s) — at least if it is used as a "stand alone" strategy without sanctions. This is because self-regulatory standards are often weak, enforcement is commonly (although not invariably) ineffective, and punishment is secret and mild.

Voluntary Agreements

At a general level this category embraces agreements between governments and individual businesses or industry sectors, taking the form of "non-mandatory contracts between equal partners, one of which is government, in which incentives for action arise from mutual interests rather than from sanctions". However, the variety of such agreements makes precise classification difficult. The most common categories are (a) public voluntary agreements such as "challenge" programmes and (b) negotiated voluntary agreements between governments and industry. There is very little evidence to suggest the former has a positive impact on innovation and for present purposes we focus on the latter.

Negotiated agreements involve specific commitments to environmental protection elaborated through bargaining between industry and a public authority. In Europe they are usually entered into by an industry association and government against a backdrop of threatened legislation: the tacit bargain being that if the industry will commit to reach given environmental outcomes through its own initiatives, government will hold off on legislation it would otherwise contemplate enacting to address the problem.

Unfortunately, the empirical literature on negotiated agreements is very limited. Many existing agreements lack clear targets, and have inadequate reporting requirements and deadlines, making evaluation of their success extremely difficult. Indeed, one of the few things upon which almost all analysts of voluntary agreements seem to agree is that far too little attention has so far been given to evaluating either their economic or environmental benefits. However, preliminary assessments of the value of the early voluntary agreements are not encouraging.

Informational Regulation and Civic Environmentalism

An increasingly important alternative or supplement to conventional regulation is what is becoming known as "informational regulation". As the OECD (1994: 8) puts it: "People and businesses often care deeply about contributing responsibly to the public good (businesses also care about 'reputation'), and governments can use information, communication, encouragement, peer pressure, and education strategies to convince the public of the need for change". In contrast to command and control, informational regulation involves the state encouraging (as in corporate environmental reporting) or requiring (as with community right to know) information about environmental impacts but without directly requiring a change in those practices. Rather, this approach relies upon economic markets and public opinion as the mechanisms to bring about improved performance.

Informational regulation is growing rapidly, partly because of the success of some of the early initiatives, partly because it offers a cost effective and less interventionist alternative to command and control in a period of contracting regulatory resources, partly because of its capacity to empower communities and NGOs, and partly because changes in technology make the use of such strategies increasingly viable and cost-effective.

Probably the most successful and best known form of information regulation is the use of community right to know (CRTK) and pollution inventories.

Space precludes a discussion of other forms of informational regulation such as the use of corporate reporting on environmental (and on ethical and social) performance, and product labeling and certification. Suffice it to say that informational regulation strategies work better in some circumstances than others. The evidence suggests that they work best with respect to large companies and environmentally aware communities.

A related development is the growth of "civic regulation", whereby various manifestations of civil society act in a variety of ways to influence corporations, consumers and markets, often by-passing the state and rejecting political lobbying in favour of what they believe to be far more effective strategies . . . Market campaigning focusing on highly visible branded retailers is a particularly favoured strategy. Less so are campaigns that seek to provide a market premium for "environmentally preferred" produce, due largely to the unwillingness of consumers to support such a strategy. More recently, certification programmes such as the Forest Stewardship Council are "transforming traditional power relationships in the global arena. Linking together diverse and often antagonistic actors from the local, national and international levels . . . to govern firm behaviour in a global space that has eluded the control of states and international organizations".

. . . the evolving role of civic regulation has not taken place entirely divorced from state intervention. On the contrary, either in response to pressure from the institutions of civil society or in recognition of the limits of state regulation, governments are gradually providing greater roles for communities, environmental NGOs and the public more generally. Thus a number of second-generation policy instruments are geared to empower various institutions of civil society to play a more effective role in shaping business behaviour, thus facilitating civic regulation. These include not only the sort of CRTK legislation described above, but also a variety of other mechanisms that seek to empower third parties, for example, by giving environmental NGOs or communities a "seat at the table" (and enabling them to influence directly planning or licensing conditions), by providing them with the standing to bring a legal action, or the information with which to threaten the reputation capital of large corporations.

Notes and Questions

1. As Gunningham suggests, "policy instruments can be located on a continuum from the least to the most interventionist" as measured in terms of government involvement. At one end of the spectrum are what many would refer to as "command and control"-based approaches which typically take the form of licences or permits that specify what technology a regulated party must employ or what environmental outcome they must achieve (specified either in terms of permissible discharges or resulting environmental quality). At the other end of the spectrum are approaches where government involvement is modest or absent altogether. Within this category are approaches in which industry (and sometimes civil society organizations) take the lead: including voluntary codes of practice, educative programs and some information and certification-based approaches of the type Gunningham describes above. Towards the middle of this spectrum lie what are often referred to as market-based approaches such as cap and trade regimes, and environmental taxes. A defining feature of these approaches is that while they are established and administered by government, firms retain considerable autonomy in terms of whether and how they participate in such regimes.

2. To date, Canadian governments have shied away from emissions trading (often called cap and trade) approaches. Cap and trade systems require government to establish a maximum "cap" on emissions/discharges into a specific air or watershed. Firms are then each allocated an emission or discharge entitlement. This entitlement then becomes a tradeable commodity. Depending on its needs, the firm can deploy its entitlement to meet its legal obligations, bank it for future use, or sell it on the open market. By pricing pollution in this way, the theory is that firms will have a strong incentive to reduce their environmental footprint. As Freeman and Farber describe, while a cap and trade regime established under the US *Clean Air Act* to combat acid rain has enjoyed some success, such regimes are by no means an environmental panacea. Bearing this in mind, it is intriguing to note that several Canadian provinces are on the verge of establishing GHG cap and trade regimes as a means of responding to climate change: see further discussion in Chapter 10.

Part IV — An Overview of Canadian Regulatory Models

In this part, we focus on two of the most of important federal environmental protection laws: the *Fisheries Act* and the *Canadian Environmental Protection Act* (CEPA). In keeping with the preceding discussion, these exemplars have been chosen as illustrations of "first generation" (the *Fisheries Act*) and "second generation" (CEPA) approaches to environmental protection. They are also the two federal statutes that have the generated the most attention to date in terms of compliance and enforcement, the topic to which we turn in Chapter 5. An in-depth examination of the *Canadian Environmental Assessment Act* (CEAA) and the *Species at Risk Act* (SARA) follows, respectively, in Chapter 7 and 9.

The *Fisheries Act*

The federal *Fisheries Act* is one of Canada's oldest statutes, providing broad federal regulators with a range of powerful tools to protect the environment. Over 100 years old and not substantially amended since the 1970s, the Act has been under Parliamentary review since 2005. Through this review process, it has become apparent that there are widely divergent views on the efficacy of the legislation and the need for reform. While environmentalists are strong supporters of the Act, they have frequently raised concerns about its efficacy in terms of compliance and enforcement. In contrast, many in the business community, particularly in British Columbia, regard the *Fisheries Act* and the Department of Fisheries and Oceans (historically known as "DFO"; more recently renamed Fisheries and Oceans Canada) as unduly impeding environmentally responsible resource development; imposing costly and inconsistent costs and requirements on legitimate ongoing and planned business operations.

A multi-faceted and complex piece of legislation with many accompanying regulations, its two key sections relevant to environmental protection are its habitat protection and its pollution prevention provisions contained in subsection 35(1) and section 36, respectively.

Habitat Protection: Subsection 35(1)

The provision of the *Fisheries Act* that most squarely addresses the protection of habitat has come to be known colloquially as "HADD", an acronym for the Act's broad prohibition on the "harmful alteration, disruption or destruction" of fish habitat.

Section 35 states:

> 35. (1) No person shall carry on any work or undertaking that results in the harmful alteration, disruption or destruction of fish habitat.
>
> (2) No person contravenes subsection (1) by causing the alteration, disruption or destruction of fish habitat by any means or under any conditions authorized by the Minister or under regulations made by the Governor in Council under this Act.

Violation of subsection 35(1) is an offence unless the HADD occurs under an authorization provided under subsection 35(2). Various interpretive uncertainties have arisen in the application of this provisions: these include what is "work or undertaking" [see the *Ecology Action Centre*, *infra* this chapter]; and whether "harmful" modifies simply "alteration" or also "disruption and destruction".

In the terminology introduced above, subsection 35(1) is a performance standard; it aims to regulate the impact of firms on the environment by focussing on the "results" of their activities on the environment. As such, it does not tell firms how to achieve compliance (by specifying approved technologies or management systems). For firms interested in certainty and minimizing liability risk, therefore, there is a strong incentive to secure advance DFO approval for proposed new works or undertakings.

While business has raised many concerns about the *Fisheries Act*'s HADD provision, efforts by environmental organizations to invoke subsection 35(1) proactively, as a means of exercising control over DFO decisions, have generally been unsuccessful as the following case illustrates.

Ecology Action Centre Society v. Canada (Attorney General)
9 C.E.L.R. (3d) 161

[Application by the Ecology Action Centre Society seeking judicial review of a Variation Order issued by the Regional Director-General, Maritimes Region, of the Department of Fisheries and Oceans. The Variation Order revoked an earlier Variation Order that had provided for a one-year ban on groundfish fishing in a region. The later Variation Order provided that the ban on groundfishing would be limited as set out in the Regulations. The Society sought orders declaring that the later Variation order was contrary to law because it allowed for the harmful alteration, disruption, or destruction of fish habitat. The Society further claimed that the later Variation Order was beyond the jurisdiction of the Director-General because it permitted the harmful alteration, disruption, or destruction of fish habitat.]

HENEGHAN J.:

The Applicant is concerned about the harmful effects of dragging in the area covered by the Variation Order. It does not advocate a total ban on dragging . . . The area affected by the Variation Order is the Canadian portion of Georges Bank. Georges Bank is a shallow submerged fishing bank that has been divided between Canada and the United States of America . . .

Dragging is a fishing method that uses mobile gear. That gear, also known as an "otter trawl", consists of wires, boards or doors and a net that is hauled behind the fishing vessel. The doors are used to spread connecting wires and to hold the net open horizontally. Weights on the bottom keep the net open vertically. The end of the net is called the "codend" which traps the fish and anything else that is picked up from the ocean floor during the dragging operations.

The Applicant says that this method of fishing indiscriminately picks up undersized fish and plant forms that are necessary to nourish and maintain the marine environment. It says that dragging has long-term serious negative consequences and in this regard, provided annotated bibliographies of peer reviewed scientific papers that address those effects.

The Respondent filed [an affidavit] that addresses the application of the various regulations enacted pursuant to the Act, as well as the general requirements for fishing on Georges Bank. The essential elements for lawful fishing in that area are receipt of a groundfish licence permitting fishing on Georges Bank, upon payment of all associated fees.

The Applicant here challenges the Variation Order as being ultra vires its enabling statute, that is the Act. Although the statute has no purpose section, it has been recognized by the Courts as conferring a broad power to regulate and manage the fisheries. The Act confers an absolute discretion upon the Minister in the matter of issuing licences.

When these provisions of the [Act and regulations] are considered, it is apparent that the Regional Director-General was authorized to make the Variation Order and the Order itself was authorized under the Regulations. The Variation Order did no more nor less than open the area 5Z for fishing. There is no basis for saying that the Regional Director-General acted beyond his jurisdiction since he did what he was authorized to do.

The Applicant argues that the Variation Order is "otherwise contrary to law" because it will cause HADD, as the result of fishing by means of dragging on the Georges Bank. HADD caused as the result of fishing is not permitted, according to the Applicant, in light of section 35 of the Act [*Ed note*: The text of this provision is set out in the note preceding this excerpt.]

The Applicant suggests that the terms "work" or "undertaking", which are undefined in the Act, should be given their ordinary meaning and be interpreted as any human endeavour. Since fishing involves human activity, it falls within the ambit of section 35(1).

The Respondent, on the other hand, submits that this view is inconsistent with the purpose of the Act. The words "work" or "undertaking" appear in sections 36 and 37, as well as section 35. These three provisions are found in the part of the Act that addresses protection of habitat and pollution prevention. The Respondent argues that the words "work or undertaking" and "fishing" are used in different parts of the Act because the terms do not carry the same meaning and are not included in each other.

In the present case, the Applicant is attempting to show that fishing falls within section 35(1) of the Act, in order to demonstrate that the Regional Director-General acted "contrary to law" in making Variation Order 2001-074. Underlying this argument is the allegation that the use of trawl gear will inevitably cause HADD in Area 5Z.

There are problems with this argument. In the first place, the Regional Director-General was acting within his lawful authority when issuing the Variation Order. The Variation Order is silent as to the type of gear that may be used in fishing during the permissible time frames; that issue is governed by whatever conditions that may be attached to any licence issued by the Minister and in accordance with the applicable regulations.

There is no evidence that the making of the Variation Order itself had any particular effect on the benthic environment in area 5Z. I agree with the submissions of the Respondent that if there was an "effect", it was due to something other than the Variation Order.

Furthermore, it is noteworthy that section 35 does not impose a blanket prohibition against HADD. HADD may occur with the authorization of the Minister or pursuant to regulations enacted by the Governor-in-Council . . . Fishing is permitted, subject to obtaining a licence and complying with any applicable conditions imposed under the Regulations. It is incongruous to say that fishing activity will be prohibited for the purpose of section 35 unless further authorization is obtained. Section 35 is a prohibition which may, in certain cases, lead to a prosecution under the Act. If Parliament intended that the words "work or undertaking" in section 35 should include fishing, it could and should have made that intention clear by importing words of limitation in the definition or elsewhere in the Act.

I endorse the Respondent's argument that, in any event, section 35 is not an absolute bar against causing HADD but only unauthorized activities that may lead to such result. It is clear from the statutory and regulatory framework that any legal fishing is subject to Ministerial authorization by means of a licence. As well, the *Fishery (General) Regulations*, supra, contain provisions concerning requests for authorization pursuant to section 35(2). Schedule VI of these Regulations details a number of specific activities for which an authorization is required, including bridges, culverts, dams, mining and erosion control. These types of activities do not fall within the definition of "fishing", although they may be ancillary to that endeavour.

The Applicant referred to the parliamentary debates relating to the amendment of the Order in 1977 which introduced provisions dealing with pollution prevention. Section 35 is found in the section of the Act that is introduced by the heading "Fish Habitat Protection and Pollution Prevention". Section 34 sets out various definitions for the purposes of sections 35 to 43. Section 34 defines "fish habitat" as follows: "fish habitat" means spawning grounds and nursery, rearing, food supply and migration areas on which fish depend directly or indirectly in order to carry out their life processes.

Reference to Parliamentary Debates can be useful for the purpose of interpreting a statute. It is clear from the material submitted by the Applicant that preservation and conservation of the fishery resource was an important consideration for the then Minister of Fisheries and indeed, that goal was supported by other members of Parliament who participated in the debate. However, the language of the Parliamentary Debates does not support the Applicant's argument that fishing activity authorized by the Minister or pursuant to the Regulations was meant to be encompassed by the words "work or undertaking" in section 35. . . . The jurisprudence cited by the Applicant in relation to "work or undertaking" in section 35 are decisions arising from prosecutions under that section. They are not relevant to the present case. In my opinion, section 35 does not apply to the Variation Order here in issue . . .

In the result, the application for judicial review is dismissed.

Notes and Questions

1. You will be introduced to the principles governing judicial review in Chapter 6. A key feature of this case, indeed many challenges to Ministerial decisions, is a high degree of judicial deference. To what extent, does this deference inform the court's conclusion that fishing (in particular, dragnet fishing) is not a "work or undertaking" under s. 35?

2. Does this decision stand for the proposition that fishing-related activities can never cause a HADD contrary to s. 35? Ought we to assume that this is Parliament's intent? If not, is this a problem in the form of standard that Parliament has employed, or in the manner in which the standard is drafted?

3. Notice that the court did not address the petitioner's argument about the precautionary principle. Recall, in this regard, the discussion in Chapter 1. Could the court, had it applied the principle, reached the same conclusion?

4. The petitioners also raised another interpretive argument that the court did not address. They contended that, for the purposes of s. 35, the adjective "harmful" only modifies noun "alteration". Do you agree? Why or why not?

Pollution Prevention: Section 36

Provisions in the *Fisheries Act* concerning pollution prevention have likewise been the subject of academic and public controversy. Section 36 has been described by critics as being overbroad, creating a "zero-tolerance" regime for marine pollution, even where the "deleterious substance" that has been discharged has caused no actual harm to the environment.

Subsection 36(3) provides that

> (3) subject to subsection (4) [*Ed. note:* Deposits authorized by regulation], no person shall deposit or permit the deposit of a deleterious substance of any type in water frequented by fish or in any place under any conditions where the *deleterious substance* or any other deleterious substance that results from the deposit of the deleterious substance may enter any such water (emphasis added)

The term "deleterious substance" is defined in subsection 34(1) as including:

> (a) any substance that, if added to *any water*, would degrade or alter or form part of a process of degradation or alteration of the quality of that water so that it is rendered or is likely to be rendered deleterious to fish or fish habitat or to the use by man of fish that frequent that water (emphasis added)

Like subsection 35(1), therefore, subsection 36(3) takes the form of a performance-based standard, prescribing that firms shall not release into "any water" a substance would affect the quality of that water to support fish or fish habitat. To avoid liability, however, a firm may rely on regulations that authorize such discharges. Subsection 36(5) of the Act enumerates the scope of these regulations which currently exempt certain substances (or classes of substances), as well as specific sites, works and undertakings. If, however, a project or activity being undertaken by a firm falls outside the scope of these regulations, it is by default subject to the requirements of subsection 36(3). This is even the case if the discharge is provincially permitted, though a defence of statutory authority may exist.

In this situation, courts — including two provincial Courts of Appeal — have been called upon in several leading cases to interpret to what the reference to "any water" in the definition of "deleterious substance" in subsection 34(1) refers. Both the British Columbia and Ontario Courts of Appeal have arrived at the same, "zero-tolerance" conclusion. In their view, "any water" is not a reference to the water into which the discharge actually occurred but rather, literally, any water whatsoever; regardless of quantity or other characteristics including whether it actually is frequented by fish. In the words of a critic, according to this approach, it therefore "does not matter whether the deposit actually disturbs any fish. All that counts is whether the substance itself is deleterious, meaning that, when added to any water in a laboratory, it makes that water deleterious". [*Ed note*: See Richler, *infra*.]

R. v. MacMillan Bloedel (Alberni) Ltd.

(1979), 47 C.C.C. (2d) 118 (B.C. C.A.)

SEATON J.A.: — The appellant was charged that it did unlawfully deposit a deleterious substance in water frequented by fish, contrary to s. 33(2) of the *Fisheries Act* [now s. 36(3)]. It was acquitted in the Provincial Court but an appeal was taken to the County Court where the acquittal was set aside and a conviction entered. This appeal from conviction is restricted to a question of law alone.

The appellant says that the County Court judge erred in his interpretation of the phrase "water frequented by fish", in his interpretation of the phrase "deleterious substance", and in denying the appellant's application to reopen the case.

The charge arose out of a spill of about 170 gallons of bunker C oil during unloading at the appellant's deep sea dock at Alberni Inlet. A suction valve was not closed when it ought to have been and the oil spilled beneath the dock. The appellant was prepared for this sort of accident and the response was prompt. Very little oil spread beyond the dock and the cleanup was carried out relatively quickly. If an offence was committed when the oil was spilled, the containment of the oil and the prompt cleanup would be relevant to the sentence but not the conviction . . .

I turn now to what is meant by "deleterious substance". It is the appellant's submission that to prove this charge the Crown must show that after the spill the water was made deleterious.

. . . Section 33(2) prohibits the deposit of a deleterious substance, not the deposit of a substance that causes the water to become deleterious. The argument to the contrary is based on the definition of "deleterious substance" . . .. in terms of this case, oil is a deleterious substance if, when added to any water, it would degrade or alter or form part of a process of degradation or alteration of the quality of that water so that that water is rendered deleterious to fish or to the use by man of fish that frequent that water. Applying that test to the findings of fact here, bunker C oil is a deleterious substance. Once it is determined that bunker C oil is a deleterious substance and that it has been deposited, the offence is complete without ascertaining whether the water itself was thereby rendered deleterious.

The appellant says that the purpose of this legislation is to prevent waters being rendered deleterious to fish and that if given the plain meaning of the words, an absurdity will result. It is said that if a teaspoon of oil was put in the Pacific ocean and oil was a deleterious substance, that would constitute an offence. In its submission that absurdity can be avoided by reading the Act to require that the water be made deleterious. There are some attractions to that reasoning, but I think that the result would be at least as unsatisfactory. Nothing could be done to prevent damage to the water that fell short of rendering the water deleterious. To prove that the damage had gone that far would be difficult indeed.

Had it been the intention of Parliament to prohibit the deposit of a substance in water so as to render that water deleterious to fish, that would have been easy to express. A different prohibition was decided upon. It is more strict. It seeks to exclude each part of the process of degradation. The thrust of the section is to prohibit certain things, called deleterious substances, being put in the water. That is the plain meaning of the words used and is the meaning that I feel bound to apply. . . .

I would dismiss the appeal.

R. v. Kingston (City)

(2004), 70 O.R. (3d) 577 (Ont. C.A.)

[The City of Kingston operated a municipal dump site on the west shore of the Cataraqui River, adjacent to Belle Island, from the early 1950s to the early 1970s. The landfill was created in a marsh in the Cataraqui River and formed a peninsula of garbage. After its closure, the landfill site was transformed into a recreational area but little was done to address the possibility of leachate generation and migration.

The charges in the instant case arise from alleged contaminants emanating from the landfill site and entering the Cataraqui River. Ms. Fletcher laid charges by means of a private citizen's information. The Ministry laid separate charges by means of its own information. Both the private prosecutor and the Ministry took and tested samples of leachate entering the Cataraqui River from the landfill site. See discussion of private prosecutions in Chapter 6.]

GILLESE JA:

All the experts at trial agreed that ammonia was the main toxicant rendering the samples acutely lethal. Ammonia is a naturally occurring substance which, at certain concentration levels, is necessary for life. Ammonia is composed of unionized ammonia (NH3) and ionized ammonia (NH4+). Unionized ammonia is much more toxic than ionized ammonia. . . . Some species of fish are more sensitive to unionized ammonia than others. . . .

On an ordinary and plain reading of paragraph (a) [of section 34(1)], a substance is deleterious if, when added to *any water*, it would alter the quality of the water such that it is likely to render the water deleterious to fish, fish habitat or to the use by man of fish that frequent the water. There is no stipulation in paragraph (a) that the substance must be proven to be deleterious to the receiving water. There is no reference to the receiving water in paragraph (a). On the contrary, the language makes it clear that the substance is deleterious if, when added to any water, it degrades or alters the quality of the water to which it has been added. The "any water" referred to in paragraph (a) is not the receiving water. Rather, it is any water to which the impugned substance is added, after which it can be determined whether the quality of that water is rendered deleterious to fish, fish habitat or the use by man of fish that frequent that water. (Emphasis in original)

Approving the BCCA's approach in *MacMillan Bloedel*, the Ontario Court of Appeal went on to conclude that was s. 36(3) prohibits is the deposit of a deleterious substance in water frequented by fish, not "the deposit of a substance that causes the receiving water to become deleterious".

Notes and Questions

In the following article, Ian Richler argues that subsection 36(3) is constitutionally overbroad contrary to section 7 of the *Charter*. Invoking the *BC Motor Vehicle Reference* (SCC, 1985), he contends that this is because it risks criminalizing conduct that is not harmful. Thus, even though protection of fish and fish habitat is a worthy and pressing objective, "If the state, in pursuing a legitimate objective, uses means which are broader than is necessary to accomplish that objective, the principles of fundamental justice will be violated because the individual's rights will have been limited for no reason". Richler then proceeds to consider a variety of counter-arguments to his contention.

Ian Richler, "*R. v. Kingston* and the Criminalization of Harmless Pollution", Case Comment

(2005) 15 J Env. L. & Prac. 319

I anticipate several challenges to my argument that s. 36(3), as interpreted in *MacMillan Bloedel* and *Kingston*, is unconstitutionally overbroad. One is that my argument has already been rejected by the courts. . . . In *R. v. Leveque* the Ontario Superior Court held that s. 35(1) of the *Fisheries Act* [*Ed. note:* The HADD provision considered above], which prohibits carrying on "any work or undertaking that results in the harmful alteration, disruption or destruction of fish habitat", is not overbroad . . .

That reasoning does not apply to s. 36(3) because the two provisions are very different. For one thing, s. 35(1) requires proof of harm to fish habitat, whereas s. 36(3) does not look at real-world effects. Also, the Court in *Leveque* held that s. 35(1) "does not attract [penal] consequences for trivial or minimal impacts on fish habitat". By contrast, *MacMillan Bloedel* made it clear that the extent of the injury to fisheries is of no consequence. Finally, unlike s. 36(3), s. 35(1) has a built-in pre-authorization process whereby anyone wishing to do something that might harm fish habitat may apply for permission. For the Court in *Leveque*, this process was another reason that s. 35(1) is not overbroad. . . .

The second challenge to my overbreadth argument is that it makes no sense to assess s. 36(3) based on its impact on what Peter Hogg calls the "most innocent possible offender". My response is that the Supreme Court has expressly endorsed the notion of using "reasonable hypotheticals" when determining whether a law is overbroad — after all, the B.C. Court of Appeal said that a conviction could result from a teaspoon of oil in the ocean. . . . Indeed there is no need to resort to imagining, because *Kingston* provides a perfect illustration of the problem. The Ontario Court of Appeal noted that ammonia is a natural substance that is actually beneficial to aquatic life in some circumstances. Should someone who deposits a demonstrably benign amount of ammonia face a conviction? Zero-tolerance for such substances is not only illogical, it may actually be counterproductive.

The third challenge is related to the second one. It says that s. 36(3) is not overbroad because prosecutors and environmental investigators have enough good sense never to charge people with trivial breaches of the provision. But this notion is directly at odds with . . . *R. v. Smith*, where the SCC held that a law cannot be saved just by showing that its unfair applications are in fact avoided due to the discretion of officials: even if no one is likely ever to be charged with depositing a minute amount of pollution, it is entirely conceivable that charges will be laid in situations where the actual or likely harm to fisheries is unclear. Indeed that is exactly what happened in *MacMillan Bloedel* and *Kingston*. It is also worth noting that *Kingston* started as a private prosecution. The discretion argument loses much of its force when any concerned citizen can investigate and prosecute an alleged offence.

The fourth challenge was raised by the B.C. Court of Appeal in *MacMillan Bloedel*: it would be too onerous for the Crown to have to prove that the deposit in question caused harm. My response is simply that it *should* be onerous for the Crown to make out a criminal or quasi-criminal conviction. It is true that regulatory offences are subject to a lower standard of *Charter* scrutiny than purely criminal ones. But the rationale for that lower standard does not fully apply to s. 36(3). In particular, it cannot be said that everyone charged under s. 36(3) made a conscious decision to enter a regulated arena: s. 36(3) applies in the same way to the recreational canoeist as it does to a chemicals manufacturer or to a municipality. Besides, the s. 7 rights of anyone charged with depositing a deleterious substance are reduced in other respects. That is, the Crown already gets a break. Most notably, there is no need for the Crown to prove *mens rea*. A lower standard of *Charter* scrutiny does not mean that the accused has no *Charter* rights at all. While requiring proof of harm would make prosecutions harder (and thus, presumably, rarer) than they are today, it should not be seen as being unduly harsh on the Crown. Such a requirement is, after all, imposed on the Crown when prosecuting several other environmental offences, including s. 35(1) of the *Fisheries Act* and s. 30(1) of the OWRA.

The fifth challenge to my overbreadth argument is that a broad law is necessary in order to deter pollution. This can easily be rebuffed. There is simply no value in deterring harmless pollution. An overbroad law will not deter harmful pollution any more effectively than a law that captures only harmful pollution. An overbroad law may even lead to disrespect and disregard for that law.

The sixth challenge is that s. 36(3) already has enough built-in safeguards for the accused. In particular, imprisonment is not available as a punishment for someone's first conviction under s. 36(3), but rather only for subsequent convictions. Also, the accused can always raise a defence of due diligence. That is, someone charged with spilling a deleterious substance could be acquitted if it were shown that he or she took all reasonable care to prevent the spill. The problem with this line of reasoning is that just because an offence is not as draconian as it could be does not mean that it is not draconian.

The seventh challenge is that the courts should not second-guess Parliament when it decides to enact broad laws . . . Drafting pollution laws is especially tricky because, as the Court held in *Canadian Pacific*, environmental protection "is not conducive to precise codification". The Court elaborated:

> Environmental protection is a legitimate concern of government, and as I have already observed, it is a very broad subject-matter which does not lend itself to precise codification. Where the legislature is pursuing the objective of environmental protection, it is justified in choosing equally broad legislative language in order to provide for a necessary degree of flexibility.

This challenge is not convincing because it presupposes that s. 36(3) means what *MacMillan Bloedel* and *Kingston* say it means. That is, it merely begs the question. But, as I will argue later on, s. 36(3) is open to another, better interpretation. A court that opted for that alternative interpretation would have at least as good a claim to judicial deference as the courts in *MacMillan Bloedel* and *Kingston*.

The eighth and strongest challenge to my argument is that s. 36(3) must be very broad because only then could it capture deposits that, though seemingly innocuous on their own, can lead to real harm when combined with similar deposits over time. As the Law Reform Commission of Canada noted 20 years ago when it examined the notion of adding a pollution offence to the *Criminal Code*, "A lake can finally lose the ability to cope with accumulated acid rain, and will die". The problem with this challenge is that its logic does not extend to all types of substances. While it may be true that even a tiny amount of a substance like PCBs — which is persistent and bio-accumulative — is harmful or forms part of a process of harm, the same does not hold for, say, ammonia, which dissipates quickly in water and is actually beneficial to aquatic life in some concentrations. It is simply irrational to adopt a zero-tolerance policy towards substances like ammonia. But that is precisely what *Kingston* has done.

One solution to this problem is the one devised in *Inco*: a distinction is drawn between "inherently toxic" substances, for which there is zero-tolerance, and all other substances, for which there is some tolerance based on the circumstances of the discharge . . . the Superior Court in *Kingston* adopted this solution only to be overturned by the Court of Appeal. This solution is sensible because it refocuses s. 36(3) on harm to the receiving water. That is, it draws a clear nexus between the prohibition and the objective.

Notes and Questions

1. Do you agree that *Fisheries Act* offences should be framed as performance based? What are some of the reasons why subsection 35(1) and subsection 36(3) are drafted as they are? How might their effectiveness be enhanced?

2. When businesses lobby government for performance-based regulations that optimize their ability to decide how they will comply with regulatory requirements are these sections akin to what they have in mind?

3. Earlier, the originators of the Smart Regulation concept suggested that where the regulated community is composed of "heterogeneous enterprises facing heterogeneous conditions" there is a strong theoretical justification exists for management-based standards, all other things being equal (Gunningham and Sinclair, 2002). How, if at all, does this conclusion apply to pollution prevention in the fisheries context?

4. Can it be said that subsections 35(1) and 36(3) are forms of prescriptive regulation? Consider, in this regard, the discussion of concept of "prescriptiveness" *infra* in this chapter. Why or why not?

The *Canadian Environmental Protection Act*

While the *Fisheries Act* is Canada's oldest and arguably still Canada's most rigorous federal environmental law, the *Canadian Environmental Protection Act* (CEPA) is broadly seen as the cornerstone of federal environmental law and policy. Originally enacted in 1988, CEPA was the first serious attempt to provide a coordinated response to the growing range of environmental challenges confronting Canada at the national level. A key feature of the CEPA, from its origins to date, is its focus on the classification, identification, and regulation of the thousands of chemical substances currently, or proposed for use in Canada. While development of Toxic Substances List proceeded at a relatively slow (some might even say "leisurely") pace during CEPA's early years, in recent years (particularly after the Act was amended in 1999) additions to the "List" have accelerated.

However, CEPA's ambit extends far beyond the regulation of harmful substances. In recent years, it has become the implementation tool of choice for a variety of international obligations Canada has undertaken including ozone layer depletion (the *Montreal Protocol*), ocean dumping (the *London Convention*), and the movement of hazardous goods and substances (the *Basel Convention*). It also seems poised to serve as a key vehicle for implementing the Kyoto Protocol on Climate Change.

CEPA is divided into 12 parts. Key among these are its provisions relating to public participation (Part 3); information gathering (Part 4); pollution prevention (Part 4); toxic substance categorization and control (Part 5); biotechnology (Part 6); pollution control (Part 7); emergency orders and measures (Part 8); and enforcement (Part 10).

Various Parts of the Act are substantially integrated. For instance, the provisions on biotechnology in Part 6 mirror the categorization process set out in Part 5. And the pollution prevention provisions in Part 4 are likewise closely linked to the pollution control provisions found in Part 5.

Public participation plays a central role in CEPA's architecture. CEPA contains a variety of provisions aimed at keeping the public informed about administrative decisions made under its provisions. These include a variety of informational measures including mandating of a public registry and requirements on decision-makers to provide "notice and comment" opportunities to the public. There are also several "action-forcing" provisions including a provision that allows for members of the public to trigger an investigation into violations of CEPA, and, in limited circumstances, to commence an environmental protection in their own right where the Minister has failed to conduct or report on an investigation. There is also a provision that entitles members of the public to commence an action for damages resulting from losses arising from violation of CEPA. However, no environmental protection actions or actions seeking damages for harm to the environment have been brought to date.

In many respects, the "heart and soul" of CEPA is Part 5 which focuses on the control of toxic substances. As set out in Chapter 3, federal jurisdiction in this area was confirmed in the well known S.C.C. decision of *R. v. Hydro-Québec*, [1997] 3 S.C.R. 213. In this case, albeit in a split decision, the court upheld the validity of this aspect of CEPA under the "criminal law power" which it opined not only vested the federal Crown to regulate to protect public health (in this case by means of an interim order banning the release of PCBs) but also, more broadly, to protect the environment.

Part 5 contemplates a two step procedure for regulating toxic substances. The first involves an assessment of the risks associated with the substance in question. If this analysis leads to a conclusion that a substance is "toxic", a second stage of analysis is triggered that involves consideration of potential means through which the risks identified can be managed, reduced or eliminated through regulation, alternative measures or a combination of both.

CEPA provides that all substances used or proposed to be used in Canada must initially be listed on either the Domestic Substances List or the Non-Domestic Substances List. The former category consists of some 23,000 substances being used domestically within Canada when CEPA was first enacted. Substances on the Domestic List were "grandfathered"; as such, they were not subject to CEPA regulation until such time as they could be appropriately reviewed and categorized. Substances on the Non-Domestic List are prohibited from import into or manufacture in Canada until they are approved under CEPA.

Given the large number of substances on the Domestic List, this review process has in many cases proceeded at a rate that has given rise to criticism. [*Ed note*: See, for example, the M'Gonigle *et al.* article, *infra* this chapter.] This process of review can be convoluted, contested and time consuming. It commences with a classification stage; a screening level assessment; possible assessment for inclusion on the Priority Substances List (a list of substances identified as being priorities for listing due to their potential toxicity); control or virtual elimination of the substance by virtue of listing under the Toxic Substances list; or alternatively a confirmation that the substance should remain unregulated on the Domestic Substances List.

Once a substance has been identified as toxic under the Part 5 review process, the Ministers of Health and Environment are given two years to pass regulations controlling its import, manufacture and use. PCBs (polychlorinated biphenyls) were among the first substances designated for regulation under this process. Initially this was done by means of an interim order that gave rise to the jurisdictional challenge in *R. v. Hydro Québec*. Subsequently, the use, storage and export of PCB have come under a variety of purpose-specific regulations enacted under CEPA including the *Chlorobiphenyls Regulations*, SOR/91-152 (governing permitted and prohibited uses); the *Federal Mobile PCB Treatment and Destruction Regulations*, SOR/90-5 (governing treatment and destruction of PCB waste on federal land); the *Storage of PCB Material Regulations*, SOR/92-507 (governing the storage of PCB waste awaiting destruction and disposal); and the *PCB Export Regulations*, SOR/97-109 (governing the export of PCB abroad). New regulations designed to update and consolidate existing regulations relating to PCB use and storage have been drafted and are expected to come into force in the near future.

One of the most controversial episodes in the history of Part 5 arose in 1995 when then Minister of the Environment Sheila Copps, acting under subsection 35(1) of CEPA, made an interim order banning the export of PCB waste from Canada. This order led to a claim under the investor protection provisions of NAFTA chapter 11 by S.D. Myers, an Ohio-based PCB disposal company. [*Ed note*: See Chapter 1 for an overview of interplay between investor rights and environmental protection.]

The company contended that the order was politically motivated and, as such, primarily designed to protect Canadian business interests, particularly those of Canadian-based companies with which it was in competition for PCB waste disposal contracts. The Canadian government rejected this argument, claiming that the order was motivated by a *bona fide* desire to comply with international obligations it had undertaken as a signatory to the *Basel Convention on the Transboundary Movement of Hazardous Wastes*. A NAFTA investment tribunal disagreed and awarded S.D. Myers damages of over $6 million, a decision that was later upheld on judicial review to the Federal Court.

Sanford Gaines, "Environmental Policy Implications of Investor-State Arbitration under NAFTA Chapter 11"[3]

This story concerns a claim for compensation by a US company, S.D. Myers, Inc. (SDMI), against Canada for measures affecting the export of polychlorinated biphenyls (PCBs) from Canada to the United States for incineration. In this case, environmental policy and economic policy decisions in both the United States and Canada converged and diverged in ways that undercut a business plan by SDMI to compete for PCB remediation business in Canada through a Canadian subsidiary.

PCBs are a family of chemical compounds that are nonflammable and do not conduct electricity. For that reason, they were marketed and used widely as a dielectric fluid for electricity transformers and other heavy duty electrical equipment. In the late 1960s and early 1970s, toxicity studies showed high human and environmental toxicity from polychlorinated compounds such as PCBs. As early as 1973, the Organisation for Economic Cooperation and Development called on member governments to reduce use of PCBs.

In 1976, when the US Congress enacted the *Toxic Substances Control Act*, it included a separate article on PCBs, calling for an immediate halt to their manufacture and sale in the United States and banning importation of PCBs. In 1977, Canada also moved to phase out use of PCBs. Nevertheless, Canada had already imported 40,000 metric tonnes of high-concentration PCBs, resulting in an enormous inventory of electrical equipment containing PCBs. This presented a long-term challenge about how to dispose of the PCBs as this equipment was taken out of service.

SDMI, based in Tallmadge, Ohio, started as a family-owned electrical equipment repair and maintenance company. In the 1980s, as an outgrowth of its core business, it developed a separate business of remediation of PCB-contaminated electrical equipment through incineration of PCBs. By 1990, SDMI was a leading company in US PCB disposal, and had established PCB remediation operations in Australia, Mexico, and South Africa

. . . in the early 1990s, only one Canadian PCB disposal and destruction facility was available, the Alberta Special Waste Treatment Centre in Swan Hills, Alberta, northwest of Edmonton. SDMI decided that the eastern Canada PCB wastes presented an attractive business opportunity for SDMI with its Ohio incineration facility close to eastern Canada. But it faced a legal obstacle in the US ban on imports of PCBs.

In 1993, SDMI began a concerted effort to overcome this obstacle and obtain the Canadian business . . . and began lobbying both US and Canadian environmental officials.

The terms of the bilateral Agreement on the Transboundary Movement of Hazardous Wastes between the United States and Canada allowed for cross-border movement of waste for environmentally-sound disposal and Canadian PCB waste export regulations authorized export to the United States with the consent of the US EPA. Myers was supported in this

---

3 (2006: CEC research paper #5), online: <<http://www.cec.org/files/PDF/ECONOMY/Final-Gaines-T-E-Symposium05-Paper_en.pdf>>.

effort by many eastern Canadian firms who believed that disposal of their PCBs by SDMI in Ohio would be less expensive than shipping to Swan Hills.

EPA began public consideration of SDMI's request for a relaxation of the US import ban in early 1995. SDMI had an excellent performance record in incineration of US PCB wastes and the transportation risks of bringing PCBs from Canada to Ohio were slight, so EPA searched for options to allow the PCBs to be imported. On 26 October 1995, EPA issued to SDMI a written notice of "enforcement discretion" under which EPA promised, in effect, not to enforce the import ban for PCBs from Canada for disposal (by destruction) by SDMI in the United States between 15 November 1995 and 31 December 1997.

Canadian environmental officials, as well as the commercial company operating the Swan Hills treatment center, Chem-Security, had been monitoring the EPA developments closely. In July 1995, before final EPA action, Canada's environment minister responded to a parliamentary question by enunciating a government position that, "the handling of [Canada's] PCBs should be done in Canada by Canadians".

No sooner had EPA announced its "enforcement discretion" policy than Chem-Security wrote to the minister urging a quick Canadian response to the imminent opening of the US border to trade in PCBs. On 16 November 1995, one day after the border was "opened" under the EPA policy, the Environment Minister signed an Interim Order in Council amending Canada's PCB *Waste Export Regulations* to prohibit the export of Canadian PCBs, thus effectively closing the border from the Canadian side. The Privy Council confirmed the Interim Order on 28 November 1995 . . .

[Ultimately, SDMI sued Canada for damages under NAFTA Chapter 11 in 1998] . . . SDMI alleged four violations of Chapter 11: failure to afford national treatment to S.D. Myers Canada; failure to afford S.D. Myers Canada fair and equitable treatment; imposition of improper performance requirements; and effective expropriation of the [Canadian] investment . . . as a result of the first three violations.

[T]he arbitral tribunal found that the actions of Canada in closing the border to PCB waste exports were not grounded in or justified by concerns about environmental risks of export of PCBs or considerations of environmental policy, but were motivated instead by an interest in maintaining the flow of waste materials to the Swan Hills facility. The tribunal refers, for example, to an internal briefing paper of Department of the Environment officials recommending support for the EPA enforcement discretion proposal "because it represents a technically and environmentally sound solution for the destruction of some of Canada's PCBs". The tribunal sums up its review of the evidence as follows:

> Insofar as intent in concerned, the documentary record as a whole clearly indicates that the Interim Order and the Final Order were intended primarily to protect the Canadian PCB disposal industry from U.S. competition. CANADA produced no convincing witness testimony to rebut the thrust of the documentary evidence. The tribunal finds that there was no legitimate environmental reason for introducing the ban. Insofar as there was an indirect environmental objective — to keep the Canadian industry strong in order to assure a continued disposal capability — it could have been achieved by other measures.

In its final award on damages, the tribunal awarded SDMI CAN$6.05 million plus interest for its lost business opportunity during the period of the Canadian closure of the border to PCB exports.

When SDMI . . . sought to do business in Canada, the two primary options for disposal of the PCB wastes in eastern Canada that the Canadian government had in view were the SDMI option of export for incineration in Ohio or the shipment of the waste to Swan Hills, Alberta for treatment and destruction at the Alberta Special Waste Treatment Center. Several additional facts are pertinent to an evaluation of the relative environmental merits of the two options.

. . . In terms of proximity, shipment of PCB wastes from eastern Canada to Swan Hills, 160 kilometers northwest of Edmonton, Alberta, requires transport over 3000 kilometers or more. This clearly presented a higher transportation hazard than shipment some hundreds kilometers to Tallmadge, Ohio. In fact, in 1985 there had already been a serious spill of PCBs during transport from Ontario to Swan Hills.

Another environmental factor is the reliability and performance of the disposal facilities. The US EPA provided SDMI with its "enforcement discretion" exemption after having determined that SDMI had operated its Ohio facility in an exemplary fashion and that the PCB destruction capability of its incinerator was extremely high, above 99.9999% destruction. The Swan Hills facility also featured high-temperature incineration capability, but its performance history had been uneven. When it first opened, Swan Hills was a joint venture between the province of Alberta and a private company, and focused on treatment and disposal of Alberta wastes. In 1995, just as SDMI was beginning its effort to do business in Canada, the facility was authorized to import PCB wastes from other Canadian provinces, though Alberta has maintained a prohibition on imports of PCB wastes from outside Canada.

In the hands of private contractors, however, operational controls were not fully maintained. Local citizens, workers, and First Nations complained of contamination of the workplace and the environment from facility operations, including PCB incineration. In 1996, during the period of Canada's export ban, a mechanical failure at Swan Hills led to a release of PCBs, and formal government charges against the facility. A few months later, the Provincial Health Officer issued an advisory against eating wild game from within a 30 kilometer radius of the facility. In July 1997, an explosion at an incinerator forced it to be shut down. Eventually, the private company sold its share back to the province, and operations were temporarily contracted out to another firm.

Other facilities in Canada have an equally sketchy history. A PCB incineration facility was built in Ontario in 1999 by SRBP Resource Recovery, but the facility has been the target of investigation and legal charges regarding air pollution. Another US company operates PCB remediation at Kirkland Lake, Ontario, but does not provide PCB destruction capability. This company was recently found guilty of an environmental violation in 2001 in attempting to send an illegal shipment of "mixed waste" including PCBs to Swan Hills.

In hindsight, technological developments since the S.D. Myers case have eroded the very premises of the two-option analysis of the mid-1990s. PCB remediation technology has advanced away from large fixed incinerators toward smaller mobile units. Consequently, in 1999, less than a year after submitting its Chapter 11 claim, SDMI sold its US and Canada-based PCB remediation business and its Tallmadge, Ohio facility to Safety-Kleen Corporation, in order to focus on mobile PCB remediation services in other countries.

Canada claimed that the export ban was based on environmental policy, in particular the Basel Convention on the Transboundary Movement of Hazardous Wastes and Their Disposal, to which Canada is a party . . . The Convention articulates a self-sufficiency principle (Article 4(2)(b), "ensure the availability of adequate disposal facilities, to the extent possible, within its own boundaries") and a principle of minimizing transboundary movements of waste (Article 4(2)(d), "ensure that the transboundary movement of hazardous wastes and other waste is reduced to the minimum consistent with the environmentally sound and efficient management of such wastes").

Notwithstanding these provisions, Canada had long maintained a policy of allowing PCB waste exports to the United States even after suspending export to other countries in 1990. This policy accorded with the consistent advice of senior officials in Environment Canada that the allowance of PCB waste exports was consistent with Canada's interpretation of the *Basel Convention*, with Canada's bilateral *Agreement on the Transboundary Movement of Hazardous Wastes* with the United States, and with an objective assessment of the relative environmental risks of shipment of PCB wastes to Ohio as compared to Alberta. Canada had also consistently expressed the view in international negotiations that Article 4(2) should not be construed to bar environmentally sound transboundary movements of waste.

The strongest environmental policy argument for the Canadian export ban was the Basel self sufficiency principle, the obligation to assure adequate domestic disposal capability. To begin with, the United States had, for many years, maintained a strict prohibition on import of PCB wastes, even from Canada. The Canadian government doubted, rightly as it turned out, that EPA's "enforcement discretion" for SDMI offered a durable or reliable alternative to PCB waste disposal in Canada. If Canada had allowed its inventory of PCB wastes to be shipped to Ohio, Chem-Security might have been left with an insufficient volume of waste to sustain its continued operation. As it is, the facility has never made a profit for its commercial operators. On this point, the tribunal simply asserted that Canada's objective "could have been achieved by other measures". . . . the tribunal's analysis is too glib on this point.

When faced with a shortage of local wastes for disposal, commercial operators exert tremendous pressure on their government regulators to relax import restrictions so that the facility can tap a broader market. This was what S.D. Myers was doing when it lobbied EPA to allow it to import Canadian PCB wastes for destruction in Ohio. Similarly, the operators of Swan Hills had already persuaded Alberta to allow import of wastes from outside the province . . . In the face of SDMI's competitive advantage in handling eastern Canada PCB waste, it is not obvious that there were practical "other measures" to foster and maintain PCB disposal capacity in Canada.

That still leaves the question of how best to manage a complex situation like the environmentally sound management of Canada's stockpile of PCB wastes. In the end, given the operational deficiencies at Swan Hills and its remoteness from the wastes in eastern Canada, the S.D. Myers option had substantial environmental advantages for Canada, as well as offering major cost savings to those having the burden of getting their wastes destroyed. S.D. Myers might have been able to expedite destruction of high-level PCB wastes in Canada. Even after the reclosing of the border from the U.S. side, Swan Hills has remained an unattractive option. Only recently have mobile incinerators have begun to offer reliable and cost-effective options for eastern Canadian companies and government agencies still holding these wastes.

Even if there are some environmental arguments to be made in defense of maintaining a source of PCB wastes to develop Canadian disposal capacity, the NAFTA arbitrators in the S.D. Myers case should not be castigated for undue interference or second-guessing of a legitimate government decision. The paper trail of the decision to close off exports to the United States vividly showed that it was taken against the advice of professional staff experts at Environment Canada and was closely linked to personal interventions by Chem-Security at the highest political levels. Even in the face of that record, the tribunal made meticulously clear their disinclination to pass judgment on Canada's environmental policy discretion:

> When interpreting and applying the "minimum standard", a Chapter 11 tribunal does not have an open-ended mandate to second-guess government decision-making. Governments have to make many potentially controversial choices. In doing so, they may appear to have made mistakes, to have misjudged the facts, proceeded on the basis of a misguided economic or sociological theory, placed too much emphasis on some social values over others and adopted solutions that are ultimately ineffective or counterproductive. The ordinary remedy, if there were one, for errors in modern governments is through internal political and legal processes, including elections.

Moreover, the tribunal concluded that Canada's action in this case did not constitute an "expropriation" under NAFTA Article 1110. In so holding, the tribunal took a view of regulatory expropriation very much along the lines advocated by environmental law commentators. In particular, the tribunal held that, in general, "expropriation" connotes a "taking" of private property by, and the transfer of such property's ownership to, a government. Expropriations involve the deprivation of ownership rights or a lasting removal of private economic rights. Regulations involve a lesser interference with economic rights. Regulatory action does not generally amount to expropriation, so regulatory conduct by a government is unlikely to support a legitimate complaint under Article 1110.

. . . . .

As with the other NAFTA Chapter 11 cases, it is difficult to discern from the record of the arbitration or from the response of the government to the findings of the arbitral tribunal any extra burden on the normal processes of environmental regulatory decision making. When Canada adopted the export ban, it had not established, or even thought of establishing, any scientific foundation for the ban through health studies, environmental evaluation, risk assessment, or other evidence showing that exporting PCBs for disposal by S. D. Myers created a health or safety risk different from or greater than the risk associated with shipment to Swan Hills. Within less than a year, Canada reversed the export ban for its own reasons, long before SDMI filed its Chapter 11 claim. Finally, the NAFTA tribunal did not care whether the measure bore an "environmental" or an "economic" label, but looked to the documented intent of the officials involved and the demonstrable effect of the regulations on the environment as well as on trade and investment.

Notes and Questions

1. The *S.D. Myers* case remains a source of controversy and debate. Critics of NAFTA argue that it and other tribunal decisions under chapter 11 of NAFTA and analogous bilateral investment treaties underscore the extent to which such agreements represent a threat to national sovereignty and environmental protection. On the other hand, proponents of NAFTA (including the previous author) and similar investor protection regimes cite the decision as an illustration of how such regimes provide a salutary form of market discipline in cases where governments take action for questionable protectionist reasons. Indeed, in many such cases, they would argue, protectionism is at odds with prudent environmental stewardship. For further discussion of related trade and environment-related issues see Chapter 1.

2. The case has also been interpreted by some as illustrating an economic analysis of regulation often referred to as the "Baptist-bootlegger" theory. This theory contends that lobbying efforts to secure favourable regulatory action will most often be successful if at least two quite different interest groups are working in the same direction: "bootleggers" and "Baptists". An advocate of this approach explains that this theory originated

> . . . in the southern United States where, in places, Sunday closing laws prevent the legal sale of alcoholic beverages. This is advantageous to bootleggers, who sell alcoholic beverages illegally; they get the market to themselves on Sundays. Baptists and other religious groups support the same laws, but for entirely different reasons. They are opposed to selling alcohol at all, especially on Sunday. They take the moral high ground, while the bootleggers persuade politicians quietly, behind closed doors. Such a coalition makes it easier for politicians to favor both groups. In other words, the Baptists lower the costs of favor-seeking for the bootleggers because politicians can pose as being motivated purely by the public interest even while they promote the interests of well-funded businesses (see B. Yandle, "Bootleggers, Baptists and the Climate Warming Battle" (2002) 26 Harv. Envtl. L.R. 177 at 188).

In the *S.D. Myers* case, this theory would postulate that what made it plausible and possible for the Canadian government to enact the ban on PCB exports was its ability to disguise the politically motivated protectionism underlying the decision, by clothing it in "green". Yandle argues that the actions of Canadian and European governments around Kyoto implementation can also be explained by this theory.

3. Canada has only rarely banned the cross border movement of toxic substances. Another high profile illustration arose in 1998 when on ostensibly environmental grounds, it banned the international and interprovincial transport of the fuel additive Methylcyclopentadienyl Manganese Tricarbonyl (MMT). In this case, the ban took the form of a stand-alone statute because MMT was not on CEPA's Toxic Substances List. As in *S.D. Myers*, the ban

led to a lawsuit under chapter 11 of NAFTA. Before the case was argued, the Canadian government settled the claim (brought by Ethyl Corp., the main US producer of the additive) for close to $20 million dollars; it also recanted its position that MMT was environmentally harmful and lifted its ban. Like *S.D. Myers*, it has been argued that the *Ethyl* case is an illustration of the Baptist-bootlegger thesis. See Soloway, "Environmental Trade Barriers under NAFTA: The MMT Fuel Additives Controversy" (1999) 8 Minn. J. Global Trade 55. Soloway contends that the ban was intended jointly to appease Canadian producers of ethanol (a competitor fuel additive) and vocal environmental interests.

4. How convincing is the Baptist-bootlegger theory of regulation? Is a key determinant of government action on the environment whether such action advances the need of key business players? If so, what implications does this have for environmental organizations' law and policy reform strategies?

References

We thank the copyright holders for their permission to reproduce their materials.

C. Coglianese & D. Lazar, "Management-based Regulation: Prescribing Private Management to Achieve Public Goals" (2003) 37 Law & Soc'y Rev. 691–730

C. Coglianese, J. Nash & T. Olmstead, "Performance-based Regulation: Prospects and limitations in Health, Safety and Environmental Protection" (2003) 55 Admin. L. Rev. 705–728

D. Paul Emond, "The Greening of Environmental Law" (1991) 36 McGill L.J. 742

M.A.H. Franson, R.T. Franson & A.R. Lucas, *Environmental Standards: A Comparative Study of Canadian Standards, Standard Setting Processes, and Enforcement* (Edmonton: Environmental Council of Alberta, 1982)

J. Freeman & D. Farber, "Modular Environmental Regulation" (2005) 54 Duke L.J. 795–912

N. Gunningham & D. Sinclair, *Leaders and Laggards: Next Generation Environmental Regulation* (Sheffield: Greenleaf, 2002)

N. Gunningham & P. Grabosky, *Smart Regulation Designing Environmental Policy* (Oxford: Oxford University Press, 1998)

K. Harrison, "Talking with the Donkey: Cooperative Approaches to Environmental Protection" (1999) 2 Journal of Industrial Ecology 51. Copyright © 1999, Yale University. Reproduced with the permission of Canada Law Book, A Division of the Cartwright Group, Ltd. (1-800-263-3269, www.canadalawbook.ca)

R.M. M'Gonigle, T.L. Jamieson, M.K. McAllister & R.M. Peterman, "Taking Uncertainty Seriously: From Permissive Regulation to Preventative Design in Environmental Decision Making" (1994) 32 Osgoode Hall L.J. 99

I. Richler, "*R. v. Kingston* and the Criminalization of Harmless Pollution", Case Comment, (2005) 15 J.E.L.P. 319

J. Soloway, "Environmental Trade Barriers under NAFTA: the MMT Fuel Additives Controversy" (1999) 8 Minn. J. Global Trade 55

C. Tollefson, F. Gale & D. Haley, *Setting the Standard: Certification, Governance and the Forest Stewardship Council* (UBC Press, 2008). Reprinted with permission of the Publisher from *Setting the Standard: Certification, Governance and the Forest Stewardship Council* by Chris Tollefson, Fred Gale and David Haley © University of British Columbia Press 2008. All rights reserved by the Publisher.

C. Tollefson, "Games without Frontiers: Investor Claims and Citizen Suits under the NAFTA Regime" (2002) 27 Yale J. Int'l L. 217

B. Yandle, "Bootleggers, Baptists and the Climate Warming Battle" (2002) 26 Harv. Envtl. L. Rev. 177

5

COMPLIANCE AND ENFORCEMENT

Introduction

A key measure of the effectiveness of environmental regulation is compliance by the regulated community. Where compliance is not forthcoming, regulators must respond by taking enforcement action or risk undermining the legitimacy and credibility of the regulatory regime. This chapter surveys a range of compliance and enforcement-related issues that arise in the environmental law context.

Part I provides definitions for some of the key concepts in this area, and reflects on the difficulties associated with assessing the efficacy of compliance and enforcement efforts. It also seeks to provide an overview of the current state of environmental compliance and enforcement "on the ground". In Part II, we consider the ongoing debate over the relative merits of cooperative versus adversarial approaches to environmental enforcement. The focus of Part III is on the legal principles and leading cases in this area. It considers a variety of topics, including:

- The role of the *Criminal Code* in environmental prosecutions
- The nature and role of the regulatory offence under federal and provincial legislation and related jurisprudence
- Sentencing in environmental cases
- Directors and officers' liability and
- Administrative monetary penalties (AMPs)

The chapter concludes, in Part IV, with reflections on the current and potential future role of citizens in environment enforcement. This section considers citizen suit provisions, avenues for citizen participation in enforcement actions under EBR (Environmental Bill of Rights) provisions; and private prosecutions.

Part I — Regulatory Compliance and Enforcement Strategies

Defining and Measuring Compliance and Enforcement

Joseph Castrilli, "Canadian Policy and Practice with Indicators of Effective Environmental Enforcement", Annex 3 to Indicators of Effective Environmental Enforcement Proceedings of A North American Dialogue

(CEC: 1999) Online: « http://www.cec.org/files/pdf/LAWPOLICY/indic-e.pdf »

In recent years, international recognition of the importance of compliance and enforcement to environmental management has reinforced interest at the national and sub-national level in ensuring compliance and enforcement with domestic environmental laws. In Canada, at both the federal and provincial levels, the concepts of "compliance" and "enforcement" have been developed at the policy level in most of the jurisdictions under consideration. In general, **"compliance"** has been defined as **"the state of conformity with the law"**. Measures that governments use to ensure compliance include written and verbal communication, consultation, monitoring, inspection, data review, and enforcement. In general, **"enforcement"** has been defined as **"activities that compel offenders to comply with their legislative requirements"**. Enforcement activities are seen to include investigations of alleged violations, imposition of corrective measures, administrative responses to compel compliance, and prosecution.

Overview of Federal and Provincial Roles in Compliance Measurement

There are several characteristics of federal and provincial environmental legislation which have implications for developing performance measures of compliance. First, a key characteristic of federal law (CEPA and the *Fisheries Act*), is that compliance is considered primarily in relation to the regulations promulgated under both laws.

Second, in comparison to federal environmental law, a key characteristic of provincial law is that compliance must be measured to a substantial degree in relation to approvals, licenses and permits as well as prohibitions, administrative orders and regulations. This broad regulatory authority can be a greater challenge to provincial governments in developing measures of compliance performance in the large areas of responsibility encompassed by provincial law, particularly during a period of resource constraints and government cutbacks.

Third, differences in the place where compliance is to be measured under federal and provincial law can have implications on how performance measures of compliance, such as inspections and self-monitoring and reporting, will be employed in determining overall levels of compliance.

Fourth, whereas federal regulations, with some exceptions, tend to be either substance-specific, without regard to medium or industrial sector, or substance-industrial sector-medium specific, provincial regulations may be substance-medium specific, without regard to industrial sector, or industrial sector-medium specific, without regard to substance. This divergence in regulation type has the potential to produce a different approach to measuring compliance, as well as the potential to produce different conclusions about the status of compliance at the same facility or class of facility.

These various differences in legislative and regulatory regimes, which may simply indicate a rich, if complex, framework in which to test compliance, also suggests the potential for a confusing, fragmented, and inconsistent approach to assessment of compliance performance. Moreover, these differences may take on greater significance in the future, either in terms of resolving or exacerbating potential inconsistencies, to the extent that federal-provincial agreements result in provincial responsibility for ensuring compliance with federal requirements or become a substitute for federal requirements.

Overview of Federal and Provincial Roles in Enforcement Measurement

One of the earliest policies in Canada on the subject of environmental enforcement was the 1988 Environment Canada enforcement and compliance policy developed in conjunction with the coming into force of *CEPA*. The policy had been preceded by concern expressed over the years by federal advisory bodies that there was "an inadequate level of enforcement of statutes and regulations which were designed to protect the quality of the environment". The policy established enforcement principles, identified enforcement personnel and their responsibilities, listed criteria for responding to violations, and set out the enforcement measures available for responding to violations. Similar policies, preceded by similar public concerns, have also been developed at the provincial level for defining enforcement, enforcement principles, and enforcement activities. Several characteristics of federal and provincial environmental legislation have implications for developing performance measures of enforcement.

First, a key characteristic of federal law (*CEPA* and the *Fisheries Act*) is that enforcement of environmental standards primarily involves the use of command and control statutory prohibitions or regulations, violations of which are prosecuted in the courts in virtually the same manner as criminal offenses. This process is expensive, time-consuming, and requires intensive preparation and resources.

Second, in comparison to federal environmental law, a key characteristic of provincial law is that enforcement mechanisms for violations are more multi-faceted and include, besides prosecutions: administrative orders, directives, minor offense ticketing, cancellation of permits or approvals and, in some provinces, administrative monetary penalties. This authority to respond to violations in a variety of ways gives the provinces more enforcement options, the ability to deal with less serious violations before they become more serious, and a wider variety of forums in which to proceed against offenders. These differences in legislative and regulatory regimes may take on greater significance in the future to the extent that federal provincial agreements result in provincial responsibility for enforcing federal requirements, or where provincial requirements become a substitute for federal requirements.

Correlating Compliance and Enforcement Outcomes with Environmental Results

The ultimate goal of federal and provincial compliance and enforcement efforts is to achieve environmental goals and objectives. However, the ability of governments in Canada to measure the relationship between compliance and enforcement outputs and outcomes on the one hand, and the overall state of the environment on the other is still rudimentary. Environment Canada has noted, for example, in its compliance and enforcement report on six regulations under *CEPA* and the *Fisheries Act* that: "Care should be taken in drawing conclusions from the state of compliance information . . . even a 100 [percent] compliance level does not equate to a 100 [percent] protection of the environment. The reason for this is that regulations and their provisions do not necessarily consider every aspect of a regulated product, substance, or activity. Nor do regulations cover all aspects of environmental protection. Consequently, the [six regulations] report is not about describing the state of the environment".

This begs the question of whether government should attempt to determine the relationship between changes in the behavior of the regulated community and overall environmental quality. Moreover, in a period of reduced government resources, making this link would appear to be increasingly difficult, especially if government efforts to report on compliance rates and trends diminish.

Conclusions

Compliance and enforcement indicators may be a combination of: (1) outputs (2) outcomes and (3) resulting improvements in environmental quality. While initiatives are occurring with respect to some of these matters, the overall development of comprehensive environmental compliance and enforcement performance measures is still in its early stages in most jurisdictions in Canada. Moreover, as one moves along the spectrum from reporting outputs to measuring resulting environmental quality, the efforts of governments appear less developed and more fragmentary.

This is not surprising, but does indicate where greater governmental effort should be directed in future. Historically, federal and provincial governments have focused on reporting compliance and enforcement outputs such as numbers of inspections conducted, or prosecutions initiated. This traditional approach is itself not old in Canada, and is by no means uniformly undertaken at the federal and provincial levels, as some governments still do not regularly report this information, or have discontinued doing so. Moreover, such traditional reporting measures may be undergoing significant change arising from trends such as: (1) targeting "chronic offenders" for inspection; (2) requiring self-monitoring and reporting, as well as encouraging voluntary compliance by the regulated community; and (3) providing "single window" inspection and enforcement pursuant to emerging federal-provincial arrangements.

. . . it is difficult to correlate compliance and enforcement outcomes with environmental results. Efforts of governments in Canada to measure the relationship are in their infancy. The few government reports that discuss the issue are quick to disclaim a relationship between compliance performance and overall environmental quality . . . Perhaps the single most important approach governments in Canada should undertake in this area is to establish performance objectives and measures and develop methods for evaluating their effectiveness for compliance and enforcement outputs, outcomes and environmental quality goals.

With respect to outcomes, these initiatives could include annual reporting of such matters as: compliance rates by permit, regulation, industrial sector, environmental media, geographic region, or a combination thereof; companies in significant non-compliance; progress in returning chronic and significant offenders to compliance as a result of compliance or enforcement efforts; rate of recidivism among significant or chronic offenders following compliance or enforcement efforts; compliance rates of companies employing voluntary compliance measures; and compliance rates of companies where public liaison committees exist. With respect to environmental quality goals, these initiatives could include annual reporting of such matters as: emission or discharge reductions by company, environmental media, permit category, regulation, substance, industrial sector, geographic region, or a combination thereof; and state of the environment by company, environmental media, regulated substance, industrial sector, geographic region, or combination thereof. The above does not constitute an exhaustive list of what might be included in such a program, but could contribute to a more systematic approach to evaluating compliance and enforcement measures than is currently used in Canada.

Notes and Questions

1. Castrilli draws and elaborates on the important distinction between "compliance" and "enforcement". What are some of the various activities undertaken by governments in these two realms? What differences exist between the federal and provincial levels in the type of compliance-related activities that are carried out? What differences are there in the way that federal and provincial regulators carry out their enforcement duties?

2. How do governments measure the efficacy of their compliance and enforcement activities? What measurement challenges exist?

. . . . .

Regulatory Enforcement: the Canadian Record

Jerry V. DeMarco & Toby Vigod, "Smarter Regulation: The Case for Enforcement and Transparency"
(2007) 17 J. Env. L. & Prac. 85

Historically, there was a shift in the mid 20th century from a reliance on the common law to address environmental issues to increased involvement by governments in regulatory activities. This signified a shift from a focus on private rights between parties to a focus on public law. This was coupled with an understanding that the environment was a public resource worthy of protection. The increase in government regulation commenced in the 1950s and continued with the establishment of Departments and Ministries of the Environment and the coming into force of a considerable amount of environmental legislation in the 1970s and 1980s. However, regulatory activity did not necessarily mean that these regulations were aggressively enforced. In Ontario, for example, from the early 1970s to the mid 1980s, the focus shifted to the use of administrative tools, such as permits and orders to obtain compliance. There was some success in dealing with 'conventional' pollutants during this period, but the negotiation approach favoured during these years had limited effectiveness. During this period, fines were criticized as being too low, too few, and too uncertain. A 1984 study for the Law Reform Commission of Canada described the regulatory process of the 1970s as somewhere between "cautious" and "captured".

The period of the late 1980s to the early 1990s was a period of increased regulatory activism and concern about the environment at the federal level and in some provinces, notably Ontario. Beginning in 1985, there was a major change of focus in Ontario, with increasing emphasis on prosecution. A special branch of professional investigators was created, prosecutions staff increased, and higher fines provided for in legislation. As a result, by 1988-89, the number of prosecutions had increased 500 per cent, and fines had greatly increased. The World Commission on Environment and Development's publication of *Our Common Future* in 1987 led to the embracing of the need to move towards 'sustainable development', however ambiguous that concept has subsequently become. There was a new emphasis on the need to address greenhouse gasses and toxic pollutants that did not respect jurisdictional boundaries. The 1992 United Nations Conference on the Environment and Development (the Rio Earth Summit) was a highpoint of public concern for the environment. In Ontario, the period of emphasis on regulatory enforcement occurred from 1985–1994, while in British Columbia there was a period of regulatory activism in the mid-1990s.

In some jurisdictions toward the end of the 1980s, and increasingly during the 1990s, there was a considerable backlash against regulatory activity and aggressive enforcement. This was coupled with an increasingly prevalent view that governments were, first of all, too large, and second, too interventionist in the affairs of industry, resulting in a lack of competitiveness in an increasingly global economy. Former Prime Minister Brian Mulroney's infamous comment when he ran for office in 1984 that there would be "pink slips and running shoes" for bureaucrats may have been the start of a rash of politicians running on anti-government platforms, which culminated in former Ontario Premier Mike Harris's Common Sense Revolution in 1995. Deregulation and regulatory "reform" became key themes of election platforms and government agendas.

The shift in emphasis to more voluntary approaches usually occurs in jurisdictions where the governing party has been elected primarily on a platform of fiscal restraint and the need to reduce the size of government. These governments often adopt the view that government needs to be dramatically restructured and that it should not be actively competing with private business interests, or at least should develop partnerships with industry in order to encourage economic growth and cut its costs . . .

In Ontario, a Red Tape Review Commission was established and issued its Final Report in January 1997. Coupled with "deregulation" initiatives was the trend towards use of self-regulation as a means of attaining environmental protection. Self-regulation can include voluntarism, codes of practice and administrative agreements. Yet at the same time, there has been growing public concern about the failure of regulators to regulate properly, whether they be government or self-regulating entities, particularly in the areas of public health, safety and the environment. While Ontario had been the most aggressive with its deregulatory agenda, in 2001, the British Columbia government established a "Deregulation Framework" with the objective of cutting regulations by one-third within three years . . .

Obviously, not every environmental objective can be accomplished by a binding standard and a strong enforcement approach. Many situations are better suited to education or incentives, especially for motivating the good actors who want to lead, rather than deterring the bad actors seeking to take advantage of a situation. However, for those areas of environmental management that are predicated on a traditional approach of binding government-imposed standards, such as water pollution, and for which there is a risk of opportunistic behaviour by bad actors, a strong enforcement regime should be a key part of an effective compliance toolkit alongside other measures. If enforcement measures are unlikely to be used by regulators, bad actors or free riders may take advantage of the situation. For these actors, violating environmental standards may appear to be justified vis-à-vis the possible positive impact on the bottom line. An over-emphasis on voluntary measures without maintaining a strong enforcement system may thus compromise compliance efforts. Regulators, therefore, have a responsibility to make sure that enforcement measures are strong enough to ensure that pollution does not pay. A strong enforcement system can help implement the polluter pays principle, which is widely accepted in Canadian environmental law. Public disclosure of environmental performance creates an additional, strong incentive for pollution control.

Notes and Questions

Concerns about the efficacy with which Canadian governments have enforced environmental laws have led to a number of citizen complaints under the North American on Environmental Cooperation (NAAEC), established under the umbrella of the North American Free Trade Agreement (NAFTA). Under the NAAEC, a citizen or NGO from any of the three Party countries (Canada, the US or Mexico), is entitled to file a submission with the NAAEC Secretariat alleging that a Party is "failing to effectively enforce its environmental laws". If the submission satisfies certain procedural requirements, the governing council of the NAAEC may decide to order the Secretariat to investigate and produce a "factual record". The main benefit of this unique "citizen submission" process is to serve a "spotlighting" function; factual records are neither adjudicative nor binding in nature. Moreover, they can only address failures to enforce existing environmental laws not gaps or deficiencies in a Party's environmental laws. Nonetheless the process has deployed with considerable frequency (and some success) particularly by Canadian and

Mexican environmental organizations: see C. Tollefson, "Games without Frontiers: Investor Claims and Citizen Submissions under the NAFTA Regime" (2002) 27 Yale J of Int'l Law 217; and David L. Markell & John H. Knox, eds., *Greening NAFTA: The North American Commission for Environmental Cooperation* (Stanford: Stanford University Press, 2003).

Part II — Cooperative versus Adversarial Enforcement Approaches

A key tension in environmental enforcement is the challenge of defining the respective roles of adversarial approaches and more cooperative strategies. Most commentators concur that both "sticks" and "carrots" can be useful. Beyond this general consensus, however, views diverge over when and how to deploy these varying approaches.

Matthew D. Zinn, "Policing Environmental Regulatory Enforcement: Cooperation, Capture and Citizen Suits"
(2002) 21 Stan. Envtl. L.J. 81

Advocates of adversarial enforcement emphasize the importance of general and specific deterrence: adversarial enforcement discourages targeted defendants and regulated entities at large from violating the law. They argue that only substantial, predictable, and public sanctions for noncompliance can achieve adequate compliance in the long run by making violation uneconomic: proper penalties make the expected cost of noncompliance higher than its expected economic benefit. The expected cost is equal to the probability that a penalty actually will be imposed multiplied by the dollar value of the penalty. The economic benefit from noncompliance is the avoided cost of attaining and maintaining compliance, including the capital and operating costs of pollution control equipment, the opportunity cost of reduced or less efficient production, and the transaction costs of compliance, such as ascertaining regulatory requirements or applying for a permit.

Deterrence advocates reject cooperative enforcement as insufficiently punitive and insufficiently certain. Cooperative enforcement often eschews penalties altogether, and where penalties are imposed, they may be small. As a result, violators face minimal material incentives to avoid noncompliance. Instead, the deterrent effect of cooperative enforcement is limited to the transaction costs of bargaining with the agency plus the expected costs of incremental compliance, which include the cost of reaching compliance over months or years and the amount of any minimal penalties imposed along the way (multiplied by their low risk), all discounted to present value. A firm may often be able to reduce the cost of incremental compliance by absorbing the cost of minor penalties along the way, allowing the firm to remain noncompliant for years.

A few values unrelated to deterrence also support adversarial, punitive enforcement. First, punishment may shore up the moral authority of the regulatory rule and the enforcement agency. For instance, formal, publicly visible enforcement actions validate the compliance decisions of voluntary compliers who might see failure to enforce vigorously against noncompliant firms as unfair. Failure to sanction violators publicly may delegitimize the rule violated and actually encourage noncompliance by others who would otherwise comply voluntarily. Second, penalties and formal administrative or judicial orders also simply express public disapprobation of polluting activity. Where enforcement is negotiated "under the table", the ethical message that polluting is "wrong" is not delivered. Finally, by forcing violators to disgorge the ill-gotten gains of noncompliance, penalties also prevent unjust enrichment. Regardless of the incentives created for future compliance, we might view profits derived from lawbreaking as "tainted" and demanding forfeiture.

Advocates of cooperative enforcement reject the unstated premise of deterrence theory that all regulated firms are "amoral calculators" that will consciously choose to violate where economically reasonable. Professors Robert Kagan and John Scholz argue that the "amoral calculator" model of firm behavior is inaccurate in many cases and that two other "types" of regulated firm are also common: the "political citizen" and the "incompetent". The citizen-firm will voluntarily comply with the subset of legal rules that the firm's decision makers view as legitimate, but will shirk compliance with rules that are considered "unreasonable". The incompetent firm, on the other hand, may be noncompliant due to ignorance of the rule, incapacity to comply (technical or fiscal), or failure of intraorganizational process.

Advocates of cooperative enforcement also advance a broader critique of adversarial enforcement, based on the ongoing relationship of regulator and regulatee inherent in much regulatory enforcement. Because pollution discharges will continue at one level or another as long as the polluting firm is in operation, the firm will necessarily interact repeatedly with the regulatory agency. In this kind of ongoing relationship, regulators must carefully assess the impact of their enforcement strategy on the agency's long-term relationship with regulated firms. Cooperative enforcement, advocates argue, is necessary to reduce (and thus avoid the costs of) the friction otherwise inherent in the regulatory process.

In this regard, cooperative enforcement may provide at least four distinct benefits in comparison to an adversarial approach. First, cooperative enforcement may lower an agency's administrative costs in each individual enforcement action, reducing transaction costs in the short run. In formal enforcement actions, agencies devote enormous resources to provide notice, develop evidence, and prosecute the enforcement action and judicial appeals. The agency can avoid these costs if it can secure voluntary compliance through informal action. The savings may be especially significant where small sources are involved: the administrative cost of adversarial enforcement may outweigh the benefits of compliance in such cases. Nevertheless, given the variation among "types" of violator discussed above, informal or negotiated enforcement might induce compliance from some firms but not others. Amoral calculators could feign compliance or withhold compliance, knowing that the costs of formal action make any threat of action merely a bluff. A general strategy of cooperation can actually undermine compliance by such firms.

Second, cooperative enforcement may also enable agencies to mitigate the perceived irrationality and unfairness of generally applicable regulations. Regulatory policy making frequently results in "overinclusiveness" — rules that are too general, stringent, and costly, if fully enforced. Faced with uniform rules, regulated firms may experience what Professors Bardach and Kagan call "site-level unreasonableness", in which the generic legal rule applies to factual settings that fail to advance the goal of the rule or do so with apparently unbalanced costs and benefits. Cooperative enforcement may mitigate this perceived unfairness and irrationality by encouraging regulators to exercise their broad discretion equitably. The regulator can withhold sanctions where the policy of the legal rule is not advanced by its application to a particular regulated firm. Avoiding irrationality and unfairness also carries significant utilitarian benefits by boosting the Agency's credibility and legitimacy. Unfairness may inspire recalcitrance in regulated firms that would otherwise comply voluntarily . . . This resistance will raise the agency's transaction costs in the long run, as firms try to hide noncompliance or fight future enforcement efforts because of past unfairness. Cooperative enforcement may reduce these long-run transaction costs by legitimating the rule and agency in the eyes of some firms. Further, by reducing perceived unfairness, cooperative enforcement may dissuade regulated firms from making political attacks on the statutory regime or the agency's authority and budgets and may shore up general public support for the agency's regulatory mandate.

Third, the greater flexibility afforded by cooperative enforcement may help remove barriers to investment in environmentally beneficial new technologies. For instance, consider a manufacturing firm that falls within the terms of a rule — say, an end-of-pipe, pollution control technology specification standard — but which, because of the peculiarities of the firm's production process, would produce none of the pollution that the rule seeks to avoid. Application of the rule to this firm may make the process uneconomic, discouraging investment in an environmentally sound production process. Sanctioning noncompliance only where doing so in fact advances the rule's purpose might solve this problem but the flexibility that makes such enforcement attractive also makes it unreliable. The mere possibility that an enforcement officer down the line may withhold sanctions is unlikely to provide sufficient confidence to stimulate capital investment.

Finally, cooperative enforcement may allow "trades" in which an agency accepts under-compliance with a legal mandate in one area in exchange for a regulatee's commitment to over-compliance in another. In exchange for permission to reduce the level of compliance required in a regulatory area where marginal pollution control costs are high (call the area x), the regulated firm can offer to reduce pollution in an area in which the firm is already in compliance but where further pollution avoidance can be readily achieved (area y). In theory, the firm will make the trade where the marginal control costs associated with x are higher than those associated with y, and the agency will agree to the trade if the marginal pollution control benefits in area x are lower than in area y.

In practice, however, allowing regulators such broad discretion places great faith in their ability to recognize and represent public interests. The enforcer must determine that the benefits to the public from a reduction in area y are as great or greater than those accruing from a reduction in area x. We may have reason to question whether an enforcement official can adequately carry out the necessary informal cost-benefit analysis, or at least whether her analysis is better than that underlying the regulation as written. While an enforcer may be better placed than a rulemaker to understand the compliance costs of particular firms, that officer will likely have less information about the public costs of pollution: she will not have available the broad public input and time for reflection available in notice and comment rulemaking. To ask agencies to make such decisions on a case-by-case basis during enforcement may assume considerable capacity that the agency lacks and may leave the agency at the mercy of an industry's superior knowledge of its own processes.

Synthesis

The basic lesson of the debate between advocates of cooperative and adversarial enforcement is that neither strategy is completely satisfactory. Although adversarial enforcement is essential to ensure that strategic profit-maximizing firms internalize external costs, the process of deterrence may in some settings raise administrative costs and create simple injustice. To strike the proper balance, an agency's enforcement tactics should depend heavily on the particular violator involved and the agency's past interactions with it . . . Agencies should cooperate with cooperators and punish evaders.

Many commentators have made the deceptively simple argument that regulators should treat different firms differently and like firms alike. The argument derives, in part, from firms' differing marginal-pollution-control-cost functions. Differences in control-cost functions may color the response of regulated firms to particular enforcement tools. That response may also vary with the less tangible, sociological variables of firm culture and the attitudes of management. In fact, not all firms with identical control-cost functions will respond to a legal rule in the same way. Some firms will always or nearly always comply with a legal rule regardless of cost, others will comply only where doing so is cost-effective, some will not comply simply out of ignorance or incapacity, and yet others will comply so long as managers consider the rule "reasonable". Accordingly, a uniform legal rule with uniform enforcement will not produce uniform results, and some flexible or "state-dependent" enforcement is justifiable.

The agency's enforcement approach should depend on where the agency and firm are in the enforcement process. Professor Scholz recommends this approach on the theory that regulatory enforcement involves the regulator and regulatee in an ongoing series of prisoner's dilemma games. Because the regulatory "game" is played repeatedly, the agency's optimal enforcement strategy is "tit-for-tat", in which the regulator chooses its action based on the regulatee's behavior in the prior round. If the regulatee has cooperated, the agency should cooperate, but if the regulatee "defects", the agency should punish until the regulatee again adopts a cooperative posture.

If a new violation is discovered, the agency should review the firm and agency's course of dealing, to determine whether the firm is in general an "incompetent", a "political citizen", or an "amoral calculator". The agency's choice of enforcement tools — cooperative or adversarial — should be based on the firm's history of reasonable cooperation with the agency, good faith, and patterns of compliance. The agency should forgive violations (and withhold penalties) if the regulatee has cooperated with the agency, such that the violation appears to have occurred notwithstanding the firm's best efforts. Where there are indicia of strategic behavior or knowing or negligent violation, however, the agency should apply punitive sanctions to each violation until the regulatee adopts a compliant strategy evidenced by continual compliance with agency orders. In other words, the agency must be willing to shift a firm from the category of "incompetent" or "political citizen" to "amoral calculator" until the firm shows a durable willingness to cooperate. When the firm returns to the fold, it may be treated again as something other than an amoral calculator.

After an individual enforcement interaction — informal negotiations or formal proceedings — has begun, the agency should be cognizant of the course of performance in that particular encounter. If the firm is dragging its feet in implementing a compliance bargain or administrative order, the agency should respond by imposing sanctions and escalating the formality of the enforcement action. Again, the severity of sanctions and the speed of their imposition should vary according to overall courses of performance and dealing.

To be sure, this approach is not perfect. Its greatest weakness is the substantial information it demands from agencies and firms. With adversarial enforcement, enforcers might reduce information costs by reducing monitoring while dramatically increasing penalties to raise the expected cost of noncompliance. Flexible enforcement, on the other hand, requires the agency to ascertain whether a penalty is justified based on more than the mere fact of a violation. Accordingly, agencies employing flexible enforcement must devote considerable resources to monitoring to learn of the regulatee's compliance status, efforts, and history, in circumstances of asymmetric information. To the extent that a flexible approach provides transaction-cost savings in individual enforcement actions and in the long run, those monitoring costs might be shouldered without substantial new resources. But in any event, agencies should impose strict monitoring and reporting terms in any negotiated compliance agreement and should remorselessly penalize all but entirely accidental violations of any such terms or statutory monitoring and reporting requirements.

The regulatee may also lack adequate information about the regulator's behavior. Because a firm will have little incentive to adopt a compliant strategy if it cannot be confident that the agency will also cooperate, the agency must broadcast its enforcement strategy. Dissemination of the agency's enforcement policy is also important to secure the legitimacy gains promised by cooperative enforcement: the agency must develop a reputation for cooperative enforcement to prove that it will not punish firms' good deeds and that good-faith compliers will not be competitively penalized by repeated violators' getting off scot-free.

Consequently, agencies should formalize their enforcement strategy in an enforcement policy and communicate that policy to firms. Although this raises the specter of inflexibility, the costs of that inflexibility must be weighed against the benefits of increased certainty that such a policy would provide. Given that this model strategy involves treating firms differently that are in many respects similarly situated, an enforcement policy may be necessary to describe to a firm why it and its competitors will be treated in particular ways.

Finally, this model of enforcement concededly does not in every case effectuate the "moral" or "expressive" function of regulation. Penalties will not be applied in every case to register societal moral outrage. Nevertheless, the tit-for-tat strategy calls for severe penalties where the violation is intentional or negligent. An agency should also impose penalties where the firm's polluting behavior causes significant effects on human health or environmental quality. Where those compelling circumstances are absent, however, the tit-for-tat strategy remains appropriate.

Notes and Questions

1. Empirically, the Zinn article draws heavily on the US experience with respect to environmental enforcement where the federal Environmental Protection Agency (EPA) has taken a strong leadership role in prosecuting environmental offences. As the Vigod and DeMarco excerpt underscores, the Canadian experience differs significantly in several key respects. What, in your view, are the key differences?

2. Do you agree with Zinn that it is possible, and desirable, to develop an approach to enforcement that blends cooperative and adversarial elements? Are there parallels between the approach he advocates and the "Smart Regulation" approach advocated by Gunningham et al. outlined in Chapter 4?

Part III — Issues in Environmental Law Enforcement

In this Part, we canvass some of the key issue-areas in environmental law enforcement, including:

- Use of the criminal law as an enforcement tool
- The role and nature of the regulatory offence
- Sentencing in environmental cases
- Directors and officers liability
- The emerging role of administrative monetary penalties (AMPs)

The Role of the Criminal Law in Environmental Protection

In many cases where serious environmental harm has occurred, prosecutors have the option of proceeding by way of a *Criminal Code* prosecution or, alternatively, by way of prosecution under applicable federal (typically, *CEPA* or *Fisheries Act*) or provincial regulatory provisions. The *Criminal Code* does not contain any specific environmental offences although their inclusion has been advocated from time to time: see Law Reform Commission of Canada "Crimes Against the Environment" (1985). As a result, if criminal prosecutions for environmental harm must be framed in terms of more generic offences such as criminal negligence (s. 427) or nuisance (s. 180).

Stanley David Berger, "The Future of Environmental Prosecutions in Ontario"
(2006) 19 C.E.L.R. (3rd) 32

The *Criminal Code* will remain the "big-stick" when negligence or deliberation causes a major environmental event resulting in serious injury or the loss of life. [*Ed note*: In offering this conclusion, the author acknowledges that that in many provinces parallel regulatory provisions empower courts to impose multi-million dollar fines and jail terms of up to 5 years.]

Under the *Criminal Code*, if the Crown proceeds summarily, the maximum fine available against corporate organizations is $100,000 and only $2,000 for individuals. The maximum imprisonment is a paltry 6 months for summary conviction offences. Moreover, the fine is not specified to be daily, as it is for provincial offences. Federal prosecutors would have to proceed by indictment to achieve comparable fines and jail terms to those under the provincial regulatory regime, but this alone would not present any difficulty, since the offences of criminal negligence and common nuisance applicable to cases of death or bodily injury can be prosecuted only by indictment. Prosecution by indictment will, however, create additional delay and complexity in the proceedings, should the defence opt, as is its right, for a preliminary hearing and/or a jury. Regardless of whether the prosecution has the luxury of proceeding by summary conviction or indictment, the Crown bears the added burden of proving negligence, unlike traditional regulatory prosecutions before the courts where this burden is assumed by the defence. Finally, in the case of criminal negligence, the prosecution will need to meet the more exacting standard of a "marked and substantial" departure from the standard of a reasonable person.

Despite these drawbacks, prosecution under the *Criminal Code* will remain attractive for more serious offences . . . There are two compelling reasons for this prosecution strategy. First, regulatory environmental prosecutions have not yet achieved the stigma of criminal prosecutions. When there is death, serious injury, or the real potential for either, the public expects government authorities to bring the full force of the law to bear on the perpetrators. Announcement of criminal charges demonstrates that the authorities have not shrunk from their responsibility, or have in any way been intimidated by events. The second reason is that the investigation in such serious cases is likely to be detailed and time-consuming. The short two-year limitation periods for laying regulatory charges will remain too confining to the authorities; when the Crown proceeds by indictment, there is no limitation period on bringing charges.

[*Ed note*: The author then discusses amendments to the *Canadian Criminal Code (Bill C-45)* that were proclaimed into force in 2004.]

These amendments dispensed with the identification theory of criminal liability, whereby a corporation could be found guilty of a criminal offence only if the offence could be proven against "a directing mind" of the corporation. The directing mind or minds of the corporation were those individuals within the corporation with decision-making authority over matters of corporate policy, as opposed to operational matters.

The amendments followed on the heels of the less-than-successful outcomes of the *Criminal Code* prosecutions of those responsible for the 1992 Westray Mining explosion in Nova Scotia, which had resulted in the deaths of 26 miners. The amendments now enable prosecutors to obtain criminal convictions against corporations, including partnerships, municipalities, trade unions and public bodies, for the acts or omissions of management; decision-making authority over corporate policy is no longer a prerequisite to corporate liability. Significantly, with respect to the criminal act, the law now acknowledges the compartmentalization of corporate functions, enabling the prosecutor to rely on the collective acts or omissions of one or more corporate representatives, including contractors, providing the prosecution can prove that the work that is alleged to have amounted to a crime was directed or negligently supervised by one or more senior officers. Thus, the amendments further create a positive legal duty on management to prevent bodily harm arising from supervised work. Finally, probation orders now apply to corporate defendants, including partnerships, municipalities, trade unions and public bodies, with creative conditions previously available only for regulatory offences such as restitution, the establishment of policies, standards and procedures, preventative or remedial orders, reporting requirements and public acknowledgement of responsibility.

. . . Criminal charges, primarily common nuisance, will become a more attractive enforcement tool with the passage of Bill C-45, as it has become easier to prove the criminal culpability of corporate organizations and as the legal duty of corporate managers has increased. When the investigation is time-consuming, regulatory limitation periods are compromised and the consequences of the offence are, or could be, grave, nothing less will do.

Regulatory Prosecutions in Environmental Cases: Strict versus Absolute Liability

Most environmental prosecutions proceed on charges filed pursuant to regulatory offence provisions set out in federal and provincial statutes. In the context of regulatory offences, a key issue concerns what evidence of "fault" must be established, and who bears the burden of proof with respect to this issue. In this context, courts have been called upon to balance prosecutorial efficacy and protection of the public against competing concerns with respect to fairness to the accused.

John Swaigen, "Absolute Liability Revisited: *Lévis v. Tétrault*", Environmental Law: Year in Review 2006
(Canada Law Book)

The Development of Absolute and Strict Liability Offences

By the beginning of the 19th century it was "the accepted view" that the need for *mens rea* was a principle of natural justice, and few offences at that time were punishable without proof of fault. As a result of this recognition that punishing the morally innocent is wrong, it became a fundamental tenet of the common law that no one could be convicted of a crime without *mens rea*.

Yet, faced with the reality that regulatory offences are often committed unintentionally, and therefore, it is frequently impossible to establish intent, but it is still necessary to protect the public against harmful acts, the courts began to treat these offences as an exception to the general rule that *mens rea* is an essential element of an offence.

For regulatory offences, some courts held that *mens rea* was required, but permitted a defence of mistake of fact or reasonable care. However, others treated regulatory offences as a type of "crime" for which a conviction could be registered without any evidence of fault. This was most often referred to as "strict liability", but since *Sault Ste. Marie* liability without any fault, of course, is known as "absolute liability".

By the time regulatory offences began to proliferate in the mid-19th century, what we now call "absolute liability" had become widely recognized as unjust. Nevertheless, some advocated permitting a degree of injustice to enter the system on utilitarian grounds in relation to this particular kind of offence. They argued, in effect, that as long as absolute liability was limited to relatively minor offences, carrying a relatively small penalty, for which conviction carried little stigma, the injustice to the individual or company charged and convicted of a regulatory offence was outweighed by the potential injustice to victims of these offences and to the public at large from ineffective or inefficient enforcement that would result if proof of fault was required.

In 1978, in the seminal decision *R. v. City of Sault Ste. Marie*, a unanimous Supreme Court of Canada, speaking through Justice Dickson (as he then was), resolved to a great degree, . . . the question of whether regulatory offences are based on *mens rea* or are matters of absolute liability by recognizing three categories of offences — "true" crimes, requiring proof beyond a doubt of both the *actus reus* and subjective *mens rea*; strict liability offences, in which the prosecutor was required to prove the *actus reus* beyond a reasonable doubt but the accused could exonerate himself or herself by establishing on a balance of probabilities a defence of reasonable care; and absolute liability offences, for which neither *mens rea* nor negligence was required to obtain a conviction. For offences of absolute liability, it is not open to the accused to exculpate himself or herself by showing that he or she was free of fault. Moreover, the Court determined that there is a presumption that regulatory offences fall into the middle category, strict liability, unless the legislature has made it clear that it intended *mens rea* or absolute liability.

This new regime applies to all regulatory offences, but has been particularly important in the environmental area, largely because of the creation of many of new environmental offences in the 1980s and 1990s, the increased reliance on prosecution as a method of enforcing these laws, the heightened inducement to alleged polluters to fight charges resulting from stronger penalties, and the increasing stigma associated with conviction for environmental offences.

Notes and Questions

After *Sault Ste. Marie*, particularly outside the motor vehicle context, most regulatory offences came to be interpreted by courts as falling within the strict liability category. The trend became even more pronounced after enactment of the Charter: see *Reference re: s. 94(2) of the Motor Vehicle Act (British Columbia)* (S.C.C., 1985). Absolute liability as a form of regulatory liability continued to dwindle until 1995, when the SCC rendered its decision in *R v. Pontes*. For a time, this case was seen by some as heralding a revival of absolute liability offences. In *Lévis (City) v. Tétrault* (S.C.C., 2006), however, the Court reaffirmed its commitment to the approach it adopted in *Sault Ste. Marie*.

. . . . .

Lévis (City) v. Tétrault; Lévis (City) v. Québec Inc.
[2006] 1 S.C.R. 420

LeBEL J.: —

Categories of Criminal Offences and Approach to Classification

The offences with which the respondents are charged belong to a vast category of offences known as regulatory offences. Legislatures enact such offences as incidental sanctions whose purpose is to enforce the performance of various duties, thereby safeguarding the general welfare of society (*Sault Ste. Marie*, at p. 1310, *per* Dickson J.). Establishing their legal framework gave rise to uncertainty because they are not always perfectly compatible with the fundamental principles of criminal law and because of the difficulty in defining the defences available to the accused. It was these problems that were addressed in *Sault Ste. Marie*.

Classifying the offence in one of the three categories now recognized in the case law thus becomes a question of statutory interpretation. Dickson J. noted that regulatory or public welfare offences usually fall into the category of strict liability offences rather than that of *mens rea* offences. As a general rule, in accordance with the common law rule that criminal liability ordinarily presupposes the existence of fault, they are presumed to belong to the intermediate category:

> Public welfare offences would *prima facie* be in the second category. They are not subject to the presumption of full *mens rea*. An offence of this type would fall in the first category only if such words as "wilfully", "with intent", "knowingly", or "intentionally" are contained in the statutory provision creating the offence. (*Sault Ste. Marie*, at p. 1326)

Absolute liability offences still exist, but they have become an exception requiring clear proof of legislative intent. This intent can be deduced from various factors, the most important of which would appear to be the wording of the statute itself:

> On the other hand, the principle that punishment should in general not be inflicted on those without fault applies. Offences of absolute liability would be those in respect of which the Legislature had made it clear that guilt would follow proof merely of the proscribed act. The overall regulatory pattern adopted by the Legislature, the subject matter of the legislation, the importance of the penalty, and the precision of the language used will be primary considerations. . . .
>
> (*Sault Ste. Marie*, at p. 1326)

The categories established by this Court were thus based on a presumption of statutory interpretation. Developments in constitutional law since the *Canadian Charter of Rights and Freedoms* came into force have reinforced their legal foundations. Without abolishing the category of absolute liability offences, the Court decided that imposing penal liability of this nature would violate the principles of fundamental justice protected by the *Charter* where a conviction would expose the accused to imprisonment (*Re B.C. Motor Vehicle Act*, [1985] 2 S.C.R. 486 at pp. 515-16; *R. v. Vaillancourt*, [1987] 2 S.C.R. 636 at p. 652, *per* Lamer J.).

This Court reconsidered the approach to classifying regulatory offences in *R. v. Pontes*, [1995] 3 S.C.R. 44. In that case, in which the Court had to decide whether a traffic offence was one of absolute liability, Cory J., writing for the majority, appeared to propose a two-stage test for determining whether an offence is an absolute liability offence. First, the analytical approach and presumptions of interpretation proposed by Dickson J. in *Sault Ste. Marie* would have to be considered (para. 27). However, it might also be determined whether the legislature intended to make a due diligence defence available (para. 28). This added refinement to the classification approach established in *Sault Ste. Marie* does not make it easier to apply. The objective of the interpretive approach adopted in *Sault Ste. Marie* is in fact to determine the nature of the defences available to the accused. To say that it is necessary to determine whether the accused can plead due diligence amounts simply to restating the very purpose of this juridical exercise. It would therefore be better to return to the clear analytical framework and classification approach adopted in *Sault Ste. Marie*.

Sentencing in Environmental Cases

The following case remains a leading decision with respect to the principles of sentencing in cases of environmental harm involving corporate accused. At the same time, it contains some intriguing observations about the limitations of prosecutions that solely target a corporate accused, and the correlative need to explore new ways to achieve corporate behaviour-modification.

R. v. United Keno Hill Mines Ltd.
[1980] Y.J. No. 10

[United Keno Hill Mines Limited "Keno" pled guilty to depositing waste in Yukon waters on May 1, 1979, in excess of the waste discharge limits prescribed by a water licence and thereby contravening the *Northern Inland Waters Act*. Keno operated a combined open pit and underground mine. During the period of the infraction the accused was operating under a licence that specified a maximum allowable concentration of contaminants in the effluent discharged by the accused into Flat Creek.]

STUART C.J.

Before considering what sentence is appropriate, some preliminary questions should be addressed. Are there unique considerations to bear in mind in sentencing for environmental offences? Are there sentencing principles peculiar to sentencing a corporation as opposed to an individual offender?

Based on a review of American and Canadian authorities, I submit the answer to both questions is clearly — yes. In sentencing corporations and in dealing with environmental offences courts on both sides of the border have evolved a body of sentencing law that is a special application of common sentencing principles. *In R. v. Kenaston Drilling (Arctic) Ltd.* (1973), 12 C.C.C. (2d) 383, the Court explicitly acknowledges a "special approach" is required in sentencing corporate environmental offenders. What is this special approach? Why is there a need for a special approach in the case of corporate offenders committing breaches of environmental laws?

Special Considerations — Nature of Environmental Damage

In sentencing assault cases the courts consider the nature of the victim (relative ability to defend, provocation) and the degree of injury (permanent or temporary disability, etc.). Similarly, in environmental cases, the courts do and should vary the severity of punishment in accord with the nature of the environment affected and the extent of damage inflicted.

Nature of Environment

A unique ecological area supporting rare flora and fauna, a high-use recreational watershed, or an essential wildlife habitat, are environments calling upon users to exercise special care. Any injury to such areas must be more severely condemned than environmental damage to less sensitive areas.

Extent of Injury

Penalties should reflect the degree of damage inflicted. The resiliency of the environment or the capacity to repair the damage is a crucial consideration. If the damage is irreparable, extensive, persistent or has numerous consequential adverse effects, the penalty must be severe. In some instances not only the actual damage caused but the potential damage that might have emanated from the polluter's activities must be considered.

As in assault offences the more severe the beating the greater the condemnation expressed in sentencing. Similarly, evidence of injury should be tendered in environmental cases. Thus the Crown should place before the Court any evidence touching upon the special nature of the environment affected, the degree of damage inflicted, the consequential or peripheral adverse impacts, the prospects and cost of repairing the damage, the duration of the damage, and the potential damage that might have been caused if the actions of the offenders had been allowed to continue.

Courts have taken and should take judicial notice to the seriousness of environmental damage, but appropriate sentencing distinctions cannot be made in the absence of Crown evidence depicting the specific damage in issue. In the absence of Crown evidence the estimates of damage presented by the offender are persuasive and to a great extent restrict any severity of sentence prompted by judicial notice. . . . Most sentencing dispositions in environmental cases necessitate expert and technical evidence to describe the extent of environmental harm caused by the offence.

The Offender — Corporations

The size, wealth, nature of operations and power of a corporation necessitate a special approach in sentencing. The activities of one corporation can reach into the lives of people and communities in many parts of the world. The scope of corporate activities has a multiplier effect on the extent and severity of risk potential flowing from corporate action.

Considerations in Sentencing of Corporations for Environmental Offences

Criminality of Conduct

The severity of punishment should be directly related to the degree of criminality inherent in the manner of committing the offence. Accidents, innocent mistakes, and not reasonably foreseen events are less damnable than wilful surreptitious violations. If a corporation surreptitiously dumps toxic waste in wilful disregard of regulations, a harsh sanction is required. Similarly, if a corporation is aware of the environmental damage being caused by their operations and does nothing to rectify or abate the problem, the Court is justified in accrediting such corporate conduct with a high degree of criminality.

Extent of Attempts to Comply

A corporation should not be harshly punished if evidence indicates diligent attempts to comply with government regulations. The diligence of a corporation can be measured by the duration of non-compliant operation, the cost of compliance contrasted with corporate profits, the general co-operative and frank nature of communication with responsible government agencies, and the actual investment of resources, time, and money in seeking to achieve compliance. If the responsible government agency is not pressing for compliance, or its actually encouraging non-compliance through tacit or explicit agreements to permit non-compliant operations, the corporation cannot be severely faulted.

Remorse

Talk is cheap, action speaks much clearer to the courts about the degree of corporate contrition than the smoothest of apologies enunciated by counsel. The actions underlying genuine contrition can take three principal forms.

Speed and efficiency of corporate action to rectify the problem or clean up the pollution is the clearest indication of corporate remorse

Voluntarily reporting the violation to authorities indicates a genuine desire to act responsibly. The bulk of environmental regulation depends upon the integrity of corporations to provide full disclosure of the impact of their operation on the environment. Voluntarily reporting breaches must be acknowledged as a mitigating circumstance by the courts in sentencing. Pleas of guilty are not of any significance if detection and conviction were inevitable.

The personal appearance of corporate executives in Court and their personal statement outlining the company's genuine regret and stating future plans to avoid repetitions of such offences is another indication of genuine corporate contrition. Too often corporations appear solely by agents, through their lawyer, or through a lesser functionary of the company. This practice suggests the lack of significance the company accords the offence. If the Court is to properly assess the degree of sanctions required to effect the full rehabilitation of the offending corporation, the governing or guiding mind, in the person of senior executive officers, should be present and give evidence.

Size of Corporation

Courts take judicial notice to the size and wealth of a corporation. The larger the corporation, the larger the fine. Conversely, smaller operations are not fined as severely for similar offences. This approach is principally motivated by the desire to ensure the fine imposed in the case of large corporations is not readily absorbed as a simple cost of doing business, or as a mere slap on the wrist. In the case of smaller corporations, the courts attempt to avoid destroying the economic viability of the corporation by imposing a crippling fine. Large corporations cannot avoid large fines by establishing a network of small corporations as courts seem prepared to hear evidence of corporate connections or simply to take judicial notice of such corporate relationships

. . . What amount will be an effective deterrent? To fairly determine a deterrent fine, the capacity of each corporate offender to deflect or absorb a fine should be assessed. Thereby such matters as profits, assets, current financial status, and characteristics of the relevant market must be before the Court.

Profits Realized by Offence

Courts attempt to ascertain the amount of profit or savings realized by the corporation as a consequence of the offence. Thus the amount of illegally realized windfall should establish in almost every case, in the absence of other outstanding mitigating circumstances, the minimum fine. Other matters considered should increase the amount of the fine. Establishing the quantum of illegal gains should reside with the defendant corporation as they are privy to the information and to the processes appropriate for determining the quantum of illegal gains. In the absence of conclusive evidence from the corporation the Court may rely on any reasonable estimate the Crown submits.

The assessment of a fine based on illegally obtained gains is essential to ensure that non-complying corporations do not acquire an economic advantage over complying competitors. It may be appropriate for the courts to hear evidence from complying competitors on the extent of economic advantages the offending corporation derived from non-compliance.

. . . In most cases restitution is a better means of attacking illegal gains than a fine. Restitution might embrace losses to corporate competitors, damage to public and private property, and the cost of prosecution. Restitution orders are best suited to compensate victims of criminal conduct; fines are more appropriately employed to sanction criminal conduct.

Criminal Record

A prior criminal record is especially important in sentencing corporations. Similar recidivistic conduct raises an assumption that the corporation is more concerned about profit than compliance.

Moral opprobrium and public censure of corporations arising from criminal prosecutions has questionable potential in promoting effective deterrence. Public censure directed at corporate criminality is diluted by the dispersal of responsibility throughout the hierarchy of the corporation and by the anonymity afforded by acting in the corporate name. Any corporation whose operations involve little or no direct contact through sales with the general public is probably only peripherally concerned about a public image. In such cases and particularly if the offence is a subsequent similar offence, the fine should be severe.

Evaluation of Sentencing Tools

In recent years the courts have relied upon substantial fines as the principal means of sanctioning corporations. This tactic assumes if the fine is significantly harsh, compliance will be assured. I disagree. Fines alone will not mould law abiding corporate behaviour. Fines are only one part of a necessary sentencing arsenal to foster responsible corporate behaviour. A greater spectrum of sentencing options is required to ensure effective deterrence and prevent illegal economic advantages accruing to corporations willing to risk apprehension and swallow harsh fines as operating costs.

Fines are inadequate principally because they are easily displaced and rarely affect the source of illegal behaviour. Usually fines can be ultimately passed on in the form of higher prices to either the consumer or the taxpayer. Sentencing, to be effective, must reach the guiding mind — the corporate managers: be they directors or supervisors. They are the instigators of the illegality either through wilfullness, wilful blindness, or incompetent supervisory practices.

Fining corporations leaves the upper echelon policy makers relatively unscathed. Fining corporate policy makers reduces somewhat the impotency of levying fines against corporate assets . . . People who value their standing in the community are likely to be extremely sensitive to the stigma emanating from criminal conviction. In the United States the imposition of criminal sanctions against corporate officials has been an effective deterrent. . . .

The American courts have partially resolved the problem of determining individual fault for corporate activities by laying the blame at the top of the corporate hierarchy. As a result, the courts imposed a duty upon upper echelon corporate officials to discover and control all corporate activities. After a few corporate presidents are prosecuted, it is likely senior executives will make it their business to know what all subordinates are doing and effective policies and checks against illegal activities will be implemented.

Upper echelon corporate officials should first prove the existence of a reasonable system of control before liability can be passed to a subordinate. This may impose hardships on some senior executives, but they are in the best position to act in protecting the public interest. The subordinate may deny liability if the matter is either outside his actual authority or was not a consequence of his lack of reasonable care. By placing the onus on senior corporate officials to identify the author of the illegal act the propensity may arise to affix responsibility to a "fall guy" or middle level manager who is stuck with the dilemma of losing his job by denying responsibility of ultimately facing criminal prosecution for activities he was powerless to oppose. Only time will take the real measure of this problem, but a court that begins with assuming corporate executives are liable will be sceptical of any evidence seeking to shift blame to lower management levels. In some cases, the answer may be a finding of joint responsibility.

Society is abruptly learning of the potentially dire consequences of some environmental regulatory violations. The authors of such environmental catastrophes, if criminally responsible, should be prosecuted with the full force of the law. A corporate veil should never afford the slightest measure of special protection to anyone for criminal conduct. By diverting corporate criminal conduct into conciliatory processes or by ignoring the criminality of responsible corporate officers, the criminal law process is offering concessions to one class of offender not afforded to others. This practice can only engender a public perception of bias and unjustifiable discrimination.

The imposition of personal responsibility necessitates an ability to identify the culpable corporate official. To do so, the Court must have power to require complete access to internal corporate allocations of responsibility.

I do not intend to suggest that fining or incarcerating corporate officials will ensure compliance; it will simply enhance the prospects of a positive criminal law contribution to the regulation of corporate activities. There must be further development of sentencing options and the use of non-criminal government tools to cope with the multifaceted requirements of corporate regulation.

The use of criminal sanctions for resource management can promote cooperation but will never by itself resolve the polycentric conflicts in resource use. Effective criminal sanctions can provide leverage for prompt and universal cooperation in negotiating, implementing and operating comprehensive resource use management schemes. In the United States, reliance on criminal sanctions encouraged voluntary compliance with pollution abatement programs and "halted the pattern of delay which was commonplace".

Notes and Questions

1. The years following the *Keno* decision have seen, as set out earlier, some important developments in legal framework governing corporate criminal liability: see discussion in Berger (2006 *infra* this chapter). Arguably, there has also been an evolution in social values with respect to the need for corporate accountability. Apart from law reform in the realm of corporate liability, there has also been a significant broadening of the liability of corporate officials, most notably directors and officers. The leading case in this regard, and one that is commonly considered to have served as a wakeup call for many corporate officials, is the decision in *Bata Industries Ltd.* excerpted below.

2. The sentencing judge in *Keno* observes that to be effective, sentencing ". . . must reach the guiding mind — the corporate managers: be they directors or supervisors. They are the instigators of the illegality either through wilfullness, wilful blindness, or incompetent supervisory practices". Do you agree?

Directors and Officer's Liability

During the 1980s and 90s, many Canadian jurisdictions broadened the ambit of legal liability for corporate directors and officers for corporate wrongdoing in the environmental context and beyond. The judgment below remains a leading articulation of the nature and scope of this emerging form of liability.

R. v. Bata Industries Ltd.
[1992] O.J. No. 236

ORMISTON J.

On August 1, 1989, two officers of the Ontario Ministry of the Environment attended at the shoe manufacturing facility of Bata Industries Limited (hereinafter Bata) located at Batawa, Ontario. They wanted to speak to the business officer in charge of the environment on an unrelated matter.

The plant was closed that day and its 700 workers were absent. They drove through an open gate looking for the business office. In the yard while turning around, they saw a large chemical waste barrel storage site. There were a large number of containers of various sizes and in varying stages of decay. Many were uncovered and exposed to the elements. Many were rusting. There was evidence of staining on the ground.

They entered the plant and spoke to the officer in charge. Eventually a series of charges were laid under the Ontario *Water Resources Act*, R.S.O. 1980, c. 361 (now R.S.O. 1990, c. O.40), as amended (hereinafter OWRA) and the *Environmental Protection Act*, R.S.O. 1980, c. 141 (now R.S.O. 1990, c. E.18), as amended (hereinafter EPA), and R.R.O. 1980, Reg. 309 under the EPA (hereinafter Reg. 309).

. . . . .

In three separate informations, Keith Weston, the on-site director/general manager; Douglas Marchant, the president of Bata Industries Limited and a director; Thomas G. Bata, chief executive officer of Bata Shoe Organization (International), chairman of the board of Bata Industries Limited and a director were charged as directors with failing to take all reasonable care to prevent a discharge contrary to the . . . OWRA and the . . . EPA. [. . .]

The Legal Standard

There is very little Canadian judicial guidance on these sections at this time. The courts of the United States have had much more experience in dealing with the issue of directors' liability . . .

The parties in this action have asked the court to clarify a more exact legal standard by which corporate officers and directors may be held personally liable . . . A court under the circumstances before me should weigh the factors of the corporate individual's degree of authority in general and specific responsibility for health and safety practices, including hazardous waste disposal. These factors should be applied in order to answer the question of whether the individual . . . could have prevented or significantly abated the hazardous waste discharge that is the basis of the claim . . .

This court will look to evidence of an individual's authority to control, among other things, waste handling practices — evidence such as whether the individual holds the position of officer or director, especially where there is a co-existing management position: distribution of power within the corporation, including position in the corporate hierarchy and percentage of shares owned. Weighed along with the power factor will be evidence of responsibility undertaken for waste disposal practices, including evidence of responsibility undertaken and neglected, as well as affirmative attempts to prevent unlawful waste disposal. . . .

Both parts of this test boil down to corporate and societal responsibility — implicitly undertaken by the acquisition of increased power or authority within the corporation and responsibility explicitly undertaken by job description or agreement. Such a liability standard here will encourage increased responsibility as an individual's stake in the corporation increases . . . As power grows, the ability to control decisions about waste disposal increases, and second, as one's stake in the corporation increases, the potential for benefiting from less expensive (and less careful) waste disposal practices increases as well. . . .

This standard will encourage increased responsibility with increased authority within a corporation. I take this to be a positive result, and thus a better standard than one which measures only the most direct knowledge or involvement in waste disposal activity, because it encourages responsible conduct instead of causing high level corporate individuals "not to see" and "to avoid getting involved with waste disposal at their facilities" . . .

I ask myself the following questions in assessing the defence of due diligence:

(a) Did the board of directors establish a pollution prevention "system" as indicated in *R. v. Sault Ste. Marie.* i.e., was there supervision or inspection? was there improvement in business methods? did he exhort those he controlled or influenced?

(b) Did each director ensure that the corporate officers have been instructed to set up a system sufficient within the terms and practices of its industry of ensuring compliance with environmental laws, to ensure that the officers report back periodically to the board on the operation of the system, and to ensure that the officers are instructed to report any substantial non-compliance to the board in a timely manner?

I reminded myself that:

(c) The directors are responsible for reviewing the environmental compliance reports provided by the officers of the corporation, but are justified in placing reasonable reliance on reports provided to them by corporate officers, consultants, counsel or other informed parties.

(d) The directors should substantiate that the officers are promptly addressing environmental concerns brought to their attention by government agencies or other concerned parties including shareholders.

(e) The directors should be aware of the standards of their industry and other industries which deal with similar environmental pollutants or risks.

(f) The directors should immediately and personally react when they have notice the system has failed.

Within this general profile and dependent upon the nature and structure of the corporate activity, one would hope to find remedial and contingency plans for spills, a system of ongoing environmental audit, training programs, sufficient authority to act and other indices of a pro-active environmental policy.

The Bata Organization

The Bata Shoe Organization comprises some 80 companies around the world. Thomas G. Bata is the chief executive officer. The one company which is located in Canada and headquartered at Toronto is Bata Industries Limited. This company has four divisions. Each division operates autonomously under a general manager and each general manager is a vice-president and director of Bata Industries Limited. The president, also a director, of Bata Industries Limited during the material time, was Douglas Marchant. Thomas G. Bata, who functioned chiefly in an advisory capacity, was chairman of the board and a director of Bata Industries Limited.

The division of Bata Industries Limited that this case involves was the shoe manufacturing division located at Batawa, Ontario. The general manager/director/vice-president on site was Keith Weston.

The prosecution involves only three directors of Bata Industries Limited, namely, Thomas G. Bata, the chief executive officer, Douglas Marchant, the president, and Keith Weston, vice-president of Bata Manufacturing, a division of Bata Industries Limited located in Batawa, Ontario.

In my opinion, the principle of delegation in environmental matters is aptly summarized as follows: Delegation is a fact of life. The *Environmental Enforcement Amendment Act* is not intended to prevent a reasonable degree of delegation. However, the Legislature has clearly declared that environmental protection is too important to delegate entirely to the lower levels of a corporation. Although the Legislature does not expect the Board of Directors or the officers of the Corporations to make all environmental decisions, it is not acceptable for them to insulate themselves from all responsibility for environmental violations by delegating all aspects of compliance to subordinates.

Re Thomas G. Bata

Thomas G. Bata was the director with least personal contact with the plant at Batawa. His responsibilities were primarily directed at the global level of the Bata Shoe Organization. It was established in the evidence that TAC 298, the environmental alert, had been distributed to his companies throughout the world.

He attended on site in Batawa once or twice a year to review the operation and performance goals of the facility. He was a walk-around director while on the site. The evidence of Mr. Riden establishes that the plant managers could not orchestrate a visit for Mr. Bata: "You never knew where Mr. Bata was going to go, believe me. He had a habit of trying to outguess where you wanted him to go". There is no evidence that he was aware of an environmental problem.

Mr. Riden also established that when the Bata Engineering chemical storage problem was brought to Mr. Bata's attention, he immediately directed the appropriate resources ($20,000) to minimize the effect on the environment. The evidence also establishes that when a water problem was identified and funds were required to construct the water treatment plant for the town of Batawa, he (the family) authorized the expenditure of $250,000.

In short, he was aware of his environmental responsibilities and had written directions to that effect in TAC 298. He did personally review the operation when he was on site and did not allow himself to be wilfully blind or orchestrated in his movements. He responded to the matters that were brought to his attention promptly and appropriately. He had placed an experienced director on site and was entitled in the circumstances to assume that Mr. Weston was addressing the environmental concerns. He was entitled to assume that his on-site manager/director would bring to his attention any problem as Mr. Riden had done. He was entitled to rely upon his system as evidenced by TAC 298 unless he became aware the system was defective.

Bata Industries Limited is a privately held Ontario corporation. It complied with the minimal statutory requirements. However, unlike a public company, much of the business done at directors' meetings or between the board and the divisions was informal with no record kept. It is very difficult in the ordinary course for a director to establish due diligence if there is no contemporary written record.

Although the burden of establishing due diligence was onerous in the absence of more recorded corporate documentation, he has done so in my opinion and is not guilty of the offences charged.

Re Douglas Marchant

Mr. Marchant presents another variation in directors' liability. His responsibility is more than Mr. Bata, but less than Mr. Weston's. This "doctrine of responsible share" is well accepted in American jurisprudence (*United States v. Park*, supra) and is applicable in this case.

He was appointed to the Board as president on January 26, 1988. Mr. Richer testified that Mr. Marchant was "down in Batawa once a month" and these visits included a tour of the plant. Mr. Richer brought the storage problem to his personal attention around February 15, 1989.

The evidence, therefore, establishes that for at least the last six months of the time alleged in the charges (February 15, 1989 to August 31, 1989), he had personal knowledge. There is no evidence that he took any steps after having knowledge to view the site and assess the problem. There is no evidence that the system of storage was made safer or temporary steps were taken for containment until such time as removal could be affected.

The evidence establishes that $100,000 had been reserved for disposal in March 1988. On January 25, 1989, Mr. De Bruyn wrote to Tricel requesting quotes for disposal. By April

14, 1989, all the quotes were received. There was still no action until August 11 when the Ministry officials were on site, Tricel was contacted and told "to get the waste out as soon as possible".

In the circumstances, it is my opinion that due diligence requires him to execise a degree of supervision and control that "demonstrate that he was exhorting those whom he may be normally expected to influence or control to an accepted standard of behaviour": *R. v. Sault Ste. Marie*, supra, and *R. v. Southdown Builders Ltd.* (1981), 57 C.P.R. (2d) 56 (Ont. G.S.P.), p. 59.

He had a responsibility not only to give instruction but also to see to it that those instructions were carried out in order to minimize the damage. The delay in clean-up showed a lack of due diligence: *R. v. Canadian Cellulose Co.* (1979), 2 F.P.R. 256 (B.C. Co. Ct.) and *R. v. Genge* (1983), 44 Nfld. & P.E.I.R. 109 (Nfld. T.D.). There is no corporate documentation between February 15, 1989 and August 31, 1989 to assist him in his defence of due diligence. In my opinion, he has not established the defence of due diligence on the balance of probabilities and is therefore guilty as charged.

There will be a conviction registered pursuant to s. 75(1) of the OWRA. The charges under s. 147 a of the EPA are stayed for reasons previously given.

Re Keith Weston

I have considered the fact that during Mr. Weston's tenure at Batawa, the company committed $250,000 to the building of a water treatment system for the village. This would seem inconsistent with the commission of the environment offence on the site of the plant. However, I note from the evidence that in this circumstance, Mr. Weston advised the Bata family of the village's needs. The Bata family agreed to donate the land, then established further financial limits for assistance over the period of five years. Why Mr. Weston did not pursue this course of action with the environmental problem on site has not been explained. The evidence establishes that Mr. Riden had no difficulty receiving such approval from Mr. Bata.

In my opinion, this evidence is not evidence of Mr. Weston's personal attention to environmental concerns, but rather an example of the personal and sentimental attachment that the Bata family had to the area.

Keith Weston's responsibilities as an "on-site" director make him much more vulnerable to prosecution. He demanded the authority to control his work environment before he took the job. He had experience in the production side and was aware toxic chemicals were used in the process. He was reminded of his environmental responsibilities by TAC 298. In my opinion, Keith Weston has failed to establish that he took all reasonable care to prevent unlawful discharge.

In addition to the evidence previously related in respect to the due diligence of Bata Industries, it is my opinion, red flags should have been raised in his environmental consciousness when the first quote of $58,000 was obtained. Instead of simply dismissing it out of hand, he should have inquired why it was so high and investigated the problem. I find that he had no qualms about accepting the second quote of $28,000 and he had no further information other than it was cheaper. This was not an informed business judgment, and he cannot rely upon the business judgment rule, which at its core recognized that a business corporation is profit-oriented and that an honest error of judgment should not impose liability provided the requisite standard of care is met:

I find confirmation in this opinion by the fact that when he was transferred in November, he allotted $100,000 to waste disposal, again without any further knowledge. One cannot help but wonder if his diminished incentive package was a motivating factor in the allotment of $100,000 at this time. This expense would only affect him personally to the amount of

$500 because the company was now in a profit position and his salary incentive based on reducing losses was minimal.

It is my finding that Keith Weston cannot shelter behind the advice he received from Mr. De Bruyn. As Bata was "cut to the bone" by Mr. Weston, the additional responsibilities fell upon Mr. De Bruyn and grossly overloaded him. The problem was aggravated by the inference from the evidence that Mr. De Bruyn was not given the authority to expend the $58,000 or $28,000 on his own. He required the approval of Mr. Weston. In my opinion the failings of Mr. De Bruyn fall on the shoulders of Mr. Weston who stands in sad comparison to Mr. Riden who occupied the same position and responsibilities at the plant next door.

As the "on-site" director Mr. Weston had a responsibility in this type of industry to personally inspect on a regular basis, i.e., "walk-about". To simply look at the site "not too closely" 20 times over his four-year tenure does not meet the mark. He had an obligation if he decided to delegate responsibility to ensure that the delegate received the training necessary for the job and to receive detailed reports from that delegate.

There will be a conviction registered pursuant to s. 75(1) of the OWRA. The charges under s. 147 a of the EPA will be stayed for reasons previously given.

Notes and Questions

The trial judge fined Bata Industries $120,000 and imposed fines of $12,000 each on Marchant and Weston as corporate directors. In addition, the trial judge ordered that Bata Industries be prohibited from indemnifying the directors for their fines. An initial sentencing appeal resulted in the fines being reduced to $90,000 and $6,000 respectively, although the order prohibiting indemnification of Marchant and Weston was affirmed. On a further appeal to the Ontario Court of Appeal, the decision to reduce the fines was affirmed while the order prohibiting indemnification of the directors was vacated.

The Emergence and Role of Administrative Monetary Penalties (AMPs)

The *Bata* case underscores that criminal and regulatory prosecutions can be costly, time-consuming and unpredictable. As government budgets for environmental enforcement were cut back in Canada, the US and the UK during the 1980s and 1990s, regulators began to explore alternative enforcement mechanisms.

Stepan Wood & Lynn Johannson, "Six Principles for Smart Regulation"
(2008) 46 Osgoode Hall L.J. 345

Ontario borrowed the idea of environmental penalties from the United States, where similar tools have been available since the 1970s, usually under the name "administrative penalties" (APs). APs were introduced to allow government officials to issue relatively modest financial penalties for minor environmental violations without incurring the time and expense of a full-blown investigation, prosecution, and trial. Before APs, environmental law enforcement boiled down to a choice between voluntary industry compliance or the blunt instrument of criminal or quasi-criminal prosecution, with the latter reserved only for the most egregious cases. Investigations and prosecutions would often drag out for years before reaching a final conclusion. As a result, many violations were not investigated or prosecuted at all.

APs were one of several innovative enforcement tools introduced to get away from this often unsatisfactory binary choice. APs do away with the need for formal court proceedings altogether. In theory, this may reduce enforcement costs for governments, regulated firms, and interested third parties alike, and increase the level of enforcement of environmental laws. Research indicates that APs have a credible deterrent effect at very modest administrative cost. For these reasons many governments embraced APs enthusiastically.

Regulated industries, on the other hand, dislike them. One concern is absolute liability: the government may impose APs without proving the elements of the offence. Another concern is double jeopardy: in some jurisdictions, payment of an AP may not bar prosecution for the same offence. Industry also objects to the relative lack of judicial scrutiny of AP determinations, the high level of administrative discretion over some APs, and the one-size-fits all approach of others. Some environmental non-governmental organizations (ENGOs) have embraced APs, but others have condemned them as trivializing what should properly be considered crimes. These concerns notwithstanding, APs have proliferated in the US and have been introduced in several other countries. They are one of the US Environmental Protection Agency's favourite enforcement tools, increasing dramatically in the last few years.

Notes and Questions

1. Following the lead of many US jurisdictions, several Canadian provinces have now implemented AMP regimes. The first province to do so was Alberta, which incorporates an AMP regime into its *Environmental Protection and Enhancement Act*. AMPs also play a key role in British Columbia legislation governing forest practices. Recently, Ontario has joined the AMP bandwagon through amendments in 2004 to its *Environmental Protection Act* (Bill 133). And now the federal government appears poised to do likewise under provisions of what is being popularly referred to as the "Environmental Enforcement Bill" (Bill C-16 introduced in March 2009) which contemplates enactment of the *Environmental Violations Administrative Monetary Penalties Act* (MPA). Under the MPA, the Governor in Council would be empowered to pass regulations to create AMPs under nine federal statutes including *CEPA*, the *National Parks Act*, the *Migratory Birds Convention Act* and the *National Marine Conservation Areas Act*.

2. A detailed survey into current research into AMPs in the environmental law context concludes that:

> Studies done on use of administrative penalties indicate that they can result in greater efficiencies for governments. These studies reveal that regulators are more likely to take enforcement action when administrative sanctions are available as opposed to when prosecution is the only enforcement tool. The lower standard of proof and the less stringent evidentiary rules under the administrative process means that enforcement action can be taken more readily and at lower cost than when criminal prosecution is the only option. There is also evidence that utilizing administrative sanctions has been effective in promoting regulatory compliance: see Ramani Nadarajah, "Environmental Penalties: New Enforcement Tool or the Demise of Environmental Prosecutions?", *Environmental Year in Review 2007* (Canada Law Book).

While empirical evidence documenting the impact of implementing AMPs on compliance is surprisingly sparse, Nadarajah notes since the Canadian Food Inspection Agency introduced AMPs, industry compliance has risen from between 60 to 70% to over 90%.

3. One key benefit of AMPs is that they can encourage regulators to undertake enforcement action in instances in cases where — due to resource constraints as well as standard of proof and evidentiary requirements — they might otherwise shy away from mounting a criminal prosecution. This, in turn, can have a positive deterrent effect on the behavior of individuals and firms being regulated. Research done by Professor Brown suggests that certainty of punishment is the most significant single factor in promoting compliance: see R. Brown, "Administrative and Criminal Penalties in the Enforcement of Occupational Health and Safety Legislation" (1992) 3 Osgoode Hall LJ 691.

4. Commentators warn, however, of the need to ensure that for serious offences criminal prosecution remains the preferred enforcement instrument. A key design issue, therefore, when establishing an AMP system is to determine which offences should be enforceable via AMPs alone, which should potentially be enforceable via AMPs or criminal prosecution, and which should be enforceable exclusively by way of criminal prosecution. In this vein, Chris Rolfe argues that

> .. for many offences such as willful dumping, interference with enforcement officials, falsifying records etc. the criminal court system is the only appropriate remedy. These are true crimes. The solemnity and stigma of the criminal court system are appropriate for these offences: see "Administrative Monetary Penalties: A Tool for Ensuring Compliance" (unpublished: West Coast Environmental Law Association, 1997).

To reduce the potential that regulators will gravitate towards over-reliance on AMPs in appropriately serious cases, Professor Brown thus recommends that a two-track system that clearly specifies a list of offences for which criminal prosecution is the only available enforcement option.

5. A final consideration is the relationship between AMP regimes and rights guaranteed under the *Charter of Rights and Freedoms*. Some commentators predict that AMP regimes, particularly those which incorporate substantial fines and rely on reverse onus or absolute liability, will be challenged under the *Charter*: see Berger (2006) *infra* this chapter. Whether such challenges will succeed will depend heavily on specifics of the regime in question and upon whether the court concludes the penalty in question as "administrative" or "criminal" in nature: see *R. v. Wigglesworth*, [1987] 2 S.C.R. 541 and S. Berger, *The Prosecution and Defence of Environmental Offences* (Aurora: Canada Law Book, 2006)

Part IV — Citizen Enforcement

Some would argue that vesting in governments an exclusive monopoly over environmental law enforcement is shortsighted and doomed to fail. As we have seen, there are a variety of reasons why governments may elect not to pursue a rigourous enforcement policy. These can range from budgetary constraints (costs and availability of prosecutorial resources); political factors (including "protecting jobs", maintaining a positive investment climate, and avoiding inter-governmental conflict) as well as legal considerations (including the apparent strength of the case and likelihood of conviction). Historically, the notion that the Crown, and in particular, the office of the Attorney General, should have broad discretion to make enforcement decisions has rested on a variety of rationales (as described by the Ferguson article below). Perhaps paramount among these is the idea that the Attorney General is in the best position to assess whether the "public interest" will be served by mounting a prosecution.

Critics argue, however, there are many "public interests" and that both democracy and the rule of law are well-served by promoting more competition in the business of law enforcement: see, for example, K. Roach & M. Trebilcock, "Private Enforcement of Competition Laws", (1996) Osgoode Hall L.J. 461. It is largely on this basis that the US Congress has incorporated "citizen suit" provisions in many federal environmental statutes. These provisions provide citizens with standing to bring enforcement actions as a "private attorneys general". Where such actions succeed, the citizen is rewarded by a requirement that they be indemnified for the costs of the action.

Canadian legislators have been extremely reluctant to follow the US lead by enacting analogous provisions. For example, unlike its US federal counterpart, the Canadian *Species at Risk Act* has no citizen provisions, despite concerted lobbying efforts by environmental organizations to have them included in the legislation. [*Ed note*: See further discussion in Chapter 9.] And while some Canadian laws have environmental rights provisions (*CEPA*; the Ontario *Environmental Bill of Rights*; and analogous provisions in Yukon and NWT legislation) that allow citizens to trigger investigations into environmental wrongdoing, and in some instances commence suit for environmental damages, to date these laws have been extremely circumscribed in both scope and application.

To remedy this, environmental groups have recently drafted a Canadian Environmental Bill of Rights, which would substantially enhance the role of citizens in environmental law enforcement. Until such a statute is enacted, however, the principal means for citizens to prosecute environmental offences remains the private prosecution. In some Canadian jurisdictions (most notably Ontario) this vehicle has proven in recent years to have significant value. Elsewhere, however, most notably in BC and Alberta, government policies have effectively precluded citizens from having access to this important enforcement tool.

In this Part, we provide a brief overview of the state of the law with respect to citizen environmental rights in Canada and emerging law reform proposals, accompanied with a snapshot of parallel US provisions. We then turn to a more detailed exploration of the current status and future prospects of the private prosecution as an environmental law enforcement tool.

Citizen Suits and Environmental Bills of Rights

South of border, there has been a long tradition of rights-based approaches to environmental protection. Many states have enacted Environmental Bills of Rights (EBRs) explicitly designed to allow citizens to litigate environmental protection issues. An early illustration is the Michigan EBR discussed in the preceding chapter: see M'Gonigle, *et al.*, in Chapter 4. These laws have provided the inspiration for a variety of successors including the proposed new Canadian Environmental Bill of Rights that we shall examine shortly. Of even greater systemic importance in terms of environmental law enforcement in the United States has been the prevalence, primarily at the federal level, of the citizen suit.

Chris Tollefson, Jerry DeMarco & Darlene Gilliland, "Towards a Costs Jurisprudence in Public Interest Litigation"
(2004) 83 Can. Bar Rev. 473

Recognition of the benefits associated with encouraging private litigants to enforce public rights has been a central feature of the American legal tradition since at least the New Deal era. Over sixty years ago, Judge Jerome Frank is said to have coined the term "private Attorney General" to describe the mantle taken on by citizens who are statutorily empowered to initiate enforcement action. The private attorney general mechanism has emerged, over the last quarter century, as a primary instrument for securing compliance with federal law. It plays a key role in a variety of important U.S. laws including: all (but one) of the major anti-pollution laws enacted by Congress since 1970; virtually all modern civil rights statutes; most anti-trust and securities laws; and in the *Equal Access to Justice Act* (which governs non-tort suits brought against federal government departments and agencies if there is no other "fee shifting" statute applicable).

Private attorney general provisions allow citizens and public interest groups to commence enforcement actions against any person alleged to be in violation of one or more specified provisions of a designated statute or regulation or to sue governments alleged to have failed to perform nondiscretionary duties. Where such enforcement proceedings culminate in judgment for the plaintiff or otherwise prevail as reflected in a negotiated settlement of the action, courts are empowered to order that the defendant(s) reimburse the citizen attorney-general for their litigation costs including "reasonable" attorney fees. If a public interest attorney with conduct of the matter has been acting *pro bono*, courts have held that they should be compensated at the rate their services would have been billed in a private law firm.

A key design feature of the private attorney-general model is its adoption of a one-way costs rule (also known as fee-shifting) . . .. this represents a fundamental departure from the common law-based, no-way American costs rule that ordinarily governs judicial costs allocation. In its place is substituted a regime under which a private attorney-general pursues enforcement actions on the expectation of being rewarded if they succeed, without risk of costs liability if they do not.

In the environmental law context, these so-called "citizen suits" have been hailed as "a defining theme of the modern environmental era". According to one commentator, the existence of environmental citizen suits has "brought competition, with its attendant virtues, to the business of environmental enforcement". As a result, the robustness and quality of environmental law enforcement has been significantly enhanced. The spectre of private enforcement has reportedly had a salutary effect in terms of governmental accountability for prosecutorial policy and compliance with environmental regulations by public and private bodies. It has also been credited with promoting broader democratic values including facilitating citizen involvement in environmental policy making, influencing judicial interpretation of key environmental provisions, and enhancing the legitimacy of environmental laws and law-making processes.

Not all commentators are as unequivocally supportive of private attorney general suits as a policy instrument. Some argue, for instance, that state enforcement is more efficient and that private enforcement can disrupt or conflict with state compliance strategies. However, . . . Roach and Trebilcock conclude that, on balance, the benefits of the American private attorney general model outweigh its drawbacks. In their view, many of the putative disadvantages identified with the model can be largely addressed or mitigated through design measures . . .

Although from time to time there have been legislative initiatives [mounted in the US] aimed at curtailing or eliminating the citizen suits and private attorney general provisions, these have almost invariably failed. In part, this result may in part be attributable to the fact that such provisions have a strong appeal to a variety of political constituencies:

> Liberals promote the private attorney general, in part, as an antidote to what they view as a conservative administration's reluctance to aggressively enforce various regulatory laws. Conservatives find virtue in the private attorney general concept because of its function in 'privatizing' law enforcement pursuant to the ideals of economic efficiency.

[*Ed note*: The authors then go onto examine the Canadian approach to citizen enforcement, which departs markedly from the American experience.]

Canadian governments . . . have also been relatively timid in pursuing legislative reforms [that support citizen environmental law enforcement] . . . To date, no Canadian laws contain "private attorney-general" or "citizen-suit" provisions modeled on those prevalent in American law. Federally, while the *Canadian Environmental Protection Act* contemplates the right of a citizen to commence an environmental protection action, due to the limited and constrained nature of this right it has never been used. Likewise, while in some provincial jurisdictions similar statutory causes of action exist, these provisions have been used only rarely. The same is true with respect to private prosecutions of environmental laws despite the existence, in some jurisdictions, of provisions allowing courts to award legal fees to successful citizen-prosecutors.

In Ontario, for example, under the *Environmental Bill of Rights, 1993* S.O.1993, c. 28 citizens are given statutory standing to enforce environmental laws under two distinct procedures. Section 84 gives a private citizen the right to commence an action to protect a public resource in Ontario from harm caused by a violation of environmental legislation. This provision, however, has only been used twice in the past ten years. One of those actions is still at the discovery stage, and the other was dismissed without costs when the plaintiffs discontinued their action. Likewise, section 103 gives an individual the right to bring an action on the basis of having suffered individual harm caused by a public nuisance. Only six actions have been brought under section 103; most of these have been class actions that have not made it past the certification stage. In assessing costs with respect to actions brought under either of these provisions, courts are given discretion to consider "any special circumstance", including whether or not a case is a test case or raises a novel point of law: see s. 100 of the *EBR*. Similar citizen suit provisions with analogous costs provisions are also in place in the Northwest Territories (*Environmental Rights Act*, R.S.N.W.T. 1988 c. 83 (Supp.), s. 5) and the Yukon (*Environment Act*, S.Y. 1991, c. 5, s. 1). To date, however, neither of the provisions has been utilized.

The paucity of citizen-led private prosecutions is likely the result of a cluster of factors. Private prosecutors in Canada must establish guilt beyond reasonable doubt whereas American citizen suits are governed by a civil standard of proof. Private prosecutions frequently also impose much more daunting legal and scientific challenges than do citizen suits, in part due to the differing burden of proof and the strictness with which American courts have interpreted many of the obligations citizen suits exist to enforce. Finally, in several provinces, the potential to pursue private prosecutions has effectively been nullified by the government policies that oblige the Attorney General, as a matter of course, to assume conduct of all such cases; a practice that almost invariably culminates in the prosecution being stayed.

Notes and Questions

1. What accounts for the differing national approaches to citizen law enforcement in Canada and United States? As the above article notes, these differences prevail across a wide range of areas of legal regulation. To what extent is resistance to the notion of citizen enforcement related to notions about citizen participation more generally?

2. Recently, as part of a broader advocacy campaign, environmental organizations have drafted a model federal citizen rights-based EBR for consideration by Parliament: see *An Act to Establish a Canadian Environmental Bill of Rights*. Its stated purpose (s. 3) is to:

(a) safeguard the rights of present and future Canadians to a healthy and ecologically balanced environment;

(b) confirm the Government of Canada's public trust duty to protect the environment under its jurisdiction; and

(c) ensure all Canadians have access to:

i. adequate environmental information;

ii. access to justice in an environmental context;

iii. effective participatory mechanisms in environmental decision-making; and

iv. adequate legal protection for employees who take action in respect of environmental harm.

Under the proposed law, the EBR "must be interpreted consistently with existing and emerging principles of environmental law" including the precautionary principle, the polluters principle and the principles of sustainable development and intergenerational equity (s. 4).

A key feature is statutory recognition that "every Canadian has a right to a healthy and ecologically balanced environment" and that the Government of Canada is legally obligated to protect this right (s. 7). The Government of Canada is also declared to be the "trustee of Canada's environment" and is obliged to "conserve it in accordance with the public trust for the benefit of present and future generations (s. 8).

The model bill incorporates a variety of substantive and procedural citizen rights, to promote compliance with its requirements. These include the right to sue to the federal Crown for failing to enforce the public trust or violating the right to a "healthy and ecologically balanced environment". It also creates a right to sue private parties where, due to a past or impending violation of federal law, "significant environmental harm" has or is likely to result: see generally s. 17. And, it broadens the ambit of judicial review of environmental decision-making, by eliminating standing and other constraints on the review of governmental decisions that "arise in the context of environmental protection" (s. 16).

It also proposes to enshrine a variety of procedural citizen rights, including the right to seek Ministerial review of any current federal law, regulation or policy (s. 12); the right to trigger an investigation of violations of federal law or regulations (ss. 13-14); the right to access environmental information (s. 10); the right to participate in environmental decision-making (s. 11); and the right to protected from federal employer reprisals (aka whistleblower protection) where the employee has exercised rights protected by the model bill (ss. 24–26).

3. Are there any citizen rights that this model bill has omitted? We discuss the concept of the public trust elsewhere in the context of our chapters on the common law (Chapter 2) and parks and protected areas (Chapter 8). To what extent do the provisions in this model bill build on existing common law and statutory public trust concepts?

4. What reception is this proposal likely to receive in Ottawa? Which of its provisions are likely to be the most contentious?

Private Prosecutions

While the jurisprudence and debate surrounding EBRs remains very much in its infancy, private prosecutions are another matter. Here, the legal tool is ancient in origin, and one that in many jurisdictions has been constrained both by governmental policy and judicial precedent. In this section, we provide a critical account of the history and competing rationales relating to the role of private prosecutions in the environmental context, followed by excerpts from *Kostuch v. Alberta*, one of the leading appellate decisions in this area of the law.

Keith Ferguson, "Challenging the Intervention and Stay of an Environmental Private Prosecution"

(2004) 13 J. Env. L. & Prac. 153

Starting around the thirteenth century in England, private prosecutions played a prominent role in the enforcement of public wrongs. In fact "it was not only the privilege but the duty of the private citizen to preserve the King's Peace and bring offenders to justice". When English law came to Canada, similar rights to conduct private prosecutions came with it. Such rights and duties began to change, however, in the nineteenth century in response to the profound societal shifts resulting from the industrial revolution. A centralized bureaucracy was gradually formed to administer and enforce a broad new range of social regulation. Thus the dominance of the private prosecution began to wane, and there has been an ongoing "process of gradual and incremental erosion of private prosecutorial authority". Indeed, in recent years assessments have been undertaken to determine whether private prosecutions should be kept at all.

Although there are significant practical difficulties in bringing a private prosecution, especially in a technical arena such as environmental law enforcement, private prosecutions retain important roles to play. These include:

- Providing a cure to the "working entente" that "too often" evolves between "an overworked bureaucracy" and "the persons subject to their regulation"
- Providing an "important safeguard in our society against real or perceived corruption in Crown prosecution decisions"
- Avoiding laws being rendered "nugatory" or becoming "paper tigers" due to government non-enforcement

- Providing reassurance to those who do comply with the law that their competitors will not benefit by non-compliance
- Providing "an important civil liberty" in a participatory democracy.

Despite these benefits, once a private prosecution has been brought, the Attorney General's office will often intervene and stay the prosecution. Indeed, in some provinces there is a policy to always intervene, such as in Alberta where, according to Duncan (in discussing environmental private prosecutions), it "has been the experience of private informants that regardless of the legal basis for their case or the strength of the evidence collected on their own accord, the Crown has intervened to stay the proceedings". In addition to being highly frustrating for a private prosecutor, this can raise suspicions that partisan politics have improperly interfered with the workings of law enforcement. Although the private prosecutor may attempt to seek judicial review of such an intervention and stay, courts have given the Attorney General's office a very high degree of deference, resulting in such attempts being "spectacularly unsuccessful".

[A key] rationale for the limited review of prosecutorial discretion is protection of the public interest and the accused. As noted by the Alberta Court of Appeal in *Kostuch* (1995) (in upholding the stay of a private prosecution):

> The criminal process is not the preserve of the private individual. The fundamental consideration in any decision regarding prosecutions must be the public interest . . . In deciding whether to prosecute, the Attorney General must have regard not only to the interest of the person laying the charges, but also to the rights of the person charged with an offence, and to the public interest . . . He or she is answerable to the Legislature and finally to the electorate, for decisions made. [see case excerpt below]

Avoiding frivolous, malicious or hopeless private prosecutions is an important part of the rationale for the Attorney General to be able to intervene and stay private prosecutions.

However, the public interest requires a balance be struck between avoiding the legal system being used for improper purposes by private prosecutors (such as "for personal gratification, private gain or malice"), termed **"zealousness error"** by Thompson, and avoiding under enforcement, termed **"leniency error".** (emphasis added). Judicial hesitancy to review a Crown counsel decision to stay a private prosecution certainly recognizes the important function of the Attorney General's office to oversee private prosecutions in order to avoid zealousness error, but appears to give little weight to the equally compelling public interest in avoiding leniency error.

Avoiding zealousness error is of course important, but this need not entail a blanket high standard of review that results in acceptance of unreasonable and even patently unreasonable decisions of the Attorney General to stay private prosecutions (and thus increasing leniency error). Given the time and expense to bring a private prosecution and the need to convince a judge or designated justice to first issue process or to give a written order for an indictment, the scale of zealousness error should first be questioned. If Crown counsel believes a private prosecution has been brought for improper motives, there should be little difficulty for them to provide a reasonable justification for their intervention and stay. If zealousness error remains a problem, punitive costs awards would appear the obvious solution.

Another important public interest factor is the democratic value of private prosecutions. In the U.S., for example, citizens have been given the right to enforce environmental laws through statutory citizen suits. Thompson suggests that:

> If citizen suits were not permitted, individual members of society would be placed in a position subservient to government enforcement officials, undermining the horizontal power structure of particular value to an effective democracy.

Such subservience well describes the current situation in Canada. Although courts have occasionally noted the important citizenship right to bring a private prosecution, they have ruled, for example, that the stay of a private prosecution does not generally violate *Charter* rights, and even if it did it would be saved by s. 1 (*i.e.* it would be "demonstrably justified in a free and democratic society") due to the added objectivity Crown counsel can bring. However, it makes little sense to allow unreasonable or patently unreasonable stays of private prosecutions if enhanced objectivity and democracy is part of the rationale. As Tingle put it: "The courts have simply not allowed the field of prosecutorial discretion to be 'democratised'."

Allowing such democratic citizenship rights to be frustrated can have adverse consequences against the public interest. As noted by the Law Reform Commission for Canada, "individuals, frustrated by the law, may seek to accommodate themselves by unlawful means", and "the form of retribution which is exacted by the citizen's resort to legal processes is clearly preferable to other unregulated forms of citizen self-help".

Courts have countered such democratic arguments with the idea that the Attorney General is accountable to the legislature and the electorate. However, this too is fraught with difficulties. For example, as noted by Tingle:

> One defect in this argument is that most decisions of the Attorney General are virtually invisible and, while they may dramatically affect the accused, they have a negligible impact on the voting public. The obscurity and political unimportance of prosecutorial discretion makes the legislature an ineffective oversight mechanism . . . [especially] when the people who benefited from the Attorney General's exercise of his discretion are the leaders of the current government.

Kostuch v. Alberta (Attorney General)
(1995), 128 D.L.R. (4th) 440 (Alta. C.A.)

[The dispute at the centre of this litigation related to construction of the Oldman River Dam, a controversy which was previously considered in another context in Chapter 3. This case arises as an appeal from the dismissal of the appellant's application for an order setting aside the entry of a stay of proceedings by the Attorney General of Alberta "AG" with respect to a private prosecution she had filed. Kostuch alleged that the provincial Crown and others involved in the construction of the Oldman River dam were in violation of subsections 35(1) and 40(b) of the *Fisheries Act*. She claimed further that the AG's decision to intervene and stay her prosecution constituted a violation of section 7 of the *Charter*. She also submitted that the power of the court to review the exercise of prosecutorial discretion by the Attorney General was not limited to cases of flagrant impropriety.]

Hetherington, Mcfadyen & Russell JJ.A.

This matter involves the construction of the Oldman River Dam by the Province of Alberta. The information in question was the last in a series of eight informations sworn by Dr. Martha Kostuch against those involved in the construction of this dam . . .. each of the informations alleged that either the Government of Alberta, its ministers, or the Crown in Right of Alberta and various construction companies breached the *Fisheries Act* by constructing and operating river diversion channels at the dam site which interfered with fish habitat, without the required authorization of the Federal Minister of Fisheries and Oceans. The first of these informations had been sworn by the appellant on August 2, 1988. The first seven informations were stayed by the Attorney General or were otherwise disposed of by the Courts for a variety of reasons, none of which have any relevance here.

Following the laying of the first information, the Attorney General intervened. On his instructions, the R.C.M.P. commenced an investigation. Inspector Duncan was responsible for this investigation. In referring the matter to the R.C.M.P., the Attorney General's department, being concerned about conflicts of interest, advised the R.C.M.P. to seek instructions regarding the investigation and prosecution from the Federal Department of Justice.

The prosecution policy established by the Attorney General of Alberta contains a two-fold test: (1) the evidence must be such that there is a reasonable likelihood of conviction when the evidence as a whole is considered; and (2) whether the public interest requires prosecution . . .

In the course of the investigation, Inspector Duncan interviewed the appellant on at least two occasions, and obtained from her a statement of facts, as well as a summary of her position on the matter. Dr. Kostuch advised Duncan that she believed that the dam construction interfered with fish habitat, that the construction had never been approved by the Minister of Fisheries, and that any delegation of administrative authority under the *Fisheries Act* to the Province of Alberta was unconstitutional. The prosecution was one of many legal avenues being pursued by the group called the Friends of the Oldman River Society in its efforts to stop the construction of the Oldman River Dam.

Following an initial investigation, Duncan concluded that while it appeared that the construction of the dam had interfered or would interfere with fish habitat, serious questions of the availability of a defence under s. 35(2) of the *Fisheries Act* also had to be addressed [*Ed note:* Ultimately, agents for the AG Alberta concluded that there was no reasonable likelihood of conviction and stayed the prosecution]

By Notice of Motion dated March 22, 1993, the appellant brought an application for an order setting aside the intervention and the stay of proceedings of the Attorney General and prohibiting the Attorney General from again intervening in the prosecution. The application was dismissed and the appellant appeals to this court.

The learned Chambers Judge reviewed the agreements between federal and provincial departments, correspondence between departments responsible for fisheries and the environment, and statements by federal ministers in correspondence with others regarding the transfer of jurisdiction to the Province of Alberta. He concluded: "From the statement contained in the letter of the Minister, one could conclude that the Minister authorized the project under s. 35(2) of the *Fisheries Act*".

The learned Chambers Judge found that the Provincial officials had carried out a complete investigation of the effect of the dam on fish habitat, and they were satisfied that adequate plans had been put in place to protect fish. Therefore no net loss of fish would result from the project. In 1977/78, the Federal Minister of Fisheries and Oceans and the Minister of the Environment confirmed their understanding that Alberta had authority to deal with matters involving fish habitat in Alberta. The Province of Alberta and the Government of Canada entered into another agreement in 1987, confirming Alberta's assumption of responsibility for enforcement of the *Fisheries Act*. Alberta did not thereafter seek permission from the Federal Minister with respect to projects located in this province. Federal officials were aware of the plans for the Oldman River Dam, the investigations by the Provincial authorities and the plans which had been put into place to protect fish and the environment, and voiced no objections to the construction of the dam. Federal Ministers of Fisheries and Oceans, had expressly declined to intervene, and the Agents of the Federal Department of Justice refused to prosecute.

The learned Chambers Judge found that the Alberta Government had acted in good faith in approving the construction of the dam. On this ground, the Crown in the Right of Alberta and the corporate defendants who acted on the authorization had a complete defence to any prosecution. These findings were supported by the evidence.

Section 7 of the *Charter*

The appellant claims that her rights under s. 7 of the *Charter* have been breached in that "she has not been able to have a court adjudicate on a matter of concern to her" thus causing her emotional stress.

In other words, the appellant claims that she has a right to prosecute another person, that s. 7 of the *Charter* protects that right, and that the Attorney General cannot interfere with a private prosecution without according the informant an opportunity of examining the reports on the investigation conducted, and giving her an opportunity to address those facts before an impartial person.

Section 7 of the *Charter* provides: "Everyone has the right to life, liberty and security of the person and the right not to be deprived thereof except in accordance with the principles of fundamental justice".

In *Reference re s. 94(2) of Motor Vehicle Act* the Supreme Court of Canada established a two-stage test for the application of s. 7. First, the appellant must demonstrate a deprivation of her right to life, liberty and security of the person; and secondly, she must demonstrate this deprivation occurred in a manner not consistent with principles of fundamental justice.

However broadly the right to "liberty and security of the person" in s. 7 of the *Charter* may come to be interpreted, it is my view that it will not and cannot include the unrestricted right on the part of a private prosecutor to continue a criminal prosecution in the face of an intervention by the Attorney General. The criminal process is not the preserve of the private individual. The fundamental consideration in any decision regarding prosecutions must be the public interest. The function of protecting the public interest in prosecution matters has been granted by Parliament to the Attorney General of a province, and in some cases to the Federal Minister of Justice.

In deciding whether to prosecute, the Attorney General must have regard not only to the interests of the person laying the charges, but also to the rights of the person charged with an offence, and to the public interest. By the provisions of the *Criminal Code*, the Attorney General is given a discretionary power to intervene in private prosecutions. The Attorney General of a province is a member of the Executive who is charged with responsibility for the administration of justice in the province. He or she is answerable to the Legislature and finally to the electorate, for decisions made. The courts have understandably been very hesitant to intervene in the exercise of that discretion.

The right, if any, of a private prosecutor to prosecute another person is very limited and is clearly restricted by the provisions of the *Criminal Code* to cases where the Attorney General opts not to intervene.

The Extent of the Power of Review

Assuming that the court has power to review prosecutorial discretion, that power will be exercised only in cases where there has been flagrant impropriety in the exercise of the prosecutorial discretion. This rule has been clearly established by the Courts, and we accept it as correct. In *R. v. Balderstone et al.* (1983), 8 C.C.C (3d) 532 at 539 (Man. C.A.); leave to appeal refused [1983] 2 S.C.R. v, Monnin C.J.M. stated as follows:

> The judicial and executive must not mix. These are two separate and distinct functions. The accusatorial officers lay informations or in some cases prefer indictments. Courts or the curia listen to cases brought to their attention and decide them on their merits or on meritorious preliminary matters. If a judge should attempt to review the actions or conduct of the Attorney General — barring flagrant impropriety — he could be falling into a field which is not his and interfering with the administrative and accusatorial function of the Attorney General or his officers. That a judge must not do.

[In our view] . . . flagrant impropriety can only be established by proof of misconduct bordering on corruption, violation of the law, bias against or for a particular individual or offence. The test for review of prosecutorial discretion remains that of flagrant impropriety, and is not unreasonableness as suggested by counsel for the appellant.

Flagrant Impropriety

The appellant . . . alleges improper interference in the investigation by the Federal Department of Justice. She asks this Court to infer that the Department so directed the investigation as to predetermine the result, referring to such action as an abuse of power. There is no evidence to support any such suggestion. The appellant asks that an inference of impropriety be drawn from the fact that after the submission of the initial report, the investigation changed direction and focused on issues of mitigation and due diligence. The appellant appears to suggest that the police investigation and the prosecutors' concerns must be limited to evidence supporting the charge, and the possibilities of valid defences ought not to be explored by the investigator or the prosecutors in arriving at their decision. Needless to say, this argument is rejected as completely unfounded in law and on the evidence.

The appellant also suggests that the Attorney General was guilty of flagrant impropriety in deciding to intervene in a case in which the Province had an interest, prior to the receipt of the opinion from the independent prosecutors. For reasons more fully stated in the analysis of the argument on bias, we agree with the finding of the learned Chambers Judge that the Attorney General for Alberta acted appropriately in this case.

Bias

Faced with possible allegations of conflict of interest, the Attorney General of Alberta instructed that the file be directed to the Federal Department of Justice, in the event that Department wished to exercise its discretion and take over the prosecution. He also directed that the file be referred to the Manitoba Attorney General's Department for decision. The Manitoba Attorney General's Department had authority to decide whether to prosecute or to stay proceedings. Counsel for the appellant suggests that the Alberta Attorney General should have waited for the decision of the Manitoba Attorney General's Department before deciding to intervene in the prosecution, and alternatively that the decision by the Manitoba Department is tainted because of its association with the Attorney General of Alberta.

The Attorney General of Alberta acted appropriately in referring the decision on the prosecution to experienced prosecutors from another province. There is no suggestion that those prosecutors were influenced in any manner by the Attorney General of Alberta or by his agents in this province. In fact, such a suggestion would be contrary to the clear indication by Mr. Dangerfield, as an officer of the Court, that he and another prosecutor from Manitoba had reviewed the file and formed their own opinions.

Further, the appellant does not suggest that the authorization and approval by the Alberta Fish and Wildlife officials was granted otherwise than in good faith. The appellant merely suggests that the delegation of authority to the province is unconstitutional. The overwhelming evidence presented which establishes that over a period of time commencing with the agreement in 1930, correspondence in 1977-78 and ending with the agreement in 1987, the Federal Minister of Fisheries and Oceans and the Minister of the Environment were consistent in the position that jurisdiction for enforcement of the *Fisheries Act* had been transferred to the province. It is difficult to see how one could conclude otherwise than that Alberta acted in good faith in authorizing the construction in question.

Flagrant impropriety has not been established.

The appeal is dismissed.

References

We thank the copyright holders for their permission to reproduce their materials.

Stanley David Berger, "The Future of Environmental Prosecutions in Ontario" (2006) 19 C.E.L.R. (3rd) 32

Joseph Castrilli, "Canadian Policy and Practice with Indicators of Effective Environmental Enforcement" in Annex 3 to *Indicators of Effective Environmental Enforcement Proceedings of A North American Dialogue* (CEC: 1999)

Jerry V. DeMarco & Toby Vigod, "Smarter Regulation: The Case for Enforcement and Transparency" (2007) 17 J. Env. L. & Prac. 85

Keith Ferguson, "Challenging the Intervention and Stay of an Environmental Private Prosecution" (2004) 13 J. Env. L. & Prac. 153

David L. Markell & John H Knox, eds., *Greening NAFTA: The North American Commission for Environmental Cooperation* (Stanford: Stanford University Press, 2003)

Ramani Nadarajah, "Environmental Penalties: New Enforcement Tool or the Demise of Environmental Prosecutions?" in *Environmental Year in Review 2007* (Canada Law Book)

John Swaigen "Absolute Liability Revisited: *Lévis v Tétrault*" in *Environmental Law: Year in Review 2006* (Canada Law Book)

Chris Tollefson, Jerry DeMarco & Darlene Gilliland, "Towards a Costs Jurisprudence in Public Interest Litigation" (2004) 83 Can. Bar Rev. 473

C. Tollefson, "Games without Frontiers: Investor Claims and Citizen Submissions under the NAFTA Regime" (2002) 27 Yale J. Int'l L. 217

Stepan Wood & Lynn Johannson, "How Not to Incorporate Voluntary Standards into Smart Regulation: ISO 14001 and Ontario's *Environmental Penalties Regulations*" CLPE Research Paper 07/2008 • Vol. 04 No. 02

Matthew D. Zinn, "Policing Environmental Regulatory Enforcement: Cooperation, Capture and Citizen Suits" (2002) 21 Stan. Envtl. L.J. 81

6

JUDICIAL REVIEW OF ENVIRONMENTAL DECISION-MAKING

Introduction

This chapter provides an overview of the nature and role of judicial review in the environmental law context. Judicial review challenges courts to balance their role as protectors of the rule of law against the need to show appropriate deference to decisions that emerge through operation of the democratic process. The inherent tension between these competing imperatives and, at times, the confusing and conflicting jurisprudence that it has generated has recently led a senior member of the Supreme Court of Canada to opine that, "Judicial review is an idea that has lately become unduly burdened with law office metaphysics". See *New Brunswick (Board of Management) v. Dunsmuir*, 1 S.C.R. 190 per Binnie J. (para. 122).

The chapter is in six Parts. Part I commences with a reflection on the role and nature of judicial review, with particular attention to the environmental law context, drawing upon recent ruminations on this theme by the Supreme Court in its landmark judgment in *Dunsmuir*. Among other things, this Part introduces the doctrinal means employed by courts to determine the level of scrutiny they will employ in reviewing a challenged administrative decision, a task commonly referred to as the "standard of review analysis". Part II then looks at how courts have dealt with this issue in the environmental law context, with a view to considering the implications of *Dunsmuir* in future cases. And in Part III, we provide an overview of the grounds upon which judicial review may be sought, using illustrations from the environmental law jurisprudence.

We then consider the growing impact on this jurisprudence of cases championed by public interest environmental organizations. In recent decades, cases of this kind have raised intriguing questions about access to justice and the rules and principles that have traditionally governed judicial review of administrative decision-making. One area that has seen significant developments is the law of public interest standing, reviewed in Part IV. Public interest environmental litigants have also pressed the courts to revisit and renovate the law governing injunctions (Part V), and costs (Part VI) that apply in judicial review proceedings.

Part I — Administrative Law and Judicial Review

An Overview of Administrative Law in the Environmental Context

Administrative law is a body of law that is concerned with defining and governing the relationship between citizens and the state. As is underscored in *Dunsmuir*, administrative law is thus "intimately connected" with the rule of law: the notion that the state derives its power to make decisions that affect individual rights through law, and as such is legally accountable for the exercise of that power.

The range of state actors and actions governed by administrative law is impressively broad. All state actors that derive their power to act from statute (*statutory decision makers*) exercise these powers subject to the principles of administrative law. As such, whether the statutory decision-maker is a Cabinet minister, a civil servant, a tribunal or a municipal council, in all instances the power in question must be exercised in a manner consistent with applicable administrative law principles. Likewise, administrative law principles govern a far-reaching range of forms of state action. In other words, administrative law not only governs specific decisions, but also the delegated power *to make regulations* that are of more general application. In the environmental context, for example, this means that administrative law defines and governs the exercise of powers to grant project-or firm-specific licences, permits and other approvals, and the power (usually vested in Cabinet) to enact regulations that address broader subject matters including generally applicable rules with respect to air, land and water protection.

As with many other areas of law, administrative law is an evolving amalgam of common law and legislation. As such, both the common law and applicable statutes define the procedures that statutory decision-makers must follow in the exercise of their powers, the means through which affected parties may seek to have input into and ultimately challenge the exercise of these powers, and the type of remedies that are available where a court determines that a decision-maker has acted unlawfully.

A key feature of modern regulation is that responsibility for making key decisions and enacting regulations is delegated by statute. As with other areas of regulation, this is an inevitable function of the complexity and scope of the state's mandate to protect the environment. The power to enact regulations is typically vested in the Minister of Environment or other Cabinet-level official. On the other hand, the power to make permitting, licencing or issue other environmental-related approvals is normally vested in a civil servant designated by statute and employed by the ministry responsible for regulating the activity in question. Most statutes provide for an internal process of appeal from decisions made at this level, either to a more senior decision-maker within the ministry or to an environmental or resource appeal tribunal.

All such decision-makers must comply with legally mandated procedures when exercising their statutory powers. Usually, these procedures are set out in some detail in the statute from which they derive their powers. However, their actions are also governed by the common law principles of *procedural fairness*. What these principles require in any particular case depends on three main factors: the nature of the decision being made, the relationship between the decision-maker and the party affected, and the effect of the decision on the rights of the party in question. Generally, procedural fairness at common law will require, at minimum, that the affected party be given notice of the impending decision and an opportunity to comment; a dual requirement commonly referred to as *notice and comment*.

Judicial Review

Ultimate responsibility for supervising administrative action lies with the superior courts. This function is referred to as *judicial review*. A key challenge for the courts is to determine how rigorously they should scrutinize administrative actions, whether in the form of the exercise of a regulation-making power or the exercise of a statutory power of decision. This judicial calculation is often referred to in terms of assessing the level of judicial *deference* should be accorded in the case in question.

A key factor in making this determination is legislative intent. Where the legislation contains language intended to signal that judicial deference should be paid (often referred to as a *privative* clause), this is ordinarily a message that courts will take seriously. As will be discussed, shortly, the rigour with which courts review administrative action is determined on a sliding scale of deference by reference to what is referred to as the "standard of review".

Courts will not, however, defer to administrative action that is beyond the powers of the statutory decision-maker in question. Such decision-makers, as creatures of statute, can only exercise the power they have been given. Where they take action falling outside their statutory *jurisdiction*, the action is *ultra vires* and, as such, may entitle the challenging party to a remedy.

The rules with respect to how and when an aggrieved party may seek judicial review (including standing requirements, forms of pleading, time limitations and available remedies) are, for the most part, set out in federal and provincial statutes that have been enacted for this purpose. Judicial review of decision-makers falling under federal jurisdiction (including decisions taken and regulations enacted under CEPA, CEAA, the *Fisheries Act* and SARA) is governed by the *Federal Courts Act* and proceeds in the Federal Court. Judicial review in all other cases, falls under analogous provincial statutes and takes place in the provincial superior courts.

In undertaking judicial review, courts frequently emphasize that their task is to review the legality of administrative action, not its merits. In Part III of this chapter, we provide illustrations of some of the common grounds upon which judicial review is sought, employing cases arising in the environmental law context. These grounds include:

- Substantive *ultra vires* (administrative action that is beyond the jurisdiction of a statutory decision maker, as discussed above);
- Failure to take account of relevant considerations (or consideration of irrelevant ones);
- Unlawful fettering of statutory discretion;
- Unlawful delegation of a statutory decision making power;
- Real or apprehended bias;
- Exercising statutory discretion for an improper or discriminatory purpose or in bad faith;
- Breach of procedural fairness; and
- In limited circumstances, errors of law and/or fact

Even where the aggrieved party establishes that there are legitimate grounds for questioning administrative action on one or more of these grounds, this will not necessarily entitle them to a remedy. Whether a remedy will be granted remains in the discretion of the reviewing court. In deciding whether to grant a remedy, courts will consider a variety of factors including equitable ones (has the aggrieved party come with "clean hands") and the appropriateness of the remedy sought (including whether the dispute is now moot). Another remedial consideration is the form of remedy sought. The main forms of remedy in the judicial review context are: (1) orders quashing administrative action (relief known historically as *certiorari*); (2) orders requiring the authority to act (relief in the nature of *mandamus*); (3) orders prohibiting the authority from acting (relief in the nature of *prohibition*); and (4) orders seeking a judicial declaration of existing rights, duties or powers (*declaratory* relief).

In many cases, an important and closely related procedural issue concerns whether, pending the hearing of their application for judicial review, the aggrieved party should be entitled to interim injunctive relief. As we shall see, *infra*, for a variety of reasons, it is difficult for public interest litigants to secure a remedy of this kind even where continuation of the *status quo* pending hearing may cause irreparable harm to the subject matter of the litigation.

The following decision of the Supreme Court of Canada offers a useful overview of many of the concepts discussed above.

New Brunswick (Board of Management) v. Dunsmuir
[2008] 1 S.C.R. 190

BASTARACHE and LeBEL JJ. (for the majority):

As a matter of constitutional law, judicial review is intimately connected with the preservation of the rule of law. It is essentially that constitutional foundation which explains the purpose of judicial review and guides its function and operation. Judicial review seeks to address an underlying tension between the rule of law and the foundational democratic principle, which finds an expression in the initiatives of Parliament and legislatures to create various administrative bodies and endow them with broad powers. Courts, while exercising their constitutional functions of judicial review, must be sensitive not only to the need to uphold the rule of law, but also to the necessity of avoiding undue interference with the discharge of administrative functions in respect of the matters delegated to administrative bodies by Parliament and legislatures.

By virtue of the rule of law principle, all exercises of public authority must find their source in law. All decision-making powers have legal limits, derived from the enabling statute itself, the common or civil law or the Constitution. Judicial review is the means by which the courts supervise those who exercise statutory powers, to ensure that they do not overstep their legal authority. The function of judicial review is therefore to ensure the legality, the reasonableness and the fairness of the administrative process and its outcomes.

Administrative powers are exercised by decision makers according to statutory regimes that they are themselves confined. A decision maker may not exercise authority not specifically assigned to him or her. By acting in the absence of legal authority, the decision maker transgresses the principle of the rule of law. Thus, when a reviewing court considers the scope of a decision-making power or the jurisdiction conferred by a statute, the standard of review analysis strives to determine what authority was intended to be given to the body in relation to the subject matter. This is done within the context of the courts' constitutional duty to ensure that public authorities do not overreach their lawful powers . . .

In addition to the role judicial review plays in upholding the rule of law, it also performs an important constitutional function in maintaining legislative supremacy. . . . In essence, the rule of law is maintained because the courts have the last word on jurisdiction, and legislative supremacy is assured because determining the applicable standard of review is accomplished by establishing legislative intent.

The legislative branch of government cannot remove the judiciary's power to review actions and decisions of administrative bodies for compliance with the constitutional capacities of the government. Even a privative clause, which provides a strong indication of legislative intent, cannot be determinative in this respect (*Executors of the Woodward Estate v. Minister of Finance*, [1973] S.C.R. 120 at p. 127. The inherent power of superior courts to review administrative action and ensure that it does not exceed its jurisdiction stems from the judicature provisions in ss. 96 to 101 of the *Constitution Act, 1867*.

Notes and Questions

As noted earlier, a threshold question to which courts must advert when embarking on judicial review concerns the *standard of review* they should employ when assessing administrative action. This is a vexed and difficult contextual question that the Supreme Court in *Dunsmuir* seeks to clarify as set out in the excerpt that follows.

. . . . .

New Brunswick (Board of Management) v. Dunsmuir
[2008] S.C.J. No. 9

BASTARACHE and LeBEL JJ. (for the majority):

The current approach to judicial review involves three standards of review, which range from correctness, where no deference is shown, to patent unreasonableness, which is most deferential to the decision maker, the standard of reasonableness *simpliciter* lying, theoretically, in the middle. In our view, it is necessary to reconsider both the number and definitions of the various standards of review, and the analytical process employed to determine which standard applies in a given situation. We conclude that there ought to be two standards of review: correctness and reasonableness.

The operation of three standards of review has not been without practical and theoretical difficulties, neither has it been free of criticism. One major problem lies in distinguishing between the patent unreasonableness standard and the reasonableness *simpliciter* standard. The difficulty in distinguishing between those standards contributes to the problem of choosing the right standard of review. An even greater problem lies in the application of the patent unreasonableness standard, which at times seems to require parties to accept an unreasonable decision.

We therefore conclude that the two variants of reasonableness review should be collapsed into a single form of "reasonableness" review. The result is a system of judicial review comprising two standards correctness and reasonableness. But the revised system cannot be expected to be simpler and more workable unless the concepts it employs are clearly defined.

Reasonableness is a deferential standard animated by the principle that underlies the development of the two previous standards of reasonableness: certain questions that come before administrative tribunals do not lend themselves to one specific, particular result. Instead, they may give rise to a number of possible, reasonable conclusions. Tribunals have a margin of appreciation within the range of acceptable and rational solutions. A court conducting a review for reasonableness inquires into the qualities that make a decision reasonable, referring both to the process of articulating the reasons and to outcomes. In judicial review, reasonableness is concerned mostly with the existence of justification, transparency and intelligibility within the decision-making process. But it is also concerned with whether the decision falls within a range of possible, acceptable outcomes which are defensible in respect of the facts and law.

The move towards a single reasonableness standard does not pave the way for a more intrusive review by courts. Deference in the context of the reasonableness standard therefore implies that courts will give due consideration to the determinations of decision makers . . . In short, deference requires respect for the legislative choices to leave some matters in the hands of administrative decision makers, for the processes and determinations that draw on particular expertise and experiences, and for the different roles of the courts and administrative bodies within the Canadian constitutional system.

As important as it is that courts have a proper understanding of reasonableness review as a deferential standard, it is also without question that the standard of correctness must be maintained in respect of jurisdictional and some other questions of law. This promotes just decisions and avoids inconsistent and unauthorized application of law. When applying the correctness standard, a reviewing court will not show deference to the decision maker's reasoning process; it will rather undertake its own analysis of the question. The analysis will bring the court to decide whether it agrees with the determination of the decision maker; if not, the court will substitute its own view and provide the correct answer. From the outset, the court must ask whether the tribunal's decision was correct.

An exhaustive review is not required in every case to determine the proper standard of review. Here again, existing jurisprudence may be helpful in identifying some of the questions that generally fall to be determined according to the correctness standard (*Cartaway Resources Corp. (Re)*, [2004] 1 S.C.R. 672, 2004 SCC 26). This simply means that the analysis required is already deemed to have been performed and need not be repeated. For example, correctness review has been found to apply to constitutional questions regarding the division of powers between Parliament and the provinces in the *Constitution Act, 1867*.

Administrative bodies must also be correct in their determinations of true questions of jurisdiction or vires. . . .

"Jurisdiction" is intended in the narrow sense of whether or not the tribunal had the authority to make the inquiry. In other words, true jurisdiction questions arise where the tribunal must explicitly determine whether its statutory grant of power gives it the authority to decide a particular matter. As mentioned earlier, courts must also continue to substitute their own view of the correct answer where the question at issue is one of general law "that is both of central importance to the legal system as a whole and outside the adjudicator's specialized area of expertise" *Toronto (City) v. C.U.P.E.*, at para. 62, per LeBel J.). Because of their impact on the administration of justice as a whole, such questions require uniform and consistent answers.

In summary, the process of judicial review involves two steps. First, courts ascertain whether the jurisprudence has already determined in a satisfactory manner the degree of deference to be accorded with regard to a particular category of question. Second, where the first inquiry proves unfruitful, courts must proceed to an analysis of the factors making it possible to identify the proper standard of review.

The analysis must be contextual. As mentioned above, it is dependent on the application of a number of relevant factors, including: (1) the presence or absence of a privative clause; (2) the purpose of the tribunal as determined by interpretation of enabling legislation; (3) the nature of the question at issue, and; (4) the expertise of the tribunal. In many cases, it will not be necessary to consider all of the factors, as some of them may be determinative in the application of the reasonableness standard in a specific case.

Notes and Questions

1. As the excerpt above underscores, *Dunsmuir* should not be interpreted as signaling a new, more interventionist approach by the courts to judicial review. Whether, and how, the decision will affect judicial review in other respects has already prompted considerable scholarly commentary. According to Professor Sossin, while *Dunsmuir* represents an advance on the "pragmatic and functional" approach [commonly associated with *Pushpanathan v. Canada (Minister of Citizenship and Immigration)*, [1998] 1 S.C.R. 982, cited in many of the cases in Part III, *infra*] and has "happily abandoned" the dual reasonableness standards, uncertainties as to its broader implications remain.

> *Dunsmuir* is a step in the right direction. From the overly formalistic pragmatic and functional approach, we have now entered an era of what I would characterize as the contextual and transparent approach. The sometimes necessary but never tenable distinction between patent unreasonableness and reasonableness *simpliciter* has been happily abandoned. The dilemmas of complexity and inconsistency which plagued the standard of review analysis, however, likely have not been resolved. Courts will now puzzle over different degrees of deference *within* each standard and in what circum-

stances more or less exhaustive applications of the standard of review analysis might be appropriate. (L. Sossin, "*Dunsmuir* — Plus ça change" Blog, 2008)

2. As you read the cases excerpted in Part II, consider whether any of them would have been differently decided under the *Dunsmuir* approach.

Part II — Standard of Review in the Environmental Law Context

Overview

The cases selected for consideration below illustrate that where the reviewing court concludes that the issue presented is one that presents a "pure question of law" (see *Wier v. British Columbia (Environmental Appeal Board)*, 2003 BCSC 1441) or goes to the jurisdiction of the decision-maker (*Algonquin Wildlands League v. Ontario (Minister of Natural Resources)*, [1998] O.J. No. 419 (Ont. Div. Ct.)), it is likely to apply a correctness-based standard of review even where the decision-maker is the responsible Minister. However, where the issue on review entails the exercise of discretion, particularly at a Ministerial level, courts have tended to apply a highly deferential standard of review (see *Canadian Parks & Wilderness Society v. Canada (Minister of Canadian Heritage)*, [2003] 4 F.C. 672). Determination of the appropriate standard of review is also affected by the nature of the statutory provision in question; where the provision vests a broad discretion, as it often the case under the *CEAA*, courts have tended to adopt a deferential standard of review (*Prairie Acid Rain Coalition v. Canada (Minister of Fisheries & Oceans*, [2006] 3 F.C.R. 610, "*TrueNorth*"). Finally, as we shall see, where the challenged decision raises questions about the Crown's constitutional duty to consult First Nations, courts have developed special judicial review principles (*Dene Tha' First Nation v. Canada (Minister of Environment)*, [2006] FSC No. 1677).

Wier v. British Columbia (Environmental Appeal Board)
2003 BCSC 1441

[The petitioner sought judicial review of a decision of the Environmental Appeal Board (EAB) holding that the Supreme Court of Canada's decision in *114957 Canada Ltée (Spray-Tech, Société d'arrosage) v. Hudson (Ville)*, *infra* Chapter 1, specifically its discussion of the role of the precautionary principle, was of no legal relevance to the test to be applied in determining whether a permit should be issued under the BC *Pesticide Control Act*. In the result, the BC Supreme Court concluded that the EAB erred in its interpretation of the legal implications of the *Spraytech* decision.]

ROSS J.

In considering the appropriate standard of review, the court is to adopt the pragmatic and functional approach described in *Pushpanathan v. Canada (Minister of Citizenship and Immigration)*, [1998] 1 S.C.R. 982, in which the central inquiry in determining the standard of review is to determine the legislative intent of the statute creating the tribunal whose decision is being reviewed.

Four factors are relevant in determining the intent of the legislature:

a) the presence or absence of a privative clause or statutory right of appeal;

b) the tribunal's expertise relative to that of the reviewing court on the issue in question;

c) the general purpose of the statute and the particular purpose of the provision in question; and

d) the nature of the question — law, fact, or mixed law and fact

See *Dr. Q v. College of Physicians and Surgeons of British Columbia*, 2003 S.C.C. 19, ¶26.

The proper focus of the reviewing court is on the relative expertise of the court and decision maker in relation to the particular issue in question; see *Barrie Public Utilities v. Canadian Cable Television Association*, 2003 S.C.C. 28, ¶12. In the case at bar, there are no privative clauses and no statutory rights of appeal under the *[BC Pesticide Control] Act* or the *Environment Management Act*, R.S.B.C. 1996, c 118, which creates the Board. This factor is therefore neutral with respect to the level of deference. There are three dimensions to evaluating the second factor: the tribunal's expertise; the reviewing court's expertise relative to the tribunal's; and the nature of the issue relative to the tribunal's expertise, see (*Pushpanathan*, *supra*, para. 33; *Dr. Q*, *supra*, para. 28).

The issue in this case is whether the Environmental Appeal Board erred in its articulation of the two-step legal test as required by s. 6(3)(a)(ii) of the *Act* as interpreted in *Earthcare*. This is a pure question of law. The Board does not enjoy greater expertise relative to the court with respect to this issue. Its factual expertise will not assist in the interpretation of the decision of the Court of Appeal in *Earthcare*. Thus, the second factor suggests that the appropriate standard is correctness.

With respect to the third factor, in my view, the purpose of the statute is to an extent polycentric in that it contemplates the consideration of numerous interests and the balancing of benefits and costs for many parties or interests. Again however, this aspect is, in my view, less engaged with respect to the issue on this application for judicial review; namely did the Board err in its interpretation of the test under *Earthcare*?

The final factor is the nature of the question. Less deference is generally associated with pure questions of law and in circumstances in which the determination has the potential to apply widely to many cases. The question here is a pure question of law. The petitioner has provided a brief of decisions of the Board in other cases. Review of these decisions shows that the issue of the Board's interpretation of the test is one that has the potential to apply to many other cases. Thus the final factor favours the standard of correctness.

In my view, having considered the relevant factors, the appropriate standard of review is that of correctness.

Algonquin Wildlands League v. Ontario (Minister of Natural Resources)
[1998] O.J. No. 419 (Ont. Div. Ct.)

[Two environmental NGOs sought judicial review of six timber and forest management plans and associated work schedules. They claimed that the Minister approved the plans in violation of the *Crown Forest Sustainability Act* (CFSA). The CFSA required all plans and associated work schedules to comply with the Forest Management Planning Manual. Prior to the Manual being completed, the Minister approved forest management plans directly affecting over 7 million acres of land.]

SAUNDERS J.

The respondents say that the standard of review, of the Minister's conduct in relation to his statutory duties, is one of extreme judicial deference and that the Minister's approvals of the plans and associated work schedules should not be interfered with unless they are patently unreasonable.

The applicants say that the Minister's failure to comply with his legal obligations is a jurisdictional failure and that the standard of review is jurisdictional correctness — was he correct that he had the legal power to approve the plans.

The statutory provisions in issue limit the Minister's jurisdiction to approve plans and work schedules. The statute limits the Minister's jurisdiction by establishing the jurisdictional condition precedent of compliance with the Manual before the Minister can approve the plans. Because these provisions limit the Minister's jurisdiction, the standard of review for the Minister's compliance with them is the standard of correctness. *Pezim v. B.C. (Superintendent of Brokers)* (1994), 114 D.L.R. (4th) 385, per Iacobucci J. at p. 405.

The respondents say the court should defer to the judgment of the Minister in approving the plans.

If the Act simply required the Minister to be satisfied in his own mind that the plans and work schedules provide for sustainability, a good deal of deference might be required. But it is not the Minister's idea of sustainability that has to be satisfied. It is the Manual's criterion of sustainability that has to be satisfied. When the Ministry does not even consider the Manual or draft manual, required by the statute as the sole publicly accountable index of sustainability, the Minister so completely exceeds his jurisdiction that the court cannot accord deference to his opinion.

This is not a case like *Reese v. Alberta (Minister of Forestry, Lands and Wildlife)* (1992), 87 D.L.R. (4th) 1 (Q.B.) where the issue was the reasonableness of the substance of the Minister's decision that the Daishowa forest management agreement was designed to provide for a perpetual sustained yield and the court, because the Minister's viewpoint was not on the evidence unreasonable, refused to intervene.

The object and purpose of this statute, centered on the objective measurement indicators provided by the Manual, is to avoid the very kind of argument that arose in *Reese*, the argument whether one person's subjective idea of sustainability was more reasonable than another person's. In order to replace these subjective decisions with decisions based on the objective decision-making process centered on the Manual, the C.F.S.A. made it a jurisdictional condition precedent that plans and schedules had comply with the Manual.

This is not a case where the court should defer to the decision maker, as in the case of an expert administrative tribunal protected by a privative clause. The Minister is not a tribunal and there is no privative clause. The question of compliance with the manual is a jurisdictional question and not an exercise of discretion.

This is not case where we are required to decide whether the Minister, in considering the compliance of the Plans with the Manual, got it exactly right or erred somewhat in his interpretation of the requirements of the manual as applied to the plans before him. In this case it is clear that neither the Minister nor his delegates considered or even addressed their minds to the question of the compliance of the Plans with the manual. The things missing from the plans, that are required by the Manual are not minor details. The things missing here are the objective indicators of sustainability at the heart of the new legal structure.

The Minister's duty to ensure that the plans and work schedules comply with the Manual is not discretionary. It is a mandatory jurisdictional condition precedent of the validity of the plans and work schedules. The Minister may have a degree of discretion in deciding in close cases whether or not a particular plan complies with the manual. But when the Minister by regulation decrees unlawfully that the plans did not have to comply with the manual, and approves without any consideration of the Manual the plans which omit the essential sustainability indicators required by the manual, it cannot be said that the Minister is exercising any discretion according to law.

In asking the court to defer to the Minister, the respondents are asking the court to defer to the Minister in the performance of a task he did not perform. The standard of review of the Minister's approval of the plans and associated work schedules is the standard of jurisdictional correctness and no curial deference to the Minister's decision is appropriate in the circumstances of this case.

Notes and Questions

In *Algonquin Wildlands*, the court rejects the suggestion that judicial deference should be accorded to the Minister's decision to approve forest development plans. In the next case, however, the court adopts a far more deferential posture. In *Canadian Parks & Wilderness Society v. Canada (Minister of Canadian Heritage)* (2001), the federal court was called upon to consider, for the first time, the meaning of an amendment to the *Canada National Parks Act* (CNPA) that imposed a new obligation requiring that "ecological integrity" be the "first priority" in parks management. The case arose as a result of a challenge to a Ministerial decision that allowed construction of a winter road through sensitive habitat in a national park on the ground that the decision was inconsistent with this statutory obligation. The Federal Court concluded that this decision should be reviewed on a "patently unreasonable" standard.

Canadian Parks & Wilderness Society v. Canada (Minister of Canadian Heritage)
[2003] 4 F.C. 672

EVANS J.A. (for the Court)

The first question to be decided is the standard of review that the Court should apply to determining if the Minister complied with subsection 8(2) [of the CNPA]. As Gibson J. noted (at para. 53), since subsection 8(2) provides that ecological integrity is the first priority, there must be other priorities to which the Minister may also have regard when considering the administration and management of the parks.

Hence, if the Minister has had regard to ecological integrity, her decision to approve the road is reviewable on the ground that she failed to treat ecological integrity as the first priority. However, it is not the function of a reviewing court to determine whether, giving the maintenance of ecological integrity the first priority, it would have approved the road. That would be to subject the Minister's exercise of discretion with respect to competing priorities to a standard of correctness which, counsel agreed, was not the appropriate standard of review. Whether the relevant standard of review is patent unreasonableness or simple unreasonableness is the question. A pragmatic or functional analysis leads me to conclude that patent unreasonableness is the applicable standard of review.

The exercise of discretion involved in this case is properly characterized as bearing on issues of a polycentric nature: weighing competing and conflicting interests, and determining the public interest from among the claims and perspectives of different groups and individuals, on the understanding that first priority must be given to restoring or maintaining ecological integrity. This is not a zero sum game.

Thus, on the one hand, residents in the Park believe that a winter road will reduce the isolation, which is particularly burdensome in the long northern winters by enabling them to visit, and be visited by, family and friends who live in or near the Park. Others support the road because it will significantly shorten the travelling time to destinations south of the Park region.

On the other hand, the road comes at a price: the difficult-to-quantify risks that it poses to wildlife and vegetation in the Park and the integrity of the Park's ecology, as well as to the livelihoods of those whose traditional traplines may be adversely affected by the road.

In addition, the fact that Parliament has conferred on the Minister broad responsibility for the administration, management and control of national parks, along with the powers necessary for its discharge, is another indication of a legislative intent that the standard of review should be at the most deferential end of the range. The duty of the Minister to justify her conduct to Parliament is the primary mechanism for holding the Minister accountable for the way that she balances competing interests and claims with respect to the use of park lands. While political accountability is often dismissed as an inadequate check on the abuse of power, in my opinion this view is not compelling in the context of the present case for at least three reasons.

First, as counsel for CPAWS argued, Parliament has always taken a close interest in the creation and protection of Canada's national parks. The establishment of a winter road in Canada's largest national park, a scheme that has been the subject of a vigorous public debate, is therefore very likely to register on the political radar.

Second, the political accountability of ministers to the public, both through Parliament and more directly, tends to be more effective when a minister's action engages with competing public interests than when it primarily concerns the interests of an individual.

Third, the decision-making processes employed in the consideration of the road proposal and its approval by the Minister render the decision transparent, in the sense that the bases of the decision and the countervailing arguments and evidence are part of the public record. This, too, is a factor that tends to enhance ministerial accountability through the political process.

Finally, reviewing the reasonableness of the Minister's exercise of discretion in the light of the applicable statutory criterion is, to an extent, fact-oriented. Thus, in so far as this application for judicial review involves the Minister's findings of fact about the environmental impacts of the road, the standard of review is that contained in paragraph 18.1(4)(d) of the *Federal Court Act*, R.S.C. 1985, c. F-7. Further, it has been held, determining whether an erroneous finding of fact has been made by the decision-maker in a perverse or capricious manner or without regard for the material before her is the practical equivalent of determining whether the finding was patently unreasonable. . . .

Thus, in reviewing the Minister's approval of the road on the ground that it was in breach of her duty under subsection 8(2), the Court must ask whether, on the basis of both the factors that the Minister had to consider and the material before her, it was patently unreasonable to have concluded that the road proposal was incompatible with maintaining as the first priority the ecological integrity of the Park through the protection of natural resources and natural processes.

Notes and Questions

1. To what extent are the approaches to standard of review in *Algonquin Wildlands* and *CPAWS* inconsistent? Can they be reconciled?

2. The Federal Court has also adopted a deferential approach to the review of decisions made by federal authorities in connection with assessments done under the *Canadian Environmental Assessment Act* (CEAA). As is discussed in Chapter 7, a key issue in CEAA litigation has been the breadth of the discretion afforded to federal authorities charged with responsibility for doing environmental assessments (responsible authorities or "RAs") under CEAA.

Prairie Acid Rain Coalition v. Canada (Minister of Fisheries and Oceans)
[2006] 3 F.C.R. 610 (FCA)

[The petitioner in this case sought judicial review of a decision by the responsible authority ("RA") with respect to the scoping of environmental assessment of a proposed forest development in northern Alberta that involved significant road construction in a wilderness area. The RA in this case was the Department of Fisheries and Oceans ("DFO"). We return to this case when we consider the topic of environmental assessment in Chapter 7.]

ROTHSTEIN J.A. (for the court)

In *Friends of the West Country Assn. v. Canada (Minister of Fisheries and Oceans)*, [2000] 2 F.C. 263 (C.A.), it was held that questions of interpretation of the CEAA were reviewable on a standard of correctness.

The same considerations apply in this case. There is no applicable privative clause. The CEAA is a statute of general application. It is administered by a broad range of federal authorities. There is no particular expertise in the DFO relative to that of the Court in respect of the interpretation of the CEAA. The interpretation issues are legal. While there is a general public interest in matters concerning the environment, the absence of relative expertise and the nature of the question being legal suggest a correctness standard of review in respect of the interpretation by the DFO of the CEAA.

However, the exercise of discretion by a responsible authority will normally be reviewed on a more deferential standard. As long as the responsible authority takes into account relevant considerations and does not take into account irrelevant considerations, the Court should not engage in a reweighing process. Here, assuming its statutory interpretations were correct, considerations involving the destruction of fish habitat and relevant mitigative measures fall within the expertise of the DFO. In these circumstances, the discretionary decisions of the DFO should be reviewed on a reasonableness standard.

Russell J. [the trial judge] conducted his review applying the correctness standard to questions of statutory interpretation and reasonableness to discretionary decisions. In doing so, he did not err.

Notes and Questions

While the decision in the preceding case (commonly known as "*TrueNorth*") is consistent with federal court CEAA jurisprudence, this jurisprudence has been criticized as immunizing, from meaningful judicial review, critical "scoping" and other decisions made by RAs who, arguably, often lack expertise in environmental matters and are frequently seen as having an interest in minimizing the breadth of the EA process by virtue of being the proponent of the project or due to close inter-agency relationships with government departments that are supportive of the project under review. Illustrative of this critique is the following article.

Andrew Green, "Discretion, Judicial Review, and the *Canadian Environmental Assessment Act*"
(2002) 27 Queen's L.J. 785–807

Vagueness in the *Canadian Environmental Assessment Act* (CEAA) has led to unnecessary litigation and confusion over the respective roles of courts, Parliament, and especially responsible authorities. The CEAA is intended to provide an assessment regime to balance the possible economic and other benefits of various types of projects against their potential environmental harm.

As highlighted in several recent cases, the CEAA provides only vague guidance in determining the scope of the project itself and the scope of the assessment of the immediate and cumulative environmental effects. It gives the responsible authority (which may be any federal body related to the project) near-complete discretion in making these determinations. This creates the danger that political or economic factors might unduly influence decision making in this sensitive area, resulting in either unnecessarily high costs on the proponent or inadequate protection against environmental harm. Federal courts have done little to improve this situation, adopting a "reasonableness simpliciter" standard of judicial review that defers to responsible authorities as long as they have followed the statutory process.

For the CEAA assessment regime to be meaningful and consistent, both Parliament and the courts must take a more active part in defining the role of responsible authorities. Parliament, currently in the process of reviewing the CEAA, should make amendments to provide more specific criteria for decisions under the Act. It should also consider creating an expert administrative tribunal that would undertake a more detailed substantive review of these decisions. If the principles governing environmental assessments were clarified, courts could undertake more meaningful reviews of decisions; in the absence of a substantially amended CEAA, courts should require responsible authorities to set out clear reasons for their decisions. If Parliament and courts take some of these steps, the CEAA regime will gain much-needed clarity and accountability.

Notes and Questions

Increasingly, in the wake of the Supreme Court's landmark decisions in *Haida Nation v. British Columbia (Minister of Forests)*, [2004] S.C.J. No. 70 and *Taku River Tlingit First Nation v. British Columbia (Project Assessment Director)*, [2004] S.C.J. No. 69, judicial review of government decisions in the environmental and resource management law areas is being sought on the ground that the Crown has failed to comply with its duty to consult as guaranteed under section 35 of the Constitution: see Chapter 3. This has prompted significant judicial reflection on how cases framed in this fashion should be analyzed in terms of standard of review.

Dene Tha' First Nation v. Canada (Minister of Environment)
[2006] FSC No. 1677

[The petitioner challenged the federal Crown, alleging a breach of the duty to consult in relation to its exclusion from discussions and decisions regarding the design of the regulatory and environmental review processes related to the Mackenzie Gas Pipeline ("MGP"). The proposed pipeline was to originate in Inuvik in the far north of the Northwest Territories and terminate just south of the Northwest Territories-Alberta border, traversing through the petitioner's traditional territory.]

PHELAN J.

The Ministers identified as the theme of its submissions the overall reasonableness of the Crown's behavior, asserting that this was the appropriate standard of review for the Court to adopt on this judicial review.

The Ministers further used the language of deference, imposing the pragmatic and functional approach from *Dr. Q v. College of Physicians and Surgeons of British Columbia*, [2003] 1 S.C.R. 226 that dominates administrative law onto the case at hand. This approach is not particularly helpful in this case where the core issue is whether there was a duty to consult and when did it arise.

The pragmatic and functional approach and the language of deference are tools most often used by courts to establish jurisdictional respect vis-à-vis statutorily created boards and tribunals. The law of aboriginal consultation thus far has no statutory source other than the constitutional one of s. 35. Therefore, to talk of deference and/or impose a test, the goal of which is to determine the level of deference, is inappropriate in this context.

In respect of the Ministers' "theme" of reasonableness, comments by the Chief Justice in *Haida* are illuminating. At paragraphs 60–63 of her judgment in *Haida Nation*, McLachlin C.J.C. concisely addresses the issue of administrative review of government decisions vis-à-vis first nations:

- Where the government's conduct is challenged on the basis of allegations that it failed to discharge its duty to consult and accommodate pending claims resolution, the matter may go to the courts for review. To date, the Province has established no process for this purpose. The question of what standard of review the court should apply in judging the adequacy of the government's efforts cannot be answered in the absence of such a process. General principles of administrative law, however, suggest the following.
- On questions of law, a decision-maker must generally be correct: for example, *Paul v. British Columbia (Forest Appeals Commission)*, [2003] 2 S.C.R. 585, 2003 SCC 55. On questions of fact or mixed fact and law, on the other hand, a reviewing body may owe a degree of deference to the decision-maker. The existence or extent of the duty to consult or accommodate is a legal question in the sense that it defines a legal duty. However, it is typically premised on an assessment of the facts. It follows that a degree of deference to the findings of fact of the initial adjudicator may be appropriate. The need for deference and its degree will depend on the nature of the question the tribunal was addressing and the extent to which the facts were within the expertise of the tribunal: *Law Society of New Brunswick v. Ryan*, [2003] 1 S.C.R. 247, 2003 SCC 20; *Paul*, supra. Absent error on legal issues, the tribunal may be in a better position to evaluate the issue than the reviewing court, and some degree of deference may be required. In such a case, the standard of review is likely to be reasonableness. To the extent that the issue is one of pure law, and can be isolated from the issues of fact, the standard is correctness. However, where the two are inextricably entwined, the standard will likely be reasonableness: *Canada (Director of Investigation and Research) v. Southam Inc.*, [1997] 1 S.C.R. 748.
- The process itself would likely fall to be examined on a standard of reasonableness. Perfect satisfaction is not required; the question is whether the regulatory scheme or government action "viewed as a whole, accommodates the collective aboriginal right in question": *Gladstone*, supra, [1996] 2 S.C.R. 723, at para. 170. What is required is not perfection, but reasonableness. As stated in *Nikal*, supra, [1996] 1 S.C.R. 1013, at para. 110, "in . . . information and consultation the concept of reasonableness must come into play . . . So long as every reasonable effort is made to inform and to consult, such efforts would suffice". The government is required to make reasonable efforts to inform and consult. This suffices to discharge the duty.
- Should the government misconceive the seriousness of the claim or impact of the infringement, this question of law would likely be judged by correctness. Where the government is correct on these matters and acts on the appropriate standard, the decision will be set aside only if the government's process is unreasonable. The focus, as discussed above, is not on the outcome, but on the process of consultation and accommodation.

It thus follows that as the question as to the existence of a duty to consult and or accommodate is one of law, then the appropriate standard of review is correctness. Often, however, the duty to consult or accommodate is premised on factual findings. When these factual findings cannot be extricated from the legal question of consultation, more deference is warranted and the standard should be reasonableness.

These two standards of review dovetail onto the questions of whether there is a duty to consult and if so, what is its scope. The further question of whether the duty to consult has been met attracts a different analysis. From McLachlin C.J.C.'s reasons, it is clear that the standard of review for this latter question is reasonableness. To put that matter in slightly different terms, the government's burden is to demonstrate that the process it adopted concerning consultation with First Nations was reasonable. In other words, the process does not have to be perfect.

In this case, all parties agree that there is a duty to consult and accommodate the Dene Tha'. The disagreement centers on when this duty arose and whether the government's failure to consult the Dene Tha' on issues of design of the consultation process constituted a breach. The federal government's efforts made after the determination as to the scope and existence of the duty to consult may be reviewed on the reasonableness standard. The issue of when the duty to consult arose is, however, one that goes to the definition of the scope of this duty, as such, as it is considered a question of law, it would attract the correctness standard of review.

In my view, the question posed by the Dene Tha' is whether the duty to consult arose at the stage of process design — that is, from late 2000 to early 2002. The questions of fact involved in this issue — what the precise Aboriginal interests of the Dene Tha' are and what are the adverse effects of this failure to consult — are better contemplated in determining the content of the duty to consult, not its bare existence. As the question posed by Dene Tha' is a question of law focused on whether the duty to consult extends to a time period prior to any decision-making as to land use, the appropriate standard of review for this inquiry is correctness.

Whether or not the government's actions/efforts after the duty to consult arose complied with this duty, however, would be judged on a reasonableness standard, assuming that it actually engaged in consultation. The issue would be whether it had engaged in reasonable consultation or made reasonable efforts to do so.

Part III — Grounds for Judicial Review

As described in Part I, applications for judicial review must specify the grounds upon which relief is being sought. The petitioner must also identify the administrative action or decision for which review is being sought, the responsible decision-maker, and form(s) of remedy being sought. In this Part, we canvass a series of cases selected to illustrate frequently invoked grounds for judicial review in environmental cases. We commence with two cases where the petitioner argued that the impugned decision was defective due to a reliance on irrelevant considerations *Wimpey Western Ltd. v. Alberta (Department of the Environment)*, 28 Alta. L.R. (2d) 193 (Alta. C.A.) and *Imperial Oil Ltd. v. British Columbia (Ministry of Water, Land & Air Protection)*, [2002] B.C.J. No. 295. The latter case also illustrates that decision-makers are precluded from delegating (directly or by implication) their power to decide without clear statutory authority. Next we consider the principles governing challenges based on allegations of discrimination *Moresby Explorers v. Canada (Attorney General)*, 2007 FCA 273. We then reflect on the challenges based on procedural fairness *Le Chameau Exploration Ltd. v. Nova Scotia (Attorney General)*, [2007] N.S.J. No. 574, before concluding with an examination of whether, and to what extent, administrative decisions may be impugned on the basis of a failure to give reasons *Pembina Institute for Appropriate Development v. Canada (Attorney General)*, 2008 FC 302.

Reliance on Irrelevant Considerations/Fettering Discretion

Wimpey Western Ltd. v. Alberta (Department of the Environment)
28 Alta. L.R. (2d) 193 (Alta. C.A.)

[The appellants sought a declaration compelling the Director of the Division of Standards and Approvals of the Department of the Environment to issue a permit for the construction of a waste water treatment facility. The appellants owned a property in Municipal District of Sturgeon. After obtaining subdivision approval to develop the land in stages as an industrial park, their application for a permit to construct a waste water treatment facility under the *Clean Water Act* was rejected. Their application for judicial review was dismissed by the Alberta Court of Queen's Bench, from which decision this appeal was brought.]

HARRANDENCE J.A.

The issues on this appeal are:

1. Whether the Director of the Standards and Approvals Division of the Department of the Environment (the "Director"), in exercising his discretion to grant a permit to construct a waste water treatment facility under the *Clean Water Act*, may consider the Minister's policy of not granting permits for major facilities until a "long-term servicing option" is operational.
2. Whether the Director fettered or refused to exercise his discretion in applying this policy to the appellant's application . . .

The appellants contend that the Director exceeded his jurisdiction by taking into account an irrelevant consideration, namely, the Minister's policy of deferring individual water treatment facilities in favour of larger Regional facilities. They argue that the Director's discretion is limited by the *Clean Water Act* to consideration of technical matters such as amounts, concentrations and rates of discharge of contaminants from waste water treatment facilities.

In determining the scope of the Director's discretion, one must start with the Act granting it — the *Clean Water Act*. Section 3(4) gives the Director a broad discretion as follows:

> The Director of Standards and Approvals may issue or refuse to issue a permit or may require a change in location of the water facility or a change in the plans and specifications as a condition precedent to giving a permit under this section.

The Act places no limitation on the Director's power to refuse to issue a permit. This does not mean, however, that his discretion is unfettered. As was stated by Lord Reid in *Padfield v. Minister of Agriculture, Fisheries & Food*, [1968] A.C. 997 (H.L.), at 1030:

> Parliament must have conferred the discretion with the intention that it should be used to promote the policy and objects of the Act; the policy and objects of the Act must be determined by construing the Act as a whole and construction is always a matter of law for the court.

While the Act does not set out the criteria which the Director must consider in making his decision, it is implicit that he may consider those items set out in subsections (2), (4) and (5) of section 3. The Act does not, however, require the Director to issue a permit once he is satisfied as to those items. It is reasonable to conclude that the Legislature intended that the Director have a discretion to refuse to issue a permit notwithstanding such satisfaction.

In de Smith, *Judicial Review of Administrative Action* (4th Ed.) at p. 340-341, it states:

> In determining what factors may or must be taken into account by the competent authority, the courts are faced with problems of statutory interpretation . . . If relevant factors are specified in the enabling Act it is for the courts to determine whether they are factors to which the authority is compelled to have regard and, if so, whether they are to be construed as being exhaustive. If the relevant factors are

> not specified . . . it is for the courts to determine whether the permissible considerations are impliedly restricted, and, if so, to what extent . . .

The factors which are relevant need not be limited to those implicit in the enabling Act. The test is whether the consideration in question is within the intent and purpose of the Act.

It is clear that the purpose of this enactment is to create an effective and focal means of controlling and eliminating the problems created by exploitation or misuse of the environment. The Minister is given far-reaching powers and in my view it is within the scope of these powers to devise policies aimed at limiting the number of points of discharge of contaminants into Alberta's waterways for ease of monitoring. It is relevant for the Director to consider the policies of the Minister keeping in mind that he must neither act under dictation nor fetter his discretion.

Imperial Oil Ltd. v. British Columbia (Ministry of Water, Land & Air Protection)
[2002] B.C.J. No. 295

ROSS J.

These proceedings arise from the attempts by the petitioner, Imperial Oil Limited ("Imperial"), to obtain an approval from the Ministry of Water, Land and Air Protection (the "Ministry") of a proposal to remediate certain lands in Salmo, British Columbia which have become contaminated with hydrocarbons.

Imperial alleges that the settlement of the civil claims was the sole reason that the respondent withheld the AIP and that this was an irrelevant consideration. Therefore, Imperial seeks an order of mandamus requiring the respondent to issue the AIP.

Imperial submits that, in this case, the only reason for the decision maker's failure to issue the approval is one which is an improper consideration under the enabling legislation; namely, the consideration of the settlement of the civil claims of the Owners [of the contaminated lands]. In such cases, it submits, an order for mandamus is appropriate . . .

[Review of applicable BC *Waste Management Act* provisions omitted.] These provisions do not confer jurisdiction upon the respondent with respect to tort claims, nor with respect to compensation for anything other than costs of remediation. The claims in question of the Owners were tort claims and not claims for the costs of remediation.

Under the *[Waste Management] Act* the respondent does not have the authority to order compensation to be paid with respect to such claims, nor is he empowered under the Act to adjudicate such claims. It follows that he cannot do indirectly what he is not entitled to do directly. Compensation for third parties, other than compensation for the costs of remediation, is therefore not a relevant factor for the respondent to consider in the exercise of his discretion with respect to an application for an AIP. Where he does so, he has exceeded his jurisdiction.

Further, where, as in this case, the irrelevant consideration is stated to be the only reason for the failure to issue the AIP, mandamus is appropriate, see *McKeown v. Port Moody (City)*, [2000] B.C.J. No. 185, per Skipp J. It is not, in my view, an appropriate or adequate remedy in this case to send Imperial back to repeat some or all of the process with another decision maker.

Counsel for the respondent has argued that mandamus is not appropriate in this case even if the consideration of compensation for the civil claims of the Owners was an irrelevant consideration because there must be further consultation with the Owners prior to an AIP being issued. That submission, however, ignores the respondent's position, which was that he was prepared to issue the AIP, subject only to the settlement of the civil claims. In other words, he had come to a decision and was satisfied that there had been sufficient consultation with the concerned parties with respect to the content of the AIP.

There is a further problem. The respondent decided to issue the AIP upon confirmation from the Owners and the Village of Salmo that they had an acceptable agreement with Imperial. This effectively put the Owners and the Village in control of the decision to issue or withhold the AIP. In my view, this constituted an improper delegation of the Deputy Director's discretion and an improper fettering of his discretion, see *Vic Restaurant Inc. v. The City of Montreal*, [1959] S.C.R. 58 at 82, per Locke J.

Counsel for the Owners opposes the application for mandamus. Much of his submission was directed to matters that may well be appropriate considerations were this hearing to be an appeal or a hearing de novo with respect to the merits of the AIP. This, however, is not such a hearing.

[In the result, the court made the order for mandamus sought by Imperial. The other relief sought by Imperial was denied because it was moot and had no practical application on the parties' rights.]

Discrimination/Exercise of Regulation-making Power

Moresby Explorers v. Canada (Attorney General)
2007 FCA 273

PELLETIER J.A. (for the court)

This dispute arises out of the management of the Gwaii Haanas National Park Reserve (the Park) by the Archipelago Management Board (the AMB). The AMB is a structure adopted to permit the Government of Canada and the Council of the Haida Nation to collaborate in the management of the Park without prejudice to either's position in the negotiation of the Haida land claim over a territory which includes the Park. For the details of the AMB's structure and its legal underpinnings, see *Moresby Explorers Ltd. v. Canada (Attorney General)*, [2001] 4 F.C. 591, ¶67 (T.D.).

In the exercise of its mandate, the AMB has adopted a group of policies limiting access to the Park with a view to protecting its natural and cultural resources. The starting point for those policies was the determination that the Park's carrying capacity was 33,000 user-day/nights per year. The AMB then allocated those user-day/nights equally between three groups, namely, independent users, Haida tour operators, and non-Haida tour operators. As a result, a maximum allocation of 11,000 user-day/nights was available to each group. The AMB also adopted a "Business caps" policy to limit the maximum number of user-day/nights available to any tour operator: 22 client-days per day, and 2,500 user-day/nights per year. This policy is designed to prevent any single operator from monopolizing Park resources.

The difficulty with the policies adopted by the AMB is that there are no Haida tour operators, while the non-Haida quota of user-day/nights is oversubscribed. Moresby alleges that the 11,000 user-day/nights limitation on non-Haida tour operators is unlawfully restricting the growth of its business.

Moresby attacks the Haida Allocation Policy and the Business caps on the ground of administrative discrimination, that is "delegated powers exercised by a subordinate authority (*e.g.* a National Parks superintendent) must be exercised strictly within the ambit of the empowering legislation, particularly where they restrict employment or the right to work".: Moresby's Memorandum, at para. 27.

This argument is succinctly summarized at paragraph 31 of Moresby's Memorandum where the following appears:

> There is nothing in either the *Canada National Parks Act* or *Businesses Regulations* that remotely authorizes a power to discriminate based on race or business size. The *Act*, in s. 4, expressly refers to *all* the people of Canada. The *Businesses Regulations*, ss. 4.1 and 5, proscribe the licensing discretion in relatively restrictive terms. All statutory provisions focus on the Park and none on the personal characteristics of the licensee. The most that can be said is that a subordinate licensing authority may, by necessary implication, assess the merits and qualifications of individual licence applicants with respect to their competence to carry out the purposes of the legislation. However, the legislation nowhere indicates an intention to allow the Superintendent to fence out or restrict a whole class of applicants on the basis of their race or the size of their businesses. This is not within the ambit of this legislation.

The only question remaining is whether the Superintendent has the legislative authority to distinguish between, or to create, different classes of businesses. An analogous issue was raised in *Sunshine Village Corp. v. Canada (Parks)* (F.C.A.)2004 FCA 166, [2004] 3 F.C.R. 600 (*Sunshine Village Corp.*), where Sunshine Village argued that setting building permit fees in Banff and Jasper National Parks at a higher rate than in other national parks was unlawful discrimination as it was *ultra vires* the Governor in Council. The Trial Division of the Federal Court of Canada (as it then was) accepted Sunshine Village's argument and held that the differential setting of business fees was discriminatory (in the administrative law sense) and was not authorized expressly or by necessary implication by the governing legislation: see *Sunshine Village Corp. v. Canada (Parks)*, [2003] 4 F.C. 459 (T.D.).

This Court allowed the Crown's appeal on the basis that the legislation authorizing the making of the Regulations which were allegedly discriminatory was broad enough to permit the Governor in Council to draw distinctions between users of different national parks. The Court distinguished the situation before it from the usual rule in municipal law cases, where discriminatory by-laws are prohibited, as follows:

> 18. Unlike the historic practice of the provinces granting specific powers to municipalities, these words, on their face, confer broad authority on the Governor in Council. There is no indication that they are subject to any limitation. The Court must take the statute as it finds it. In the absence of limiting words in the statute, the Court will not read in limitations.
>
> 22. The courts have historically required express or necessarily implied authorization in municipalities' governing statutes before the municipalities will be allowed to enact discriminatory by-laws. Conversely, when Parliament confers regulation-making authority on the Governor in Council in general terms, in respect of fees for Crown services, the courts approach the review of such regulations in a deferential manner. That is simply a matter of interpreting, in context, the words Parliament has used in accordance with their ordinary and grammatical meaning: *Sunshine Village Corp. v. Canada (Parks)*, ¶18 and 22.

Since there was no limitation in the governing legislation restricting the Governor in Council's power to set different scales for building fees in different parks, the Court was not prepared to read them in. The situation is therefore the exact opposite of that which prevails in municipal law where discrimination is prohibited unless it is expressly allowed. In the context of legislation conferring broad regulation making power on the Governor in Council, discrimination (in the administrative law sense) is permitted unless it is expressly prohibited.

In this case, we are not dealing with a challenge to the Governor in Council's regulation making power, but rather with the exercise of the power conferred upon the Superintendent by those Regulations. The respondent alleges . . . that because the object of Moresby's challenge is a policy adopted pursuant to the Regulations rather than the Regulations themselves, the application cannot succeed, since mere policies (as opposed to decisions based on policies) are not subject to review.

The grounds on which a policy may be challenged are limited. Policies are normally afforded much deference; one cannot, for example, mount a judicial challenge against the wisdom or soundness of a government policy *Maple Lodge Farms Ltd. v. Canada*, [1982] 2 S.C.R. 2 at 7-8. This does not, however, preclude the court from making a determination as to the legality of a given policy *Canada (Attorney General) v. Inuit Tapirisat of Canada*, [1980] 2 S.C.R. 735 at 751-752; *Roncarelli v. Duplessis*, S.C.R. 121 at 140. Because illegality goes to the validity of a policy rather than to its application, an illegal policy can be challenged at any time; the claimant need not wait till the policy has been applied to his or her specific case *Krause v. Canada*, [1999] 2 F.C. 476, ¶16 (C.A.).

The regulation making power found in the *Canada National Parks Act* contains no limitation which would prohibit the drawing of distinctions between various classes of businesses. The Regulations promulgated pursuant to that power deal with the regulation of business by means of the licensing power. That power is very broad. The Regulations do not contain any explicit limitation on the Superintendent's power to distinguish between classes of businesses. In fact, subsection 5(3) permits the Superintendent to impose conditions on a business license which depend upon the type of business. Those conditions include matters related to "the preservation, control and management of the park". I have no difficulty concluding that the legislation and the regulations are sufficiently broad to permit the Superintendent to impose conditions on business licenses which vary with the kind of business.

Moresby's argument is that it is one thing to distinguish between a hardware store and a restaurant but quite another to distinguish between a Haida owned business and a non-Haida owned business. The nature of the business being regulated may require special conditions to be imposed; the personal characteristics of the owner of the business do not impose a similar requirement. In fact, given human rights legislation and the equality provisions of the *Charter*, conditions or limitations based on race are generally contrary to public policy.

In my view, the question of administrative discrimination resolves itself as follows. The regulation making power conferred upon the Governor in Council by the *Canada National Parks Act* is not limited so as to prohibit discrimination between classes of business. Thus the Governor in Council is competent to promulgate regulations which authorize discrimination (in the administrative law sense) between individuals and businesses. This, in itself, sets the present case apart from the municipal law cases relied upon by Moresby where the delegated authority, the municipal council, lacks the power to discriminate unless it is specifically conferred by the legislation.

The Regulations passed by the Governor in Council contemplate distinctions being drawn between businesses, but not, says Moresby, the type of distinction being drawn in this case. As noted earlier, administrative law discrimination deals with drawing distinctions, as opposed to the basis on which such distinctions are drawn. Unless the distinction drawn by the Superintendent can be shown to be contrary to public policy, there is nothing in the Regulations which would preclude the type of distinction being drawn here. In the end the question is whether the allocation of access to the Park between Haida and non-Haida tour operators is contrary to public policy.

Public policy takes its color from the context in which it is invoked. Discrimination on the basis of race is contrary to public policy when the discrimination simply reinforces stereotypical conceptions of the target group. However, there is legislative support for the proposition that discrimination designed to ameliorate the condition of a historically disadvantaged group is acceptable. See, for example, section 16 of the *Canadian Human Rights Act*, R.S.C. 1985, c. H-6, where Parliament authorizes the adoption of special programs designed to prevent or reduce disadvantages suffered by groups when those disadvantages are based on prohibited grounds of discrimination. See also the *Employment Equity Act*, S.C. 1995, c. 44, which mandates programs designed to increase the representation of visible and other minorities in the workplace. Even the *Charter of Rights and Freedoms* contains a reservation at subsection 15(2) to the effect that the constitutional guarantee of equality "does not preclude any law, program or activity that has as its object the amelioration of conditions of disadvantaged individuals or groups". Consequently, the proposition that discrimination based on race is contrary to public policy is too broad. Discriminatory provisions designed to ameliorate the condition of the historically disadvantaged are not contrary to public policy.

[*Ed note*: Discussion of the remedial nature of the policy has been omitted.]

In the end result, I conclude that the Regulations authorize the Superintendent to discriminate between classes of businesses and that the distinction drawn on the racial or ethnic origin of the owners of commercial tour businesses is not a distinction which is void on public policy grounds.

It follows from this that Moresby's argument with respect to administrative discrimination fails. As a result, I would dismiss Moresby's appeal.

In conclusion, I am of the view that the distinction drawn by the Superintendent, acting through the AMB, between Haida and non-Haida tour operators is not *ultra vires* the Superintendent on the basis that it results in discrimination between classes of businesses which is not authorized by the governing legislation. In my view, the Regulations are wide enough to include the power to draw such distinctions or, following this Court's decision in *Sunshine Village Corp.*, there is nothing in the Act or the Regulations which would prohibit such a distinction.

Procedural Fairness

In the administrative law context, courts have long prided themselves as defenders of the procedural fairness. Illustrative of the judicial perception of this role are the following comments of Binnie J. in *Dunsmuir*:

> . . . a fair procedure is said to be the handmaiden of justice. Accordingly, procedural limits are placed on administrative bodies by statute and the common law. These include the requirements of "procedural fairness", which will vary with the type of decision maker and the type of decision under review. On such matters, as well, the courts have the final say. The need for such procedural safeguards is obvious. Nobody should have his or her rights, interests or privileges adversely dealt with by an unjust process. Nor is such an unjust intent to be attributed easily to legislators. Hansard is full of expressions of concern by Ministers and Members of Parliament regarding the fairness of proposed legislative provisions. There is a dated hauteur about judicial pronouncements such as that the "justice of the common law will supply the omission of the legislature" (*Cooper v. Wandsworth Board of Works* (1863), 14 C.B. (N.S.) 180, 143 E.R. 414 at p. 420 (Eng. C.P.)). Generally speaking, legislators and judges in this country are working with a common set of basic legal and constitutional values. They share a belief in the rule of law. Constitutional considerations aside, however, statutory protections can nevertheless be repealed and common law protections can be modified by statute . . .

Bearing these sentiments in mind, consider the following case.

Le Chameau Exploration Ltd. v. Nova Scotia (Attorney General)
[2007] N.S.J. No. 574

[The petitioner, a company engaged in exploring and recovering artifacts from shipwrecks off the coast of Nova Scotia, sought an order quashing the decision of the Executive Director of the Nova Scotia Museum to deny a permit pursuant to the *Special Places Protection Act*, R.S.N.S. 1989, and an order in the nature of mandamus, to compel the Director to issue the permit. The applicant also alleged that the Director acted in excess of jurisdiction and erred in law by determining that the government of the United Kingdom owned a wreck thought to be in the area covered by the Permit. In the alternative, it argued that the Director breached the rules of natural justice and procedural fairness by denying the Applicant the opportunity to be heard with respect to the claim to ownership of the wreck asserted by the government of the United Kingdom]

MacADAM J.

The Applicant is of the view that the *Special Places Protection Act* and the *Treasure Trove Act* do not permit the Director to determine ownership of a vessel or artifact purportedly lying in an area covered by a treasure trove license. It says both statutes imply that the Province of Nova Scotia owns cultural and heritage property. It appears, however, from the correspondence noted above, that the director accepted the British claim of ownership. If there are other laws that are relevant to heritage and cultural property, over which the province claims constitutional jurisdiction, these determinations should be made in a proper forum, according to the Applicant.

The Applicant also says the Director failed to observe the rules of natural justice and procedural fairness in deciding not to issue the requested permit. An administrative decision-maker has a duty of procedural fairness, including an obligation to give a party who will be affected by the decision an opportunity to put forward their views.

Existence of a Duty of Procedural Fairness

The existence of a common law duty of procedural fairness has long been recognized and in *Real Cardinal and Eric Oswald and Director of Kent Institution*, [1985] 2 S.C.R. 643, Le Dain, J. in delivering the judgment of the Court, at p. 653, stated:

> This Court has affirmed that there is, as a general common law principle, a duty of procedural fairness lying on every public authority making an administrative decision which is not of a legislative nature and which affects the rights, privileges or interests of an individual: . . .

Here the decision of the Director was an administrative decision, not of a legislative nature, that affected the "rights, privileges or interests" of the Applicants.

Scope and Conduct of the Duty

L'Heureux-Dubé J. reviewed several factors relevant to determining the content of the duty of procedural fairness in *Baker v. Canada (Minister of Citizenship and Immigration)*, [1999] 2 S.C.R. 817:

> Although the duty of fairness is flexible and variable, and depends on an appreciation of the context of the particular statute and the rights affected, it is helpful to review the criteria that should be used in determining what procedural rights the duty of fairness requires in a given set of circumstances. I emphasize that underlying all these factors is the notion that the purpose of the participatory rights contained within the duty of procedural fairness is to ensure that administrative decisions are made using a fair and open procedure, appropriate to the decision being made and its statutory, institutional, and social context, with an opportunity for those affected by the decision to put forward their views and evidence fully and have them considered by the decision-maker.
>
> Several factors have been recognized in the jurisprudence as relevant to determining what is required by the common law duty of procedural fairness in a given set of circumstances. One important consideration is the nature of the decision being made and the process followed in making it. . . . The more the process provided for, the function of the tribunal, the nature of the decision-making body, and the determinations that must be made to reach a decision resemble judicial decision making, the more likely it is that procedural protections closer to the trial model will be required by the duty of fairness . . .
>
> A second factor is the nature of the statutory scheme and the 'terms of the statute pursuant to which the body operates' . . . The role of the particular decision within the statutory scheme and other sur-

> rounding indications in the statute help determine the content of the duty of fairness owed when a particular administrative decision is made. Greater procedural protections, for example, will be required when no appeal procedure is provided within the statute, or when the decision is determinative of the issue and further requests cannot be submitted.
>
> A third factor in determining the nature and extent of the duty of fairness owed is the importance of the decision to the individual or individuals affected. The more important the decision is to the lives of those affected and the greater its impact on that person or those persons, the more stringent the procedural protections that will be mandated.
>
> Fourth, the legitimate expectations of the person challenging the decision may also determine what procedures the duty of fairness requires in given circumstances. Our Court has held that, in Canada, this doctrine is part of the doctrine of fairness or natural justice, and that it does not create substantive rights: . . . [it] is based on the principle that the 'circumstances' affecting procedural fairness take into account the promises or regular practices of administrative decision-makers, and that it will generally be unfair for them to act in contravention of representations as to procedure, or to backtrack on substantive promises without according significant procedural rights.
>
> Fifth, the analysis of what procedures the duty of fairness requires should also take into account and respect the choices of procedure made by the agency itself, particularly when the statute leaves to the decision-maker the ability to choose its own procedures, or when the agency has an expertise in determining what procedures are appropriate in the circumstances.

The Applicant notes the Director did not inform it that it was in receipt of the British Diplomatic Note or the correspondence from the Department of Foreign Affairs, and says it had no opportunity to respond to any competing ownership claim before its application for the Heritage Research Permit was rejected . . . The Applicant had a legitimate expectation that the Director would consider and decide this administrative question issue according to the standard procedures set out in the legislation, and according to the principles of natural justice and procedural fairness. The Applicant had a significant interest in having the Permit issued.

Conclusion

The issue on this judicial review application is not the merits of the decision made by the Director, but rather the matter of procedural fairness. In reviewing the procedure used by a decision-maker, it is not the Court's role to substitute its own decision for that of the decision-maker. The Court's role is to determine whether the decision-maker accorded procedural fairness.

I am satisfied that an order in nature of certiorari is appropriate here. The Applicant was denied the opportunity to make submissions on the legal claim to ownership of the wreck of the Fantome, even though this claim was precisely the basis upon which the Applicant was denied a Heritage Research Permit. Regardless of the merits of the British claim, it was a fundamental error for the Director to accept it, without question, and without allowing the Applicant an opportunity to be heard.

Failure to Give Reasons

Failure of an administrative decision-maker to provide reasons for their decision is a rarely invoked and even more rarely successful ground for judicial review. In some measure, this is likely due to the fact that at least some decision makers (Cabinet ministers, for example) are under no duty to provide reasons. Nor is it entirely clear in what circumstances civil servants are bound by this duty. The absence of such a duty can present serious evidentiary problems for a party seeking to challenge a decision on other administrative law grounds.

On the other hand, quasi-judicial entities such as tribunals are under a duty to provide reasons as are their judicial cousins. The precise origin of this duty can sometimes be murky. Certainly it can be argued that it is an incident of procedural fairness. It may also, as in the case that follows, flow from a consideration of the legislative scheme within which the decision takes place.

Pembina Institute for Appropriate Development v. Canada (Attorney General)
2008 FC 302

[The petitioner sought judicial review with respect to a report by the Joint Review Panel established by the Alberta Energy and Utilities Board and the Government of Canada to complete environmental impact assessment of the Kearl Oil Sands Project. The Panel recommended to the responsible federal authority, the Department of Fisheries and Oceans ("DFO"), that the Project be authorized to proceed. The petitioner submitted that the environmental assessment conducted by the Panel did not comply with the mandatory steps in the *Canadian Environmental Assessment Act* and in the Panel's Terms of Reference.]

TREMBLAY-LAMER J.

Greenhouse Gas Emissions

The applicants submit that the Panel erred by failing to provide a cogent rationale for its conclusion that the adverse environmental effects of the greenhouse gas emissions of the Project would be insignificant, and by failing to comment on the effectiveness of intensity-based "mitigation". According to Imperial Oil's EIA, the Project will be responsible for average emissions of 3.7 million tonnes of carbon dioxide equivalent per year, which equals the annual greenhouse gas emissions of 800,000 passenger vehicles in Canada, and will contribute 0.51% and 1.7% respectively, of Canada and Alberta's annual greenhouse gas emissions (based on 2002 data).

The respondent, Imperial Oil, argues that the EIA that was before the Panel set out the annual greenhouse gas emissions, as well as the intensity of greenhouse gas emissions on a per barrel basis for the Project during the operating period. Further, the Project Application sets out Imperial Oil's approach to greenhouse gas management including the requirement that the most energy efficient, commercially proven and economic technology be selected to minimize emissions. There is no evidence to suggest that the Panel failed to consider all the evidence that was before it, and while it did not comment specifically on the effects of the greenhouse gas emissions . . . the EARPGO (predecessor to the CEAA) does not specify a particular form for the report and thus, it is not the role of this Court to insist on a particular form in the present case. At the hearing, Imperial Oil's counsel added that for the Panel to comment on the proposed intensity based mitigation measures would shift its role into the realm of policy recommendation.

While I agree that the Panel is not to engage in policy recommendation, nevertheless, it is tasked with conducting a science and fact-based assessment of the potential adverse environmental effects of a proposed project. In the absence of this fact-based approach, the political determinations made by final decision-makers are left to occur in a vacuum.

I recognize that placing an administrative burden on the Panel to provide an in-depth explanation of the scientific data for all of its conclusions and recommendations would be disproportionately high. However, given that the Report is to serve as an objective basis for a final decision, the Panel must, in my opinion, explain in a general way why the potential environmental effects, either with or without the implementation of mitigation measures, will be insignificant.

Should the Panel determine that the proposed mitigation measures are incapable of reducing the potential adverse environmental effects of a project to insignificance, it has a duty to say so as well. The assessment of the environmental effects of a project and of the proposed mitigation measures occur outside the realm of government policy debate, which by its very nature must take into account a wide array of viewpoints and additional factors that are necessarily excluded by the Panel's focus on project related environmental impacts. In contrast, the responsible authority is authorized, pursuant to s. 37(1)(a)(ii), to permit the project to be carried out in whole or in part even where the project is likely to cause significant adverse environmental effects if those effects "can be justified in the circumstances". Therefore, it is the final decision-maker that is mandated to take into account the wider public policy factors in granting project approval.

I am fully aware of the level of expertise possessed by the Panel. The record shows that they had ample material before them relating to the issue of greenhouse gas emissions and climate change, and thus any articulated conclusions drawn from the evidence should be accorded a high measure of deference. However, this deference to expertise is only triggered when those conclusions are articulated. Instructively, in *Canada (Director of Investigation and Research, Competition Act) v. Southam Inc.*, [1997] 1 S.C.R. 748, [1996] S.C.J. No. 116 (QL), at para. 62, Iacobucci J. cited with approval the following excerpt from Kerans, R. P., Standards of Review Employed by Appellate Courts (Edmonton: Juriliber, 1994) . . .:

> Experts, in our society, are called that precisely because they can arrive at well-informed and rational conclusions. If that is so, they should be able to explain, to a fair-minded but less well-informed observer, the reasons for their conclusions. If they cannot, they are not very expert. If something is worth knowing and relying upon, it is worth telling. Expertise commands deference only when the expert is coherent. Expertise loses a right to deference when it is not defensible. That said, it seems obvious that [appellate courts] manifestly must give great weight to cogent views thus articulated.

Thus, deference to expertise is based on the cogent articulation of the rational basis for conclusions reached.

The evidence shows that intensity-based targets place limits on the amount of greenhouse gas emissions per barrel of bitumen produced. The absolute amount of greenhouse gas pollution from oil sands development will continue to rise under intensity-based targets because of the planned increase in total production of bitumen. The Panel dismissed as insignificant the greenhouse gas emissions without any rationale as to why the intensity-based mitigation would be effective to reduce the greenhouse gas emissions, equivalent to 800,000 passenger vehicles, to a level of insignificance. Without this vital link, the clear and cogent articulation of the reasons behind the Panel's conclusion, the deference accorded to its expertise is not triggered.

While I agree that the Panel is not required to comment specifically on each and every detail of the Project, given the amount of greenhouse gases that will be emitted to the atmosphere and given the evidence presented that the intensity based targets will not address the problem of greenhouse gas emissions, it was incumbent upon the Panel to provide a justification for its recommendation on this particular issue. By its silence, the Panel short circuits the two step decision making process envisioned by the CEAA which calls for an informed decision by a responsible authority. For the decision to be informed it must be nourished by a robust understanding of Project effects. Accordingly, given the absence of an explanation or rationale, I am of the view that the Panel erred in law by failing to provide reasoned basis for its conclusion as mandated by s. 34(c)(i) of the CEAA.

As this error relates solely to one of the many issues that the Panel was mandated to consider, I find that it would be inappropriate and ineffective to require the entire Panel review to be conducted a second time . . . Accordingly, the application for judicial review is allowed in part. The matter is remitted back to the same Panel with the direction to provide a rationale for its conclusion that the proposed mitigation measures will reduce the potentially adverse effects of the Project's greenhouse gas emissions to a level of insignificance.

Notes and Questions

What is the source and scope of the duty to provide reasons that the court in this case found was violated? Does the decision in this case provide a basis for extending the duty to provide reasons to other environmental decision makers who, to date, it has been assumed are exempt from such a duty? Why or why not?

Part IV — Public Interest Standing

Benefits of Public Participation

As a prelude to our consideration of public interest standing, it is worthwhile to reflect upon the reasons why public participation is generally seen as a public good. The article excerpted below is an important early articulation of the case for public participation in environmental decision-making.

Raj Anand & Ian Scott, "Financing Public Participation in Environmental Decision Making"
(1982) 60 Can. Bar Rev. 81

Access to Justice

The objection that encouraging public participation would have the effect of stirring up unmeritorious litigation is only one aspect of a wider attack on "public interest" advocacy that is commonly mounted by critics who argue that conflict resolution is the sole legitimate purpose of civil actions. Another aspect of this approach is the assumption that when claims are not enforced through litigation, it is because they are unimportant to the affected individuals . . .

It is clear that the failure to advance a particular cause in a given piece of litigation often results from barriers to legal redress that have nothing to do with the merit of the cause or the relative importance of the harm that is perceived by the "victim". Economic barriers to participation in decision-making are well documented in all forms of litigation, and apply most severely to those who suffer in addition from social, psychological and cultural impediments to the redressing of their grievances.

Additional barriers present themselves in the case of public interest groups. Professor Michael Trebilcock, in a 1975 critique of the modern regulatory system and its effects on consumer interests, has identified three such barriers that have analogous effects on environmental groups. Firstly, the environmental concerns of the average citizen are spread across a great range of projects, issues and locations. On the other hand, a business interest that is concerned with the particular project, issue or location has "a sufficiently concentrated stake in any prospective regulation of it to make [its] views known very forcefully to government".

. . . . .

Secondly, unlike highly concentrated producer interests, environmental interests are not generally homogeneous. Most environmentalists are also both consumers and producers of goods and services, and in these roles will often see things differently.

. . . . .

The third barrier — is commonly known as the "free rider" phenomenon. Olson, for example, argues that unless the membership in a public interest group is small, or unless some special incentive is provided to encourage individuals to act in the common interests of the group, rational and self-interested individuals will not act to achieve their common or group interests. Olson cites the nation state as an extreme example of a large group that cannot survive on voluntary contributions but must resort to coercive taxes.

In the result, public interest groups never achieve the strength that their number of potential beneficiaries would indicate, since many of the possible contributors of money, time and expertise either require or are permitted to take a "free ride" at the expense of existing members. It is by overcoming these "barriers to litigation" that the encouragement of public participation achieves the significant benefit of obtaining confidence in our system of civil justice. A significant "process" value is attached by the community to enhanced public involvement in collective decision-making.

Private Enforcement of Public Rights

A common response to the argument for increased citizen involvement in environmental decision-making is the assertion that intervenors have no useful purpose to serve, given that the public agencies such as administrative tribunals and courts have been entrusted with the dual roles of regulators of industry and representatives of the public interest. Yet, enforcement of public policies can be achieved by private individuals by supplementing the work of the various tribunals or by "energizing the agencies" . . .

Professor Gellhorn has identified three principal factors which combine to produce what has become known as agency "capture" by regulated interests. Firstly, the limited resources that are allocated to administrative agencies, considered in relation to the sheer mass of activity that is required to monitor and test proposals and applications, necessitates close co-operation between the regulator and the regulated industry. Administrative boards thus become dependent upon industry as providers of information. A second cause of industry orientation is the dependence of regulatory agencies on the regulated interests for political support. Independent tribunals cannot rely upon the government to protect them from legislative attack and must therefore develop their own constituencies that are capable of generating support in the legislatures. In this regard, a natural ally can often be found in the regulated interests.

Most importantly, two other characteristics of the administrative process have combined to form a third source of agency deference to industry positions. At the very least, even if the interests of the regulated industry and the adjudicator do not fully coincide, it is clear that the "public interest" which is the theoretical mandate of the decision-maker is not unitary. It has diverse and indeed countervailing components, and so the environmental tribunal or court cannot be, expected to become its guardian with unqualified success. Public intervention "softens the artificial two-sidedness which is often a by-product of the adversarial adjudicative process".

Improvement of the Administrative and Judicial Processes

Four distinct benefits accrue to the investigative and adjudicative processes as a result of increased public participation. Firstly, public participation provides decision-makers with a greater range of ideas and information on which to base their decisions. This input has important implications for what is essentially a decentralized, pluralistic system of adjudication by courts and tribunals; that is, one that, by delegation, performs the legislative function of balancing the concerns of competing interest groups. . . . The second element of substantive contribution is the presentation of a viewpoint or perspective that is not otherwise available to the decision-maker. Intervenors are often able to put forward a legal or factual argument which places a unique emphasis or interpretation upon existing issues or causes the tribunal to examine a new issue . . .

The second major benefit is that public participation can enhance public acceptance of judicial and administrative decisions . . . Public acceptability, in turn, can be expected to ease the implementation and enforcement of judicial and administrative decisions that rely upon public co-operation . . .

Third, problems of agency dependence on industry for political support may be alleviated by the broad participation of other parties. Such participation may promote the actual autonomy of the agency, both by giving it a broader perspective from which to view its own role, and by providing alternative potential bases of political support.

Fourth, the presentation of alternative view points at the board or lower court level is said to induce these decision-makers to be more thorough in their analyses and to articulate more clearly and precisely the reasons for their decisions. These improvements may in turn contribute to the building of a record on which a reviewing or appellate court might reverse the initial decision

Notes and Questions

If some public participation is a good thing, is more public participation always a better thing? What critiques of public participation are particularly compelling? Does this depend on the nature of the forum?

Public Interest Standing

During the 1970s and 1980s, the rules of public interest standing were liberalized as courts became increasingly mindful of the benefits associated with public interest litigation. Students of constitutional law will be familiar with the SCC's public interest standing trilogy from this period of *Thorson*, *McNeil* and *Borowski*. Also important to this development was the enactment of the Canadian *Charter of Rights and Freedoms* in 1982, and the SCC's extension of public interest standing to non-constitutional cases in *Finlay* in 1986. Currently, the test for public interest standing has three elements:

1. Is there a justiciable and serious issue to be tried?
2. Does the applicant have a genuine interest in the subject matter?
3. Is there another reasonable and effective manner for the case to be brought forward?

While standing is not the barrier to public interest litigation that it once was, as a legal issue it is by no means irrelevant in environmental cases and other public interest spheres. This was underscored by the 1992 decision in *Canadian Council of Churches* where the Supreme Court of Canada offered the following cautionary comments:

> . . . I would stress that the recognition of the need to grant public interest standing in some circumstances does not amount to a blanket approval to grant standing to all who wish to litigate an issue. It is essential that a balance be struck between ensuring access to justice and preserving judicial resources. It would be disastrous if the courts were allowed to become hopelessly overburdened as a result of the unnecessary proliferation of marginal or redundant suits brought by well-meaning organizations pursuing their own particular cases certain in the knowledge that their cause is all-important. . . . (per Cory J.)

In the following section, we canvass several illustrative cases decided in the years since *Canadian Council of Churches*. As you will discern, while this decision did not usher in a more restrictive era in terms of public interest standing as some predicted, standing remains very much a live issue in many public interest environmental cases.

Shiell v. Canada (Atomic Energy Control Board)
(1995), 98 F.T.R. 75 (Fed. T.D.)

[This was an application for judicial review of a decision by the Atomic Energy Control Board (the Board) approving an amendment to an operating licence and for mandamus to review a waste management plan. The corporate respondent operated a uranium mine and mill. An environmental impact study had been done. The corporate respondent questioned the applicant's standing. She lived in the province several hundred miles from the mine and had participated in a number of hearings and inquiries concerning the uranium industry. She had previously been denied standing in injunction proceedings in a related matter based on lack of a direct personal interest in the subject matter at issue.]

HEALD D.J.

The respondent, Cameco, raises a number of issues. The first . . . [is] whether the applicant has standing to bring this application for judicial review.

The applicant was born in England and married a Canadian soldier in 1946. She came to Canada with her husband and son. The family farmed near Govan Saskatchewan for many years. The applicant moved to Nipawin Saskatchewan in 1994. Since 1976, the applicant has been interested in the various proposals for developing Saskatchewan's high-grade uranium. In 1977, she participated in the Cluff Lake Inquiry. In 1980, she fully participated in the Key Lake Inquiry. In 1981, she participated in hearings concerning a uranium mine at Rabbit Lake. As noted supra, she has been very interested in the proposed changes at Key Lake involving the respondent, Cameco.

Cameco submits that the applicant is in the same position on this application as she was in the case of *Shiell v. Amok Ltd. et al.*. In that case, this same applicant sought an injunction preventing the respondent Amok from reprocessing leach tails produced by a uranium mining operation pursuant to a Ministerial decision authorizing such processing. After a careful review of the relative jurisprudence, Barclay J. stated (page 14):

> I am satisfied that the plaintiff does not have a direct personal interest in the alleged improper granting of the ministerial approval under section 16 of the *Environmental Assessment Act*. If it was sufficient for the plaintiff to be interested in the sense that she is concerned about the environment and environmental issues, then it is difficult to conceive of cases where this criteria would not be met. In my respectful view, to be afforded standing the plaintiff must be affected in the sense that the issue has some direct impact on her. This is clearly distinguishable from the Finlay case in which the respondent had a direct personal interest in the issue as deductions were being made from his cheques.

As in *Amok*, the applicant does not have a direct personal interest in these proceedings and, accordingly, the decision in *Finlay v. Canada (Minister of Finance)* has no relevance. She lives at Nipawin Saskatchewan, several hundred miles from the respondent's Key Lake operation. Her interest is neither direct nor personal. The decision a quo will not affect her in any way different from that felt by any other member of the general public. In *Finlay*, Le Dain J. stated:

> The judicial concern about the allocation of scarce judicial resources and the need to screen out the mere busybody is addressed by the requirements affirmed in *Borowski* that there be a serious issue raised and that a citizen have a genuine interest in the issue.

This concern expressed by the Supreme Court of Canada has been repeated in the more recent decision in *Canadian Council of Churches v. The Queen*, where Cory J. stated:

> I would stress that the recognition of the need to grant public interest standing in some circumstances does not amount to a blanket approval to grant standing to all who wish to litigate an issue. It is essential that a balance be struck between ensuring access to the Courts and preserving judicial resources; It would be disastrous if the Courts were allowed to become hopelessly overburdened as a result of the unnecessary proliferation of marginal or redundant suits brought by well-meaning organizations pursuing their own particular cases certain in the knowledge that their cause is all important. It would be detrimental, if not devastating, to our system of justice and unfair to private litigants.

On the basis of the jurisprudence cited *supra*, I have reluctantly come to the conclusion that this applicant does not enjoy the necessary standing to make this application for judicial review. I say "reluctantly" because I have no doubt about the applicant's bona fide interest and concern relative to the issues raised by this application. However, that interest and that concern do not *per se*, confer the requisite "standing" entitling her to continue with this application.

For these reasons, the application for judicial review is dismissed.

Notes and Questions

The approach adopted by the Court in *Shiell* is inconsistent with the more liberal posture adopted by most other courts. The next two cases excerpted below are illustrative of this more liberal approach to standing.

Algonquin Wildlands League v. Ontario (Minister of Natural Resources)
93 O.A.C. 228 (Ont. Div. Ct.)

SAUNDERS J.

The application is brought by Algonquin Wildlands League and the Friends of Temagami. As can be seen, they are asserting a public right or interest by the institution of proceedings for declaratory or injunctive relief. That is generally done by the Attorney General. These applicants have no standing as of right to apply for the relief sought as there is no evidence that they fall within the recognized exceptions to the general rule. They may however, in the discretion of the court, be granted standing as public interest applicants. See: *Minister of Finance of Canada v. Finlay* (1986), 33 D.L.R. (4th) 321.

It is uncontradicted that both applicants are nonprofit public interest environment organizations with a history of responsible involvement in forest and land use planning issues in the Temagami area. The issues raised by the applicants are justiciable and in my opinion there is no other reasonable or effective manner in which the issues are likely to be brought before the court. It was suggested that the Minister of the Environment might attack the decisions but that seems to me to be highly unlikely. It was also suggested that members of the community could have brought the matter before the court and had not done so. It is also uncontradicted that the members of the applicants include many persons, who either live in Temagami or frequent the area for pleasure or business. It is clear from the material that there is considerable controversy in the area and that may members of the community support or at least do not oppose the government actions. As I have said it seems to me that unless someone, like the applicants, bring these issues to the court, the court will not be asked to address them. Accordingly if the applicant can overcome the hurdle that these are serious issues to be tried, I would be prepared to grant them standing to bring the application.

[*Ed note*: In the result, the Saunders J. granted public interest standing. The case, as we shall see, is also notable for its discussion of injunction law: see Part V, *infra* this chapter.]

Miningwatch Canada v. Canada (Minister of Fisheries & Oceans)
[2007] F.C.J. No. 1249

MARTINEAU J.

With respect to standing, the Proponent contends that the Applicant has not raised a serious issue, that it does not have a genuine interest in the subject matter and that there are other directly affected parties who chose not to come forth with an application for judicial review.

The Proponent submits in this regard that the Applicant has not challenged the substantive outcome of the Course of Action Decision and that the issues raised by the Applicant have already been decided by this Court and the Federal Court of Appeal in the *True North* case, above. The Proponent notes that the Applicant is an advocacy group headquartered in Ottawa who does not represent any group of local citizens or interest groups directly affected by the Project. First Nations groups who are directly affected by the Project have not made an application for judicial review. Moreover, the Proponent stresses that the Applicant has chosen not to participate in the cooperative environment assessment process. Indeed, the Applicant has not made any submissions on the merits of the Project [prior to bringing this petition].

Tri-part test

The jurisprudence of the Supreme Court of Canada establishes that standing will be granted to a public interest group who wishes to challenge the exercise of administrative authority, as well as legislation, where the following tri-part test is met: a serious issue is raised; the Applicant shows a genuine interest; and there is no other reasonable and effective manner in which the issue may be brought to the Court (*Thorson v. Attorney General of Canada et al.*, [1975] 1 S.C.R. 138; *Minister of Justice of Canada v. Borowski*, [1981] 2 S.C.R. 575 at pages 339-340; *Canadian Council of Churches v. Canada*, [1992] 1 S.C.R. 236, ¶33 and following).

In applying this tri-part test, this Court has consistently rejected the proposition that the words "directly affected" used in subsection 18.1(1) of the FCA should be given a restricted meaning. Indeed, it has been decided in the past that an applicant who satisfies the requirements of discretionary public interest standing may seek relief under subsection 18.1(1) of the FCA even though not "directly affected", when the Court is otherwise convinced that the particular circumstances of the case and the type of interest which the applicant hold justify status being granted . . .

Exercise of the Court's discretion to allow standing

I accept the arguments submitted in writing and orally at the hearing on behalf of the Applicant. In the exercise of my discretion, I have considered all three factors of the tri-part test, as well as the purpose of the CEAA and the particular circumstances of this case.

The fundamental purpose of the CEAA is to ensure that projects requiring an EA are considered in a careful and precautionary manner before federal authorities take action in connection with them, in order to ensure that such projects do not cause "significant adverse environmental effects" (paragraph 4(a) of the CEAA). Another underlying purpose is to ensure that there are opportunities for timely and meaningful public participation throughout the environmental assessment process (paragraph 4(d) of the CEAA) [emphasis added].

Therefore, operational provisions found in the CEAA and its regulations must be interpreted and applied in a manner consistent with these purposes.

For the purpose of facilitating public access to records related to environmental assessments and providing notice in a timely manner of the assessments, there is a registry called the Canadian Environmental Assessment Registry (the Registry), consisting of an Internet Site and projects files (subsection 55(1) of the CEAA). Within fourteen days after the commencement of an EA under the CEAA, notice of its commencement must be posted on the Agency's Internet site (paragraph 55.1(2)(a) of the CEAA). The notice shall include a description of the scope of the project in relation to which an EA is to be conducted, as determined under section 15 of the CEAA (see paragraph 55.1(2)(c) of the CEAA). In the preceding section (see IV — Factual Background, particularly subsection B. Federal Assessment), I have examined the measures taken by the RAs and/or the Agency to inform the general public.

In addition to any requirement to notify the public or opportunities for public participation flowing from the provisions of the CEAA, an obligation on the Crown (though not on private companies or individuals) to consult First Nations exists where aboriginal rights may be affected by a project (see *Taku River Tlingit First Nation v. British Columbia (Project Assessment Director)*, [2004] S.C.J. No. 69; *Haida Nation v. British Columbia (Minister of Forests)*, [2004] S.C.J. No. 70).

A serious issue is raised by the Applicant with respect to the legality of the Course of Action Decision which is a final decision for the purpose of the present judicial review. In this instance, the Applicant is contesting that the impugned decision represents a departure from a positive duty to consult the public. To this effect, the issue of public participation is of import, not just in this case, but for future projects across Canada. Comprehensive studies as stated, mandate public consultation.

Section 21 of the CEAA which the Applicant alleges to be applicable in the case at bar, has been amended substantially in 2003. The current and enhanced version of this provision was introduced by section 12 of the Act to amend the *Canadian Environmental Assessment Act*, S.C. 2003, c.9 (the Bill C-9 amendments). The former text of section 21 of the CEAA is also reproduced at the end of the present reasons for order (see Appendix "A"). The Bill C-9 amendments came into effect on October 30, 2003 and apply to the Project.

The *True North* decisions invoked by the Respondents to sustain the legality of the impugned actions or decisions are based on the law as it read prior to the Bill C-9 amendments.

Section 21 of the CEAA now makes public consultation mandatory when conducting an EA by means of a comprehensive study. Specifically, the new provision provides that "[w]here a project is described in the comprehensive study list, the RA shall ensure public consultation with respect to the proposed scope of the project for the purposes of the environmental assessment, the factors proposed to be considered in its assessment, the proposed scope of those factors and the ability of the comprehensive study to address issues relating to the project".

A duty to consult the public at an early stage on key aspects of the environment assessment process is, therefore, one fundamental aspect introduced by the Bill C-9 amendments. Another one is participant funding. Previous subsection 58(1.1) required the Minister to establish a participant funding program to facilitate the public's participation in mediations and assessment by a review panel. The Bill C-9 amendments expand this program by extending participant funding to comprehensive studies and also clarifies that the participant funding program applies to joint assessment by a review panel as well . . .

The Notice of Commencement which was posted on the Registry on May 23, 2004, announced that DFO would conduct a comprehensive study commencing on May 19, 2004. It can seriously be argued by the Applicant that this created a legitimate expectation that the general public would be consulted in accordance with section 21 of the CEAA. Moreover, at the time that the RAs changed "track" and chose to proceed by way of a screening, the documentation on file shows that the public consultation process under the provincial EA was well underway. Indeed, it was completed prior to the announcement made on the Registry of the Scoping Decision of March 2005.

In the end result, there was no public consultation with respect to the screening report prepared in 2006 under the purported authority of section 18 of the CEAA. This contrasts sharply with the evidence on file that the public has been consulted by the RAs with respect to the comprehensive study prepared in the case of the Galore Creek Gold — Silver — Copper mine, which is also located in the area where the Red Chris property is situated . . .

I defer to the reasoning of Justice Cory in *Canadian Council of Churches v. Canada*, [1992] 1 S.C.R. 236, at para. 38 wherein it was elucidated that the issues of standing and of whether there is a reasonable cause of action are closely related and indeed tend to merge. In the case at bar, compliance with the CEAA raises a serious and justiciable question of law.

The Applicant also shows a genuine interest in the issues raised in this application for judicial review. More than a mere bona fide interest and concern about social and environmental issues is necessary to obtain public interest standing. In Citizens' Mining, above, at para. 30, this Court determined that an applicant seeking public interest standing must demonstrate: ". . . a longstanding reputation and it must do significant work on the subject-matter of the challenge, and its interest must be greater than that possessed by a member of the general public".

Based on the evidence before me, MiningWatch clearly satisfies this requirement. It is a federally-registered non-profit society that functions as a coalition of environmental, social justice, aboriginal and labour organizations from across Canada. By focusing on federal aspects of mining development, the Applicant enjoys the highest possible reputation and has demonstrated a real and continuing interest in the problems associated mine development. Indeed, MiningWatch has made submissions before the House Committee on Bill C-19, the predecessor of the 2003 amendments to the CEAA, and has published studies critical of failed mitigation plans in relation to mine development.

The Applicant's lack of participation in the provincial environment assessment process is not a barrier to the granting of standing in this judicial review as the provincial forum would not have been to appropriate place for the Applicant to raise its concerns about the conduct of the RAs, all of whom are federal departments. Further, this Court has ruled that the lack of participation in an assessment does not preclude an interested party from seeking standing: *Sierra Club*, above, at para. 68. Finally, I am also of the view that since Ms. Kuyek raised the Applicant's concerns with various delegates or employees of the Ministry of Environment, DFO and the Agency throughout 2005, this suggests an involvement with the Project that prevents the striking out of the application on the ground of lack of standing.

Although the Applicant raises a serious issue and has a genuine interest in the subject matter of this application, public interest standing may still be denied if there are other persons who are more directly affected than the Applicant, and are reasonably likely to institute proceedings to challenge the administrative action in question. The rationale for this final requirement is that those most directly affected by administrative action are often in the best position to bring to the court the information necessary for an appropriate resolution of the dispute.

It is obvious that members of the general public as well as aboriginal groups/individuals living geographically proximal to the Project may have an interest in this judicial review. However, given the complexities and interconnectedness of modern society (as discussed by the Supreme Court in *Canadian Council of Churches*, above, at para. 29), I am not persuaded that geographical proximity ought to be the determinative factor when assessing public interest standing.

Instead, I import the reasoning of Justice Mackay in Citizens' Mining that public interest standing should be accorded "where the applicant has a genuine interest and there is no evidence of another or others with a genuine interest that could reasonably be expected to bring a challenge". I disagree that that just because others might share the Applicant's concerns, but have not commenced legal action, the Applicant should be denied standing. In the case at bar, there is no evidence to suggest that others might raise the important issue raised by the Applicant concerning both the scope of section 21 of the CEAA, as amended by Bill C-9, and its application in relation to the Project.

In sum, MiningWatch represents a coalition of approximately twenty groups that express a communal concern and seek to challenge a decision that might otherwise be essentially beyond review. In my view, the Applicant is the only one to demonstrate sufficient interest or the means to launch this judicial review.

Therefore, standing is accorded to the Applicant under the doctrine of public interest.

Notes and Questions

1. Can *Shiell* be reconciled with *Algonquin Wildlands League* and *Miningwatch*? To what extent, if at all, can the outcome in these cases be explained on the basis differing statutory language or other contextual factors?

2. As we shall see, the litigation in *Miningwatch* is ongoing. The trial decision above was reversed by the Federal Court on other grounds; as of the date of publication, the case is awaiting hearing at the Supreme Court of Canada: see Chapter 7.

Part V — Interim Injunctive Relief

At stake in many environmental cases are apprehended harms that cannot be readily compensated for, if at all, by monetary damages. As such, the spectre of "irreparable harm" plays an especially prominent role in this area of the law. As Professor McLeod-Kilmurray has argued:

> Interlocutory injunctions are not merely procedural motions at the periphery of the main litigation. In many environmental cases, they *are* the litigation . . . Doctrinally, injunctions can affect the substantive law . . . Granting an injunction, even an interlocutory one, reveals the value placed on the protected interest, and that the interest is important enough to prevent, rather than compensate, harm to it. (*The Process of Judging the Environment*: Ph.D. thesis, 2007.)

The corollary to McLeod-Kilmurray's point is, of course, that where interim injunctive relief is denied this likewise speaks powerfully as to how we value competing interests.

C. Tollefson, "Advancing an Agenda: Reflections on Recent Developments in Public Interest Environmental Litigation"

(2002) 51 U.N.B.L.J. 175

A common stumbling block faced by environmental and other organizations that have sought recourse to the courts to protect natural areas from development has been their inability to obtain interlocutory injunctive relief. Even where courts have acknowledged that their legal claims have significant merit, judicial application of the prevailing test with respect to the availability of injunctions under *RJR-MacDonald Inc. v. Canada (Attorney General)* has frequently led to a denial of interim relief sought. *RJR-MacDonald* established a threefold test: (1) is there a serious issue to be tried?; (2) would the applicants suffer irreparable harm if the injunction were refused? and (3) does the balance of convenience between the parties to the application justify the relief sought? In addition, courts have traditionally deemed it necessary for the applicant to undertake to indemnify the respondent for damages in the event that the claim is ultimately dismissed . . .

The two primary difficulties environmental groups have encountered in securing interlocutory relief have related to this undertaking requirement, and judicial interpretation of the "irreparable harm" arm of the test under *RJR-MacDonald*. Many if not most such groups lack the financial resources to make an undertaking as to damages. As such, it seems appropriate that courts employ the undertaking requirement flexibly to ensure that the right to a remedy is not dictated solely by economic considerations. This is especially so insofar as one of the traditional reasons for imposing the undertaking requirement is to ensure that an applicant who secures interim relief is not unjustly enriched at the expense of the party against whom the relief has been granted, a rationale that seemingly has little application in the context of public interest litigation.

American courts have been alive to this concern and have been generally unwilling "to close the courthouse door in public interest litigation by imposing burdensome security requirement(s)". As such the usual practice in the United States has been to require public interest litigants seeking injunctive relief to post a nominal bond . . .

Recent Canadian authority suggests that our courts are beginning to re-evaluate the appropriateness of invariably imposing an undertaking requirement on public interest litigants. For example in *Friends of Stanley Park et al. v. Vancouver Parks and Recreation Board*, Davies J. observed that

> If an applicant who applies for injunctive relief in a matter concerning serious public interests is able to establish a serious question to be tried, and that the balance of convenience, including the public interest, favours the granting of injunctive relief, such relief should not generally, at the interlocutory stage, be rendered ineffectual by reason of the fact that the applicant may not have the financial wherewithal to provide a viable undertaking as to damages.

Davies J. went to state that had the applicant succeeded in meeting the test to obtain an interim injunction, he would have issued the injunction without an undertaking as to damages. The decision in this case appears to accord with emerging authority [*Ed note*: See for example *Friends of Stanley Park v. Vancouver (City)* (2000), 10 MPLR (3d) 25 (B.C. S.C.)]

The other barrier faced by public interest environmental litigants in securing interim injunctive relief has been the judicial treatment of the second arm of the *RJR-MacDonald* test: the requirement that the applicant demonstrate that they will suffer irreparable harm if relief is not granted. In private litigation, this inquiry has traditionally focused on the risk to the applicant of physical injury or economic loss. Where the applicant has been granted standing as a public interest litigant this risk is, by definition, absent; instead, in such cases, it has been argued that the relevant "irreparable harm" is harm to the environment.

The meaning of "irreparable harm" has been considered in a variety of cases that have sought to challenge the legality of proposed logging on public lands, often in old growth areas. In several cases, despite evidence that it can take hundreds of years for trees to reach mature (old growth) status, courts have concluded that the logging of old growth does not constitute irreparable harm. In *Wilderness Society v. Banff*, the court concluded that "irreparable harm" would not result from clear-cut logging of three hundred year old trees in Banff National Park, despite expert evidence that logging would have precisely this effect . . .

Recent cases have been more responsive to the argument that natural resource extraction, in particular clear-cut logging, can constitute "irreparable harm". Indeed, the Supreme Court's decision in *RJR MacDonald*, rendered in 1994, tends to support this view. There the Court relied on a case where logging was enjoined on an island claimed by First Nations to illustrate the meaning of irreparable harm. In its words, "irreparable" refers to the nature of the harm, not its magnitude: examples include where a permanent loss of natural resources will be the result when a challenged activity is not enjoined".

Over time, American courts have come to conclude that harm to the environment will almost always be "irreparable". In the words of the U.S. Supreme Court: "Environmental injury, by its nature, can seldom be adequately remedied by money damages and is often permanent or at least of long duration, i.e. irreparable. If such injury is sufficiently likely, therefore, the balance of harms will usually favour the issuance of an injunction to protect the environment".

Three recent decisions involving interim applications to enjoin logging activities in or near parklands suggest that Canadian courts may be coming to a similar realization. In 1998, Monnin J.A. (in chambers) upheld an interim injunction prohibiting construction of a road through a provincial park noting that "damages will not compensate for a destroyed forest", and observing that failure to grant the relief sought would "trigger a non-reversible process". In a similar vein, Lamek J. concluded that "absent an injunction, the clearing of the road will proceed and the trees will be gone, if not forever, at least for decades". Most recently, the Federal Court Trial Division held that because the proposed logging would result in the loss of trees that "could not be replaced in a person's lifetime" this meant that nature of the harm "could not be quantified in monetary terms".

Our first illustrative injunction case arises in the *Algonquin Wildlands* litigation noted earlier.

Algonquin Wildlands v. Ontario (Minister of Natural Resources)
[1996] O.J. No. 3355

SAUNDERS J.

The stay order sought is analogous to an injunction. There is no dispute as to the general nature of the test to be applied. It is the test set out in *RJR-MacDonald Inc. v. The Attorney General of Canada* (1994), 111 D.L.R. (4th) 385. It is a threefold test:

(i) Is there a serious issue to be tried?;

(ii) Would the applicants suffer irreparable harm if the stay were refused?; and

(iii) What is the balance of convenience? That is which of the parties would suffer the greater harm from the granting or refusing the interim relief.

Serious Issue to Be Tried

Initially this is the test with the lowest threshold. As stated in *RJR-MacDonald* at p. 411 unless the case on the merits is frivolous or vexatious or is a pure question of law, the judge as a general rule should go on to the next stage. The nature of the issues may be revisited at the end of the day when reaching a conclusion on the balance of convenience test. In dealing with this issue, the court should do no more at this stage than make a preliminary investigation of the merits. Indeed it is undesirable to go into the merits in any detail, having regard for the fact that they will be fully canvassed by the panel.

The applicant's attack on the municipal action is based on a noncompliance with the *Crown Forest Sustainability Act*, S.O. 1994, c. 25 and the conditions imposed by the Environmental Assessment Board. In my opinion the applicants have raised issues of statutory interpretation and ministerial conduct which are not frivolous and which require consideration before they can be determined. It is accordingly appropriate to pass to the second stage.

Irreparable Harm

The applicants allege irreparable harm, in effect, on the simple straightforward position, that once you cut down a tree you cannot put it back. The extent or even the existence of the harm is disputed by the respondents. Furthermore the Minister submits that even if there were to be harm demonstrated, there has been no harm to these applicants, which the Minister submits is a necessary element of the test. In support of this proposition the Minister relies on a passage from Beetz J. in the Supreme Court of Canada in *Metropolitan Stores (MTS) Ltd. v. Manitoba Food & Commercial Workers, Local 832* (1987), 38 D.L.R. (4th) 321 which is quoted in the *RJR-MacDonald* at p. 405 to the effect that only the harm to the applicant should be considered at this stage and the harm to the respondents and to the public interest, should be considered at the third or balance of convenience stage.

The cases suggest that the three tests should be considered in order and that if the applicant fails at any stage, that should be the end of the matter. It is important to note that neither the applicants in *Metropolitan Stores* nor the applicants in *RJR-MacDonald* were public interest applicants. The cases cited by the Minister in support of the submission that the irreparable harm must be suffered by the applicants either involved the issue of standing or were not binding on this court. It would be a rare case where a public interest applicant such as the organizations which are making this application would directly suffer irreparable harm. It would be illogical to grant these applicants standing and then turn around and deny them relief because they had not suffered harm. It would seem to me that a better approach would be to consider the public interest harm alleged by the applicants along with the harm to the respondents at the third stage of the inquiry. In my opinion there is nothing in the passage of Mr. Justice Beetz that would be inconsistent with that approach, bearing in mind that in *Metropolitan Stores* there was no public interest applicants. In short, in this situation, we should skip stage two and move to stage three.

The Balance of Convenience Stage

The third stage is the balance of convenience or as it is sometimes called the balance of inconvenience. The factors to be considered vary from case to case. In this case the public interest is very much involved. The applicants say there would be irreparable harm to the public interest if this stay is not grated. Conversely the respondents say there would be irreparable harm to the public interest if the stay were to be granted.

As I have said the applicants take the simple and straightforward position that if you cut down the trees you cannot put them back. The respondents dispute there will be any significant harm or indeed any harm at all. There is considerable conflicting evidence on this point and it is not possible to make any meaningful determination. For the purpose of this motion, I am prepared to assume there will be some irreparable harm to the natural growth and wildlife in the area in spite of the efforts to keep it to a minimum.

The harm to the respondents is of a different nature. The Crown will be hampered in pursuing its policy for the use of Crown lands. Crown revenue will be at least deferred and perhaps lost. It is uncontradicted that needed wood supply will be unavailable and the Goulard mill will not be able to operate at full capacity. It is also uncontradicted that if this occurs there will be loss of employment which will have a ripple effect in the community. Again it is hard to quantify the extent of the harm, but it must be assumed that there will be some harm.

What is going on here is part of a world wide controversy or debate carried on in an effort to achieve a sustainable environment. In assessing the balance of convenience it is suggested in *RJR-MacDonald* that the court in determining whether to grant or withhold interlocutory relief should have regard not only to the harm which the parties contend they will suffer, but also to the nature of the relief sought, the nature of the legislation which is under attack, and where the public interest lies. To this I would add the nature of the authority of the Ministry which is under attack. . .

For a number of years the Ministry and interested segments of the public have been struggling with the issue of forest management. It is the obvious goal of all to achieve and maintain a sustainable environment while balancing the interests of the various segments. It is a complicated, ongoing and developing process. The details are set out in the material filed. In the course of argument it was not suggested that there had been anything other than good faith on the part of all parties to this application. The cutting of the forest at Owain Lake is clearly part of a comprehensive government policy with respect to the use of its land carried out in accordance with the principles I have tried to describe. While the applicants raised serious issues with respect to the compliance with the legislation and with the Environmental Assessment Board conditions they have not, as submitted by the respondents for the industry, demonstrated anything that is substantially inconsistent with the draft manual or any connection between the alleged deficiencies and the alleged harm. The government action has been consistent with its declared policy.

In all of the circumstances I considered the balance favours the respondents. In my opinion it would be inappropriate to interfere with the action of the government, even for a short time. The motion therefore will be dismissed.

Notes and Questions

1. Ultimately, the petitioners prevailed at trial, a decision that underscored the strength of their claim for injunctive relief: (1998), 26 C.E.L.R. (N.S.) 162. They also received a substantial award of costs. If on these facts interim relief is unavailable, what does this suggest generally about the prospects of securing such relief in environmental cases? For further ruminations on this theme see Stewart Elgie, "Injunctions, Ancient Forests and Irreparable Harm", (1991) 25 U.B.C.L.R. 387.

2. The next case we will look at arises in litigation with respect to the environmental assessment of the Kearl Oil Sands Project, discussed previously in Part III of this chapter.

Imperial Oil Resources Ventures Ltd. v. Canada (Minister of Fisheries and Oceans)

[2008] F.C.J. No. 541

de MONTIGNY J.: — This is an application for a stay of application or, alternatively, for an injunction prohibiting the Minister from revoking an authorization given under subsection 35(2) of the *Fisheries Act*, R.S.C. 1985, c. F-14 (the "Authorization") to Imperial Oil allowing work to be done as part of the Kearl Oil Sands (KOS) Project. . . .

Facts

The course of events leading to the present motion can be briefly summarized. Imperial Oil wishes to construct the KOS Project, an oil sands mine, in a location approximately 70 kilometres north of Fort McMurray, Alberta, on the east side of the Athabasca River. This is a huge project, consisting of four open pit truck and shovel mines providing for an average of 24,750 tonnes per hour mining capacity, corresponding ore preparation and bitumen separation facilities, a cogeneration plant, a bitumen froth processing plant, a terminal to deliver the oil sands products to a pipeline system, and utilities and off-site facilities to support the mining and processing operations. The operations at the KOS Project are expected to continue until approximately 2060 and will be followed by final reclamation of the KOS Project site. The total project is designed to produce a maximum capacity of 55,000 cubic meters of partially deasphalted bitumen per day for a period of 50 years.

The Project is subject primarily to regulation established by Alberta Environment pursuant to the *Environmental Protection and Enhancement Act*, R.S.A. 2000, c. E-12 and by the Alberta Energy & Utilities Board pursuant to the *Oil Sands Conservation Act*, R.S.A. 2000, c. O-7. It also falls within federal jurisdiction as a result of the need for Imperial Oil to obtain an authorization from the federal Minister of Fisheries and Oceans pursuant to subsection 35(2) of the *Fisheries Act*. Accordingly, the Project was subject to the environmental assessment processes of both the Governments of Alberta and Canada. . . .

On January 18, 2006, the Department of Fisheries and Oceans, after consulting with other federal departments and agencies, recommended to the Minister of Environment that the KOS Project be assessed under the *Canadian Environmental Assessment Act*, S.C. 1992, c. 37 (the CEAA). More specifically, it was to be referred to a review panel due to the potential for the proposed project to cause significant adverse environmental effects. On July 14, 2006, Canada entered into an agreement with the government of Alberta to conduct a joint review panel.

> . . . the Joint Panel concluded that the proposed Project was not likely to result in significant adverse environmental effects, provided that the proposed mitigation measures and the recommendations of the Joint Panel were implemented (7).

Subsequent to the issuance of the Joint Panel Report, the Alberta Department of Environment and the Alberta Energy & Utilities Board issued the approvals required in connection with the KOS Project to Imperial Oil. On August 14, 2007, the Government of Canada issued a response to the Joint Panel Report, stating that it accepts all the conclusions and recommendations of the Joint Panel as presented in its Report.

On March 29, 2007, an application for leave and judicial review was filed by various non-profit organizations concerned about the environmental effects of the KOS Project (File T-535-07). They submitted that the environmental assessment conducted by the Joint Panel did not comply with the mandatory steps in the CEAA and in the Panel's Terms of Reference. The hearing took place from January 15 to 17, 2008.

Despite this challenge to the Joint Panel's Report, the Minister of Fisheries and Oceans issued Imperial Oil an authorization under subsection 35(2) of the *Fisheries Act* on February 8, 2008.

On the basis of that authorization, Imperial Oil immediately commenced its work on the Project.

Madam Justice Tremblay-Lamer issued her Reasons and Order on March 5, 2008 (*Pembina Institute for Appropriate Development v. Canada (Attorney General)*, [2008] F.C.J. No. 324, 2008 FC 302). She allowed the application for judicial review in part, and remitted the matter back to the same Panel with the direction to provide a rationale for its conclusion that the proposed mitigation measures will reduce the potentially adverse effects of the Project's greenhouse gas emissions to a level of insignificance. She refrained, however, from requiring the entire Panel review to be conducted a second time, as the error related solely to one of many issues that the Panel was mandated to consider . . .

On March 11, 2008, the Chief Executive Officer for Imperial Oil wrote to the Minister of Fisheries and Oceans, articulating concerns over the impact of the Judgment on the Project work then underway, and on the Authorization issued on February 12, 2008, pursuant to subsection 35(2) of the *Fisheries Act*.

On March 13, 2008, two of the Applicants in the judicial review of the Joint Panel's Report initiated a new judicial review application (File T-418-08). Imperial Oil is named as a Respondent, as is the Minister of Fisheries and Oceans. This new judicial review application is directed to the Authorization issued on February 12, 2008, pursuant to subsection 35(2) of the *Fisheries Act*. It seeks relief which included an Order quashing the Authorization, and interlocutory injunctive relief enjoining all or part of the KOS Project until the final resolution of the issues raised.

On March 20, 2008, the Department of Fisheries and Oceans delivered a letter to Imperial Oil, stating their opinion that the Authorization had been rendered a nullity as a result of the decision of Madame Justice Tremblay-Lamer. On the same day, Imperial Oil filed Judicial Review Application T-460-08 which underlies the present motion for a stay of the Minister's decision to revoke the Authorization given on February 8, 2008.

Analysis

The test for issuing a stay of proceedings is well known, and has been set out by the Supreme Court of Canada in *RJR-MacDonald Inc. v. Canada (Attorney General)*, [1994] 1 S.C.R. 311. The applicant must establish a) a serious issue to be tried, b) that it will suffer irreparable harm if the stay is not granted, and c) that the balance of convenience favours the applicant.

In this case, I think it is beyond dispute that a serious issue to be tried has been established. Briefly stated, the arguments of the parties can be summarized in the following way. The applicant contends there is nothing in the *Fisheries Act* allowing the Minister to revoke the subsection 35(2) authorization or revisit his decision to grant the authorization. As to the argument that the authorization has been rendered a nullity as a legal consequence of the judgment of Madam Justice Tremblay-Lamer, the applicant further argues, first of all, that the Joint Panel's Report was not quashed or set aside, but was merely sent back for the Panel to better explain its recommendations with respect to the problem of greenhouse gas emissions and to provide a basis for its conclusion on this particular issue. In any event, counsel for the applicant submits that section 37 of the CEAA directs the Minister to take into account the Panel Report, not to rely solely on its rationale. While it was conceded that the result might be different if the Court had quashed the Report, it is argued that the authorization cannot fall merely because the reasoning of the Panel was found defective on one aspect of its findings.

The respondents, on the other hand, take the view that the Minister has not revoked the Authorization, but that it has become void as a legal consequence of the decision made by Madam Justice Tremblay-Lamer. If one is to follow their argument, the regulatory regime put in place in the CEAA emphasizes that environmental assessment is a process in which environmental assessment precedes and informs regulatory decision making. Since there has been a material flaw in the environmental assessment process which, to use Madam Tremblay-Lamer's words, "short-circuits" this sequence, the Authorization is a nullity. In other words, the CEAA makes it clear that the Minister cannot proceed until a completed environmental assessment is over, one that meets all the requirements of the CEAA, and a report that as described in section 34 has been submitted to the Minister. Since the Court found a material error in the Panel's Report, it nullifies the Authorization as a condition precedent to the exercise of the authority has not been fulfilled. The responsible authority could not proceed because it could not make an informed decision.

It would be inappropriate, at this stage, to go any further into the arguments presented by counsel from each side. They are better left to the judge who will be seized of the underlying Application for Judicial Review, who will be in a much better position to rule on this legal issue after having considered a full record and more comprehensive written and oral arguments. Suffice it to say that, for the purposes of this Motion for a stay of application, I am satisfied the applicant has a case which deserves to be heard by the Court.

I am not convinced, however, that the applicant will suffer irreparable harm if the stay is not granted, especially if the Application for Judicial review is heard on an expedited basis. Indeed, counsel for the applicant conceded that much during his oral submission by teleconference. In his affidavit, Mr. Christopher Douglas Allard, Senior Project Manager for the KOS Project, stated that if work is to be stopped, there will be a domino effect on the timeline set for the work to be completed by 2012. While this is no doubt true, I also note that there is some vagueness in that schedule. For example, the ditching work will continue through "the first quarter or half of 2008" (para. 40 of the affidavit). Dewatering would then commence, and Imperial Oil "believes" it must start in the summer of 2008, as there are many different factors that can impact the pace of dewatering (para. 41 of the affidavit). If the ditching stops and dewatering cannot occur as planned, "that may extend the Project out one or more years" (para. 44 of the affidavit).

In light of these crude estimates, and in the absence of any cross-examination on the affidavits, it is difficult to assess with any degree of certainty the damage that would result from a long term stay. Imperial Oil also argued that if it wishes to commence operation of the KOS Project on schedule, it must order certain equipment, execute an engineering procurement and construction management contract and execute an earthworks construction contract. Many equipment items must be ordered 3 to 4 years prior to delivery, and the cost and availability of this equipment could change during this time. Moreover, the hundreds of engineers that have been mobilized for this project would likely be redeployed to other projects, and it would be impossible to say how many would be able to rejoin the KOS Project upon recommencement.

These are no doubt costs to be taken into consideration, but the amount of which is difficult to assess. How much of these costs would Imperial Oil be able to recoup is also difficult to foresee. What appears to be clear, however, is that a short term delay will most likely not be a major impediment in the overall schedule of the project. Moreover, Imperial Oil stands to lose a lot more if they were to do more work and expand further capital investment, only to see their Application for Judicial Review dismissed by the Court in a year or so.

It is true that from a compensation standpoint, Imperial Oil has committed to a No Net Loss Plan under the subsection 35(2) authorization such that any fish habitat that is altered, disrupted or destroyed must be replaced on a ratio of 2 to 1. I am also mindful of the undertaking given by the applicant as to damages that may be caused as a result of the granting of a stay. But these are only some of the considerations that must be taken into account. Of far more significance, it seems to me, is the crucial importance to resolve all the uncertainties, legal and otherwise, before embarking upon such an important project. This can only be done when the issues will have been fully canvassed, and when all the interested parties will have had an opportunity to be heard.

For all these reasons, the application for interim relief shall be denied.

Part VI — Costs in Judicial Review Proceedings

Judicial review can be a risky proposition for any litigant due to the potential for adverse costs liability. Public interest environmental litigants are especially at risk by virtue of the fact that if they are unsuccessful they may not only be liable for the costs of the governmental agency whose decision was challenged but also the costs of any private parties that may have joined (or been granted permission to be joined) in the litigation to uphold the decision in question. It is not surprising therefore that a recent survey of public interest environmental practitioners has revealed that the spectre of adverse costs liability is the most pressing access to justice issue confronted in their practice area: see C. Tollefson "Costs and the Public Interest Litigant: *Okanagan Indian Band* and Beyond", (2006) 40 C.J.A.L.P. 39–61 at 49. The following article canvasses recent developments in law of costs relating to public interest litigants.

Chris Tollefson, "Costs in Public Interest Litigation: Recent Developments and Future Directions"

(2009) 35 Advocates' Q. 181

When counseling public interest clients on the prospect of pursuing litigation, the spectre of adverse costs liability invariably looms large. Even where the case is strong, has compelling public interest features and adequate legal resources are available to mount the claim, a litigator is duty-bound to ensure that their client is fully mindful of and reflects carefully on the risks of proceeding in terms of costs liability. These risks are significantly enhanced if the contemplated litigation, as it often does in environmental cases, involves government as well as other private parties, either at the outset or potentially down the road.

Across the Commonwealth world, it is broadly recognized that the application of traditional costs rules presents a formidable barrier to access to justice. Indeed, as Lord Justice Brooke has observed in a recent lecture on public interest environmental litigation, costs rules ". . . above all, the risk of having to pay one's opponent's costs if one loses, and the uncertainty at the outset of litigation as to how large those costs will be" are arguably the most substantial barrier to access to justice. This conclusion is one that has equal force in the Canadian setting, as a recent study of access to justice in public interest litigation tends to confirm.

In Canada, the allocation of costs, although governed by statute, remains largely a matter of judicial discretion. The breadth of this discretion has, in public interest cases, created a costs jurisprudence that has been characterized by what one trial judge has described as yielding "erratic and unpredictable results". Given the central role of costs in promoting access to justice, academics have argued that establishing a more coherent and predictable public interest costs jurisprudence is "the most critical variable affecting the long-term health of public interest litigation".

While progress towards this goal has been slow, there are some hopeful signs on the horizon. Overall, it would appear that courts are becoming increasingly attuned to costs as an access to justice issue. Moreover, appellate level decisions both in Canada and England suggest at least a modest appetite for renovating the law of costs in public interest cases. But transforming this rhetorical appreciation of the importance of access to justice into legal principles that measurably reduce the risks (real and perceived) associated with pursuing public interest litigation has been hobbled by a variety of judicial concerns. These include difficulties associated with developing a workable definition of "public interest"; concerns about the "fairness" implications of special public interest costs rules in litigation involving private parties; and a general apprehensiveness about eroding the historically broad judicial discretion that has existed in this realm.

The Costs Landscape in Public Interest Cases: Trends and Terminology

In general, the law of costs in Canada, both common law and statutory, establishes a presumption that costs will ordinarily "follow the event" on a partial indemnity basis. The entitlement of the victor to costs rests on a variety of rationales including compensation (ensuring that the prevailing party is compensated for defending the suit), deterrence (as a measure to deter wrongful conduct) and spoils (the notion that entitlement to costs accompanies victory *per se*). Courts also possess a broad discretion to depart from this practice in special circumstances. Thus, the victor may be denied its costs on equitable grounds, for example, to discipline bad faith or sharp conduct. Alternatively, a court may refuse to award costs in recognition of the public benefits associated with the litigation (for example, where the case involves consideration of a novel legal point or an issue of public significance) or on an access to justice rationale (where an adverse award would visit undue hardship on a responsible public interest litigant). In contrast, public interest intervenors are conventionally regarded as being outside normal costs rules, although there are exceptions to this general practice . . .

In other Commonwealth jurisdictions, costs law follows these same basic contours and reflects analogous policy considerations. There is, however, one material difference that distinguishes Canadian costs law from that prevailing in England and some other Commonwealth jurisdictions. While in Canada the victor is presumptively entitled to be compensated on a partial indemnity basis (that may, depending on the jurisdiction, cover only half of their actual legal costs), in England the prevailing judicial policy is that the victor should be fully indemnified. This, of course, makes the stakes even higher for unsuccessful public interest litigants seeking relief from adverse costs liability.

In the academic literature, the Commonwealth approach to costs is typically referred to as a "two-way" costs regime. This terminology refers to the fact that at the conclusion of litigation costs can flow in two distinct directions, with a litigant either receiving or being liable for costs depending on which party has prevailed on the merits. This is in contrast to prevailing common law practice in the United States where the default position is a "no-way" regime in which parties bear their own legal costs regardless of the outcome. But while unsuccessful American litigants are not normally liable for adverse costs, this no-way model has been statutorily modified to allow for the recovery of costs in successful citizen suit actions. Thus, where a party (typically a public interest litigant) has been granted standing as a "private attorney general" to enforce a legal obligation against government (including under many federal environmental and civil rights laws) they are entitled to recover their costs on a full indemnity basis if their suit ultimately succeeds. This form of costs regime is known as a "one-way" model; an approach under which public interest litigants are shielded from adverse costs liability if they lose but are compensated for their costs if they prevail.

Understandably, many in the Canadian public interest bar are somewhat envious of the American one-way costs model, an approach that has not only served to sustain public interest law as a robust practice area but is also reported to have significantly enhanced the efficacy of federal law enforcement under legislation containing citizen suit provisions. North of the border, however, efforts to secure comparable citizen suit laws have met with political resistance. As a result, and perhaps to some extent by default, the principal venue for advocacy with respect to costs law reform in Canada has been the courts.

In this setting, reformers have argued for judicial recognition of a "public interest costs exception" that would serve to shield responsible public interest litigants from adverse costs liability where they have unsuccessfully litigated an issue of public importance. Recognition of this exception would, in effect, institute a one-way costs model for Canadian public interest litigation. To date, Canadian courts have been reluctant to carve out a judicial exception to the prevailing two-way model for public interest litigation, preferring to deal with such cases under the ambit of their general discretion to afford relief from adverse costs liability in appropriate cases.

One area of costs law where Canadian courts have displayed an appetite for innovation is with respect to advance funding orders. In the landmark case of *Okanagan Indian Band*, [2003] 3 S.C.R. 371, the Supreme Court of Canada affirmed that superior courts have an inherent jurisdiction to order government to pay an impecunious litigant its legal costs in advance of the litigation where such an order is mandated by access to justice considerations and the applicant meets a rigourous eligibility test

While subsequent cases have emphasized the highly exceptional nature of this form of order, *Okanagan Indian Band* remains strong authority for the proposition that judicial discretion over costs should be exercised in a manner that promotes access to justice. Indeed, a seldom appreciated dimension of *Okanagan Indian Band* is its importance in underscoring that in public interest cases courts should be prepared to depart from their traditional practice of addressing costs as an *ex post facto* issue, to be considered only when litigation has concluded.

To the extent that one goal of public interest costs law reform is to provide prospective public interest litigants with enhanced predictability as to the financial risks and consequences of proceeding, the timing of the adjudication of the costs issue is obviously critical. From a public interest litigant's perspective, *ex post facto* adjudication of costs, even under a regime that recognizes the existence of a public interest costs exception, generates a significant and ever-increasing deterrent to proceeding, particularly for parties that are risk averse or of modest means.

Despite compelling access to justice reasons for moving the exercise of this judicial function to an early stage in public interest cases (as is already done in applications for advance funding under *Okanagan Indian Band*), a variety of objections are likely to be raised if this were to become a more general practice. These objections, many of which underpin the policy that *Okanagan Indian Band* funding orders should be sparingly made, include concerns about pre-judging the merits of a pending claim, attenuation of the disciplinary function of costs, and the spectre of over-subsidizing public interest litigation. Nonetheless, despite these various concerns, English courts have recently forged ahead in this direction by crafting a new form of costs order for deployment in appropriate public interest cases: what have become known as "PCOs" or protective costs orders: see *R (Corner House Research) v. The Secretary of State for Trade and Industry*, [2005] EWCA Civ. 192, [2005] 1 W.L.R. 2600..

Current Canadian Public Interest Costs Caselaw

Even a cursory examination of the prevailing public interest costs caselaw reveals a jurisprudence that is rife with uncertainty and inconsistency. A highly instructive and thorough overview of this caselaw and related principles has recently been provided by Justice Perell in *Incredible Electronics* (2006), 80 O.R. (3d) 723. . . . [*Ed note:* Discussion of Perell J.'s detailed discussion of the relevant caselaw has been omitted].

Perell J. commences his analysis by acknowledging that since costs are a matter of judicial discretion one would not expect the caselaw to "demonstrate a consistent pattern". Still, even bearing this caveat in mind, in his view the caselaw reveals "erratic and unpredictable results". To lend greater coherence and predictability to this caselaw, he opines that in the costs setting "public interest litigation requires special treatment" and that this should be a guiding principle in the exercise of judicial discretion over costs allocation.

As a stand-alone proposition, this suggestion should be relatively non-controversial. Indeed it is entirely consistent with emerging judicial authority, as cogently articulated in *Okanagan Indian Band* [where the Supreme Court of Canada] opines at some length on the role of costs as a policy instrument in public interest cases to promote access to justice. To date, however, with some notable exceptions, courts have done little to translate this notion into a coherent and predictable approach to the allocation of costs in public interest cases.

In the balance of this paper, I explore both the obstacles impeding progress towards the development of such an approach and some of potential avenues through which these obstacles can be surmounted. To do so, I will consider how and to what extent potential reforms in the exercise of judicial discretion over costs at two junctures in the litigation process — at the *ex post facto* stage and at the outset of litigation — might advance the goal of creating a more coherent and predictable public interest costs jurisprudence.

***Ex post facto* Costs Orders**

Traditionally, the issue of costs has been addressed at the conclusion of litigation once the dust from trial has settled. From this *ex post facto* vantage point, courts are well poised to assess whether the ordinary rule as to costs should apply (i.e. that the victor should be awarded its costs on a partial indemnity basis) or alternatively whether there are reasons to depart from this approach.

When considering the question of costs in the public interest context, the Supreme Court of Canada has urged trial courts to be mindful of the desirability of promoting access to justice and of the public benefits that often flow from litigation of this kind. In the words of Lebel J. in *Okanagan Indian Band*, in public interest cases:

> . . . the more usual purposes of costs awards are often superseded by other policy objectives, notably that of ensuring that ordinary citizens will have access to the courts to determine their rights and other issues of broad social significance. Furthermore, it is often inherent in the nature of cases of this kind that the issues to be determined are of significance not only to the parties but to the broader community, and as a result the public interest is served by a proper resolution of those issues.

While trial courts have, I would argue, displayed an appreciation of the access to justice and public benefit dimensions of public interest litigation, to date few have analyzed these issues, in a systematic fashion in the costs setting. This has tended to lead to an undervaluation of the public benefit rationale for special costs rules in public interest litigation. It has also contributed to a tendency by at least some courts to narrow the availability of special costs treatment to only those cases where it can be concluded that the applicant possesses no "personal, proprietary or pecuniary interest" in the outcome of the proceeding.

Critics have weighed in on both of these fronts. For example, McCool has urged courts to adopt a more contextual approach in determining whether and how the public interest is engaged. She and others have also advocated for the need to avoid categorical approaches to the definition of "public interest litigant" that would exclude those who may possess some special or direct interest in the litigation.

The reasons of Perell J. in *Incredible Electronics* offer some intriguing ruminations on how these concerns might be addressed. He argues that the overarching question ought to be whether it can be properly concluded that the case at bar constitutes "public interest litigation". To answer this question, he proposes that courts employ two sequential tests.

The Public Importance Test

Perell J. proposes that the first question for a court to consider when adjudicating costs following trial concerns the nature and significance of the issue(s) at stake in the litigation. This inquiry — what might be termed the "public importance" test — focuses on the broader implications for and benefits flowing to the public-at-large from litigation. The existing costs caselaw underscores the diversity of situations that might qualify under this test. While resolution of a fresh or novel legal issue may help to tilt the balance in arguing that the test is met, I would argue that the test should also be deemed to have been met where the applicant demonstrates that the case raises for consideration a public policy of broad social concern or importance.

In Perell J.'s formulation what is critical is that the party seeking a special order as to costs is thus a partisan "in a matter of significance not only to the parties but to the broader community". Once this is established, the inquiry then shifts to a consideration of whether the litigant in question should properly be deemed a "public interest litigant".

The Public Interest Litigant Eligibility Test

Clearly, not all partisans in matters of broad public significance should be deemed public interest litigants. The purpose of this second stage of the inquiry is thus to determine whether the litigant seeking special costs treatment is more properly characterized as a public or a private interest litigant.

In tackling this question, it is instructive to note that the Supreme Court of Canada has opined that the concept of public interest litigant embraces two types of public interest litigants: (a) those that have no direct, pecuniary or other material interest in the proceeding (i.e. non-profit NGOs); and (b) those litigants that possess a private or pecuniary interest that is modest in comparison to the cost of mounting the proceeding (i.e. an interest that ordinarily would make it uneconomic to litigate the case): see *Odhavji Estate v. Woodhouse*, [2003] 3 S.C.R. 263.

The conventional view is that public interest litigants must, as Perell J. puts it, "manifest unselfish motives". Illustrative of this approach is a recent BCSC judgment in *OPEIU v. BC (Hydro and Power Authority)*, [2004] B.C.J. No. 623. In this case, Neilson J. rejected the submission by a union that it should be insulated from an adverse costs award arising from an unsuccessful challenge to out-sourcing legislation on the basis that the litigation was brought primarily to protect union job security.

But should courts invariably insist that all prospective public interest litigants manifest "altruism" or have "little to gain financially" from the litigation? In Perell J.'s view, a somewhat more flexible approach is merited; in his view, these characteristics "work better as indicia than as criteria for qualification as a public interest litigant". In support of a more flexible approach he notes that some litigants (social welfare claimants challenging eligibility rules and First Nations asserting aboriginal rights and title) may well stand to gain significantly from a favourable litigation outcome. In his view, the existence of this pecuniary interest should not automatically exclude them from invoking the mantle of public interest litigant. Indeed, he asserts that, in appropriate cases virtues other than altruism "such as courage, loyalty, patriotism, dedication to a worthy cause and the pursuit of justice" may suffice to qualify a party as a public interest litigant for costs purposes.

A related and contentious issue that often arises is the relevance of a party's financial resources and its bearing on their ability to support litigation (including paying adverse costs awards) and to withstand the financial and related risks of litigation. In many costs cases, the presumed existence of "deep pockets" and/or the availability of *pro bono* or government sponsored representation have been relied on as factors militating against special costs treatment. Here again, Perell J. advocates for a non-categorical approach: "it seems to me that the point is not so much whether the public interest litigant is affluent or impecunious but whether having regard to the benefit of securing their participation, they ought to be immunized from an adverse costs award".

But if altruism, having little to gain financially, and impecuniosity should be seen as indicia rather than criteria to acquiring the status of "public interest litigant" what other factors are relevant in tipping the balance in difficult cases? Here Perell J. contends courts should strive to keep an open mind, recognizing the reality, that as he puts it:

> At this point in its legal development, there is a certain je-ne-sais-quoi quality to the nature of the public interest litigant . . . a relevant but not determinative feature is that the public interest litigant is either the "other", a marginalized, powerless or underprivileged member of society, or [a litigant that] speaks for the disadvantaged in society, even if he or she has his or her own selfish reasons for litigating . . .

Costs liability of Public Interest Litigants to Private parties

Where a party has met the requirements of the preceding two tests, according to Perell J. they should ordinarily be excused from adverse costs liability in relation to governmental and public agencies. This, he asserts, is consonant with the obligation of such agencies to act in the public interest and provides symmetry between that obligation and the conclusion that the proceeding at bar is "public interest litigation". This leaves unanswered one final question, however: when and to what extent should a victorious private party drawn into public interest litigation be compelled to subsidize its losing opponent?

Many courts have tended to treat as self-evident the notion that a prevailing private litigant in these circumstances should receive its costs. Illustrative is the well-known decision in *Sierra Club v. BC (Chief Forester)*, [1994] 83 D.L.R. (4th) 708. In this case, while Smith J. concluded that the NGO petitioner had acted responsibly in raising for determination an issue of public importance (i.e. whether the Chief Forester had properly interpreted the term "sustainable" in establishing allowable annual cut rates) and that petitioner qualified as a public interest litigant, he nonetheless awarded costs to a large forest company that had been joined in the litigation at its request in support of the provincial government's position. According to Smith J., this conclusion flowed from the fact that "MacMillan Bloedel is a private citizen, not a public agency. It is entitled to go about its business within the law . . . [and] had no practical option but to defend against the petitioner's application. It was not drawn into the fray by any fault of its own".

The approach adopted by Smith J. has been criticized both for characterizing MacMillan Bloedel as merely a "private citizen" going about its business and, in the process, for neglecting the broader context in which underlying dispute arose. In particular, it has been argued that where large corporations enjoy broad state-conferred entitlements (i.e. over the extraction of natural resources or with respect to other public goods), courts should be careful not to deter "regular and careful public supervision" of these arrangements by imposing adverse costs awards against responsible public interest litigants.

In the case before him, Perell J. considered that this criticism, by analogy, was persuasive. In his view, to exempt public interest litigants from adverse costs liability to government but then to impose an adverse award in favour of a corporation operating with the benefit of a state-conferred monopoly (in the case before him, Bell ExpressVu), would undermine the policy imperatives that justify special treatment for public interest litigants. In his words, "from the perspective of the public interest litigant, not having to pay costs to the Attorney General but having to pay costs to Bell ExpressVu would be similar to avoiding a car only to be hit by a train".

Perell J.'s judgment in *Incredible Electronics* is impressive in scope and ambition. Indeed, I suspect that many in the public interest legal community would argue that its comprehensive judicial critique of this troubling area of law is long overdue. But whether and to what extent the judgment offers a roadmap towards a more coherent and predictable public interest costs jurisprudence is more difficult to assess. Perhaps part of the problem lies in the inherent tension between these two goals. The goal of coherence mandates a nuanced approach that recognizes and makes sense of the complex challenges surrounding the definition of public interest and the identification of those who should be deemed to be litigating under this mantle. Conversely, the goal of predictability implies the need for bright line, readily applicable legal tests or principles for adjudicating costs issues in real cases.

I would argue that overall Perell J.'s judgment takes us further down the road to coherence than predictability. In no other judgment in this area, does a court more clearly and convincingly critique the prevailing judicial tendency to equate public interest litigation with altruism or the absence of "private" motivations or values. His judgment is equally insightful in its recognition of the dangers of treating corporate actors, particularly those endowed with broad state-conferred rights or powers, as mere private citizens for costs purposes. However, while his judgment exposes the indeterminacy of the private-public distinction, it also seems ultimately to concede that determining who is a "public interest litigant" is an inherently subjective exercise that defies clear legal definition. Indeed, if this is true, if as Perell J. puts it at the end of the day there is "a je-ne-sais-quoi quality to the nature of the public interest litigant", one might well wonder whether the rendering the caselaw in this realm more predictable is a plausible or realistic goal. . . .

The Next Frontier: Anticipatory Costs Orders in Public Interest Cases

The main reason greater predictability in the rules governing costs is important to public interest litigants is the deterrent effect of the uncertainty surrounding the nature and quantum of their adverse costs liability in the event that their claim fails. A simple way to eliminate or reduce this risk is for courts to decide the allocation of costs at the outset of litigation. As discussed previously, this reform is a significant procedural departure from prevailing practice and one that triggers various judicial and extra-judicial objections including concerns about prejudging the merits of pending cases, attenuation of the disciplinary function of costs and inappropriate or over-generous subsidization of public interest cases.

Intriguingly, however, there are signs that it may well be an idea whose time has come. To date, the jurisdiction where anticipatory costs orders in public interest cases have evolved the furthest is England. There, jurisdiction to make protective costs orders (PCOs) in public interest cases was first recognized by Dyson J. in the 1999 case of *R v. Lord Chancellor ex parte CPAG*. In that case, three NGOs sought an advance order immunizing them from costs in the cause. While Dyson J. declined to make the order sought, he affirmed that in exceptional circumstances such orders were available. Applications for PCOs have since now been made in close to a dozen cases with a relatively high rate of success.

In 2005, the availability and nature of PCOs was argued for the first time in the Court of Appeal in what has come to be known as the *Corner House* case. The applicant, Corner House, was a small NGO involved in advocacy work around government corruption issues. The matter came on for hearing on an expedited basis, by way of an appeal from a denial of a PCO at first instance. The Court granted the appeal, ordering that the applicant be immunized from liability for adverse costs on the condition that its entitlement to recover its costs if successful would be capped by subsequent order of a costs judge.

In written reasons that followed, the Court affirmed that courts have a broad discretion to grant a PCO where:

> 1. the issues are of general public importance;
> 2. the public interest requires that those issues be resolved;
> 3. the claimant has not private interest in the outcome of the case;
> 4. having regard to the financial resources of the parties and the amount of costs likely to be involved, it is fair and just to make the order; and
> 5. if the order is not made, the claimant will probably discontinue the proceedings and will be acting reasonably in so doing. . . .

Canadian courts have not, as yet, pronounced upon the principles governing the availability and nature of PCOs under Canadian law. That this remains the case is somewhat surprising given the considerable attention that has surrounded what in many ways is an analogous form of anticipatory costs order: namely the advance funding order approved by the Supreme Court of Canada in its 2003 decision in *Okanagan Indian Band*. In this landmark case, the Court expounds at some length on the role of costs as a vehicle for promoting access to justice. In its view, this value is of such importance that in exceptional cases courts should be prepared to order government to pay the public interest litigant's costs in advance. To secure an award of this kind, the Court held that an applicant must meet the following test:

1. that it genuinely could not afford to pay for the litigation and that there was no realistic option for bringing the issues to trial;

2. that its claim was prima facie meritorious; and

3. that the issues raised by the case were of public importance and not resolved in previous cases.

If an applicant satisfied this test, a court may make the order sought unless it concludes that to do so is contrary to the interests of justice.

While some observers offered rather dire predictions about this potential impact of *Okanagan Indian Band* on government coffers and judicial dockets, in the three years immediately following the case funding applications were only brought in about a dozen instances and in most cases were unsuccessful. Nonetheless in 2006, the Court granted leave in one of the few cases where a funding order was secured, with a view to revisiting the principles surrounding such orders: see *Little Sisters II*, [2007] S.C.J. No. 2 In this case, concluding that the trial judge had erred in making a funding order, the Court took pains to emphasize the exceptional nature of such orders. And while the decision does not alter the nature of the test articulated in *Okanagan Indian Band*, it exhorts trial courts to regard such orders as a last resort.

Yet while the Supreme Court in *Little Sisters II* has confirmed that its reasons in *Okanagan Indian Band* should not be interpreted as the first volley in a judicially-led revolution in public interest costs reform, a little-noticed passage in the majority's reasons offers some hope for a more modest evolutionary approach. In this regard, it endorses the approach taken in *Corner House*:

> Finally, different kinds of costs mechanisms, like adverse costs immunity, should also be considered. In doing so, courts must be careful not to assume that a creative costs award is merited in every case; such an award should be an exceptional one, to be granted in special circumstances. Courts should remain mindful of all options when they are called upon to craft appropriate orders in such circumstances. Also, they should not assume that the litigants who qualify for these awards must benefit from them absolutely. In the United Kingdom, where costs immunity (or "protective orders") can be ordered in special circumstances, the order may be given with the caveat that the successful applicant cannot collect anything more than modest costs from the other party at the end of trial: see *R (Corner House Research) v. Secretary of State for Trade and Industry*, [2005] 1 W.L.R. 2600, [2005] EWCA Civ 192, ¶76. We agree with this nuanced approach.

Since *Little Sisters II*, successful advance funding orders have, not surprisingly, been rare. More surprising is the fact that public interest litigants have been so slow to take up the opportunity to advocate for PCOs given the opportunities that *Corner House* creates and the endorsement the English approach has received in *Little Sisters II*. . . .

Conclusion

The road to a more predictable and coherent public interest costs jurisprudence will undoubtedly have twists and turns. Indeed, it may be true that — given the amorphous nature of the concept of public interest litigation and the fact-specific nature of this area of judicial discretion — predictability will remain a somewhat elusive goal. Cases like *Incredible Electronics* . . . underscore, however, the need for a deeper level of engagement by trial courts with these issues before it can be concluded that this is the case. For this to happen, public interest lawyers must redouble their efforts to ensure that courts are mindful of the rationale for and importance of this engagement.

Meanwhile, public interest lawyers also have an opportunity to advance the law by encouraging trial courts to take up the Supreme Court's invitation in *Little Sisters II* to craft creative anticipatory costs orders, drawing on the lead of the English Court of Appeal in *Corner House* and the emerging English PCO jurisprudence. Undoubtedly, this must be done cautiously and strategically, and will require some hard, up-front work. Arguably, however, at least some of the heavy lifting has already been done in *Okanagan Indian Band*. In the process, one would hope that, at the very least, in cases where such orders are made, public interest litigants will enjoy the not insignificant benefit of greater predictability in the final reckoning as to costs.

Notes and Questions

1. To what extent is the reluctance of courts to depart from the traditional approach to costs allocation in public interest cases a function of their discomfort with the malleability of the concept of the "public interest"? Does this depend upon one's confidence on whether one assumes that the role of the office of the Attorney General is to represent the public interest?

2. In *St. James' Preservation Society v. Toronto (City)*, Ducharme J. offers a somewhat different approach to addressing costs issues in public interest cases: (2006), D.L.R. (4th) 149. Review the approach adopted by Ducharme J. and compare it with the approach employed in *Incredible Electronics*. Which approach do you prefer?

3. The trial judge's decision to award costs to MacMillan Bloedel in *Sierra Club* (discussed in the above article) on the basis of its status as a "private citizen" has been criticized as conclusory. Should all "private citizens" including corporate persons be presumptively entitled to their costs when "drawn into" public interest litigation to defend their interests? To what extent, if at all, should the financial situation of the public interest plaintiff be taken into account? If you are not in favour of the categorical approach adopted in *Sierra Club*, should the matter simply be left to judicial discretion or can you identify interpretive principles that could be of assistance in guiding the exercise of this discretion?

4. Compare the prevailing *ex post facto* Canadian approach to costs determinations to the approach adopted by the English House of Lords in *Corner House*. Should Canadian courts adopt the *Corner House* approach or some modified version of the approach it approves? How far would its adoption mitigate access to justice concerns in public interest environmental cases and in public interest litigation more generally?

References

We thank the copyright holders for their permission to reproduce their materials.

Raj Anand & Ian Scott, "Financing Public Participation in Environmental Decision Making" (1982) 60 Can. Bar Rev. 81

Andrew Green, "Discretion, Judicial Review, and the *Canadian Environmental Assessment Act*" (2002) 27 Queen's L.J. 785–807

David Phillip Jones & Anne S. de Villars, *Principles of Administrative Law* (4th ed) (Toronto: Thomson Carswell, 2004)

David J. Mullan, *Administrative Law* (Toronto: Irwin Law, 2001).

L. Sossin, "*Dunsmuir* — Plus ça change" (Blog: March 17, 2008) http://www.thecourt.ca/2008/03/17/dunsmuir-%E2%80%93-plus-ca-change/

C. Tollefson, "When the 'Public Interest' Loses: the Liability of Public Interest Litigants for Adverse Costs Awards" (1995) U.B.C.L. Rev. 303

C. Tollefson, D. Gilliland & J. DeMarco, "Towards a Costs Jurisprudence in Public Interest Litigation" (2004) 83 Can. Bar Rev. 607

C. Tollefson, "Costs and the Public Interest Litigant: *Okanagan Indian Band* and Beyond" (2006) 40 Can. J. Admin. L. & Prac. 39–61

C. Tollefson, "Costs in Public Interest Litigation: Recent Developments and Future Directions" (2009) 35 Advocates' Q. 181. Reproduced from 35 Advocates' Quarterly with the permission of Canada Law Book, A Division of the Cartwright Group, Ltd. (1-800-263-3269, www.canadalawbook.ca).

7

Federal Environmental Assessment

Introduction

Environmental assessments (EAs) differ from many other regulatory tools in that they seek to anticipate, prevent or reduce environmental impacts of proposed new activities rather than try to manage the impacts of existing activities. This ability to anticipate potential environmental effects and influence decision makers to take steps to avoid them has been the great promise of environmental assessment and, at the same time, its greatest challenge. It remains to be seen whether environmental assessment can deliver on this promise.

Most of Canada's environmental assessment laws are of fairly recent vintage. While Canada's first EAs were carried out in the early 1970s, it was not until the 1990s that most Canadian jurisdictions enacted mandatory EA legislation. The *Canadian Environmental Assessment Act* (CEAA) is a case in point, coming into force in 1995.

Due to the diversity of EA regimes across Canada, in this chapter we focus on federal environmental assessment and, in particular, on CEAA. To this end, in Part I we provide short history of EA at the federal level and an introduction to the key concepts and elements of the CEAA. In Part II we then turn to one of the key legal issues that has emerged in the application and interpretation of CEAA, namely, the principles surrounding the "scoping" of projects that are subject to CEAA review. In this Part, we review four of the leading scoping cases under CEAA: *Alberta Wilderness Assn. v. Cardinal River Coals Ltd.*, 1999 CarswellNat 511 (F.C.T.D.); *Friends of the West Country Assn. v. Canada (Minister of Fisheries & Oceans)*, 1999 CarswellNat 2081 (Fed. C.A.); *Prairie Acid Rain Coalition v. Canada (Minister of Fisheries & Oceans)*, 2006 FCA 31; and *Miningwatch Canada v. Canada (Minister of Fisheries & Oceans)*, 2007 FC 955. Finally, in Part III, we consider some of the key challenges that lie ahead under CEAA including scoping; public participation; engagement with First Nations; strategic environmental assessments; and sustainability-based environmental assessment.

Part I — Overview of Federal Environmental Assessment

Environmental assessment has been an important environmental policy tool since the early 1970s. One of the earliest illustrations of EA becoming a legally regulated requirement was under the 1969 *National Environmental Policy Act* (NEPA) in the US. Since the mid 1980s, federal and provincial EA processes in Canada have gradually moved in this direction, evolving from their discretionary roots to towards a more legalized form. In some jurisdictions in Canada, the focus has also shifted from pollution control to a more proactive and comprehensive consideration of proposed activities and alternatives in light of the overall risks and benefits. Many legislated processes have tended to focus on physical projects while some have started to include policies, plans and programs.

Approaches to environmental assessments proposed in Canadian literature have also clearly evolved. The characteristics of a sound EA process are now generally recognized to include several key features. A strong legislative foundation helps to ensure clarity, certainty, fairness and consistency. Procedures, in order to be suitable, have to be able to adapt to the needs of a particular project or activity to be assessed. At the same time, the procedures have to be consistent with basic principles of fairness and openness, and they have to be as consistent and predictable as possible to facilitate public engagement. Public involvement is recognized as an important principle, both in terms of access to the process and the opportunity to influence the decision. All this suggests that EA processes should be orientated toward problem-solving, and that there should be a clear link between the process and decision making. The importance of monitoring and feedback capabilities, to ensure compliance and to evaluate the process and the project, are also increasingly recognized in the literature.

In moving from these principles to the design and implementation of EA processes, there are a number of key issues to be explored. The first is *what human activities are to be covered* by the process. Most EA processes in Canada focus on project based assessments. Projects to be assessed can be listed, they can be identified through a threshold test, or they can be determined through the exercise of either professional or political judgment. However decided, some EA processes are limited to government projects, but most include private developments. Some have focused on large-scale projects, whereas others have included smaller projects. A few have gone beyond projects to provide for assessments of policies, plans and programs.

Closely related to the question of coverage is *the nature of the EA process.* Where the process only applies to large-scale government projects, it may be reasonable to design a "one size fits all" process. Where it includes a broad range of projects, and perhaps even policies, plans and programs, designing processes that are sufficiently flexible to accommodate the range of activities to be assessed while remaining true to the fundamental principles of a sound EA process becomes a challenge. A key challenge is to design processes that identify appropriate roles for the proponent, the public, non-governmental organizations, regulators, other departments within the level of government initiating the assessment, governments other than the level initiating the process, proponents of alternatives, and aboriginal communities.

Another critical issue in the design and implementation of EA processes is the *scope of the assessment* to be carried out. Scope in this context refers to the substance of the assessment. As a starting point, this involves often difficult decisions about the scope of the project, policy, plan or program to be assessed. Does the assessment include the whole activity proposed, or just one component? Does it include only what is proposed by one particular proponent, or does it extend to other activities made possible by allowing a particular proposed activity to proceed? The scope of the assessment also refers to the issues to be addressed. Does the EA focus on biophysical impacts, or include socio-economic effects? What is the role of values, ethical considerations, traditional and aboriginal knowledge in the assessment?

Another key issue in the design and implementation of EA processes is the *nature and implications of the final outcome.* Some EA processes result in binding decisions on the activities assessed, with the decision made by the tribunal responsible for the EA process. At the other end of the spectrum, the EA process can be an information gathering process that is completely separate from the decision-making process. Under such a process, the results of the EA process are simply made available to the decision maker, together with information and a range of possible decisional options.

History of Federal EA in Canada

The federal Cabinet decided in the early 1970s to establish the Federal Environmental Assessment Review Office to oversee the newly established non-legislative EA process. The focus was on a screening process to identify proposed federal projects that had the potential to cause unacceptable pollution. Proposed projects identified through the screening process were expected to go through a more thorough environmental assessment process.[4]

The initial Cabinet decision was followed with a broader Cabinet policy directive in 1973 to carry out an environmental assessment of significant new proposals. The main implication of the 1973 directive was to broaden the application of the act from federal projects to private projects with federal involvement in the form of federal financial support, land, or regulatory oversight. Federal EAs continued to be non-legislative. The determination of whether a full assessment was needed, as well as the design and implementation of the EA process was left in the hands of those responsible for the ultimate project decision.

It was the period from 1974 to 1980 that brought about the first evolution of federal EAs in Canada. A catalyst for this evolution was the Berger Inquiry on the proposed Mackenzie Valley Pipeline, which took place between 1974 and 1977. In many respects, the Berger Inquiry process looks very familiar to anyone who has followed federal EA panel reviews over the past two decades.

In parallel with the Berger Inquiry from 1974 to 1977, the federal EA process was gradually strengthened and formalized as the Environmental Assessment and Review Process (EARP). Some of the changes include encouraging earlier public consultations and not including federal decision makers on review panels if they were involved in proposing the activity to be assessed. Nevertheless, it was still common for major projects to be approved before the environmental assessment was completed or without any assessment.

In the early 1980s, further events influenced the evolution of federal EA. First among these was a proposed new approach to environmental impact assessment published by Beanlands and Duinker in 1983. It has become the most cited, if not always followed, methodology for environmental assessments in Canada. Around the same time, Charles Caccia became the federal Environment Minister and convinced his Cabinet to formalize the EARP process as a guidelines order issued by Cabinet. The guidelines order is drafted in mandatory language. However, federal departments did not consider themselves bound until a series of court cases confirmed the binding nature of the EARP Guidelines Order.

The EARP Guidelines Order was passed in 1984, following both an internal and external review. The guidelines order applies to proposals that are "initiatives, undertakings, and activities" for which the federal government has a "decision making responsibility". During the implementation of the EARP Guidelines Order, it became clear that proposals include not only physical projects and activities, but also policies, plans and programs. At the same time, the requirement that there has to be a "decision making responsibility" for something to be considered a proposal was interpreted narrowly, to mean a legal duty. This duty, for EARP purposes, can relate to the federal government as proponent, financial contributor, land owner, or regulator.

In response to ongoing criticism of the federal EA process under the EARP Guidelines Order and the growing number of successful court challenges involving the federal EA process, the government introduced a bill in 1990 to entrench the federal EA process in legislation in the form of the *Canadian Environmental Assessment Act* (CEAA). The Act was passed in 1992 by the Conservative Government, but proclamation was delayed pending the

---

4 For a more detailed assessment of the federal EA process, see M. Doelle, *The Federal Environmental Assessment Process: A Guide and Critique* (Markham, Ont.: LexixNexis Butterworths, 2008). Portions of this overview are adapted from this publication.

development of key regulations. A change in government in 1993 resulted in further changes by the new Liberal Government and led to proclamation of CEAA in January, 1995.

CEAA Overview

CEAA differs from the EARP Guidelines Order in a number of important ways. The most obvious distinction is that CEAA is set out in legislation. This makes the process less susceptible to interference by government without the approval of Parliament, but also more difficult to update in light of changing circumstances. CEAA is limited in its application to undertakings and physical activities, whereas the EARP Guidelines Order included the assessment of policies, plans and programs. This type of assessment is now left to a separate process under a Cabinet Directive on Strategic Environmental Assessments (SEA).

The so called Law List regulations are also new. They list all regulatory decisions that trigger an environmental assessment under CEAA. The comprehensive study process is an added process option under CEAA. It is designed to be a hybrid between self-assessment in the form of a screening and independent public review in the form of a review panel. The independence of panel members, mediation, more direction on the scope of the assessment, and provision for the assessment of projects with transboundary impacts are among other key features of CEAA.

The preamble of CEAA sets out the key objectives of the federal government in passing the Act:

- to achieve sustainable development
- to conserve and enhanced environmental quality directly
- to promote economic development that conserves and enhances environmental quality
- to integrate environmental factors into planning and decision making that promotes sustainable development
- to facilitate public participation and to provide access to information
- to exercise leadership in anticipating and preventing environmental degradation
- to ensure economic development is compatible with the high value Canadians place on environmental quality

Section 4(1) of CEAA identifies the following purposes:

- to ensure that projects are considered in a careful and precautionary manner
- to ensure that such projects do not cause significant adverse environmental effects
- to encourage responsible authorities to take actions that promote sustainable development
- to ensure EAs are carried out by responsible authorities in a coordinated manner with a view to eliminating unnecessary duplication
- to promote cooperation and coordinate action with provincial governments
- to promote communication and cooperation with Aboriginal peoples
- to ensure that projects do not cause significant adverse environmental effects outside the jurisdiction

- to ensure opportunities for timely and meaningful public participation throughout the environmental assessment process

These provisions suggest an EA process that is fully integrated into decision making, implemented cooperatively with provinces and Aboriginal peoples, engages members of the public in a meaningful manner, is efficient, is precautionary, and leads to sustainable development in Canada. This is the standard set for federal EA in the preamble and purpose sections.

Does the Act Apply?

For many EA processes at the provincial level in Canada, activities which trigger the process are identified through a project list or are left to the discretion of a Minister. A combination of the two is also very common. The application of CEAA, however, is determined through a fairly complex combination of definitions and project lists. There were three principle reasons for the approach taken in CEAA.

The dominant influence on the approach was constitutional. It was thought to be difficult to come up with a list of all projects, or all types of projects, that warrant an environmental assessment and for which there is a sufficient federal role to justify a federal assessment. The second was a concern that a list would tend to exclude unanticipated and new projects, which are sometimes the projects most in need of environmental assessments. The third consideration was to ensure consistent and predictable application of the process, rather than a discretionary one influenced by political considerations.

The definition of "project" is central to determining whether the CEAA process applies. If a proposed activity does not meet the definition of project in section 2 of the Act, the process does not apply. If the proposed activity does meet the definition, the process applies only if additional requirements discussed below are met. The definition has two branches, one for undertakings in relation to a physical work, and one for physical activities not in relation to a physical work.

For those related to a physical work, undertakings (such as construction, operation modification and abandonment) are considered to be projects unless they are excluded through exclusion list regulations. For those not related to a physical work, physical activities are only considered to be projects if they are listed in an inclusion list regulation. Not all activities that meet the definition of project are assessed. Some are excluded for national security reasons, some in case of emergencies, and some can be excluded due to minimal federal involvement in the project.

Projects that are not excluded require an assessment before a federal authority, as defined in section 2, makes a decision under section 5 of the Act. The requirements of section 5 are central to the application of the CEAA process. They identify the federal decisions that trigger an assessment under the Act. They also set a minimum expectation of the timing for the completion of the EA process. If no section 5 decision is required, the project does not trigger an assessment under CEAA.

The requirements of section 5 have created practical difficulties in cases where it was unclear for one reason or another whether a section 5 decision would be required. For example, section 35 of the *Fisheries Act* requires an approval in case of alteration of fish habitat. Whether a project causes an alteration of fish habitat may not be known for certain until the late design stages of the project, much later than an EA process should ideally be initiated.

Alternative triggers to section 5 are available in sections 46 to 48, generally referred to as the transboundary provisions of the Act. Under these sections, the Minister can, in certain circumstances, initiate an environmental assessment of a project even in the absence of a section 5 decision, if the project is expected to have environmental effects across provincial or international boundaries or on federal lands.

In summary, the Act applies to projects that involve decisions by one or more federal authority. Some projects are specifically excluded. The terms "federal authority" and "project" are defined in Section 2. Some projects are excluded from the application of the Act, either through exclusion lists in regulations or through statutory provisions. Not all decisions of federal authorities that relate to projects trigger an environmental assessment. Only decisions included in Section 5 of the Act trigger assessment of a project. Sections 46 to 48 provide alternative triggers for projects with transboundary implications.

Scoping Basics

The term "scoping" refers to the process of deciding what will be included in, and excluded from, an environmental assessment. Scoping involves determining both the scope of the activity to be assessed and the scope of the assessment to be carried out. In other words, scoping requires decision makers to determine exactly what is to be assessed, and what questions are to be answered through the assessment. Under CEAA, the pre-condition for the scoping process is a determination that there is a project, as defined in the Act, for which a federal authority is exercising a duty, power, or function included in section 5. Section 5, in combination with the definitions of project and federal authority, determines whether an assessment of a given project is to be carried out. Sections 15 and 16 determine the scope of the project and the scope of the assessment to be carried out under the Act respectively.

Decisions on scope are critical to the environmental assessment process. They determine how the project is defined for purposes of the assessment, what issues can be raised, and what impacts will be considered. As a result, scoping can have a fundamental impact on the assessment process and on the final decision. The narrower a project is scoped, the narrower will be the range of environmental impacts considered. For example, the environmental impacts of an entire forestry operation will be far broader than the environmental impacts of only a stream crossing. The broader the scope, the more time and resources will likely be required to complete the assessment.

Scoping has been the subject of much litigation over CEAA since its entry into force in 1995. Some of the central cases are included in Part II of this chapter. In particular, these cases explore the limits of the discretion of federal decision makers in determining the scope of the project to be assessed, the factors to be considered in the assessment and the scope of those factors. Key among the many issues explored in the long line of cases on scoping are the interpretation of section 15(3) on the scope of the project, cumulative effects, the consideration of alternatives and alterative means, and the role of the public in the scoping process.

Process Options

There are four process options under the Act. Assessments can be carried out by way of a screening, a comprehensive study, a panel review, mediation, or some combination of these four processes. Screenings and comprehensive studies are generally regarded as alternative forms of self assessment, whereas mediation and panel reviews are more independent forms of assessment. It is important to remember, for all process options, that they only apply if the Act is triggered as described above.

More than 99% of all projects that trigger the EA process under CEAA undergo a screening level assessment only. The screening process is designed to impose minimal process and substantive requirements, thereby offering maximum flexibility to federal decision makers responsible for the EA process of a particular project. At any time before, during or after a screening of a project, a responsible authority or the Minister of the Environment can decide that a panel review is the more appropriate process option and refer the project to a panel. Screening level assessments can be further streamlined through the use of model and replacement class screening options.

Key mandatory steps in the screening process include public notice of commencement of the assessment, determination of the scope of project and assessment, preparation of the screening report, and the final project decision. Coordination among federal decision makers and with other jurisdictions depends on the nature and extent of the involvement of multiple decision makers and jurisdictions. Transparency and public engagement obligations are limited to certain notice requirements and minimum waiting periods before decision making. Active public engagement in scoping, the preparation of the screening report and the final decision is discretionary.

Follow-up is also within the discretion of federal decision makers on a project by project basis. Process and final project decisions are made by responsible authorities. These are federal decision makers with section 5 responsibilities for the project being assessed. Responsible authorities are required to make final decisions in light of the outcome of the EA process. A fundamental question in this process is whether the project is likely to cause significant adverse environmental effects. Depending on the answer to this question, responsible authorities have different options to exercise their powers, duties or functions, to refuse to do so, or to impose conditions.

About 5 to 10 comprehensive studies are carried out under the Act in an average year. Comprehensive studies are required as the minimum level of assessment for all projects that meet the description of projects listed in the comprehensive study regulations. A comprehensive study, while still considered a form of self assessment, is really a hybrid between a screening and a panel review. It is similar to a screening in the sense that the responsible authorities retain control over much of the process and the final project decision. It is similar to a panel review in that it includes mandatory public engagement at all critical steps in the process, as well as a participant funding program. The minimum standard for the scope of the assessment of a comprehensive study is also the same as for a panel review.

Key mandatory steps in the comprehensive study include and build on those required for a screening. After the notice of commencement of the EA, a comprehensive study includes mandatory public engagement at the scoping stage, during the preparation of the environmental assessment report and before the project decision. In addition, a comprehensive study involves a final track decision. This means that contrary to the screening process, a formal decision is made early in the comprehensive study process to either continue with the comprehensive study or refer the project to a review panel. The decision is usually made in conjunction with the scoping decision. The public has to be given an opportunity to comment before the decision is made, and the decision, once made, is final.

All comprehensive studies are coordinated by the CEA Agency. This is the agency that coordinates various responsible authorities and with other jurisdictions interested in the federal EA. Coordination includes the identification of responsible authorities, the scoping decisions, the preparation and review of the environmental assessment report and the project decision. It is important, however, to note that the power of the Agency as coordinator is generally limited to process. It cannot impose decisions on whether a federal decision maker is a responsible authority. It cannot make scoping decisions, and it cannot prescribe final project decisions for responsible authorities.

The Minister of the Environment, who is not involved in a screening other than to decide whether a panel review is warranted, is given an enhanced role in a comprehensive study. Most notably, the Minister is required to review the comprehensive study report, seek public input, and essentially determine whether the process is ready for responsible authorities to make final project decisions. Responsible authorities are then required to make final decisions in light of the outcomes of the EA process, and in particular, considering whether the project is likely to cause significant adverse environmental effects. As is the case for screenings, responsible authorities have different options to exercise their powers, duties or functions, to refuse to do so, or to impose conditions. Follow-up is mandatory for all comprehensive studies.

Panel reviews make up between one and five assessments initiated under the Act in a given year. Key differences between comprehensive studies and panel reviews include the following:

- The process is taken out of the hands of responsible authorities and placed in the hands of independent panel members
- Panel reviews have, as a matter of practice, always involved public hearings, something that is less clear for comprehensive studies
- Panel reviews involve an enhanced role for the Minister of the Environment, most notably with respect to scoping
- The final project decision is subject to Cabinet approval.

The key process decisions in a panel review are made by the Minister, while the implementation of the process is left to an independent panel. Once the decision to refer a project to a panel is made, the Minister determines the scope of the project, the scope of the assessment, sets the terms of reference of the panel, and appoints panel members. In practice, the panel is often involved in the scoping process, and frequently will hold scoping hearings. Once the scoping determination is made, the review panel takes control over the process in accordance with the terms of reference issued by the Minister. It establishes procedures, holds hearings, reviews oral and written submissions, and prepares recommendations for decision makers. Section 34 outlines the key responsibilities of the panel:

- Ensure that the required information is obtained and made available to the public.
- Hold hearings in a manner that offers the public an opportunity to participate in the assessment.
- Prepare a report that includes conclusions, recommendations and a summary of comments received from the public.
- Submit the report to the Minister and the responsible authority.

A review panel may summon any person to appear as a witness to give evidence and produce documents considered necessary for the assessment. The panel has the same powers as a court of record, and its orders can be enforced in the Federal Court.

At the conclusion of the EA process, the panel prepares a final report on the results of the environmental assessment. The report will usually identify whether the project is likely to cause significant adverse environmental effects, and whether it should be allowed to proceed. If the panel recommends that the project be permitted to proceed, it will usually propose conditions and make other recommendations on how to minimize any adverse effect and maximize expected benefits. Panels, commonly, also comment on the contribution the project is expected to make to sustainable development.

The Minister has the responsibility to make the panel report available to the public. The report is then used by the responsible authority, with the approval of the Governor in Council, to determine whether to exercise its powers, duties and functions to allow the project to proceed. The determination that the project can proceed can be made either on the basis that the project is not likely to cause significant adverse environmental effects, or that significant effects are justified in the circumstances. If the Governor in Council decides that the project can proceed based on the environmental assessment carried out by the panel, responsible authorities may still have discretion to decide whether to exercise their powers, duties and functions under section 5. The panel's recommendations, beyond applying the "likely significant" test, can be invaluable in assisting responsible authorities to make determinations consistent with the purposes of the Act.

Public participation is a key feature of panel reviews. The importance of public participation is reflected by additional transparency measures. Included in the concept of transparency are public notices of important steps in the process, direct access to the panel through hearings, and access to relevant information and documentation through the electronic and paper registries. Intervenor funding and the ability to adjust the nature of the hearing to the cultural norms or preferences of those interested in participating are other strengths of the public participation process for panel reviews.

In addition to the standard panel review process, CEAA provides for joint panel reviews with other jurisdictions and for panel substitutions. A joint panel process allows for cooperation between the federal government and other jurisdictions, such as provinces. It generally involves each jurisdiction appointing some of the panel members and an agreement on how the joint process will meet the legal requirements of the jurisdictions involved. Issues covered in such agreements for joint panel reviews commonly include the scope of the assessment, timelines, intervenor funding, and other procedural issues. These agreements have most commonly taken the form of project-specific memorandums of understanding, but they can also be in the form of generic harmonization agreements.

Panel substitution is different from joint panels in a number of ways. First of all, substitution is only possible under the Act with suitable federal processes. Secondly, a substitution is only possible if the Minister of the Environment is of the opinion that a federal process is suitable and will adequately address the factors required for a panel review under section 16. The power to accept a substitute process is set out in subsection 43(1) of CEAA.

Mediation is available informally in most EA processes. Its function in those circumstances is to complement rather than replace the formal process. Most EA processes can accommodate a mediation process as part of the traditional EA process. In CEAA, for example, there is nothing in the Act to prevent a responsible authority in the context of a screening or a comprehensive study, or a panel in case of a panel review, from appointing a mediator to resolve a particular issue. In addition to this informal use of mediation, CEAA also provides for mediation as a separate process option. In such cases, mediation replaces any other process requirements and the mediation report is used like any other EA report by the responsible authority to make its final project decision. The discretion to refer a project to mediation rests with the Minister of the Environment. The Minister can exercise this discretion if the interested parties have been identified and are willing to participate in the mediation.

It is instructive to consider mediation in comparison to the traditional CEAA process options. Mediation is similar to a panel review in a number of ways. First, the process is taken out of the hands of responsible authorities and placed in the hands of someone independent of proponent, intervenors and government decision makers. As is the case for panel members, the mediator is appointed by the Minister of the Environment, not by responsible authorities. Responsibility for scoping decisions also rest with the Minister of the Environment.

Furthermore, responsible authorities retain control over the substantive outcome in the form of the final project decision.

A key difference between mediation and a panel review is the form of interaction among participants, and the role of the mediator versus the panel. The mediator seeks consensus among participants, the panel evaluates the information and positions put forward and applies its own judgment to provide advice to the project decision makers. Furthermore, the role of intervenors is very different.

On the one hand, an intervenor is, subject to resources and capacity, an equal participant in the mediation process, whereas its role in a panel review is to provide information and take positions without any control over how that information is used. On the other hand, panel reviews can accommodate very different levels of involvement from intervenors, whereas mediation can only accommodate full participation. This means that, practically, opportunities for public engagement are limited to those who can commit to the level of engagement necessary to make a mediation process work.

Finally, there is no guarantee that there will be any result from a mediation process. In a panel review, the panel will make its recommendations regardless of whether participants can agree on whether and under what conditions a project should proceed.

Notes and Questions

1. Do you think the process for determining whether CEAA applies is effective? Assuming you have to operate within the existing constitutional structure, is there a better way to decide which projects trigger the CEAA process? What about a "list" approach as is used in many provinces?

2. A critical term in the definition of project is the term "physical work", yet there is no definition in the Act. Consider whether the following are physical works and the implications for the application of the two branches of the definition: an air plane, a vessel, a mobile incinerator, a beaver dam. Based on this, can you come up with a working definition of "physical works"?

3. Carefully consider the strengths and weaknesses of the four process options under CEAA. Is there one that you think should be applied to all projects? Why? If not, which process is best suited for what type of project? How would you legislate the selection of the appropriate process for the appropriate project?

4. Assuming that screenings are intended for small and routine projects, comprehensive studies for medium size projects and panel reviews for large and controversial projects, how can each process be improved to achieve greater efficiency, greater effectiveness, or both?

5. When do you think the mediation process should be used? How can its use be encouraged?

6. The design of the four process options is based in part on the assumption that federal decision makers who have decision making responsibilities for a project, such as those set out in Section 5, are not always in the best position to make process and substantive decisions on the EA process. Do you agree? Would you distinguish between the four categories of federal decisions identified in section 5? Explain.

Part II — The Evolution of Scoping under CEAA

Scoping is a critical step in any EA process. It is also likely the most contentious aspect of the federal EA regime due to the perception that, in some cases, the scoping power has been manipulated by responsible authorities (RAs) to shield projects from meaningful public review. Likewise, some have argued that courts have compounded this problem by being overly deferential when called upon to review RA scoping decisions.

It is at the scoping stage that decisions are made about what is assessed during the course of an assessment under CEAA, and in how much detail. These decisions are central to the capacity of the process to deliver on the principles and purposes set out in the Act, most notably to deliver an effective and efficient process that informs decision making consistent with sustainable development.

It is not surprising, therefore, that much of the litigation over the first decade of CEAA has been over scoping decisions. A key issue throughout has been the exercise of discretion by responsible authorities and the Minister of the Environment in determining the scope of a project under section 15 and the scope of the assessment under section 16. Much of the litigation has sought to determine what limits these and related provisions of the Act impose on the discretion of decision makers to determine the appropriate scope of the project and the assessment.

One of the challenges with the use of discretion in the scoping process has been the wide range of perspectives different RAs have brought to the process. RAs range in their core responsibilities from environmental protection to resource management, transportation, economic development and industry promotion. The implication for the exercise of discretion on scoping is not surprising. Nevertheless, as evident from the cases to follow, courts have tended to apply a high degree of judicial deference when reviewing scoping decisions.

Judicial review of scoping decisions under CEAA has, to date, been inconsistent. For its part, the Federal CA has a highly deferential approach to reviewing scoping decisions made by RAs under the Act. This non-interventionist approach is evident in *TrueNorth* (C.A., 2004) and most recently *Red Chris* (F.C.A., 2008). On the other hand, at the trial level, the Federal Court has been significantly more receptive to scoping-related challenges: see *Sunpine* (T.D., 1998); *Cheviot* (T.D., 1999); and *Red Chris* (T.D., 2007). Key scoping issues addressed in the caselaw include the nature of the discretion vested in the RA to determine the *scope of a project* under s. 15. This issue plays a key role in *TrueNorth* (C.A., 2004) excerpted below. Another set of scoping-related issues arises in the interpretation of the requirements of s. 16 which mandates consideration of cumulative effects and, in some circumstances, an analysis of alternatives to a project, alternative means of carrying out a project, and the need for the project. Judicial treatment of this set of issues, that pertain to the *scope of the assessment*, is addressed in the other two cases excerpted in this Part: namely, *Cheviot* (T.D., 1999) and *Sunpine* (C.A., 1999).

. . . . .

Alberta Wilderness Assn. v. Cardinal River Coals Ltd.
1999 CarswellNat 511 (F.C.T.D.)

[This litigation, often referred to as the "Cheviot" case, gave rise to one of the earliest yet still influential decisions under CEAA. In this case, the Alberta Wilderness Association (AWA) challenged the adequacy of an environmental assessment carried out by one of the first-ever review panels to be established under CEAA. The proposed Cheviot Coal Project was an open pit coal mine that the proponent, Cardinal River Coals Ltd., planned to construct and operate near the eastern boundary of Jasper National Park. The mine's lifespan was projected to be 20 years. As such, the AWA argued it would have significant ongoing environmental effects on the surrounding environment. The main issues presented by the case were the duties of a (joint) review panel, and requirements under section 16 to consider the cumulative effects of the proposed mine and alternative means of carrying out the project.]

. . . . .

Campbell J.:

In March 1996, Cardinal River Coals Ltd. ("CRC") submitted applications to obtain Alberta regulatory approvals and a Federal Department of Fisheries and Oceans ("DFO") authorization to construct a 23 km. long and 3.5 km. wide open pit coal mine in its mine permit area located 2.8 km. east of the Jasper National Park boundary.

The applicants have voiced substantial concerns about the Cheviot Coal Project ("the Project"), and commenced this judicial review to challenge the DFO authorization ("the Authorization") issued which allows work to begin on the Project. The challenge attacks the Authorization itself, and the environmental assessment which is a pre-condition to its issuance, with the intention of having the public environmental assessment process re-opened to address environmental concerns which, they argue, were not properly considered.

Factual Background and Issues

The Project involves excavating a series of 30 or more open pits, and the construction of associated infrastructure which includes roads, rail lines and the installation of a new transmission line for the supply of electricity. The undertaking will generate millions of tonnes of waste rock which will be deposited on site in stream valleys and other areas.

The Project, being undertaken on the Eastern Slopes of the Rocky Mountains close to the eastern boundary of Jasper National Park, is located in an environmentally rich area that is home to a variety of wildlife. It is argued that the construction and operation of the Project, which is expected to be in operation for 20 years, will have a dramatic impact on the immediate and surrounding environment.

Section 35(2) of the federal *Fisheries Act* requires that an authorization be obtained from the Minister prior to the alteration, disruption, or destruction of fish habitat. In May 1996, CRC applied to DFO for the appropriate authorizations required under the *Fisheries Act*, in connection with the Project. However, before the Minister of Fisheries and Oceans (the "Minister") may issue an authorization for a project in compliance with the *Fisheries Act*, an environmental assessment must be conducted pursuant to s. 5(1)(d) of the *Canadian Environmental Assessment Act* (*CEAA*) Accordingly, the Minister became the responsible authority for the project pursuant to s. 11(1) of *CEAA*.

A comprehensive study was commenced but, before it was completed, the Minister concluded that the Project may potentially result in significant adverse environmental effects and, therefore, should be referred to a panel under *CEAA*. Since an environmental review was also required under Alberta legislation, the federal Minister of Environment and the Alberta Energy and Utilities Board ("EUB") agreed to hold a joint federal and provincial review as is provided for under *CEAA*, and, to that end, signed the "Agreement for the Cheviot Coal Project", dated October 24, 1996 ("Joint Panel Agreement").

The Joint Panel Agreement set out the terms of reference for the EUB-*CEAA* Joint Review Panel ("the Joint Review Panel"), including the factors that they were required to consider in conducting the environmental assessment.

The Project was referred to the Joint Review Panel in the fall of 1996 and hearings were conducted from January 13, 1997 to February 20, 1997, with an additional hearing date on April 10, 1997.

On June 17, 1997, the Joint Review Panel issued its report and recommendations entitled "*Report of the EUB-CEAA Joint Review Panel: Cheviot Coal Project, Mountain Park Area, Alberta*" ("the Joint Review Panel Report") which recommended that the Minister approve the Project by providing CRC with the necessary regulatory authorizations under the *Fisheries Act*. [. . .]

On August 17, 1998, the Minister, pursuant to s. 35(2) of the *Fisheries Act*, issued the Authorization, which is the first of a series of authorizations required for the Project. The Authorization allowed CRC to begin construction of the access corridor for the Project.

[*Ed note*: The AWA then brought on this application for judicial review. Its main argument was that the Joint Review Panel erred in failing to comply with its obligations under s. 16 of the *CEAA* and with Joint Panel Agreement. In the following excerpt, the trial judge addresses this argument by first by considering the nature of the duties vested in the JRP, and secondly by considering whether the JRP had complied with those duties.] [. . .]

Legal Context

The Provisions of CEAA

An overview of duties under *CEAA* is conveniently expressed as follows:

- **Information-gathering**: the review panel must ensure that all information required for an assessment is obtained and made available (s. 34(a)) and hold hearings to foster public participation (s. 34(b)).
- **Considerations**: the panel must conduct an environmental assessment (EA) of the project which includes, *inter alia*, an assessment of all related operations and undertakings (s. 15), and consideration of cumulative environmental effects and their significance (ss. 16(1)(a) and (b)), mitigation measures (s. 16(1)(d)), the need for and alternatives to the project (s. 16(1)(e)), alternative means of carrying out the project and the environmental effects of those alternatives (s. 16(2)(b)), and the capacity of affected renewable resources to be sustained (s. 16(2)(d)).
- **Report**: the panel must prepare a report which includes the rationale, conclusions, and recommendations of the panel regarding the matters considered in the EA, and a summary of any public comments (s. 34(c)).
- **Decision**: the responsible authority (RA) must respond to the report, with the approval of the Governor in Council (s. 37(1)(a)). Then, the RA (in this case the Minister of Fisheries and Oceans) may take a course of action under s. 37(1), i.e. make a decision. If the project is likely to cause significant adverse environmental effects, the RA may approve the project only if its effects "can be justified in the circumstances" (s. 37(1)(a)). [. . .]

Precedent Interpreting the Provisions of CEAA

Two decisions clearly define the legal importance of the environmental assessment and the standard to be applied respecting its sufficiency.

1. — The Appeal Division decision in A-430-98 respecting T-2354-97

Adapted to the present application, the points that emerge from Sexton J.A.'s decision are these: the environmental assessment carried out by the Joint Review Panel in accordance with *CEAA* is a pre-condition to the issuance of the Authorization; the assessment must be conducted in accordance with the *CEAA*, including the requirements of s. 16; and a "proper" assessment is one conducted in accordance with *CEAA*. I take this last statement to mean that an assessment which is not conducted in accordance with *CEAA* is one conducted in error of law.

2. — Alberta Wilderness Assn. v. Express Pipelines Ltd.

The principle that an environmental assessment can be challenged and found not to be in accordance with *CEAA* on an error in law was previously established in *Alberta Wilderness Assn. v. Express Pipelines Ltd.* Adapted to the present application, the points that emerge from Hugessen J.A.'s decision are these: the Joint Review Panel's failure to comply with a requirement of s. 16 of *CEAA* can constitute an error of law; it is important to appropriately characterize a perceived failure to comply as a question of law or merely an attack on the "quality" of the evidence and, therefore, the "correctness" of the conclusions drawn on that evidence; if a perceived failure is in the latter category, no question of law arises and, therefore, the conclusions of the Joint Review Panel stemming from an uncontested high degree of expertise in environmental matters, must not lightly be interfered with; determining the "significance" of an environmental effect under s. 16(1)(b) of *CEAA* involves a subjective determination by the Joint Review Panel and does not involve an interpretation leading to possible error in law; the "alternative means" to be considered under s. 16(2)(b) are circumscribed by the scope of the environmental assessment set by the Joint Panel Agreement; and mitigation measures and environmental effects are properly considered together.

It is important to note that, in *Alberta Wilderness Assn. v. Express Pipelines Ltd.* the Appeal Division found that the joint review panel in that case conducted a "full and thorough environmental assessment". This is, therefore, a qualitative finding which, as a practical matter, contributed to arguments on the sufficiency of the panel report to be rejected. In effect, the Appeal Division found that the panel in that case met its statutory duties of information gathering and reporting.

Therefore, the primary question is whether the Joint Review Panel in the present case has met its statutory information gathering and reporting duties. If a duty is found to be breached, as a misinterpretation of a legal requirement, it is an error of law. It is uncontested that if such a finding is made, the standard of review of the error is correctness.

The Joint Review Panel: Duties

Section 35(2) of the *Fisheries Act* requires that an authorization be obtained from the Minister of Fisheries and Oceans prior to the alteration, disruption, or destruction of fish habitat. Under the CEA Act, prior to issuing such an authorization, an environmental assessment of the project must be undertaken. Following notification by CRC as to its intention to apply for the above authorization, the DFO, as a Responsible Authority under the CEA Act, initiated a review of the proposed project. In a letter dated 26 August 1996 to the Minister of the Environment, the Minister of Fisheries and Oceans stated that, following a review of CRC's environmental information, the DFO had determined that the project may potentially result in significant adverse environmental effects. In order to expedite the review process, the Minister of Fisheries and Oceans recommended that the Cheviot Coal Project should be referred by the Minister of the Environment for review by a panel and further recommended, in the spirit of the 1993 Canada/Alberta Harmonization Agreement for Environmental Assessment, that the CEAA attempt to integrate this panel review through a Joint Review Panel, with any hearing process required by the EUB.

Sections 40 and 41 of the CEA Act provide for the establishment and appointment of a Joint Review Panel and for the factors to be considered by a Joint Review Panel.

Decision Making and Recommendation Duty

As can be seen, the two distinct Alberta and Federal regulatory processes set different obligations for the Joint Review Panel to meet. The difference between the two is clearly set out in the following passage from the Joint Review Panel Report:

> There are significant differences worth noting in the role of the Panel in a combined provincial and federal decision-making process. Under the Alberta provincial statutes, the Panel is charged with determining whether a proposed energy development is in the public interest. In making its determination as to whether a project is in the public interest, the Panel is required to consider a range of factors, including resource conservation, safety, economic and social impacts of the project, and effects on the environment. Its decision, including reasons, is documented in a Decision Report.
>
> Under the CEA Act, the Panel is required to submit to the Minister of the Environment and to the Responsible Authority (in this case DFO) a report which provides its rationale, conclusions, and recommendations relating to the environmental assessment of the project, including any mitigation measures and follow-up programs. No decision on federal issues is made by the Panel. Section 37 of the CEA Act authorizes the Responsible Authority to exercise its power to allow a project to proceed if,

> taking into account the report submitted by a review panel and any mitigation measures, its adverse environmental effects are deemed to be insignificant or, if they are significant, felt to be justified in the circumstances.
>
> As per the agreement between the EUB and CEAA, the Panel intends to issue a single Decision Report designed to meet the requirements of both levels of government.

Therefore, in the present case, the Joint Review Panel has two roles to fulfill: Alberta decision making, and Federal recommending. The statutory schemes leading to the review reflects this difference. The Alberta scheme has the Joint Review Panel decision as the last step in a process which has first tested for deficiencies in the Environmental Impact Assessment (EIA) produced by CRC, whereas the Federal process has the Joint Review Panel recommendation as the first step in the decision making to be conducted thereafter. Under *CEAA*, apart from the determination that the project may result in significant adverse environmental effects, prior to the Joint Review Panel's review activities, no pre-determination of sufficiency had occurred.

Therefore, the essential point is that, to satisfy the Minister's concern about the Project, the *CEAA* information gathering investigation can reasonably be expected to go farther than that necessary to meet Alberta requirements.

Consideration, Information Gathering, and Reporting Duties under CEAA and the Joint Panel Agreement

Consideration duty

The general duty set out in s. 16(1) and s. 16(2) is as follows:

> 16. (1) Every screening or comprehensive study of a project and every mediation or assessment by a review panel *shall include a consideration* of the following factors: . . .
>
> (2) In addition to the factors set out in subsection (1), every comprehensive study of a project and every mediation or assessment by a review panel *shall include a consideration* of the following factors: . . . [Emphasis added]

Section 41 of *CEAA* requires that a joint panel agreement include the factors required to be considered under s. 16(1) and (2), and also provides that additional "requirements" can be set out. [. . .]

With regard to the scope of the consideration to be undertaken by the Joint Review Panel, s. 41(c) of *CEAA* requires that the Minister "shall fix or approve the terms of reference for the panel". Schedule 1 to the Joint Panel Agreement in the present case, named "Terms of Reference for the Panel of the Cheviot Coal Project", sets out the terms of reference for consideration of the Project, and requires that: The Panel will include in its review of the Cheviot Coal Project consideration of the factors identified in Appendix 1. The Joint Review Panel's consideration of the factors listed in Appendix 1 shall be reflected in the Final Report.

With regard to the s. 16 *CEAA* factors to be considered by the Joint Review Panel, it is not contested that, in somewhat different wording, Appendix 1 to Schedule 1 of the Joint Panel Agreement requires that the factors listed in the following sections of *CEAA* are to be considered by the Joint Review Panel: s. 16(1)(a): environmental effects, including cumulative effects; s. 16(1)(b): significance of the effects; s. 16(1)(c): public comments; s. 16(1)(d): mitigating measures; s. 16(1)(e): need for the project and alternatives to the project; and s. 16(2)(b): alternative means of carrying out the project.

In addition, the opening words of Appendix 1 to the Joint Panel Agreement require as follows:

> For the purposes of the EUB, the Panel shall determine whether the Cheviot Coal Project is in the public interest, having regard to the social and economic effects of the project and the effects of the project on the environment and shall consider but not be limited to the factors itemized below. These

> factors will also be considered by the Panel in developing and substantiating conclusions and recommendations for federal decision makers: . . .

I find that in the present case, given the Minister's conclusion that "the project may potentially result in significant adverse environmental effects", and the just identified need for information to be gathered to meet *CEAA* requirements as opposed to Alberta requirements, to meet the "consideration" duty in s. 16 of *CEAA* the Joint Review Panel is required to perform to a high standard of care.

Information gathering duty

A mandatory requirement of a *CEAA* environmental assessment is set out in s. 34(a) as follows:

> 34. A review panel shall, in accordance with any regulations made for that purpose and with its term of reference,
>
> > (a) ensure that *the information required for an assessment by a review panel is obtained* and made available to the public; . . . [Emphasis added]

However, Schedule 1 of the Joint Panel Agreement states:

> 4. The Panel will ensure that *all information required for the conduct of its review is obtained* and made available to the public, which will include, but is not necessarily limited to:
>
> > a) existing technical, environmental or other information relevant to the review, including documents filed in connection with applications No. 960313, and 960314 to the EUB and comments and critique on these documents,
> >
> > b) supplementary information including a description of any public consultation program, its nature and scope, issues identified, commitments made, and outstanding issues,
> >
> > c) the terms of reference for the EIA, dated January 23, 1995, for the Cheviot Coal Project and documentation generated by the proponent, and other interested parties, in response to these terms of reference,
> >
> > d) *any other available information that is required to assess the significance of the Environmental Effects.* [Emphasis added]

I find that the italicized words of paragraph 4 of Schedule 1 have an amplifying effect on the requirements of s. 34(a) of *CEAA* and create a clear and onerous evidence gathering duty on the Joint Review Panel in the present case, being the duty to obtain *all available information* that is required to conduct the environmental assessment.

Respecting the use of the phrase "all information required" in paragraph 4, with respect to the *CEAA* aspect of the Joint Review Panel's duty, I find that what is "required" is that which will meet the just found high standard of care respecting consideration of the s. 16 factors, and the onerous evidence gathering duty on the Joint Review Panel.

I also find that the information gathering duty of the Joint Review Panel does not depend on the Project proponent CRC's information gathering success, nor does it depend on that of any intervenor or interested party. The duty is the Joint Review Panel's to meet.

The Joint Review Panel is provided with ample powers to compel the production of evidence . . . [under] section 35 of *CEAA*. [*Ed note*: Recitation of s. 35 omitted.]

Reporting duty

The opening words of Appendix 1 to the Joint Panel Agreement quoted above require that "[the factors listed in Appendix 1] will also be considered by the [Joint Review] Panel in developing and *substantiating conclusions* and recommendations for federal decision makers". Therefore, by these words, I find it is reasonable to conclude that the Joint Review Panel is required to substantiate the recommendations made for the purposes of *CEAA*. [. . .]

Obviously, the Joint Review Panel Report has a multifaceted advisory purpose. First, the public has a right to know the basis for recommendations made in order to know how to respond legally or politically; similarly, federal decision makers must know the evidentiary basis for any recommendation made in order to assign it weight in formulating an appropriate response.

Granted, there might be gaps in the evidence about cumulative environmental effects. Where such is the case, the *Canadian Environmental Assessment Act Responsible Authority Guide* properly suggests that the professional expertise of the panel members can be applied to fill the gaps.

However, in my opinion, the suggestion that gaps in the evidence can be filled by expert opinion only applies where the evidence is not available; that is, where either it does not exist or is inaccessible.

By the provisions of s. 35 of *CEAA*, which provide production of evidence powers, including confidential evidence, I find that the Joint Review Panel has a duty to use these powers to the full extent necessary to, in the words of paragraph 4 of Schedule 1, obtain and make available "all information required for the conduct of its review".

I find that to meet this duty it is incumbent on the Joint Review Panel to require the production of information which it knows exists, and which is apparently relevant to one or more of the s. 16 factors. In my opinion, it is not sufficient to withdraw from this duty to fill a gap in the evidence with subjective, albeit, expert opinion, when actual information is known to be available. [. . .]

I find that to meet its reporting obligations, the Joint Review Panel must clearly state its recommendations in the Joint Review Panel Report, including the evidence it has relied upon in reaching each recommendation. I also find that if the Joint Review Panel decides to fill a gap in the evidence with its own expert opinion, it must clearly state this to be the case and give an explanation for why doing so is necessary. In this way, the *CEAA* decision maker, and the public, will be able to decide the weight to be placed on each recommendation reached. [. . .]

The Joint Review Panel: Breach of Duty?: Cumulative Effects

Extent of the Duty to Consider Cumulative Effects

CEAA and Joint Panel Agreement requirements

The duty set under *CEAA* is contained in s. 16(1)(a) as follows:

> 16. (1) Every screening or comprehensive study of a project and every mediation or assessment by a review panel shall include a consideration of the following factors:
>
> > (a) the environmental effects of the project, including the environmental effects of malfunctions or accidents that may occur in connection with the project and any cumulative environmental effects that are likely to result from the project in combination with other projects or activities that have been or *will be carried out*; . . . [Emphasis added]

In addition, paragraph 3 of Appendix 1 of the Joint Panel Agreement reads as follows:

> The Environmental Effects of the Cheviot Coal Project including the Environmental Effects of malfunctions or accidents that may occur in connection with the Cheviot Coal Project and any cumulative Environmental Effects that are likely to result from the Cheviot Coal Project in combination with other projects or activities that have been or *are likely to be carried out*. [Emphasis added]

By comparing the above two provisions it can be seen that the requirements of *CEAA* are amplified by the Joint Panel Agreement: that is, in the former, the cumulative effects that are likely to result from the Project are to be considered in combination with others that "have been or *will be carried out*", while in the latter, cumulative effects are to be considered in combination with others that "have been or *are likely to be carried out*". Thus, the Joint

Panel Agreement requires that certain projects which have not yet been approved are to be considered.

Federal concerns

In its submission to the Joint Review Panel, the DFO clearly stated that one of its concerns relating to the Project is "the loss/degradation of stream habitat due to mine development which in conjunction with creation of multiple pit lakes in the area may affect the function and integrity of the aquatic ecosystems involved". In particular, DFO cited as an effect of loss/alteration of stream habitat the cumulative impacts of "multiple developments (e.g., the proposed mine development and forestry)".

The Joint Review Panel Report acknowledges that Parks Canada expressed concern that "the Cheviot Coal Project, as proposed, clearly has the potential to adversely impact the ecological integrity of Jasper National Park". In this respect Parks Canada recommended that "the cumulative effects/core area assessment should be expanded to include other planned or foreseeable human activities (eg. timber harvesting, mineral and oil and gas exploration and development, recreation, etc.) in the larger analysis area .."..

Therefore, the Joint Review Panel was certainly on notice that consideration of cumulative effects should include forestry and other mining development. On the basis of the above analysis of the requirements of *CEAA* in combination with the Joint Panel Agreement, I find that the Joint Review Panel had a duty to obtain all available information about likely forestry and mining in the vicinity of the Project, to consider this information with respect to cumulative environmental effects, to reach conclusions and make recommendations about this factor, and to substantiate these conclusions and recommendations in the Joint Review Panel Report.

Meeting the Duty

Forestry

Respecting forestry activities in the vicinity of the Project, the Joint Review Panel made the following statement:

> The Panel also notes that CRC, in attempting to carry out an assessment of potential cumulative effects (CEA), stated that it was unable to obtain the necessary information from other industry sources, particularly forestry. The Panel can appreciate the difficulty that this creates for an applicant. Given that a CEA is a requirement of both the provincial and federal EIA process, the Panel believes that the government has a responsibility for ensuring either that needed data can be collected or alternatively, that the current legislation is amended to recognize the limitations that lack of cooperation between industry sectors or companies within a sector can create for a CEA. In this particular case, the Panel notes that CRC was able to use data from the Tri-Creeks watershed as a surrogate measure of the likely effects of modern forestry practices on both discharge rates and water quality, and found little evidence of impact. Therefore, the Panel does not expect the cumulative effects of coal mining and forestry at present/predicted levels to have a significant impact on regional fisheries resources, or reduce their capacity as renewable resources, to meet either present or future needs.

I find that this statement proves two facts: the Joint Review Panel did not obtain "necessary information", and the Joint Review Panel determined that it was not its obligation to obtain the information.

In fact, information respecting likely future forestry activities in the vicinity of the Project site is available. Subsequent to the judicial review hearing of T-2354-97 before McKeown J., the Appeal Division allowed the filing of new evidence to prove this point.. The same evidence has been filed in the present application.. The evidence conclusively proves that extensive logging and road building activities are likely to the northeast, east and southeast of the mine site over at least the next seven years. [. . .] it is evident that the Joint

Review Panel, while displaying concern about ungulate habitat in the mine area, operated on the apparently erroneous assumption that forest cover would be maintained in that area.

Therefore, I find that the Joint Review Panel breached its duty to obtain all available information about likely forestry in the vicinity of the Project, to consider this information with respect to cumulative environmental effects, to reach conclusions and make recommendations about this factor, and to substantiate these conclusions and recommendations in the Joint Panel Report.

Mining

Of primary concern in this application is the cumulative environmental effects of coal mining on carnivores. The geographic area about which concern exists is called the "Coal Branch" planning area, which is a large area on the eastern slopes of the Rocky Mountains which contains the Project's "Carnivore Cumulative Effects Assessment" area, which in turn contains the Project mine site.

Alberta government information describes coal mining in the Coal Branch as follows:

> *Coal* — Coal development in the Coal Branch dated back to the turn of the century and increased until the 1950's when railways converted to diesel fuel. Major coal development then occurred, as the demand for both metallurgical and thermal coal grew in the late 60's and 70's. Coal production in 1984 was just under eight million tonnes (about half metallurgical coal and half thermal). The extent of existing coal deposits presently proven in the planning area contains a total of nearly three billion tonnes of coal. Much of the coal rights are under disposition. Today, there are three, coal-mines operating in the Coal Branch. Two other projects have been issued mine permits and are awaiting growth and stabilization of both world and domestic coal markets. Preliminary disclosures of six coal projects have been recognized by the government as being consistent with government policies or intentions for these areas. With exploration, the more promising coal deposits are proven and reserves are increased.

The Coal Branch area is important for the development of high quality coals because of geology and the existing infrastructure. [*Ed note*: The applicants led evidence that the Government of Alberta had granted approvals in principal to five other coal mining operations in the same planning area. They asked the Joint Review Panel to compel disclosure from the government of the nature of these proposed operations so that this information could be incorporated into the EA.]

About the application to compel the "approvals in principle", the Joint Review Panel said this:

> The AWA Coalition requested that the Panel require the Government of Alberta to produce copies of the preliminary disclosure documents, prepared under the requirements of the Coal Development Policy of Alberta, for a number of other surface coal mines which had been proposed in the region. The Government of Alberta advised the Panel that those documents had, in its view, been submitted in confidence and so could not be released, except perhaps under a request under the *Freedom of Information and Protection of Privacy Act*. The Government also noted that the documents were dated, with some being submitted in the mid-1970's, and that without someone to speak to them, it would not be possible to determine if the various proposals remained relevant.
>
> The Panel determined that, given the expectation of the parties that the documents were submitted in confidence and, more importantly, the inability of anyone, including the applicant, to test the relevance of the documents, it was not prepared to attempt to compel that the documents be submitted to the hearing.

I find that this statement proves that the Joint Review Panel failed to compel the production of the mining information because it misconstrued its power to do so, and it misconceived that it has the obligation to decide on its relevance once produced.

Therefore, with respect to the two projects for which permits have been granted and the five projects which have received approvals in principle, I find that the Joint Review Panel breached its duty to obtain all available information about likely mining in the vicinity of the

Project, to consider this information with respect to cumulative environmental effects, to reach conclusions and make recommendations about this factor, and to substantiate these conclusions and recommendations in the Joint Review Panel Report.

The Joint Review Panel: Breach of Duty?: Alternate Means

Extent of the Duty to Consider Alternate Means

Section 16(2)(b) provides as follows:

> (2) In addition to the factors set out in subsection (1), every comprehensive study of a project and every mediation or assessment by a review panel shall include a consideration of the following factors:
>
> .. (b) alternative means of carrying out the project that are technically and economically feasible and the environmental effects of any such alternative means; . . .

In the present case, with respect to the method of mining, I find that the requirements of this section are properly restricted to the alternate means to open pit mining being underground mining.

With respect to alternative means, the [. . .] the Joint Review Panel limited its consideration because of CRC's practical and economic concerns [in particular, the CRC's reticence to seriously consider underground mining techniques] and, consequently, the terms of its proposal. As noted above, CRC applied for Alberta regulatory approval for an open pit coal mine, and the scope of its Environmental Impact Assessment (EIA) was limited accordingly. It appears that, as a result of this limitation, the Joint Review Panel's consideration was similarly limited.

While the alternative means of underground mining is generally considered in the Joint Review Panel Report, the effects of this alternative means, as compared to the effects of open pit mining, are not considered in any meaningful way. I agree with the applicant's argument that simply identifying potential "alternative means" without discussing their comparative environmental effects fails to provide any useful information to decision makers, and fails to meet the requirements of s. 16(2)(b) of *CEAA*.

While it is true that, as the Joint Review Panel asserts, CRC has the right to carry out the extraction of the coal resources within the applied for mine permit boundary, I find that it does not have the right to do it by open pit mine.

Thus, I find that a comparative analysis between open pit mining and underground mining at the Project site is required to comply with the provisions of s. 16(2)(b).

During the course of the hearing, counsel for CRC tactfully pointed out that, prior to the Joint Review Panel's consideration of the Project under *CEAA*, all detailed Alberta regulatory approvals leading to a final decision had been given. The point made was that, in the face of these approvals, the Minister's concern and, therefore, the requirements of *CEAA* are incidental to this almost completed process. My response to this assertion is that *CEAA*, as well as Alberta resource and environmental protection legislation, serves the interests of Albertans, and consequently, its terms must be met as framed.

Conclusion

. . . during the course of argument, I expressed the opinion that, if the environmental assessment conducted by the Joint Review Panel is found not to be in compliance with the requirements of *CEAA*, the least intrusive approach to reaching compliance would be adopted. [. . .]

In view of my findings . . . it is clear that the Project cannot proceed until the Joint Review Panel's environmental assessment is conducted in compliance with *CEAA*. Therefore . . . in my opinion the Minister has authority and responsibility to direct the Joint Review Panel to reconvene and, having regard to my findings, direct that it do what is necessary to make adjustments to the Joint Review Panel Report so that the environmental assessment conducted can be found in compliance with *CEAA*. For this result to occur, in my opinion, the following directions must be met:

(1) Obtain all available information about likely forestry in the vicinity of the Project, consider this information with respect to cumulative environmental effects, and, accordingly, reach conclusions and make recommendations about this factor, and substantiate these conclusions and recommendations in the Joint Review Panel Report;

(2) Obtain all available information about likely mining in the vicinity of the Project, consider this information with respect to cumulative environmental effects, and, accordingly, reach conclusions and make recommendations about this factor, and substantiate these conclusions and recommendations in the Joint Review Panel Report;

(3) With respect to alternative means, do a comparative analysis between open pit mining and underground mining at the Project site to determine the comparative technical and economic feasibility and comparative environmental effects of each, consider this information, reach conclusions and make recommendations about this factor, and substantiate these conclusions and recommendations in the Joint Review Panel Report.

Notes and Questions

1. What are the information gathering duties of a review panel?

2. What are the reporting obligations of a review panel?

3. Under what circumstances can a review panel apply its own expertise and judgement to fill information gaps?

4. In the case of *Sharp v. Canada (Transportation Agency)*, [1999] F.C.J. No. 948 (Q.L.), the Federal Court of Appeal dealt with the issue of alternatives to a project in the context of a railway line. The Transportation Agency was asked to consider approving a railway line. The decision triggered CEAA under paragraph 5(1)(d), a licensing provision on the Law List. The Transportation Agency made a decision to consider needs and alternatives under 16(1)(e), but was restricted under its own licensing provisions regarding the extent to which it was to consider needs and alternatives. The court challenge was initiated to require the Transportation Agency to study in detail the need for, and alternatives to, the line under CEAA. The court decided that the Transportation Agency should strive to exercise its discretion under CEAA in a manner consistent with regulatory decisions that triggers EA, should only consider needs and alternatives if the proposed project has serious adverse environmental effects. How does this decision fit with the Cheviot Mine decision of the Federal Court Trial Division?

. . . . .

Friends of the West Country Assn. v. Canada (Minister of Fisheries & Oceans)
1999 CarswellNat 2081 (C.A.)

[This case, commonly known as "*Sunpine*" was the first significant CEAA case to be decided at Federal Court of Appeal. The case arose as a result of a challenge brought by the Friends of the West Country or "FCW" with respect to the adequacy of an EA done by an RA in relation to a forestry-related project being proposed by Sunpine Forest Products. The proposed development involved construction of a logging road (known as the Mainline

Road) and two bridges: over Ram River and Prairie Creek. FCW challenged the RA's decision to scope the project as being the two bridges, seeking to have the scope expanded to include the entire logging road the construction of which, in its view, would have significant environmental effects.

Gibson J., the trial judge, held that the RA had not erred in scoping *the project* under subsection 15(1). However, in scoping *the environmental assessment* of the project (for the purposes of considering *inter alia* cumulative effects), he held that the RA failed to apply subsection 15(3) which, in his view, required the assessment to also consider the environmental effects of the Mainline Road.

The relevant statutory provisions are set out below.

> 15. (1) The scope of the project in relation to which an environmental assessment is to be conducted shall be determined by
>
> (a) the responsible authority
>
> (3) All proposed undertakings to be considered — Where a project is in relation to a physical work, an environmental assessment shall be conducted in respect of every construction, operation, modification, decommissioning, abandonment, or other undertaking in relation to that physical work that is proposed by the proponent or that is, in the opinion of
>
> (a) the responsible authority . . . likely to be carried out in relation to that physical work.
>
> 16. (1) Every screening or comprehensive study of a project and every mediation or assessment by a review panel shall include a consideration of the following factors:
>
> (a) the environmental effects of the project, including the environmental effects of malfunctions or accidents that may occur in connection with the project and any cumulative environmental effects that are likely to result from the project in combination with other projects or activities that have been or will be carried out;
>
> (3) Determination of factors — The scope of the factors to be taken into consideration pursuant to paragraphs (1)(a), (b) and (d) and (2)(b), (c) and (d) shall be determined
>
> (a) by the responsible authority

In concluding that subsection 15(3) required that the Mainline Road should form part of this environmental assessment, Gibson J. relied on an "independent utility test" that had previously been employed under US environmental assessment law. This test turned on whether the project, as scoped (the bridges), had utility independent of larger works being constructed (most notably the Mainline Road). Since, in his view, the bridges failed the independent utility test, the Mainline Road should therefore have been considered, pursuant to subsection 15(3), as part of the RA's cumulative effects analysis under section 16. As we shall see in the following excerpt, the Federal Court of Appeal, while disagreeing with Gibson J.'s analysis with respect to subsection 15(3) and the need for an independent utility analysis, upheld his conclusion that the EA was flawed.]

. . . . .

ROTHSTEIN J.A.:

Sunpine Forest Products Limited harvests timber in an area of over one thousand square miles in west central Alberta. It processes the timber at mills in Alberta, including a mill at Strachan, Alberta. In 1994, Sunpine identified a need for a permanent road to transport logs to its Strachan mill. After consultation involving Sunpine, the Province of Alberta and the Municipal District of Clearwater, a Strachan Area Transportation Network study was prepared. Public input on the study was sought. A Forest Advisory Committee was established with representation from Sunpine, the Province of Alberta Environmental Protection and the Municipality. The respondent was also represented on the Committee. In May 1995, the Committee, with the respondent dissenting, approved a new "Mainline Road" rather than upgrading the existing "North Fork Road". In August 1995, the Province of Alberta Environmental Protection approved a revised Mainline Road submission from Sunpine subject to several environmental conditions.

In December 1995, Sunpine submitted an application for approval under section 5 of the *Navigable Waters Protection Act (NWPA)*. to construct bridges across the Ram River and Prairie Creek along the Mainline Road corridor. As a result of the requirement to obtain federal approval to construct the bridges over navigable waters, federal environmental assessments were triggered pursuant to paragraph 5(1)(d) of the *CEAA*. No approvals for the bridges could be issued under the *NWPA* until environmental assessments requirements of the *CEAA* had been met. The Canadian Coast Guard acted on behalf of the Minister of Fisheries and Oceans as the responsible authority to carry out the environmental assessments.

The Coast Guard defined the projects subject to environmental assessment as the Ram River Bridge and the Prairie Creek Bridge. On July 18, 1996, the Coast Guard issued Screening Environmental Assessment Reports for each project. The decisions contained in each Report determined that the proposed bridges were "not likely to cause significant adverse environmental effects".

Following issuance of the Screening Reports, public comments were solicited. Following receipt of public comments, the Coast Guard issued an addendum to its Screening Environmental Assessment Reports. The conclusion was that taking into account the implementation of certain mitigative measures, the proposed bridges were "not likely to cause significant adverse environmental effects". Approvals to construct the bridges were issued on August 18, 1996.

Subsequently, Sunpine revised its Ram River Bridge plans to provide for a clear span bridge rather than one with a pier to be constructed within the active channel of the Ram River. On December 3, 1996, the Coast Guard issued a further Screening Environmental Assessment Report for the Ram River Bridge project, concluding that taking into account the implementation of certain mitigative measures, the revised bridge design was "not likely to cause significant adverse environmental effects". On December 12, 1996, the Minister of Fisheries and Oceans issued an approval for the revised Ram River Bridge.

The respondent sought judicial review in the Federal Court Trial Division from the July 18, 1996 decisions of the Coast Guard. At the hearing before Gibson J., the respondent "refine(d) the reliefs sought ..". to include judicial review of the August 16 and December 3, 1996 decisions of the Coast Guard and to ask that approvals issued under the *NWPA* to authorize the construction of the Prairie Creek and Ram River Bridges be quashed.

On July 7, 1998, Gibson J. allowed the judicial review. He set aside the approvals granted by the Coast Guard and referred the matter back to the Minister of Fisheries and Oceans or other appropriate minister for consideration and redetermination in a manner consistent with the *CEAA*, the *NWPA* and his reasons.

At this point, we are dealing with a question of statutory interpretation. The independent utility principle originated in the United States where questions of constitutional jurisdiction and the applicable statutory scheme of the relevant environmental protection legislation undoubtedly differ from those in Canada. I do not find the independent utility principle or the portions of the Guide which may reflect the independent utility principle helpful for the purpose of interpreting subsection 15(3) of the *CEAA*. The intent and meaning of subsection 15(3) may be adequately discerned from a consideration of the context of sections 15 and 16 and the logical reason for the words "in relation to" in subsection 15(3).

I conclude, as a matter of statutory interpretation, that once the responsible authority scoped each project under subsection 15(1), subsection 15(3) did not require that the environmental assessment include construction, operation, modification, decommissioning, abandonment or other undertaking outside the scope of the projects.

Subsections 16(1) and 16(3)

I turn to subsections 16(1) and 16(3). Gibson J. was of the view "that subsection 16(1) clearly reflects, on the facts of this case, an obligation on the part of the responsible authority to apply the independent utility principle in the definition of the scope of the assessment". He found that the Coast Guard erred in law in failing to include consideration of the cumulative environmental effects likely to result from the combination of the Mainline Road and the bridges.

Again, it is necessary to focus on the question of statutory interpretation. Subsection 16(1) is indeed mandatory. It requires consideration of the factors enumerated in paragraphs 16(1)(a) to (e). In particular, paragraph 16(1)(a) states that the environmental assessment shall consider the environmental effects of the project as scoped and "any cumulative environmental effects that are likely to result from the (scoped) project in combination with other projects or activities that have been or will be carried out". However, the scope of the factors to be taken into consideration pursuant to paragraph 16(1)(a) is to be determined by the responsible authority under subsection 16(3). This scoping is a discretionary decision on the part of the responsible authority.

The process involves two aspects. The first is for the responsible authority to consider the applicability of all of the factors in paragraphs 16(1)(a) to (e) to the project being assessed. The use of the word "shall" in subsection 16(1) indicates that some consideration of each factor is mandatory. Under paragraph 16(1)(a), the relevant factor is the environmental effect of the project which includes, *inter alia*, cumulative environmental effects. This requires the responsible authority to consider environmental effects that are likely to result from the projects scoped under subsection 15(1), in combination with other projects or activities that have been or will be carried out.

The second aspect involves the exercise of the discretion vested in the responsible authority by subsection 16(3) to determine the scope of this part of the paragraph 16(1)(a) factor, i.e. the cumulative environmental effects that will be considered. By necessary implication, a decision as to the cumulative environmental effects that are to be considered requires a determination of which other projects or activities are to be taken into account. It is, therefore, within the discretion of the responsible authority to decide which other projects or activities to include and which to exclude for purposes of a cumulative environmental effects assessment under paragraph 16(1)(a).

The learned motions judge makes no mention of s. 16(3) in his reasons and it appears that it may not have been brought to his attention. . . . When it is taken into account, it is plain that while it is mandatory in the sense that it requires a scoping of certain factors in s. 16(1) by the responsible authority, that scoping is left to the discretion of the responsible authority . . . The scoping of other projects or activities under ss. 16(3) and paragraph 16(1)(a) places no mandatory duty in that regard on the responsible authority.

Application of Subsections 15(1), 15(3), 16(1) and 16(3) of the CEAA

I turn now to the actions of the Coast Guard in relation to sections 15 and 16. Under subsection 15(1), in the exercise of its discretion, the responsible authority scoped each project. The learned motions judge found no error in that exercise of discretion. He states:

> I can find no reviewable error in the manner in which the responsible authority here exercised his discretion in defining the projects subject to environmental assessment review. More specifically, I find no error on the part of the responsible authority in failing to include within the scope of the bridge projects the road to which the principle [sic] projects, that is to say the bridges and the related abutments, could be said to be accessory and the proposed forestry operations to which the bridges might also, on the facts of this matter, be considered to be accessory.

No cross-appeal was taken from this finding. Accordingly, no question of error by the Coast Guard arises with respect to subsection 15(1). Once the bridge projects were scoped under subsection 15(1), there was no obligation on the Coast Guard to include the Mainline Road or the Sunpine forestry operations in its environmental assessment by reason of subsection 15(3).

In the case of section 16, Gibson J. found that the responsible authority erred in failing to include consideration of the Mainline Road in its cumulative effects analysis. From his reasons, he seems to treat the error as one of either misinterpreting paragraph 16(1)(a) or perhaps misapplying it to the facts of the case.

The Coast Guard's Screening Environmental Assessment Reports of July 18, 1996 address cumulative effects. With respect to the Ram River Bridge, the Report states:

> **Scope of Environmental Assessment**
>
> The scope of the environmental assessment includes the environmental effects at and downstream of the bridge site, identified in paragraph 16(1)(a) and section 2 of *CEAA* of the bridge and any works related to the construction and maintenance of the bridge.
>
> **Cumulative Effects**
>
> The Ram River Crossing is isolated from other man-made structures by several kilometers. The accumulated hydraulic effects of this bridge with other structures on the waterway are related to the distance upstream or downstream that other in-water structures are located. These hydraulic effects are insignificant and have been addressed by the design of the bridge structure itself.
>
> The potential of cumulative effects from ice and log jamming is also related to the bridge's distance from other structures. To further reduce any jamming-related effects, the design and location of the pier structure on the midstream gravel bar has decreased the potential for ice or log jamming to occur.
>
> Siltation related cumulative effects are considered insignificant as the sediments affected by construction will not be allowed to enter the waterway directly without prescreening through geotextile filters placed prior to construction.

With respect to the Prairie Creek Bridge, the Report states:

> **Scope of Environmental Assessment**
>
> The scope of the environmental assessment includes the environmental effects at and downstream of the bridge site, identified in paragraph 16(1)(a) and section 2 of *CEAA* of the bridge and any works related to the construction and maintenance of the bridge.
>
> **Cumulative Effects**
>
> The Prairie Creek Crossing is a single-span bridge, with no in-water components, isolated from other man-made structures by several kilometers. The accumulated hydraulic effects of this bridge with other structures on the waterway are related to the distance upstream or downstream that other in-water structures are located. These hydraulic effects are insignificant and have been addressed by the design of the bridge structure itself.
>
> Siltation related cumulative effects are considered insignificant as the sediments affected by construction will not be allowed to enter the waterway directly without prescreening through geotextile filters placed prior to construction.

These reasons make no mention of the Mainline Road or forestry operations.

The only reference in the material that is more explicit as to the reasons why the Mainline Road and forestry operations were not mentioned in the July 18, 1996 Screening Reports is a government memorandum of August 16, 1996, written after public comments were received following the issuance of these Reports. This memorandum appears to have accompanied the August 16, 1996 Screening Environmental Assessment Reports Addenda. The memo states in part:

> Comments that identified areas of federal jurisdiction that were within the scope of project that were not already addressed within the Canadian Coastguard Screening Report have been utilized in the preparation of an Addendum to the Report.

. . . . .

The remaining submissions were related to

- areas outside the defined scope of project for these crossings,
- outside of federal jurisdiction.

The July 18, 1996 Reports address only the bridges and work related to the construction and maintenance of the bridges and the accumulated hydraulic effects of the bridges and other structures on each of the two waterways. From the absence of any reference to the Mainline Road or forestry operations in the Screening Reports and having regard to the August 16, 1996 memo, it is apparent that the Coast Guard declined to consider matters that were outside the defined scope of the projects and that were outside federal jurisdiction. In declining to consider matters outside the scope of the projects and outside federal jurisdiction, I think it misinterpreted paragraph 16(1)(a) and subsection 16(3). It construed the boundaries of the exercise of its discretion more narrowly than those provisions permit and, therefore, declined to exercise the discretion conferred on it.

Under paragraph 16(1)(a), the responsible authority is not limited to considering environmental effects solely within the scope of a project as defined in subsection 15(1). Nor is it restricted to considering only environmental effects emanating from sources within federal jurisdiction. Indeed, the nature of a cumulative effects assessment under paragraph 16(1)(a) would appear to expressly broaden the considerations beyond the project as scoped. It is implicit in a cumulative effects assessment that both the project as scoped and sources outside that scope are to be considered. Further, nothing in paragraph 16(1)(a) or subsection 16(3) limits the assessment to sources within federal jurisdiction. In order to trigger a federal environmental assessment, some aspect of federal jurisdiction must be engaged. However, once engaged, the federal responsible authority is to exercise its cumulative effects discretion unrestrained by its perception of constitutional jurisdiction. As was stated by LaForest J. in *Friends of the Oldman River v. Canada (Minister of Transport)*:

> What is important is to determine whether either level of government may legislate. One may legislate in regard to provincial aspects, the other federal aspects. Although local projects will generally fall within provincial responsibility, federal participation will be required if the project impinges on an area of federal jurisdiction . . .

During the course of argument, it was pointed out that the Mainline Road passed over a number of non-navigable waters that were in some way connected to the two navigable waterways over which there was federal jurisdiction. It was suggested that the construction or operation of a road or bridges over non-navigable waterways could have a cumulative adverse environmental effect, together with the effect of the construction and operation of the bridges over the navigable waters. It is, of course, not for the Court to speculate as to whether such suggestion is well-founded. However, the example demonstrates why it is logical that a cumulative effects assessment under paragraph 16(1)(a) not be restricted to the scope of the federal project or to projects only under federal jurisdiction. Having said this, I emphasize that it is within the discretion of the responsible authority to determine the scope of factors to be taken into consideration pursuant to paragraph 16(1)(a). Provided the responsible authority does not decline to exercise its discretion by misinterpreting paragraph 16(1)(a) and subsection 16(3), it is open to it to include or exclude other projects — in this case, the Mainline Road or forestry operations as it considers appropriate.

Of course, in saying that a responsible authority may consider factors outside federal jurisdiction, I am restricting my comments to paragraph 16(1)(a) and subsection 16(3) and to where, once a project under federal jurisdiction has been scoped, the requirement to consider cumulative environmental effects is engaged.

Nor do I ignore subsection 12(4) of the Act which provides:

> (4) Where a screening or comprehensive study of a project is to be conducted and a jurisdiction has a responsibility or an authority to conduct an assessment of the environmental effects of the project or any part thereof, the responsible authority may co-operate with that jurisdiction respecting the environmental assessment of the project. [. . .]

The Province of Alberta conducted certain environmental assessments. I see no reason why it would not be open to the Coast Guard to have regard for the work done by the Province of Alberta in its cumulative effects assessment under paragraph 16(1)(a). I do not read paragraph 16(1)(a) or the discretion to be exercised under subsection 16(3) as inviting or requiring duplication of environmental assessments.

I need make no finding as to the type of environmental effects that the responsible authority may take into consideration in its cumulative effects assessment. However, it is clear that although the responsible authority in this case has jurisdiction over navigable waters, it must consider environmental effects touching upon all areas of federal jurisdiction. In *Friends of the Oldman River v. Canada, supra*, LaForest J. states:

> I should make it clear, however, that the scope of assessment is not confined to the particular head of power under which the government of Canada has a decision-making responsibility within the meaning of the term "proposal". Such a responsibility, as I stated earlier, is a necessary condition to engage the process, but once the initiating department has thus been given authority to embark on an assessment, that review must consider the environmental effect on all areas of federal jurisdiction. . . .. Here, the Minister of Transport, in his capacity of decision maker under the *Navigable Waters Protection Act*, is directed to consider the environmental impact of the dam on such areas of federal responsibility as navigable waters, fisheries, Indians and Indian lands, to name those most obviously relevant in the circumstances here.

Although the Court in *Oldman River* was dealing with the federal environmental assessment regime which the *CEAA* replaced, the principle is equally applicable here notwithstanding the different terminology of the current legislation. However, given the divided constitutional jurisdiction over environmental assessments between the federal government and the provinces, it follows that the federal responsible authority is to focus its environmental assessment on effects within federal jurisdiction — such as in this case, the effects on Navigation and Shipping, Inland Fisheries, and Indians, and Lands reserved for the Indians. It appears that this was the focus of the assessments in this case and I see nothing inappropriate in that regard.

I note that the decision of the Coast Guard is that the bridge crossings, when mitigative measures are taken into account, are determined to have an insignificant effect on the environment. Implicit in a cumulative effects assessment under paragraph 16(1)(a) are effects from both the project as scoped and other projects or activities. Sunpine argued that if there were no adverse environmental effects from the project as scoped, there could be no cumulative effects as envisaged by that paragraph. While on its face this argument is compelling, I am not sure it is possible to rule out that a federal project, while creating no adverse effects itself, could exacerbate adverse effects of other projects. In any event, a finding of insignificant effects as was made here still implies some effects from the bridge projects themselves. It is not illogical to think that the accumulation of a series of insignificant effects might at some point result in significant effects. I do not say that is the case here. I only observe that a finding of insignificant effects of the scoped projects is sufficient to open the possibility of cumulative significant environmental effects when other projects are taken into account. For this reason, I do not think the insignificant effects finding precludes the application of the cumulative effects portion of paragraph 16(1)(a) or subsection 16(3) in this case.

For these reasons, I am of the opinion that the Coast Guard erred in declining to exercise the discretion conferred on it in its cumulative effects analysis under paragraph 16(1)(a) by excluding consideration of effects from other projects or activities because they were outside the scoped projects or were outside federal jurisdiction.

Conclusion

The appeal will be dismissed. The matter is to be redetermined in accordance with the reasons of the learned motions judge as modified by these reasons. The respondent will be entitled to costs.

Appeal dismissed.

Notes and Questions

1. Why did the Court of Appeal reject the independent utility test? What is the implication of this decision for responsible authorities' discretion to determine the scope of a project to be assessed?

2. Do you agree with the court that the life cycle approach is more consistent with the provisions of CEAA? What would be the implication for scoping if the court had accepted the independent utility test instead? Would its application unduly broaden the scope of projects so as to make the process unmanageable?

3. To what extent does the court consider in its deliberations whether it would be appropriate, in the case before it, to include the road or the logging operations in the scope of the project?

4. To what extent is the court influenced by the fact that aspects of the logging operation excluded from the scope of project are still included under cumulative effects? What are the implications of considering the logging road and logging operations under cumulative effects rather than as part of the project?

. . . . .

Prairie Acid Rain Coalition v. Canada (Minister of Fisheries and Oceans)
2006 FCA 31

[The third case we consider in this Part, commonly known as "*TrueNorth*", is one of a series of cases that test the application of the CEAA process to major oil sands developments in western Canada. It is also a critical decision with respect to judicial review of project scoping decisions under section 15 of *CEAA*. The proponent proposed to construct and operate a major oil sands facility in Alberta. The operation required the destruction of a watercourse. This, in turn, required approval under the *Fisheries Act* and triggered an EA under *CEAA*. The RA determined the scope of the project to be the destruction of the watercourse, not the oil sands development. This scoping decision was challenged in a lawsuit filed by the Prairie Acid Rain Coalition. Consider when reviewing the Court of Appeal's decision excerpted below whether you agree with its approach to the scope determination, to the role of the provincial assessment, and to the constitutional context for the exercise of discretion with respect to the scope of project and scope of assessment.]

. . . . .

ROTHSTEIN J.A.:

The issue in this appeal involves the scoping of a "project" under the *Canadian Environmental Assessment Act*, S.C. 1992, c. 37 (CEAA).

Facts

The respondent TrueNorth Energy Corporation is the proponent of the "Fort Hills Oil Sands Project" (oil sands undertaking) which consists of an open pit mine, a crude bitumen extraction plant, a bitumen froth processing plant, a terminal to deliver oil sands to a pipeline system and utilities and off-site facilities to support the mining and processing operations.

The oil sands undertaking is primarily subject to regulation by the Province of Alberta. Pursuant to its *Environmental Protection and Enhancement Act*, R.S.A. 2000, c. E-12, an environmental impact assessment was conducted. Public hearings were held by the Alberta Energy and Utilities Board. Representatives of the federal government were present and cross-examined witnesses giving evidence on behalf of TrueNorth. Environment Canada made submissions to the Board on issues including cumulative effects, air quality, migratory birds and other related environmental issues. The Department of Fisheries and Oceans (DFO) made submissions on the effect on fish and fish habitat. The DFO concluded that any direct loss in fish habitat could be compensated or mitigated.

On October 22, 2002, the Alberta Energy and Utilities Board issued its decision approving the oil sands undertaking. Shortly thereafter, Alberta Environment granted TrueNorth approvals under the *Environmental Protection and Enhancement Act* and the *Water Act*, R.S.A. 2000, c. W-3.

Because the oil sands undertaking would require the destruction of Fort Creek, a fish-bearing watercourse, TrueNorth was required to obtain authorization of the Minister of Fisheries, pursuant to subsection 35(2) of the *Fisheries Act*, R.S.C. 1985, c. F-14. TrueNorth's application for authorization under subsection 35(2) of the *Fisheries Act* triggered the CEAA pursuant to paragraph 5(d) of that Act.

The DFO, as the "responsible authority" under the CEAA, determined that, pursuant to subsection 15(1) of the CEAA, the scope of the project that was to be subject to a federal environmental assessment was the destruction of Fort Creek and ancillary or subsidiary works and activities . . .

The appellants are "not for profit" associations concerned with the preservation of the environment and in particular, adverse environmental effects of developments such as the oil sands undertaking. They applied to the Federal Court from the scoping decision of the DFO, which they considered to be too narrow. They are of the view that the environmental assessment to be conducted under the CEAA, notwithstanding the Alberta hearings and decision (paragraphs 3 and 4), should cover the entire oil sands undertaking and that such federal environmental assessment should consider all areas of federal jurisdiction and not just the destruction of fish habitat. They say that the oil sands undertaking could adversely affect such matters under federal authority as migratory birds, Aboriginal peoples and water and fisheries in the Athabasca River.

Russell J. dismissed the appellants' application for judicial review. They now appeal to this Court from the decision of Russell J.

Standard of Review

In *Friends of the West Country Assn. v. Canada (Minister of Fisheries)* (1999), 248 N.R. 25 at paragraph 10, it was held that questions of interpretation of the CEAA by the Coast Guard were reviewable on a standard of correctness.

The same considerations apply in this case. There is no applicable privative clause. The CEAA is a statute of general application. It is administered by a broad range of federal authorities. There is no particular expertise in the DFO relative to that of the Court in respect of the interpretation of the CEAA. The interpretation issues are legal. While there is a general public interest in matters concerning the environment, the absence of relative expertise and the nature of the question being legal suggest a correctness standard of review in respect of the interpretation by the DFO of the CEAA.

However, the exercise of discretion by a responsible authority will normally be reviewed on a more deferential standard. As long as the responsible authority takes into account relevant considerations and does not take into account irrelevant considerations, the Court should not engage in a re-weighing process. Here, assuming its statutory interpretations were correct, considerations involving the destruction of fish habitat and relevant mitigative measures fall within the expertise of the DFO. In these circumstances, the discretionary decisions of the DFO should be reviewed on a reasonableness standard.

Russell J. conducted his review applying the correctness standard to questions of statutory interpretation and reasonableness to discretionary decisions. In doing so, he did not err.

Analysis

Power of the DFO Under Subsection 15(1)

The appellants say the DFO misdirected itself as to its discretion under subsection 15(1) of the CEAA and wrongly limited the scope of the project in respect of which an environmental assessment was to be conducted to the destruction of the Fort Creek fish habitat. They submit that the DFO was required to scope the project as the entire oil sands undertaking.

The definition of "project" in section 2 of the CEAA provides:

> "project" means
>
> (a) in relation to a physical work, any proposed construction, operation, modification, decommissioning, abandonment or other undertaking in relation to that physical work, or
>
> (b) any proposed physical activity not relating to a physical work that is prescribed or is within a class of physical activities that is prescribed pursuant to regulations made under paragraph 59(b);

Subsection 15(1) provides:

> The scope of the project in relation to which an environmental assessment is to be conducted shall be determined by
>
> (a) the responsible authority; or
>
> (b) where the project is referred to a mediator or a review panel, the Minister, after consulting with the responsible authority.

The appellants' argument that the DFO was obliged to scope the project for environmental assessment purposes as the entire oil sands undertaking ignores the words of subsection 15(1), which empower the responsible authority, the DFO in this case, to determine the scope of the project. In *Friends of the West Country* at paragraph 12, this Court described the powers of a responsible authority under subsection 15(1) in the following words:

> Subsection 15(1) is straightforward. It confers on the responsible authority . . . the power to determine the scope of the project in relation to which an environmental assessment is to be conducted. The appellants' approach would deprive the DFO of any discretion in respect of the scoping of a project contrary to the words of subsection 15(1).

Nonetheless, the appellants refer to other provisions of the CEAA to support their view. They refer to paragraph 5(1)(d) and in particular to the words "in whole or in part". Paragraph 5(1)(d) provides:

> 5. (1) An environmental assessment of a project is required before a federal authority exercises one of the following powers or performs one of the following duties or functions in respect of a project, namely, where a federal authority . . .
>
> (d) under a provision prescribed pursuant to paragraph 59(f), issues a permit or licence, grants an approval or takes any other action for the purpose of enabling the project to be carried out in whole or in part. [Emphasis added.]

As I understand the argument, it is that the words "in whole or in part" imply that a project must consist of an entire physical work or physical activity, although the federal power may only apply to a part of that work or activity.

The appellants have misconstrued paragraph 5(1)(d). The project referred to in paragraph 5(1)(d) is the project as scoped by the responsible authority under subsection 15(1).

The words "in whole or in part" recognize that within a project as scoped by a responsible authority, the power to be exercised by a federal authority under subsection 5(1)(d) may relate only to a part of that project. In this case, TrueNorth requires authorization from the Minister of Fisheries and Oceans of Canada under subsection 35(2) of the *Fisheries Act* for the destruction of the Fort Creek fish habitat. However, the project, as scoped, involves more than the destruction of Fort Creek: for example, construction of camps and storage areas required to carry out the destruction of Fort Creek. Although the construction camps and storage areas are scoped as part of the destruction of the Fort Creek project, TrueNorth will not require permits under paragraph 5(1)(d) for them.

Next, the appellants say the power of a responsible authority to impose mitigative measures under provisions such as subsections 20(2) or 37(2) of the CEAA would be rendered superfluous if the scope of a project does not include the entire physical work or activity. Subsections 20(2) and 37(2) provide:

> 20. (2) When a responsible authority takes a course of action referred to in paragraph (1)(a), it shall, with respect to any mitigation measures it has taken into account and that are described in paragraph (1.1)(a), ensure their implementation in any manner that it considers necessary and, in doing so, it is not limited to its duties or powers under any other Act of Parliament.
>
> 37. (2) Where a responsible authority takes a course of action referred to in paragraph (1)(a), it shall, notwithstanding any other Act of Parliament, in the exercise of its powers or the performance of its duties or functions under that other Act or any regulation made thereunder or in any other manner that the responsible authority considers necessary, ensure that any mitigation measures referred to in that paragraph in respect of the project are implemented. [. . .]

This argument is based on a reading of these provisions in isolation, without regard for the scheme of the Act. Provisions under which a responsible authority may require mitigative measures to be taken are predicated on the scoping of a project under subsection 15(1). In this case, the mitigative measures that the DFO may impose will pertain to the project as scoped, here, the destruction of Fort Creek. It was the environmental impact assessment conducted by the Province of Alberta that considered the oil sands undertaking and imposed such mitigative measures as it thought necessary in respect of that undertaking.

The appellants' next argument is based on the *Comprehensive Study List Regulations*, SOR/94-438. Many of the projects listed in these Regulations are under provincial jurisdiction with a limited federal role. Nonetheless, they argue that projects listed in these Regulations must be subject to an environmental assessment under the CEAA.

The purpose of the Regulations appears to be that when a listed project is scoped under subsection 15(1), a comprehensive study, rather than a screening, will be required in respect of that project. But it does not purport to impose on a responsible authority exercising its discretion under subsection 15(1) of the CEAA the requirement to scope a work or activity as a project merely because it is listed in the Regulations. In this case, the oil sands undertaking is subject to provincial jurisdiction. The *Comprehensive Study List Regulations* do not purport to sweep under a federal environmental assessment undertakings that are not subject to federal jurisdiction. Nor are the Regulations engaged because of some narrow ground of federal jurisdiction, in this case, subsection 35(2) of the *Fisheries Act*. See *Friends of the Oldman River Society v. Canada (Minister of Transport)*, [1992] 1 S.C.R. 3 at pages 71-72.

The appellants are making a policy argument that "many of the sections of the Regulations will wither away from disuse" and "management of the federal aspects of these projects will devolve by default to the provinces". However, subsections 12(4) and (5) of the Act recognize that an environmental assessment may be carried out under provincial jurisdiction and that a federal responsible authority may cooperate with the province in that environmental assessment. Subsection 12(4) and paragraph 12(5)(a) provide:

> (4) Where a screening or comprehensive study of a project is to be conducted and a jurisdiction has a responsibility or an authority to conduct an assessment of the environmental effects of the project or

any part thereof, the responsible authority may cooperate with that jurisdiction respecting the environmental assessment of the project.

(5) In this section, "jurisdiction" means

(a) the government of a province;

The appellants may not be satisfied with a province conducting an environmental assessment, but the subject of the environment is not one within the exclusive legislative authority of the Parliament of Canada. Constitutional limitations must be respected and that is what has occurred in this case.

The appellants' final argument in respect of subsection 15(1) is that environmental concerns should be assessed "unconfined by any parsing of the natural world into provincial and federal pieces". In making this argument, the appellants are addressing the scope of an assessment under section 16 and not the scope of the project under section 15. Paragraph 16(1)(a) provides:

16.1 (1) Every screening or comprehensive study of a project and every mediation or assessment by a review panel shall include a consideration of the following factors . . .

(d) the environmental effects of the project, including the environmental effects of malfunctions or accidents that may occur in connection with the project and any cumulative environmental effects that are likely to result from the project in combination with other projects or activities that have been or will be carried out [. . .]

Once a project has been scoped, it is possible that the effects of other projects or activities may impact the environmental assessment of the scoped project. This was dealt with in *Friends of the West Country*. At paragraph 34, this Court stated:

Under s. 16(1)(a), the responsible authority is not limited to considering environmental effects solely within the scope of a project as defined in s. 15(1). Nor is it restricted to considering only environmental effects emanating from sources within federal jurisdiction. Indeed, the nature of a cumulative effects assessment under s. 16(1)(a) would appear to expressly broaden the considerations beyond the project as scoped. . . .

However, the power to consider factors outside federal jurisdiction was expressly limited:

Of course, in saying that a responsible authority may consider factors outside federal jurisdiction, I am restricting my comments to s. 16(1)(a) and s. 16(3) and to where, once a project under federal jurisdiction has been scoped, the requirement to consider cumulative environmental effects is engaged.

The consideration of cumulative effects enables a responsible authority to consider environmental effects emanating from sources outside federal jurisdiction. However, this involves the scope of an assessment, not, as the appellants argue, the scope of a project.

Definition of Project

The appellants argue that DFO incorrectly interpreted the definition of "project" in section 2 of the CEAA. For ease of reference, the definition of project is repeated here:

"project" means

(a) in relation to a physical work, any proposed construction, operation, modification, decommissioning, abandonment or other undertaking in relation to that physical work, or

(b) any proposed physical activity not relating to a physical work that is prescribed or is within a class of physical activities that is prescribed pursuant to regulations made under paragraph 59(b);

The *Inclusion List Regulations* SOR/94-637 are the Regulations referred to in the definition of "project". Section 3 of these Regulations provides:

> 3. The physical activities and classes of physical activities set out in the schedule are prescribed for the purpose of paragraph (b) of the definition "project" in subsection 2(1) of the *Canadian Environmental Assessment Act* except in so far as they relate to a physical work.

In her affidavit in the judicial review in the Federal Court, Dorthy Majewski, Area Chief, Habitat, DFO, stated at paragraph 29:

> In my opinion it is reasonable to scope the project as the activities or works that cause the harmful alteration, disruption or destruction (HADD) of fish habitat in Fort Creek. The issuance of a section 35(2) authorization is the CEAA trigger. Because such an activity is on the *Inclusion List Regulations*, the dewatering and partial destruction is caught, and a CEAA environmental assessment would have to be done.

The appellants say that Ms. Majewski was incorrect in referring to the *Inclusion List Regulations* as authority for scoping the project as the destruction of Fort Creek. They say that the *Inclusion List Regulations* only apply to physical activities not related to a physical work. However, the destruction of Fort Creek is related to the construction of the oil sands undertaking, which is a physical work. Therefore, they say the *Inclusion List Regulations* do not apply and Ms. Majewski misdirected herself. In the view of the appellants, the destruction of Fort Creek should be part of an environmental assessment of the entire oil sands undertaking.

The respondents concede that Ms. Majewski's reference to the *Inclusion List Regulations* as the authority for scoping the environmental assessment project as the destruction of Fort Creek was incorrect. However, they say that her reference to the Regulations did not invalidate her scoping decision. They rely on concurring reasons in *British Columbia (Milk Board) v. Grisnich*, [1995] 2 S.C.R. 895 at pages 905-906:

> There is no precedent for holding that an administrative body must consciously identify the source of power it is relying on, in order for the exercise of that power to be valid . . . Courts are primarily concerned with whether a statutory power exists, not with whether the delegate knew how to locate it.

and followed by Stone J.A. in *Dynamex Canada Inc. v. Canadian Union of Postal Workers*, [1999] 3 F.C. 349, ¶122.

I agree with the respondents. The question is whether DFO had the power to scope the project as the destruction of Fort Creek, not whether Ms. Majewski, in a subsequent explanation, correctly identified the source of the power relied upon by DFO.

It was the request from TrueNorth to obtain authorization from the Minister of Fisheries of Canada under subsection 35(2) of the *Fisheries Act* for the destruction of the Fort Creek fish habitat that was the CEAA trigger. Ms. Majewski correctly identified the subsection 35(2) authorization as the CEAA trigger. Her reference to the *Inclusion List Regulations* while incorrect is of no consequence.

If, as the appellants seem to argue, the subsection 35(2) trigger requires that the project's scope be the entire oil sands undertaking, a responsible authority would have no discretion under subsection 15(1) of the CEAA as to the scoping of a project for federal environmental assessment purposes. Any trigger would automatically require an overall federal environmental assessment of the entire proposed physical work. Nothing in the CEAA supports the view that project scoping under subsection 15(1) must always include the entire proposed physical work.

Another argument of the appellants is that each project must have measurable benefits that can be weighed against adverse environmental effects of the project. For example, they rely on subparagraph 37(1)(a)(ii) which provides:

> 37.1 (1) Subject to subsections (1.1) to (1.3), the responsible authority shall take one of the following courses of action in respect of a project . . .
>
> (a) where, taking into account the implementation of any mitigation measures that the responsible authority considers appropriate,
>
> (ii) the project is likely to cause significant adverse environmental effects that can be justified in the circumstances,
>
> the responsible authority may exercise any power or perform any duty or function that would permit the project to be carried out in whole or in part; [. . .]

They say that the justification for the adverse environmental effects of a project must arise from the project itself. Here, the destruction of Fort Creek is not in and of itself justified and therefore cannot be a project under the CEAA.

While in some circumstances, the project which causes adverse environmental effects may itself have measurable benefits, I see nothing in the words of the CEAA that makes that a requirement in every case. Indeed, the indication is to the contrary. For example, subsection 15(2) provides that there may be more than one federal project that may be triggered under the CEAA. Subsection 15(2) provides:

> For the purposes of conducting an environmental assessment in respect of two or more projects,
>
> (a) the responsible authority, or
>
> (b) where at least one of the projects is referred to a mediator or a review panel, the Minister, after consulting with the responsible authority,
>
> may determine that the projects are so closely related that they can be considered to form a single project. [. . .]

One project may produce measurable benefits while the other does not. Similarly, where a development such as the TrueNorth oil sands undertaking is assessed under provincial environmental assessment procedures, I see no reason why the benefits of that undertaking, even if not within a federally scoped project, cannot be considered as justification for adverse environmental effects of the federally scoped project.

Although the appellants did not use the term, their argument reflects what has been termed the "independent utility principle" under which, where an individual project has no independent utility but is inextricably intertwined with other projects, the agency charged with considering the environmental impacts must consider all projects. This "independent utility principle" originated in the United States where questions of constitutional jurisdiction and the applicable statutory scheme of the relevant environmental protection legislation undoubtedly differ from those in Canada. In *Friends of the West Country*, the independent utility principle was found not to be helpful (at paragraphs 21 and 22). I see nothing that suggests that the independent utility principle is one that is applicable to this case.

In oral argument, the appellants argued that a narrow scoping of a project would preclude the Minister from referring to a mediator or a review panel, transboundary adverse effects or adverse effects on lands in which Indians have an interest (as well as other matters in respect of Indians) under subsections 46 and 48 of the CEAA. Subsections 46(1) and 48(1) provide:

> 46. (1) Where no power, duty or function referred to in section 5 is to be exercised or performed by a federal authority in relation to a project that is to be carried out in a province and the Minister is of the opinion that the project may cause significant adverse environmental effects in another province, the Minister may refer the project to a mediator or a review panel in accordance with section 29 for an assessment of the environmental effects of the project in that other province.

> 48. (1) Where no power, duty or function referred to in section 5 is to be exercised or performed by a federal authority in relation to a project that is to be carried out in Canada and the Minister is of the opinion that the project may cause significant adverse environmental effects on
>
> (e) lands in respect of which Indians have interests,
>
> the Minister may refer the project to a mediator or a review panel in accordance with section 29 for an assessment of the environmental effects of the project on those lands. [. . .]

The argument is that the Minister cannot act under subsections 46(1) and 48(1) when a responsible authority is already performing an environmental assessment. If that environmental assessment is scoped narrowly, there is no possibility for addressing adverse environmental effects on other provinces or lands in which Indians have an interest.

Again, the appellants' concern arises from a misinterpretation of the CEAA. The appellants' concern relates to the scoping of the environmental *assessment* under section 16 of the CEAA, not the scoping of a *project* under subsection 15(1). Under paragraph 16(1)(a), every screening or comprehensive study of a project must include "the environmental effects of the project". If the destruction of Fort Creek caused adverse transboundary effects or adverse effects on lands in which Indians have an interest, those concerns may be taken into account in the screening or comprehensive study being undertaken. It is not necessary to rescope the project.

Improper Delegation

The appellants say the DFO improperly delegated the assessment of project impacts in federal matters to the Province of Alberta. This argument is unsupported by the facts. Delegation involves the transfer of federal power to the province. That has not occurred here. The oil sands undertaking is subject to provincial jurisdiction. The province conducted an environmental assessment of that undertaking.

The DFO proposed to scope the project as the destruction of Fort Creek. It circulated its proposal and received comments from other government departments and from the appellants. It exercised its discretion to maintain the scope of the project as the destruction of Fort Creek. This decision is a valid exercise of discretion by the DFO. It does not imply a delegation of federal responsibility to the province.

Was the Discretionary Decision of the DFO Reasonable?

Finally, the appellants say that if there was no interpretive error by DFO, the scoping decision was unreasonable. The DFO circulated its proposed scoping and received submissions. It concluded that the area of federal responsibility that was triggered was the destruction of the Fort Creek fish habitat and that TrueNorth was required to obtain authorization from the Minister of Fisheries for that project. It took account of the fact that the oil sands undertaking had been environmentally assessed by the Province of Alberta. There is no basis for the argument that the scoping decision was unreasonable.

Conclusion

As a matter of policy it is sensible that undertakings with potential adverse environmental effects be subject to only one environmental assessment. The Governments of Canada and Alberta are parties to agreements that express this policy. The Canada-wide Accord on Environmental Harmonization signed January 29, 1999 and the Sub-agreement on Environmental Assessment share the objectives of efficiency and effective use of resources. The Sub-agreement on Environmental Assessment has the particular objective of ensuring that there is a "single environmental assessment and review process for each proposed project".

In this case the Alberta provincial authorities were conducting an environmental assessment. It would be inefficient for two assessments to be performed. It was both legally appropriate and efficient from a policy perspective for the DFO to rely on Alberta's performance of an environmental assessment.

For all these reasons, the appeal should be dismissed with costs to the Minister of Fisheries and Oceans of Canada and TrueNorth Energy Corporation.

Notes and Questions

1. Did the court apply the legal principles established in the *Sunpine* case, or did it go further in establishing the discretion for RAs to determine the scope of project?

2. In light of *TrueNorth*, what are the legal limits on the exercise of discretion to determine the scope of project by an RA?

3. How does the timing of the provincial assessment affect whether it was appropriate for the RA to be influenced by it in setting the scope of the federal assessment?

4. Are the comments on constitutional issues consistent with the SCC in the *Oldman River* case?

5. Based on *TrueNorth*, can you come up with a fact situation where the court is likely to interfere with an RA's scoping decision?

Miningwatch Canada v. Canada (Minister of Fisheries & Oceans)
2007 FC 955

[Our last illustrative case, commonly known as "*Red Chris*", is a trial decision of the Federal Court. It is the first case involving the post-2003 version of the CEAA. In this case, the proponent was proposing to construct and operate a mine in British Columbia. On its face, the nature and size of mine proposed would have required it to undergo a comprehensive study. Instead, however, the RA "re-scoped" the project as the tailing ponds and commenced a project screening without seeking public input into its scoping decision. The applicants challenged the failure to consult with the public before determining the scope of the project be limited to the tailing pond arguing that the project should be required to undergo a comprehensive study.]

MARTINEAU J.:

A notice of application for the present judicial review was filed by the Applicant on June 9, 2006. Essentially, the Court is asked to determine whether the RAs have been under the legal duty, since the EA was announced on the Registry in May 2004, to conduct a comprehensive study and to consult the public prior to taking a course of action decision in respect of the Project.

At issue in this case, is the right of the RAs to make the Course of Action Decision under the purported authority of paragraph 20(1)(a) of the CEAA. The Applicant claims that section 20 of the CEAA does not apply to the EA of the Project. The Applicant states that pursuant to section 13 of the CEAA, any course of action decision taken in this case must be made under section 37 of the CEAA before the Project is allowed to proceed and before authorizations or licences are given or issued by the RAs in accordance with the *Fisheries Act* and the *Explosives Act* respectively. Finally, the applicant contends that the Governor in Council ought to amend Schedule 2 of the MMER.

The Applicant has abandoned its earlier request for a declaration that the Project falls under item 9 of the CSL, as it exceeds the water diversion volume threshold of 10 million

m^3 per year. However, the Applicant maintains its request that the Project be declared a "project" for which a comprehensive study is required as it exceeds the ore production capacities provided in items 16(a) and/or 16(c) of the CSL. It also seeks an order in the form of a declaration declaring, *inter alia*, that the RAs were under a legal duty pursuant to subsection 21(1) of the CEAA to ensure public consultation with respect to the proposed scope of the Project, the proposed factors to be considered in its assessment, the proposed scope of those factors and the ability of the comprehensive study to address issues relating to the Project. The Applicant further seek an order declaring that the RAs erred in law or acted without jurisdiction in failing to perform their legal duty pursuant to subsection 21(1) of the CEAA.

Furthermore, the Applicant requests an order in the nature of *certiorari* quashing and setting aside the Course of Action Decision. It also seeks an order prohibiting the exercise of any powers under paragraph 5(1)(d) or subsection 5(2) of the CEAA that would permit the Project to be carried out in whole or in part. Alternatively, it seeks an order in the nature of a *mandamus* compelling the RAs, the Minister of Fisheries and Oceans, the Minister of Natural Resources and the Governor in Council, as represented by the Attorney General, to refrain from exercising any power, duty or function that would permit the Project to be carried out in whole or in part until a course of action has been taken in relation to the Project in accordance with paragraph 37(1)(a) of the CEAA, in performance of their duty to conduct an EA under section 13 of the CEAA. [. . .]

VIII — Merits of the Case

Essentially, the Court is faced with a "chicken or the egg" conundrum. Once an EA has been "triggered" pursuant to section 5 of the CEAA, does a RA have jurisdiction to re-scope a project listed in the CSL in a manner that will prevent the RA from conducting a comprehensive study? [. . .]

I will now analyze the two *TrueNorth* decisions rendered by this Court in 2004 and the Federal Court of Appeal in 2006. The relevant facts of that case, as set out by my colleague Justice Russell in *TrueNorth* — first instance, are explained below. Like the cases mentioned above, the *TrueNorth* decisions are also based on the provisions of the CEAA as they read prior to the Bill C-9 amendments. However, the text of section 15 has remained the same. [. . .]

It is interesting to note that in these passages, no direct mention is made by Justice Rothstein to former section 21. Justice Rothstein's reasoning in *TrueNorth* suggests that the word "project" which is broadly defined at section 2 of the CEAA must have a more restrictive meaning when it is used in paragraph 5(1)(d) of the CEAA: "[t]he project referred to in paragraph 5(1)(d) is the project as scoped by the responsible authority under subsection 15(1)" [emphasis added]. However, this leaves the question whether the word "project" used elsewhere in other provisions of the Act should be read as the project scoped by the RA or as the project proposed by the proponent. In other words, does the scope of the project proposed by the proponent or determined by the RA have an effect on the level of assessment itself?

Without directly answering this question, Justice Rothstein rejected the applicants' argument that projects listed in the CSL must be subject to an EA under the CEAA, stating at para. 23 and 24:

> The appellants' next argument is based on the *Comprehensive Study List Regulations*, SOR/94-438. Many of the projects listed in these Regulations are under provincial jurisdiction with a limited federal role. Nonetheless, they argue that projects listed in these Regulations must be subject to an environmental assessment under the CEAA.
>
> The purpose of the Regulations appears to be that when a listed project is scoped under subsection 15(1), a comprehensive study, rather than a screening, will be required in respect of that project. But

> it does not purport to impose on a responsible authority exercising its discretion under subsection 15(1) of the CEAA the requirement to scope a work or activity as a project merely because it is listed in the Regulations. In this case, the oil sands undertaking is subject to provincial jurisdiction. The *Comprehensive Study List Regulations* do not purport to sweep under a federal environmental assessment undertakings that are not subject to federal jurisdiction. Nor are the Regulations engaged because of some narrow ground of federal jurisdiction, in this case, subsection 35(2) of the *Fisheries Act*. See *Friends of the Oldman River Society v. Canada (Minister of Transport)*, [1992] 1 S.C.R. 3 at pages 71-72.
>
> . . .
>
> The appellants may not be satisfied with a province conducting an environmental assessment, but the subject of the environment is not one within the exclusive legislative authority of the Parliament of Canada. Constitutional limitations must be respected and that is what has occurred in this case. [emphasis added]

Indeed, in *TrueNorth*, Justice Rothstein stated:

> In this case the Alberta provincial authorities were conducting an environmental assessment. It would be inefficient for two assessments to be performed. It was both legally appropriate and efficient from a policy perspective for the DFO to rely on Alberta's performance of an environmental assessment.

I read these passages to mean that the mere fact that a particular undertaking appears to be covered by the CSL, does not mean that an EA must be conducted under section 5 of the CEAA. There must always be a federal trigger present. However, I am not sure that Justice Rothstein meant by this that a RA could use section 15 to discard the application of former section 21 where it has already been decided that a joint assessment of the project proposed by a proponent, as in this case, would be conducted by the provincial and federal authorities. In the case at bar, it was initially announced by the RA in spring 2004 and subsequently recognized by the BCEAO that the Project would be jointly assessed at the level of a comprehensive study, and in this regard, a draft working plan was jointly developed during the autumn of 2004 in accordance with the Agreement (see paragraph 58 above).

Leave for appeal to the Supreme Court of Canada of the judgment of the Court of Appeal in *TrueNorth* was dismissed without reasons on July 20, 2006.

D. — Course of Action Decision Reviewable

In May 2004, based on the information provided by RCDC, the Notice of Commencement posted on the Registry announced that a comprehensive study *commencing* on May 19, 2004 would be conducted with respect to the Project. It is apparent in the correspondence and various documents emanating from DFO and the Agency that while DFO, "had not yet formally identified the scope of the project for the purposes of the comprehensive study", the RAs would consult the public on the proposed scope of the project and other aspects mentioned at section 21 of the CEAA (see DFO's Notice to Federal Authorities, the Briefing Book and the Draft Work Plan).

As stated in the Briefing Book addressed to the minister of the Environment in July 2004, the tracking decision taken by DFO in May 2004 was consistent both with the scheme of the CEAA and Bill C-9 amendments which now oblige the RAs to consult the public on their proposed approach, report on this consultation to the minister of the Environment, and recommend to the latter whether the EA be continued by means of a comprehensive study, or the project be referred to a mediator or a review panel.

The decision taken in December 2004 to suddenly re-track the Project appears to have been based on inexistent "new" fisheries data. This contrasts sharply with the decision made in January 2005 to conduct a comprehensive study commencing on January 22, 2005, of the Galore-Creek Gold-Silver-Copper mine, where the Agency has established a $50,000 participant funding program to assist groups and/or individuals to take part in the federal EA of the proposed project, which exceeds threshold production listed under paragraphs 16(a), (b) and (c) of the CSL. Indeed, the general public was subsequently invited to comment on the scope of the project and on the scope of the factors contained in the document entitled "Comprehensive Study Scoping Document for the NovaGold Canada Inc. Proposed Galore-Creek Gold-Silver-Copper Mine Project in North-Western British Columbia" dated November 30, 2005.

What is really at issue in this case is whether the RAs may legally refuse to conduct a comprehensive study on the grounds that the Project as re-scoped by them does not include a mine and milling facility anymore.

Overall, sections 2, 5, 13, 14, 15, 16 and 18 and the new section 21 of the CEAA, as I read them together, and having in mind the purpose of the CEAA and the intention of Parliament, support the Applicant's principal proposition that where a project is described in the CSL, the RA must now ensure public consultation with respect to the proposed scope of the project for the purposes of the EA, the factors proposed to be considered in its assessment, the proposed scope of those factors are the ability of the comprehensive study to address issues relating to the project. [. . .]

While I do not need to resort on the guidelines, I am comforted by the fact that my interpretation is in accord with same. I note that according to the guidelines, large-scale projects with potentially significant environmental effects identified on the CSL, such as marine terminals; highways; airstrips; electrical generating stations; dams and reservoirs; artificial islands for oil and gas production; oil sands processing plants and mines; oil refineries; oil and gas pipelines; metal and uranium mines; pulp and paper mills; and certain military constructions will usually undergo the rigorous assessment of a "comprehensive study".

While these guidelines are not legally binding — what counts are the actual applicable legislative and regulatory provisions — they provide a strong indication that the present project is one of these large-scale projects which Cabinet wanted to undergo the rigorous assessment of a comprehensive study. I doubt very much that Cabinet's intention in adding to the CSL mining projects exceeding any of the thresholds mentioned at items 16, 17 and 18 of the CSL, was to restrain the scope of an assessment by way of a comprehensive study to mines located on Crown lands or operated by a federal authority.

According to the original wording of paragraph 59(d) of the CEAA, which section came into force on January 19, 1995, Parliament wholly reserved to Cabinet the discretion to decide what projects to describe in the CSL. It must be assumed that this was not meant to be the project "as scoped" by the RA, otherwise the exercise of Cabinet's plenary discretion would be futile and useless. Cabinet has exercised the discretion by promulgating and amending the CSL Regulations from time to time. As I read the CSL, the EL and the IL, projects mentioned in these regulations, refer to the project described by a proponent.

Moreover, since the amendments brought by Bill C-9 in October 2003, the power to add a project in the CSL has been transferred by Parliament from Cabinet to the minister of Environment (the Bill C-9 Amendments, above, at s. 29(2.1)). Section 58(1)(i) of the amended CEAA, (the version, it bears re-iterating, that is applicable to the case at bar), now provides that the minister of the Environment may "make regulations prescribing any project or class of projects for which a comprehensive study is required where the Minister is satisfied that the project or any project within that class is likely to have significant adverse environmental effects".

The corollary to this is also true: if the minister does not wish to have mining projects, such as the present Project, to be "tracked" for the purpose of an EA as one requiring a comprehensive study, the minister may simply suppress the same from the current CSL. In my opinion, this legislative amendment is significant since, in the event that the government determines projects have been either omitted from or wrongly included in the CSL, it makes for an even easier process to rectify such an oversight.

As stated in the preamble of the CEAA, an EA is a tool used to help achieve the goal of sustainable development by providing "an effective means of integrating environmental factors into planning and decision-making processes".

I am not persuaded that once public consultation is required under section 21 of the CEAA, it is possible to avoid the entire public consultation process by narrowing the scope of the project in order to reduce it to the level of a screening. Once a project has been included in the CSL, section 21.1 grants the minister of the Environment the discretion to either continue with the comprehensive study or to refer the project to a mediator or review panel in accordance with section 29. The legislative scheme, thus, only allows the minister of the Environment to maintain a comprehensive study or to upgrade it to a more in-depth process. No provision in the CEAA empowers the minister of the Environment to downgrade a comprehensive study to a screening. Likewise and more significantly to the case at bar, no provision in the CEAA empowers a responsible authority to downgrade a comprehensive study to a screening.

Once a tracking decision had been made requiring the project to undergo a comprehensive study, it is my view that the RAs did not have the discretion to re-scope the project in such a manner as to avoid the public consultation implications of section 21. To allow them to do so would violate not only the plain meaning of the legislation in question, but also the spirit of the entire legislative scheme, as amended, which is designed to foster public participation for projects with significant potential environmental repercussions.

Counsel for the Proponent asserts that the current case is virtually on all fours with *TrueNorth* in that:

- *TrueNorth* proposed to develop an oil sands extraction mine;
- The entire mining project was the subject of a full provincial environmental assessment;
- Viewed as a whole, the mine included a processing facility with a capacity of 30 000 m^3/d and a mine with a capacity of 15 000 m^3/d, which meant that it was described on the comprehensive study list;
- The only federal authorization for the project was the *Fisheries Act* authorization for harm to the fish habitat; and
- The RA (DFO) determined pursuant to section 15(1) of the CEAA that the scope of the project that was to be subject to a federal environmental assessment was the destruction of Fort Creek and ancillary works and activities.

First, it is trite law that this Court is bound by the judgment of the Federal Court of Appeal in *TrueNorth*. While I agree with the Proponent that there are some similarities between the two cases, the Proponent fails to note a few factual differences which, in my opinion, limit its applicability to this case:

- In *TrueNorth*, the applicants were seeking the judicial review of a scoping decision made pursuant to section 15 of the CEAA. In this case, the Applicant alleges an ongoing breach of the duty to ensure public consultation in accordance with section 21 of the CEAA, which breach culminated in the communication of the Course of Action Decision Report, and whose legality must be examined in light of the factual context of the case.
- There is no evidence in *TrueNorth* to indicate the responsible authorities originally decided the project ought to be tracked as a comprehensive study, only to modify the decision at a later date. Indeed, in *TrueNorth*, the evidence before this Court and the Federal Court of Appeal was that the project was always intended to undergo a

screening and not a comprehensive study. Again, this suggests to me that the *True-North* decision should be applied cautiously and only to the extent that the facts of this case are directly on point with the facts in that case.

- There was no TIA to be constructed by the proponent in *TrueNorth*.
- There was no explosives factory and magazine involved in *TrueNorth*. Not only does a federal licence under the *Explosives Act* needs to be issued by the minister of Natural Resources, but the explosives factory and magazine will be constructed on the mine site. Indeed, the facilities are to be located approximately 400–450 m apart and 450–500 m north of the ultimate toe of the waste rock storage area.
- Physical activities in relation to the carrying of the Project go beyond the harmful alteration, disruption, or destruction of fish habitat (HADD) but contemplates the deposit of a deleterious substance (tailings) into a TIA which is also included in the Project "as scoped" by the RAs.
- The tailings in question are produced by physical activities carried on the mine site. The metals will come from milling operations and from precipitation runoff and ground water draining through the north waste dump and across and through the exposed rock in the open pit walls.

Second, given that the vast majority of the analysis of the Federal Court of Appeal in *TrueNorth* focused on section 15 of the CEAA, I find that it is of limited applicability to a case, such as this one, where an analysis of section 21 as it now reads since the coming into force of Bill C-9 amendments, is of central importance to the resolution of the issues raised by the Applicant. Upon a careful reading of the Federal Court of Appeal decision, I note that it does not once reference the former section 21 expressly in its reasons, although at paragraphs 23 and 24 of the same cited above, it dismisses the argument made by the appellants that the projects listed on the CSL must be subject to an EA under section 5 of the CEAA.

Third, and perhaps most significantly, although the *TrueNorth* decision was rendered by this Court in September, 2001, it was issued in consideration of the former section 21, which did not refer to the "proposed scope" of a project. As aforementioned, the CEAA was amended in October, 2003. All parties agree and I support their view that only the new version of the CEAA applies in this situation. Even in the decision of this Court in *True-North*, I do not find that former section 21 is rigorously scrutinized. Indeed, former section 21 seems to refer to the project as "listed" on the CSL and not to the project as "scoped" under section 15. I, therefore, do not believe I am bound by the *TrueNorth* decision to the extent that it was deciding issues outside the particular context of sections 5 and 15.

It is worthwhile to briefly highlight a few of the differences between the former and the amended versions of section 21 in order to emphasize why I am of the view that the *True-North* decision is of limited applicability to the case at bar. Firstly, while the former section 21 of the CEAA did not make public consultation mandatory, the current version does. Furthermore, it is clear that the language of "proposed scope", as added to the new section 21, mandates that public consultation must take place prior to the actual scoping decision. Finally, under the new CEAA, once a "project" that has been proposed is set out in the CSL, the environmental assessment must be carried out by means of a comprehensive study.

Accordingly, I am of the opinion that the *TrueNorth* decision of the Federal Court of Appeal remains the law with respect to a scoping decision made pursuant section 15, if such an EA were commenced prior to October, 2003. However, I am not of the view that it applies to assessments commenced after October 2003 pursuant to section 21 of the CEAA.

Therefore, I do not view the discretion to scope a project under section 15 of the CEAA as the "full discretion" alleged by the Respondents. Instead, the RAs are bound *procedurally* by the requirements of new section 21 of the CEAA, such that if the project proposed by a proponent is on the comprehensive study list, there is a duty to consult the public, assuming that there is a section 5 trigger. After public consultations, the scoping exercise shall set the parameters for the comprehensive study and provide a rationale for the design of the studies which may be required, on a case-by-case basis.

It is not entirely clear to the Court why, once it had been determined the Project, as described by the RCDC, was included in the CSL, the decision was subsequently made to downgrade the extent of the assessment required to that of a screening. To this effect, the only affiant to submit an affidavit on behalf of the Crown was an individual who was employed by DFO as the acting manager of the Major Projects Review Unit for the Pacific Region from February to August 2005.

This affiant was only involved in the Project for approximately six months out of an approximately twenty-four month environmental assessment, and interestingly, was not involved in the Project during the time in question when the re-tracking decision of December 2004 was made. Nevertheless, according to the cross-examination of the affiant on his affidavit, he was aware the Project would no longer be addressed as a comprehensive study within the initial weeks of his tenure as acting manager.

The Project is currently based on the mill production rate of 30 000 tonnes of ore per day for sale to the export market, over a projected mine life of 25 years. I do not need to rest my decision on the fact that the re-scoping of the Project has all the characteristics of a capricious and arbitrary decision which was taken for an improper purpose. It is sufficient to declare that DFO correctly determined in the initial tracking decision of May 2004 that the Project would require a comprehensive study level review based on a proposed ore production capacity of up to 50 000 tonnes/day which exceeds the threshold of 600 tonnes/day threshold under item 16(c) of the CSL. In view of this conclusion, I do not need to determine whether the proposed construction, decommissioning or abandonment of the Red Chris porphyry copper-gold mine also falls under item 16(a) of the CSL as it is a metal mine, other than a gold mine, with an ore production capacity of 3 000 tonnes or more per day.

Therefore, in sidestepping statutory requisites mentioned in section 21 of the CEAA as amended in 2003, in the guise of a decision to re-scope the Project, the RAs acted beyond the ambit of their statutory powers. Thus, in my opinion the RAs committed a reviewable error, which error culminated in the communication of the Course of Action Decision, by deciding to forego the public consultation process that the Project was statutorily mandated to undergo under section 13 of the CEAA. This is not to suggest that the RAs do not have the discretion to amend the scope of projects. To the contrary, such a ruling would be absurd, given the language of section 15(1) which clearly imparts discretion to the responsible authority. Further, such a ruling would violate the case law (see section C. Case law, above) which emphasizes that section 15 of the CEAA grants RAs wide latitude to scope projects in the manner they deem appropriate on a case-by-case basis.

The consequences of downgrading the Project from a comprehensive study to a screening were known and understood by the RAs at all relevant times. According to the evidence on record, the RAs were well aware that environmental groups, including the Applicant, would be unhappy with the re-tracking decision. Likewise, the RAs understood that the minister of the Environment would no longer have any decision-making power with respect to the Project and that, as a consequence of the decision to re-track the Project, the general public would not have the opportunity to submit comments with respect to the proposed scope of the Project, the factors proposed to be considered in its assessment, the proposed scope of those factors and the ability of a comprehensive study to address issues relating to the Project.

Setting aside the Course of Action Decision will therefore endorse a fundamental purpose of the CEAA, which premises that public participation is meant to improve the quality and influence the outcome of an EA. Public consultation on the parameters mentioned in section 21 of the CEAA as it now reads since the Bill C-9 amendments, undoubtedly improves the EA and decision-making process.

I must take into account the fact that there was no public consultation whatsoever by the RAs prior to the taking of the Course of Action Decision with respect to the draft screening report. While I recognize that the public was invited to make comments in the 65 day period mentioned in the Provincial Notice, this concerned exclusively the provincial EA process. Again, considering the particular and very unusual circumstances of this case which have been set out in great detail above (IV — Factual Background), I find that judicial intervention is necessary and in the public interest.

In *Friends of Oldman River Society*, above, by the time the application was heard, the dam at issue was 40% completed. By the time the appeal got to the Supreme Court, the dam was almost entirely completed. Despite these facts, the Supreme Court rejected the respondents' arguments that granting prerogative relief would be futile.

The facts in the case at bar are more favourable to relief, as construction has not started on the Project. A comprehensive study will involve public participation, additional section 16 considerations, and mandatory follow-up, and thus cannot be said to be futile.

Conclusion

Having considered the particular circumstances of this case, the conduct of the parties and the representations made by counsel, I am satisfied that relief should be granted in the exercise of the Court's remedial powers under section 18 and 18.1 of the FCA.

Accordingly, the present application shall be allowed [. . .]

Notes and Questions

1. On appeal, the Federal Court of Appeal held that the *TrueNorth* decision applied to the facts before the court in *Red Chris*. Consistent with the Court of Appeal's deferential approach in CEAA cases, Justice Rothstein held that the responsible authority has the discretion to determine the scope of a project, even if the effect is to downgrade a project from one requiring a comprehensive study to one subject only to a screening, thereby depriving the public of the opportunity to be consulted during the scoping process.

2. Do you agree with the trial judge that the *TrueNorth* decision can be distinguished on the basis of the changes to the comprehensive study process, or was the court required to follow *TrueNorth* as held by the Court of Appeal? Explain.

3. Consider the implication of the incorporation, in 2003, of the precautionary principle into the purpose section of the CEAA with regard to the relevance of the pre-2003 scoping cases. Should this have been judicially considered in *Red Chris*?

4. On December 18th, 2008, the Supreme Court of Canada granted Miningwatch leave to appeal. Check to see whether and how the SCC has finally decided the case.

Part III — Challenges Ahead for EA

More than a decade of EA under CEAA and close to 40 years of EA at the federal level in Canada have provided considerable experience to draw upon to improve the effectiveness and efficiency of the federal EA process. In the following sections, you will find brief discussions of a selection of concerns raised with the federal EA process in Canada. The issues covered in this section are the following:

- The Scoping Challenge;
- The Role of the Public;
- Engagement with First Nations;
- Strategic Environmental Assessments (SEAs); and
- Sustainability Assessments

The Scoping Challenge

Given the court cases discussed in the previous section, it is not surprising that scoping under the CEAA has been among the most criticized and most controversial aspect of the federal EA process. Law reform proposals on scoping started almost as soon as the process was implemented. A report prepared at the request of the Canadian Environmental Assessment Agency in 1996 was one of the first to reconsider the CEAA's approach to scoping. The report concludes that the main challenge for scoping is how to make the EA manageable without eliminating issues that are important to members of the public. The report suggests that professionals could probably agree relatively easily on what issues are important enough to be included in the EA. The problem, it is suggested, is that proponents, members of the public and public officials often have different views on what should be included than EA professionals.

As such, the report raises important questions about the relationship between the predictive and evaluative aspects of EA. To the extent that it is desirable to base scoping decisions on professional judgment rather than expression of public values, how is it practically possible to get professionals to make decisions without undue influence from proponents, the public, and government officials? Is it appropriate for scoping decisions to be made by professionals who are not accountable to the general public? What are the appropriate roles of government officials, proponents, and the public in deciding what is important enough to be part of the EA?

A number of specific recommendations for reform have been made since the 1996 report commissioned by the CEA Agency. The House of Commons Committee, for example, recommended in its 2003 review of the Act that national environmental priorities and international environmental commitments be incorporated into the EA process. This would mean that issues such as the impact of projects on climate change and biodiversity, for example, would automatically become part of the scope of a federal assessment. The Committee further recommended that cumulative effects assessment become a priority under the CEAA.

The Regulatory Advisory Committee reported on the results of its review of the Act in 2000. It recommended a more formal scoping process, the establishment of criteria, and suggested that the Agency should play a more central role in the scoping process. The Committee concluded that the scope determination must be appropriately linked to national priorities and international obligations. More generally, the report pointed out that a policy context is needed for appropriate scoping. Some commentators have suggested legislated criteria such as an interdependence test, a linkage test, a proximity test, and the shift of discretion from RAs to the Minister of the Environment or the Agency. Other reform proposals include making the consideration of the purpose, need, and alternatives to a project mandatory at the earliest stage of all EAs.

Notes and Questions

1. Three separate but related sets of issues with respect to scoping can be identified from the literature and the review of the federal EA process. One set of issues pertains to who should make the scoping decision. A second set of issues concerns the process for making the scoping decision and the appropriate roles of proponents, regulators, and members of the public in that process. The third set of issues refers to the substance of the scoping decision and establishing what level of substantive guidance or criteria should be given to decision makers.

2. In light of the cases covered in the previous section, what role do you think legally binding criteria for the determination of the scope of project could make in addressing the problems with scoping under the CEAA? Can you suggest criteria?

3. What about criteria for scope of assessment? Are the factors listed in section 16 sufficient, or is additional guidance needed? Can you suggest additional factors or criteria for setting the scope of those factors?

4. One suggestion has been to increase the role of government in cumulative effects assessments, and in needs and alternatives consideration. This is based on the concept that the proponent should only be responsible for its own project, and that it is up to government to think about alternatives and interactions with other possible human activities, past, present and future. Do you agree?

5. Who should make scoping determinations? Should proponents and intervenors be able to appeal those decisions? If so, on what basis?

6. Are final scope determinations needed, or could the EA process remain open to new issues until the final decision is made? What would be the implication of such an approach?

The Role of the Public

The role of the public is not as clearly set out in the Act as that of responsible authorities, nor is it necessarily as apparent to someone not familiar with the EA process. The Act does not impose obligations on the public. Rather, the public is recognized in the preamble and the purpose section as a valuable contributor to the process, whose participation should be facilitated and encouraged. Actual engagement of the public is discretionary for most EAs carried out under the Act.

The role of the public is nevertheless recognized in the literature and in international law to be critical for sound decision making. First, the public has a role to play both as a source of information to help predict the consequences of a proposed action, and to evaluate the range of consequences and their likelihood, to determine which set of consequences are preferable. More specifically, according to public participation literature, meaningful public participation in EA has a number of benefits, such as:

- providing access to local and traditional knowledge from diverse sources;
- enhancing the legitimacy of proposed projects;
- helping define problems and identify solutions;
- permitting a comprehensive consideration of factors upon which decisions are based;
- ensuring that projects meet the needs of the public in terms of both purpose and design;
- bringing alternative ethical perspectives into the decision making process;

- broadening the range of potential solutions considered;
- furnishing access to new financial, human and in kind resources;
- preventing "capture" of EA agencies by project proponents;
- encouraging more balanced decision making;
- increasing accountability for decisions made;
- facilitatating challenges to illegal or invalid decisions before they are implemented;
- illuminating goals and objectives, which is necessary for working through values or normative conflict;
- furnishing venues for clarifying different understandings of a resource problem or situation, which is key to resolving cognitive conflict;
- helping avoid costly and time-consuming litigation; and
- reducing the level of controversy associated with a problem or issue.

Key to effective participation, according to the literature, are early and adequate notice of an EA, full and convenient access to relevant information, assistance to ensure sufficient capacity, and meaningful opportunities to provide input into the EA and decision making processes. Other issues raised in the public participation literature include opportunities for transformative learning, and consideration of factors that lead to non-participation in EA processes. Barriers to participation are capacity and a lack of confidence in the ability to influence the outcome of the EA process.

As indicated, the importance of meaningful public participation is reflected in the preamble as well as the purposes of the CEAA. The Act also requires that members of the public be provided with convenient access to documents that are relevant to the EA process. An electronic registry is provided for under the Act, which must contain relevant documents or information on how to get them and notices about the key stages in the EA process.

Some form of public involvement is mandatory for three out of the four process options established in the Act. Only for screenings is public participation discretionary. Even for screenings, there are indications beyond the general statements in the preamble and the purpose section that public participation should play an important part in the EA process. First, subsection 18(3) sets out in some detail what is required once a determination has been made that the public should be provided with an opportunity to participate. In addition, a ministerial guideline and detailed guidance has been developed for public participation in screenings.

For comprehensive studies, the CEAA provides for mandatory public participation before scoping decisions, before a final decision is made whether to proceed by way of comprehensive study or panel review, during the comprehensive study process itself, and before the final process and project decisions are made. Panel reviews tend to involve the highest level of public participation, although the access points for members of the public are in many cases similar to comprehensive studies. A key difference is that panel reviews always involve hearings, whereas comprehensive studies are more flexible in the form of public engagement. Furthermore, in case of panel reviews, the concerns of the public are heard and considered by an independent third party, not by the federal decision maker. In mediation, the form of public participation may be different. However, mediation can only proceed if those interested in the EA process have been identified and are willing to participate in the mediation process. The opportunity for public participation in mediation is therefore assured.

In practice, however, the role of the public in environmental assessments under the CEAA has been limited. Out of about 20,000 environmental assessments carried out under the Act between 2003 and 2009, less than 100 are identified as subject to public involvement.

Notes and Questions

1. Effective public participation requires the capacity to engage, access to relevant information, access to decision makers, access to justice, and access to resources. How does the CEAA measure up in these areas?

2. It is clear that there is a considerable gap between theory and practice when it comes to public engagement in EAs. Can you think of some of the reasons for this gap?

3. How can the effectiveness of public engagement be enhanced while keeping the process manageable, in terms of time and cost, for proponents and public officials?

4. What is the role of law in encouraging constructive and effective public engagement?

5. What, if any, changes would you make to the CEAA with respect to public engagement? Explain.

Engagement with First Nations

The role of Aboriginal peoples in the federal environmental assessment process has evolved significantly over the past ten years, and the process is ongoing. When the CEAA first came into force, it contemplated Aboriginal involvement mainly through projects on, or affecting, reserves or areas subject to land claims or self government agreements. The Supreme Court of Canada has since made it quite clear that the federal Crown has a duty to consult Aboriginal peoples before making decisions that have the potential to interfere with Aboriginal rights or title, whether fully recognized or not. (See Chapter 3, *infra.*) This obligation has led to suggestions to link or integrate consultations with EA processes. It has also led to suggestions that consultations need to take place independent of EA processes, where possible in parallel processes with appropriate information exchange.

To appreciate the evolving role of Aboriginal peoples in the federal environmental assessment process, it is important to have some sense of the range of aboriginal interests involved. Some rights arise out of the *Indian Act*, involving status Indians and the reserve structure of governance. Other rights arise out of agreements entered into between Aboriginal peoples and the Crown. Historic agreements are generally referred to as treaties, whereas the modern versions are referred to as land claims and self government agreements depending on their focus and scope. Finally, Aboriginal peoples have retained certain inherent rights that reflect their pre-contact practices, customs and traditions. The main sources of Aboriginal rights are therefore inherent rights that have not been relinquished, rights under various forms of agreements with the Crown, and statutory rights. [*Ed note*: See further discussion in Chapter 3.]

Section 35 of the Constitution is central to an understanding of Aboriginal rights in the context of the federal EA process. In a long line of cases, this section and the general fiduciary duty of the Crown toward Aboriginal communities has been interpreted over the past two decades to highlight a number of critical rights and obligations that are relevant in the EA context. Whatever the source, these rights can take the form of Aboriginal title to land or more specific rights, such as a right of access to a resource. Access to a resource can be for subsistence, cultural purposes, or to earn a livelihood. The exact nature and extent of the right is often still in dispute. Only in areas that are subject to a recent land claims or self-government agreement are the rights of Aboriginal peoples generally clear and undisputed.

Against this backdrop, the CEAA includes several provisions dealing with Aboriginal issues in the federal EA process. First, there are a number of provisions that help to establish the role of Aboriginal peoples in the general EA process. The purpose section sets the tone by specifically referring to the promotion of "communication and cooperation between responsible authorities and Aboriginal peoples with respect to environmental assessment". The definition of environmental effect includes effects of biophysical changes on "physical and cultural heritage", on "the current use of lands and resources for traditional purposes by aboriginal persons", and "any structure, site, or thing that is of historical, archaeological, paleontological or architectural significance". Section 16.1 provides for the consideration of Aboriginal traditional knowledge in the EA process. These provisions combine to bring Aboriginal issues and perspectives squarely within the four corners of the EA process under the CEAA.

The CEAA provides opportunities for harmonization between the EA process under the Act and EA processes carried out under Aboriginal land claims and self government agreements. The Act provides for joint assessments or substitution with EA processes established under land claims agreements. It also provides discretion to initiate the federal EA process on the basis of a project's potential impact on land that is subject to Aboriginal rights.

In addition to these provisions dealing with the general EA process, there is a process specifically designed for projects proposed on reserves. The section provides for regulations to require band councils to carry out an environmental assessment of projects funded or proposed by band councils. This is complemented with a definition of federal lands, which includes "reserves, surrendered lands and any other lands that are set apart for the use and benefit of a band and are subject to the *Indian Act*".

It is apparent from these provisions of the CEAA that there are a number of challenges related to the potential impacts of projects on Aboriginal communities and the potential infringement of Aboriginal rights in the EA process. As a starting point, the definition of environmental effect brings the potential impacts of a proposed project on Aboriginal communities squarely within the scope of the EA process. This alone makes the active engagement of potentially affected Aboriginal communities essential. The formal recognition of Aboriginal traditional knowledge in the Act should further serve to facilitate more effective participation of affected communities.

Harmonization of processes set up under various forms of Aboriginal governance and the CEAA is a second key area. Included here are EA processes under land claims and self government agreements. The CEAA permits this harmonization, but it is left to those responsible for the EA process under the CEAA to negotiate appropriate harmonization agreements, either on a case-by-case basis, or generically. Increasingly, EA processes established under land claims agreements are incorporated into project-specific memorandums of understanding negotiated by interested jurisdictions before the formal commencement of the EA process.

A third area of interest is the role of band councils. The Act provides for a separate process in cases where the project decision is made by a band council rather than a federal authority. However, to date, there are no regulations in place to implement this varied process for projects on reserves. In the absence of regulations, there is no requirement for band councils to carry out an EA under the CEAA.

Finally, the federal Crown has constitutional obligations to protect the range of Aboriginal rights that may be affected through the approval of a project assessed under the CEAA. Where the right is proven, the obligation takes the form of a fiduciary obligation with respect to any right potentially affected. Where the right is asserted, but not proven, the obligation to consult arises out of the honour of the Crown, rather than a fiduciary obligation to protect the Aboriginal right potentially affected. This raises a number of critical questions about the relationship between the Crown's duty to consult and the federal EA process.

What is the appropriate role of the EA process under the CEAA in identifying the possible infringement of Aboriginal rights? Any impacts that arise out of biophysical changes in the environment are clearly within the scope of the EA process given the specific references to impacts on Aboriginal people in the definition of environmental effect. What is less clear is whether, and how, the EA process should deal with the nature of the Aboriginal right potentially infringed as a result of the project's impact. In other words, there are two very different areas of uncertainty to explore. One is whether the project will have an impact on Aboriginal communities. The other is whether the impacts constitute an infringement of aboriginal rights. The challenge with respect to the latter is that the exact nature of the rights that may be affected has, in many cases, been under dispute and negotiations for decades.

Most unclear and controversial is whether the EA process is an appropriate tool for consultations between the Crown and Aboriginal peoples on whether Aboriginal rights would be infringed and whether an agreement can be reached on terms and conditions under which Aboriginal communities are prepared to consent to a possible infringement. As discussed in Chapter 3, recent cases have established that the Crown has a duty to consult with potentially affected Aboriginal communities, and that the duty to consult is not limited to circumstances where the Aboriginal claim has been settled or accepted by the Crown. Arising out of the Crown's fiduciary duty toward Aboriginal peoples is a general duty to consult.

Essentially, compliance with the duty to consult is a precondition for courts accepting an infringement of an Aboriginal right, but it may not be sufficient for courts to permit the infringement. The courts have thereby separated the question of whether the Crown has the right to infringe Aboriginal rights from the question of due process in case of a possible infringement of Aboriginal rights.

In some cases, such as a proven treaty right or a right confirmed in a land claims agreement, the Crown may not be able to infringe an Aboriginal right without the consent of the Aboriginal communities affected. In other cases, such as possible interference with inherent rights, or unsettled claims, infringements may be possible without the consent of affected Aboriginal peoples.

The courts have focused, so far, on procedural protection of Aboriginal rights through the duty to consult. This means that, at a minimum, the federal Crown has a duty to consult with Aboriginal communities who have a potential claim that a proposed project will infringe their title to land or other Aboriginal rights in the form of inherent rights, treaty rights, or statutory rights. The level and form of consultation required will depend on the status of the rights involved and the nature of the possible infringement.

An open question is whether, or to what extent, the EA process can and should serve to satisfy the federal Crown's duty to consult. The SCC decisions in *Taku River* and *Haida* suggest that the EA process can serve this function in certain circumstances: see Chapter 3. At the same time, it is clear from the above that Aboriginal peoples' involvement in the EA process is essential regardless of whether there is agreement that it serves as the forum for consultations with the federal Crown. The question is whether to proceed with separate consultation and EA processes, whether to link the two, or whether to develop an integrated process. Until this issue is resolved either by the courts, through legislation, or informally, it will be critical that the role of the EA process with respect to the duty to consult be clarified on a case-by-case basis. Otherwise, there will be a disincentive for Aboriginal communities to fully participate in the federal EA process. To avoid this result, responsible authorities should seek early engagement with affected communities before scope determinations are made.

Notes and Questions

1. What role should Aboriginal traditional knowledge play in EA processes? For example, how should the EA process handle conflicting evidence on the size of the population of a certain species provided by an Aboriginal elder and a renowned scientist?

2. For an interesting set of cases that dealt with EA requirements and Aboriginal rights issues, see *Mikisew Cree First Nation v. Canada (Minister of Canadian Heritage)*, [2005] 3 S.C.R. 388, and *Canadian Parks & Wilderness Society v. Canada (Minister of Heritage)*, [2001] F.C.J. No. 1543 (T.D.). Why was the Mikisew Cree First Nation successful where the Canadian Parks and Wilderness Society failed? To answer this question, it will be helpful to refer to excerpts from these decisions found in Chapter 8.

3. Under what circumstances would you consider the EA process to be an appropriate forum for Crown consultation with Aboriginal communities?

Strategic Environmental Assessments (SEAs)

Strategic environmental assessments at the federal level in Canada are not new. There has been a Cabinet Directive in place on SEAs since 1994, and the EARP Guidelines Order did allow for the assessment of some policies, plans and programs. Some provinces have also experimented with SEAs. In short, SEA is not without precedent in Canada. At the same time, it is still very difficult to even grasp the concept of SEA, as it means different things to different people and is practiced very differently across jurisdictions. Some definitions, such as the one in the Cabinet Directive, see it primarily in the context of major Cabinet decisions. Others view SEA as an overriding concept to push EA beyond the project level.

A recent book on international experience with strategic environmental assessments offers a range of definitions for SEA.[5] The authors note that early definitions of strategic environmental assessments were closely linked to project assessments, essentially broadening the scope of environmentally focused project assessments to the environmental consequences of policies, plans and programs. The focus of these processes was on initiatives that were already proposed. More recent definitions tend to take a broader perspective. First, the trend is toward the inclusion of environmental, economic and social considerations to encourage integrated decision making. Increasingly, SEA is also seen as a tool for the development of sustainability policies, plans and programs, not just as a tool for assessing those proposed for more limited purposes. For our discussion, the concept of SEA is considered to incorporate at least the following possible elements:

- An environmental assessment that goes beyond a single project to consider an industry sector, a region, or a particular policy, plan or program.
- An SEA can be reactive in response to the proposal of a particular project, such as the first proposal to introduce a new technology or a new industry, such as an LNG facility or in-stream tidal energy technology, if it extends beyond the individual project to look at the whole technology or industry sector or region.
- An SEA can be reactive by responding to a proposed policy, plan or program initiated for economic reasons, such as the Free Trade Area of the Americas (FTAA) initiative.
- An SEA can be proactive by responding to a identified sustainable development or environmental challenge, such as an SEA leading to the development of an energy

---

5 See B. Dalal-Clayton & B. Sadler, *Strategic Environmental Assessment* (London: Earthscan, 2005).

policy that encompasses a range of environmental, social and economic concerns related to climate change, air pollution and energy security.

- An SEA can be proactive by responding to a policy gap or an outdated policy identified in the context of a project EA.

There is now growing experience with SEA around the world. SEA practice is starting to expand dramatically within the European Union as a result of its 2001 directive on SEA. Although some EU member States had experience with SEA prior to the implementation of the directive in 2004, it was limited. In the United States, experience with SEA goes back over 35 years to the early days of NEPA. Its use has, however, been limited in the United States. Other developed nations, including Australia, New Zealand, and Japan, have also experimented with SEA.

International development institutions, such as the World Bank, regional development banks, the United Nations Development Programme (UNDP), as well as international development institutions of several developed nations, have either started to implement SEA processes or carried out some SEAs on an *ad hoc* basis. SEA experience in economies in transition and developing nations is growing rapidly. Many economies in transition began to implement SEAs in the 1990s, and several developing nations are now experimenting with SEA.

In Canada, the assessment of policies, plans and programs was originally included in the EARP Guidelines Order. In return for limiting the application of the *Canadian Environmental Assessment Act* to project assessments, the initial Cabinet Directive on the assessment of policies and programs was introduced. The original Cabinet Directive has been updated periodically, most recently in 2004. Under the most current version, an SEA is expected whenever a proposal that may result in important environmental effects is submitted to a Minister or Cabinet for approval. When appropriate, SEAs are encouraged based on public concern about the possible consequences of a proposed policy, plan or program. SEAs are also encouraged to help implement sustainable development goals.

In terms of the content of an SEA, the Cabinet Directive uses language similar to the CEAA, referring to scope, mitigation and adverse environmental effects. It is not clear whether social and economic considerations are to be included in the assessment itself, but the Cabinet Directive does anticipate their equal consideration in the final decision on the proposed policy, plan and program through full integration of predicted consequences. Public participation is encouraged through the use of existing mechanisms where appropriate. In short, the Cabinet Directive does little more than communicate a general expectation to identify and consider environmental consequences of major decisions at the federal level on par with social and economic factors.

A key change in the shift from including SEAs under the EARP Guidelines Order to the Cabinet Directive was a transition from a legally-binding process to one that is not. This transition went against the trend for project EAs and against the general trend in EA worldwide, which has been toward the legalization of EA processes. The consequences of this transition were considered by Hazel and Benevides in a study which compared the implementation of the original Cabinet Directive to a strategic assessment process under the *Farm Income Protection Act*. The study considers three assessments under each process and compares compliance, scope of the assessment, assessment of alternatives, follow-up, and consultations. The study concludes that the legislative SEA process is superior in its effectiveness and the level of compliance, and attributes this in large part to its legal basis.

The federal Commissioner of the Environment and Sustainable Development carried out an audit of the implementation of the SEA Cabinet Directive in 2004. The overall conclusion reached was that the level of commitment and compliance with the Cabinet Directive was low. Departments evaluated had conducted few strategic environmental assessments, the completeness of the assessments carried out varied, and tracking of assessments carried out was found to be inadequate. The report found that there was insufficient commitment by senior management, no central responsibility for compliance and quality control, and limited integration of the results of the assessments into the decision-making process. Furthermore, few of the assessments had been made available to the public after the fact, with even fewer involving the public in the EA process.

It is clear that SEA at the federal level, in its current form under the 2004 Cabinet Directive, is far from its promise of helping to overcome the limitations of project EAs and delivering integrated decision making for sustainability. The process is not set out in legislation, it often does not involve the public, it is only applied in limited circumstances, and it appears to have limited influence on federal decision making.

There have been efforts to make better use of the SEA process. The Environment Minister's Regulatory Advisory Committee (RAC) on the CEAA identified SEA as a priority as a result of its review of the CEAA in 2000. Since then, the RAC has considered various proposals on how to make better use of SEA within the federal EA process. In addition, there have been *ad hoc* efforts to make use of SEA, such as the SEA on tidal energy in the Bay of Fundy currently underway.

Notes and Questions

1. Can you identify the key differences between the SEA Cabinet Directive and the type of process needed to make the SEA process an effective tool for the assessment of cumulative effects, needs and alternatives?

2. Do you agree that the SEA process has the potential to deal with many of the shortcomings of EA at the project level? Explain.

Sustainability Assessments

Many academics and environmentalists argue that a key flaw of the CEAA is its focus on the "significance" of biophysical environmental effects. They argue for a reformed approach that would assess in broad terms the sustainability of proposed projects. The choice between significance-based assessments and sustainability-based assessments is fundamentally a question of focus. The focus of significance-based assessments is on preventing and mitigating significant impacts on the biophysical environment. Sustainability assessments seek an integrated assessment of the social, economic, and environmental benefits and risks associated with a project. In the article that follows, a leading proponent of a sustainability-based approach to environmental assessment reflects on some of the implications of adopting this approach under the CEAA.

The article by Professor Gibson excerpted below was prompted in part by two CEAA review panel decisions in which proponents were required to provide evidence that their undertakings would make a positive contribution to sustainability, and respect the precautionary principle: see *Voisey's Bay* (1997) and *Red Hill* (1999).

Robert B. Gibson, "Favouring the Higher Test: Contribution to Sustainability as the Central Criterion for Reviews and Decisions under the *Canadian Environmental Assessment Act*"

(2000) 10 J. Env. L. & Prac. 39

At least on the face of things, this "positive contribution to sustainability" criterion [employed in the Voisey's Bay and Red Hill reviews] is substantially different from the "mitigation of significant adverse environmental effects" criterion that has been the focus of most assessments under CEAA. The panels may well be justified in favouring the higher test. But the shift raises difficult questions that will need careful and early attention.

A wide range of issues and questions is raised by [moving towards a sustainability-based approach to EA under CEAA]. I will outline only a few here for illustrative purposes.

1. — Is use of the sustainability criterion under CEAA appropriate and desirable?

This may be a matter for debate among legal scholars. However, it would seem on the surface that choice of the higher test is reasonable in logic and that pursuit of sustainability is entirely suitable in our global circumstances.

Even if this is quickly accepted, clarifying more precisely what application of the sustainability criterion should be expected to accomplish would be helpful, if only as a basis for building a better understanding of how to specify the relevant requirements for proponents and other assessment participants.

2. — How should the criterion be specified?

All decision criteria involve definitional difficulties posed by the value laden terms ("significant", "acceptable", etc.) that are unavoidable in assessment work. Adopting contribution to sustainability should not present overwhelming difficulties. The need for a working understanding of what sustainability means as an effective criterion was not among the recognized problems of the Voisey's case and, so far at least, is not among the pressing concerns of those who are unhappy about the Red Hill assessment. Nevertheless, there are some important areas of potential confusion to address. These include the following:

(i) Tradeoffs: very generally, pursuit of sustainability entails integrated pursuit of ecological and socio-economic ends, rather than some sort of "balancing". In specific cases, however, the acceptability of tradeoffs (between short and long term gains, between ecological and socio-economic improvements, and between onsite losses and offsets elsewhere) must be considered.

(ii) Losses/unsustainable activities: adoption of a sustainability criterion does not entail rejection of all undertakings that involve losses or unsustainable activities, but may limit the kinds of losses and unsustainable activities that are tolerable (e.g. mining may be acceptable where its immediate negative effects are largely corrected through remediation and its socio-economic benefits are designed to provide a bridge to a more sustainable future for the local community).

(iii) Gains: because most assessment work has focused on avoidance of significant adverse effects, we will need expanded consideration of how to design for gains, and how to assess potential benefits.

(iv) Precaution: the panels have properly emphasized the precautionary aspect of commitment to sustainability, and the implications of uncertainty have been receiving considerable scholarly and some practical attention in various fields, recently, but little of this has yet been interpreted for application to assessment work (e.g. in *47 considering implications for risk avoidance versus reversibility versus replacability; or in specifying how adaptability is to incorporated into the design of undertakings).

3. — How should broader application of the criterion to cases subject to CEAA be managed?

It might be desirable to extend implementation of the approach gradually through CEAA decision making, beginning with the most important and promising applications. But consistency in legal interpretation of the Act's requirements would seem to demand a more comprehensive transition. Since the Voisey's Bay panel has already applied the sustainability criterion in a completed review, there will be reasonable expectations for further and expanded use. Perhaps a case could be made for application of the sustainability criterion first to cases at the comprehensive study, mediation or panel review level. The purposes commitment to sustainability is, however, not limited to any particular set of assessed cases and would seem to be generally applicable to all work under the Act.

4. — What happens to ecological concerns in a broader sustainability process?

Under CEAA, assessment and review have often remained on the periphery of decision making. They are commonly viewed as an addendum to deliberations on the central economic and political considerations. Adoption of the sustainability criterion expands the agenda of environmental assessment and necessarily pushes it closer to a position as the main governmental process for addressing broad public interest considerations in project decision making.

This seems both realistic and desirable. Already environmental assessment under CEAA is typically the only process for rigorous and open attention to public concerns about proposed undertakings. Exclusion of direct social effects and other sustainability considerations from CEAA assessment proceedings (as is suggested by the CEAA definitions of "environment" and "environmental effects") is unrealistic as well as inappropriate from a sustainability perspective. But expanding the scope can be risky.

A shift from narrow environmental assessment to broader sustainability assessment would be retrogressive if it allowed loss of the old environmental assessment focus on ecological considerations and opened the door to reassertion of the traditional emphasis on immediate economic priorities. In theory, sustainability assessment should focus on the longer term where ecological, social and economic imperatives tend to coincide. In practice, however, short term imperatives are driven by powerful economic and political interests and are difficult to resist. This suggests that transition to sustainability assessment will be helpful only if the sustainability criterion is clearly specified and imposed in ways that stress the long term and prevent ecological sacrifices for short term gain.

5. — Where should sustainability-focused assessment fit in federal decision making?

If sustainability-centred assessments are be the main public vehicles for open evaluation of proposed undertakings (and their alternatives), it is not clear that the process should report to or through the Minister of the Environment. Such assessment might be more credible and powerful within government if the process reported to Cabinet or Parliament, as representatives of the broad public interest, rather than to a single minister who will be unavoidably associated with a narrower mandate. But like the more general shift away from a narrow environmental focus, this move raises concerns about loss of attention to ecological issues.

6. — How would sustainability-focused assessment at the project level fit with decision making on broader matters?

The move towards adoption of the broad sustainability criterion can be seen as part of a larger trend to expand the scope and application of environmental assessment. The trend is also evident in the gradual introduction assessment requirements at the strategic level (policies, programs, plans, etc.) and in the growing recognition of needs for more attention to the cumulative and regional effects of multiple activities rather than just to the particular effects of individual projects.

Because many sustainability considerations are more evident at a larger scale and perhaps best addressed there, application of the sustainability criterion in assessments at the project level will need to be much better linked with assessments at the strategic assessment level. As noted above, it is convenient that The 1999 Cabinet Directive on the Environmental Assessment of Policy already includes useful steps towards a sustainability-based approach to assessment. However, it remains a non-legislated directive with weak provisions for public accountability and participation. Until strategic assessment also has a credible legislative foundation, strong integration of strategic and project level assessment will be problematic.

7. — Does CEAA need amendment to facilitate application of the sustainabililty criterion?

The Voisey's and Red Hill cases suggest that CEAA as presently drafted can serve as a base for public sustainability assessments of significant undertakings within federal jurisdiction. But if CEAA is to serve this function effectively, several aspects of the current law would seem to need attention. For example,

(i) CEAA now applies complex and minimally workable definitions of "environment" and "environmental effects" that are open to various interpretations but seem intended to discourage consideration of direct social, economic and cultural effects. More explicitly comprehensive definitions of these two terms would seem to be appropriate for assessments focused on sustainability effects.

(ii) The current definitions of "environment" and "environmental effects" implicitly include both positive and negative effects, as is appropriate for sustainability considerations. However, as noted above, some CEAA provisions (e.g. section 37 (1)(a)) stress attention only to "significant adverse environmental effects". As well, the current opening to accept even significant adverse effects if these are "justified in the circumstances" is not defined. In both cases, amendments seem to be needed to clarify the implications of commitment to encouraging sustainability. This would entail mandatory attention to both positive and adverse effects and to ensuring that projects are approved only if there is good reason to expect overall positive contributions to sustainability.

(iii) As suggested above, integration of assessment at the strategic and project levels is desirable but will remain problematic so long as there is no legislative base for strategic level assessments. At minimum, it would seem reasonable to extend CEAA to provide for strategic assessments that meet CEAA standards and that can be used as appropriate frames for relevant project assessments.

(iv) Probably the most difficult challenge is to specify the meaning and implications of the sustainability criterion, addressing the areas of potential confusion listed under question 2, above, and ensuring that the process is not made more vulnerable to narrow interests and short term pressures. The first step here may be to develop appropriate guidelines under section 58(1)(a).

The sustainability-based approach advocated for by Professor Gibson has since been employed in two more recent panel reviews — Kemess North and White's Point — as chronicled in the article that follows.

Alberto Fonseca & Robert B. Gibson, "Kemess North Fails the Test"
(2008) 34 Alternatives Journal 4 at 10–12

Northgate Mineral Corporation's proposed Kemess North Project will not be going ahead, at least not soon and not as proposed. The project — an open pit copper-gold expansion to an existing mine in a remote, mountainous area of north-central British Columbia — was rejected by provincial and federal authorities. In his March 7, 2008 announcement, BC Environment Minister Barry Penner said that while the government recognized the mine would bring jobs and other economic benefits for an expected 13 years of construction and operation, these benefits would be "outweighed by the adverse social, environmental and cultural effects and risks". In denying Northgate's application, Penner accepted the recommendation of a federal-provincial environmental assessment panel that had held public hearings and applied a "contribution to sustainability" test to the proposed project.

While environmental assessment processes are often presented as a means of contributing to sustainability, the longstanding tradition has been to focus only on how to mitigate significant adverse effects. Instead, the Kemess North panel took the sustainability requirement seriously. They asked whether the project would leave a positive overall legacy, not just whether the immediate effects would be minimally damaging.

In its September 2007 final report, the panel concluded that the project was not likely to bring lasting gains, especially because of the long term effects of the mine wastes on ecological and Aboriginal interests. The project as proposed would have dumped 700 million tonnes of acid-generating mine tailings and waste rock into nearby Amazay Lake (also called Duncan Lake), a body of water that is spiritually significant for local First Nations. The company said that using Amazay Lake for tailings disposal was the safest and least costly option. But the panel noted that after the mine closed, the wastes would have to be managed for thousands of years. First Nations, the region's main residents and who have unresolved land claims in the area, would be most at risk.

For its assessment review, the Kemess panel adopted a sustainability-based evaluation framework based on recent mining industry initiatives and on the BC government's 2005 Mining Plan. The framework focused on five sustainability considerations: environmental stewardship, economic benefits and costs, social and cultural benefits and costs, fair distribution of benefits and costs, and present versus future generations. After evaluating the project in light of these considerations, individually and in combination, the panel concluded that "overall, from a public interest perspective, the benefits of project development do not outweigh the costs".

Although the Kemess panel was the first in Canada to recommend the outright rejection of a mining project, it was not the first to apply a sustainability test. The pioneering case was the mid-1990s environmental assessment of the Voisey's Bay nickel mine-mill project in Labrador. The Voisey's Bay panel, established under a joint agreement involving two Aboriginal organizations as well as the federal and provincial governments, examined "the extent to which the undertaking may make a positive overall contribution towards the attainment of ecological and community sustainability, both at the local and regional levels". In the end, the panel found that the proposed project was generally acceptable if the project proponent met certain conditions.

The Kemess North panel report took a similar approach, though with an analysis based on five key sustainability considerations, and with less favourable results for the proponent.

In October 2007, only a month after the Kemess North decision, a federal-provincial panel on the other side of the country released its sustainability-based review, also concluding that the project proponent had failed to meet the test. The White's Point panel reviewed a proposal for a large basalt quarry and marine terminal in Nova Scotia. The panel found the immediate economic gains from the project would accrue mostly to the proponent and would compromise long term qualities and opportunities, in this case sustainable community economic development based on tourism and fishing. The Nova Scotia government accepted the panel's recommendation to reject the project, though the proponent, a US firm, has since initiated an appeal under NAFTA.

Whether the Voisey's Bay, Kemess and White's Point cases represent the future of environmental assessment in Canada is not yet clear. But Anthony Hodge, a professor of mining and sustainability at Queen's University, believes the writing is on the wall. He says, "It's inevitable that this is going to happen more and more". It is not an issue of whether sustainability tests will be increasingly applied in environmental assessment reviews, but, says Hodge, "how fast it will happen".

Joan Kuyek, the national co-ordinator of MiningWatch Canada, is less optimistic. While Kuyek hopes that the higher test will prevail, she fears that the Kemess and White's Point results may trigger industry lobbying against panel reviews with sustainability expectations. Last year MiningWatch took Fisheries and Oceans Canada (DFO) to court for dodging a full assessment of the proposed Red Chris Copper-Gold Mine in Northern BC. Federal Court Justice Luc Martineau ruled in favour of MiningWatch, agreeing that DFO had unlawfully evaded the required comprehensive study of the Red Chris proposal in favour of a simple screening process. But that ruling was appealed and has since been overturned by a higher court. Kuyek believes industry lobbying lay behind DFO's efforts to minimize assessment obligations and is likely to focus now on preventing entrenchment of the Voisey's Bay, Kemess and White's Point precedents. Such lobbying contradicts the global mining industry's commitment to the principles of sustainable development. An example of the mining industry's official stand is the Sustainable Development Framework of the International Council on Mining and Metals, which has been embraced by the world's top mining corporations and associations.

The BC and Nova Scotia governments' acceptance of the Kemess and White's Point panel recommendations appears to corroborate Hodge's optimism. Other Canadian and International cases also point to the spread of sustainability-based tests. Applications have been reported in Australia, Hong Kong, Ghana, South Africa and the United Kingdom, among others. In 2006, the international *Journal of Environmental Assessment Policy and Management* dedicated an entire issue to the "new" field.

Approaches vary. Some consider economic, social and ecological effects (the "three pillars" of sustainability) separately, while others attempt to address interrelationships and overlapping concerns such as livelihood effects, and the distribution of gains and losses. But they all share a broader agenda and a longer vision than has been the common practice. It is an innovation that brings to mind the sensible words of Henry David Thoreau: "In the long run, men hit only what they aim at. Therefore, though they should fail immediately, they had better aim at something high".

Notes and Questions

1. Some within the mining industry reacted to the Kemess panel review and the White's Point Quarry panel review in Nova Scotia by claiming that the panels' reliance on sustainability criteria is not authorized by the CEAA. Do you agree?

2. Do you think sustainability assessments should be formally adopted in the CEAA? What advantages and disadvantages can you identify when compared to the currently prevailing approach of focussing the process on significant adverse environmental effects?

3. What legal and/or policy changes, if any, would be necessary to shift the focus of federal EA under the CEAA from significant environmental effects to sustainability?

References

We thank the copyright holders for their permission to reproduce their materials.

E. Beanlands Gordon & Peter N. Duinker, *An Ecological Framework for Environmental Impact Assessment in Canada* (Halifax: Institute for Resource and Environmental Studies, Dalhousie University, 1983)

Hugh J. Benevides, "Real Reform Deferred: Analysis of Recent Amendments to the *Canadian Environmental Assessment Act*" (2004) 13 J. Env. L. & Prac. 195

J. Benedickson, *Environmental Law*, 3rd ed. (Toronto: Irwin, 2008)

T.R. Berger, *Northern Frontier, Northern Homeland: The report of the Mackenzie Valley Pipeline Inquiry* (Ottawa: Ministry of Supply and Services Canada, 1977).

A.P. Diduck & A. J. Sinclair. "Public Involvement in Environmental Assessment: The Case of the Non-participant" (2002) 29:4 Environ. Manage. 578

B. Dalal-Clayton & B. Sadler, *Strategic Environmental Assessment* (London: Earthscan, 2005)

M. Doelle & A. J. Sinclair, "Time for a New Approach to Environmental Assessments: Promoting Cooperation and Consensus for Sustainability" (2006) 26:2 Environ. Impact Assess. Rev. 185

M. Doelle, *The Federal Environmental Assessment Process: A Guide and Critique* (Markham, Ont.: LexisNexis Butterworths, 2008)

Robert B. Gibson, "Favouring the Higher Test: Contribution to Sustainability as the Central Criterion for Reviews and Decisions under the *Canadian Environmental Assessment Act*" (2000) 10 J. Env. L. & Prac. 39

Robert B. Gibson, "Sustainability Assessment: Basic Components of a Practical Approach" (2006) 24 Impact Assessment and Project Appraisal 170–182

Robert B. Gibson, "Favouring the Higher Test: Contribution to Sustainability as the Central Criterion for Reviews and Decisions under the *Canadian Environmental Assessment Act*" (2000) 10 J. Env. L. & Prac. 39

Andrew Green, "Discretion, Judicial Review, and the *Canadian Environmental Assessment Act*" (2002) 27 Queen's L.J. 785

Kevin S. Hanna, ed., *Environmental Impact Assessment: Practice and Participation* (Oxford: Oxford University Press, 2005).

J. Hanebury, "Cooperative Environmental Assessments: Their Increasing Role in Oil and Gas Projects" (2001) 24 Dal. L.J. 87

S. Hazel & H. Benevides, "Federal Strategic Environmental Assessment: Toward a Legal Framework" (1997) 7 J. Env. L. & Prac. 349

S.A. Kennett, *Toward a New Paradigm for Cumulative Effects Management* (Calgary: Canadian Institute for Resources Law, 1999)

A. Kwasniak, "Slow on the Trigger: The Department of Fisheries and Oceans, the *Fisheries Act* and the *Canadian Environmental Assessment Act*" (2004) 27 Dal. L.J. 347

Susan Rutherford & Karen Campbell, "Time Well Spent? A Survey of Public Participation in Federal Environmental Assessment Panels" (2004) 15 J. Env. L. & Prac. 71

8

Parks and Protected Areas

Introduction

Parks and protected areas play a central and rapidly evolving role in Canadian environmental law and policy. Canadians are deservedly proud of their parks system which, over the last 40 years, has grown and evolved significantly. At the same time, our parks and broader network of protected areas are under growing pressure to deliver an ever broadening range of values as species loss, climate change and environmental degradation across the broader landscape escalates. As a result, it is increasingly recognized that greater attention needs to be given to the role of parks and protected areas in mitigating wider landscape level changes. This is especially true, as we will see, in the marine environment. Another critical challenge is to identify strategies that protect the marine and terrestrial environments that are consistent with the constitutional imperative to recognize and respect First Nations rights and title; a goal that, in the past, has been seldom achieved or even fully appreciated.

This chapter is in four Parts. In Part I, we offer a snapshot of recent developments in, and current status of, parks and protected areas in Canada. We then consider, in Part II, the values that parks and protected areas promote, how those values may be quantified or conceptualized, and the respective roles of the provincial and federal governments as parks stewards. In Part III, we address four key issues in protected areas law and policy that are of particular interest from a legal perspective. These include:

- The challenges associated with fulfilling Canada's international commitments to complete a marine protected area system;
- Legal and policy issues relating to the need for greater integration within our protected areas network to, among other things, enhance species protection;
- The unresolved tension between competing "use" and "preservation" mandates under the *Canadian National Parks Act* (CNPA) and the role of "ecological integrity" in Parks Canada decision making; and
- The implications of recognizing and respecting Aboriginal rights and title for management and expansion of parks and protected areas.

Finally, in Part IV, we reflect on two more "prospective" issues of relevance to protected areas law and policy moving forward: the potential role of the public trust doctrine as a means of enhancing protection outcomes within our parks system; and the possibilities for law reform that may exist, drawing on new parks legislation recently enacted by the province of Ontario.

Part I — History and Overview of Parks and Protected Areas in Canada

Executive Summary, Canadian Protected Areas Status Report 2000–2005

http://www.cws-scf.ec.gc.ca/publications/habitat/cpa-apc/sum_e.cfm

Since Canada's first park was created in 1872, almost 100 million hectares of terrestrial protected areas have been set aside, an amount equal to 10% of this country's total land mass. Over 3 million hectares or 0.5% of Canada's oceans have been secured as marine protected areas. These protected areas play a central role in preserving our country's greatest asset — our natural capital. They also provide a variety of social and economic benefits to Canadians by creating both direct and tourism-based employment opportunities for many communities. In addition, protected areas offer world class opportunities for nature appreciation, learning, research, spiritual enrichment and outdoor recreation, with resulting benefits to personal health and national identity. Protected areas are an important means of demonstrating Canada's commitment to a sustainable environment, society and economy. Finally, maintaining a healthy and dynamic protected areas system responds to recent polling which consistently indicates that Canadians rank protection of the environment next to health and education as priority issues.

Canadians can be proud of the progress that has been achieved over the last five years to preserve and manage the wealth of natural capital within the country's protected areas networks. Canada's protected areas family has grown by roughly 19% since Parks Ministers last gathered in Iqaluit in 2000. All governments have contributed to this progress, and have strengthened their respective protected areas programs. Over the last five years progress has included:

- developing and implementing protected areas strategies;
- increasing management effectiveness of protected areas;
- updating protected areas legislation; and
- allocating increased resources to protected areas programs.

Also since 2000, five important policy advances and shifts in industry practice promise to provide significant new opportunities to safeguard Canada's natural capital:

- Integrated landscape and oceans management is emerging in Canada as a means of ensuring that resource allocation decisions are made in concert with conservation planning.
- Leading resource industries are increasingly becoming partners and advocates for innovative conservation solutions as a proactive means to enhance competitiveness and demonstrate corporate social responsibility, while providing greater investment certainty.
- Land claim settlements and other cooperative agreements are providing means to preserve lands of ecological and cultural importance, that in turn provide economic and social benefits to Aboriginal communities.
- The federal government has initiated the Oceans Action Plan, a roadmap to integrated management for five Large Oceans Management Areas, and has adopted a government wide strategy to establish a federal marine protected area network.
- Canada has committed to the Convention on Biological Diversity's Programme of Work on Protected Areas, with an overall international objective of completing com-

prehensive global networks of terrestrial and marine protected areas by 2010 and 2012 respectively.

Philip Dearden, "Progress and Problems in Canada's Protected Areas: Overview of Progress, Chronic Issues and Emerging Challenges in the Early 21st Century"
(unpublished, 2008)

... in 1992 Canada's federal, provincial and territorial Ministers of Environment, Parks and Wildlife signed *A Statement of Commitment to Complete Canada's Network of Protected Areas*. Terrestrial systems were to be completed by 2000 whereas marine designation was to be "accelerated". Despite impressive growth, Canada is still far from meeting these commitments. ... In terms of overall protection of Canada's ecoregions, 29% are provided a high level of protection (ie over 12% of their area), 12.4% moderate protection (6 to 12%), 41.9% low protection (<6%) and 16.6% have no protected areas (Environment Canada 2006).

Parks Canada's performance targets for creating and expanding new parks were to increase the number of represented terrestrial regions from 25 in March 2003 to 34 by March 2008, and increase the number of represented marine regions from two in March 2003 to eight by March 2008 (Parks Canada 2007). Neither of these were met and currently 28 terrestrial regions are represented by national parks. Progress was made on several candidate national parks but funding limitations and the complicated nature of the park establishment process resulted in a reduction of performance expectation for representation to 30 terrestrial regions represented by March 2008.

The marine target was also not met. Currently 2 of 29 marine regions are represented, but these are from existing areas and not new acquisitions protected under the NMCA Act. As a result, the goal was reduced to 4 of 29 in the 2007/2008 Corporate Plan, but as yet no areas have been designated, although progress is being made on several areas. Under 0.5% of Canada's marine area is set aside in protective designation and Canada ranks 70th globally in terms of the percentage of oceans protected (Environment Canada 2006). Projections suggest that Canada will optimistically achieve perhaps 33% of its international target goal by 2012 (Roff and Dearden 2007).

Figure 1: National parks system plan showing current state of representation

There have also been major increases at the provincial level. In 1968, Ontario had 90 regulated protected areas totalling 1.6% of the province by area. Currently, Ontario has 632 protected areas totalling over 9.4 million ha, 8.7% of the province (Davis, pers com). Nova Scotia in 2007 passed the *Environmental Goals and Sustainable Prosperity Act* requiring the province to protect 12% of its terrestrial area by 2015 (Government of Nova Scotia 2007). In BC the area of parkland doubled between 1977 and 2005 and now totals over 12 million ha. BC is the only jurisdiction to accomplish the 12% target set by the WCED (1987). However, no provincial government has completed the 1992 Statement of Commitment to complete a representative network of protected areas (Environment Canada 2006).

To date, about 10% of Canada's terrestrial area has been awarded protective designation, well short of the average 14.6% protected by OECD countries (Environment Canada 2006). However, 95% of Canada's terrestrial protected areas fall within IUCN categories I–IV and hence have a strong protective mandate. Amongst OECD countries Canada ranks 16th out of 30 in terms of the proportion of land protected (the US, for example protects almost 25% compared with our 10%), yet ranks 4th in terms of proportion of land with strong protection (IUCN I–IV). Furthermore, Canada has some two-thirds of its protected area within a small number of sites that are in excess of 300,000 ha in size. Few countries have the ability to preserve such large intact landscapes.

The question of progress in terms of establishing a greater extent of protected area in Canada is clearly answered in the affirmative. The protected area system has grown enormously within the last forty years. Parks Canada is inching towards completion of the system plan and many provincial jurisdictions have set aside significant areas under their jurisdiction as PAs. However, much remains to be done. Canada is signatory to the UN Convention on Biological Diversity which calls for "the establishment and maintenance by 2010 for terrestrial and by 2012 for marine areas of comprehensive, effectively managed, and ecologically representative national and regional systems of protected areas ..". Canada will not be able to meet these international commitments for quite some time after the target dates. The marine system is in its infancy and getting off to a very slow and underfunded start. A significant number of the ecoregions of Canada still remain unprotected. Canada is not a world leader in term of the proportion of area set aside, yet we have some of the largest and wildest PAs on Earth. Progress has undoubtedly been made, but much remains to be done.

Part II — The Role of Parks and Protected Areas

Phil Dearden & Rick Rollins, "Parks and Protected Areas in Canada" in P. Dearden & R. Rollins, eds., *Parks and Protected Areas in Canada*, 3rd ed.,
(Oxford University Press, 2009)

Protected Area Values

We expect protected areas to play a variety of roles in the landscape. These roles represent the values that we wish to see maintained within the landscape that, without protection, would not be able to withstand market forces. That is why they are protected. These values [may be] depict[ed] as . . . different locations and institutions in a city. The purpose of [this metaphor] ... is to illustrate that PAs are not 'single use' areas, any more than all the functions of specific urban locations could be united into one, and to illustrate the diversity of values represented in PAs.

- *Art gallery*: Just as people visit an art gallery for aesthetic reasons, many parks were designated for their scenic beauty. When Banff was first established, Canadian Pacific Railway President, William Van Horne declared that 'since we can't export the scenery we shall have to import the tourists' and appreciation of scenery is still a major reason why people visit parks.
- *Zoo*: Parks are usually easy places to watch wildlife in relatively natural surroundings. Park wildlife, at least in the national parks, is protected from hunting, and not, therefore, as shy of humans as wildlife outside parks.
- *Playground*: Parks provide excellent recreational settings for many outdoor pursuits and provision of recreational opportunities has been one of the main functions of parks over the years. However, in keeping with the quote from the first Commissioner of National Parks, J.B. Harkin, park recreation should be thought of in a more profound sense of 're-creation' of self, rather than merely playing games.
- *Movie theatre*: Like a movie, parks are able to transport us into a different setting from our everyday existence. We go there to do different things than we would normally do. This is one of the arguments against having golf courses in our parks. Golf might be a fine recreational pursuit but it is not dependent upon being in a park to play it and, furthermore, it introduces everday activities into the park environment at the cost of discovering new activities that are dependent upon a park environment. An excellent treatise on this topic, is *Mountains Without Handrails*, (Sax, 1980)
- *Cathedral*: Many people derive spiritual fulfillment from nature, just as others go to human-built structures, such as churches, temples, and mosques. Such sites, irrespec-

tive of denomination, help us appreciate the existence of forces more powerful than ourselves and remind us that humility is a virtue.

- *Factory*: The first national parks in Canada were designated with the idea of generating income through tourism. Since these early beginnings, the economic role of parks has been recognized, although it is a controversial one due to the potential conflict with other roles. A study by Eagles et al. (2000) on national parks, wildlife areas and provincial parks in Canada calculated total daily economic impact of between $120.47 to $187.69 per park visitor. Overall the economic impact was between $13.9 and $21.6 billion dollars for the year. Although these totals are high, of perhaps greater significance is the distribution of the benefits. As Walton and Simon (2003) point out in poor, northern, Aboriginal communities, income potential is extremely limited and the factory role of parks takes on great significance, perhaps requiring a different perspective on park policies than those extant in the south.
- *Museum*: Parks protect the landscape as it might have been when European colonists first arrived in North America. As such, parks act as museums to remind us of these conditions. Nash (1967), in his well-known history of the wilderness movement, describes this as a main reason behind the early growth of the parks' movement in the US, although it is certainly a less prominent motivation now. These museums also serve a valuable ecological function as they provide important areas against which to measure ecological change in the rest of the landscape, often known as the *benchmark* role. Davis et al. (2006) provide a review of this role and a Canadian example of a comparative monitoring system, Environment Canada's Ecological Monitoring and Assessment Network (EMAN) is described in more detail by Craig *et al.* (2003).
- *Bank*: Parks are places in which we store and protect our ecological capital, including threatened and endangered species. From these accounts we can use the interest to repopulate areas with species that have disappeared. Examples include the musk-oxen from the Thelon Game sanctuary that have recolonized terrain outside the Sanctuary, and the elk and bison from Elk Island National Park outside Edmonton that have been used to start herds elsewhere.
- *Hospital*: Ecosystems are not static and isolated phenomena but are linked all over the planet. Protected areas constitute some of the few places where these processes still operate in a relatively natural manner. As such, they may be considered ecosystem 'hospitals' that help to maintain processes that may be damaged and not working effectively elsewhere. Much attention, for example, is now focused on the carbon cycle as imbalances caused by the burning of fossil fuels contribute to global warming. Forests are major carbon 'sinks' where carbon dioxide is taken in from the atmosphere and stored in organic form. Thus forests that are protected play a major role in maintaining some balance in the carbon cycle. Kulshreshtha and Johnston (2003), for example, calculate that Canada's national parks have sequestered 4.43 gigatonnes of carbon that would cost society between $72–$78 billion to replace. In a more modest but also interesting example of the *hospital role* Knowler et al. (2003) calculate the value to salmon of protecting freshwater habitat in protected areas on Canada's west coast. Although the hospital function is a commonly overlooked role of protected areas, it is becoming one of increasing interest to scientists.
- *Laboratory*: As relatively natural landscapes, parks provide outside laboratories for scientists to unravel the mysteries of nature. For example, Killarney Provincial Park in Ontario provided an important laboratory for early research on acid precipitation in Canada.

- *Schoolroom*: Parks can play a major role in education as outdoor classrooms. Direct physical contact with the complexities of the natural environment help inspire awe, humility, and respect. This function can also play a key role in helping influence visitors to change behaviours to more environmentally benign practices in their everyday lives.

It is useful to bear this full range of values in mind as the emphasis amongst them can change over time. As already mentioned, when Canada's national parks were inaugurated there was an overwhelming emphasis on the playground and factory roles. As the rest of the landscape became dominated by market forces for forestry, agriculture and urban uses, the ecological roles became increasingly recognized. For many years, Parks Canada legislation and policies laboured under what was known as the 'dual mandate' which required making full use of the parks for the enjoyment and benefit of the people while ensuring that they were unimpaired for future generations. Various administrators interpreted this balance in differing ways, but finally, in 1988 the *National Park Act* was amended to clear priority to protection of ecological integrity over human use, and this has been further emphasized in more recent policy and legislation ...

Similar changes are evident at provincial levels as the need for more protection becomes evident. For example, the oldest and one of the most significant provincial parks in the country, Algonquin, some 260 km northeast from Toronto has been subject to extensive logging activity over the years and contains over 8,000 km of logging roads. The Ontario Parks Board recommended in 2007 that the area protected from logging needed to be raised from 22 per cent to 54 per cent of the park in order to increase protection for park ecosystems.

There are also further nuances regarding changes in role priority. For example, historically within the ecological context most emphasis was placed on the *bank role*. Recently increasing interest has been shown in the *hospital role* and the value of ecosystem services provided by PAs. This interest reflects greater scientific understanding of ecosystem linkages and heightened public and political awareness of environmental degradation in general ...

Notes and Questions

1. How would you rank in importance the various roles that the authors above ascribe to parks? Is ranking possible without embarking on an economic valuation of the various functions that parks can potentially perform?

2. For a more skeptical approach to the rationale for parks, which raises these and related questions, consider the following article.

Robert W. Turner, "Market Failures and the Rationale for National Parks"
(2002) 33 Journal of Economic Education 4 at 347–356

The most fundamental question is whether the government should provide things like national parks or, said another way, if private markets would provide them efficiently. If there is a case for national parks, the next question is whether the current size of the national park system is appropriate. Answering either question requires the identification of market failures that would justify national parks. After describing the market failures that may provide a rationale for national parks, I summarize what evidence is needed to make a strong case for a national park system. A large body of evidence arising from Krutilla's (1967) analysis of conservation relates to the conservation or preservation of nature or wilderness in general and in specific areas, sometimes including national parks. Nonetheless, the justification for national parks is based largely on assertions that, although reasonable, cannot be supported strongly by existing empirical evidence. This article is related to a large body of economic literature about "the amenities associated with unspoiled natural environments", to use the words of Krutila (1967, 778), which many consider the seminal article on the subject. Most of this literature concerns the recreational value of parks and other natural areas. My main focus in this article is on the existence of national parks, whereas most of the literature either uses national parks as examples of a broader class of natural areas or considers changes in particular attributes of specific national parks; I emphasize the importance of the nonrecreational aspects of parks. [...]

The clearest rationale for government provision of national parks is the case of pure public goods. Pure public goods are both nonrival (some economists use the terms nondepletable or indivisible) and nonexcludable. Nonrival refers to the property that the same unit of the good can be consumed by more than one person whereas nonexcludable refers to the inability to prevent anyone from consuming the good once it is produced. National defense is the quintessential textbook example of a pure public good, and public health and safety examples are also common. Nonexcludability leads to free (or easy) riding, where individuals refuse to pay (or understate their willingness to pay) for the good because they know that they can consume the good even if they do not pay (fully) for it. This provides the usual justification for government provision; because of the free rider problem, no company could profitably produce and sell the good [...]

National parks are not themselves pure public goods, however. Most national parks, at least the parts of them most heavily visited, are clearly excludable, as shown by the existence of entrance gates where visitors are asked to pay a fee. Club goods are excludable goods that are nonrival except for congestion. The provision of club goods is characterized by two decisions. First, the membership of the club is determined. Membership might be restricted or it might be open to the entire public; there may or may not be a membership fee. Second, when members visit the club, goods or services are provided; these goods or services are nonrival except for congestion.

National parks are more than recreational areas, however. They are also places where natural and historic resources are conserved for future generations. If the purpose of this conservation is to allow future visitors to enjoy the resources, this is viewed better as a club good than as a pure public good. If private owners know that future generations will want to visit the parks, they will conserve the parks' resources accordingly, just as the owner of any nonrenewable resource saves some of it to sell in the future. [...]

Park advocates maintain that national parks provide large benefits in addition to the recreational benefits received by present and future visitors. These benefits can be described as various kinds of nonuse or existence values of the parks. National parks have nonuse values if people get satisfaction from knowing that parks exist, even if they have never visited them and never plan to visit them. By their nature, goods with nonuse values are pure public goods: There is no way to exclude individuals from getting nonuse values, and one individual's value is unaffected by the fact that others are also getting nonuse values from the same resource. [...]

To the extent that the park system provides pure public goods, its existence may be justified on that basis. But a benefit-cost analysis is still required: The public goods provided by the parks must create enough benefits to offset the associated costs. These costs include the direct operating costs of the park system plus the opportunity costs of using land for this purpose. In addition, a case needs to be made that direct government provision is more effective than private provision with government subsidies or regulation. [...]

Another possible reason that private markets would not provide the efficient amount of places like national parks is that some visitors to the national parks create spillover effects on other people; that is, there are externalities. Students of economics are used to thinking of negative externalities, such as pollution, when market activities create direct harmful effects on third parties. Negative externalities certainly exist in national parks: One person's use of the park creates congestion externalities; alternative uses in parks conflict; and some uses harm the resources of the park, reducing the enjoyment of future park visitation and also reducing the nonuse values associated with the resources. None of these provide a justification for government provision of parks, however, except for the effects on nonuse values, all of these externalities would be taken into account by a private owner of a club good. [...]

Another possible argument for positive externalities is that national parks act as natural laboratories for scientific research of various kinds. Like other forms of research, the research activities may benefit society as a whole in addition to creating private benefits for the researchers ... [...]

Another way in which externalities might justify government provision of national parks is that government provision may be an efficient response to external threats. Most national park units are threatened by negative externalities created by activities outside the parks. Mining, drilling, and electricity generation outside the parks can lead to water and air pollution in the parks, reducing visibility and creating health hazards to visitors as well as degradation of the ecosystem; the operations have also been known to cause seismic disturbances that threaten park ecosystems. Logging on adjacent lands can impair a park's scenic attractiveness and its ecosystem. [...]

National parks may potentially be justified on the basis of several market failures, but none of the possible explanations is compelling without some sense of the magnitude of the associated market failure. In the context of public-good provision, the magnitude of existence values for the resources conserved in national parks needs to be estimated and compared with the economic costs of conservation, including the opportunity cost of using the land for this purpose. To know if the park system as currently configured is justified, existence values and costs for the specific resources conserved in each park are needed, or else the existence values and costs must be related to the overall size of the park system so that marginal benefits can be compared with marginal costs. If positive spillover effects of visitation are to be used as the rationale for national parks, an estimate of their magnitude is required and a convincing argument must be made that government provision is administratively the best form of government intervention, rather than, for instance, government subsidies. [...]

Theoretical arguments can, in principle, justify some level of public provision of parks. More evidence needs to be marshaled, however, before the size and scope of the U.S. national park system can be clearly supported on economic grounds. Although this evidence will be difficult to obtain, it is hard to give an economic rationale for national parks without it.

Notes and Questions

In federal states, both national and sub-national levels of government play in role in parks creation and maintenance. This complicates the task of parks and protected areas management, as it does in many other area of environmental management. The following excerpt highlights some of the key differences between provincial and national parks.

Chris Malcolm, "Provincial Parks" in P. Dearden & R. Rollins, eds., *Parks and Protected Areas in Canada*, 3rd ed.
(Oxford University Press, 2009)

Provincial versus National Parks

What is the difference between a provincial and national park? At first glance, they both protect habitat and often provide recreational opportunities, including vehicle camping. Many people may not realize that they are in one type or the other. However, at the most fundamental level, national parks protect landscape of national significance. That being said, because of the vast size of Canada there are many provincial parks that are also of national significance. National parks are established by Parks Canada, a federal government agency within the Ministry of the Environment, through the *National Parks Act*. National Parks are placed on federal Crown land and can be in any province or territory of Canada. Parks Canada has developed a National Parks System Plan (Parks Canada, 1997), in which National Parks are organized into 39 terrestrial natural regions. As mentioned above, the provincial governments own most of the land in Canada's 10 provinces. This means that in order to establish a national park, the federal government usually has to negotiate with the provincial government to obtain the land; this can often be a tedious and expensive process.

Provincial parks are established and managed by the provincial governments in which the parks are situated. Similar to the federal natural region classification, all provinces have divided their lands into regions based on natural features. However, the method by which the classifications are determined may differ from province to province. Some of the first provincial parks in Canada were established based on similar reasoning to the first national parks, mainly as tourism destinations for economic profit. It is easy to understand, then, why provinces historically have been and can be reluctant to cede land to the federal government, as they lose potential long-term economic revenue. Sometimes, a better option for the provincial governments is to retain the land and create a provincial park. In doing so the province retains tourism revenue, as well as options for resource extraction, such as logging or mining, in the future. Income from these activities can be put towards operating the provincial park system.

There are advantages and disadvantages, beyond economics, to development of provincial park systems. Some of the advantages may include:

- The provinces assess their landscapes at a smaller scale than does the federal government and, consequently, identify more 'natural regions' within their boundaries. As a result the provinces can identify a greater number of representative areas in which to place protective areas. As such, provincial protected area systems may be more ecologically diverse and therefore more resilient.
- Local management (provincial government), as opposed to federal management, based in Ottawa, can mean that local concerns are more likely to be taken into account, and local communities may be more able to take part in management issues.

There are potential disadvantages as well:

- There can be less emphasis on ecological conservation within provincial systems than is the cae for national parks. Some provincial governments have weak conservation mandates and, therefore, provincial park systems are often less prone to protect against recreation and extraction activities (which can counteract the first advantage above).
- Multiple protected area agencies (e.g., Parks Canada, Environment Canada, Fisheries and Oceans Canada, as well as provincial government agencies) may cause ineffi-

ciencies in protected area establishment and management on a national scale, due to lack of communication, duplication of protected area types, and diverse conservation goals.

- The general public may not be aware whether they are visiting a national or provincial protected area. This can weaken the conservation message.
- National parks have very strong legislation, policy, management capability, and accountability mechanisms. Provincial parks often find themselves at the whim of provincial politicians and may lack adequate resources for effective protection.

The issue of multiple agencies being responsible for habitat protection in Canada is particularly important due to the number of difficult management issues that exist in our attempts to create efficient protected area networks.

Part III — Current Issues and Challenges

Marine Conservation

In this Part, we consider four challenges currently at the forefront of parks and protected areas law and policy reform. These are:

- fulfilling Canada's international commitments to complete its marine protected area system;
- promoting greater integration and coordination within our protected areas network to, among other things, enhance species protection;
- grappling with the unresolved tension between competing "use" and "preservation" mandates under the *Canadian National Parks Act* (CNPA) and operationalizing the concept of 'ecological integrity' in Parks Canada decision making; and
- recognizing and respecting Aboriginal rights and title in the management and expansion of our parks and protected areas system.

As discussed in Part I, in 1992 Canada's federal, provincial and territorial Ministers of Environment, Parks and Wildlife signed *A Statement of Commitment to Complete Canada's Network of Protected Areas*. Under this agreement, the Ministers committed to completing the terrestrial park system by 2000, and to "accelerating" the marine designation process. While significant progress has been achieved on the terrestrial front, less headway has occurred with respect to marine designations.

P. Dearden & R. Canessa, "Marine Protected Areas" in P. Dearden & R. Rollins, eds., *Parks and Protected Areas in Canada*, 3rd ed.
(Oxford University Press, 2009)

Internationally, marine protected areas are defined as 'any area of intertidal or subtidal terrain, together with its overlying waters and associated flora, fauna, historical and cultural features, which has been reserved by legislation or other effective means to protect part or all of the enclosed environment' (Kelleher and Rechia, 1998). The potential contributions of MPAs include:

- protection of marine biodiversity, representative ecosystems and special natural features (Sobel, 1993);

- support rebuilding of depleted fish stocks, particularly groundfish, by protecting spawning and nursery grounds (e.g., see Wallace *et al.*, 1998);
- insurance against current inadequate management of marine resources;
- provision of benchmark sites against which to evaluate human impacts elsewhere and undertake scientific research;
- recognition of cultural links of coastal communities to biodiversity;
- provision of opportunities for recreation and education.

The effectiveness of marine reserves in providing for these benefits is largely conditional on size, how they are linked to other reserves, the kinds of activities allowed within the borders, the co-operation of local communities in supporting the reserve, the vulnerability to polluting influences from outside, and the ability to mitigate these negative impacts.

The Canadian Context

Canada has the longest coastline of any country in the world along three oceans and the second largest area of continental shelf. For over 30 years Canada has sought to gradually extend its jurisdiction over these waters and was a significant contributor to the UN Law of the Sea Convention (UNCLOS) between 1974 and 1982. Nevertheless, it was not until 2003 that Canada ratified UNCLOS. Ratification allows Canada to extend its sovereign rights over the seabed to the edge of the continental shelf, where it extends beyond the 200 nautical mile (370.4 km) exclusive economic zone (EEZ) thus adding 1,750,000 km^2 (an area equivalent to the size of Canada's three prairie provinces). Once declared, Canada's jurisdiction will cover approximately 7 million km^2, some 2 per cent of the world's oceans. This vast area and diversity of habitats give rise to a spectacular marine life wherein all major groups of marine organisms are represented. There are some 1,100 species of fish and globally important populations of many marine mammals, including gray, bowhead, right, beluga, minke, humpback and killer whales. Unfortunately several of these species are also on Canada's endangered and threatened lists including northern abalone, leatherback sea turtle, some salmon populations, Atlantic cod, and the beluga, bowhead, right and Georgia Strait killer whales (COSEWIC, 2007).

These pressures on marine species, at least in part, are a result of the high proportion of the Canadian population living in the coastal zone. Manson (2005) suggests that almost 40 per cent of Canada's population lives within 20 km of a coast (including the Great Lakes) and this will increase by 5 million people by 2015.

Canada's biophysical diversity is paralleled by its jurisdictional complexity. The federal government, for example, is empowered to deal with navigation, fisheries and general law-making and has a raft of legislation (e.g., the *Fisheries Act*, the Canada *Shipping Act*, the *Canadian Environmental Protection Act*, the *Coastal Fisheries Protection Act*), to enable it to do so. However, coastal provinces can also have considerable influence and have jurisdiction over activities such as aquaculture, fish processing and marketing, and ocean bed mining and drilling. In offshore areas the seabed is under federal jurisdiction, but in 'internal' waters, it is provincial. A 'federal' gray whale can enter a provincial marine park, and while still federal in the water column it may disturb the provincial substrate and eat a provincially protected amphipod that spent a short time as a free-swimming federally controlled larva, that subsists on federally supplied detritus from the water column. In subsequent years gray whales can enter a biosphere reserve in Mexico, a port authority in California, cross federal and state marine protected areas, become a target for Makah traditional fisheries, or even become a member of the International Whaling Committee sanctioned hunt in the Chuckchi

Sea. Or wash up in a municipality on southern Vancouver Island and confound authorities as to who exactly is responsible for disposing of this once great and wonderful animal.

Speed of Establishment

The most fundamental problem besetting MPAs in Canada is that given such a vast and rich marine area within its jurisdiction, only 0.4 per cent of this area is designated for marine protection. The federal government has made commitments at both the international level (at the World Summit on Sustainable Development in Johannesburg in 2002 and under the Convention in 2004) and at the national level (in the throne speech of October 2004) to complete a network of MPAs by 2012. Clearly, we will be a long way from meeting these commitments. It is over 20 years since the MPA initiative began at the federal level. Although progress is occurring, the quality of the marine environment continues to deteriorate. It was more than 15 years ago when the Canadian Council of Ministers of the Environment, Canadian Parks Ministers Council of Canada and Wildlife Ministers' Council of Canada signed the Tri-Council statement of Commitment to 'accelerate the protection of areas representative of Canada's marine natural regions'. Fisheries and Oceans Canada, Parks Canada and Environment Canada all have struggled since the mid-1990s to designate protected areas on the water. The Commissioner of the Environment and Sustainable Development was critical of the speed of progress by DFO in establishing MPAs. DFO did not meet its commitment to establish five MPAs by 2002. In fact, not one MPA had been designated by that time. The Commissioner's report noted that the MPA evaluation process alone was taking five to seven years (Office of the Auditor General of Canada, 2005). The report questioned the effectiveness of inter-departmental committees and the challenges DFO faces in shifting its focus from fisheries management to oceans management as mandated by the *Oceans Act*. It also cited the lack of performance expectations and accountability for the Oceans Action Plan and an anticipated higher level of funding by DFO to meet its goals. DFO is not alone. Parks Canada's proposed NMCAs and Environment Canada's proposed MWAs have similarly long gestation periods. This lack of performance puts into question the political will to create effective MPAs. Unfortunately the second phase of the Oceans Action Plan once again received minimal support in the 2007 budget emphasizing the lack of political support.

Level of Protection

Current levels of protection in existing MPAs are inadequate to ensure ecological integrity. MPAs are only effective in protecting ecological integrity insofar as the species and habitats are protected from destructive and disturbing activities. Large-scale habitat disturbance such as that caused by dredging, mining, oil or gas drilling, dumping, bottom trawling, dragging, finfish aquaculture or other extractive activities have to be excluded if MPAs are to achieve minimum standards of protection. Watling and Norse (1998), for example, compare the impacts of bottom trawling with that of clear-cutting and conclude that it is both more destructive and more widespread.

It is hard to generalize on the level of protection afforded to MPAs since this depends on individual regulations and site-specific planning for each MPA. Most of the sites held either provincially or by the CWS have little legal protection from destructive activities. The Canadian and BC governments, as part of the Marine Protected Areas Strategy for the Pacific coast of Canada, have set minimum protection standards for all sites within their jurisdictions, including the prohibition of ocean dumping, oil and gas exploration and development, and dredging. This strategy does not, however, have any legal basis and has remained under discussion since it was prepared in 1998. These restrictions are also applied to Parks Canada's NMCAs. Removal of living marine organisms and mineral resources in DFO's MPAs are only permitted as part of a formal research plan to better conserve, protect and understand the area. Prohibiting commercial fishing is a particularly contentious issue for MPAs and is usually accommodated with the trend towards zoned multiple-used MPAs.

Aboriginal Interests

... the obligations of the government of Canada in taking into account the needs and aspirations of Aboriginal peoples ... [needs to] be particularly emphasized with respect to coastal peoples whose cultures and sustenance have been dependent upon the sea for thousands of years. In many cases governments have failed to consult meaningfully with Aboriginal people or have altered agreements after consultations had been held. The proposed Race Rocks MPA was to be announced as Canada's first under the *Oceans Act*, but was withdrawn after it was revealed First Nations no longer supported the proposal following changes that had been made after they had given their initial approval (Leroy et al., 2003).

Aboriginal peoples often have different perspectives on conservation principles and mechanisms (Ayers, 2005), and it is essential that governments are open to addressing these different world views through meaningful consultation. However there are also examples where Aboriginal interests seem to have been incorporated in a genuinely collaborative fashion. The Montagnais Essipit Band, for example is a strong supporter of the Saguenay-St Lawrence Marine Park and a member of the park co-ordinating committee. In Gwaii Hanaas National Park Reserve, there is successful co-management between the Haida and the federal government, and it is anticipated that a similar structure will be put in place for the proposed NMCA. Aboriginal peoples are more than another stakeholder group, and present a major challenge to governments in trying to establish MPAs. However, without their consent any MPAs that did result would be functionally meaningless.

Stakeholder Involvement

The level of protection is often a function of local wishes. Globally, protected area agencies are falling over backwards to 'include the local community'. It has become, and deservedly so, the mantra of the new century. Many parks were created in the days of Big Government when local populations had little say in their establishment and often contributed subsequently to making the park as ineffective as possible (Kessler, 2004). Those times are gone. Today stakeholder involvement is viewed as a necessary condition for a successful MPA ... There is a difference, however, in paying due heed to local stakeholders and in compromising the fundamental goals of protected area establishment as a commons resource for the good of all of society both now and in the future. In their efforts to appease local stakeholders, protected agencies are now reluctant to emphasize their responsibilities to a broader range of stakeholders. As a result, often MPAs are stymied, such as the attempts by Parks Canada to establish them in the West Isles in New Brunswick and also in Bonavista/Notre Dame Bay in Newfoundland, due to objections from local resource extractors. On this basis it is doubtful whether scarcely a terrestrial park, would have been created anywhere in the country, as some segment of society is almost always involved with resource extraction in the area. Indeed, Yellowstone, the world's first national park, would never have been established had the government of the US listened to the local stakeholders who were there to slaughter the last of the mighty plains bison.

Even where MPA establishment might run the gauntlet of local opposition, all legislation allows such flexibility in terms of regulations, that actual protection might be nominal. When the Memorandum of Understanding was signed to establish Pacific Rim National Park Reserve, for example, crab fishing was allowed to continue, and has now grown to an extractive industry of over five times its original size. This kind of situation might in fact be more damaging than not having a park established. . . .

The foregoing is not to argue against local input by resource extractors into MPA designation and management. It is to point out that there are also broader societal responsibilities of protected area agencies and that the latter should not be uniformly sacrificed to the former as is currently the case. This situation is not unique to Canada, nor MPAs. As Ray and McCormick-Ray (1995: 37) point out: 'Unfortunately, there is an expedient tendency to speak to the lowest common denominator in proposing MEPAs (marine and estuarine protected areas) and their management, resulting from consensus-based participatory processes. This is self-defeating in the end, perhaps sooner than later'. However, it should be emphasized that the optimal situation is to establish MPAs that are ecologically viable and yet enjoy strong support from local communities. A case-sensitive approach is called for, but one that holds strong to conservation principles, one that invests in conservation education and actively tries to develop sustainable alternative futures for communities whose economic livelihoods are threatened.

"Networking" our Parks and Protected Areas System

A current challenge faced by many countries is the need to secure greater integration of their parks and protected areas. As development pressures continue to encroach on these areas, their ability to provide ecological services is undermined. This is particularly true with respect to the provision of habitat and range for species at risk, a phenomenon that speaks to the need for better coordination between policymaking and implementation in the realms of parks and endangered species protection. Below we provide an excerpt from an article by Dearden and Dempsey that provides an overview of this increasingly important issue. We return to this topic in Chapter 9, where we profile research on this question recently completed by Deguise and Kerr.

P. Dearden & J. Dempsey, "Protected Areas in Canada: Decade of Change"
(2004) 48 Canadian Geographer 225–239

Habitat fragmentation and isolation of parks as 'islands' is an ongoing problem. Banff is flanked to the east by Canmore, which is outside the legislative power of Parks Canada and whose population doubled between 1988 and 1998, with estimates as high as 30,000 by 2015 (Bachusky 1998). Applications for seismic lines and mining are being considered near Nahanni National Park in NWT by the local resource board. Over the last few years, the rapid pace of development in the NWT is creeping closer to the park, with 12 applications for the development of mines, oil and gas activities around the park and near streams that flow into the park. In Waterton National Park, proposed housing developments on park boundaries threaten to fragment previously contiguous landscapes (Parks Canada Agency 2000a). These external developments are widely recognised as major impacts on park integrity. Recent research by Landry et al. (2001) shows that virtually all protected areas are too small to maintain ecological integrity on their own. In the 1997 State of the Parks survey, 24 of 36 parks reported major or severe impacts from external sources.

The need to think of protected areas as networks is widely recognised in parks' literature. Networks allow for wildlife movement beyond the boundaries of parks, most of which are too small to maintain viable populations over the long term. The Greater Yellowstone initiative, or Yellowstone to Yukon, which aims to build a contiguous area of land for the Rocky Mountain ecosystem across borders, is one example of such a connected system. In addition to building networks of protected habitat for wildlife, limiting fragmentation and the 'island effect' through sustainable land management and ecosystem-based management outside parks is central to these networks. However widely recognised these approaches are, the co-ordination across borders (internationally, national-provincial and private-public) has been difficult, if not impossible, to obtain.

Many external threats stem from jurisdictional problems between the provinces and the federal government, or between departments within governments. Provinces have jurisdiction over much of the land base outside the parks, control resource tenure on them and gain taxation revenue from development activities on them and are therefore reluctant to limit development anywhere in their boundaries, including near parks. This is a political problem embedded in Canada's federal system and therefore requires solutions beyond what Parks Canada itself can provide. Even more broadly, at the centre of this problem are land use and resource-extraction practices outside parks driven by a type of economic development that fails to recognise the value of ecological health. This is a problem that is obviously not going to be solved by Parks Canada alone. There are signs of hope that ecosystem-based management may materialise in small steps. Pending resources, Parks Canada Agency supports recommendations made by the First Minister's Roundtable on Parks Canada to support greater ecosystem management, advance regional partnerships in at least three national parks and advance a strategy to manage at least one contiguous network of protected areas. However, these partnerships and networks are still considered lower-priority needs for Parks Canada and "will be further evaluated as opportunities to pursue these approaches arise at a later date".

Conflicting Mandates? Use, Preservation and Ecological Integrity in our National Parks

Throughout the 1990s, there was growing concern about development and visitor use impacts on the ecological health of Canada's national parks. In 1998, this prompted the federal government to appoint an expert panel to provide recommendations on conserving ecological integrity throughout the national parks system. The Panel concluded that, in light of growing stresses on the system, Parks Canada should "ensure ecological integrity is the first priority in all aspects of park management". This key recommendation was implemented through amendments to the *Canadian National Park Act* (CNPA), which came into force in early in 2001.

At the time of the Panel's report, the relevant legislation (then the *National Parks Act*) provided that maintenance of ecological integrity was first priority only "in relation to park zoning and visitor use": see s. 5(1.2) NPA. The 2001 amendments broadened this mandate to require that the "[m]aintenance or restoration of ecological integrity, through the protection of natural resources and natural processes, shall be the first priority of the Minister *when considering all aspects of the management of parks*" (emphasis added). In addition, the CNPA added a new definition of the term "ecological integrity"; namely, "... a condition that is determined to be characteristic of its natural region and likely to persist, including abiotic components and the composition and abundance of native species and biological communities, rates of change and supporting processes": s. 2(1) CNPA.

Unaltered was the provision that is commonly known as the CNPA's "dedication" clause. This provision directs that "[t]he national parks of Canada are hereby dedicated to the people of Canada for their benefit, education and enjoyment ... and the parks shall be maintained and made use of so as to leave them unimpaired for the enjoyment of future generations": see s. 4 CNPA. A key question, therefore, was how these "ecological integrity" amendments would be reconciled with the tension, inherent in this dedication language, between "use" versus "preservation". Shortly after the 2001 amendments came into force, the Federal Court was called upon to offer its views on this question. As we shall see, in the *CPAWS* case, excerpted below, environmentalists argued that the new CNPA's "ecological integrity" provisions imposed important new fetters on the exercise of ministerial discretion over parks policy and management. The facts of the case also gave rise to a legal challenge brought by the Mikisew Cree, discussed later in this chapter.

Canadian Parks & Wilderness Society v. Canada (Minister of Canadian Heritage)

[2003] F.C.J. No. 703 (C.A.)

EVANS J.A.: —

Wood Buffalo National Park is the biggest national park in Canada and one of the world's largest. Situated mainly in northern Alberta, and partly in the Northwest Territories, the Park measures nearly 45,000 square kilometres. It was established in 1922 especially to protect the resident bison and today remains home to the largest herd of free-roaming bison in the world. The Park also contains the last known nesting area of the endangered whooping crane, the finest example of gypsum karst landforms in North America, and vast undisturbed boreal forests. In recognition of its ecological importance, Wood Buffalo National Park was declared a UNESCO world heritage site in 1987.

These proceedings arise from the approval of a proposal to establish a winter road in the Park. The road would occupy less than 1% of the park's total area. The Canadian Parks and Wilderness Society ("CPAWS") applied for judicial review of the approval of the road by the Minister of Canadian Heritage, acting through her delegate, the Director General, Western and Northern, Parks Canada Agency. The Minister made the decision to approve the road after considering an environmental screening assessment report and concluding that the proposed road was "not likely to cause significant adverse environmental effects".

[At trial, CPAWS challenge was dismissed: see *Canadian Parks and Wilderness Society v. Canada (Minister of Canadian Heritage)* (2001), 212 F.T.R. 1, 2001 FCT 1123, per Gibson J. On appeal, CPAWS framed one of its principal grounds of appeal as follows:

> ... in approving the construction of the road, the Minister failed to discharge the statutory duty imposed by subsection 8(2) of the CNPA to make the "maintenance or restoration of ecological integrity ... the first priority of the Minister when considering all aspects of the management of parks". In her reasons for decision, the Minister did not expressly take into account the maintenance of ecological integrity as the first priority, but referred only to the absence of significant adverse environmental effects. The Minister thus erred in law in the exercise of her discretion by failing to take into consideration a relevant factor or, in the alternative, the decision was unreasonable in light of the material before her.]

The applicant for judicial review and appellant in this proceeding, CPAWS, is a national environmental group with a sizeable membership across Canada. It is active in the promotion and protection of parks and wilderness areas in Canada, and has opposed the proposal to construct a road in Wood Buffalo National Park by participating in the public consultative processes held in connection with it.

The Minister of Canadian Heritage is a respondent to the application. The Minister is responsible for the direction of the Parks Canada Agency and for the management of national parks. The other respondent is the Thebacha Road Society. The Society is a non-profit group established by residents in and adjacent to the Park to promote the development of the road. Its members include the town of Fort Smith (population 2,500), which is located just outside the Park, Fort Smith Métis, the Salt River First Nation who live in Fort Smith,

Smith's Landing First Nation, and the Little Red River Cree. If the road goes ahead, the Society, not Parks Canada, will be responsible for financing, constructing and maintaining it.

The construction of a road along the route of a previous winter road, which was built in 1958 and abandoned in 1960, has been contemplated since the early 1980s, and was accepted in principle in 1984 by the Wood Buffalo National Park Management Plan. The present road proposal emerged from meetings in 1999 at Fort Smith between the Minister and supporters of a road.

The road will be for winter use only and is unlikely to be open for more than about four months each year. It will be constructed mostly of compacted snow and ice and, except for two one-lane bailey bridges, ice bridges will be constructed to take the road across rivers in the Park. The road will be 118 kilometres in length, with a right-of-way of 10 metres in width. The road itself will be 8.4 metres wide, which will allow two vehicles to pass and snow to be stored on each side of the road.

The road proposal has proved to be very controversial. Opposition has come from environmental groups and some local residents, including Aboriginal people who are concerned that the road may adversely affect their traplines in the Park. Indeed, the Mikisew Cree First Nation, some of whose members live on the Peace Point Reserve, has successfully challenged the approval of the road on the ground that, in the absence of adequate consultation, the decision will unjustifiably interfere with their treaty rights to trap and hunt in the Park: *Mikisew Cree First Nation v. Canada (Minister of Canadian Heritage)* (2001), 214 F.T.R. 48, 2001 FCT 1426. [*Ed note:* Later in this chapter we consider the decision of the Supreme Court of Canada, which upheld this decision.]

CPAWS' objections to the road are pitched at different levels. First is what I would term the "in principle" objection to any development in a national park that is not demonstrably required either for reasons of sound ecological management or for increasing public access to the wilderness without endangering it. In CPAWS' view, the proposal to construct a road does not meet these criteria because it is not required for any of the purposes for which the Park was created, but is merely a means of satisfying a perceived regional transportation need.

Second, CPAWS' opposition to the road is driven by a fear that incremental degradation poses a major threat to the integrity of the ecology of Canada's parks. That is, while an individual project may in itself cause no great environmental damage, the approval of one project makes others more difficult to resist. A park may thus be more vulnerable to death from a thousand small blows than from a single lethal attack.

In accordance with the *Canadian Environmental Assessment Act*, S.C. 1992, c. 37, section 18 ("CEAA"), Parks Canada developed terms of reference for independent consultants to subject the road proposal to an environmental screening assessment. In addition, Parks Canada initiated public hearings, surveys and workshops to consider the proposal. Reports from the screening assessment process became available in April and August 2000. They indicated that, because it was proposed to construct a narrow road mostly within the route of the previous road, little clearance would be required. Thus, re-establishing a winter road would cause minimal loss of habitat and fragmentation of the existing boreal forest. CPAWS no longer challenges the validity of the environmental assessment process.

On the basis of these reports, the Minister's approval of the winter road was announced on May 25, 2001. The decision stated that any adverse environmental impact of the road would be insignificant, both because of its design and limited use, and because of the measures that would be taken to monitor and mitigate any unforeseen problems through "adaptive management" techniques.

The decision to approve the road was purportedly made pursuant to subsection 8(1) of the CNPA, which confers on the Minister responsibility for the administration, management and control of the Park, including the administration of the public lands within it. One other component of the administrative process should also be mentioned. In 1998, the Minister established a Panel on Ecological Integrity to advise on the development of new legislation, which ultimately became the CNPA. After the Act was passed, the Panel was disbanded. Before its demise, the Panel listed the road as one of the environmental stressors on national parks that it had visited.

The Panel's particular achievement with respect to the CNPA appears to have been securing the expansion of the application of the principle of ecological integrity in subsection 8(2) of the Act, a provision that assumes considerable importance in this litigation. Under subsection 5(1.2) of the previous statute, the *National Parks Act*, R.S.C. 1985, c. N-14 ("NPA"), "the maintenance of ecological integrity" was "the first priority ... when considering park zoning and visitor use in a management plan". The Panel was of the view that the scope of this provision was too narrow and that Parks Canada had not always been sufficiently committed to implementing a policy of maintaining and restoring ecological integrity. In an attempt to ensure the necessary change in the Agency's culture, subsection 8(2) was added to the CNPA and provides that the maintenance or restoration of ecological integrity shall be the first priority of the Minister when considering "all aspects of the management of parks".

[At trial] ... Gibson J. held that the approval of the road was not inconsistent with the duty imposed on the Minister by subsection 8(2) of the CNPA to give "the first priority" to the "maintenance or restoration of ecological integrity" of the Park "when considering all aspects of the management of parks". He observed that ecological integrity is not the only statutory priority of the Minister and that the Minister is required to engage in a "delicate balancing of conflicting interests" identified in the purposes provisions in subsection 4(1) of the CNPA.

Was the Minister's approval of the road in breach of the statutory requirement that "ecological integrity" shall be the "first priority" of the Minister when considering all aspects of park management?

The duty in question is contained in subsection 8(2) of the CNPA which, for convenience, I set out again.

> 8. (2) Maintenance or restoration of ecological integrity, through the protection of natural resources and natural processes, shall be the first priority of the Minister when considering all aspects of the management of parks.

Also relevant is the definition of "ecological integrity" provided in subsection 2(1), which reads as follows:

> "ecological integrity" means, with respect to a park, a condition that is determined to be characteristic of its natural region and likely to persist, including abiotic components and the composition and abundance of native species and biological communities, rates of change and supporting processes.

The standard of review

The first question to be decided is the standard of review that the Court should apply to determining if the Minister complied with subsection 8(2). As Gibson J. noted (at para. 53), since subsection 8(2) provides that ecological integrity is the first priority, there must be other priorities to which the Minister may also have regard when considering the administration and management of the parks.

Hence, if the Minister has had regard to ecological integrity, her decision to approve the road is reviewable on the ground that she failed to treat ecological integrity as the first priority. However, it is not the function of a reviewing court to determine whether, giving the maintenance of ecological integrity the first priority, it would have approved the road. That would be to subject the Minister's exercise of discretion with respect to competing priorities to a standard of correctness which, counsel agreed, was not the appropriate standard of review. Whether the relevant standard of review is patent unreasonableness or simple unreasonableness is the question. A pragmatic or functional analysis leads me to conclude that patent unreasonableness is the applicable standard of review.

The exercise of discretion involved in this case is properly characterized as bearing on issues of a polycentric nature: weighing competing and conflicting interests, and determining the public interest from among the claims and perspectives of different groups and individuals, on the understanding that first priority must be given to restoring or maintaining ecological integrity. This is not a zero sum game.

Thus, on the one hand, residents in the Park believe that a winter road will reduce the isolation, which is particularly burdensome in the long northern winters by enabling them to visit, and be visited by, family and friends who live in or near the Park. Others support the road because it will significantly shorten the travelling time to destinations south of the Park region.

On the other hand, the road comes at a price: the difficult-to-quantify risks that it poses to wildlife and vegetation in the Park and the integrity of the Park's ecology, as well as to the livelihoods of those whose traditional traplines may be adversely affected by the road.

In addition, the fact that Parliament has conferred on the Minister broad responsibility for the administration, management and control of national parks, along with the powers necessary for its discharge, is another indication of a legislative intent that the standard of review should be at the most deferential end of the range. The duty of the Minister to justify her conduct to Parliament is the primary mechanism for holding the Minister accountable for the way that she balances competing interests and claims with respect to the use of park lands. While political accountability is often dismissed as an inadequate check on the abuse of power, in my opinion this view is not compelling in the context of the present case for at least three reasons.

First, as counsel for CPAWS argued, Parliament has always taken a close interest in the creation and protection of Canada's national parks. The establishment of a winter road in Canada's largest national park, a scheme that has been the subject of a vigorous public debate, is therefore very likely to register on the political radar.

Second, the political accountability of ministers to the public, both through Parliament and more directly, tends to be more effective when a minister's action engages with competing public interests than when it primarily concerns the interests of an individual.

Third, the decision-making processes employed in the consideration of the road proposal and its approval by the Minister render the decision transparent, in the sense that the bases of the decision and the countervailing arguments and evidence are part of the public record. This, too, is a factor that tends to enhance ministerial accountability through the political process. [...]

Thus, in reviewing the Minister's approval of the road on the ground that it was in breach of her duty under subsection 8(2), the Court must ask whether, on the basis of both the factors that the Minister had to consider and the material before her, it was patently unreasonable to have concluded that the road proposal was incompatible with maintaining as the first priority the ecological integrity of the Park through the protection of natural resources and natural processes.

Failure to Consider a Relevant Consideration

Counsel for CPAWS submitted that, in exercising her discretion, the Minister failed to take into account a relevant consideration. The reasons for decision do not state that, in deciding whether to approve the road, the Minister had as her first priority the restoration or maintenance of the ecological integrity of the Park. I agree that the Minister ought to have referred explicitly to the "ecological integrity" test, which had become applicable to decisions made under subsection 8(1) only three months before the date of the decision, and after the preparation of the environmental screening assessment report on which the decision relied.

The failure of a decision-maker to consider a factor that she or he was required in law to consider in the exercise of discretion is an indication that the decision was patently unreasonable: *Suresh v. Canada (Minister of Citizenship and Immigration)*, [2002] 1 S.C.R. 3, ¶37-38. However, I am not persuaded that the Minister committed a reviewable error when she failed to refer specifically to the need to ensure that the maintenance of ecological integrity was the first priority when exercising her power to approve the road under subsection 8(1).

That a decision-maker does not expressly mention a relevant consideration in the reasons for decision does not necessarily mean that it was not in fact considered.

In the present case, it is difficult to believe that both the Minister and Parks Canada had overlooked the very recent and much heralded enactment of the expanded duty to ensure as the first priority in all aspects of decision-making relating to national parks the restoration or maintenance of the ecological integrity of the Park.

Indeed, the environmental assessment report, on which the Minister relied in making her decision, quoted as follows from the report of the Panel on Ecological Integrity:

The overriding objective behind every recommendation in our report is to firmly and unequivocally establish ecological integrity as the core of Parks Canada's mandate.

The environmental assessment report went on to observe:

> although it is not yet clear how, and to what extent, Parks Canada will implement the panel's recommendation, it is likely that the panel's findings will significantly influence Parks Canada's approach to future human development within the national parks.

In addition, the Minister acknowledged the receipt of a letter from the Chair of the Panel raising the issue of ecological integrity prior to the screening process. By the time that the Minister made her decision, of course, the Panel's recommendation respecting the pre-eminence of the principle of ecological integrity in decision-making had received the enthusiastic support of the Minister and had become law. And, even before subsection 8(2) was added to the legislation, paragraph 3.1.2 of Parks Canada Guiding Principles and Operational Policies stated: "Human activities within a national park that threatens the integrity of park ecosystems will not be permitted".

Moreover, counsel for CPAWS was unable to identify items that would be pertinent to the restoration or maintenance of ecological integrity through the protection of natural resources and natural processes that were not considered in the Minister's reasons for decision or in the environmental screening assessment report prepared by independent consultants that the Minister had before her when deciding to approve the road. Rather, his argument was that the "restoration or maintenance of ecological integrity" was a higher standard than "significant adverse environmental effects". However, he could not explain in what respects, or by how much, the standard was higher.

Since, in this case, the same facts are relevant to both statutory standards, and the standards seem not call for very different kinds of assessment, the Court can review the Minister's exercise of discretion by asking whether the material before her was sufficient in law to support her decision. On the basis of the statutory definition in subsection 2(1) of the CNPA, failure to maintain the "ecological integrity" of a park seems to be simply a sub-set of "significant adverse environmental effects", but one to which first priority must be given in the making of decisions.

Moreover, as explained below, I am satisfied that, on the material before her, the Minister's carefully considered and fully reasoned decision was not patently unreasonable. Indeed, in my opinion it would also survive review on the more demanding standard of reasonableness *simpliciter*.

For these reasons, I would dismiss the appeal and award the Thebacha Road Society its costs as against CPAWS. The Minister did not seek costs and none are awarded.

Notes and Comments

1. Consider the discussion of "standard of review" in this case in light of the subsequent judgment (discussed in Chapter 6) of the Supreme Court of Canada in *Dunsmuir* (2008). Would the principles in *Dunsmuir* have led to the same conclusion?

2. On what basis does the Federal Court conclude that the Minister gave appropriate priority to "ecological integrity" as required by section 8 of the CNPA? Do you agree with this conclusion?

3. The Federal Court seems to equate the determination of whether a proposed project fails to give priority to "restoration or maintenance of ecological integrity" as required by the CNPA, with a legal standard employed under CEAA, namely, whether there the project would create "significant adverse environmental effects". Recalling the material covered in Chapter 7, do you agree?

4. Some further reflections on the implications of the *CPAWS* are offered in the commentary below. Do you agree with the author's critique and prescription?

Shaun Fluker, "Maintaining ecological integrity is our first priority" — Policy Rhetoric or Practical Reality in Canada's National Parks? A case comment on *Canadian Parks & Wilderness Society v. Canada (Minister of Canadian Heritage)*

(2003), 13 J. Env. L. & Prac. 131

Both Federal Court [the FCA and FCTD] judgments significantly undermine the *Parks Act* s. 8(2). They interpret ecological integrity as simply another factor for parks management consideration, despite the language of s. 8(2) and the Ecological Integrity Panel Report proposal that ecological integrity be an "overriding" priority. The Court of Appeal, without any analysis, interprets the ecological integrity standard as equivalent to that of a federal environmental assessment screening. Finally, both judgments suggest that the Minister's parks management decisions, despite *Parks Act* s. 8(2), need not make any explicit reference to ecological integrity at all ...

Why did the Court of Appeal go to such lengths to defend the Minister's decision, undermining the *Parks Act* s. 8(2) in the process? The obvious reason is that the Court applied the established policy of judicial deference to administrative or discretionary decisions. Unfortunately in this instance, the Minister made it very awkward for the Court to be deferential simply because she failed to expressly consider ecological integrity in her decision. The question remains as to why the Minister failed to reference ecological integrity in her decision.

Arguably, the *Parks Act* ecological integrity definition was the source of trouble for both the Minister and the Court. For the Minister, the definition makes s. 4(1) and s. 8(2) incompatible: that is, the *Parks Act* ecological integrity definition renders the s. 8(2) ecological integrity "first priority" incompatible with the s. 4(1) national parks dedication to the enjoyment of Canadians. In this case, the Minister chose to avoid discussing "ecological integrity". For the Court, the definition allows for a conceptual separation between humans and *nature*: that is, the Trial Division separated human community concerns from "ecological integrity" and the Court of Appeal interpreted "ecological integrity" as another way of describing "environmental effects". Accordingly, both the Minister and the Court asked themselves how to resolve a conflict between the needs of humans and those of *nature* (understood as non-humans). Viewing a decision as conflict resolution may be familiar territory for the law, however it is an impediment towards solving difficult value-based problems concerning Canada's national parks.

There are various perspectives on ecological integrity which debate whether ecological integrity and humans can co-exist. Some commentators, represented by the work of James Karr, Stephen Woodley, and Laura Westra, believe ecological integrity can exist only in the absence of human influence. Ecological integrity is independent from humans — (*natural ecological integrity*). In contrast, others such as James Kay, Henry Regier, and Eric Schneider, reject the hypothesis that human activity and ecological integrity are mutually exclusive. From their perspective, ecological integrity represents a desirable socio-ecological relationship wherein social and ecological systems are understood as mutually dependent self-organizing entities — (*socio-ecological integrity*).

The *Parks Act* ecological integrity definition refers to natural ecological integrity. In fact the Ecological Integrity Panel Report which led to this statutory definition explicitly associated ecological integrity with a natural state "... where humans do not dominate the ecosystem". Together, natural ecological integrity and its place as the first priority in management decisions should significantly restrict or eliminate human activity within national parks. Management decisions consistent with *Parks Act* s. 8(2) require national parks to be managed as core preservation areas within the larger context of a core/buffer land conservation strategy. The parks are a place where the preservation of *nature* is the first priority, with human interests of secondary concern. The effect of s. 8(2) is to elevate ecological integrity, as a *natural* condition, to a position of dominance over humans. This is the troublesome underlying rationale of the *Parks Act* s. 8(2), one that breeds a false perception of conflict between humans and the rest of nature.

Critics suggest natural ecological integrity, by failing to acknowledge that nature means different things to different persons, will remain an unpersuasive policy goal: "Tempting as it may be to play nature as a trump card in this way, it quickly becomes a self-defeating strategy: adversaries simply refuse to recognize each others" trump and then go off to play by themselves". Moreover, why should public decision-makers take natural ecological integrity seriously? Human society inevitably alters its ecological context. As William Rees notes, humans are "patch disturbers" like many other species. "Human ecology begins with recognition that the mere existence of people in a given habitat implies significant effects on local ecosystems' structure and function". Accordingly some commentators reject the preservation of natural ecological integrity as a desirable public policy goal generally.

The mandate to maintain or restore *natural* ecological integrity is particularly troublesome for the Minister because the *Parks Act* s. 4(1) dedicates the parks to the use and enjoyment by people. The preservation of natural ecological integrity, where humans are *not* understood as natural, inevitably places decisions that conform with s. 8(2) in conflict with the s. 4(1) dedication. Natural ecological integrity, as a management priority, is simply too rigid for the majority of Canada's national parks.

Natural ecological integrity, and the underlying rationale of the *Parks Act* s. 8(2), will necessarily exclude humans from places where they want to be. Furthermore it promotes language of conflict rather than relationship between humans and the rest of nature. In this case, it led the Minister and the Federal Court to ask how to balance "competing" social and ecological interests, rather than ask the more difficult value-laden question of what socio-ecological relationship is desirable for the park. Decisions concerned with maintaining ecological integrity (in this case "socio-ecological integrity") should seek to answer the latter question.

Social and ecological interests co-exist rather than compete. Human social systems rely upon the energy and components of their surrounding ecological systems for sustenance. In the process of sustaining themselves, social systems alter the structure and processes of ecological systems. In turn, these alterations influence the structure and processes of social systems in desirable or undesirable ways. Feedback loops are created and eliminated as social and ecological systems self-organize and influence each other. Socio-ecological integrity represents a desirable relationship between these systems.

The primary policy attribute of socio-ecological integrity is that it requires decision-makers to seriously consider the *mutual* influences between social and ecological systems. Within the outer bounds of limiting human activity to leave our ecological context unchanged, and fostering human activity which results in ecological collapse, is a range of socio-ecological relationships both desirable and undesirable. Our management challenge is to implement the desirable relationships by making inclusive, value-based decisions. The maintenance of socio-ecological integrity, achieved by meeting this challenge, can lead the way as a policy goal in public decision-making. Socio-ecological integrity must, however, govern our decisions rather than simply be taken into account. Given the presence of "ecological integrity" in the *Parks Act*, Canada's national parks represent an ideal starting point for this form of decision-making in today's society.

Parliament made a choice in selecting natural ecological integrity to lead the way in Canada's national parks. Parliament chose a decision-making tool that, as presently interpreted, separates humans from the rest of *nature* and leads to park management decisions that exclude people from national parks. As it currently stands, the *Parks Act* s. 4(1) dual mandate simply cannot co-exist with the rationale of s. 8(2). Accordingly in this case, it seems that s. 8(2) was overlooked by the Minister.

To overcome this problem, either the *Parks Act* definition of ecological integrity should be amended to represent socio-ecological integrity (for example, by including humans and their values as important components of ecological integrity), or the *Parks Act* s. 4(1) should be amended to assert that parks are a place where the preservation of natural ecological integrity is the first priority, with human interests of secondary concern.

Reconciling Parks and Protected Areas Policy with Aboriginal Rights and Title

The implications of recognizing and respected Aboriginal rights and title as guaranteed by section 35 of the Constitution is, as we have seen, an overarching concern for Canadian environmental law and policy. While this issue frequently arises out of Crown resource allocation decisions, particularly in the forestry and mining contexts, it is also an important consideration in the context of parks and protected areas. Many of Canada's parks and protected areas were created without consultation with First Nations. The Supreme Court of Canada's decisions in *Haida* and *Taku* underscore the Crown's duty to consult and accommodate where a proposed decision or action might infringe a section 35 protected right: see Chapter 3. As we shall see, this principle has important implications not only for future designation decisions but, more generally, for parks and protected areas management. Among them is recognition of the need, where parks conservation objectives overlap with traditional territories of First Nations, to develop new management structures and policies that ensure First Nations' community economic development goals are accommodated.

P. Dearden & S. Langdon, "Aboriginal Peoples and National Parks" in P. Dearden & R. Rollins, eds., *Parks and Protected Areas in Canada*, 3rd ed., (Oxford University Press, 2009)

... On 1 March 1872 over 810,000 ha of north-western Wyoming were designated as the world's first national park — Yellowstone. The park was set aside during an effort to subdue Plains Indian tribes, and the traditional inhabitants of the park moved to reservations or were forced out by the United States Army. In 1885, Banff National Park was established in Alberta, seven years after the Siksika (Blackfoot) and Nakoda (Stoney) tribes ceded much of southwestern Alberta to the Crown. The treaty allowed the tribes to continue hunting in the region, but the federal government decided these rights would not apply to Banff National Park. Since the establishment of these early national parks, thousands of new protected areas have been created throughout the world. Many of these protected areas have been designated on lands traditionally used by Aboriginal peoples. Often, they have been established without the participation of Aboriginal peoples living in the regions affected. In many instances, the Aboriginal people have been forcibly removed from regions in which protected areas were established. Early establishment of national parks in Canada followed the same pattern, but in more recent times (post 1982) rights have been recognized and traditional activities have been allowed to continue.

The practice of establishing protected areas without regard for the needs of Aboriginal people has sometimes adversely affected both Aboriginal societies and protected area conservation initiatives. In effect, 'indigenous people have borne the costs of protecting natural areas, through the loss of access for hunting, trapping or other harvesting activities'. Displacement of Aboriginal people often disrupts traditional social and economic systems and results in serious social problems, such as malnutrition and loss of cultural identity. At the very least, such negative impacts may reduce popular support among Aboriginal peoples for protected areas. Consequently, the effectiveness of conservation in protected areas has been compromised because of poaching, clandestine exploitation of resources, or other forms of non-compliance with regulations governing protected areas.

In response to these problems, it became clear there was a need to understand Aboriginal perspectives on parks, involve Aboriginal peoples in protected-area planning and management, and further, to allow exploitation of resources in protected areas for subsistence purposes.

The role of Aboriginal people in national parks has become an important area of concern globally for Aboriginal organizations, as well as for protected area managers and social scientists. In the last 30 years, the relationship between Aboriginal people and national parks in Canada has changed fundamentally, although these changes are uneven across the country. Aboriginal peoples in northern Canada have played a significant role in national park planning and development, while in southern Canada their role has varied from park to park. In general, national parks established since the Constitution Act, 1982, with its entrenchment of Aboriginal and treaty rights have working relationships with Aboriginal people. Steady progress is being made in parks established before that date, as the value of strong working relationships is recognized by Parks Canada in its corporate plan. A number of northern national parks have been established in conjunction with Aboriginal land claim . . . settlements, while park reserves await claims set-tlement before attaining full park status. Overall, more than 50 per cent of the land area in Canada's national park system has been protected as a result of Aboriginal peoples' support for conservation of their lands and 17 formal co-operative management agreements exist in addition to numerous informal agreements. Dearden and Berg (1993) suggest that First Nations have emerged as the most dominant force influencing the establishment of national parks in Canada over the years since the 1982 Constitution Act . . .

Many of Canada's national parks were designated at a time when both the federal and provincial governments did not acknowledge Aboriginal rights and title. Aboriginal peoples utilizing traditional lands or occupying reserves encompassed by newly designated parks were given little, if any, input in park planning and management. Indeed, when Riding Mountain National Park was established in 1933, the Keeseekoowenen Band was evicted and their houses burned (Morrison, 1995). Aboriginal people with reserves in proposed park areas were encouraged by Parks Canada to sell or trade their reserves for lands outside proposed parks, and were prevented from hunting and trapping within them. There was little appreciation within government that parks could be used to support and maintain the land uses of Aboriginal peoples, and hence protect their land-based cultures. Instead, Parks Canada stressed the need for the parks system to represent biophysically defined natural areas. Adherence to the natural areas framework may have contributed to the estrangement of parks from Aboriginal peoples. Parks identified through the framework might have been excellent choices to represent natural areas, but were sometimes irrelevant to protecting vital wildlife habitat, the element of parks legislation that interested many Aboriginal groups. To Aboriginal peoples dependent on hunting, fishing, and trapping, the location of a park was the key to its utility and political acceptability.

The attitude of Parks Canada began to change in the 1970s as the aspirations of Aboriginal peoples became better known and appreciated by the Canadian public and political leaders. This process was aided by public hearings into oil and gas megaprojects, which brought representatives of Aboriginal peoples and environmental and other groups into the same camp. The Berger inquiry of 1974–7 into a proposed gas pipeline from the Mackenzie Delta and northern Alaska, for example, noted the need for parks and conservation areas to be planned simultaneously with non-renewable resource development. In addition, Justice Thomas Berger, who earlier had acted as chief counsel to the Nisga'a, proposed a new type of park, a 'wilderness park', to preserve wildlife, wildlife habitat, and natural landscapes in northern Yukon, and to under-pin the still-vibrant renewable resource economy of Inuvialuit and Dene. This recommendation is now an acknowledged milestone in the debate that connects Aboriginal peoples with national parks. [...]

In 1994, Parks Canada revised its policies, with a new and strong emphasis on ecological integrity, improved regional integration through co-operation with other jurisdictions, and a more comprehensive approach to working with Aboriginal peoples. The 1994 *Guiding Principles and Operational Policies* sets out several polices with respect to Aboriginal interests:

- negotiation of comprehensive claims based on traditional uses and occupancy of land;
- rights and benefits in relation to wildlife management and the use of water and land, and the opportunity for participation on advisory or public government bodies;
- respect for the principles set out in court decisions, such as Sparrow v. The Queen, where existing Aboriginal or treaty rights occur within protected areas;
- at the time of new park establishment, respect for Canada's legal and policy framework regarding Aboriginal rights as affirmed by section 35 of the Constitution Act, and consultation with affected Aboriginal communities. [. . .]

While Parks Canada still faces many legal situations related to the interpretation of legal rights, the organization is recognized as a national and international leader in cooperative management of protected areas.

The most recent *National Parks System Plan* reflects implementation of Parks Canada's policies with respect to Aboriginal people by endorsing, 'a new type of national park where traditional subsistence resource harvesting by Aboriginal people ... continues and where cooperative management approaches are designed to reflect Aboriginal rights and regional circumstances' (Parks Canada, 1997b).

Amendments to the *National Parks Act* in 1988 and 2000 also recognize the importance of traditional resource harvesting to Aboriginal peoples. The 1988 amendments allowed specific Aboriginal groups to carry out such harvesting in certain parks. It also extended, at the minister's discretion, traditional renewable resource harvesting rights in wilderness areas of national parks to Aboriginal peoples with land claim settlements, and allowed for regulation of traditional renewable resource harvesting in national parks by Order-in-Council.

The Canada *National Parks Act* of 2000 extend harvesting rights to a larger number of parks, including all those established by agreement. Section 10(1) of the Act also supports co-operative agreements with a wide range of organizations, including Aboriginal governments, for carrying out the purposes of the Act. The Act specifies that the federal cabinet may 'make regulations respecting the exercise of traditional renewable resource harvesting activities' in Wood Buffalo, Wapusk, and Gros Morne national parks, any park established in the District of Thunder Bay in the Province of Ontario; and 'any park established in an area where the continuation of such activities is provided for by an agreement between the Government of Canada and the government of a province respecting the establishment of the park' (s. 17(1)). For the first time, the *National Parks Act* also provides for the removal of non-renewable resources in the form of carving stone, in order to support traditional economies.

The new *National Parks Act* does not guarantee co-operative management for Aboriginal peoples whose traditional lands fall within national parks; however, on a policy basis, Parks Canada has been very active in developing not only a formalized consultative process but also co-operative management arrangements as well. The Gulf Islands National Park Reserve is a good example of how Parks Canada, in advance of treaty settlements, has developed three co-operative management arrangements with Aboriginal groups to ensure consultation and input into major park decisions that affect them. In the case of Gwaii Haanas, the *National Parks Act* specifies in Section 41(1), that, 'the Governor in Council may authorize the Minister to enter into an agreement with the Council of the Haida Nation respecting the management and operation of Gwaii Haanas National Park Reserve of Canada'. Section 41(2), further allows for 'regulations, applicable in the Gwaii Haanas National Park Reserve of Canada, respecting the continuance of traditional renewable resource harvesting activities and Haida cultural activities by people of the Haida Nation to whom subsection 35(1) of the *Constitution Act, 1982* applies.

Aboriginal people are permitted to harvest plants and animals in many national parks based on land claim settlements or on other policy-related arrangements. All national parks in the North have harvesting regimes, as do several in southern Canada. Some examples are Pukaskwa in Ontario, Gulf Islands, Gwaii Haanas, and Pacific Rim in BC. Animals that are harvested range from large mammals such as moose to fur bearers such as mink. Harvesting activities happen primarily in the northern parks, although exact records of harvest activities are not kept. Although rights or granted access may exist, the level of harvest is relatively low. This may reflect the Aboriginal perspective that these jointly protected areas are special and, therefore, that harvesting should be minimized. It is also known that, in some situations, access to resources is easier in areas outside of national parks

Perhaps the most important accommodation the *National Parks Act* makes to Aboriginal peoples lies in the term 'national park reserve', introduced through amendment to the statute in 1972. This designation applies, for example, to Nahanni, and Pacific Rim, which are to become full national parks upon settlement of comprehensive land claims. The 'reserve' designation allowed Parks Canada to treat and manage the areas in question as national parkland, but did not extinguish any Aboriginal rights or title to the areas. Importantly, this designation does not prejudice the ability of Aboriginal peoples to select parkland in the course of land claim negotiations.

Canadian legislators seem to have chosen an ad hoc approach to accommodating the needs of Aboriginal peoples in national parks. Wood Buffalo National Park and Auyuittuq National Park Reserve provide examples of this ad hoc approach. The area around Wood Buffalo National Park was a favoured hunting ground of Aboriginal people for many years prior to its establishment as a park in 1922 (Lothian, 1976). When the park was established, Aboriginal people who had previously hunted and trapped in the area continued these activities under permit. In 1949, special district game regulations for Wood Buffalo National Park were instituted, which superseded the National Parks Game Regulations and allowed for traditional hunting, trapping, and fishing by Aboriginal people (*ibid.*). The *National Parks Act* also enables the appointment of a Wildlife Advisory Board for the traditional hunting grounds of Wood Buffalo National Park, and this Board has a role, for example in bison management and hunting, fishing, and trapping regulations (*Canada National Parks Act*, s. 37). Auyuittuq National Park Reserve, located on Baffin Island, was established in 1972 long before the Nunavut Agreement. Public park planning meetings in the early 1970s resolved that the Inuit, who had inhabited the region for almost 4,000 years, would retain traditional resource extraction rights within the park. When Auyuittuq National Park Reserve was established there was provision for a "park advisory committee". This represented one of the first co-operative efforts by Parks Canada. All of the national parks found in Nunavut currently have park advisory committees, and they have evolved into an effective means for the Inuit people to participate in the planning and management of the national parks found in their traditional territories.

The interaction between Aboriginal peoples and National Parks in Canada is not as clear as might be suggested by National Park Policy and legislation. Land claim settlements, in addition to Parks Canada policy and legislation and legal precedent, determine the role of Aboriginal peoples in planning for, and managing, national parks. This has given rise to subtly different kinds of parks in northern and southern Canada, for a significant park planning and management role is accorded Aboriginal peoples in northern Canada where parks are tied to settlement of land claims. Land claims in northern Canada will likely be completed sooner than many of those, for example, in British Columbia. In addition, many Aboriginal peoples in the south must look to treaties, legal precedent and the *National Parks Act* and Parks Canada's *Guiding Principles and Operating Policies*, rather than to comprehensive land claim settlements, to protect their interests.

In response to this variation in approaches to working with Aboriginal organizations, the Panel on the Ecological Integrity of Canada's National Parks recommended that, 'Parks Canada adopt clear policies to encourage and support the development and maintenance of genuine partnerships with Aboriginal peoples in Canada'. The Panel also outlined key steps to foster trust and respect between Parks Canada and Aboriginal peoples, such as initiating a process of healing; providing adequate resources to maintain genuine partnerships; integrating Aboriginal culture, knowledge, and experience into education and interpretation programs; and ensuring protection of cultural sites, sacred areas, and artifacts. In an effort to move beyond the constraints of strict government legal positions, Parks Canada established an Aboriginal Secretariat in 1999, with the task of improving relationships with Aboriginal organizations throughout the national park system. Under the direction of the chief executive officer of the day, the Parks Canada corporate plan was also modified to better reflect the need for strong relationships with Aboriginal people and the important role they play in delivery of the Parks Canada mandate of protection, memorable experiences and educational opportunities.

Notes and Comments

The *Mikisew* decision, below, arose in litigation that was pursued in parallel with the *CPAWS* case discussed above. Consider what lessons can be drawn from the *Mikisew* case, in terms of the evolution of Parks Canada policy with respect to First Nations rights and interests?

Mikisew Cree First Nation v. Canada (Minister of Canadian Heritage) [2005] S.C.J. 71

BINNIE J.: — The fundamental objective of the modern law of aboriginal and treaty rights is the reconciliation of aboriginal peoples and non-aboriginal peoples and their respective claims, interests and ambitions. The management of these relationships takes place in the shadow of a long history of grievances and misunderstanding. The multitude of smaller grievances created by the indifference of some government officials to aboriginal people's concerns, and the lack of respect inherent in that indifference has been as destructive of the process of reconciliation as some of the larger and more explosive controversies. And so it is in this case.

Treaty 8 is one of the most important of the post-Confederation treaties. Made in 1899, the First Nations who lived in the area surrendered to the Crown 840,000 square kilometres of what is now northern Alberta, northeastern British Columbia, northwestern Saskatchewan and the southern portion of the Northwest Territories. Some idea of the size of this surrender is given by the fact that it dwarfs France (543,998 square kilometres), exceeds the size of Manitoba (650,087 square kilometres), Saskatchewan (651,900 square kilometres) and Alberta (661,185 square kilometres) and approaches the size of British Columbia (948,596 square kilometres). In exchange for this surrender, the First Nations were promised reserves and some other benefits including, most importantly to them, the following rights of hunting, trapping, and fishing:

[In 2001], the federal government approved a 118-kilometre winter road that, as originally conceived, ran through the new Mikisew First Nation Reserve at Peace Point. The government did not think it necessary to engage in consultation directly with the Mikisew before making this decision. After the Mikisew protested, the winter road alignment was changed to track the boundary of the Peace Point reserve instead of running through it, again without consultation with the Mikisew. The modified road alignment traversed the traplines of approximately 14 Mikisew families who reside in the area near the proposed road, and others who may trap in that area although they do not live there, and the hunting grounds of as many as 100 Mikisew people whose hunt (mainly of moose), the Mikisew say, would be adversely affected. The fact the proposed winter road directly affects only about 14 Mikisew trappers and perhaps 100 hunters may not seem very dramatic (unless you happen to be one of the trappers or hunters in question) but, in the context of a remote northern community of relatively few families, it is significant. Beyond that, however, the principle of consultation in advance of interference with existing treaty rights is a matter of broad general importance to the relations between aboriginal and non-aboriginal peoples. It goes to the heart of the relationship and concerns not only the Mikisew but other First Nations and non-aboriginal governments as well.

In this case, the relationship was not properly managed. Adequate consultation in advance of the Minister's approval did not take place. The government's approach did not advance the process of reconciliation but undermined it. The duty of consultation which flows from the honour of the Crown, and its obligation to respect the existing treaty rights of aboriginal peoples (now entrenched in s. 35 of the *Constitution Act, 1982*), was breached.

The Mikisew appeal should be allowed, the Minister's approval quashed, and the matter returned to the Minister for further consultation and consideration.

Facts

About 5 percent of the territory surrendered under Treaty 8 was set aside in 1922 as Wood Buffalo National Park. The Park was created principally to protect the last remaining herds of wood bison (or buffalo) in northern Canada and covers 44,807 square kilometres of land straddling the boundary between northern Alberta and southerly parts of the Northwest Territories. It is designated a UNESCO World Heritage Site. The Park itself is larger than Switzerland.

At present, it contains the largest free-roaming, self-regulating bison herd in the world, the last remaining natural nesting area for the endangered whooping crane, and vast undisturbed natural boreal forests. More to the point, it was been inhabited by First Nation peoples for more than over 8,000 years, some of whom still earn a subsistence living hunting, fishing and commercial trapping within the Park boundaries. The Park includes the traditional lands of the Mikisew. As a result of the *Treaty Land Entitlement Agreement*, the Peace Point Reserve was formally excluded from the Park in 1988 but of course is surrounded by it.

The members of the Mikisew Cree First Nation are descendants of the Crees of Fort Chipewyan who signed Treaty 8 on June 21, 1899. It is common ground that its members are entitled to the benefits of Treaty 8.

The Winter Road Project

The proponent of the winter road is the respondent Thebacha Road Society, whose members include the Town of Fort Smith (located in the Northwest Territories on the northeastern boundary of Wood Buffalo National Park, where the Park headquarters is located), the Fort Smith Métis Council, the Salt River First Nation, and Little Red River Cree First Nation. The advantage of the winter road for these people is that it would provide direct winter access among a number of isolated northern communities and to the Alberta highway system to the south. The trial judge accepted that the government's objective was to meet "regional transportation needs".

The Consultation Process

According to the trial judge, most of the communications relied on by the Minister to demonstrate appropriate consultation were instances of the Mikisew's being provided with standard information about the proposed road in the same form and substance as the communications being distributed to the general public of interested stakeholders. Thus Parks Canada acting for the Minister, provided the Mikisew with the Terms of Reference for the environmental assessment on January 19, 2000. The Mikisew were advised that open house sessions would take place over the summer of 2000. The Minister says that the first formal response from the Mikisew did not come until October 10, 2000, some two months after the deadline she had imposed for "public" comment. Chief Poitras stated that the Mikisew did not formally participate in the open houses, because "... an open house is not a forum for us to be consulted adequately".

On May 25, 2001, the Minister announced on the Parks Canada website that the Thebacha Road Society was authorised to build a winter road 10 metres wide with posted speed limits ranging from 10 to 40 kilometres per hour. The approval was said to be in accordance with "Parks Canada plans and policy" and "other federal laws and regulations". No reference was made to any obligations to the Mikisew.

The Minister now says the Mikisew ought not to be heard to complain, about the process of consultation because they declined to participate in the public process that took place. Consultation is a two-way street, she says. It was up to the Mikisew to take advantage of what was on offer. They failed to do so. In the Minister's view, she did her duty.

The proposed winter road is wide enough to allow two vehicles to pass. Pursuant to s. 36(5) of the *Wood Buffalo National Park Game Regulations*, SOR/78-830, creation of the road would trigger a 200-metre wide corridor within which the use of firearms would be prohibited. The total area of this corridor would be approximately 23 square kilometres.

The Mikisew objection goes beyond the direct impact of closure of the area covered by the winter road to hunting and trapping. The surrounding area would be, the trial judge found, injuriously affected. Maintaining a traditional lifestyle, which the Mikisew say is central to their culture, depends on keeping the land around the Peace Point reserve in its natural condition and this, they contend, is essential to allow them to pass their culture and skills onto the next generation of Mikisew. The detrimental impact of the road on hunting and trapping, they argue, may simply prove to be one more incentive for their young people to abandon a traditional lifestyle and turn to other modes of living in the south.

Analysis

The post-Confederation numbered treaties were designed to open up the Canadian west and northwest to settlement and development. Treaty 8 itself recites that "the said Indians have been notified and informed by Her Majesty's said Commission that it is Her desire to open for settlement, immigration, trade, travel, mining, lumbering and such other purposes as to Her Majesty may seem meet". This stated purpose is reflected in a corresponding limitation on the Treaty 8 hunting, fishing and trapping rights to exclude such "tracts as may be required or taken up from time to time for settlement, mining, lumbering, trading or other purposes". The "other purposes" would be at least as broad as the purposes listed in the recital, mentioned above, including "travel".

There was thus from the outset an uneasy tension between the First Nations' essential demand that they continue to be as free to live off the land after the treaty as before and the Crown's expectation of increasing numbers of non-aboriginal people moving into the surrendered territory.

As Cory J. explained in *Badger*, at para. 57, "[t]he Indians understood that land would be taken up for homesteads, farming, prospecting and mining and that they would not be able to hunt in these areas or to shoot at the settlers' farm animals or buildings".

The Process of Treaty Implementation

Both the historical context and the inevitable tensions underlying implementation of Treaty 8 demand a *process* by which lands may be transferred from the one category (where the First Nations retain rights to hunt, fish and trap) to the other category (where they do not). The content of the process is dictated by the duty of the Crown to act honourably. Although *Haida Nation* was not a treaty case, McLachlin C.J. pointed out, at paras. 19 and 35:

> The honour of the Crown also infuses the processes of treaty making and treaty interpretation. In making and applying treaties, the Crown must act with honour and integrity, avoiding even the appearance of "sharp dealing" (*Badger*, at para. 41). Thus in *Marshall, supra*, at para. 4, the majority of this Court supported its interpretation of a treaty by stating that "nothing less would uphold the honour and integrity of the Crown in its dealings with the Mi'kmaq people to secure their peace and friendship"
>
> But, when precisely does a duty to consult arise? The foundation of the duty in the Crown's honour and the goal of reconciliation suggest that the duty arises when the Crown has knowledge, real or

> constructive, of the potential existence of the Aboriginal right or title and contemplates conduct that might adversely affect it.

The Mikisew Legal Submission

The appellant, the Mikisew, essentially reminded the Court of what was said in *Haida Nation* and *Taku River*. This case, the Mikisew say, is stronger. In those cases, unlike here, the aboriginal interest to the lands was asserted but not yet proven. In this case, the aboriginal interests are protected by Treaty 8. They are established legal facts. As in *Haida Nation*, the trial judge found the aboriginal interest was threatened by the proposed development. If a duty to consult was found to exist in *Haida Nation* and *Taku River* then *a fortiori*, the Mikisew argue, it must arise here and the majority judgment of the Federal Court of Appeal was quite wrong to characterise consultation between governments and aboriginal peoples as nothing more than a "good practice"

The Minister's Response

The respondent Minister seeks to distinguish *Haida Nation* and *Taku River*. Her counsel advances three broad propositions in support of the Minister's approval of the proposed winter road.

1. In "taking up" the 23 square kilometres for the winter road the Crown was doing no more than Treaty 8 entitled it to do. The Crown as well as First Nations have rights under Treaty 8. The exercise by the Crown of *its* Treaty right to "take up" land is not an infringement of the Treaty but the performance of it.
2. The Crown went through extensive consultations with First Nations in 1899 at the time Treaty 8 was negotiated. Whatever duty of accommodation was owed to First Nations was discharged at that time. The terms of the Treaty do not contemplate further consultations whenever a "taking up" occurs.
3. In the event further consultation was required, the process followed by the Minister through Parks Canada in this case was sufficient.

For the reasons that follow, I believe that each of these propositions must be rejected.

In "taking up" Land for the Winder Road the Crown Was Doing No More than it was Entitled To Do Under the Treaty

The Minister ... assert[s] ... that the test ought to be "whether, after the taking up, it still remains reasonably practicable, within the Province as a whole, for the Indians to hunt, fish and trap for food [to] the extent that they choose to do so" (emphasis added). This cannot be correct. It suggests that a prohibition on hunting at Peace Point would be acceptable so long as decent hunting was still available in the Treaty 8 area north of Jasper, about 800 kilometres distant across the province, equivalent to a commute between Toronto and Quebec City (809 kilometres) or Edmonton and Regina (785 kilometres). One might as plausibly invite the truffle diggers of southern France to try their luck in the Austrian Alps, about the same distance as the journey across Alberta deemed by the Minister to be an acceptable fulfilment of the promises of Treaty 8.

The "meaningful right to hunt" is not ascertained on a treaty-wide basis (all 840,000 square kilometres of it) but in relation to the territories over which a First Nation traditionally hunted, fished and trapped, and continues to do so today. If the time comes that in the case of a particular Treaty 8 First Nation "no meaningful right to hunt" remains over *its* traditional territories, the significance of the oral promise that "the same means of earning a livelihood would continue after the treaty as existed before it" would clearly be in question, and a potential action for treaty infringement, including the demand for a *Sparrow* justification, would be a legitimate First Nation response.

Did the Extensive Consultations with First Nations Undertaken in 1899 at the Time Treaty 8 Was Negotiated Discharge the Crown's Duty of Consultation and Accommodation?

The Crown's second broad answer to the Mikisew claim is that whatever had to be done was done in 1899. The Minister contends:

> While the government should consider the impact on the treaty right, there is no duty to accommodate in this context. The treaty itself constitutes the accommodation of the aboriginal interest; taking up lands, as defined above, leaves intact the essential ability of the Indians to continue to hunt, fish and trap. As long as that promise is honoured, the treaty is not breached and no separate duty to accommodate arises. [Emphasis added]

This is not correct. Consultation that excludes from the outset any form of accommodation would be meaningless. The contemplated process is not simply one of giving the Mikisew an opportunity to blow off steam before the Minister proceeds to do what she intended to do all along. Treaty making is an important stage in the long process of reconciliation, but it is only a stage. What occurred at Fort Chipewyan in 1899 was not the complete discharge of the duty arising from the honour of the Crown, but a rededication of it.

The Crown has a treaty right to "take up" surrendered lands for regional transportation purposes, but the Crown is nevertheless under an obligation to inform itself of the impact its project will have on the exercise by the Mikisew of their hunting and trapping rights, and to communicate its findings to the Mikisew. The Crown must then attempt to deal with the Mikisew "in good faith, and with the intention of substantially addressing" Mikisew concerns (*Delgamuukw*, at para. 168). This does not mean that whenever a government proposes to do anything in the Treaty 8 surrendered lands it must consult with all signatory First Nations, no matter how remote or unsubstantial the impact. The duty to consult is, as stated in *Haida Nation*, triggered at a low threshold, but adverse impact is a matter of degree, as is the extent of the Crown's duty. Here the impacts were clear, established and demonstrably adverse to the continued exercise of the Mikisew hunting and trapping rights over the lands in question.

In summary, the 1899 negotiations were the first step in a long journey that is unlikely to end any time soon. ...

Was the Process Followed by the Minister Through Parks Canada in this Case Sufficient?

I should state at the outset that the winter road proposed by the Minister was a permissible purpose for "taking up" lands under Treaty 8. It is obvious that the listed purposes of "settlement, mining, lumbering" and "trading" all require suitable transportation. The treaty does not spell out permissible "other purposes" but the term should not be read restrictively:

The question is whether the Minister and her staff pursued the permitted purpose of regional transportation needs in accordance with the Crown's duty to consult. The answer turns on the particulars of that duty shaped by the circumstances here. In *Delgamuukw*, the Court considered the duty to consult and accommodate in the context of an infringement of aboriginal title (at para. 168):

In *Haida Nation*, the Court pursued the kinds of duties that may arise in pre-proof claim situations, and McLachlin C.J. used the concept of a spectrum to frame her analysis (at paras. 43–45):

The determination of the content of the duty to consult will, as *Haida* suggests, be governed by the context. One variable will be the specificity of the promises made. Where, for example, a treaty calls for certain supplies, or Crown payment of treaty monies, or a modern land claims settlement imposes specific obligations on aboriginal peoples with respect to identified resources, the role of consultation may be quite limited. If the respective obligations are clear the parties should get on with performance. Another contextual factor will be the seriousness of the impact on the aboriginal people of the Crown's proposed course of action. The more serious the impact the more important will be the role of consultation. Another factor in a non-treaty case, as *Haida* points out, will be the strength of the aboriginal claim. The history of dealings between the Crown and a particular First Nation may also be significant. Here, the most important contextual factor is that Treaty 8 provides a framework within which to manage the continuing changes in land use already foreseen in 1899 and expected, even now, to continue well into the future. In that context, consultation is key to achievement of the overall objective of the modern law of treaty and aboriginal rights, namely reconciliation.

The duty here has both informational and response components. In this case, given that the Crown is proposing to build a fairly minor winter road on *surrendered* lands where the Mikisew hunting, fishing and trapping rights are expressly subject to the "taking up" limitation, I believe the Crown's duty lies at the lower end of the spectrum. The Crown was required to provide notice to the Mikisew and to engage directly with them (and not, as seems to have been the case here, as an afterthought to a general public consultation with Park users). This engagement ought to have included the provision of information about the project addressing what the Crown knew to be Mikisew interests and what the Crown anticipated might be the potential adverse impact on those interests. The Crown was required to solicit and to listen carefully to the Mikisew concerns, and to attempt to minimize adverse impacts on the Mikisew hunting, fishing and trapping rights. The Crown did not discharge this obligation when it unilaterally declared the road realignment would be shifted from the reserve itself to a track along its boundary.

Had the consultation process gone ahead, it would not have given the Mikisew a veto over the alignment of the road. As emphasized in *Haida Nation*, consultation will not always lead to accommodation, and accommodation may or may not result in an agreement. There could, however, be changes in the road alignment or construction that would go a long way towards satisfying the Mikisew objections. We do not know, and the Minister cannot know in the absence of consultation, what such changes might be.

In the result I would allow the appeal, quash the Minister's approval order, and remit the winter road project to the Minister to be dealt with in accordance with these reasons.

Notes and Questions

1. The importance of *Mikisew* extends far beyond the interactions between First Nations with treaty rights in Canadian parks and the federal government. In many ways, the decision sheds new light on the obligations of government generally when making land or resource use decisions that potentially affect treaty rights. In this vein, Professor Bankes argues that three features of Mikisew are especially important:

> First, it confirms that the First Nation signatories to the numbered treaties have a continuing interest in their traditional territories and that the provincial Crown cannot ignore this interest. Although expressed in formal terms as a hunting right, the Court protects this interest by imposing on the Crown a duty to consult in relation to any disposition or regulatory decision that may affect the quality or quantity of that right. The case will have implications not only for Crown disposition policies but also, and perhaps more importantly, for the regulatory activities of government departments and regulatory tribunals such as the Energy and Utilities Board. Second, the case confirms that the treaty right to hunt is not exhausted by its use as a defence to a charge of illegal harvesting of wildlife or other natural resources. *Mikisew* therefore adds to the body of case law in which First Nations have used the treaty right to hunt as a sword to contest competing land use policies. Third, by severing the source of the duty to consult from a rights infringement, and by locating that duty in the honour of the Crown rather than the particular language of the treaty, the court has indicated its willingness to develop a body of constitutional common law to apply to the intersocietal relationship between indigenous and settler societies in order to further the objective of reconciliation enshrined in s.35 of the

Constitution Act, 1982 (See N. Bankes, "Mikisew Cree and the Lands Taken Up Clause of the Numbered Treaties" (2005-2006) 92 *Resources* 1–8, at 7).

2. In many provinces, an emerging issue is balancing the goals of promoting biodiversity protection and conservation with the Crown's constitutional obligation to recognize and respect Aboriginal rights and title. This is particularly true in British Columbia, where much of the land base with high conservation values currently facing resource development pressures is subject to unresolved Aboriginal rights and title claims.

A key venue in which this challenge has played out is BC's Central and North Coast; a region whose future, for much of the last decade, has been the subject of intense negotiations involving provincial government, First Nations and conservation organizations. The size of the area in question is approximately 6.4 million hectares, or more than twice the size of Vancouver Island. Included in the area was a large intact coastal old growth area, dubbed by conservationists as the 'Great Bear Rainforest'.

Ultimately, as a result of a collaborative process that involved First Nations, industry, environmentalists, local governments and other stakeholders, a comprehensive plan for the management of the area was developed. One of the prerequisites to implementing this plan was amendments to BC's *Parks Act*, to create a new protected area designation known as "conservancies": see the *Park (Conservancy Enabling) Amendment Act* (SBC, 2006).

This new designation addresses First Nations' concerns about their traditional territories being designated for protection under predecessor provincial legislation. These concerns included the need to maintain and protect Aboriginal food, social and ceremonial rights and the need to ensure that opportunities for low impact, compatible economic activities were not lost.

As the result of government-to-government negotiations between First Nations and the provincial government on the Central and North Coast, the amendments explicitly recognize the importance of maintaining and protecting First Nations values related to social, ceremonial and cultural uses. At the same time, a wider range of low impact, compatible economic opportunities may be permitted in a conservancy than in a Class A park. In a Class A park, economic activities are limited to those related to recreation and tourism. Compatible economic activities in conservancies must be consistent with the legislation and are determined through a management planning process. Commercial logging, mining, and hydro electric power generation, other than local run-of-river (micro-hydro) projects, is not be allowed in conservancies. A park use permit may be issued for local run-of-river projects within conservancies, for the purposes of supplying power for approved uses in a conservancy or to nearby communities that do not have access to the power grid.

Currently, North and Central Coast First Nations are developing Collaborative Management Agreements with the province, which specify how the conservancies in each First Nations' territory will be managed collaboratively in a government-to-government relationship.

Part IV — Emerging Issues in Parks and Protected Areas Law

In this concluding Part, we offer some prospective thoughts on the future of protected areas law in Canada. Two themes, in our view, are especially deserving of attention in this regard. The first concerns the potential for citizens to secure greater protection for protected areas using the public trust doctrine. In Chapter 3, we provided an overview of the doctrine and discussed the implications of *British Columbia v. Canadian Forest Products* (SCC, 2004) ("*Canfor*"), a decision that observers suggest may portend a more robust role for the doctrine in Canadian law in the years ahead. This is especially true, we would argue, in the context of securing enhanced protection for protected areas. The second theme concerns the potential and options for law reform. To manage our expanding protected areas network, both provincially and nationally, many have argued that we need to enhance the legal regimes under which they are governed. In order to consider some of the law reform options that present themselves, we examine the key features of Ontario's new *Parks Act*, enacted in 2006.

The Public Trust Doctrine

Chapter 2 introduced the public trust doctrine as a common law principle, vesting in the Crown a trust-like duty to protect public resources for the benefit of the public at large. In its common law guise, the doctrine has ancient roots. And in more modern times, especially in the United States, it has proven to be a powerful tool to advance the goals of environmental stewardship. In contrast, until recently, in Canada, the doctrine has been relatively quiescent. Academic commentators, however, believe that the decision in *Canfor* may create an opportunity for the doctrine to blossom.

One realm in which the doctrine could play a particularly important role is in the context of public resources that are governed by parks legislation. In this setting, it is argued that such resources are not only protected by a common law public trust but also a statutory one. The argument that the Crown is under a statutory public trust in managing parks derives from the dedication language that is frequently present in parks legislation. For example, as discussed infra, the CNPA states that:

> The national parks of Canada are hereby dedicated to the people of Canada for their benefit, education and enjoyment, subject to this Act and the regulations, and the parks shall be maintained and made use of so as to leave them unimpaired for the enjoyment of future generations: s. 4(1)

Comparable, although in some instances less unequivocal language, is contained in most provincial parks laws.

Both in the United States and Canada, environmental organizations have sought to compel governments to take action to protect public resources within parks, contending that analogous dedication provisions create an actionable right to enforce a statutory public trust. Below we offer excerpts from two early cases where this argument was mounted. The differing analysis and outcomes are illustrative of the general trajectory of the public trust doctrine to date.

Sierra Club v. Department of the Interior
376 F. Supp. 90 (N.D. Cal. 1974)

SWEIGERT District Judge:

This is an action by plaintiff, Sierra Club, against the Department of the Interior, and officials of the Department, to obtain judgment of this court directing defendants to use certain of their powers to protect Redwood National Park from damage allegedly caused or threatened by certain logging operations on peripheral privately-owned lands.

[The] complaint alleges in substance and effect as follows:

> That subsequent to the establishment of the Redwood National Park in 1968 plaintiff learned that logging operations on slopes surrounding and upstream from the park were seriously endangering the park's resources, and that these dangers were reported to defendants
>
> That on September 24, 1971, plaintiff formally petitioned the Secretary of the Interior to take immediate action pursuant to his authority under the *Redwood National Park Act* to prevent further harm to the park's resources, and that a task force was then created by the Department of the Interior to make intensive field investigations of the threatened and actual damage to the Redwood National Park and to prepare a report of its findings;
>
> That defendants have taken no action to prevent damage to the park from the consequences of logging on lands surrounding or upstream from the park, except to request the voluntary cooperation of timber companies to reform their operations on minor portions upstream and upslope from the park; that the timber companies have not effectively cooperated with this request and that defendants manifest no intent to protect the park from further damage to the park's trees, soil, scenery and streams;
>
> That past and present logging operations on privately-owned steep slopes on the periphery of the park leave the park vulnerable to high winds, landslides, mudslides and siltation in the streams which endangers tree roots and aquatic life.

Plaintiff, citing the *National Park System Act* and the *Redwood National Park Act* contends that defendants have a judicially-enforceable duty to exercise certain powers granted by these provisions to prevent or to mitigate such actual or potential damage to the park and its redwoods as is alleged in the complaint.

The *National Park System Act* provides for the creation of the National Park Service in the Department of the Interior which Service shall:

> promote and regulate the use of Federal areas known as national parks, monuments, and reservations ... by such means and measures as conform to the fundamental purpose of said parks, monuments, and reservations, which purpose is to conserve the scenery and the natural and historic objects and the wild life therein and *to provide for the enjoyment of the same in such manner and by such means as will leave them unimpaired for the enjoyment of future generations* (emphasis added)

In addition to these general fiduciary obligations of the Secretary of the Interior, the Secretary has been invested with certain specific powers and obligations in connection with the unique situation of the Redwood National Park.

The Redwood National Park was created on October 2, 1968 by the *Redwood National Park Act*,

> to preserve significant examples of the primeval coastal redwood (Sequoia sempervirens) forests and the streams and seashores with which they are associated for purposes of public inspiration, enjoyment, and scientific study ...

Congress limited the park to an area of 58,000 acres; appropriated 92 million dollars to implement the Act, of which, according to the Second Claim of the Amended Complaint, 20 million dollars remain unspent; and conferred upon the Secretary specific powers expressly designed to prevent damage to the park by logging on peripheral areas.

The question presented is whether on the allegations of the amended complaint, considered in the light of these statutory provisions, this court can direct the Secretary to exercise the powers granted under [the *National Parks Systems Act*].

Good sense suggests that the existence, nature and extent of potentially damaging conditions on neighboring lands and the effect thereof on the park, and the need for action to prevent such damage are matters that rest, primarily at least, within the judgment of the Secretary. However, neither the terms nor the legislative history of the *Redwood National Park Act* are such as to preclude judicial review of the Secretary's action or inaction.

In *Rockbridge v. Lincoln*, 449 F.2d 567 (9th Cir. 1971) our Circuit ... held that, in view of the trust relationship of the Secretary toward the Indians ... such discretion as was vested in the Secretary was not an unbridled discretion to refuse to regulate but only a discretion to decide what specific regulations to promulgate and, therefore, a cause for judicial relief ... was stated ...

In view of the analogous trust responsibility of the Secretary of the Interior with respect to public lands ... and the analogous legislative history indicating a specific set of objectives which the provisions of the *Redwood National Park Act* were designed to accomplish, we consider *Rockbridge, supra*, to be strongly persuasive to the point that a case for judicial relief has been made out by plaintiff.

We are of the opinion that the terms of the statute ... impose a legal duty on the Secretary to utilize the specific powers given to him whenever reasonably necessary for the protection of the park and that any discretion vested in the Secretary concerning time, place and specifics of the exercise of such powers is subordinate to his paramount legal duty imposed, not only under his trust obligation but by the statute itself, to protect the park.

Notes and Questions

1. Litigation aimed at protecting Redwood National Park from the impacts of adjacent logging continued for several more years after this decision. In 1975, the court found that the Interior Secretary was in violation of his

statutory public trust obligations even though, after the decision excerpted above, his Department had entered into various agreements with logging companies to mitigate impacts on the Park: *Sierra Club v. Department of the Interior*, 398 F. Supp. 284 (US Dist. Crt., 1975). The Court criticized the adequacy of these agreements and ordered the Secretary to develop a protection plan for court approval. Ultimately, in the late 1970s, the controversy was resolved when the US government expanded the Park's boundaries by buying out affected logging interests.

2. The next case provides an interesting counterpoint. As you read *Green v. Ontario*, decided just as the Redwood litigation was gearing up, consider the factual and analytic differences between the two cases.

Green v. Ontario
(1972), [1973] 2 O.R. 396

LERNER, J.: — These reasons are the result of separate motions by each defendant ... wherein they seek orders striking out the statement of claim as it relates to each of them and dismissing the action ...

From the statement of claim it appears that the plaintiff, Larry Green, is a Canadian citizen residing in Metropolitan Toronto and a researcher in the employ of "Pollution Probe" at the University of Toronto. ... Lake Ontario Cement Limited, entered into a written lease on January 12, 1968, with the Province of Ontario for a parcel of land containing 16.02 acres and forming part of the sand banks and some lands under the waters of West Lake in the Township of Hallowell, Prince Edward County ... for 75 years ... to remove and carry away, from time to time and without charge, sand in unlimited quantities from the lands ...

Some two years and three months later, pursuant to the authority of the *Provincial Parks Act*, the Province of Ontario established the "Sandbanks Provincial Park" as a provincial park ... consisting of 1,802 acres ... adjacent to and adjoining the 16.02 acres previously leased to Lake Ontario Cement before any park was ever in existence. The 16.02 acres have never been nor are they now, part of the said park lands so dedicated.

The statement of claim sets out s. 2 of the *Provincial Parks Act* which states:

> All provincial parks are dedicated to the people of the Province of Ontario and others who may use them for their healthful enjoyment and education, and the provincial parks shall be maintained for the benefit of future generations in accordance with this Act and the regulations.

and on the basis of s. 2 alleges that it imposes a trust upon the Province of Ontario with regard to Sandbanks Provincial Park so designated, to maintain that park in keeping with the "spirit" of s. 2 and that by permitting the use of the adjoining lands which the Province of Ontario had legally conveyed by leasehold to the other defendant were in breach of the trust implicit in s. 2 set out above.

This plaintiff was careful not to frame the action in public nuisance. Counsel for the plaintiff conceded in argument that on the basis of a public nuisance, the action could not succeed because there is no suggestion of any damage or injury to the plaintiff, Larry Green, beyond that which might be alleged by any other member of the public ...

The plaintiff, in fact, is seeking a declaration of breach of a statutory trust which is not open to him unless he has a special interest above that of the general public ...

It was also admitted by counsel for the plaintiff that but for the existence of s. 2 of the *Provincial Parks Act* there would be no basis for bringing the action. Notwithstanding the philosophical and noble intentions (my expression) of the Legislature to express in the pertinent section an ideological concept, no statutory trust has been created. It becomes necessary to break down the wording thereof: "All provincial parks are dedicated to the people of the Province of Ontario and others who may use them ..".. This simply makes it clear that all persons (and I presume that includes those lawfully in Canada) are entitled to make use of the parks without the inhibitions or restrictions of race, religion, creed or other prejudicial implications inimical to the welfare of society and particularly the people of Ontario. "... and the provincial parks shall be maintained for the benefit of future generations in accordance with this Act and the regulations" implies that the Province of Ontario is required to physically maintain the parks so dedicated. This view is confirmed and amplified by the provisions of s. 3(1) and all the subsections of s. 19 covering such things as the issuing of permits, the fees for the right to enter and use the parks, which are so complete as to make the power of the Province in the whole concept of park lands, absolute.

A reading of s. 2 together with s. 3(2) makes it clear that the subject-matter of the trust is not certain. Section 3(2) empowers the Province to increase, decrease or even put an end to or "close down" any park. There cannot be a trust as is alleged by the plaintiff herein unless the subject-matter of the trust is of certainty.

... considered in the light of s. 3(2) and when coupled with s. 2 should make it clear that the Province of Ontario cannot be held to be a trustee. Section 3(2) cannot be construed as compelling the Province to hold these lands or for that matter any park lands, for any certain period of time or forever for the purposes that are alleged by the respondent to be read into s. 2 of the *Provincial Parks Act*.

... [Moreover] s. 19 of the *Provincial Parks Act* ... gives unfettered and wide ranging powers to the Province in the operation and use of its parks and their ancillary or collateral benefits not only for the public but it also permits the use of same for private business enterprises, other gainful activities for special "classes", e.g., amusement operators, tourist accommodation operators, retail and wholesale stores and all manner of trades and businesses all of which would depend upon the discretion of the government. The action therefore as framed for breach of trust discloses no reasonable cause of action.

No one can be critical of resort to the Courts to remedy social wrongs or injustices by way of interpretation of law, either statutory or by precedent. This is desirable in our rapidly changing society and preferable to the lawless or anarchial way of seeking rectification of real as well as unreal injustices, inequities and abuses as practised in other jurisdictions. Nevertheless, if resort to the Courts is to be had, care must be taken that such steps are from a sound base in law otherwise ill-founded actions for the sake of using the Courts as a vehicle for expounding philosophy are to be discouraged.

Having first concluded that the plaintiff has no status to maintain this action and that the statement of claim discloses no reasonable cause of action, on reflection, I do not think it improper for me to find also that the action is vexatious and frivolous. I say this because the plaintiff had to know of the existence and terms of the lease and that it pre-dated by a substantial period of time, the establishment of Sandbanks Provincial Park.

... the applications of both defendants are allowed and the action against all defendants is dismissed with costs ...

Notes and Questions

1. Identify the factual and legal distinctions between the two preceding cases. Which of these distinctions are most important to explaining the differing legal results?

2. One key distinction between the cases is the level of judicial comfort with the public trust doctrine, particularly one that provides its beneficiaries with a right of action. In the *Canfor* decision, Binnie J. refers to American public trust caselaw, including the seminal decision of the U.S. Supreme Court in *Illinois Central Railroad Co. v. Illinois*, 146 U.S. 387 (1892), in the course of concluding that "there is no legal barrier to the Crown suing for compensation as well as injunctive relief in a proper case on account of public nuisance, or negligence causing environmental damage to public lands, and perhaps other torts such as trespass". Notably, however, he stops short of recognizing a stand-alone Crown right to sue based on the public trust. And he deliberately leaves open what he refers to as some "important and novel policy questions". These questions, in his view, include:

> ... the Crown's potential liability for *inactivity* in the face of threats to the environment, the existence or non-existence of enforceable fiduciary duties owed to the public by the Crown in that regard, the

> limits to the role and function and remedies available to governments taking action on account of activity harmful to public enjoyment of public resources, and the spectre of imposing on private interests an indeterminate liability for an indeterminate amount of money for ecological or environmental damage.

Clearly, then, while the door has been opened to renewed attempts by individual litigants to pursue relief akin to that sought in *Green*, the future of the public trust doctrine — whether in its common law or statutory forms — is by no means clear.

3. If the *Green* case was litigated today, in a Canadian court, what result would you expect? What if a case, with facts similar to those in *Sierra Club v. Department of the Interior*, were filed in response to duly authorized, private logging on provincial Crown lands adjacent to Pacific Rim National Park?

Reforming Ontario Parks Legislation: the Ontario Experience

Christopher J.A. Wilkinson, "Protected Areas Law in Ontario, Canada: Maintenance of Ecological Integrity as the Management Priority"

(2008) 28 Natural Areas Journal 180–186

... Ontario's system of protected areas includes 329 provincial parks, 292 conservation reserves, and 10 wilderness areas, all of which are managed by the Ministry of Natural Resources. These areas combine to cover approximately 9% of the province's land base, totalling 8.7 million hectares.

Provincial parks, formerly regulated under the *Provincial Parks Act*, R.S.O. 1990, account for 88% of the total land base of protected areas in Ontario (Ministry of Natural Resources 2004:4). Provincial parks range from small areas intended mainly for recreation, such as Devil's Glen Provincial Park covering just 61 hectares, to huge wilderness parks, such as Woodland Caribou Provincial Park encompassing more than 450,000 hectares. Many of these provincial parks are actively operated to provide recreational opportunities — 105 operating parks provide facilities or services on a formal basis. These operating parks offer 18,810 vehicle-accessible campsites and 7000 interior campsites accessible by foot or canoe. Ontario's provincial parks host more than 10 million visits each year and generate an economic impact of approximately 380 million a year. At the same time, these protected areas are meant to conserve habitat for many of Ontario's 2900 species of vascular plants, 160 species of fish, 80 species of amphibians and reptiles, 400 species of birds, and 85 species of mammals.

Conservation reserves make up about 12% of the protected areas network. This type of protected area was created in 1994 under the authority of the *Public Lands Act*. Conservation reserves were intended primarily to protect significant features and provide recreational opportunities. These areas had fewer restrictions on recreational and commercial uses than provincial parks, although they did exclude logging and mining. However, the Environmental Commissioner of Ontario (2004:46) previously reported that "the *Public Lands Act* was not intended or designed to protect natural heritage features such as sensitive habitats or important species, and thus it is not a good public policy mechanism for protecting these values in conservation reserves".

Wilderness areas, regulated under the *Wilderness Areas Act* of 1959, make up about 0.001% of the protected areas network. A total of 33 wilderness areas were established in

Ontario, although no new wilderness areas have been established since the early 1960s and only 10 areas are located outside existing provincial parks or conservation reserves.

... The primary statute at issue, the *Provincial Parks Act* was introduced in 1954 when there were only eight provincial parks in Ontario. Indeed, many different stakeholders, independent experts, and government panels and agencies have called for such reforms over the years, stating that the law did not reflect modern science, planning, or environmental realities (Swaigen 1978, 1982, 2001; Eagles 1984; Michels et al. 1998; Campbell 2000: Wilkinson and Eagles 2001; Environmental Commissioner of Ontario 2002; Wilkinson 2002; Bell 2002). As Bell (2002:19) observes,

> The legislative changes needed to set an unequivocal conservation mandate for the Provincial Parks system have been discussed for twenty years now, and there is general agreement that these must include, at the very least, a provision for public consultation, the prohibition of industrial activities and a clear statement of purpose and guiding principles. ... The province should act now, in the public interest, to protect the ecological integrity of the Provincial Parks system.

Protected areas are the very foundation of any concerted effort to conserve biodiversity in Ontario (Campbell 2000; Wilkinson 2002). The loss of natural areas is one of the greatest threats to biodiversity worldwide, including within Ontario (Environmental Commissioner of Ontario 2002). Protected areas are places meant to maintain and restore ecological and natural heritage values. They should be havens for wild species, conserving the diversity among and within them. Ideally, these areas serve a crucial conservation role at a local level, but equally as important, they also should function as an interconnected network at a landscape level. The degree to which the law actually protects these areas is critical, marking the difference between them existing as simple lines on a map or places where biodiversity is truly safeguarded.

Wilkinson and Eagles examined the need for legislative reform of Ontario's protected area legislation, concluding that a new statute should contain: "(1) the recognition of biodiversity conservation as the primary goal; (2) the need for management plans for each park, and (3) the requirement for an open consultative process". This examination also raised the issues of better regulating appropriate and prohibited activities, the necessity of adequate funding and staffing for protected areas by the provincial government, and the need to address increasing recreational demands on the system (Wilkinson and Eagles 2001).

The Environmental Commissioner of Ontario (2004:46) has also noted that "only 38 out of 548 protected areas (7 per cent) in Ontario have approved plans that involved public consultation and that are not in need of review. Without sound planning and conscientious management, Ontario's protected areas are little more than "paper parks — simple lines on a map" A similar set of concerns previously was expressed by another independent officer of the Legislative Assembly of Ontario (Auditor General of Ontario 2002:208–225).

Discussion

All provincial parks, formerly regulated by the *Provincial Parks Act*, and all conservation reserves, formerly regulated under the *Public Lands Act*, will now be administered under the *Provincial Parks and Conservation Reserves Act, 2006*. The Ministry of Natural Resources will also evaluate the 10 wilderness areas, regulated under the *Wilderness Areas Act*, that are outside provincial parks and conservation reserves. Where natural values justify protection, the ministry will regulate these areas through a public consultation process as either provincial parks or conservation reserves.

This new legislation repeals the *Provincial Parks Act*, the *Wilderness Areas Act* and *the Algonquin Provincial Park Extension Act, 1960-61*. It also makes minor amendments to the *Algonquin Forestry Authority Act*, the *Crown Forest Sustainability Act, 1994*, the *Historical*

Parks Act, the *Kawartha Highlands Signature Site Park Act, 2003*, the *Mining Act*, and the *Off-Road Vehicles Act.*

Principles to Guide the Management of Protected Areas

Section 1 of the *Provincial Parks and Conservation Reserves Act, 2006* stales that the purpose of this statute is "to permanently protect a system of provincial parks and conservation reserves that includes ecosystems that are representative of all of Ontario's natural regions, protects provincially significant elements of Ontario's natural and cultural heritage, maintains biodiversity and provides opportunities for compatible, ecologically sustainable recreation". This purpose statement is notable because, for the first time, Ontario's protected areas are expressly mandated to maintain biodiversity. Further, it also recognizes that provincial parks and conservation reserves are intended to be managed as a system, rather than as isolated areas. Swaigen (2001:226) comments that such purpose sections within a statute are important in "setting the tone for those agencies that implement it and for the Courts that interpret it".

The most significant change to the governance of Ontario's protected areas is that ecological integrity is now the guiding purpose for planning and management. Subsection 3(1) of the statute states that the "maintenance of ecological integrity shall be the first priority and the restoration of ecological integrity shall be considered" for all provincial parks and conservation reserves. Unlike its legislative predecessor, the *Provincial Parks and Conservation Reserves Act, 2006* also explicitly recognizes in subsection 3(2) that opportunities for public consultation shall be provided in the planning and management of protected areas.

Importantly, the new statute defines ecological integrity in subsection 5(2) as "a condition in which biotic and abiotic components of ecosystems and the composition and abundance of native species and biological communities arc characteristic of their natural regions and rates of change and ecosystem processes are unimpeded". The inclusion of a definition of ecological integrity is of fundamental importance, for both ministry staff in administering the Act and for the public to clearly understand the purpose of Ontario's protected areas (see Panel on the Ecological Integrity of Canada's National Parks 2000). The *Provincial Parks and Conservation Reserves Act, 2006* also further defines ecological integrity in subsection 5(3) as including "healthy and viable populations of native species, including species at risk, and maintenance of the habitat on which the species depend" and "levels of air and water quality consistent with protection of biodiversity and recreational enjoyment". This encompassing definition is similar to that contained in the *Canada National Parks Act*, which defines ecological integrity as "with respect to a park, a condition that is determined to be characteristic of its natural region and likely to persist, including abiotic components and the composition and abundance of native species and biological communities, rates of change and supporting processes".

In a similar fashion to the old *Provincial Parks Act*, the new statute contains relatively benign language that dedicates the parks to the people of Ontario and others for reasons such as their enjoyment and education. However, the *Provincial Parks and Conservation Reserves Act* significantly expands upon this dedication in section 6 by specifying that provincial parks and conservation reserves "shall be managed to maintain their ecological integrity and to leave them unimpaired for future generations". This language is important as it reinforces that the legal mandate of these areas is to maintain ecological integrity and that all other activities should be managed within that context.

It is noteworthy that the Ontario Parks branch of the Ministry of Natural Resources does not have an overall mandate to maintain ecological integrity, unlike its federal counterpart. The *Parks Canada Agency Act* firmly establishes in its preamble that the mandate of Parks Canada as an agency is "to maintain or restore the ecological integrity of national parks".

The *Ministry of Natural Resources Act* solely directs in section 13(1) that "the Minister may establish programs to promote and stimulate the development and management of natural resources in Ontario". Arguably, the combination of the ecological integrity provisions within the *Canada National Parks Act* and the *Parks Canada Agency Act* provide for a stronger "presumption against developments and activities that would impair the ecological integrity" of protected areas than what now exists at the provincial level in Ontario (Swaigen 2001:230).

Goals and Objectives

The legal objective of both provincial parks and conservation reserves will now be "to permanently protect representative ecosystems, biodiversity and provincially significant elements of Ontario's natural and cultural heritage and to manage these areas to ensure that ecological integrity is maintained" as stated in subsection 2(1) of the new statute. This objective is a significant improvement as the old *Provincial Parks Act* was silent in this regard and those objectives for provincial parks that did exist were both weaker and relegated to non-binding policy. Indeed, prior to this new legislation, conservation reserves lacked many basic legal protections when they were regulated under the *Public Lands Act*.

Provincial parks also have the new legal objective, in subsection 2(1), to provide opportunities for "ecologically sustainable outdoor recreation", "in addition to providing opportunities for visitors to increase their knowledge of Ontario's natural and cultural heritage. These objectives vary slightly for conservation reserves in that they may be managed to provide ecologically sustainable land uses, including traditional outdoor heritage activities", as set out in subsection 2(2) of the new statute. Provincial parks and conservation reserves also both have the objective of facilitating scientific research and serving as benchmarks to monitor ecological change on the broader landscape.

Classification and Zoning

The *Provincial Parks and Conservation Reserves Act, 2006*, akin to its predecessor, recognizes six classes of provincial parks in subsection 8(1): wilderness, nature reserve, cultural heritage, natural environment, waterway, and recreational class. However, the new statute now states the specific objectives of each of these classes, whereas previously these directions were left to ministry policy. Further, the statute also creates a new aquatic class of provincial park at a date to be proclaimed later by the Lieutenant Governor.

The new statute allows for a system of zoning to be applied to both provincial parks and conservation reserves. This is a similar approach to that of the old *Provincial Parks Act*, in which detailed policies would then apply to specific areas within a given class of park. However, the *Provincial Parks and Conservation Reserves Act, 2006* states in subsection 12(3) that zoning shall not constrain hunting in conservation reserves.

Mandatory Management Direction and State of Protected Areas Reporting

The Ministry of Natural Resources now is required by section 10 of the new statute to prepare "management direction" for all provincial parks and conservation reserves. These directions may apply to one or more protected areas and shall identify site-specific management policies to cover a 20-year period. Management directions may take one of two forms, either a detailed management plan or a management statement, when addressing non-complex issues. Unlike the old *Provincial Parks Act*, the new legislation also explicitly requires in subsection 10(6) that public consultation occur when producing, reviewing, or amending management direction. The new legislation also contains language, similar to subsection 10(1) of the *Canada National Parks Act*, which would make it possible for the Ministry of

Natural Resources to enter into co-management agreements with First Nations for specific provincial parks and conservation reserves.

The new statute does not expressly state that indicators of ecological integrity should be identified in the management plans or statements for each protected area. Ideally, the use of identified indicators and measurable objectives in each management direction would also form the basis of each protected area's ecological monitoring program. The Panel on the Ecological Integrity of Canada's National Parks (2000) has noted that the management direction should also contain a description of how visitor use stresses the protected area's ecological integrity and how such stresses arc being mitigated or eliminated.

The *Provincial Parks and Conservation Reserves Act, 2006* requires the preparation of a planning manual to replace the "Ontario Provincial Parks: Planning and Management Policies". Known as the Blue Book, it was last significantly updated in 1992, and it contains the detailed policy directions for provincial parks. Conservation reserves lacked similar detailed policies, and they will now be covered under the new manual.

The new statute requires in section 11 that the Ministry of Natural Resources produce a state-of-the-parks report every five years. This reporting requirement is similar to Parks Canada's system-wide reports for national parks as required in subsection 12(2) of the *Canada National Parks Act*. These reports will contain an assessment of the extent to which the objectives of provincial parks and conservation reserves are being achieved, including "ecological and socio-economic conditions and benefits, the degree of ecological representation, number and area of provincial parks and conservation reserves, known threats to ecological integrity of provincial parks and conservation reserves and their ecological health and socio-economic benefits" as stated in subsection 11(2). The new statute states that the Ministry of Natural Resources shall post these reports on the publicly accessible Environmental Registry, as established by section 5 and 6 of the *Environmental Bill of Rights, 1993*.

Major Industrial Uses

The *Provincial Parks and Conservation Reserves Act, 2006* explicitly prohibits in section 16 the following activities in protected areas: the commercial harvest of timber; the generation of electricity; prospecting, staking mining claims, developing mineral interests or working mines; and extracting aggregate, topsoil, or peat. The inclusion of these prohibitions is a dramatic improvement compared to the old legislative framework, as historically such details were often *left to the* discretion of non-binding policy (Swaigen 2001). However, the new statute does include numerous exceptions to these prohibitions, such as allowing for electricity generation facilities within protected areas for 'off-the-grid' communities.

The most environmentally significant exception to these prohibitions is that commercial timber operations are allowed to continue in Algonquin Provincial Park, as stated in section 17. The new statute essentially defers to subsection 11(1) of the *Algonquin Forestry Authority Act* that states that die management of this protected area be balanced between recreation and "the public interest in providing a flow of logs from Algonquin Provincial Park". The Environmental Commissioner of Ontario has urged the Ministry of Natural Resources to conduct a public review of the appropriateness of commercial logging in Algonquin and to address "how the proposed park management goal of ecological integrity would be achieved if this policy is allowed to continue".

The *Provincial Parks and Conservation Reserves Act, 2006* reasonably addresses the issue of resource access roads. In some instances, these roads are necessary as a protected area may entirely surround sites with mineral tenure, or timber operations on Crown land may be inaccessible without a road to cross a protected area. The new statute states in subsection 21(1) that such resource access roads may only be constructed if there is no reasonable alternative (lower cost is not justification), and all reasonable measures will be undertaken to minimize harmful environmental impacts and to protect ecological integrity. Further, when the road is no longer required for the purpose for which it was approved or will not be used for a period of five years or more, it will be closed, effective measures will be taken to prevent its use, and the rehabilitation and removal of any infrastructure (i.e., bridges) will be undertaken.

Non-Industrial Uses

Human use is a part of the nature of protected areas, but some forms, levels, or timings of activities are incompatible with ecological integrity. Further, what may be an appropriate activity in one protected area may not be suitable in another area. Experts also recognize that any determination of what is an appropriate activity should not be based on the need for revenue generation. With few exceptions, almost all non industrial uses are not addressed in the new statute and are left to regulation or policy.

The *Provincial Parks and Conservation Reserves Act, 2006* does distinguish, in one specific instance, the differences between classes of provincial parks and which activities are appropriate. Borrowing from ministry policy, the new statute states in subsection 8(2) that visitors to Ontario's eight wilderness class parks may only travel by "non-mechanized means" or engage in "low-impact recreation". These terms are not defined, but the Ministry of Natural Resources will presumably provide further detail in the regulations that will accompany the new statute.

The new statute does not change the manner in which hunting is permitted in Ontario's protected areas, despite Swaigen's (2001:233) recommendation that it should be limited to "necessary aboriginal hunting". By default, recreational hunting is permitted in all conservation reserves. By exception, recreational hunting is permitted in provincial parks. However, that exception has been extended to allow recreational hunting in 132 provincial parks as prescribed in Part 3 of Ontario Regulation 663/98 under the *Fish and Wildlife Conservation Act*. Consequently recreational hunting is allowed in more than two-thirds of Ontario's protected areas However, as noted by the Panel on the Ecological Integrity of Canada's National Parks (2000), the recreational harvest of species can conflict with the maintenance of ecological integrity in a protected area and can impair their utility as true ecological benchmarks. The new statute does not explicitly address commercial trapping, but existing policy dictates that it will be phased out of all provincial parks by no later than January 2010. In contrast to the provincial approach, the *Canada National Parks Act* only allows aboriginal hunting and trapping in a limited number of national parks ...

Deregulation and Disposition of Land

The *Provincial Parks and Conservation Reserves Act, 2006* establishes new conditions for the deregulation and alteration of boundaries of provincial parks and conservation reserves. The Lieutenant Governor in Council, effectively the Cabinet of the Government of Ontario, may dispose of an area of a provincial park or conservation reserve that is less than 50 hectares or less than 1% of the total area, whichever is the lesser as stated in subsection 9(3). For any larger disposition, the Minister of Natural Resources must table the disposition before the Legislative Assembly and obtain its endorsement. However, dispositions do not have to follow this process if they are part of a land claims settlement, an addition to a national park or marine conservation area, or part of a transaction that increases the size of the protected area and enhances ecological integrity as stated in subsection 9(5).

A long-standing criticism, voiced by many stakeholders over the past decade, is that protected areas may be used as floating reserves and that boundaries may be re-drawn to accommodate industrial activities such as mining. It is unfortunate that the new statute did not give the authority to the Minister to order the withdrawal of lands from mineral staking, under the *Mining Act*, for all candidate protected areas.

Conclusions

The *Provincial Parks and Conservation Reserves Act, 2006* is a significant improvement to the legislative framework governing Ontario's protected areas. While not flawless, this new legislation moves Ontario from the back of the pack to near the forefront of protected areas law in Canada. It is a promising beginning to the much-needed overhaul of how Ontario's provincial parks and conservation reserves are managed, and the new statute resolves many of the deficiencies of its legislative predecessor. As next steps, the Ministry of Natural Resources must now revise the regulations and policies that will provide many of the essential details and specific directions that will guide the planning and management of these protected areas. Further, the ministry also must begin to address the substantial backlog of protected areas that do not have a current management plan.

Despite this new statute, concerns still remain as to how Ontario's protected area system is managed overall by the Government of Ontario. These concerns serve as a valuable starring point to possible future research. Firstly, both the Environmental Commissioner of Ontario and the Auditor General of Ontario have expressed concern that the Ontario Parks branch of the Ministry of Natural Resources does not have sufficient resources to properly fulfil its mandate. Ontario is among the only jurisdictions in North America that is attempting to run its protected areas system on a cost recovery basis, and its funding is very low given the vast amount of land that is involved.

The Government of Ontario only allocates approximately $15 million (Cdn.) a year for the Ministry of Natural Resources to plan, manage, protect, and monitor approximately 94,000 km2 of protected areas in Ontario. Between 1992 and 2007, in inflation-adjusted terms, the Government of Ontario's funding for Ontario Parks decreased by 73%. Almost half of all operating provincial parks do not have sufficient staff or funding to meet existing minimum standards of operation. Further, the majority of non-operating parks are visited only once a year or not at all by ministry staff (Environmental Commissioner of Ontario 2004:43). Therefore, if a protected area is not paying for itself, there is no assurance that the law — maintaining ecological integrity — is being upheld. It will be a significant challenge for the Ministry of Natural Resources to adequately administer and enforce the *Provincial Parks and Conservation Reserves Act, 2006* unless there are significant increases to its budget.

Secondly, it is a common fallacy that protected areas are unimpaired swaths of wilderness with pristine natural conditions. In reality, Ontario's provincial parks and conservation reserves are threatened by numerous ecological stresses and threats, some of which originate beyond their boundaries. Indeed, in many cases, the boundaries of protected areas are political constructs and do not reflect natural boundaries. As such, there may be an issue of concern outside of a protected area that affects its management, but it is beyond an imaginary line and cannot be effectively addressed by Ontario Parks staff or even the Ministry of Natural Resources.

In contrast, section 48 of the federal *Canadian Environmental Assessment Act* can require that an environmental assessment be conducted for any project outside the boundaries of a national park that may adversely affect its ecological integrity. Ontario's provincial laws fail to contain any similar safeguards. Unlike national parks, the land inside and outside of most protected areas in Ontario has the benefit of being managed by the same entity; yet, the Government of Ontario has few mechanisms to restrict incompatible land uses, such as urbanization or commercial timber harvesting, near the boundaries of its own protected areas.

What is needed is an ecologically sensible landscape-level approach to the broader issue of Crown land management. Different branches or ministries — all part of the same government — should not be seen as threatening or competing against each other's interests. Protected areas should be given the priority and recognition that they deserve. Provincial parks and conservation reserves must be managed on a greater ecosystem basis in order to fulfil their mandate of protecting Ontario's ecological integrity. Wildlife and natural processes know no boundaries; therefore, failing to take this wider perspective imperils Ontario's protected areas.

Notes and Questions

1. The author concludes that *Provincial Parks and Conservation Reserves Act, 2006* "moves Ontario from the back of the pack to near the forefront of protected areas law in Canada". What are the strengths of the new legislation? What weaknesses remain?

2. Compare and contrast the new Ontario legislation with the *Canadian National Parks Act* and, if you are from a province other than Ontario, with applicable parks legislation in your province. Applicable legislation for other provinces includes:

British Columbia — *Park Act*, R.S.B.C. 1996 c. 344

Alberta — *Provincial Parks Act*, R.S.A. 2000, c. P-35

Saskatchewan — *Parks Act*, S.S. 1986, c. P-1.1

Manitoba — *Provincial Parks Act*, R.S.M. 1993, c. 39

Quebec — *Parks Act*, R.S.Q. 1977, c. P-9

New Brunswick — *Parks Act*, R.S.N.B. 1982, c. P- 2.1

Nova Scotia — *Provincial Parks Act*, R.S.N.S. 1989, c. 367

Prince Edward Island — *Natural Areas Protection Act*, R.S.P.E.I. 1988, c. N-2

Newfoundland and Labrador — *Provincial Parks Act*, R.S.N. 1990, c. P-32

Yukon — *Parks and Land Certainty Act*, S.Y. 2001, c. 46

Northwest Territory — *Territorial Parks Act*, R.S.N.W.T. 1988, c. T-4

Nunavut — *Territorial Parks Act*, R.S.N.W.T. 1988, c. T-4, (as duplicated for Nunavut by s. 29 of the *Nunavut Act*)

In 2002, David Boyd created a report card for the laws governing Canada's parks. In that report, federal legislation scored a B, but only 2 of the provinces, Nova Scotia (B) and Newfoundland (D), passed. Using Boyd's criteria (excerpted below), assess your province's current parks legislation (*Wild by Law: A Report Card on Laws Governing Canada's Parks and Protected Areas*: 2002 at p. 6–8). How does it fare?

1. Mandates conservation and ecological integrity as top priority;
2. Prohibits industrial resource use (logging, mining, etc.);
3. Protects permanently (boundaries legislated);
4. Incorporates dedication to future generations;
5. Ensures public participation in *mandatory* parks planning;
6. Requires reporting on the state of the parks;
7. Recognizes aboriginal rights;
8. Enshrines minimum 12% protection of all ecosystems within jurisdiction;
9. Provides additional protection for ecological reserves and wilderness areas; and
10. Establishes regional management responsibility.

References

We thank the copyright holders for their permission to reproduce their materials.

N. Bankes, "Mikisew Cree and the Lands Taken Up Clause of the Numbered Treaties" (2005-2006) 92 Resources 1–8

David R. Boyd, *Wild by Law: A Report Card on Laws Governing Canada's Parks and Protected Areas* (Polis Project, University of Victoria: 2002)

David R. Boyd, *Unnatural Law: Rethinking Canadian Environmental Law and Policy* (Vancouver, UBC Press: 2003)

P. Dearden & R. Canessa, "Marine Protected Areas" in P. Dearden & R. Rollins, eds., *Parks and Protected Areas in Canada*, 3rd ed. (Oxford University Press, 2009)

P. Dearden & J. Dempsey, "Protected Areas in Canada: Decade of Change" (2004) 48 Canadian Geographer 225–239. Copyright © 2004, The Canadian Association of Geographers/L'Association canadienne des géographes. Reproduced with permission of Blackwell Publishing Ltd.

P. Dearden & S. Langdon, "The Role of Aboriginal Peoples" in P. Dearden & R. Rollins, eds., *Parks and Protected Areas in Canada*, 3rd ed., (Oxford University Press, 2009)

P. Dearden & Rick Rollins, "*Parks and Protected Areas in Canada*" in P. Dearden & R. Rollins, eds., *Parks and Protected Areas in Canada*, 3rd ed., (Oxford University Press, 2009)

S. Fluker, "'Maintaining ecological integrity is our first priority' — Policy Rhetoric or Practical Reality in Canada's National Parks? A case comment on *Canadian Parks & Wilderness Society v. Canada (Minister of Canadian Heritage)*" (2003) 13 J. Env. L. & Prac. 131

C. Malcolm, "The Provincial Story" in P. Dearden & R. Rollins, eds., *Parks and Protected Areas in Canada*, 3rd ed., (Oxford University Press, 2009)

Turner, Robert W., "Market Failures and the Rationale for National Parks", Journal of Economic Education, Vol. 33, No. 4, pp. 347–356, Autumn, 2002. Reprinted with permission of the Helen Dwight Reid Education Foundation. Published by Heldref Publications, 1319 Eighteenth St. NW, Washington DC 20036-1802. Copyright © 2009.

Wilkinson, Christopher J.A., "Protected Areas Law in Ontario, Canada: Maintenance of Ecological Integrity as the Management Priority" (2008) 28 Natural Areas Journal 180–186

9

SPECIES PROTECTION

Introduction

Canada has long prided itself as an important global biodiversity storehouse. And, on the international stage, it has aspired to play a leading role in protecting biodiversity worldwide as evidenced by, among other things, being the first signatory to the Rio *Convention on Biological Diversity*. But just how effectively has Canada protected its biodiversity legacy? Is our reputation for international leadership around this issue justified? And by what measures can we assess these questions? With these questions in mind, in this chapter we explore the Canadian record with respect to species protection, a key dimension and indicator of the larger challenge of protecting biodiversity.

This chapter is in 4 parts. Part I provides an overview of the nature and magnitude of species at risk as a national and global public policy problem. It also provides an introduction to the history of Canada's *Species at Risk Act* (SARA) and some of the rationales that support using legislation to protect species at risk.

Part II is an extensive comparative overview and analysis of federal species protection in both Canada and the United States. A variety of reasons make this comparative approach useful. At the federal level, the United States has been grappling with the legal challenges of protecting species since the 1970s; about thirty years longer than we have in Canada. In many ways, the American experience under their federal *Endangered Species Act* (ESA) has profoundly shaped the architecture of our *Species at Risk Act*, enacted in 2002. It is, therefore, instructive to compare the key features of the two laws closely. To this end, we compare SARA and ESA along four dimensions: species listing; habitat designation and species recovery strategies; prohibitions on harm to species and their habitat; and compensation for affected private interests.

Building on this context, in Part III, we explore a variety of what might be termed governance-related themes in species protection. These include the challenges for species and biodiversity diversity that arise under federalism; the species protection record at the provincial and territorial levels, as measured against the aspirations of the 1996 *National Accord for the Protection of Species at Risk*; and the legal relationship between the aspirations and principles set out in SARA and provincial land and resource-use decision-making. This Part concludes with an overview of Canada's newest species protection law: the Ontario *Endangered Species Act, 2007*.

Finally, in Part IV, we conclude by offering some emerging and critical perspectives on the relationship between species and biodiversity protection.

Part I — Overview of the Magnitude and Nature of the Problem

P. Wood & L. Flahr, "Taking Endangered Species Seriously? British Columbia's Species-at-Risk Policies"
(2004) 30 Canadian Public Policy 382

We are now in the beginning of the sixth major mass extinction event of all geological time. The major cause of the current event is well known: the alteration, fragmentation, or destruction of species' habitats by humans. Overexploitation of resource species and the introduction of destructive "exotic" species into ecosystems where they are not native are additional contributing factors. By 2050, global climate change is predicted to compete with habitat alteration as the leading cause of species extinctions.

At the current rate, "the loss of biodiversity ... has serious consequences for the human prospect in the future" (Royal Society in a joint statement with the US National Academy of Sciences 1992) because humanity in the long term is dependent on the maintenance of the world's biodiversity. Scientists recognized the beginning of the current extinction phenomenon approximately three decades ago. In response, the United Nations formulated the *World Charter for Nature* in 1982 followed by the more specific *Global Biodiversity Strategy* in 1992. The single most significant human response to date occurred in 1992 when most of the world's nations signed the *Convention on Biological Diversity* at the world's first Earth Summit in Rio de Janeiro. Canada was the first nation to sign this Convention.

A requirement of the Convention was for each signatory party (nation) to develop domestic legislation to protect biodiversity. Biodiversity conservation legislation can be classified into three broad categories. The first category encompasses legislation that authorizes governments to legally designate large protected areas in which species and natural processes may persist relatively undisturbed by human activities. The Canada *National Parks Act* and the several provincial equivalents are examples.

In the second category are those pieces of legislation that stipulate preventative measures to protect biodiversity and other specified environmental values on the matrix of public or private lands beyond the boundaries of protected areas. British Columbia's *Forest and Range Practices Act* is an example. Its purpose is to mitigate harmful environmental consequences that can result from forest harvesting operations on public lands.

The third category encompasses legislation aimed at protecting from further harm those species that are already at risk of extinction. In addition, this type of legislation usually requires the recovery of species at risk in order to rectify past harms. Recovery usually entails repopulating the number of individuals in a species' natural habitat and/or re-habilitating its habitat. The US *Endangered Species Act* was an early example and the recently passed Canadian federal *Species at Risk Act* is another.

Kate Smallwood, *A Guide to Canada's Species at Risk Act*
(Vancouver, Sierra Legal Defence Fund: 2003)

Canada is internationally renowned for its natural beauty. One of the largest countries on the planet, Canada is home to about 20% of the Earth's wilderness, 24% of its wetlands, 20% of its freshwater and 10% of its forests.

This incredible biodiversity is under threat. Over 400 species have been identified as being at risk in Canada, although the number is in fact much higher. A report by the Canadian Endangered Species Council, *Wild Species 2000, The General Status of Species in Canada*, examined the status of over 1,600 Canadian species. Of these species, only 65% were considered to be secure, while 10% were considered to be at risk or potentially at risk. Canada's list of plants and animals at risk includes Canadian icons like the Grizzly Bear, Killer Whale, Polar Bear and Eastern Cougar, as well as species like the Burrowing Owl, the Salish Sucker, the Northern Leopard Frog and the Small White Lady's Slipper.

Species loss and decline is not limited to Canada. Globally, we are now experiencing an unprecedented loss of species and genetic diversity — the sixth major period of extinction in the history of the Earth. In 1992, the international community sought to address this problem by passing the United Nations *Convention on Biological Diversity* (the "Rio Convention"). Article 8 of the Convention, which addresses "in situ" or "on the ground" conservation, includes the specific commitment to pass legislation for the protection of species at risk. Although Canada was the first industrialized nation to ratify the Rio Convention, it has taken Canada nearly a decade to address this commitment. Bill C-5, the *Species at Risk Act* ("SARA"), was the government's fourth attempt at passing endangered species legislation. SARA passed through the Senate without amendment on December 12, 2002 ...

SARA took nearly ten years to pass for a variety of reasons, including jurisdictional wrangling between the federal and provincial governments; major policy debates over how habitat should be protected and whether scientists or politicians should decide which species would be legally protected; fears about "US style" litigation over endangered species, concerns about private land issues and compensation, and two federal elections. SARA is the clearly the product of these policy and jurisdictional debates. As a policy decision, the federal government has elected to protect species and habitat only within a very narrow interpretation of federal jurisdiction and leave the primary role for species and habitat protection in Canada to the provinces and territories. The federal government has also consciously chosen to rely on voluntary conservation and stewardship initiatives as the primary approach for habitat protection, especially on private land.

The end result is a law that is largely restricted to federal lands, aquatic species and migratory birds under the *Migratory Birds Convention Act*. The majority of species listed under the Act will only be protected if they are found on federal land — a mere 5% of Canada outside the territories. Elsewhere in Canada, species at risk will be subject to a patchwork of protection. Significant gaps exist in the legislative framework for species and habitat protection from East to West. Neither BC nor Alberta, for example, has their own species legislation. Other provinces that do have endangered species legislation have consistently failed to list and protect species at risk listed by COSEWIC (the Committee on the Status of Endangered Wildlife in Canada). None of the provinces or territories is meeting all the requirements for species and habitat protection outlined in the *National Accord for the Protection of Species at Risk*, the primary national policy document on species at risk in Canada.

J. Kunich, "Preserving the Womb of the Unknown Species with Hotspots Legislation"

(2001) 52 Hastings L.J. 1149

Why Should We Care About Species We Have Never Identified?

In a world dominated by humans, in which the needs of humans are, not surprisingly, seen as preeminent by most members of that species, it is important to examine the question of why we should be concerned with the extinction of other life forms. The ESA certainly has been controversial, in part because of the perceived conflict it generates between people and other living things. If the ESA or other pieces of legislation are to be given a chance of making a difference, people will need to understand the benefits they can expect to derive from the bargain. The reasons for humans to attempt to prevent the extinction of other creatures can be bundled into four main groups: (1) present practical value; (2) potential future practical value; (3) intangible value; and (4) moral duty. I will summarize each of these briefly.

First, many species of plants and animals currently provide Homo sapiens with a variety of tangible, practical benefits of real value to people. A host of domesticated animals and crop plants are obvious examples, directly supplying nutrients for the human diet. People can derive this nutrition directly, by consuming all or part of the plant or animal itself, or indirectly, by eating substances produced by the plant or animal, such as eggs, milk, honey, fruit, grains, vegetables, and foods made therefrom. In addition to food, plants and animals are the producers of essentials such as cotton, wool, silk, leather, wood, paper, dyes, and their ancillary commodities. However, only twenty species provide ninety percent of the global food supply today, and three species (corn, wheat, and rice) contribute more than half of the total. Countless other species, currently known or unknown, could perhaps "be bred or provide genes to increase production in deserts, saline flats and other marginal habitats" to feed the world's expanding population in the future.

Plants are the source of many medicinal drugs, and about half of all prescription drugs in the United States come from wild organisms, of a total value estimated to exceed $14 billion per year. Our antibiotics, anti-cancer agents, pain killers, and blood thinners have been derived thus far from only a few hundred species, leaving the biochemistry and genetic components of millions of other species unexplored and untapped as a potentially colossal reservoir of new medicines and healing agents ...

The role of animals in medical and other scientific research has been of inestimable worth, and largely the contribution of otherwise insignificant or despised creatures such as the common mouse, rat, and fruit fly. Less obvious but still practical benefits come from creatures that facilitate the production of other plants or animals which in turn are consumed or otherwise used. This includes a vast array of insects, which pollinate many flowering plants, including fruit-bearing varieties, and which are the primary food source for many birds; it also includes annelids (earthworms) and other burrowing organisms which similarly play an unobtrusive yet vital role in aerating soil, making it suitable for producing plant life.

Ecological benefits conferred by living things are sometimes overlooked by laypersons, but are of paramount importance. In addition to all of the human-centered practical reasons for preserving species as individual species, there are tangible synergistic benefits produced by species interactions on an ecosystem level. The concept of "ecosystem services" is fairly new, but several enormously significant examples have been identified. These include the decomposition and detoxification of organic matter and other wastes, which is mostly performed by the smallest, least charismatic organisms in any ecosystem. Without the microorganisms and insects that effectuate the decomposition process for organic material, the world would quickly be buried in its own waste. Other examples are generation and renewal of soil, mitigation of floods, purification of air and water, and partial stabilization of climate.

Among the most fundamental of ecosystem services is the photosynthetic process of most plants, which not only fixes, or converts, solar energy into usable nutrients, but also converts carbon dioxide into oxygen, literally the life-breath of our species. And the exquisitely intricate natural system of checks and balances by which various species keep one another's populations-including those of pest and disease-causing organisms-within manageable limits is far more effective and safe than any pesticide program.

Most previously-identified species that provide obvious, practical benefits to humans are not in danger of extinction. In fact, many are actively safeguarded, raised, cultivated, and otherwise managed to maximize their productivity. There have been some cases of overharvesting of such species, but for the most part this type of species is safe, due to our own self-interest. Of course, this presupposes that humans have (1) discovered the species and (2) learned of the benefits the species has to offer. In the case of the myriad unidentified species inhabiting the world's hotspots, neither of these presuppositions obtains.

The species that are less ostentatious about their value to people, moreover, may be even less fortunate. In some cases, for example, it is not even known which species of insects pollinate which useful plants, or which species are depended on by birds, fish, and other creatures for their sustenance, so humans may destroy or allow the destruction of these insects without realizing the consequences.

A second basic reason for humans to preserve species is that they may have future practical value to people. New uses are continually being discovered for living things, often transforming apparently inconsequential species into valuable assets. By definition, of course, it is impossible to know which or how many species fall into this category at any point in time. But it should be evident that modem technology and research methods are powerful tools for unleashing the power of helpful genies from the most unassuming, unlikely magic lamps. Given some of the important benefits now being derived from uncharismatic and previously unimportant species, it would be wise to preserve as many as possible to provide future investigators with the raw material for their experiments.

Each living species can be viewed as the end product of countless years of research and development, the culmination of eons of experimentation in nature's laboratory. As Edward O. Wilson has stated, "each species of higher organism is richer in information than a Caravaggio painting, Bach fugue, or any other great work of art".

Each species represents a successful set of strategies for meeting some of life's challenges and threats. Much can be learned from the collective experience of these myriad generations in assisting people with their own problems. And with the advent of genetic engineering, wherein it is increasingly possible to transfer genetic material from one taxonomic group to another (even across the kingdom barrier) to confer previously lacking biological traits, each species is potentially a significant genetic, resource. This genetic wealth, in millions of different forms, could be as vital in tomorrow's society as wood and paper in today's.

It is possible, and even probable, that some currently "insignificant" species could take on a crucial role in the ecosystems of the future. Wild relatives of current crop species can be an invaluable source of genetic diversity in the event the monoculture cultivated plants fall prey to disease or other environmental conditions. And if environmental conditions change, through global warming, increased pollution, or other habitat alterations, some other species may possess traits that will prove pre-adapted to these new circumstances. Some species that occupy key positions in today's ecosystems may be unable to adapt, and unless other species are available to fill their niche, the ecosystems may suffer catastrophic degradation. The redundancy provided for by millions of years of natural selection cannot be fully understood and appreciated unless and until it is needed. It is not necessarily the large, obvious life forms that play these pivotal roles; in fact, the "lower" levels of the food web are the foundation upon which all other components of each ecosystem depend.

The biosphere that is the planet earth may be conceptualized as an exceedingly complex "computer program" with millions of parts, each of which is evolving. It would be foolish indeed to destroy, or to allow the destruction of, the program's codes, because we do not and cannot know their importance, whether at present or in some unforeseeably altered world of the future. Extinction shuts doors and deprives us forever of the option to discover value in that which we previously found valueless.

A corollary of this principle is that some species may be valuable precisely because they are endangered or threatened. A particularly vulnerable species within a given habitat may someday provide an early warning signal that there are problems that may eventually affect far more species. This has been termed the "canary in the mine" syndrome. For such species, their strength is in their weakness.

A third main reason to preserve species is their intangible value. Although less practical, and less susceptible to being reduced to monetary worth, there is real wealth in living things.

Many people find great beauty in nature, and nowhere else is the maxim more true that beauty is in the eye of the beholder. Depending on one's individual preferences, species as diverse as a house cat, a fern, a goldfish, a beetle, and a paramecium can be works of art, supplying emotional sustenance. Entire industries are tailored for the loyal human aficionados of these living art forms.

Finally, fourth, and least pragmatic, is the moral duty not to exterminate our fellow passengers on this planet. With its origins at least as ancient as the biblical injunction to "replenish" the earth as its caretakers, this moral duty has strong precedential support. Although most people accept the propriety of human use of other species for food, clothing, and other purposes, they likely would draw the line at exploiting these species into extinction. The moral duty may be seen as an obligation to refrain from "murdering" another species, because that species has in some sense a right to exist. Additionally, people may want to preserve other species as a living legacy for their children and grandchildren, feeling it is wrong to deprive their posterity of a heritage their own ancestors had passed down for their enjoyment.

Notes and Questions

1. In most countries, legislation to protect species is fairly new. The world's first purpose-built species protection legislation was enacted by the United States in 1966. Dubbed the "pitbull" of American environmental law, the federal *Endangered Species Act* (ESA) remains one of that county's most powerful environmental laws. Substantially strengthened through amendments in 1973, it has weathered various attempts in Congress to scale back its potent protection provisions which include, among other things, well-used citizen suit enforcement provisions (see Chapter 5). While two Canadian provinces (Ontario and New Brunswick) also enacted species protection in this early period, these laws were considerably less rigourous than ESA. Ontario, as we will discuss, has recently enacted endangered species legislation that commentators have heralded as the strongest law of its kind in Canada.

2. At the federal level, Canada did not have species protection legislation until late 2002, when the *Species at Risk Act* received Royal Assent. [*Ed note*: SARA's provisions came into force in three stages, coming fully into force on June 1, 2004]. The law reform process that preceded the enactment of SARA lasted almost a decade. In the early 1990s, environmental groups mounted a concerted campaign for a federal law. In 1994, the government committed to enacting federal legislation. The next eight years saw often heated debates over the philosophy and content of the proposed law both in Ottawa and across the country. Environmentalists fought hard for a law akin to ESA (see Smallwood above *infra*). Many other interests, however, were intent on developing a law that was quite different from its American cousin. In the balance of this chapter, we will return to this theme by means of comparisons between ESA and Canada's SARA.

Part II — Federal Endangered Species Legislation in Canada and the United States

Most species protection law address four key issues. A threshold issue is the identification of what species the law should protect. This is commonly known as the *species listing* process. A second key issue is to determine what measures should be taken to protect the species and allow it to recover to healthy and sustainable populations. Here, two related processes are relevant: the *designation of critical habitat* and the development and implementation of *recovery plans*. A third feature of such laws are provisions making it an offence to harm species or species habitat. The provisions are often referred to as species *"taking" prohibitions*. Finally, in developing species protection laws, lawmakers are usually under significant political pressure to provide *compensation* to land and resource tenure holders affected by implementation of the law.

The balance of this section is devoted to reviewing how these four issues are addressed under SARA and ESA.

Species Listing

A key legislative design issue in developing species protection legislation is the listing process. At stake, as is often the case in environmental law regimes, is the relationship between science and politics. A fundamental precept of the ESA is that listing determinations are made on the basis of credible science alone. While Canadian environmentalists urged the federal government to adopt a similar approach, this position met with considerable political resistance. In the end, as chronicled by Smallwood, SARA reflects a compromise which, for species identified in need of protection after enactment of the law, vests in Cabinet the power to veto a scientific listing recommendation.

Species Listing under SARA

Kate Smallwood, A *Guide to Canada's Species at Risk Act*
(Vancouver, Sierra Legal Defence Fund: 2003)

Listing is the prerequisite to protection under SARA. ... [a key] debate has been whether the federal government should adopt a scientific listing process or a political listing process. Under a *scientific listing process*, the national list of species at risk prepared by the Committee on the Status of Wildlife in Canada ("COSEWIC") would become the legal list under the Act. Under a *political listing process*, COSEWIC's role would be advisory only — federal Cabinet would have the ultimate decision as to which species would be listed under the Act. Political listing has been a proven failure provincially, as most species listed by COSEWIC are not listed provincially.

At third reading, the government finally agreed to the compromise solution supported by the House Standing Committee on Environment and Sustainable Development — "negative option" or "reverse onus" listing. Under this approach, the COSEWIC list becomes the legal list under the Act unless Cabinet takes contrary action within nine months. This process will ensure that no species will be ignored or indefinitely deferred through Cabinet inaction ..

The Legal List

The List of Wildlife Species at Risk (the "legal list") is contained in Schedule 1 of the Act and constitutes the legal list under the Act. Unless a species is included in the legal list, it will not be protected under SARA. Under the listing process ..., COSEWIC listing assessments will be included on the legal list in Schedule 1 unless within nine months after receiving the assessment federal Cabinet takes contrary action. ... once federal Cabinet has received an assessment from COSEWIC, it has nine months to review the assessment (s. 27). During that time period, Cabinet may, on the recommendation of the Minister of the Environment, take one of three courses of action:

(a) accept the assessment and add the species to the list;

(b) decide not to add the species to the List; or

(c) refer the matter back to COSEWIC for further information or consideration.

If federal Cabinet decides not to add the species to the legal list or decides to refer the matter back to COSEWIC, the Minister of Environment, after the approval of Cabinet, is required to include a statement in the public registry setting out the reasons for the decision. If Cabinet takes no action within nine months after receiving an assessment, the Minister of Environment is required to amend the legal list in accordance with COSEWIC's assessment. Before making a recommendation to Cabinet in respect of a wildlife species, the Minister of the Environment must take into account COSEWIC's assessment in respect of the species, and must consult with the competent minister or ministers (the Minister of Fisheries and Oceans and the Minister of Canadian Heritage). If the species is found in an area governed by a wildlife management board under a land claims agreement, the Minister of the Environment must consult with the wildlife management board before making a recommendation to Cabinet.

Listing Categories

There are four different listing categories under SARA (s. 2):

- *Extirpated species*: means a wildlife species that no longer exists in the wild in Canada, but exists elsewhere in the wild.
- *Endangered species*: means a wildlife species that is facing imminent extirpation or extinction.
- *Threatened species*: means a wildlife species that is likely to become an endangered species if nothing is done to reverse the factors leading to its extirpation or extinction.
- *Species of special concern*: means a wildlife species that may become a threatened or endangered species because of a combination of biological characteristics and identified threats.

The listing categories are important because the risk category under which a species is listed dictates the level of protection it will receive under the Act. In general, species of special concern receive a much lower level of protection under the Act and in certain circumstances, extirpated species will only be covered if a recovery strategy has recommended the reintroduction of the species into the wild in Canada.

The three key areas where the difference in listing category becomes important are:

- *Basic prohibitions* — There are two basic prohibitions in SARA. Section 32 prohibits killing, harming, harassing, capturing or taking a listed species as well as possession or trading of a listed species or any part of a listed species. Section 33 prohibits damaging or destroying a listed species' "residence". The basic prohibitions only apply to listed extirpated, endangered or threatened species. Species of special concern are not covered. Both sets of prohibitions are limited to federal jurisdiction only, i.e. federal lands, aquatic species and migratory birds under the *Migratory Birds Convention Act*.
- *Critical Habitat Prohibition* — Section 58 prohibits the destruction of critical habitat within federal jurisdiction (federal lands, federal waters, aquatic species and migratory birds under the *Migratory Birds Convention Act*). The critical habitat prohibition applies to listed endangered and listed threatened species. Listed extirpated species

are only covered if a recovery strategy has recommended the reintroduction of the species into the wild in Canada. Species of special concern are not covered.

- *Recovery Process* — Recovery strategies must be prepared for all listed extirpated, endangered and threatened species. The recovery process for species of special concern is addressed through a separate and less prescriptive process involving management plans.

Notes and Questions

1. The newly-enacted Ontario species protection legislation adopts an approach to listing that is much closer to the ESA than the SARA approach: see *infra* this Chapter.

2. There has been considerable controversy in the implementation of species listing since SARA's enactment. These controversies include the federal government's attempts to extend the nine month time limit; and the Minister of Environment's practice of referring out for consultation COSEWIC listing recommendations with the result that these recommendations are being analyzed through a "socio-economic" lens: see Ecojustice Legal Defence Fund's SARA enforcement complaint to the CEC at 2–6: see CEC Citizen Submission SEM-06-05 "Species at Risk" cited at end of this chapter.

3. Authors of a recent scientific study of Cabinet listing decisions claim that the listing process displays bias: see A. Mooers et al., "Biases in Legal Listing under Canadian Endangered Species Legislation" 21 Conservation Biology (2007) 572–576. When SARA came into force in 2003, all 233 species previously assessed by COSEWIC as imperiled were automatically included on the legal list. Since then, the authors claim that Cabinet listing decisions made between 2003 and 2006 display a pronounced bias against listing marine and northern species. According to the authors:

> .... two factors ... seem to have contributed to the taxonomic and geographic biases in legal listing decisions under Canada's endangered species legislation. The first is a reluctance by wildlife management boards and the Department of Fisheries and Oceans to accept the additional stewardship responsibilities required by SARA. The second pertains to deficiencies in the cost-benefit analyses that precede the legal listing decisions.
>
> Wildlife management boards (WMBs), whose responsibilities are primarily in the north, are involved in the legal listing decisions for species in their jurisdictions. The stated governmental reason for not listing northern mammals is to allow for further consultation with WMBs, notably the Nunavut WMB. The SARA provides no timelines for such post-assessment consultations, and the WMBs are consulted by COSEWIC before each assessment. The resulting delays may elevate the extinction risk for some species. For example, Bourdages et al. (2002) estimated that current harvesting rates of the eastern Hudson Bay beluga whale population, which was denied listing, will lead to its extinction within 10–15 years. These consultations also affect populations outside Nunavut insofar as Nunavut-based delays have prevented the listing of the wolverine, grizzly bear, and polar bear elsewhere in Canada.
>
> Although not made explicit in SARA, the legal listing process includes something called a regulatory impact analysis (RIAS). The RIASs are cost-benefit analyses undertaken by the federal government, promulgated under the *Financial Administration Act*. A RIAS typically take place during the 9 months that immediately precede a listing decision, prior to the development of any form of recovery strategy or action plan. This timing is clearly problematic; A RIAS will be unable to provide a complete assessment of the costs and benefits of species recovery, potentially biasing the perception of the socioeconomic impact of a listing decision. In addition, these cost-benefit analyses are not subject to external review.
>
> A major deficiency of RIAS is that relatively little effort is expended in estimating benefits. By one estimate, half of all RIASs examined do not quantify benefits at all. Quantifying the benefits of recovering species is obviously critical if cost-benefit analyses are to be taken seriously. Globally, the loss of habitats and populations deprives humanity of goods and services with a net worth of perhaps US$250 billion annually. In Canada failure to take meaningful action to reduce fishing mortality on Newfoundland's northern Atlantic cod in the late 1980s led to a subsequent expenditure of C$2-C$3 billion for income support, buy outs of commercial fishing licenses, and training for alternative em-

> ployment for displaced fishers and processors. Benefits to listing must also account for nonuse economic values. These are the benefits of conservation that can be reflected in part by the value that society holds for the preservation of species.
>
> Biodiversity conservation would be best served by strict, transparent, legislated timelines for all aspects of the listing process following receipt by the Minister of the Environment of the status assessments undertaken by COSEWIC. We also recommend that, within the RIAS framework, SARA require that the full costs of extinction and the full benefits of recovery be quantified in externally reviewed reports so that they can be fairly weighed against the impacts of legal protection.

Drawing on this research, the David Suzuki Foundation has published "Left off the List: A Profile of Marine and Northern Species Denied Listing under SARA" (2007). Among the species discussed in this report are the Peary caribou, polar bear, wolverine, grizzly bear, Beluga whale, Coho salmon, Atlantic cod and the Porbeagle shark. The work of Mooers et al. has recently been reviewed and elaborated in C. Scott Finlay, Stewart Elgie, Brian Giles and Linda Burr, "Species listing under Canada's Species at Risk Act: A Follow-up to Mooers et al." (forthcoming: Conservation Biology).

4. The Minister of Environment has an "emergency power" under SARA to list a species: see s. 80. To date, this power has never been used. As part of ongoing efforts to secure protection in British Columbia for the Northern Spotted Owl ("spotted owl"), Sierra Legal (now Ecojustice Canada) commenced legal action to compel the exercise of this power. [*Ed note*: As of 2008, it is believed that there are only six spotted owls now remaining in the wild in BC.] Ecojustice argued was that the Minister was aware of the owl's plight and was unreasonably delaying taking action due to behind the scenes negotiations with the provincial government. In support of its lawsuit, Ecojustice sought discovery of documents under Rule 317 of the Federal Court Rules. The federal government took the position that it was not subject to the rule, since there was no decision or order being challenged. The Federal Court upheld the Minister's contention: see *Western Canada Wilderness Committee v. Canada (Minister of the Environment)*, 2006 FC 786, 2006 CF 786, 23 C.E.L.R. (3d) 290.

Through analogous efforts in the United States, the spotted owl secured listing under ESA in 1990: see *Northern Spotted Owl et al. v. Hodel*, excerpted below. When reading the case, bear in mind that it is typical for the species in question to be listed as the lead plaintiff in the style of cause; it is also noteworthy that the surname of the first defendant in such cases typically belongs to the occupant of the Cabinet post legally responsible for administering the ESA (usually, the Secretary of Interior for terrestrial species and the Secretary of Commerce for marine ones).

Species Listing under ESA

While listing decisions under ESA are effectively made at the Cabinet level, as they are in Canada, under American law the statutory discretion to decide "not to list" is much narrower. The ESA mandates that these listing decisions be based "solely" on the best available scientific and commercial data regarding a species' extinction risk, without reference to possible economic impacts or other non-biological factors. As a result, the opportunity to challenge a decision not to list species under ESA is greater than it is under SARA, as the following case underscores.

Northern Spotted Owl et al. v. Hodel
716 F. Supp. 479 (W.D. Wash., 1988)

ZILLY District Judge:

A number of environmental organizations bring this action against the United States Fish & Wildlife Service ("Service") and others, alleging that the Service's decision not to list the northern spotted owl as endangered or threatened under the *Endangered Species Act of 1973*, as amended, ("ESA" or "the Act"), was arbitrary and capricious or contrary to law.

Since the 1970s the northern spotted owl has received much scientific attention, beginning with comprehensive studies of its natural history by Dr. Eric Forsman, whose most significant discovery was the close association between spotted owls and old-growth forests.

This discovery raised concerns because the majority of remaining old-growth owl habitat is on public land available for harvest.

In January 1987, plaintiff Greenworld ... petitioned the Service to list the northern spotted owl as endangered. In August 1987, 29 conservation organizations filed a second petition to list the owl as endangered both in the Olympic Peninsula in Washington and in the Oregon Coast Range, and as threatened throughout the rest of its range.

In July 1987, the Service announced that it would initiate a status review of the spotted owl and requested public comment. The Service assembled a group of Service biologists, including Dr. Mark Shaffer, its staff expert on population viability, to conduct the review. The Service charged Dr. Shaffer with analyzing current scientific information on the owl. Dr. Shaffer concluded that:

> the most reasonable interpretation of current data and knowledge indicate continued old growth harvesting is likely to lead to the extinction of the subspecies in the foreseeable future which argues strongly for listing the subspecies as threatened or endangered at this time.

The Service invited a peer review of Dr. Shaffer's analysis by a number of U.S. experts on population viability, all of whom agreed with Dr. Shaffer's prognosis for the owl, although each had some criticisms of his work.

The Status Review was completed on December 14, 1987, and on December 17 the Service announced that listing the owl as endangered under the Act was not warranted at that time. This suit followed ...

The Court will reject conclusory assertions of agency "expertise" where the agency spurns unrebutted expert opinions without itself offering a credible alternative explanation. Here, the Service disregarded all the expert opinion on population viability, including that of its own expert, that the owl is facing extinction, and instead merely asserted its expertise in support of its conclusions.

The Service has failed to provide its own or other expert analysis supporting its conclusions. Such analysis is necessary to establish a rational connection between the evidence presented and the Service's decision. Accordingly, the United States Fish and Wildlife Service's decision not to list at this time the northern spotted owl as endangered or threatened under the *Endangered Species Act* was arbitrary and capricious and contrary to law.

The Court further finds that it is not possible from the record to determine that the Service considered the related issue of whether the northern spotted owl is a threatened species. This failure of the Service to review and make an express finding on the issue of threatened status is also arbitrary and capricious and contrary to law.

In deference to the Service's expertise and its role under the *Endangered Species Act*, the Court remands this matter to the Service, which has 90 days from the date of this order to provide an analysis for its decision that listing the northern spotted owl as threatened or endangered is not currently warranted.

Notes and Questions

1. Ultimately, in June 1990, the Service finally listed the spotted owl as "threatened". However, as we shall see later in this chapter, litigation over spotted owl protection continued for many years to come.

2. Based on the same body of evidence, but under SARA listing legislation, how likely would it be that a Canadian court would make a ruling akin to that made in the preceding case? What evidentiary and procedural barriers would a litigant seeking to compel Cabinet to make a listing decision under SARA encounter?

Critical Habitat Designation and Recovery Strategies

Ultimately the efficacy of species protection legislation turns on the efficacy of its provisions designed to protect critical habitat and implement recovery measures. While Canadian and US legislation differ in some important respects, in both cases the implementation record to date has been poor as we discuss below.

Under ESA, the general rule is that critical habitat must be designated concurrently with species listing unless it can be shown that it is (1) not determinable; or (2) not prudent (designation could actually lead to adverse impacts on species). In contrast to the listing decision, critical habitat determinations may take socio-economic factors into account. There is also a parallel obligation, upon listing, to develop and implement recovery plans for the conservation and survival of listed endangered and threatened species, unless such a plan will not promote the conservation of the species in question.

The approach adopted under SARA is much more discretionary. Under SARA there is no necessary or presumptive linkage between a listing decision and the requirement to protect critical habitat. Instead, whether critical habitat will be designated is subject to a highly discretionary process that commences with the development of a "recovery strategy" and culminates in implementation of an "action plan" stage. Critical habitat is defined in SARA as "the habitat that is necessary for the survival or recovery of a listed wildlife species and that is identified as the species' critical habitat in the recovery strategy or in an action plan for the species": see s. 2. As such, for the purposes of Act, the critical habitat of a species does not exist and is not protected, unless it is identified in the recovery strategy or action plan. Recovery strategies are intended to set out the overall scientific framework within which recovery is to be implemented, while action plans describe the specific actions to be taken to implement the recovery plan. Recovery plans are intended to be exclusively science-based, while action plans may take socio-economic factors into account.

Critical Habitat Protection and Species Recovery under SARA

Upon species listing, *SARA* requires recovery planning to commence. Recovery strategies are the primary main tool for mapping and bringing about the actions needed to reverse the decline of species at risk and lay the groundwork for their recovery. Newly listed species must have recovery strategies posted on the SARA public registry within 1 year of listing, whereas endangered species that were listed when the Act came into force must have recovery strategies posted within 3 years of the section coming into force, which was June 3, 2003. As of July 2008, only 66 of the 218 recovery strategies that were due had been completed: see SARA public registry. In addition to delays in completing recovery plans, environmentalists have criticized the adequacy of many of the completed plans. SARA provides that recovery plans must identify critical habitat "to the extent possible, based on the best information": see s. 41(1)(c). In a complaint filed with the NAFTA Commission for Environmental Cooperation in 2006, Ecojustice claimed that:

> ... to date (September 2006), of the 23 recovery strategies posted on the *SARA* registry, only 3 identify critical habitat, and 5 partially identify critical habitat. There is little certainty as to whether the prohibitions in the *SARA* apply where critical habitat has been identified only partially. Moreover, the 3 species where recovery plans identify critical habitat are located within protected areas (Aurora Trout and Horsetail Spike-rush), or have restricted distribution (Barrens Willow). Further, research into two of the plans indicates that where habitat was not identified, or only partially identified, science for full identification does exist but has not been incorporated into the strategy (see recovery plans for the Piping Plover and Spotted Owl).

On March 6th, 2008, the Office of the Auditor General of Canada released the 2008 status report of the Commissioner of the Environment and Sustainable Development, which stated: "Departments and organizations are also required under the Act to identify to the extent possible, critical habitat necessary for the survival or recovery of species at risk. This document identified that as of June 2007, critical habitat had been identified for only 16 of the 228 species at risk for which recovery strategies were due".

Once a recovery strategy has been completed, SARA requires an action plan(s) to be developed, which specifies measures that are to be taken to carry out the proposed recovery strategy. The overall procedure for preparation of action plans is very similar to the procedure for preparation of recovery strategies. There are mandatory requirements for consultation and cooperation, the proposed plan must be filed in the public registry, there is a public comment period, existing plans may be used in whole or part and the competent minister may amend the action plan or plans. Unlike recovery strategies, however, SARA does not prescribe a time period for the completion of actions and, as noted above, action plans may incorporate socio-economic factors.

One of the reasons for the apparent reluctance of federal officials to identify critical habitat in the recovery strategies issued to date are concerns about potential impacts on private landowners. The failure to identify critical habitat in recovery strategies is documented in an independent report commissioned by the federal government, which evaluated the federal government's implementation of the SARA. According to this report, authored by the consulting firm of Stratos Inc.:

> Core departments have made very limited, and less than anticipated progress in identifying critical habitat through the recovery planning process ... Policy considerations are also a factor [in not identifying critical habitat]. Where provinces/territories are leading recovery planning efforts, they report a reluctance to identify critical habitat on non-federal lands until the supporting policy framework is clarified. (2006)

An even more worrisome pattern appears to be emerging at the provincial level. In BC, over 90% of recovery plans completed to date do not identify critical habitat. Critics claim this is due in large measure to the fact that the Provincial government has instructed government scientists not to include such geo-spatial data in plans of this kind. On behalf of a coalition of conservation organizations, in late 2008, the UVic Environmental Law Centre asked BC's Auditor General to investigate this practice, contending that the species in question are "vital public resources" that the Province is failing to manage in accordance with the public interest.

The only recovery strategy completed under SARA to date that has identified critical habitat that impacts private lands is described below [*Ed note*: The following article uses the terminology "recovery plan" and "recovery strategy" interchangeably].

Martin Mittelstaedt, "A sweeping strategy to save a tiny fish: To rescue B.C.'s Nooksack dace, Ottawa has issued a recovery plan with broad implications for property owners"

Globe and Mail (19 March, 2008)

The Nooksack dace is an obscure variety of minnow found nowhere else in Canada but four small streams in the Fraser Valley near Vancouver.

It's a homely fish not much longer than a ballpoint pen when fully grown, and it rarely travels farther than 50 metres during its entire lifetime. But the endangered minnow has set an unusual precedent that may have the potential to help many of Canada's hundreds of species at risk of extinction. Fisheries and Oceans Canada last week quietly issued a revised recovery strategy for the minnow that covers privately owned land whose preservation will be critical if the small populations of the fish — noted for its large pectoral fins and a snout that overhangs its mouth — are to survive in Canada.

It is the first time Ottawa has issued a recovery plan identifying privately owned land as critical habitat that needs to be safeguarded to help an endangered species. In this case, here are about 650 properties lining the streams in which the endangered fish lives.

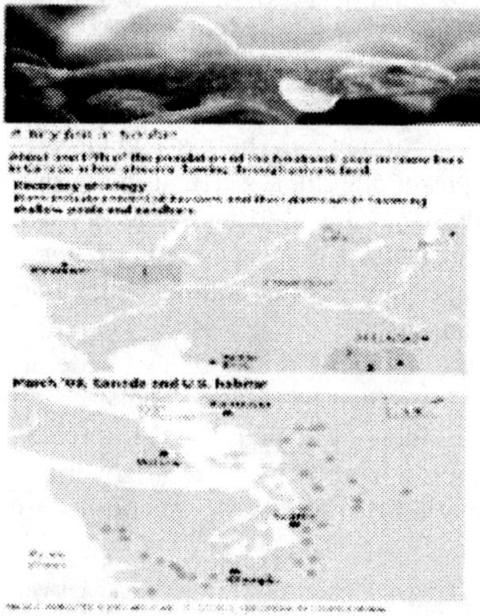

Source: Fisheries and Oceans Canada; Photo by Mike Pearson: Nooksack dace, an endangered species that can be found in only four streams in Canada.

The identification could lead to some restrictions on how land is used, something that has often emerged as a flashpoint with landowners in the United States over preservation efforts for endangered species there.

"Because it was the first time in Canada that critical habitat was proposed for private lands, it was really important for the department to ensure that we got it right", said Allison Webb, regional director of policy for Fisheries and Oceans. She said the government has tried to allay landowner concerns about the implications of living near an endangered species through consultations with those affected, mainly farmers and homeowners, and subjected its selection of habitat to a peer review to bolster its scientific validity.

Although Ottawa is required under the *Species at Risk Act* to include details of the critical habitat needed for endangered wildlife in all of its species recovery plans, it often fails to do so and didn't for the Nooksack dace last July, when it issued what it called its "final recovery strategy" for the fish.

The lack of habitat identification prompted three environmental groups last August to launch a lawsuit against the federal government over the issue. A spokesman for the groups said that the legal challenge was a factor forcing the government to issue a revised strategy. "The feds only do the right thing ... once they're sued", contended Aaron Freeman, policy director for Environmental Defence, one of the groups that launched the challenge. The groups intend to press on with their lawsuit in a bid to get a formal legal ruling that would force Ottawa to follow habitat provisions in the act in all future recovery strategies, according to Mr. Freeman. He said the federal government is reluctant to identify areas that need to be preserved because this could lead to possible conflicts with the provinces, landowners or commercial interests.

Canada has about 400 endangered species. Under the *Species at Risk Act*, the government has an obligation to draft recovery strategies that identify critical habitat "to the extent possible, based on the best available information". According to records compiled by Environmental Defence, 91 species have final recovery strategies in place, of which only 18 have some critical habitat identified. The group termed the current government's compliance record with the law as "very poor".

The preservation of habitat is considered among the most important determinants of long-term survival for endangered species. Although many species face threats from chemical pollutants and hunting, among other perils, habitat loss is considered the major factor leading to wildlife declines for about 80 per cent of species in danger of extinction.

The destruction of stream habitat through dikes, infilling and drainage projects is the biggest threat affecting the future of the Nooksack dace, according to a 2005 federal study, although beaver dams and seasonal low water flows are also harmful factors.

The Nooksack dace is an unusual breed of minnow that is thought to have evolved as a distinct species in what is now British Columbia and nearby Washington State some time during the last series of ice ages. The fish has already been extirpated, or made locally extinct, in many B.C. streams where it was abundant as recently as the 1960s. The minnow is also found in about 20 other streams in northwest Washington State, but its current status in the United States isn't known. It is thought, however, that about 20 per cent of the fish's population is in Canada and 80 per cent in the United States. The federal study said populations would recover rapidly if suitable habitat were available because the fish quickly reach sexual maturity, and breed prolifically, often more than once each year.

A small freshwater fish, the Nooksack dace takes its name from a river in Washington State. It was once plentiful in B.C. and Washington but has started to disappear as a result of construction, development and other human activities. Fully grown, the fish averages 10 centimetres in length. Adults eat insect larvae and young dace feed on midge pupae and small crustaceans. In B.C., the minnow is found in three small streams that feed into the Nooksack River in the lower Fraser Valley around Abbotsford, Aldergrove and Clearbrook. Adult members of the species are usually found in riffles — shallow parts of streams where water flows brokenly — with gravel or stony bottoms. Young dace are found most often in shallow, slow waters with sandy or muddy bottoms.

Critical Habitat Protection and Species Recovery under ESA

Under ESA, "critical habitat" must be designed for listed species, "to the maximum extent prudent and determinable", concurrently with the listing of any species as endangered or threatened. This express linkage between listing and habitat designation is a key feature of the Act, and one that distinguishes it from SARA. Another distinction is the specificity with which ESA defines "critical habitat". ESA defines critical habitat as (i) the specific areas within the geographical area occupied by the species, at the time it is listed ... on which are found those physical or biological features (1) essential to the conservation of the species; and (2) which may require special management considerations or protection; and (3) specific areas outside [such area], upon a determination by the Secretary that such areas are essential for the conservation of the species. Regulations elaborate this definition using examples of "physical or biological features" that can render a habitat critical for the survival of a listed species specifically mentioning areas important for population growth, food and water supplies, shelter from the elements, sites for mating, areas for rearing young, and habitats representative of the historic range of the species.

In contrast with ESA's listing provision, consideration of economic and "other relevant" impacts is explicitly made part of the process of designating critical habitat. However, habitat must be designated as critical if it is concluded failure to do so will result in extinction of the listed species, irrespective of any economic or other non-biological factors. As the case excerpted below discusses, critical habitat designations must generally be concurrent with (within one year of) the listing decision. However, a decision on critical habitat may be deferred for up to an additional year if such habitat is not "determinable". There must be a final decision as to whether designation is prudent or determinable within two years from the date of the proposed listing. Thus, at the end of these two years, a final decision whether to designate or deem that such a designation would not be "prudent" must be made. Despite these ostensibly firm statutory timelines, however, often these deadlines are not met. As of December 31, 2000, only 135 species had critical habitat designated, at a time when a total of 1244 United States species had been listed as threatened or endangered: see Kunich *infra*.

As with SARA, under ESA recovery planning is also intended to play a key role in species protection. The ESA requires recovery plans to be developed and implemented for all listed species unless this will not promote the conservation of the species in question. Recovery plans must contain site-specific management actions and "objective, measurable criteria" designed to monitor a species' progress toward delisting, along with an estimated timetable for this recovery process. However, ESA provides little guidance as to contents of such plans nor does it impose deadlines for their completion or implementation. As a result, recovery plans have not kept pace with listing decisions. As of December 31, 2000, recovery plans had only been completed for a total of 947 species out of 1802 listed species: see Kunich *infra*

Northern Spotted Owl et al. v. Lujan
758 F. Supp. 621 (W.D. Wash., 1991)

ZILLY District Judge:

In May 1988, twenty-two environmental organizations filed suit against the Secretary of the Interior, the U.S. Fish and Wildlife Service ("Service"), and other federal defendants, alleging the Service's decision not to list the northern spotted owl under the *Endangered Species Act of 1973* ("ESA"), was arbitrary and capricious, and contrary to law. After extensive briefing and argument by counsel, this Court ruled in favor of plaintiffs and remanded this matter to the Service for further proceedings: *Northern Spotted Owl v. Hodel*, (1988, see *infra* text, this chapter).

On June 23, 1989, the Service proposed to list the northern spotted owl as a "threatened" species under the *Endangered Species Act*. On June 26, 1990, the Service published its final rule confirming that listing decision. In both the proposed and final listing rules, the Service expressly deferred designation of critical habitat for the spotted owl on grounds that it was not "determinable".

Plaintiffs move this Court to order the federal defendants to designate "critical habitat" for the northern spotted owl. As defined under the ESA, "critical habitat" refers to geographic areas which are essential to the conservation of the spotted owl and which may require special management considerations or protection. Thus, even though more extensive habitat may be essential to maintain the species over the long term, critical habitat only includes the minimum amount of habitat needed to avoid short-term jeopardy or habitat in need of immediate intervention.

The initial determination of what areas constitute critical habitat is to be made on the basis of "the best scientific data available". This requires identifying geographic areas containing the physical and biological features considered to be essential to the conservation of the species. In addition, Congress directed the Secretary of the Interior to consider the probable economic or other impacts on human activities resulting from the critical habitat designation. The Secretary is expressly authorized to exclude any area from critical habitat if he determines that the benefits of such exclusion outweigh the conservation benefits, unless to do so would result in the extinction of the species.

Plaintiffs challenge the Service's decision, on behalf of the Secretary, to defer designation of critical habitat for the northern spotted owl. The ESA requires the Secretary, "to the maximum extent prudent and determinable", to designate critical habitat *concurrently* with his decision to list a species as endangered or threatened. When critical habitat is not determinable at the time of the final listing rule, the Secretary is authorized up to twelve additional months to complete the designation. The governing administrative regulations specify that the Secretary must state his reasons for not designating critical habitat in the proposed and final listing rules.

The Secretary, through the Service, claims that critical habitat for the spotted owl was not "determinable" when, in June 1989, the Service proposed to list the owl as threatened or when it issued its final rule one year later. The federal defendants contend that, under these circumstances, they are entitled to a twelve-month extension of time. Plaintiffs charge that the Secretary has violated the *Endangered Species Act* and the *Administrative Procedure Act* by failing to designate critical habitat concurrently with the listing of the northern spotted owl ...

Turning to the record presented, this Court is unable to find any support for the federal defendants' claim that critical habitat for the northern spotted owl was not determinable in June 1989 when the Service proposed to list the species, or when the Service issued its final rule one year later. Critical habitat received only brief discussion in both published rules ...

Indeed, the Service candidly acknowledged in its June 1989 proposed rule that it had not conducted the analyses required by section 4(b)(2) [of ESA]. This Court interprets the Service's statement one year later that it "*will* evaluate the economic and other relevant impacts", absent any evidence of having done so, as tacitly reaffirming that the studies still had not been performed. More is required under the ESA and the Service's own regulations than the mere conclusion that more work needs to be done.

This Court is mindful of the prodigious resources dedicated by the Service to the spotted owl. The listing process required a truly remarkable effort by the Service given the volume of comments received and the complexity of the issues raised. In any event, such efforts, which the Court assumes have been on going since prior to June 1989, do not relieve the Service of its statutory obligation to designate critical habitat concurrently with the species listing, or to provide a rational and articulated basis for concluding that critical habitat is not determinable.

Upon the record presented, this Court finds the Service has failed to discharge its obligations under the *Endangered Species Act* and its own administrative regulations. Specifically, the Service acting on behalf of the Secretary of the Interior, abused its discretion when it determined not to designate critical habitat concurrently with the listing of the northern spotted owl, or to explain any basis for concluding that the critical habitat was not determinable. These actions were arbitrary and capricious, and contrary to law.

Common sense dictates that the spotted owl would be poorly served by a hastily crafted or uninformed habitat plan. Congress expressly provided for periodic revisions to critical habitat plans to avoid this result. Accordingly, the Service is ordered to submit to the Court by March 15, 1991 a written plan for completing its review of critical habitat for the northern spotted owl. The Service is further ordered to publish its proposed critical habitat plan no later than forty-five days thereafter. The final rule is to be published at the earliest possible time under the appropriate circumstances.

Notes and Questions

In ensuing years, the issue of critical habitat designation has been litigated frequently; moreover, federal habitat designations have lagged far behind what the law, on its face, would require. There has also been a lack of clarity as to the respective roles of habitat designation and recovery planning. This has led to a vigourous discussion of law reform alternatives, as illustrated by the following article.

A. Hagen & K. E. Hodges, "Resolving Critical Habitat Designation Failures: Reconciling Law, Policy and Biology"

(2006) 20 Conservation Biology 399–407

The ideals intended by the U.S. Congress when it enacted the *Endangered Species Act* (ESA) in 1973 are drowning in legal issues and court cases today. Agency decisions about critical habitat designations for listed species are routinely being overturned by court decisions, leading to an agency focus on backlogged designations, high legal costs, reallocation of ESA budget appropriations to resolve court-ordered designation, and inadequate species listing.

Four major problems with critical habitat designation are evident. First, as of 2001, the U.S. Fish and Wildlife Service (FWS) and the National Oceanic and Atmospheric Administration (NOAA) Fisheries, the agencies that implement the ESA, had not designated critical habitat for approximately 90% of listed species leading to a bombardment of legal suits and court-ordered designations. As of April 2005, 74% of listed species were still without critical habitat despite a recent surge in designations. Second, many provisions of the ESA provide protection for species, leading to controversy over whether critical habitat designation provides additional species protection. Third, it is unclear at what stage within listing and recovery planning the designation of critical habitat is most useful. Fourth, transforming biological information into critical habitat determinations is often challenging, especially when data are insufficient ...

Congressional intent and judicial reviews are consistent: Critical habitat designation should be the default for listed species, with the not-prudent and not-determinable exceptions applied rarely. Agency practice has been the reverse, with the exceptions overwhelmingly more common than designation. Designation currently is judicially and politically driven rather than being routine or even based on biological priority. If the congressional intent of protecting habitat via critical habitat designation is to be upheld, the practice of designation has to change so that biological complexity can be better addressed and the continuous legal entanglement reduced. We outline several possible strategies, some of which could be combined.

One option is for congressional amendment of the ESA, removing the requirement for critical habitat designation. The major benefits would be a focus on listing and recovery planning for species at risk and elimination of the time and financial costs that occur with the critical habitat debate. We do not support this option because it would substantially weaken ESA protection for threatened and endangered species.

A second option is to amend the ESA to move the critical habitat designation process from listing to recovery planning. For example, the Canadian *Species at Risk Act* incorporates designation of critical habitat into recovery planning because listing partially protects habitat. Because U.S. critical habitat designation currently is funded within the listing budget, this rescheduling would alleviate some of the time and resource constraints associated with the current listing process. Still, many listed species lack recovery plans, so shifting critical habitat designation to recovery planning could simply delay the problem ...

Third, increasing appropriations would decrease the designation bottleneck as court-ordered and other designations could be handled more quickly. This solution, however, would not solve the pattern of litigation fully or lead to increased numbers of designations at the time of listing. The designation problem is complex and difficult even without the exacerbation of limited funding, so although we encourage improved funding, a full solution requires additional changes.

A fourth option, and one we highly recommend, is for modification of [federal agency] criteria and practice for designating critical habitat. The ESA and [associated] implementation guidelines are not providing sufficient guidance for critical habitat designation to be an efficiently implemented part of ESA, even when substantial biological information is available. This problem makes it essential to construct better systems by which existing information is used for designations ... The major litigation and funding problems with critical habitat designation arise from this central challenge, and any lasting solution to the critical habitat problems requires modifying the agency criteria to make it easier to apply existing data to delineate critical habitat.

Prohibitions on Harming Species

A critical feature of endangered species legislation is the manner and extent to which it prohibits actions that harm species or species habitat, provisions that are often referred to "takings" protections. In this respect, as in many others, the approach adopted under SARA differs considerably from that under US law. As we shall see, the key difference between the statutes lies in the scope of application of the applicable provisions.

Takings Protection under SARA

Species listed under SARAs are subject to "takings" prohibitions: it cannot be killed, harmed or traded (s. 32) nor can "its residence" be damaged or destroyed (s. 33). However, the scope of the protection afforded by these provisions is limited: applying *only* within designated areas of federal jurisdiction (i.e., federal lands, aquatic species and migratory birds under the *Migratory Birds Convention Act*). The following excerpt analyzes these provisions in more detail, describing their political and legislative history.

Kate Smallwood, *A Guide to Canada's Species at Risk Act*
(Vancouver, Sierra Legal Defence Fund: 2003)

Most species listed at risk under SARA will not be protected by the basic prohibitions unless they are found at national parks, federal agricultural lands, Indian reserves, military bases, airports, post offices, coast guard stations or other federal land [unless the federal government invokes its "safety net" order power discussed *infra*].

Section 32 prohibits two broad categories of activity — harm to a listed species, and possession or trade in a listed species or parts of a listed species:

> (1) No person shall kill, harm, harass, capture or take an individual of a wildlife species that is listed as an extirpated species, an endangered species or a threatened species.
>
> (2) No person shall possess, collect, buy, sell or trade an individual of a wildlife species that is listed as an extirpated species, an endangered species or a threatened species, or any part or derivative of such an individual.

Section 33 prohibits damage or destruction of a species' "residence". The prohibition applies to listed endangered and threatened species, and listed extirpated species provided a recovery strategy has recommended the reintroduction of the species into the wild in Canada. The term "residence" is not a biological or scientific concept. It is an artificial tool to minimize the automatic consequences of listing a species under SARA by restricting legal protection to a minimal portion of the species' critical habitat.

As originally drafted in Bill C-5, "residence" was defined to mean:

> ... a dwelling-place, such as a den, nest or other similar area, place or structure, that is occupied or habitually occupied by one or more individuals during all or part of their life cycles, including breeding, rearing or hibernating.

Various stakeholders ... objected to this definition because it was too narrow, rendering it biologically inapplicable to many species. By restricting the definition to "den, nest or other similar area", many species such as caribou that do not have a den or nest or "similar" area, would not be eligible for protection.

In response to these concerns, the House Standing Committee on Environment and Sustainable Development expanded the definition to include areas used for feeding, staging and wintering, but failed to delete the word "similar". The amended definition was then somewhat contradictory — areas used for wintering and feeding, for example, are not "similar" to a den, nest or other dwelling area.

Aside from one minor amendment, the government retained the Committee's definition. The definition — which remains somewhat contradictory, although it is clear that broader areas are meant to be covered — now reads:

> a dwelling place, such as a den, nest or other similar area or place, that is occupied or habitually occupied by one or more individuals during all or part of their life cycles, including breeding, rearing, staging, wintering, feeding or hibernating

Section 58 is the primary section under SARA for protection of critical habitat. "Critical habitat" as defined in the Act means:

> "habitat that is necessary for the survival or recovery of a listed wildlife species and that is identified as the species' critical habitat in the recovery strategy or action plan for the species".

Unlike the basic prohibitions therefore, protection of critical habitat does not apply automatically upon listing a species, but is delayed until the recovery process.

Section 58 contains an outright prohibition against the destruction of any part of the critical habitat of a listed endangered, threatened or extirpated species, if a recovery strategy has recommend the reintroduction of the species into the wild in Canada. Section 58 is limited to federal jurisdiction only i.e. federal lands, federal waters (exclusive economic zone of Canada and continental shelf of Canada), aquatic species and migratory birds under the *Migratory Birds Convention Act*.

The stated purpose of section 58 [as set out in section 57] is to ensure that within six months after critical habitat has been identified in a recovery strategy or action plan that has been filed in the public registry, that critical habitat is protected by:

- provisions in or measures under SARA, including conservation agreements under section 11;
- provisions in or measures under other federal legislation; or
- the critical habitat prohibition under section 58(1) of SARA (i.e. critical habitat within federal jurisdiction).

Section 58 protection can extend to areas within provincial or territorial jurisdiction but only where Governor in Council, at its discretion, upon the recommendation of the Minister of Environment, makes an order to that effect. This is known as a "safety net" order: see s. 61.

The Minister of Environment *must* make the recommendation if the Minister is of the opinion, after consultation with the appropriate provincial or territorial minister, that:

- There are no provisions in or measures under SARA, including conservation agreements under section 11, that protect the particular critical habitat;
- There are no provisions in or measures under other federal legislation that protect the particular critical habitat; and
- The *laws of the province or territory do not effectively protect the critical habitat.* (emphasis added)

... it is unclear at this stage how the federal government will assess whether the laws of a province or territory do provide effective protection for critical habitat.

An order made under section 61(2) lasts for five years, unless the Governor in Council, by order, renews it (s. 61(5). If the Minister of Environment is of the opinion that an order made under section 61(2) is no longer necessary to protect the critical habitat to which the order relates or that the province or territory has brought laws into force which protect that critical habitat, the Minister *must* recommend that the order be repealed.

Takings Protection under ESA

American courts have interpreted the ambit of protection against "takings" under ESA broadly. The leading case, and one that has provoked considerable ongoing controversy and debate, is excerpted below. Like the predecessor cases we have reviewed, it too arose in the context of the ongoing dispute over protection of spotted owl habitat in the US Pacific Northwest.

Babbitt v. Sweet Home Chapter of the Communities for a Great Oregon
515 U.S. 687 (1995)

STEVENS J.

Section 9 of the Act makes it unlawful for any person to "take" any endangered or threatened species. The Secretary has promulgated a regulation that defines the statute's prohibition on takings to include "significant habitat modification or degradation where it actually kills or injures wildlife". This case presents the question whether the Secretary exceeded his authority under the Act by promulgating that regulation.

Section 3(19) of the Act defines the statutory term "take": "The term 'take' means to harass, harm, pursue, hunt, shoot, wound, kill, trap, capture, or collect, or to attempt to engage in any such conduct".

The Act does not further define the terms it uses to define "take". The Interior Department regulations that implement the statute, however, define the statutory term "harm":

> *Harm* in the definition of 'take' in the Act means an act which actually kills or injures wildlife. Such act may include significant habitat modification or degradation where it actually kills or injures wildlife by significantly impairing essential behavioral patterns, including breeding, feeding, or sheltering.

Respondents in this action are small landowners, logging companies, and families dependent on the forest products industries in the Pacific Northwest and in the Southeast, and organizations that represent their interests ... Respondents [argued] ... that Congress did not intend the word "take" in s. 9 to include habitat modification, as the Secretary's "harm" regulation provides.

The text of the Act provides three reasons for concluding that the Secretary's interpretation is reasonable. First, an ordinary understanding of the word "harm" supports it. The dictionary definition of the verb form of "harm" is "to cause hurt or damage to: injure". In the context of the ESA, that definition naturally encompasses habitat modification that results in actual injury or death to members of an endangered or threatened species.

Second, the broad purpose of the ESA supports the Secretary's decision to extend protection against activities that cause the precise harms Congress enacted the statute to avoid ... As stated in s. 2 of the Act, among its central purposes is "to provide a means whereby the ecosystems upon which endangered species and threatened species depend may be conserved ...

Third, the fact that Congress in 1982 authorized the Secretary to issue permits for takings that s. 9 would otherwise prohibit, "if such taking is incidental to, and not the purpose of, the carrying out of an otherwise lawful activity" strongly suggests that Congress understood s 9 to prohibit indirect as well as deliberate takings ... This reference to the foreseeability of incidental takings undermines respondents' argument that [the 1982 amendment] covered only accidental killings of endangered and threatened animals that might occur in the course of hunting or trapping other animals. Indeed, Congress had habitat modification directly in mind ...

Compensation Issues in Species Protection

Protecting species and species habitat can be an enormously costly proposition. A key question, therefore, is how the costs of protection should be allocated. Both in Canada and United States, this issue has been a lightening-rod for controversy. In Canada, during the lengthy debate leading up to enactment of SARA, this question was of particular concern to rural and agriculture-based communities who lobbied strenuously for SARA to incorporate provisions that ensured that farmers and other rural property owners impacted by the operation of the Act received compensation from government. Compensating affected landowners has also been a longstanding issue in the ESA context. To date, however, as we shall, it is not a topic that is explicitly addressed in ESA or related federal regulations.

Compensation under SARA

To secure passage of the SARA, the federal government was under considerable pressure from rural ridings to incorporate strong compensation measures. In response, environmentalists argued that much of the rural concern regarding the need for compensation was based on an unfounded concern that the legislation would have extensive application on private land (see Smallwood, 2003). To this end, they pointed out (as seen in the preceding section) that "while SARA's basic prohibitions against harming a listed endangered, extirpated or threatened species or its residence will apply on private land in the case of aquatic species and migratory birds under the *Migratory Birds Convention Act*, the Act is otherwise primarily limited to federal lands.

Another key feature of the SARA compensation debate was a concern that incorporating such a provision into the legislation would establish an undesirable and expensive precedent. Critics argued that it "was unprecedented in Canadian environmental legislation to provide compensation for anything short of actual expropriation" (Smallwood, 2003). This argument was given credence by a report authored Dr. Peter Pearse that was commissioned by the federal government in the lead-up to enactment of the SARA. In this report, Pearse noted that:

> [Canadian] courts and governments have historically drawn a distinction between expropriation of property, for which compensation is due, and restrictions on the use of property for some public purpose, for which compensation is generally not payable. Restrictions that might be imposed under the *Species at Risk Act* are of this regulatory type, so compensation for them conflicts with long established policy in Canada.

The compromise that was ultimately brokered is contained in section 64 of the SARA. It states that the federal government "may, in accordance with the regulations, provide fair and reasonable compensation to any person for losses suffered as a result of any extraordinary impact" arising out of application of specified provisions of the Act. These include:

- The critical habitat prohibition in section 58;
- The discretionary prohibition against the destruction of habitat on federal land for species classified as endangered by a province or territory (s. 60);
- The critical habitat safety net in section 61; or
- Habitat identified in an emergency order that is necessary for the survival or recovery of a wildlife species.

To date, the federal government has yet to enact regulations elaborating how "fair and reasonable compensation" is to be calculated, or what constitutes an "extraordinary impact" arising from operation of the legislation.

Notes and Questions

1. Professor Rounthwaite has argued that against the notion of defining "extraordinary impacts" as a percentage of loss in market value or net returns from the land in favour of a principled approach for classifying losses as "extraordinary" (Rounthwaite, J.E.L.P. 2000). He contends that "although there is a dearth of judicial authority on the subject, the U.S. and Canadian jurisprudence on *de facto* expropriation may provide a starting point for a discussion of when compensation should be paid to a landowner who must bear more than a fair share of the costs of protecting and recovering our wildlife species at risk". In his view, losses should be classified as "extraordinary" after careful consideration of the following factors:

- What degree of harm does the current or proposed use of the land pose to the critical habitat of the wildlife species at risk?
- The relative ease with which the harm to the critical habitat can be avoided through cooperative measures taken by governments and landowners.
- The social utility of the landowners present or proposed use of the land taking into account the nature of the land or resource in question.
- The extent to which the regulatory restrictions take away the incidents of ownership.
- Equitable principles including whether the applicant seeking compensation has acted in good faith and has "clean hands".

He contends that if, after applying these factors, it can be concluded that the losses suffered by the private property owner are indeed "extraordinary", compensation for those losses should be paid. Moreover, he contends that in this situation compensation for the loss should be "paid in full". In his words:

> Where the landowner has voluntarily and cooperatively tried to modify his or her operations taking into account the nature of the land, the degree of harm caused to critical habitat by these operations, the ease with which his or her method of operating can be modified to accommodate the critical habitat of wildlife species at risk, has little or no other incidents of ownership left to exercise as a result of the regulatory restrictions and has made good faith attempts to accommodate the needs of

> the species at risk, compensation in full seems warranted. Such a theory of compensation would provide incentives for voluntary, cooperative approaches by government and private property owners to work together to protect the critical habitat necessary for the recovery of species at risk. Much of the existing uncertainty concerning entitlement to compensation would also be removed, to the benefit of both governments and property owners.

Do you agree with the approach proposed by Rounthwaite?

2. In a commentary on Rounthwaite's article, the Alberta Environmental Law Centre argues against statutory compensation under the SARA, which it contends, "may create a legal entitlement which does not otherwise exist at common law":

> We foresee several potentially grave consequences resulting from SARA's use of compensation. Firstly, this approach enforces the mistaken view that property entitlements grant landowners the right to forever destroy critical habitat on which species at risk depend for survival. This distorted view of property entitlements should be rejected, not promoted, by governments. Secondly, this approach may act as an incentive to encourage development and destruction of critical habitat. This is because qualifying for compensation likely will require evidence of actual intent to develop critical habitat. This in turn will promote development planning on habitat that would not have otherwise occurred. Without doubt, carrying out some of such plans would prove to be more lucrative to landowners than applying for federal compensation. Finally, this approach will set back and burden the excellent work of conservation agencies. Many activities of these organizations depend on landowners choosing not to develop habitat for reasons other than economic gain.
>
> It is our recommendation that SARA abandon the compensation approach. A perverse incentive to develop land must not be created by rewarding landowners for not destroying habitat. Rather, SARA should be used to encourage voluntary stewardship efforts by individuals. Efforts must be made to provide stewardship education and assistance, including financial assistance where appropriate, to assist landowners in enhancing habitat. Incentives — rather than compensation — are required to encourage stewardship efforts by individuals.

Compensation under ESA

Perhaps surprisingly, given the strong American individual property rights tradition, and associated constitutional guarantees found in the fourth and fifteenth Amendments to the Bill of Rights, ESA and its associated regulations do not provide for compensation to landowners affected by orders or decisions made under the ESA regime. Pressures to amend ESA to provide for such protections, however, have been. As described in the following article, in 2005, amendments to ESA that would have required mandatory compensation for affected landowners secured the approval of the House of Representatives. In 2005, this culminated in the amendments to ESA described below.

Amy Fagan, "*Endangered Species Act* updated: House approves legislation requiring compensation for landowners"

The Washington Times (30 September, 2005) at A09

The House yesterday passed Republican-backed legislation overhauling the *Endangered Species Act* that includes a provision requiring the government to compensate landowners whose property is confiscated to protect animals.

"When the law is not working, we have to respond to that, step in, reauthorize the bill, put the emphasis on recovery, protect private property owners", said House Resources Committee Chairman Richard W. Pombo, California Republican. "If you take away someone's private property — if you take away the use of it — you have to pay them for it".

The vote was 229-193, with 36 Democrats and 193 Republicans in favor, and 158 Democrats, 34 Republicans and one independent opposed. The Bush administration — in a statement by the Office of Management and Budget — voiced support for the bill, praising "the importance of protecting private property rights". But it also said that new requirements related to the creation of recovery plans for endangered species, new statutory deadlines and the new conservation aid program "could result in a significant budgetary impact" and that some language in the bill could generate new litigation. The Senate has not acted on the measure.

Supporters of the bill said the 1973 act actually has hurt the environment because the presence of an endangered species on private property brings about heavy and even prohibitive restrictions on land use, thus discouraging landowners from reporting a species' existence. Rep. Denny Rehberg, Montana Republican, said the law has scared Western landowners so much that they'd rather hide endangered species than report them. He lifted a shovel over his head yesterday and said it is "time to end the joke of shoot, shovel and shut up". Rep. Joe Baca, California Democrat, said a hospital in his district had to pay $3 million to move their building several hundred feet to protect an endangered fly. "That's ridiculous", he said.

But many Democrats said the bill would gut a valuable law that has saved many species and create a giveaway to big developers. "It's an entitlement program for landowners that want to gut the *Endangered Species Act*", said Rep. Tom Udall, New Mexico Democrat. Both support and opposition for the bill cut across party lines. Many Western lawmakers from land-rich ranching and farming states supported it, while some budget-conscious conservatives opposed it, because it would create a government entitlement by requiring compensation to landowners. ... Opponents of the bill also complained of a provision they said would make it easier to approve dangerous pesticide use and one that would create recovery plans for endangered species that they said would have no enforcement mechanism and, thus, essentially be useless.

"They're paper tigers", Bart Semcer, a D.C. representative of the Sierra Club, said of the new recovery plans. There are about 1,300 endangered species listed, and fewer than 20 have recovered and been removed from the list, Mr. Semcer said.

Supporters of the bill said those numbers are proof the law is not working and needs major change. Others said many more species would be extinct right now if the law had not been in place. 99 percent of species put on this list are not extinct", said Rep. Norm Dicks, Washington Democrat. "That is not a failure; that's an enormous success".

Notes and Questions

The 2005 amendments described above were subsequently tabled twice on the floor of the Senate, and later referred to a Senate subcommittee, where the proposal ultimately died.

Part III — Species Protection as a Governance Issue

Biodiversity protection, and more particularly species protection, poses especially difficult challenges in federal states, where jurisdiction over key powers is divided between national and sub-national levels of government [*Ed note*: For further discussion see Chapters 3 and 10, *infra*.].

In this respect, as we have seen, the debates and tensions chronicled above in developing a federal endangered species law in Canada have parallels not only in the United States, but also in other federal states, such as Australia. While on paper and in practice our constitutional arrangements differ from those in the United States and elsewhere and (as the preceding section underscores quite starkly) our federal endangered species law departs (in many ways quite deliberately) from its US counterpart, SARA and ESA represent attempts to grapple with analogous governance-related issues.

This Part commences with some ruminations on the tensions between federalism and biodiversity from a leading American environmental law scholar. We offer this excerpt to provoke discussion about the extent to which species protection may be inherently more difficult in a federation and, as such, must be viewed as a governance issue.

We then provide a brief overview of the state of endangered species protection at the provincial level. In this vein, we will canvass one of the founding principles of SARA, its commitment to promoting species protection through a cooperative approach in which the federal, provincial and territorial governments are partners. Whether the commitment to co-operation, embodied in the 1996 *Accord for the Protection of Species at Risk* and reflected in bilateral agreements (that have been concluded between the federal government and most of its provincial and territorial counterparts pursuant to section 10 of SARA), is showing results is one of the key questions addressed in this section. We also consider the interaction between SARA and provincial land use decision-making processes, and examine the role both in theory and in practice of the SARA federal safety net power.

Finally, we provide a brief overview of Canada's newest endangered species law: the Ontario *Endangered Species Act* of 2007.

Federalism and Biodiversity

A. Dan Tarlock, "Biodiversity Federalism"

(1995) 54 Md. L. Rev. 1315

Environmental protection policy is subdividing into two branches: risk minimization and biodiversity protection. Risk reduction is a difficult, if problematic, objective to accomplish because we have no reliable way to measure the magnitude of the risks that we are trying to minimize. However, this objective has been widely accepted as a legitimate public policy for the past twenty-five years. Risk prevention is consistent with the Western legal tradition because it seeks to prevent or redress human injury. Biodiversity protection on the other hand presents much more difficult problems of legitimacy and implementation within this tradition because it partially collapses the ethical dichotomy between humans and nature. As a result of scientific and popular alarm over species declines, the maintenance of biological diversity has rapidly emerged as a primary objective of both international and United States environmental law, because it provides a reasonably coherent and general principle of natural resources management.

However, the achievement of this objective remains highly contingent because biodiversity protection strategies pose greater challenges to existing legal institutions as compared with the reduction of air, water and land pollution risks. At bottom, the achievement of effective biodiversity protection is difficult because the very idea of biodiversity protection is antithetical to the Western idea of human economic progress through science, technology and the encouragement of individual initiative. These challenges vividly manifest themselves in the efforts to fit biodiversity protection into a federal system which seeks to promote values associated with economic progress.

This Article explores ongoing efforts to implement biodiversity protection programs within the United States federal system, although the problems are the same in analogous political systems such as Australia and Canada. Federalism problems are a subset of the much noticed fragmentation of biodiversity protection efforts both in the United States and other countries.

Biodiversity protection programs reflect the tension between the universality of the abstract justifications for the exercise of national power to promote this objective, and the inherently local or site-specific nature of the problems. Universal biodiversity protection goals may be easily articulated, but they cannot be applied across the board. The chief threat to biodiversity protection is habitat loss. Thus, the objective of any protection program is habitat conservation and restoration, rather than the regulation of industrial activities through the application of standard technology. As Edward O. Wilson has written, "[t]he primary tactic in conservation must be to locate the world's hot spots and to protect the entire environment they contain". In short, biodiversity protection requires strong land-use regulation and incentive schemes to induce the dedication of protected habitat, both of which are among the most difficult natural resources management or environmental objectives to achieve in a federal system.

None of the dominant models of federalism are suited to protect biodiversity or to describe the protection experiments underway. In fact, federalism principles are as likely to frustrate biodiversity protection as to promote it for three principal reasons. First, federalism is premised on the search for the optimum exclusive regulatory balance, and this can often frustrate necessary intergovernmental cooperation. Second, the maintenance of national protection floors supplemented by states is unworkable because in contrast to air and water pollution control, there are no uniform standards that one can realistically apply to biodiversity in states as different as Alaska, Arizona and Florida. Third, the national government must rely on powers ... that are traditionally and firmly lodged within state and local governments.

This misfit is critically important to biodiversity protection because the main threat to achieving this objective is local resistance that may undermine national efforts. This statement simply reflects the long standing tension between national articulation of resource management goals and local efforts to promote unrestricted access to natural resources for economic exploitation. Although the tradition of local resistance to national conservation is well into its second century, the current manifestation of this tension is the wise-use movement which seeks to tie all regulation to statutory compensation in excess of that required under federal or state constitutional law. Innovative state and local attempts to promote biodiversity are driven by the need to comply with federal mandates, primarily the *Endangered Species Act*. But, despite the constitutional power of the national government to achieve this objective, federal mandates are perceived as intrusions on state and local sovereignty ...

Biodiversity protection ... does not mesh well with federalism for a number of reasons. The most important are: (1) federalism often impedes the protection of biodiversity because the political boundaries of the federal system do not match ecosystem boundaries; (2) many of the implementation problems involve conflicts among different federal agency mandates ... (3) many of the constitutional values sought to be protected by federalism, specifically those protecting private property and individual liberty interests, are difficult to adapt to biodiversity protection; (4) federalism jurisprudence is neutral with respect to biodiversity maintenance and thus Supreme Court decisions and doctrines are as likely to hinder as promote it; and (5) the demands of biodiversity protection exceed the effective ability, as opposed to the constitutional authority, of the national government to achieve effective protection without state and local cooperation in the experiment.

Notes and Questions

To what extent, if at all, do you find Professor Tarlock's observations about the relationship between biodiversity and federalism relevant to the Canadian experience? If his arguments are generalizable beyond the US context, are some models of federalism (centralized vs. decentralized; various modes of allocating heads of power) more functional than others from biodiversity protection perspective?

Species Protection Initiatives at the Provincial Level

Seven years before SARA came into force, the federal, provincial and territorial governments jointly committed to enhancing their respective efforts to protect endangered species under the auspices of the 1996 *National Accord for the Protection of Species at Risk* (the "Accord"). Rhetorically, at least, it was on the faith that the provinces and territories were adhering to these commitments that the federal government took the position that a cooperative approach to species protection (with the provinces and territories taking the lead role subject only to federal intervention via the "emergency" and "safety net" order powers) should inform the design and operation of SARA

How effectively have the provinces and territories lived up the expectations associated with this Accord? Environmental organizations claim that, by and large, the record has not been encouraging. In the following 2004 report, Environmental Defence Canada undertook the task of grading Canadian governments against commitments set out in the Accord. While the data is now a few years old and some provinces (most notably, Ontario) have taken steps to achieve better compliance with the Accord, the report card and accompanying analysis is instructive.

Environmental Defence Canada, *Next Stop Extinction: A Report Card on the Failure of Canadian Governments to Save Endangered Species* (2004)

In 1996, Canadian federal, provincial and territorial governments agreed to "establish complementary legislation and programs that provide for effective protection of species at risk throughout Canada". Under the *National Accord for the Protection of Species at Risk*, each government committed to implement 15 principles to ensure the survival of Canadian species at risk:

- All non-domestic species covered.
- Independent process to assess Species At Risk (SAR) status.
- Legally designate species as endangered/threatened.
- Immediate legal protection for SAR.
- Protection for habitat of SAR.
- Recovery plans in one to two years that address threats to SAR and habitat.
- Ensuring of multi-jurisdictional cooperation for cross-border SAR recovery plans.
- Consideration of needs of SAR as part of environmental assessment process.
- Recovery plans implemented in a timely fashion.
- Monitoring, assessing and reporting on status of all wild species.
- Emphasis on preventative measures.
- Improvement of awareness of needs of SAR.
- Encouraging of citizen conservation/protection.
- Recognition, fostering and support for effective.

This Report Card evaluates the progress being made on these principles. On the ground, there is little doubt that the modest legislative gains at the federal and provincial level in recent years are not of the scope or scale that will make a significant difference for Canada's disappearing wild animals and plants. According to government figures, 80% of our endangered, threatened and extirpated species are showing population declines, and roughly half of listed species do not have active recovery teams.

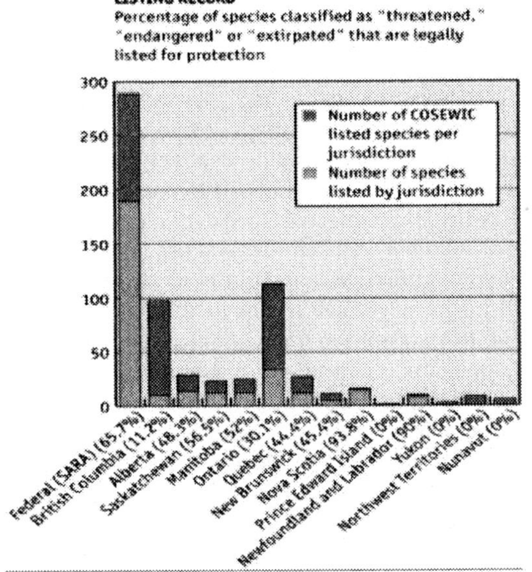

Grades for Accord Implementation

Nova Scotia **B**
Manitoba **C**
Newfoundland **C**
Prince Edward Island **C**
NewBrunswick **C**
Ontario **D+**
Quebec **D**
Nunavut **D**
Saskatchewan **D**
BC **F**
Alberta **F**
Yukon **F**
Northwest Territories **F**

Overall, the record in Canada is bleak. No jurisdiction is adhering to all of its obligations under the Accord. In fact, few are even meeting half of the Accord's criteria. As a result, Canada stands to lose many endangered animals and plants forever. On average, only 36% of species scientifically listed by the Committee on the Status of Endangered Wildlife in Canada (COSEWIC) are legally classified for protection by the provinces and territories. The various jurisdictions cannot even agree on a common legal definition of "species". Many provinces do not include plant species in this definition, with the result that a large proportion of endangered species are not even eligible for legal protection in these jurisdictions. Four jurisdictions — British Columbia, Alberta, Northwest Territories and Yukon — all receive failing grades in this report. None of these provinces or territories have stand-alone legislation protecting species at risk. In Alberta and Yukon, species at risk are even legally hunted. While British Columbia — the Canadian province containing the most biodiversity — has some legislative protections for species, the law is clear that these protections cannot significantly reduce timber cutting, and the law fails to list nearly 90% of the species classified as "at risk" in the province.

For the full report see: *http://www.environmentaldefence.ca/reports/Endangered%20Species_Final_ebook.pdf*

SARA and Provincial Land and Resource-use Decision-making

Another intriguing question is the extent to which SARA is having a direct or indirect impact on the many decisions made each day by provincial resource and environmental permitting and licencing agencies. Has SARA, the Accord or a general awareness of endangered species made any difference to these processes? Research suggests that the interstitial effect of SARA and these other legal instruments is modest at best. Consider the following case, one of the few, to date, to address this important issue.

0707814 BC Ltd. v. British Columbia (Assistant Regional Water Manager)
2008 CarswellBC 65, 34 C.E.L.R. (3d) 163 (Environmental Appeal Board)

[A provincial water approvals manager refused an application by a developer to infill a wetland in a ravine near a suburban area on the basis that it would negatively impact the habitat for several species at risk, including the Red-legged Frog (a SARA-listed species of concern) and the Oregon Forestsnail (a SARA-listed endangered species). The developer revised and resubmitted the application, which was again refused. Under both applications, the habitat of the species, and the species occupying the ravine, would be destroyed.]

The Revised Application proposes to infill the ravine which means that the habitat, and the species there at the time, will be eliminated. In terms of gravity and magnitude of harm, there are few things that could be worse: the magnitude and gravity of the harm is at the most severe end of the scale. The Appellant argues, however, that the answer is really not this simple. It submits that there is a bigger question to be answered first. That is, would the species at issue in this case persist if the ravine and Ravine Pond were left in their current state? More specifically, if the Revised Application is not granted, would those species survive in any event? If they would not persist on the property, the Appellant argues that this should change the amount of weight they are to be given in the context of the application. If they will not survive anyway, why should the Revised Application not be granted?

The Appellant submits that, based on the most credible evidence, those species at issue in this case will not persist. It maintains that the evidence shows that there are too many threats to their habitat already. It submits that the only way to ensure the species have some reasonable chance of survival is to grant its application and impose conditions to protect the most suitable habitat for them: the Ravine Pond ...

This has been a very difficult question for the Panel. The Panel's findings were particularly difficult in relation to the Oregon Forestsnail, already listed as endangered federally, as well as the Red-legged Frog. While there was some discussion about attempting to capture and relocate some of these species to other locations, the Panel finds that this is not a feasible option for most of the species involved, although salvage on the property may be feasible for some.

Like many areas of science, predicting whether a species will persist is not an exercise in certainties. When considering the ravine and Ravine Pond in their current state, and predicting what will happen to those habitats in the future, the Panel is relying on "best guesses", based on the best available evidence.

Regarding the need for further study, the Panel finds that this is not the appropriate case to make such an order. Even assuming that good habitat exists in the ravine and the Ravine Pond there is no question that threats to these species' survival already exist at the site:

- the site is not pristine,
- it is surrounded by developments,
- further development directly north of the property may occur, and more are planned up the mountain, and

- there is already evidence that at least part of the subject property is used regularly by the public.

The property is an oasis in an urban landscape.

The Panel finds that the presence of threats to the persistence of these species does not mean that they will not, or cannot, persist despite these pressures. However, in the present case, the pressures are simply too overwhelming for the Panel to have any confidence that, without the protection proposed by the Appellant, any of the species, except for the Pacific Waterleaf, is reasonably likely to persist. With the protection around the Ravine Pond, at least some will have a better chance of persisting on the property.

Unfortunately, the *Water Act* is not meant to deal with land use issues. The Participants submit that what is needed in this case is to actively protect the ravine and the Ravine Pond. The Participants state:

> Once a species is listed nationally as endangered, threatened, or special concern, or provincially as red or blue, trends need to be reversed if its path on the road to extinction (from special concern to threatened to endangered to extirpated to extinct) is to be stopped and eventually reversed. Further, it is important to implement protections as early as possible on this path, namely at the special concern (or blue) stage, rather than waiting for the problem to approach crisis proportions, namely threatened and beyond.

The Panel agrees with this statement. However, the *Water Act* is an inadequate tool to address the problems for the species on this property. Unfortunately, the protection of these species in this area needed to have occurred some time ago in order to ensure the continued survival of a viable population.

In this regard, the Panel finds that although the site is a functioning ecosystem now, ... it is no longer one of "high value". The Participants are correct that, despite the surrounding development, the species are still on the property. However, the Panel finds that the property is too cut-off from other viable populations and natural habitat. All of the experts agree generally that isolation of the site affects the quality of the habitat for the species resident there, and that development of portions of the site and surrounding area would further fragment and isolate this habitat. Thus, the species' habitat is being degraded, and more is expected.

Therefore, based on all of the evidence, the Panel finds that, with the exception of the Pacific Waterleaf, the species identified are not likely to persist in the ravine and Ravine Pond without help. That help is not coming from the City, as it is the City that is making the road a condition of development approval. As the City states in its closing submissions, "ironically, the way to protect the environment of this compromised site is to allow the application and protect the wetland and adjacent area through a covenant".

Given all of the evidence, the Panel finds that the Revised Application will not have an irreparable impact on the species at risk identified in this case.

[In the result, the appeals were allowed and the development was permitted to proceed with conditions.]

The Ontario *Endangered Species Act, 2007*

In May 2007, environmentalists celebrated the outcome of a decade-long campaign for new species protection legislation in Ontario. That month saw enactment of what is being broadly described as the strongest law of its kind in Canada. The new law, which replaced its weak and seldom-used predecessor in force since the 1970s, aims to provide much-enhanced protection for the province's 200 endangered plant and animal species; which represent over a third of the Canadian total.

Even before the law came into force, however, the celebratory mood turned sour. As the proclamation date of July 1, 2008 approached, the Ontario government announced plans to exempt the forest industry from regulation under the Act for a one-year period. This prompted a flurry of criticism from environmentalists, who contend that the decision will mean that endangered species like the woodland caribou, whose habitat is located predominantly in the 45% of the province under logging tenures, will remain at risk.

Notwithstanding these recriminations, on paper the legislation appears to offer considerable potential to protect endangered and threatened species, in many respects departing markedly from the SARA approach.

Like its U.S. counterpart, the Ontario law has a science-based mandatory listing process. In this regard, Government is obliged to act on the listing recommendations of an independent committee known as COSSARO (the Committee on the Status of Species at Risk in Ontario), subject to a power to ask COSSARO to reconsider its recommendation: sections 7 and 8. COSSARO's recommendations, in turn, are to be based on "the best available scientific information, including information obtained from community knowledge and aboriginal traditional knowledge": subsection 5(5).

There are also strong mandatory provisions with respect to the development of recovery strategies and habitat designations. The responsible Minister is obliged to prepare a recovery strategy for every endangered or threatened listed species: section 11. For endangered species this strategy must be completed within one year of its listing; for threatened species, the time limit is two years from listing: subsection 11(4). The Minister may seek to extend the time for developing a strategy (having regard to "complexity of the issues", the need for inter-jurisdictional cooperation, or to give priority to other pending recovery strategies), but in no event can the strategy be delayed for more than five years after the initial listing: subsections 11(4), (5).

The Minister must also designate critical habitat for listed species by regulation: subsection 56(1). These designations must occur within 2 years of listing for endangered species and within 3 years of listing for threatened species: subsections 56(2), (3).

The law also contains broad takings prohibitions that address both harm to listed species and their habitat: sections 9, 10. These prohibitions, however, seek to balance the traditional use rights of First Nations by allowing the Minister to offer exemptions from these provisions through agreements with specified native organizations: paragraph 19(1)(2).

The law is silent with respect to compensation for affected landowners and resource tenure holders.

Part IV — Emerging Perspectives on Species and Biodiversity Protection

In this concluding section we canvass two related questions both highly relevant to charting the course ahead in terms of the role of environmental law in biodiversity protection. The first concerns whether, and to what extent, a focus on protecting species, particularly "special species", may need to be rethought. Doremus argues that the dominance of this approach, particularly in the U.S. context, has had a variety of unintended and unfortunate consequences for biodiversity protection. In an innovative and provocative article, she argues that governments need to tackle biodiversity protection using a much broader suite of regulatory instruments and approaches than have been deployed to date.

A second set of questions pertain to the relationship between protected areas and enhancing species protection. A key assumption of the traditional approach to species protection is that, in large measure, the solution lies in setting aside habitat areas as protected reserves. But just how effectively is our current network of protected reserves functioning to protect species? New research into this question, by Deguise and Kerr, has generated some interesting conclusions, which suggest that the relationship between protecting areas and protecting species may not be as straightforward as might be assumed. Like Doremus, they conclude that while establishing protected areas is part of the answer, securing long term species protection on a national scale will require a broader, more integrated conservation strategy that incorporates agricultural and urban land-use planning outside of formally protected areas.

Holly Doremus, "Biodiversity and the Challenge of Saving the Ordinary"
(2002) 38 Idaho L. Rev. 325

Both scientists and policymakers today tout the goal of protecting biodiversity, understood to encompass the range of biotic resources. Ecologists and conservation biologists wholeheartedly endorse biodiversity protection. It is enshrined [in the mandates and policies of many federal agencies]. The protection of biodiversity has even been enshrined as a goal of international law, through the adoption of the *Convention on Biological Diversity*. Of course, as a society we are still arguing vociferously about how much biodiversity to protect, what costs we are willing to bear in the name of biodiversity, and how to divide those costs. My point is only that we seem, at least on the surface, to have a strong consensus at the policymaking level that biodiversity protection is an important goal.

Unfortunately, our dominant strategy for achieving that goal remains one developed in another era for different purposes. As we did in the earliest days of conscious nature protection, we continue to concentrate on setting aside special places and protecting dwindling special resources against exhaustion. Given today's conditions, that strategy is not likely to achieve our current goal of protecting a wide range of biotic resources over a long period of time. If we are to succeed in protecting biodiversity, we must find ways to focus the law and the public on ordinary nature rather than merely the obviously special or unique aspects of nature.

Conventional Criticisms of Current Strategies for Biodiversity Protection

We have recognized for some time that our current strategies for nature protection are not well suited to saving biodiversity. We have not yet acknowledged, however, that the root problem is our focus on the special. Instead, critics have focused on the way we identify the special elements of nature on which our strategies concentrate. Two frequently repeated criticisms of the ESA illustrate this point. The first is that biodiversity protection could be accomplished more efficiently and effectively if we emphasized the protection of ecosystems, biodiversity hot spots, or more carefully selected focal species. The second is that we delay taking protective action until it is nearly, and perhaps entirely, too late.

Protection of individual endangered species through the ESA is not effectively protecting the range of biodiversity. At first, this may seem surprising. The ESA, which is framed as a safety net for all plant and wildlife species, should in theory be capable of protecting biodiversity which, after all, equates at least roughly to the sum of all species. Indeed, the ESA should be a very sensible mechanism for biodiversity protection, covering all plant and animal species but concentrating our efforts on those in most dire need of our immediate attention. In reality, however, as the critics point out, only the most extraordinarily special species, and only those special in a very particular way, are actually helped by the ESA. Only those species with significant public appeal or tenacious human advocates are able to run the gauntlet of the ESA's listing process. Of those species that do make it to listing, a handful of the most charismatic, not necessarily the most threatened or ecologically critical, receive the bulk of the resources put into species recovery.

By interpreting specialness differently, perhaps we could use individual species more effectively as surrogates for biodiversity. It has been suggested that by setting our species protection priorities carefully, concentrating on indicator, keystone, and umbrella species, we might wind up protecting far more than the relatively small number of species that become listed. Indicator species are supposed to reflect the health of the larger ecosystem, so that by ensuring their health we ensure that of the ecosystem. Keystone species are thought to be especially important contributors to community structure, so saving them should keep the community intact. Umbrella species are those that require extremely large ranges; their protection, it is hoped, will guarantee that of many smaller-range species. Alternatively, critics suggest that we should shift our focus to protecting key ecosystems, or "hotspots"-locations that harbor unusually high levels of biodiversity.

Conservation advocates have deliberately chosen the strategy of the special for its political appeal. Threats to special places and special things attract attention and can motivate people to action. Even those who seek much more than protection of individual charismatic species have concentrated on that strategy, expecting, or at least hoping, that the political appeal of the most special places and species could be leveraged to achieve the larger goal of biodiversity protection. Our experience so far under the ESA, though, counsels to the contrary. Protection of the special has not proven an effective strategy for saving the ordinary.

Indeed, it may not be possible to use special locations or species as effective surrogates for larger systems. Ecologists have found it difficult to define the keystone concept or identify species that fit it, and umbrella species now appear far less useful than we once thought.

Even if it were possible to leverage conservation of the right set of individual species or the right collection of reserves to protect biodiversity, by adopting the strategy of the special we almost ensure that we will not choose our protected set to achieve that particular goal. Our experience to date validates this claim. We have shown little or no inclination to set our species protection priorities with a view toward biodiversity protection. When we demand that entities qualify for protection by being sufficiently special, we should not be surprised that the most charismatic or symbolically appealing species end up first in line. For species to be chosen on the basis of their ability to stand in for biodiversity protection, we would need to convince the public that biodiversity itself is special.

That is difficult to do because biodiversity is so abstract, and so ordinary. Human beings simply are not wired to care about, or even to notice, the ordinary. We cannot attend to everything that competes for our attention. We have therefore developed a variety of filtering mechanisms to help us focus effectively on some things by more or less shutting out others ...

It is therefore much easier to convince people to take action to save whales, wolves, or other specific, eye and imagination-catching creatures, than it is to persuade them that they must act to save nature as a whole, or biodiversity, which is nearly the same thing ...

The strategy of the special predisposes us, perhaps even unconsciously, to focus our efforts on government-owned lands in particular and on setting aside nature reserves in general. It almost inevitably leads us to see nature as something apart from our daily lives. That, in turn, is likely to doom our efforts to save a broad range of nature ...

The strategy of the special sends us to the public lands because those lands, and only those lands, are already special in our cultural understanding. Unlike privately-owned lands, public lands are supposed to be dedicated to some vision of the public good.

The importance of private lands for biodiversity protection poses a challenge for biodiversity advocates because our background assumption is that private lands are not particularly special. We seem culturally ingrained to assume that landowners are entitled to control their lands in most respects, including the extent of accommodation they choose to make for nature. Of course some landowners choose to dedicate their land to nature protection, and even seek out and acquire lands for the express purpose of biodiversity protection. ... Landowners assume that they are or should be free to use their land in virtually any way they please, so long as other people are not directly injured by that use. Because that assumption is widespread and politically powerful, the effort to impose the kinds of regulatory controls on land use that are essential to biodiversity protection faces particularly formidable institutional barriers. That kind of change to the legal status quo must be supported by an appealing focal point, something special enough to rally the needed political support.

The law also needs focal points for effective implementation ... [these] focal points need not be the places or things we are protecting. Instead of trying to craft a single "magic bullet" biodiversity law, we might be better off with a patchwork of federal, state, and local law focusing on things, places, and activities that affect biodiversity. We might well find that the sum of those disparate parts is greater protection than we could hope to get from any one law.

Our portfolio of biodiversity protection should include regulation that proscribes, limits, or establishes prerequisites to those activities that predictably pose a threat to biodiversity. Habitat degradation, for example, results from: air and water pollution; water diversion and storage; residential, commercial and industrial construction; extractive industries such as mining, silviculture, and agriculture; and recreation, among other activities. Regulating all of those activities seems like a tall order, but in fact many of them already are subject to some kind of federal, state, or local regulation. The trick with respect to those activities is to ensure that biodiversity considerations are adequately factored into existing regulatory schemes. That is a political problem, not an institutional one. We can take biodiversity into account if we are sufficiently motivated to do so.

Broad geographic regions can also provide useful focal points for the law ... Protecting biodiversity means keeping nature ordinary, and for that we need planning efforts that cover most of the landscape, not just isolated hotspots.

Local land use regulation, which has developed institutions for long-range area-wide planning applicable to a wide range of activities, has an important role to play in our biodiversity protection efforts. However, because of the need for coordination and a broader vision, balkanized local regulation is not likely to be effective. Multi-jurisdictional regional plans are needed.

In addition to regulations applicable to specific activities that pose special threats to biodiversity, effective biodiversity policy probably requires implementation of a large-scale planning approach applicable to all or nearly all lands. Our planning efforts should be devoted to protecting biodiversity, or as I would prefer to say, protecting nature, broadly, not just in limited locations.

The biodiversity problem sharply highlights the challenge of saving the ordinary. We are naturally drawn to the strategy of the special, but that strategy does not work to protect biodiversity, which is the entire tapestry of nature. In order to save biodiversity, we must find institutional focal points other than special places and special creatures. That is not trivial, but it can be done with some creativity.

We can use human activities and geographic regions, for example, as focal points for law. The tougher challenge is building the political support to limit human actions, saving some room on the planet for nature. That requires the development and maintenance of emotional connections to ordinary nature.

Notes and Questions

1. To what extent does Doremus's argument resonate in the Canadian context? Do we tend to value "charismatic mega-fauna" over more humble and anonymous creatures and, if so, has this skewed public policy? Or do the sagas of the Spotted Owl and Nooksack Dace suggest other conclusions?

2. The following article, like the preceding one, speaks powerfully to the need for a more integrated and holistic approach to biodiversity protection.

Isabelle Deguise & Jeremy Kerr, "Protected Areas and Prospects for Endangered Species Conservation in Canada"

(2006) 20 Conservation Biology 48–55

To be effective, reserve networks must be able to ameliorate the effects of factors that threaten species with extinction, which have been well studied. In the United States, habitat loss is a primary cause of species endangerment. Similarly ... land-use conversion to agriculture was the best predictor of numbers of endangered species in Canada. Introduced species and urbanization have also caused the decline of many species. Overhunting, even in the absence of serious land-use changes, is believed to be the primary threat to more than one-third of World Conservation Union (IUCN) red-listed mammals and birds. These and other threats can act additively, act synergistically, or interact unexpectedly to deplete biodiversity

Reserve networks represent one of the leading strategies for reducing extinction rates. The gap between the potential utility of reserves and their actual contribution, however, is sometimes substantial, largely because relatively few reserves have been designated specifically to conserve biodiversity. Many species cannot maintain viable populations even within some of the largest reserves ever established ...

As human activities continue to expand into remaining wilderness areas, the need to establish protected areas in areas where they are most needed becomes progressively more acute. In Canada, where permanent land use changes are still relatively concentrated and extensive wilderness areas persist, protected-areas networks are considered critical to the protection and recovery of endangered species and are integrated into new endangered species legislation (*Species at Risk Act 2002*). Many of Canada's endangered species are also threatened in the United States, and conserving peripheral populations of these species is particularly important for their long-term survival.

We used new data on endangered species and protected areas in Canada to address two questions. First, given the distribution of terrestrial endangered species within each of Canada's fifteen ecozones, how effectively does the existing reserve system include endangered species relative to randomly situated reserves? Second, we tested for a relationship between patterns of species endangerment and the extent of protected areas across Canada. A significant proportion of the world's remaining wilderness is in Canada, so measurements of the effectiveness of biodiversity conservation strategies there could inform conservation planning for the world's remaining wilderness frontiers.

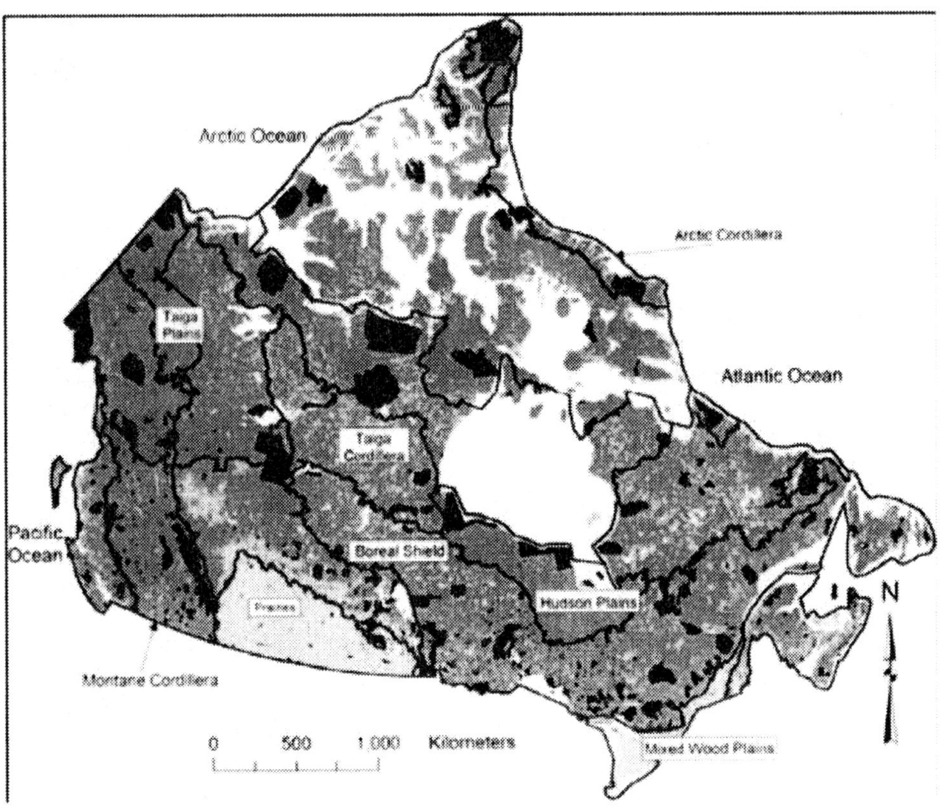

Figure 1. Protected areas (black), ecozones (black lines), extent of human-dominated lands (light gray), or lands with limited human dominance (dark gray) in Canada. Areas in white are water or outside Canadian territory. Human-dominated lands were detected using satellite-based land-use data. More information about Canada's ecozones can be found at http://www.ccea.org/ecozones/terr.html.

Among Canada's ecozones, existing reserve networks most commonly included no more endangered species than expected by chance. In the most seriously degraded ecozone, the Mixed Wood Plains, randomly generated reserve networks included more endangered species than expected by chance. This area is the most densely populated in Canada, includes extensive urban and agricultural land uses, has the greatest concentration of endangered species, and is for many taxa the most diverse region in the country. There were also many endangered species in the Montane Cordillera, where the existing reserve network included fewer endangered species than any randomly generated network. Land uses that inhibit reserve establishment in this ecozone include extensive forestry activities and agriculture, which are concentrated in the south.

The benefits of reserves in the most threatened regions of Canada are limited by their small size: mean reserve size in Canada declined sharply as numbers of endangered species per ecozone increased.

Areas with the highest diversity are now dominated by agricultural land uses, which makes it difficult to establish new reserves or expand existing, small reserves. Similar patterns of skewed reserve distributions have been found across the Western Hemisphere. Canada's *Species at Risk Act* provides little additional habitat protection in areas with the largest numbers of endangered species (and therefore the smallest reserves), although it promotes cooperative conservation measures in these areas of mostly privately owned land. These efforts have not yet been widely implemented and their effects cannot yet be evaluated.

Species in some northern ecozones (e.g., Taiga Shield and Boreal Cordillera) were included in existing reserves relatively completely, although there were few endangered species in these areas and low species richness overall ... Even in Canada's wilderness areas, however, reserve systems in three ecozones (Arctic Cordillera, Taiga Plains, and Hudson Plains) included significantly fewer endangered species than expected by chance.

Reserve networks in Canada might include unexpectedly few endangered species for two reasons. First, endangered species are concentrated in areas with extensive human land use, clearly inhibiting reserve establishment or expansion. This cannot explain why reserve networks in ecozones consisting predominantly of wilderness include fewer endangered species than expected by chance (although land claims and traditional land uses by aboriginal Canadians influence reserve placement). A second reason for poor reserve performance, however, is that protected areas have simply not been established to protect biodiversity. National parks, for example, are intended to maintain areas for the "benefit, education and enjoyment" of Canadians (*National Parks Act 2000*). It is only in the later *Species at Risk Act* that an endangered species protection role is firmly established for national parks.

Cordillera, and even some ecozones that lack extensive permanent human land uses, protected areas networks alone are unlikely to provide effective endangered species protection in Canada.

Conservation activities outside reserves, especially efforts that involve private landowners, should be a high priority. Tax incentives and conservation easements may prove effective in this respect and would reduce the land-use conflicts that would arise from — and probably scuttle — efforts to establish large protected areas in the midst of privately held lands. Even had existing reserve networks included more endangered species than expected by chance, reserve area is far smaller in areas with many endangered species. Thus, we emphasize the importance of distinguishing between inclusiveness and effectiveness. The small reserves in ecozones with many endangered species are unlikely to maintain viable populations of most endangered species. Even species that can reach high population densities (e.g., invertebrates) in small reserves cannot be reliably conserved in such areas ... Integrating conservation into agricultural and urban land-use practices will be critical for reducing the loss of species in Canada given the wide gap between the effectiveness of reserves and the needs of endangered species.

Notes and Questions

Do the findings reported above surprise you? What implications or lessons do they offer for species protection policy-makers? What about for policy-makers working in the realm of parks and protected area?

References

We thank the copyright holders for their permission to reproduce their materials.

Jamie Benidickson, *Environmental Law*, 3rd ed., (Irwin Law, 2009)

David R. Boyd, *Unnatural Law: Rethinking Canadian Environmental Law and Policy* (UBC Press: 2003)

David Suzuki Foundation, "Left off the List: A Profile of Marine and Northern Species Denied Listing under SARA" (Vancouver: 2007)

Isabelle Deguise & Jeremy Kerr, "Protected Areas and Prospects for Endangered Species Conservation in Canada" (2006) 20 Conservation Biology 48–55. Copyright © 2006, Society for Conservation Biology. Reproduced with permission of Blackwell Publishing Ltd.

Holly Doremus, "Biodiversity and the Challenge of Saving the Ordinary" (2002) 38 Idaho L. Rev. 325

Ecojustice Legal Defence Fund, "Species at Risk" Submission to the Secretariat of the Commission on Environmental Cooperation, online: <http://www.cec.org/citizen/submissions/details/index.cfm?varlan=english&ID=114>.

Stewart Elgie, "The Politics of Extinction: The Birth of Canada's Species at Risk Act" in D. Van Nijnatten & R. Boardman, eds., *Canadian Environmental Law and Policy*, 3rd ed., (Oxford University Press, 2009)

Stewart Elgie, "Statutory Structure and Species Survival: How Constraints on Cabinet Discretion Affect Endangered Species Listing Decisions" (2009) 19 J. Env. L. & Prac.

Environmental Defence Canada, *Next Stop Extinction: A Report Card on the Failure of Canadian Governments to Save Endangered Species* (2004), online: <http://www.environmentaldefence.ca/reports/Endangered%20Species_Final_ebook.pdf>. Reprinted by permission of Environmental Defence Canada and Aaron Freeman, Policy and Campaigns Director, Environmental Defence Canada.

A. Hagen & K. E. Hodges, "Resolving Critical Habitat Designation Failures: Reconciling Law, Policy and Biology" (2006) 20 Conservation Biology 399–407. Copyright © 2006, Society for Conservation Biology. Reproduced with permission of Blackwell Publishing Ltd.

J. Kunich, "Preserving the Womb of the Unknown Species with Hotspots Legislation" (2001) 52 Hastings L.J. 1149. © 2001 by University of California, Hastings College of the Law. Reprinted from Hastings Law Journal, Volume 52, Number 6, 2001, by permission.

A. Mooers, et al., "Biases in Legal Listing under Canadian Endangered Species Legislation" (2007) 21 Conservation Biology 572–576

Brenda Heelan Powell, "A Comment by the Environmental Law Centre on the Use of Compensation Under the Proposed *Species at Risk Act*" (2000) 10 J. Env. L. & Prac. 283

H. Ian Rounthwaite, "A Theory of Compensation Under the *Species at Risk Act* Bill C-5" (2000) 10 J. Env. L. & Prac. 259

Kate Smallwood, *A Guide to Canada's Species at Risk Act* (Vancouver, Sierra Legal Defence Fund: 2003)

A. Dan Tarlock, "Biodiversity Federalism" (1995) 54 Md. L. Rev. 1315

P. Wood & L. Flahr, "Taking Endangered Species Seriously? British Columbia's Species-at-Risk Policies" (2004) 30 Canadian Public Policy 382

10

CLIMATE CHANGE

Introduction

Climate change is widely regarded as the pre-eminent challenge of the twenty-first century. Jurisdictions around the world are struggling to find ways to meet this challenge. As a result, here in Canada, many of the themes we have addressed in the preceding chapters are being revisited and debated afresh in the context of climate change. These themes include:

- The implications of ratifying the Kyoto Protocol for domestic law and policy;
- Jurisdictional issues, particularly the respective roles and powers of our federal and provincial governments in tackling climate change impacts;
- Regulatory alternatives for responding to climate, change including the role of existing legislation (and related opportunities for conservation and other organizations to leverage action through judicial review), as well as growing interest in relative merits of new regulatory models including carbon taxes and cap and trade systems;
- The role of the tort system in preventing future harms associated with climate change, and in compensating adversely affected interests; and
- The implications of climate change for Indigenous communities and endangered species, and strategies for responding to these implications.

As a means synthesizing and integrating these and other themes we have covered and as a vehicle to ruminate on some important and timely questions of law and policy reform, in this concluding chapter we chose to explore what climate change may mean for Canadian environmental law and policy in the years ahead.

Part I considers the evolution and current status of climate change as a policy issue in Canada, reflecting on how the issue has emerged to become the overarching challenge of our time. Part II explores the nature of our commitments under the Kyoto Protocol, as well as domestic implementation issues. Among other things, it considers a recent federal court decision, in a case that alleged the Harper government had violated the *Kyoto Protocol Implementation Act*, S.C. 2007, c. 30. Part III considers regulatory alternatives for responding to climate change, chronicling current and emerging policy initiatives at the federal and provincial levels and the debate over the relative merits of carbon taxes versus cap and trade systems. In Part IV, we consider the implications of the foregoing for the constitutional division of powers. In Part V, we consider the current and emerging role of tort litigation as a response to the impacts of climate change. In Part VI, we offer some reflections on the interplay between climate change and environmental assessment with particular attention to the *Canadian Environmental Assessment Act* (CEAA). Part VII explores the challenges posed by climate change for endangered species protection, revisiting some of the key features of the *Canadian Species at Risk Act* (SARA) and its US counterpart the *Endangered Species Act* (ESA). Finally, in Part VIII, we consider the legal implications of, and strategies for responding to climate change impacts on Indigenous Peoples.

Part I — The Emergence of Climate Change as a Canadian Policy Priority

Steven Bernstein, Jutta Brunnée, David G. Duff & Andrew J. Green, "Introduction" in Bernstein et al., eds., A Globally Integrated Climate Policy for Canada

(Toronto: University of Toronto Press, 2007)

Canada and Climate Policy — Looking Back

In order to understand the policy options for Canada going forward, it is important to know not only where we currently stand on climate issues but also how we got to the present policy juncture. Canada was initially a significant international presence in creating the climate change regime, contributing early on to diplomacy and science. Not only has it recently backed away from this stance, it has also failed — throughout its involvement in global policy making — to back up its international position with effective domestic policies.

Hot and Cold: Canada and the Global Regime

The Canadian government and individual Canadians, especially from the early 1970s to early 1990s, were at the forefront of global environmental concerns and of sustainable development thinking. Government scientists or senior bureaucrats have led transnational or intergovernmental environmental organizations and activities, including the United Nations Environment Programme (Maurice Strong and later Elizabeth Dowdeswell), the World Climate Research Program (Gordon McBean), and the OECD Environment Directorate (Jim MacNeill), and such leadership had been encouraged within the bureaucracy. Canadians have also led major agenda-setting conferences and exercises. Notable examples include Maurice Strong, who was secretary-general of both the 1972 UN Conference on the Human Environment in Stockholm and the 1992 UN Conference on Environment and Development in Rio de Janeiro, and Jim MacNeill, who was secretary-general of the World Commission on Environment and Development. MacNeill worked closely with the chair (Gro Harlem Brundtland) and commissioners (including Strong) to produce the Brundtland Report, known for developing and popularizing the concept of sustainable development. [...]

Canada's framing of climate policy and sustainable development — that action to combat climate change must simultaneously enhance competitiveness, promote economic growth, and facilitate innovation — also found resonance in the final outcome of the UNFCCC negotiations. Among the core principles of the UNFCCC is the recognition of 'the need to maintain strong and sustainable economic growth' (Article 4.2).

Despite this early leadership, after 1992 domestic political factors conspired to make Canada a laggard internationally and in its domestic policy response. These factors included internal divisions within the federal Cabinet and between the federal government and provinces, a lack of attention from the prime minister, and resistance from powerful actors in the energy sector and industry more broadly.

As momentum gathered to negotiate a protocol with legally binding commitments, Prime Minister Jean Chretien, previously unengaged in the issue, forcefully intervened, leading to an abrupt policy change on the eve of the Kyoto meeting. While the reasons for the abrupt shift are a matter of some debate, concerns about Canada's international reputation and direct pressure from Canada's allies — including at the Denver G8 Summit in June 1997 and subsequent pressure from EU and American leaders — played a role. In November, Chretien overrode a decision of federal and provincial ministers of environment and energy to merely stabilize emissions at 1990 levels by 2010, and called initially for a three per cent reduction by 2010. Then, in Kyoto, Canada committed to a six per cent reduction of greenhouse gas (GHG) emissions below 1990 levels, one percentage point less than the U.S. commitment at the time. Canada agreed to this cut despite intensive lobbying from industry opposed to a legally binding agreement and a public campaign run by the Canadian Coal Association, which included advertisements warning of 'economic suicide' if Canada signed a deal in Kyoto.

In its public statements, the government played up Canada's position between the United States and the EU and its desire to 'help find common ground in Kyoto.' This stance reflected an attempt to reinvigorate Canada's role as a facilitator of global agreement and compromise. It has obvious parallels to the diplomatic position now asserted by Prime Minister Stephen Harper.

Following the negotiation of the Kyoto Protocol, the Chretien government maintained its firm commitment to the agreement. Further negotiations ensued to flesh out the elements of the Kyoto deal, so as to enable states to decide whether to ratify or not. Canada was active in these negotiations and signalled its intention to implement the protocol, despite the U.S. withdrawal and the concerns that this raised about Canadian competitiveness. During this period, notwithstanding ongoing opposition from a number of domestic interests, Canadian public opinion remained generally supportive of ratification.

The path toward ratification in 2002 has remarkable parallels to the run-up to Canada's commitment to emissions reductions in 1997 and the signing of Kyoto. Again, Canadian domestic policy proved woefully inadequate to shift business-as-usual emission trajectories, undercutting Canada's foreign climate policy leverage as it sought to increase its elbow room in meeting the Kyoto commitments. The government had to bargain hard to gain traction on issues such as maximizing allowable activities under the protocol's two 'carbon sink' articles, initially without having the requisite research or diplomatic leverage to convince other parties about the carbon-storage potential of land use, land use change, and forestry activities.

As it turned out, the U.S. withdrawal from Kyoto served to increase Canadian leverage. Now Canada and virtually all of its major negotiating partners in the 'Umbrella Group,' but Japan and Russia in particular, needed to ratify for the protocol to account for 55 per cent of industrialized country emissions, which Kyoto required in order to come into force. Canada thus got its way on forest sinks. Although it did not succeed in getting credits for natural gas exports to the United States, even that proposal received a more serious hearing than it previously had.

As in 1997, however, progress internationally was not matched by significant policy consensus or policy development at home. Thus, when Chretien surprised nearly everyone and signalled at the 2002 World Summit on Sustainable Development that Canada would ratify Kyoto, an even more hotly contested domestic debate erupted than in 1997. An implementation plan that showed signs of haste and lacked specifics was then put forward with strong opposition from the provinces. After Chretien made it clear that the federal plan would prevail despite provincial concerns, 'negotiations between the provinces and the federal government ground to a halt, effectively terminating the joint National Climate Change Process that the federal government had entered into with the provinces after Kyoto.

After the protocol entered into force, Canada again found itself an outlier in negotiations, with its reputation suffering owing to its poor domestic record. For a brief moment it looked as if the tide had turned in both Canadian diplomacy and domestic climate policy. At the first Meeting of the Parties (MOP 1) of the Kyoto Protocol in Montreal in 2005, then environment minister Stéphane Dion, acting as president of the conference, helped move discussions forward on a number of contentious issues, including a process to consider future commitments post-2012. Shortly thereafter, however, the defeat of the Paul Martin government and the new Conservative government's decision to shift to a 'made in Canada' climate policy brought yet another policy reversal. It also put then environment minister Rona Ambrose in the unenviable position of being the chair of the UNFCCC Conference of the Parties in 2006, while representing a government that had made clear it had no intention of adhering to its Kyoto commitments or participating in its international mechanisms.

[...] Canadian climate policy appears to have come full circle. The Canadian government is again portraying itself as a potential broker between the EU and U.S. positions on climate change. However, [...] there are some significant differences. Canada is still without a clear vision of how to reconcile contradictory trends in both its foreign and domestic climate policies and, arguably, without much credibility in this role. But it has also taken the unprecedented step of declaring itself not only unable but also unwilling to meet its commitment under the Kyoto Protocol, while simultaneously refusing to withdraw from the treaty.

The Policy Gap: The Lack of Domestic Action

Despite its initial international support for climate change action, the Canadian government has done little domestically to reduce greenhouse gas emissions. Again, it is worth taking a closer look at the policy trajectory. Prior to the Kyoto negotiations, the federal government emphasized mostly information and education programs along with voluntary measures such as a Voluntary Challenge Registry (VCR) for industries. These programs had little apparent effect on emissions, which continued to rise. Immediately following the Kyoto negotiations, the Chretien government launched a National Climate Change Process, a consultation process conducted in conjunction with provinces. As this process was not reaching consensus, the federal government released another plan, again relying on voluntary action and subsidies.

In 2002, following Chretien's decision to ratify the Kyoto Protocol, it announced another plan — the Climate Change Plan for Canada. This plan also relied heavily on voluntary programs, particularly with industry, as well as subsidies. There was very little in the way of actual regulation, no emission limits, and no taxes. There were minor allowances for the purchase of international credits. Importantly, the government also committed to capping abatement costs that industry would have to pay at $15 per tonne.

The next major policy move came from the government of Prime Minister Martin and his environment minister, Stéphane Dion. In 2005, the government proposed Project Green, which relied more heavily on spending, especially internationally. For large emitters, this plan proposed a cap-and-trade system, though it also reduced the share of the emissions reduction burden that these emitters would have to bear and provided that emissions limits could be satisfied by payments to a Technology Investment Fund. To help reach Canada's Kyoto target, Project Green also included a Carbon Fund to finance the purchase of emission credits domestically and internationally. There was also funding of 'partnership' projects with the provinces and territories aimed at reducing emissions. Finally, Project Green contained a number of voluntary measures such as an agreement with the automobile industry to improve fuel efficiency and the One Tonne Challenge encouraging individuals to reduce emissions in their everyday lives.

Project Green was never implemented. The Harper government, which came into power in early 2006, backed away from international purchases of emission credits, declared that Canada could not meet its Kyoto targets, and proposed a 'made in Canada' solution premised on the view that any regulation of greenhouse gases needed to be attentive to the economic and social realities in Canada. The government also clearly stated that it would not introduce a carbon tax. There was continued spending, such as on a tax credit for transit users, as well as continued reliance, at least in the short term, on voluntary agreements (including with the auto sector). On the regulatory side, the government cancelled the cap-and-trade system for large final emitters, instead proposing intensity targets for industry, energy efficiency standards for some products, and future fuel efficiency standards for automobiles. This plan has been criticized on a number of fronts, including that 'the Conservatives' policies for large final emitters tracked previous Liberal efforts, complete with provisions that might more accurately be described as loopholes.' [...]

The Need for Action

The recent award of the Nobel Peace Prize to the Intergovernmental Panel on Climate Change (IPCC) is only the latest signal that the scientific debate has entered a new phase, in which political discussion begins by asking how, not whether, to respond to the threat of global climate change. The latest IPCC series of reports (its fourth since being created in 1988) concluded that '[w]arming of the climate system is unequivocal, as is now evident from observations of increases in global average air and ocean temperatures, widespread melting of snow and ice, and rising global average sea level.' Moreover, the rate of increase of greenhouse gases (GHGs) in the industrial era is unprecedented in more than 10,000 years, and is 'very likely' (i.e., greater than 90 per cent certainty) the result of human activity, mostly the burning of fossil fuels.

Natural systems throughout the world are already being affected by climate change. By 2100, scientists expect increases in average surface temperatures of approximately 1.1 to 6.4°C, resulting in rising sea levels, increases in heat waves and hot days, more severe storms, and increases in areas affected by drought, among other changes to the earth's climate. Recent data suggests that the developments since the completion of the IPCC report have outpaced even its worst-case scenarios, and that dramatic changes may be underway. In particular, the global climate may be changing at a faster rate than expected, with already manifest effects, because of numerous feedback effects. For example, increasing temperatures have accelerated the melting of the arctic ice cap, leaving more of the Arctic Ocean exposed. As water absorbs more of the sun's radiation than ice, the water warms up, which, in turn, melts the ice even faster. According to the IPCC, these projected changes pose significant consequences for human health, conflict, food security, and movements of displaced populations.

Many experts and some political actors assert that, to avert dangerous climate change, global temperature increases should not exceed 2°C above pre-industrial levels. While it remains contested what constitutes 'dangerous' or 'tolerable' climate change, there is growing consensus that a stabilization target of a 2°C increase would require a 60–80 per cent cut in emissions from industrialized countries by mid-century, with a similar abatement path for developing countries in later years. Emissions must peak somewhere between 2010 and 2020 to achieve this trajectory. [...]

Canadian Policy Options and Obstacles

Quite obviously, in devising a globally integrated policy, policy choices must take into account not only the desirability of participation in a global regime, but also domestic policy options and attendant constraints. That is why we emphasize the need for a globally integrated climate policy for Canada. Thus, having canvassed the broad parameters that militate in favour of a globally integrated climate policy, we now consider what such an approach would mean in terms of policy choices for Canada, and what the constraints are on such choices.

Given that greenhouse gas emissions are a form of large-scale externality (where those who reap the benefits of an activity do not bear all of the costs), there are a range of potential policy measures that national or sub-national governments might adopt in order to reduce emissions, including the following:

- Fostering voluntary action by individuals or industry such as through agreements or challenges, hoping that underlying norms or self-interest will provide the impetus for reductions in greenhouse gas emissions;
- providing information or education to either activate a latent concern by Canadians about the environment (if such a concern exists) or develop new norms or values around the environment;
- using subsidies to encourage environmentally friendly activity;
- introducing taxes which discourage greenhouse gas emissions, either on specific activities or more broadly on the emissions of carbon;
- establishing cap-and-trade or obligation-and-certificate programs, which would allow trading of requirements amongst participants; or
- Prohibiting or regulating activities which emit greenhouse gases (for example, set energy efficiency standards for appliances or emissions standards for vehicles).

Of course, Canada should also devise adaptation policies in conjunction with mitigation measures. Such policies would foster actions that reduce the harms from climate change either in Canada or in other countries, where the consequences of climate change are likely to be worse. [...]

Federalism

The complexity of Canadian federalism in cross-cutting areas such as the environment further complicates the policy process. The Canadian constitution does not assign the power over the environment to either the federal or provincial governments. Canadian courts have been willing to find that the federal government has fairly broad powers to regulate environmental issues. However, there are limits on these federal powers. In particular, most of the powers cannot be used in a manner that infringes unduly on provincial areas of responsibility. The constitution grants the provinces jurisdiction over property and civil rights and non-renewable natural resources, with the result that provinces also have significant powers to regulate in the area of the environment.

The consequence of these potentially overlapping or conflicting powers is that the federal and provincial governments have in the past fought over who has control over environmental policy. Given the high stakes of climate policy, continued conflict seems likely. A key principle of any national strategy from the start had been that 'no region or sector [should be] asked to bear an unreasonable share of the burden.' However, making this work in a federal system has proven very difficult.

Shi-Ling Hsu & Robin Elliot, "Regulating Greenhouse Gases in Canada: Constitutional and Policy Dimensions"
(SSRN http://ssrn.com/abstract=1265365 (posted September 11, 2008))

In a 2007 speech to the Canadian Bar Association, former Alberta Premier Peter Lougheed warned of an impending constitutional crisis over the regulation of greenhouse gases. A "major constitutional battle" was brewing between the federal government, which faces increasing international and domestic pressure to regulate the emissions of greenhouse gases, and the government of Alberta, where high greenhouse emissions are produced by oil and gas development, a jealously-guarded provincial prerogative. "Public pressure", in Lougheed's view, "is likely to force the passage of strong [federal] environmental legislation", while the economic forces driving oil sands development will likely lead to resistance from Alberta in the form of conflicting legislation.

Is there really a constitutional storm on the horizon? Lougheed's most memorable political legacy is his constitutional quarrel with Prime Minister Pierre Trudeau over the National Energy Program, during which Lougheed challenged the federal government's authority to tax oil and gas production. This experience may be colouring Lougheed's view. Although there is tension between federal and provincial authority over the regulation of Canadian greenhouse gases, this tension need not be, and should not be, an obstacle to sensible greenhouse gas regulation. [...]

Canada's greenhouse gas emissions have risen sharply since 1990, the baseline year from which the commitments under the Kyoto Protocol are derived, from 596 Mt in CO2-equivalents to 747 Mt in 2005, the steepest rise of the G8 countries over this time period. It is now impractical for Canada to comply with its Kyoto commitment to lower its emissions to 563 Mt. Increases have been across almost all sectors — emissions from electricity generation, transportation, petroleum production, mining, agriculture, waste, and fugitive releases from natural gas production all increased between 1990 and 2005. Only greenhouse gas emissions from industrial processes declined slightly over that time period. It no longer makes sense for Canada to unilaterally and immediately cease the upward momentum of emissions and begin an emissions reduction of more than 25% over the next four years.

The general problem of greenhouse gas regulation pits Alberta against the rest of Canada. Alberta emits nearly one-third of Canada's greenhouse gases, and its emissions have increased the most sharply of all the provinces, from approximately 173 Mt CO2-eq to 235 due mainly to its oil sands development. Although certain promising greenhouse gas control technologies are on the horizon, Alberta's juggernaut oil sands development will make it difficult for Alberta to contain its greenhouse gas emissions. Politically, this cleave superficially appears either to preclude federal greenhouse gas emissions regulation, or to require a re-enactment of the federal-provincial showdown that marred Canada's first attempt at an energy plan ...

Notes and Questions

1. Does federalism tend, by its nature, to undermine preclude effective, coordinated responses to climate change? In this sense, is climate change any different than other policy areas we have considered (e.g. endangered species protection)?

2. To what extent are the difficulties we seem to be facing in developing an effective, coordinated response to climate change due to features unique to Canada?

Part II — Climate Change, International Law and Domestic Implementation

The UN Framework Convention on Climate Change (UNFCCC) has its roots in UNCED in Rio de Janeiro and has operated since 1994 in coordination with the Intergovernmental Panel on Climate Change (IPCC) to make up the international climate change regime. The IPCC provides the scientific basis for international negations, with major reports issued to inform each of the major steps in the development of the international regime under the UNFCCC. The UNFCCC in turn has provided the context for more substantive negotiations on how to mitigate the effects of human induced climate change and how to adapt to the impacts that cannot be mitigated.

The Kyoto Protocol was the first substantive product of negotiations under the UNFCCC. The Protocol was negotiated in 1997 and came into force in 2005. It requires developed states to reduce their emissions for the commitment period from 2008–2012. Emission reduction targets were negotiated on a state by state basis, and range from 8% below to 11% above 1990 levels of emissions. The targets in the Kyoto Protocol can be met through a combination of domestic action and reliance on a number of mechanisms. These mechanisms are available to developed nations to supplement domestic action with reductions achieved outside their own jurisdictions: the Clean Development Mechanism (CDM), Joint Implementation, and Emissions Trading. The following article explores the implications of these three Kyoto Mechanisms for climate change mitigation in Canada.

Meinhard Doelle, "Global Carbon Trading and Climate-Change Mitigation in Canada: Options for the use of the Kyoto Mechanisms" in Bernstein et al., eds., A Globally Integrated Climate Policy for Canada
(Toronto: University of Toronto Press, 2007)

Global Carbon Trading and the Kyoto Mechanisms

The Kyoto mechanisms, consisting of emissions trading (ET), the clean development mechanism (CDM), and joint implementation (JI), use the cap-and-trade system and create emission reduction credits. The emissions trading system under Kyoto is essentially a cap-and-trade system. The CDM generates credits for emission reductions below the business-as-usual baseline in developing nations, without imposing any obligation on developing countries to reduce emissions. JI is a hybrid between the two. These three Kyoto mechanisms, and the role they play in the international climate-change regime, are reviewed in this section.

Emissions Trading (ET)

The emissions trading system under the Kyoto Protocol uses emissions reduction targets for developed countries as the basis for a cap-and-trade system. These targets are implemented through an allocation of allowed emissions for the first commitment period called assigned amount units (AAUs). The emissions trading system establishes rules for trading these AAUs as well as the trading of credits generated from the other two mechanisms. ET sets the rules for trading units that are created through developed-country targets, and those accredited through the CDM and JI, thereby introducing a trading system that allows developed countries to buy and sell permission to emit greenhouse gases during a given commitment period.

Kyoto allows more-or-less unrestricted trading of AAUs and credits from CDM and JI projects, with a few largely symbolic measures to address competing concerns about compliance, liability, and the environmental integrity of the trading system. Parties are free to trade credits generated from the use of the other two mechanisms in addition to being able to trade AAUs. Trading can take place between parties or private entities. There is a limit imposed on 'banking' credits, in other words, saving credits for future commitment periods. Banking has become particularly important because a significant surplus of AAUs is expected to be available for the first commitment period, from 2008 to 2012. This is due to two factors: the sharp reduction in emissions in former Soviet Union states resulting from the collapse of their economies in the early 1990s, and the absence of the United States as a major buyer. Without banking, the price of carbon globally would likely collapse for the first commitment period.

The Clean Development Mechanism (CDM)

The CDM was a relatively late addition to the Kyoto Protocol. Its objective is twofold. It is designed to give developed nations a release valve if domestic action becomes too expensive. At the same time, the CDM can provide developing countries with much-needed development assistance in the form of technology transfer and economic activity that can help to place them on a low-emissions development path. In the process, CDM will engage developing countries in climate-change mitigation without imposing emissions reduction targets. The CDM is currently the only mechanism available under Kyoto to encourage investment in mitigation efforts in developing nations. Support for the CDM has the potential to be an effective way to engage developing nations in mitigation in a manner consistent with the principle of common but differentiated responsibilities.

The CDM reflects the view that if reductions can be achieved more cost-effectively in a developing nation without a reduction target, that country should be able to join forces with a developed nation to achieve the latter's reduction target. The reductions count toward the target of the developed country in return for providing the financial and technical assistance needed to effect reductions in the developing country that otherwise would not be achieved.

Joint Implementation (JI)

JI combines elements from ET and the CDM and is directed mainly at economies in transition. It consists of two tracks. One resembles ET, and the other is project-based and is based on the CDM. The two tracks resulted from a concern among developed nations interested in JI activities that some of the states with economies in transition would have capacity problems in implementing the eligibility requirements (e.g. monitoring and reporting requirements) for emissions trading. This resulted in one JI track that required these eligibility requirements to be met, and another track that can operate without them. The main difference between the two tracks therefore relates to the establishment of the baseline and verification of the additionality of emissions reduction units to be issued to the funding party. For track one, the emissions trading track, it is up to the host country to ensure the credits sold are in line with the reductions achieved from the project. Track two is available where the host country has not met monitoring and reporting eligibility requirements (such as annual emissions reporting), and is therefore treated more like a developing nation without an emissions reduction target.

It is too early to make accurate predictions about the amount of CDM and JI credits likely to be available for the first commitment period. JI, however, is expected to make only a relatively modest contribution to the carbon market.

Choice of Carbon Credits for Kyoto Compliance

The Kyoto mechanisms offer Canada a range of compliance alternatives to domestic action. Canada's emissions are more than 30 per cent above its Kyoto target, with the start of the commitment period only months away, and only five years left to reduce domestic emissions to comply. [*Ed note*: As of January 2009, Canada remains 30 per cent above its Kyoto target.] To achieve compliance under these circumstances, some reliance on carbon credits from the Kyoto mechanisms seems inevitable. In this section, the choice of available international credits is considered from a Canadian perspective, based on the previously stated assumption that Canada's policy goal is to meet its Kyoto commitments. The implications of choosing among AAUs, CDM credits, and JI credits are identified, as well as the implications of choices within each category of credits. Factors taken into account include the likely cost of the credits, the contribution the purchase will make to GHG emission reductions, and the impact on low-emissions sustainable development in Canada as well as globally.

The first category considered is AAUs. As they reflect the limited allowance of emissions in developed countries, one might expect that the purchase of these credits would reflect actual emission reductions beyond what was required under Kyoto in another developed nation. [...] The bottom line for AAUs is that they are a source of credible carbon credits, subject to whether the credits are available as a result of emissions reduction efforts or through unrelated circumstances. The significance of these issues for a potential buyer will depend to some extent on whether one takes a short- or long-term view of carbon trading under the international climate-change regime. If trading is to be an important part of the regime over the long term, a key feature of the Kyoto trading system is the ability to bank credits. Banking refers to the ability to hold units eligible for compliance within the first commitment period for use in a future commitment period. Given the unrestricted ability to bank excess assigned-amount credits, it is reasonable to take the position that the quality of credits purchased is immaterial, as the elimination of any credit will force additional action by the seller in the future, regardless of how the selling state acquired the credit. Such an approach would favour the purchase of the lowest-cost credits available.

An alternative view would be to focus on supporting the most meaningful emission reductions through the purchase of AAUs. This perspective would lead to an assessment of which developed countries have made the most effective efforts to move toward a low-emissions development path. Such credits are likely to be more expensive and limited. [...]

Similar issues arise with respect to credits generated through JI. The emissions trading track of JI would essentially allow parties that have excess emission credits, whether from a generous assigned-amount allocation, general emissions reduction efforts, or from specific projects, to sell those credits. JI credits from business as usual will tend to demand the lowest price. Emissions reduction credits more clearly linked to projects that are assisting economies in transition to choose a low-emissions development path will likely demand a higher price.

With respect to the CDM, the starting point is that it does offer the potential for achieving the dual function of meeting mitigation obligations and assisting developing nations in their sustainable-development efforts. For the CDM, there is a clear distinction between credits generated from a given project and any allocation of credits to developed countries with targets under the Kyoto Protocol. The reason is that CDM projects have to be located in developing party states with no emissions reduction targets and therefore no assigned-amount unit allocation. Nevertheless, there are still potential choices to be made in the purchase of CDM credits. There are considerable differences among CDM projects in terms of technology used, the baseline used to quantify reductions, the basis for establishing additionality, and the contribution the project can be expected to make to a low-emissions development path in the host nation. [...]

Canada will have to choose whether, to what extent, and how to make use of international carbon credits for compliance with the Kyoto Protocol. Given Canada's record to date on domestic emissions reductions, and the short time left to make reductions at home, it seems clear that some reliance on international credits will be required for compliance with the first commitment period. Looking at the three basic options and the range of credits available within each, one policy decision to be made is whether to purchase the lowest-cost credits available, or whether to make purchasing decisions based on which credits were generated with long-term solutions to climate change in mind. If the latter approach is chosen, criteria for selection of appropriate credits will have to be considered (see section 3 below). Furthermore, Canada will have to decide whether and how to limit access to international carbon credits to ensure some level of domestic action. Finally, Canada will have to decide to what extent it wants to integrate domestic mitigation with international carbon trading over the long term.

[Ed note: A discussion of the future of Kyoto implementation has been omitted.]

Use of the Kyoto Mechanisms Domestically

I now turn to the role of carbon trading in a domestic emissions reduction strategy that is integrated with Canada's international obligations. Three options are briefly reviewed, followed by some recommendations for a coherent domestic policy on the use of the Kyoto mechanisms. The three options are: full integration of international carbon trading with domestic mitigation efforts; no use of international credits; and the controlled use of international credits.

Option One:

Full integration of domestic emissions reduction and international carbon credits would essentially provide any domestic entity responsible for reducing emissions full access to international credits recognized under the Kyoto Protocol to meet its domestic obligations. This would mean unlimited access to credits created under JI and the CDM. It would also mean access to the AAUs of other parties. Access could be through emissions trading systems in other states or regions, such as the trading system established in the EU. It could also take the form of direct purchases of credits from CDM or JI host nations, or nations willing to sell AAUs.

Under this approach there would be no government control over how much of Canada's target is met through domestic action and how much is met through the purchase of international credits. There would similarly be no control over the source of international credits, the choice of mechanisms, or how mechanisms are used. A fully integrated approach would allow the energy sector free access to international credits eligible under the Kyoto Protocol. This, in turn, would allow each energy producer to choose whether to produce energy in a manner consistent with the target, or whether to carry on with business as usual and purchase credits to offset emissions above the emissions limit set per unit of energy produced.

Option Two:

The second option involves the rejection of international credits and a focus on domestic action. If fully implemented, it would eliminate international carbon trading as an option not only for domestic private entities with emissions reduction obligations, but also for the Canadian government. Given the significant uncertainties involved with GHG emissions reductions, this approach inevitably has a significant amount of risk associated with it. With sufficient lead time and planning, this approach can, however, result in an early start to domestic action to effectively move toward a low-emissions development path. The steps necessary to ensure that Canada can meet its first-commitment-period target through meaningful domestic action alone have not been taken.

Due to the absence of meaningful domestic action toward a low-emissions development path to date, the rejection of international credits at this late stage would force Canada to choose between two undesirable options. One would be potentially very expensive domestic action to achieve compliance in the short time left. The other would be to face the consequences of being perhaps the only country to fail to comply with its obligations under the Kyoto Protocol at a time when climate change is increasingly seen as one of the greatest threats to the global community. To do so would place Canada in the uncomfortable position of being subjected to the non-compliance procedure under the Kyoto Protocol. More importantly, perhaps, it would undermine Canada's moral basis for pushing other nations to meet the much tougher future targets needed to avoid the most dangerous consequences of climate change.

Option Three:

The third option involves the controlled use of and access to international carbon credits. Control over access can be approached in many different ways. One approach under this option would be to restrict access to the federal government. The government would determine some time before the final accounting of our emissions and credits for the first commitment period how much of the Kyoto Protocol target will be met through domestic action and would take steps to secure sufficient international credits to make up the difference. An effective way to implement this approach would be in combination with a domestic financial mechanism such as a carbon tax. An alternative might be a domestic emissions reduction target for various sectors and industries in combination with a penalty high enough to allow the federal government to purchase the international credits necessary to make up the gap from a source that meets predetermined criteria.

Another approach would be to allow domestic entities with emissions reduction obligations access to international credits, but to limit this access. One form of control could be to limit the percentage or share of emissions reductions a domestic entity can acquire through the purchase of international credits. Another form of control would be to specify the types of credit that can be purchased. This could involve a choice among AAUs, credits from the CDM, and credits from JI. The control could also be specific within one type of international credit. For example, the federal government could require that CDM credits be from projects involving certain technologies. It could also specify that AAUs from former Soviet Union states are not eligible for compliance with domestic emissions reduction targets.

Conclusion

In the short term, access to international carbon credits will be an essential component of any coherent, globally integrated domestic climate-change mitigation strategy. Given the quantity of international credits available, access to the global carbon market will ensure that Canada meets its international obligations and upholds the integrity of the international regime — the best hope for a global solution to the global climate challenge. The proposed approach will allow Canada to focus on measures needed to get to deep cuts over the long term while upholding the integrity of the international regime at the lowest cost. This approach has the best chance to serving the dual purpose of making progress at home and setting the stage for global action. As serious efforts are made to reduce emissions at home and to place Canada on a low-emissions path to sustainable development, the dominant reason for nevertheless encouraging the use of international credits is that it can be an effective way to assist developing nations in choosing a low-emissions development path in a manner that formally recognizes Canada's contribution to this effort.

As we get to long-term targets in the 70–80 per cent range of reductions below 1990 for developed nations, access to mechanisms could very well become more important than the target. In combination with access to a well-functioning CDM, and possibly other mechanisms to fund reductions in developing states to offset domestic emissions, developed nations could eventually get close to 100 per cent emissions reduction targets. It is quite conceivable that within a decade or two the international debate will shift from what developed-country targets should be, to what combination of domestic reduction and offset through Kyoto mechanism-type carbon trading will lead to 100 per cent offsets in developed nations. In other words, the debate will be about access to carbon trading and generating credits in developing countries more than about overall targets.

Notes and Questions

1. The connection between Canada's international obligations and its domestic action to mitigate climate change has been the subject of considerable debate in Canada. The current federal minority government has taken the position that it will not and cannot be legally required to meet Canada's obligations under the Kyoto Protocol to reduce emissions to 6% below 1990 levels. Opposition parties disagreed and were able to ensure passage of the *Kyoto Protocol Implementation Act* (KPIA), S.C. 2007, c. 30, to force the government to develop and implement a plan to reach Canada's Kyoto targets by the end of 2012. The KPIA sets out legal obligations that purport to bind the federal government, including the preparation of a Climate Change Plan that provides a detailed description of measures to be taken to ensure that Canada meets its Kyoto obligations; a requirement to publish draft regulations setting out proposed GGH emissions reduction targets; and mandatory timetables to implement the foregoing.

2. Following enactment of the KPIA, the federal Minister of Environment tabled a Climate Change Plan indicating that Canada was not intending to meet its Kyoto targets. In response, Friends of the Earth Canada initiated a judicial review applications seeking, among other things, declarations that the federal government was in violation of various provisions of the KPIA. The following are excerpts from the Federal Court's decision rendered in late 2008.

Friends of the Earth v. Canada (Governor in Council)
2008 CarswellNat 3763, 2008 FC 1183

BARNES J:

The Applicant, Friends of the Earth — Les Ami(e)s de la Terre (FOTE), is a Canadian not-for-profit organization with a mission to protect the national and global environment. It has 3,500 Canadian members and is part of an international federation representing 70 countries.

FOTE brings three applications for judicial review before the Court each seeking declaratory and mandatory relief in connection with a succession of alleged breaches of duties said to arise under the *Kyoto Protocol Implementation Act*, 2007, c. 30 (KPIA). All three of the applications are closely related and they were ordered to be heard consecutively by an Order of Justice Anne Mactavish dated April 17, 2008. Because these applications are all based on common material facts and involve interrelated issues of statutory interpretation, it is appropriate to issue a single set of reasons.

In its first application for judicial review (T-1683-07) FOTE alleges that the Minister of the Environment (Minister) failed to comply with the duty imposed upon him under s. 5 of the KPIA to prepare an initial Climate Change Plan that fulfilled Canada's obligations under Article 3.1 of the Kyoto Protocol .... its second application for judicial review (T-2013-07) FOTE alleges that the Governor In Council (GIC) failed to comply with s. 8 and 9 of the KPIA by failing to publish proposed regulations in the Canada Gazette with accompanying statements and by failing to prepare a statement within 120 days setting out the greenhouse gas emission reductions reasonably expected to result from each proposed regulatory change and from other proposed mitigation measures its third application (T-78-08) concerns s. 7 of the KPIA. It alleges that the GIC failed in its duty within 180 days to make, amend or repeal regulations necessary to ensure that Canada meets its obligations under Article 3.1 of the Kyoto Protocol.

FOTE argues that the language of s. 5, 7, 8 and 9 of the KPIA is unambiguous and mandatory. It says that the Respondents have refused to carry out the legal duties imposed upon them by Parliament and they have each thereby acted outside of the rule of law.

The Respondents assert that the statutory duties that are the subject of these applications are not justiciable because they are not properly suited or amenable to judicial review. In particular, the Respondents say that the KPIA creates a system of Parliamentary accountability involving scientific, public policy and legislative choices that the Court cannot and should not assess. In short, they assert that their accountability for their failure to fulfill Canada's Kyoto obligations will be at the ballot box and cannot be in the courtroom.

Legislative History and Background

Following its introduction to Parliament as a private member's bill (Bill C-288), the KPIA became law on June 22, 2007. The KPIA was not supported by the government which had earlier stated that Canada would not comply with the Kyoto Protocol targets. The KPIA thus embodies a legislative policy which is inconsistent with stated government policy. This also explains why the KPIA does not authorize the expenditure of public funds to achieve its objectives. A money bill cannot be introduced to Parliament unless it is presented by the government.

The KPIA imposes a number of responsibilities upon the Minister and upon the GIC. A central element of the legislation requires the Minister to prepare an annual Climate Change Plan which describes "the measures to be taken [by the federal government] to ensure that Canada meets its [Kyoto] obligations". Each Plan must be tabled in Parliament and referred to an appropriate standing Committee. The KPIA also directs the GIC to make, amend or repeal environmental regulations to ensure, as well, that Canada complies with its Kyoto obligations; this provision is tied to others which create additional reporting functions all tied to various timelines for action.

The Minister's initial Climate Change Plan was released on August 21, 2007. The Plan, on its face, acknowledges the responsibilities imposed by the KPIA upon the Minister and the GIC although, at least implicitly, it characterizes some of those responsibilities as discretionary. For instance, in describing the provisions of the KPIA dealing with regulatory change, the Plan states:

> With regard to Sections 6 through 8 of the Act, these call for the Government to regulate compliance with the Kyoto Protocol, but are silent on what types of regulation are expected and which sectors of society should shoulder the burden. The Governor-in-Council has discretion on whether and how best to regulate to meet legislative objectives, in order that the Government may pursue a balanced approach that protects both the environment and the economy. The Government is taking aggressive action to reduce greenhouse gases and will therefore continue to fulfil its proper role in Canada's parliamentary system by regulating where appropriate and in a balanced and responsible manner. In that context, this document elaborates on the Government's existing plan to regulate greenhouse gas emissions and air pollution, *Turning the Corner*.

The Climate Change Plan also makes it very clear that the Government of Canada has no present intention to meet its Kyoto Protocol commitments. The Climate Change Plan does confirm Canada's ratification of the Kyoto Protocol, which requires a reduction of greenhouse gas emissions between 2008 and 2012 to levels below 1990 (base year) levels. The Climate Change Plan indicates that Canada's Kyoto target for emission reduction is 6%

below 1990 levels. In March 2007 Canada declared its base year emissions to be 599 Mt CO_2 equivalent. For Canada to meet its Kyoto reduction targets its average annual greenhouse gas emissions between 2008 and 2012 are thus limited to 563 Mt CO_2 equivalent.

Canada's greenhouse gas emissions have not declined. In fact, they have steadily increased since 1990 including during the period following Canada's ratification of the Kyoto Protocol. According to the Climate Change Plan that growth, if not constrained, is projected to lead to average annual emissions levels between 2008 and 2012 of 825 Mt CO_2 equivalent. Because of Canada's increasing post-Kyoto reliance on fossil fuels, the Climate Change Plan states that Canada would have to achieve an average 33% reduction in emissions each year for five years to meet the promise of 6% below base year levels. The Climate Change Plan also describes the government's position on the challenges it faces in complying with the Kyoto Protocol:

Unfortunately, when cast against a timeframe that requires Canada to begin reducing its greenhouse gas emissions by one-third beginning in January 2008, it is evident that domestic action would have to be buttressed by some international purchase of emission credits. Even allowing for such purchases, the government would need to take further drastic action that would overwhelm the environmental and other benefits of action on climate change that Canadians are seeking. These measures would require placing the equivalent of a tax on energy, impacting both large industrial emitters of greenhouse gases and individual consumers. The Government has examined this scenario and rejected it as a viable policy option. ...

The Government's analysis, broadly endorsed by some of Canada's leading economists, indicates that Canadian Gross Domestic Product (GDP) would decline by more than 6.5% relative to current projections in 2008 as a result of strict adherence to the Kyoto Protocol's emission reduction target for Canada. This would imply a deep recession in 2008, with a one-year net loss of national economic activity in the range of $51 billion relative to 2007 levels. By way of comparison, the most severe recession in the post-World War II period for Canada, as measured by the fall in real GDP, was in 1981-1982. Real GDP fell 4.9% between the second quarter of 1981 and the fourth quarter of 1982.

All provinces and sectors would experience significant declines in economic activity under this scenario, while employment levels would fall by about 1.7% (or 276,000 jobs) between 2007 and 2009. In addition, there would be a reduction of real per capita personal disposable income levels from forecast levels of around 2.5% in 2009 (or about $1,000 per Canadian in today's dollars).

Meeting Canada's Kyoto Protocol target on the timeline proposed in the *Kyoto Protocol Implementation Act* would also have implications for energy prices faced by Canadian consumers. Natural gas prices could potentially more than double in the early years of the 2008-2012 period, while electricity prices could rise by about 50% on average after 2010. Prices for transportation fuels would also inevitably rise by a large margin — roughly 60%.

These statistics demonstrate the immense challenges associated with trying to meet our Kyoto Protocol target following a decade in which our emissions have grown steadily.

The Climate Change Plan sets new emission reduction targets well above Canada's Kyoto commitments based on a series of proposed regulatory changes, new conservation programs, research and development initiatives, incentives and collaborative action. All of these measures are projected to reduce Canada's average annual greenhouse gas emissions between 2008 and 2012 to 755 Mt CO_2 equivalent — a figure that is 34% higher than Canada's Kyoto target for those years.

In accordance with s. 10.1 of the KPIA, the Climate Change Plan was submitted to the National Round Table on the Environment and the Economy (Round Table) for its analysis and advice. As required by that provision the Round Table undertook research and gathered information with respect to the Minister's Climate Change Plan and then it issued a report. The Round Table report examined the likelihood that the Climate Change Plan and accompanying statement would be "reasonably expected" to achieve their stated objectives. The report describes the ongoing KPIA mandate of the Round Table as follows:

> The NRTEE further notes that since it is obligated to carry out this analytical function for 2007 through to 2012, its assessment must necessarily be considered an iterative one. It expects that further information and understanding about the actual versus expected outcomes set out in the government's Plan and Statement will emerge and evolve. As judgements about whether signatories to the Kyoto Protocol have met their obligations are withheld until the conclusion of the protocol's time period, so too must the NRTEE's final judgment and conclusion be cumulative. In short, this is the first word on the subject, not the last. Although the NRTEE believes that the analytical approach it has taken is pragmatic and appropriate, it should not therefore be seen in any way as comprehensive or definitive.

What is clear from the Round Table report is that the Climate Change Plan was found, in a number of instances, to overestimate projected emissions reductions between 2008 and 2012 or to contain projections based on insufficient information. The Round Table report also noted that the mandate to establish the likelihood of emission reductions in a definitive way from the policy measures proposed and from the assumptions used in the Climate Change Plan was "extremely challenging", in part, because of the short timeframe permitted by the KPIA. The Round Table report concludes with the following observation about the emissions gap between Canada's Kyoto obligations and the projections contained within the Climate Change Plan:

> Statements and information contained in the government's Plan indicate that it is not pursuing a policy objective of meeting the Kyoto Protocol emissions reductions targets. The Plan explicitly states that the government will not participate directly in the purchase of Certified Emissions Reductions (CERs), also known as international credits. Therefore, the stated emissions reductions set out in the Plan would not be sufficient for Canada to comply with the Kyoto Protocol as domestic emissions reductions alone are insufficient to achieve its Kyoto obligations. While statements in the Plan are correct — that non-compliance with the Kyoto Protocol can only be judged after the end of the commitment period in 2012 — it is unlikely that the measures and regulations in the Plan will be sufficient to meet Canada's Kyoto obligations.

As can be seen the Round Table report is a fairly robust scientific critique of the Climate Change Plan at least insofar as it challenges many of the government's projected emission reduction outcomes and confirms that the Plan will not achieve Canada's initial Kyoto commitments.

The evidence is uncontradicted that at the point of commencement of FOTE's second and third applications the GIC had not carried out any regulatory action as contemplated by s. 7, 8 and 9 of the KPIA. [...]

The Principles of Statutory Interpretation and Justiciability

The issues raised by these applications concern the interpretation of a number of the provisions of the KPIA to determine whether the responsibilities imposed respectively upon the Minister and the GIC are justiciable. Before examining the specific language of the KPIA relied upon by FOTE, it is helpful to recall some of the general principles of statutory interpretation and justiciability.

Statutory Interpretation

One of the guiding principles of statutory interpretation is that the search for the meaning of specific words or phrases is informed by the context of the entire statutory text. Words should not be construed in isolation from other surrounding language. Wherever possible the exercise is one of looking for internal consistency and harmony of the language used with the ultimate goal of advancing the intention of Parliament. A useful general statement of these points can be found in the following passage from *Ontario (Minister of*

Transport) v. Ryder Truck Rental Canada Ltd. (2000), 47 O.R. (3d) 171, [2000] O.J. No. 297 (Ont. C.A.):

> The modern approach to statutory interpretation calls on the court to interpret a legislative provision in its total context. The court should consider and take into account all relevant and admissible indicators of legislative meaning. The court's interpretation should comply with the legislative text, promote the legislative purpose, reflect the legislature's intent, and produce a reasonable and just meaning. The Supreme Court has repeatedly affirmed this approach to statutory interpretation, most recently in *R. v. Gladue*, [1999] 1 S.C.R. 688 at p. 704, 171 D.L.R. (4th) 385, where Cory and Iacobucci JJ. wrote:
>
> > As this Court has frequently stated, the proper construction of a statutory provision flows from reading the words of the provision in their grammatical and ordinary sense and in their entire context, harmoniously with the scheme of the statute as a whole, the purpose of the statute, and the intention of Parliament. The purpose of the statute and the intention of Parliament, in particular, are to be determined on the basis of intrinsic and admissible extrinsic sources regarding the Act's legislative history and the context of its enactment ...

Justiciability

The parties do not disagree about the principles of justiciability but only in their application in these proceedings. They agree, for instance, that even a largely political question can be judicially reviewed if it "possesses a sufficient legal component to warrant a decision by a court": *see Reference Re Canada Assistance Plan (B.C.)*, [1991] 2 S.C.R. 525 at para. 27, 83 D.L.R. (4th) 297. The disagreement here is whether the questions raised by these applications contain a sufficient legal component to permit judicial review. The problem, of course, is that "few share any precise sense of where the boundary between political and legal questions should be drawn": see Lome M. Sossin, *Boundaries of Judicial Review: The Law of Justiciability in Canada* (Scarborough: Carswell, 1999) at p. 133.

One of the guiding principles of justiciability is that all of the branches of government must be sensitive to the separation of function within Canada's constitutional matrix so as not to inappropriately intrude into the spheres reserved to the other branches ... Generally a court will not involve itself in the review of the actions or decisions of the executive or legislative branches where the subject matter of the dispute is either inappropriate for judicial involvement or where the court lacks the capacity to properly resolved it ...

Appropriateness not only includes both normative and positive elements, but also reflects an appreciation for both the capacities and legitimacy of judicial decision-making. Tom Cromwell (now Mr. Justice Cromwell of the Nova Scotia of Appeal) summarized this approach to justiciability in the following terms:

> The justiciability of a matter refers to its being suitable for determination by a court. Justiciability involves the subject matter of the question, the manner of its presentation and the appropriateness of judicial adjudication in light of these factors. *This appropriateness may be determined according to both institutional and constitutional standards. It includes both the question of the adequacy of judicial machinery for the task as well as the legitimacy of using it.*

While it is helpful to develop the criteria for a determination of justiciability, including factors such as institutional capacity and institutional legitimacy, it is necessary to leave the content of justiciability open ended. We cannot state all the reasons why a matter may be non-justiciable. While justiciability will contain a diverse and shifting set of issues, in the final analysis, all one can assert with confidence is that there will always be, and always should be, a boundary between what courts should and should not decide, and further, that this boundary should correspond to predictable and coherent principles. As Galligan concludes, "Non-justiciability means no more and no less than that a matter is unsuitable for adjudication".

While the courts fulfill an obvious role in the interpretation and enforcement of statutory obligations, Parliament can, within the limits of the constitution, reserve to itself the sole enforcement role: see *Canada (Auditor General) v. Canada (Minister of Energy, Mines and Resources)*, [1989] 2 S.C.R. 49, [1989] S.C.J. No. 80, ¶68 to 70. Such a Parliamentary intent must be derived from an interpretation of the statutory provisions in issue — a task which may be informed, in part, by considering the appropriateness of judicial decision-making in the context of policy choices or conflicting scientific predictions.

Are the Issues Raised by These Applications Justiciable?

The question presented by FOTE's first application is whether, under s. 5 of the KPIA, the Minister is permitted as a matter of law to tender a Climate Change Plan that, on its face, is non-compliant with Canada's Kyoto obligations. In other words, does the KPIA contemplate judicial review in a situation like this where the government declares to Parliament and to Canadians that it will not, for reasons of public policy, meet or attempt to meet the emissions targets established by the Kyoto Protocol.

The question posed by FOTE's second and third applications concerns the right of the Court to involve itself in the regulatory business of the executive branch of government.

Section 5 of the KPIA deals with the Minister's duty to prepare an annual Climate Change Plan. FOTE relies heavily on the opening language of s. 5 which speaks to a Climate Change Plan that ensures that Canada meets its Kyoto obligations. FOTE says quite simply that the Minister's Climate Change Plan does not ensure Kyoto compliance because it expressly acknowledges noncompliance.

FOTE advances much the same argument with respect to s. 7 and 9 of the KPIA. Those provisions similarly impose responsibilities on the GIC and on the Minister to ensure, by various means, that Canada meets its Kyoto obligations. Section 8 of the KPIA requires the GIC to pre-publish for consultation any proposed environmental regulations made pursuant to s. 7 with accompanying efficacy statements. Section 9 is also linked to s. 7 because it requires the Minister to prepare a statement concerning the emission reductions anticipated from any regulation created under s. 7. The justiciability of the s. 8 and 9 obligations is, therefore, dependent upon the authority of the Court to order the GIC to make, amend, or repeal the environmental regulations referenced in s.7.

The justiciability of all of these issues is a matter of statutory interpretation directed at identifying Parliamentary intent: in particular, whether Parliament intended that the statutory duties imposed upon the Minister and upon the GIC by the KPIA be subjected to judicial scrutiny and remediation.

All of the statutory provisions which are the subject of FOTE's applications are linked to one another and, in order to construe any one of them, it is necessary to consider all of them. I have added emphasis to the provisions that are of particular significance to these applications. Sections 5, 6, 7, 8, 9, 10 and 10.1 of the KPIA state the following:

> 5. (1) Within 60 days after this Act comes into force and not later than May 31 of every year thereafter until 2013, the Minister shall prepare a Climate Change Plan that includes
>
> > (a) *a description of the measures to be taken to ensure that Canada meets its obligations under Article 3, paragraph 1, of the Kyoto Protocol*, including measures respecting
> >
> > > (i) regulated emission limits and performance standards,
> > >
> > > (ii) market-based mechanisms such as emissions trading or offsets,
> > >
> > > (iii) spending or fiscal measures or incentives,
> > >
> > > (iii.1) *a just transition for workers affected by greenhouse gas emission reductions*, and

(iv) *cooperative measures or agreements with provinces, territories or other governments*:

(b) for each measure referred to in paragraph (a),

(i) the date on which it will come into effect, and

(ii) the amount of greenhouse gas emission reductions that have resulted or are expected to result for each year up to and including 2012, compared to the levels in the most recently available emission inventory for Canada;

(c) the projected greenhouse gas emission level in Canada for each year from 2008 to 2012, taking into account the measures referred to in paragraph (a), and a comparison of those levels with Canada's obligations under Article 3, paragraph 1, of the Kyoto Protocol;

(d) *an equitable distribution of greenhouse gas emission reduction levels among the sectors of the economy that contribute to greenhouse gas emissions*:

(e) a report describing the implementation of the Climate Change Plan for the previous calendar year, and

(f) a statement indicating whether each measure proposed in the Climate Change Plan for the previous calendar year has been implemented by the date projected in the Plan and, if not, an explanation of the reason why the measure was not implemented and how that failure has been or will be redressed.

(2) Provinces — A Climate Change Plan shall respect provincial jurisdiction and take into account the relative greenhouse gas emission levels of provinces.

(3) Publication — The Minister shall publish

(a) within 2 days after the expiry of each period referred to in subsection (1), a Climate Change Plan in any manner the Minister considers appropriate, with an indication that persons may submit comments about the Plan to the Minister within 30 days of the Plan's publication; and

(b) within 10 days after the expiry of each period referred to in subsection (1), a notice of the publication of the Plan in the Canada Gazette.

(4) Tabling — The Minister shall table each Climate Change Plan in each House of Parliament by the day set out in subsection (1) or on any of the first three days on which that House is sitting after that day.

(5) Committee — A Climate Change Plan that is laid before the House of Commons is deemed to be referred to the standing committee of the House that normally considers matters relating to the environment or to any other committee that that House may designate for the purposes of this section.

6. (1) Regulations — *The Governor in Council may make regulations*

(a) limiting the amount of greenhouse gases that may be released into the environment;

(a.1) within the limits of federal constitutional authority, limiting the amount of greenhouse gases that may be released in each province by applying to each province Article 3, paragraphs 1, 3, 4, 7, 8, and 10 to 12, of the Kyoto Protocol, with any modifications that the circumstances require;

(b) establishing performance standards designed to limit greenhouse gas emissions;

(c) respecting the use or production of any equipment, technology, fuel, vehicle or process in order to limit greenhouse gas emissions;

(d) respecting permits or approvals for the release of any greenhouse gas;

(e) respecting trading in greenhouse gas emission reductions, removals, permits, credits, or other units;

(f) respecting monitoring, inspections, investigations, reporting, enforcement, penalties or other matters to promote compliance with regulations made under this Act;

(g) designating the contravention of a provision or class of provisions of the regulations by a person or class of persons as an offence punishable by indictment or on summary conviction and prescribing, for a person or class of persons, the amount of the fine and imprisonment for the offence; and

(h) respecting any other matter that is necessary to carry out the purposes of this Act.

(2) Measures province considers appropriate — Despite paragraph (1)(a.1), and for greater certainty, each province may take any measure that it considers appropriate to limit greenhouse gas emissions.

7. (1) Obligation to implement Kyoto Protocol — *Within 180 days after this Act comes into force, the Governor in Council shall ensure that Canada fully meets its obligations under Article 3, paragraph 1, of the Kyoto Protocol by making, amending or repealing the necessary regulations under this or any other Act.*

(2) Obligation to maintain implementation of Kyoto Protocol — At all times after the period referred to in subsection (1), the Governor in Council shall ensure that Canada fully meets its obligations under Article 3, paragraph 1, of the Kyoto Protocol by making, amending or repealing the necessary regulations under this or any other Act.

(3) Other governmental measures — *In ensuring that Canada fully meets its obligations under Article 3, paragraph 1, of the Kyoto Protocol, pursuant to subsections (1) and (2), the Governor in Council may take into account any reductions in greenhouse gas emissions that are reasonably expected to result from the implementation of other governmental measures, including spending and federal-provincial agreements.*

8. Consultation for proposed regulations — *At least 60 days before making a regulation under this Act or, with respect to subsections 7(1) and (2), any other Act, the Governor in Council shall publish the proposed regulation in the Canada Gazette for consultation purposes with statements*:

> (a) setting out the greenhouse gas emission reductions that are reasonably expected to result from the regulation for every year it will be in force, up to and including 2012; and
>
> (b) indicating that persons may submit comments to the Minister within 30 days after the publication of the regulation.

9. (1) *Within 120 days after this Act comes into force, the Minister shall prepare a statement setting out the greenhouse gas emission reductions that are reasonably expected to result for each year up to and including 2012 from*

> (a) *each regulation made or to be made to ensure that Canada fully meets its obligations under Article 3, paragraph 1, of the Kyoto Protocol, pursuant to subsections 7(1) and (2)*; and
>
> (b) each measure referred to in subsection 7(3).

(2) Minister — The Minister shall

> (a) publish the statement in the Canada Gazette and in any other manner that the Minister considers appropriate within 10 days of the period set out in subsection (1); and
>
> (b) table the statement in each House of Parliament by the day set out in subsection (1) or on any of the first three days on which that House is sitting after that day. ...

Section 5

If the intent of s. 5 of the Act was to ensure that the Government of Canada strictly complied with Canada's Kyoto obligations, the approach taken was unduly cumbersome. Indeed, a simple and unequivocal statement of such an intent would not have been difficult to draft. Instead s. 5 couples the responsibility of ensuring Kyoto compliance with a series of stated measures some of which are well outside of the proper realm of judicial review. For instance, s. 5(1)(a)(iii.1) requires that a Climate Change Plan provide for a *just transition* for workers affected by greenhouse gas emission reductions and s. 5(1)(d) requires an *equitable distribution* of reduction levels among the sectors of the economy that contribute to greenhouse gas emissions. These are policy-laden considerations which are not the proper subject matter for judicial review. That is so because there are no objective legal criteria which can be applied and no facts to be determined which would allow a Court to decide whether compliance had been achieved: see *Chiasson v. Canada*, 2003 FCA 155 ...

It is not appropriate for the Court to parse the language of s. 5 into justiciable and non-justiciable components, at least, insofar as that language deals with the content of a Climate Change Plan. This provision must be read as a whole and it cannot be judicially enforced on a piecemeal basis. While the failure of the Minister to prepare a Climate Change Plan may well be justiciable, an evaluation of its content is not. Indeed the various obligations under the Act for the Minister and others to prepare, publish and table the required reports, regulations and statements are all coupled with the mandatory term "shall". That word is construed as imperative in a statutory context, and when used it almost always creates a mandatory obligation: see the *Interpretation Act*, R.S.C., 1985, c. I-21, s. 11. So far as I can determine, the word "ensure" found in s. 5 and elsewhere in the KPIA is not commonly used in the context of statutory interpretation to indicate an imperative.

There are other reasons for not construing the words in s. 5 "to ensure that Canada meets its [Kyoto] obligations" as creating justiciable duties. The Act contemplates an ongoing process of review and adjustment within a continuously evolving scientific and political environment. It refers to cooperative initiatives with third parties including provincial authorities and industry. These are not matters that can be completely controlled by the Government of Canada such that it could unilaterally ensure Kyoto compliance within any particular timeframe. The Act also recognizes that the implementation of any given Climate Change Plan may not be fully accomplished in any given year. This is the obvious purpose of ss. 5(1)(f), which allows for a failure to implement any of the required remedial measures for ensuring Kyoto compliance in a given year. Any such failure must be explained by the Minister in the succeeding Climate Change Plan to be tabled in Parliament, but it is implicit in this provision that strict compliance with the Kyoto emission obligations in the context of any particular Climate Change Plan is not required by s. 5.

Furthermore, if the Court is not permitted by the principles of justiciability to examine the substantive merits of a Climate Change Plan that dubiously claimed Kyoto compliance, it would be incongruous for the Court to be able to order the Minister to prepare a compliant Plan where he has deliberately and transparently declined to do so for reasons of public policy.

Section 7

That the words "to ensure" used in s. 5 of the Act reflect only a permissive intent is also indicated by the use of those words in s. 7 of the Act dealing with the authority of the GIC to pass, repeal or amend environmental regulations.

An isolated and strictly literal interpretation of ss. 7(1) would suggest that the GIC had a duty to make all of the regulatory changes required to ensure Kyoto compliance within 180 days of the Act coming into force. Such a construction is, however, incompatible with the practical realities of making such regulatory changes, and is also inconsistent with the language of ss. 7(2) which allows the GIC at any time after the passage of the Act to make further regulatory changes to also "ensure" that Canada meets its Kyoto obligations. These two provisions are difficult to fully reconcile but the apparent intent is to allow for an ongoing process to regulate Kyoto compliance, with the initial 180-day timeframe being merely directory or suggestive. I note, as well, that s. 6 of Act says only that the GIC "may" make regulations. That language is clearly not mandatory. This, I think, was the basis for the admonition by Lord Browne-Wilkinson in *R. v. Secretary of State for the Home Department*, [1995] 2 All E.R. 244 (H.L.), to the effect that without clear statutory language the courts have no role to play to in requiring legislation to be implemented. This, he said, would tread dangerously close to the area over which Parliament enjoys exclusive jurisdiction. The language of ss. 7(1) and ss. 7(2) is sufficiently unclear that I do not think that it was intended to override the clearly permissive meaning of the words "may make regulations" in ss. 6(1) of the Act.

The argument that ss. 7(1) creates a justiciable duty is further weakened by the problem facing the Court for crafting a meaningful remedy. FOTE concedes that the Court cannot dictate what it was that the GIC must have done to regulate compliance with Kyoto. Nevertheless, it argues that the GIC had a residual duty to do something of a regulatory nature within 180 days of the KPIA becoming law. It is undeniable that an attempt by the Court to dictate the content of the proposed regulatory arrangements would be an inappropriate interference with the executive role. The idea that the Court should declare that the GIC had a legal duty to make some sort of regulatory adjustment within 180 days, however insignificant that response might have been, has very little appeal and seems to me to pose an unsatisfactory role for the Court. In *R. v. Secretary of State*, above, Lord Nicholls declined to recognize as justiciable a statutory duty requiring the Secretary of State to appoint a date for the commencement of certain statutory provisions. Lord Nicholls was concerned about the judicial enforcement of a duty that was "substantially empty of content" and where the Minister's substantive decision involved consideration of a "wide range of circumstances".

Given that the Court is in no position to consider or to dictate the substance of the regulatory scheme anticipated by the Act, it seems to me to be highly unlikely that Parliament intended that the 180-day timeframe be mandatory and justiciable. Indeed, I question whether, outside of the constitutional context, the Court has any role to play in controlling or directing the other branches of government in the conduct of their legislative and regulatory functions. This was the view of Justice Barry Strayer in *Alexander Band No. 134 v. Canada (Minister of Indian Affairs and Northern Development)*, [1991] 2 F.C. 3, [1990] F.C.J. No. 1085, where he observed that the enactment of regulations must be seen as primarily the performance of a political duty which is not judicially enforceable ...

Sections 8 and 9

If s. 7 of the KPIA does not create a mandatory duty to regulate, it necessarily follows that all of the regulatory and related duties described in s. 8 and s. 9 of the KPIA are not justiciable if the GIC declines to act. If the government cannot be compelled to regulate, it cannot be required to carry out the ancillary duties of publishing, reporting or consulting on the efficacy of such measures — unless and until there is a proposed KPIA regulatory change.

Parliamentary Accountability

The issue of justiciability must also be assessed in the context of the other mechanisms adopted by the Act for ensuring Kyoto compliance. In this case, the Act creates rather elaborate reporting and review mechanisms within the Parliamentary sphere. On this point I agree with the counsel for the Respondents that, with respect to matters of substantive compliance with Kyoto, the Act clearly contemplates Parliamentary and public accountability. While such a scheme will not always displace an enforcement role for the Court, in the overall context of this case, I think it does. If Parliament had intended to impose a justiciable duty upon the government to comply with Canada's Kyoto commitments, it could easily have said so in clear and simple language. The Act, however, uses somewhat equivocal language substituting "to ensure that" for the usual mandatory term "shall". It then goes on to create an indirect scheme for "ensuring" Kyoto compliance largely through the function of scientific review and reporting to the public and to Parliament. For instance, the annual Climate Change Plan required by s. 5 must be published and subjected to public comment. The Plan must also be tabled in Parliament and referred to the appropriate Parliamentary committee for consideration. Any regulations proposed to be made under the authority of the Act must first be published for public consultation purposes in the Canada Gazette. Section 9 requires that within the first 120 days of the Act becoming law, the Minister must prepare a statement setting out the gas emission reductions that are reasonably expected to result in every year until 2012. That statement must also be published and tabled in Parliament. Both the Climate Change Plan and the Minister's statements are then required to be submitted to the Round Table for external review, advice and comment. The Round Table analysis is required to include consideration of the likelihood that the proposed measures or regulations will achieve the projected emission reductions. This report must also be published by the Minister and tabled in both the House of Commons and Senate, The Commissioner of the Environment and Sustainable Development (Commissioner) is similarly obliged to prepare, publish and table a bi-annual report which analyses Canada's progress in implementing the Climate Change Plans and in meeting its Kyoto obligations.

All of the above measures are directed at ensuring compliance with Canada's substantive Kyoto commitments through public, scientific and political discourse, the subject matter of which is mostly not amenable or suited to judicial scrutiny.

Considering the scope of the review mechanisms established by the Act alongside of the statutory construction issues noted above, the statutory scheme must be interpreted as excluding judicial review over issues of substantive Kyoto compliance including the regulatory function. Parliament has, with the KPIA, created a comprehensive system of public and Parliamentary accountability as a substitute for judicial review. The practical significance of Parliamentary oversight and political accountability should not, however, be underestimated, particularly in the context of a minority government: see *Canada (Auditor General) v. Canada (Minister of Energy, Mines and Resources)*, above, at para, 71.

I find support for this view in the comprehensive justiciability analysis carried out by Justice Richard Mosley in *Canadian Union of Public Employees*. That case involved allegations that the Minister of Health had failed to carry out certain statutory duties imposed by the *Canada Health Act*, R.S.C. 1985, c. C-6 related to provincial compliance with the national healthcare standards. Among other claims for relief, the applicants sought a declaration that the mandated *Canada Health Act* Annual Report was not sufficiently comprehensive in dealing with the issue of provincial compliance. It was also argued that the Minister had disregarded his statutory authority to compel provincial compliance and had thereby exercised his discretion in a way that frustrated the purpose of the legislation. The Minister took the position that his statutory reporting function involved a policy-laden duty owed solely to Parliament; as such it was not justiciable. The Court sided with the Minister for the following reasons;

As stated by Chief Justice Dickson in *Canada (Auditor General) v. Canada (Minister of Energy, Mines & Resources)*, *supra* at pp. 90-91, a determination of whether a matter is justiciable is:

> ... first and foremost, a normative inquiry into the appropriateness as a matter of constitutional judicial policy of the courts deciding a given issue, or instead, deferring to other decision-making institutions of the polity ... There is an array of issues which calls for the exercise of judicial judgment on whether the questions are properly cognizable by the courts. Ultimately, such judgment depends on the appreciation by the judiciary of its own position in the constitutional scheme.

In the view of this member of the judiciary, while this application raises important questions, they are of an inherently political nature and should be addressed in a political forum rather than in the courts.

The Act requires that the annual report tabled by the Minister be laid before each House of Parliament, thus indicating that Parliament's intention in creating this obligation was to provide for review and debate on the content of the reports by Parliament itself. Allegations of informational deficiencies with such reports are, therefore, to be addressed and dealt with by that branch of government, and not, in my view, by the judiciary. It is not for the courts to usurp the role of Parliament in determining the nature and quality of the information it has deemed necessary to conduct its functions. As stated by Justice McLachlin, as she then was, in *New Brunswick Broadcasting Co. v. Nova Scotia (Speaker of the House of Assembly)*, [1993] 1 S.C.R. 319 at p. 389:

> ... Our democratic government consists of several branches: the Crown, as represented by the Governor General and the provincial counterparts of that office; the legislative body; the executive; and the courts. It is fundamental to the working of government as a whole that all these parts play their proper role. It is equally fundamental that no one of them overstep its bounds, that each show proper deference for the legitimate sphere of activity of the other.

The Minister's duty to report to Parliament on an annual basis as to provincial compliance with the Act's criteria and conditions is clear. The determination of what constitutes "all relevant information" for the purpose of the reporting requirement is appropriately determined by the Minister, in consultation with the provinces, and is subject to policy and political concerns, the parameters of which it is not for this Court to determine. The Minister is accountable to Parliament for the scope and accuracy of the information the report contains. I agree with the respondent that the section 23 obligation is one owed to Parliament and not to the applicants or the public at large although requiring production of an annual report will necessarily inform public debate on the subject. Any remedy, therefore, with regards to fulfilling the section 23 obligation lies within Parliament and not with the courts.

Conclusion

I have concluded that the Court has no role to play reviewing the reasonableness of the government's response to Canada's Kyoto commitments within the four corners of the KPIA. While there may be a limited role for the Court in the enforcement of the clearly mandatory elements of the Act such as those requiring the preparation and publication of Climate Change Plans, statements and reports, those are not matters which are at issue in these applications.

Even if I am wrong about the issue of justiciability, I would, as a matter of discretion, still decline to make a mandatory order against the Respondents. Such an order would be so devoid of meaningful content and the nature of any response to it so legally intangible that the exercise would be meaningless in practical terms.

In the result, these applications must be dismissed. I will deal with the issue of costs in writing.

Notes and Questions

1. Do you agree with the Federal Court that the application raises issues that are not justiciable? In Part V of this chapter, we consider another case where justiciability was raised as a defence to a climate change-related lawsuit: see *State of Connecticut v. American Electric Power Company* (2005), 406 F. Supp. 2d 265.

2. Does it matter that the Kyoto Protocol includes three flexibility mechanisms which allow Canada to meet its emission reduction obligations without making domestic emission reductions?

3. The court seems to be influenced by the fact that the legal obligations arose out of a private members bill that was passed by opposition parties in a minority parliament. What relevance do these factors have in determining whether to require the government to comply with the provisions of the KPIA? Is the judgment consistent with the notion of parliamentary sovereignty?

4. What if the government had filed a plan that experts concluded was inadequate to meet Canada's emissions reduction obligations? What if the plan had simply stated that the government intended to purchase credits to make up for any emissions above the target?

5. Do you agree that granting the relief sought would have been meaningless in practical terms?

Part III — Regulatory Options for Responding to Climate Change

Efforts to control GHG emissions in Canada are still very much in their infancy. While all federal and provincial jurisdictions have implemented some measures to try to reduce emissions since Canada signed the UNFCCC in 1992, much of the early effort was voluntary and has proven ineffective at controlling emissions. More serious efforts to grapple with the challenge to control emissions did not get underway until Canada ratified the Kyoto Protocol in 2002. In this Part, we explore two main questions: the extent to which existing regulatory regimes can be harnessed in the fight against climate change; and the relative efficacy of proposed new regimes and policy instruments including carbon taxes and GHG cap and trade systems. In exploring these questions, we consider the landmark 2007 decision of the US Supreme Court in *Massachusetts v. EPA*, in which a coalition of states, local governments and NGOs was successful in securing an order compelling the EPA to regulate GHGs under the federal *Clean Air Act* and an analogous lawsuit filed in Canada. We also provide an overview of the various regulatory initiatives currently underway in various Canadian jurisdictions.

Regulation of GHG as an Air Pollution Issue

Both in Canada and the United States, there has been considerable debate and litigation with respect to the existence and scope of the duty of federal regulators to take steps to combat climate change under federal air quality laws. In 1999, a group of NGOs petitioned the US EPA to regulate GHG as a pollutant under the *Clear Air Act*. When the EPA declined to do so, the petitioners — now joined by various states and local governments — took the matter to court. In 2007, they won a decisive victory in the US Supreme Court.

Massachusetts et al., Petitioners v. Environmental Protection Agency et al.
59 U.S. 497 (2007)

STEVENS J.

Calling global warming "the most pressing environmental challenge of our time", a group of States, local governments, and private organizations, alleged in a petition for certiorari that the Environmental Protection Agency (EPA) has abdicated its responsibility under the *Clean Air Act* to regulate the emissions of four greenhouse gases, including carbon dioxide. Specifically, petitioners asked us to answer two questions concerning the meaning of §202(a)(1) of the Act: whether EPA has the statutory authority to regulate greenhouse gas emissions from new motor vehicles; and if so, whether its stated reasons for refusing to do so are consistent with the statute.

Section 202(a)(1) of the *Clean Air Act* provides:

> The [EPA] Administrator shall by regulation prescribe (and from time to time revise) in accordance with the provisions of this section, standards applicable to the emission of any air pollutant from any class or classes of new motor vehicles or new motor vehicle engines, which in his judgment cause, or contribute to, air pollution which may reasonably be anticipated to endanger public health or welfare.
>
> ...

The Act defines "air pollutant" to include "any air pollution agent or combination of such agents, including any physical, chemical, biological, radioactive ... substance or matter which is emitted into or otherwise enters the ambient air.. "Welfare" is also defined broadly: among other things, it includes "effects on ... weather ... and climate".

When Congress enacted these provisions, the study of climate change was in its infancy. [The court goes on to trace the evolution of scientific knowledge concerning climate change from 1959 to date]

On October 20, 1999, a group of 19 private organizations filed a rulemaking petition asking EPA to regulate "greenhouse gas emissions from new motor vehicles under §202 of the *Clean Air Act*.". Petitioners maintained that 1998 was the "warmest year on record"; that carbon dioxide, methane, nitrous oxide, and hydrofluorocarbons are "heat trapping greenhouse gases"; that greenhouse gas emissions have significantly accelerated climate change; and that the IPCC's 1995 report warned that "carbon dioxide remains the most important contributor to [man-made] forcing of climate change". The petition further alleged that climate change will have serious adverse effects on human health and the environment.

Fifteen months after the petition's submission, EPA requested public comment on "all the issues raised in [the] petition", adding a "particular" request for comments on "any scientific, technical, legal, economic or other aspect of these issues that may be relevant to EPA's consideration of this petition".

On September 8, 2003, EPA entered an order denying the rulemaking petition. The agency gave two reasons for its decision: (1) that contrary to the opinions of its former general counsels, the *Clean Air Act* does not authorize EPA to issue mandatory regulations to address global climate change; and (2) that even if the agency had the authority to set greenhouse gas emission standards, it would be unwise to do so at this time.

Petitioners, now joined by intervenor States and local governments, sought review of EPA's order ...

[*Ed note*: Apart from the next paragraph, the Court's treatment of standing has been deleted.]

In sum — at least according to petitioners' uncontested affidavits — the rise in sea levels associated with global warming has already harmed and will continue to harm Massachusetts.

The risk of catastrophic harm, though remote, is nevertheless real. That risk would be reduced to some extent if petitioners received the relief they seek. We therefore hold that petitioners have standing to challenge the EPA's denial of their rulemaking petition ...

The scope of our review of the merits of the statutory issues is narrow. As we have repeated time and again, an agency has broad discretion to choose how best to marshal its limited resources and personnel to carry out its delegated responsibilities.

On the merits, the first question is whether §202(a)(1) of the *Clean Air Act* authorizes EPA to regulate greenhouse gas emissions from new motor vehicles in the event that it forms a "judgment" that such emissions contribute to climate change. We have little trouble concluding that it does. In relevant part, §202(a)(1) provides that EPA "shall by regulation prescribe ... standards applicable to the emission of any air pollutant from any class or classes of new motor vehicles or new motor vehicle engines, which in [the Administrator's] judgment cause, or contribute to, air pollution which may reasonably be anticipated to endanger public health or welfare.". Because EPA believes that Congress did not intend it to regulate substances that contribute to climate change, the agency maintains that carbon dioxide is not an "air pollutant" within the meaning of the provision.

The statutory text forecloses EPA's reading. The *Clean Air Act*'s sweeping definition of "air pollutant" includes "*any* air pollution agent or combination of such agents, including *any* physical, chemical ... substance or matter which is emitted into or otherwise enters the ambient air. ..." §7602(g) (emphasis added). On its face, the definition embraces all airborne compounds of whatever stripe, and underscores that intent through the repeated use of the word "any". Carbon dioxide, methane, nitrous oxide, and hydrofluorocarbons are without a doubt "physical [and] chemical ... substance [s] which [are] emitted into ... the ambient air". The statute is unambiguous.

The alternative basis for EPA's decision — that even if it does have statutory authority to regulate greenhouse gases, it would be unwise to do so at this time — rests on reasoning divorced from the statutory text. While the statute does condition the exercise of EPA's authority on its formation of a "judgment", that judgment must relate to whether an air pollutant "cause[s], or contribute[s] to, air pollution which may reasonably be anticipated to endanger public health or welfare". Put another way, the use of the word "judgment" is not a roving license to ignore the statutory text. It is but a direction to exercise discretion within defined statutory limits.

EPA has refused to comply with this clear statutory command. Instead, it has offered a laundry list of reasons not to regulate. For example, EPA said that a number of voluntary executive branch programs already provide an effective response to the threat of global warming, that regulating greenhouse gases might impair the President's ability to negotiate with "key developing nations" to reduce emissions, *id.*, at 52931, and that curtailing motor-vehicle emissions would reflect "an inefficient, piecemeal approach to address the climate change issue",

Although we have neither the expertise nor the authority to evaluate these policy judgments, it is evident they have nothing to do with whether greenhouse gas emissions contribute to climate change. Still less do they amount to a reasoned justification for declining to form a scientific judgment.

Nor can EPA avoid its statutory obligation by noting the uncertainty surrounding various features of climate change and concluding that it would therefore be better not to regulate at this time. If the scientific uncertainty is so profound that it precludes EPA from making a reasoned judgment as to whether greenhouse gases contribute to global warming, EPA must say so ...

In short, EPA has offered no reasoned explanation for its refusal to decide whether greenhouse gases cause or contribute to climate change. Its action was therefore "arbitrary, capricious, ... or otherwise not in accordance with law".

Notes and Comments

Earlier we excerpted from the trial decision in a lawsuit brought by the Friends of the Earth (FOTE) to compel the federal government to comply with the *Kyoto Protocol Implementation Act* (KPIA). Prior to commencing this litigation, FOTE had sued the federal government under the *Canadian Environmental Protection Act* (CEPA) to take action on GHG emissions. This lawsuit, in abeyance while the KPIA litigation is before the courts, resembles in some key respects the *Massachusetts v. EPA* case set out above: see Christine Elwell and Grant Boyle, "*Friends of the Earth v. the Minister of Environment*: Does CEPA 166 Require Canada to Meet its Kyoto Commitments?" (2008) 18 JELP 254–277.

The lawsuit alleges that in the face of growing evidence of the impacts of climate change, the federal Minister is violating of section 166 of CEPA by failing to take appropriate remedial action to "prevent, control or correct pollution". The lawsuit claims the obligation under section 166 to take remedial action is triggered where (1) a substance is being released from a source within Canada into the air; (2) that substance creates or may be anticipated to create "air pollution"; and (3) the air pollution "violates, or is likely to violate, an international agreement binding on Canada in relation to the prevention, control or correction of pollution". FOTE contends that greenhouses are an air pollutant and the Kyoto Protocol is an international agreement binding in Canada.

What, in your view, are the strengths and weaknesses of the FOTE's lawsuit? Does *Massachusetts v. EPA* provide support for their claim?

Current Canadian Governmental Regulatory Initiatives and Alternatives

In more recent years, the focus of the regulatory debate with respect to climate change has changed from "whether" to "how". In other words, most Canadian governments are now in the midst of either developing or implementing regulatory responses to climate change. In this setting, lawyers can play an important role, both in assisting policy makers in weighing the pros and cons of various policy options and in designing policy regimes that are effective and consistent with regulatory initiatives in other jurisdictions.

In the next article, Professors Hsu and Elliot canvass recent regulatory activity at the federal and provincial levels as part of a larger article, to which we will return later.

Shi-Ling Hsu & Robin Elliot, "Regulating Greenhouse Gases in Canada: Constitutional and Policy Dimensions"

SSRN http://ssrn.com/abstract=1265365 (posted September 11, 2008)

While the many possibilities for greenhouse gas regulation have been treated extensively elsewhere, a brief review of the potential regulatory instruments would help to frame the discussion in the Canadian context. Only the most frequently discussed types of schemes are included in this brief review, as a comprehensive treatment, which would necessarily involve scores of ideas, is beyond the scope of this article.

Greenhouse gas regulation could take a traditional form of environmental regulation, sometimes referred to as command and control regulation, which typically contemplates some administrative standard that serves as a baseline for pollution control performance. The standard could be fixed, specifying a numerical expression of performance, such as in the regulations governing chlor-alkali plants under the *Canadian Environmental Protection Act*, which provide that "[t]he quantity of mercury that the owner or operator of a plant may release into the ambient air from that plant shall not exceed (a) 5 grams per day per 1,000 kilograms of rated capacity, where the source of the mercury is the ventilation gases exhausted from cell rooms. ..." Alternatively, a standard could be linked to industry practices and contain keywords that hint at how ambitious the polluter must be relative to the industry practice, such as "Best Available Technology Economically Achievable" (BATEA). The distinguishing feature of command-and-control systems is that compliance is a matter of whether an emitter has adopted the right technology or industrial practices, something that is determined administratively.

In a marked break in philosophy with the traditional means of environmental regulation, cap-and-trade programs have gained popularity as a regulatory instrument. Rather than defining compliance in terms of some administratively-set standards, cap-and-trade programs involve the issuance of allowances to emitters that permit them to emit a quantity of pollution. Compliance is thus determined solely by whether the emitter has enough allowances to cover its quantity of emissions. Allowances can be traded, and economic theory predicts that the allowances will flow to their highest and best use — to those emitters for whom emissions reduction would be the most costly. This has the effect of concentrating emissions reductions among those for whom emissions reduction would be cheapest, and thereby minimizing overall industry compliance costs. Additionally, cap-and-trade programs are thought to spur innovation because the imposition of a cost on emissions should induce emitters to undertake a self-interested effort to find ways to reduce emissions. Ideally, the total allowances issued would be fixed, producing a hard "cap", and allowances would be scarce enough to achieve a net decrease in emissions. Cap-and-trade programs in the greenhouse gas context typically involve the issuance of allowances to emit some quantity of carbon or carbon dioxide.

In the wake of concerns about the compliance costs of cap-and-trade programs, a less effective alternative has emerged, one favoured by the last two Canadian federal governments: intensity-based emissions trading. Intensity-based emissions trading involves not hard and fixed caps, but moving caps that seek only to reduce greenhouse gas emissions intensity, and not necessarily the absolute amount of emissions. Under the intensity-based emissions trading programs proposed by Canadian governments, allowances are issued to emitters on the basis of their productive output, so any emitter that becomes more efficient in operations will be given more allowances. Because the cap is dependent upon productive output, and can be ratcheted up by the achievement of productive efficiencies, there is no hard and fixed emissions "cap" per se.

[...] taxes have long been popular among economists for addressing large-scale pollution problems, leading to the idea of a carbon tax surfacing in some policy debates. A carbon tax is a payment based on the actual or anticipated quantity of carbon emissions released into the atmosphere. In practice the tax is levied upon some point of sale involving a carbon-based product that is intended for combustion. The rationales behind ... taxation and cap-and-trade programs are the same: impose a marginal cost on emissions, and those that can most cheaply reduce emissions will do so. The difference between taxation and cap-and-trade programs is that a cap-and-trade program is essentially a quantity instrument, while a taxation program is a price instrument; taxation programs offer a degree of certainty for emitters that the price of emissions will stay at a particular level, while cap-and-trade programs (if not riddled with political sweeteners) ensure a particular level of emissions, but only among those emitters covered by the cap-and-trade program.

[*Ed note*: A portion of the article in which the authors discuss employing the *Canadian Environmental Assessment Act* (CEAA) has been omitted and excerpted below.]

Federal Attempts at Greenhouse Gas Regulation

In 2007, under intense international pressure, Prime Minister Harper finally dragged the Conservative Party into the climate change discussion, announcing an intention to reduce Canada's total emissions of greenhouse gases to 20% below 2006 levels by the year 2020, and by 60% below 2006 levels by 2050. The Conservative Party plan is an intensity-based emissions trading program, covering the most greenhouse gas-emitting industries, including the electricity generation, oil and gas, aluminum, cement, and pulp and paper industries. Large facilities in existence before 2004 will have 2010 reduction targets of 18% below 2006 levels, with 2% further reductions annually. "New facilities" (with a first year of operation after 2003) will be required to achieve intensity reductions of 2% annually after the third year of operation. Oil sands facilities coming online after 2012 must install carbon capture and storage technology. As noted above, with intensity-based emissions trading programs, it is difficult to determine how much emissions reduction will actually take place, because the number of allowances is keyed to productive output. And if there is economic pressure on output (as there clearly will be with a developing industry such as oil sands production), then improvements in productive efficiency will lead to the availability of more emissions allowances, thereby lifting the ceiling on emissions.

Government projections of a 20% decrease from 2006 levels by the year 2020 are hard to evaluate, based as they are on a complicated macroeconomic model, but they do incorporate some assumptions that seem optimistic.

Despite mutual criticism between the Liberal and Conservative parties over greenhouse gas regulation, the current proposal bears an odd resemblance to a plan rolled out in 2005 by then-Prime Minister Paul Martin, in that it is an intensity-based emissions trading program that covered roughly the same set of seven hundred or so "large final emitters", and allowed contribution to a "Greenhouse Gas Technology Fund" to substitute for actually achieving the mandated emissions intensity improvements. If the current plan is, as opposition parties argue, insufficient, the previous 2005 Liberal plan was delusional. The only concrete part of the Liberal plan was the intensity-based emissions trading plan for large final emitters, which was projected to achieve only fifty-five megatons of emissions reduction, a mere one-fifth of the reductions required to comply with Kyoto. The remaining four-fifths of the emissions reductions were projected to occur as a result of a variety of ill-defined spending programs, such as the Greenhouse Gas Technology Fund. To put it bluntly, the Martin Plan consisted of a modest emissions trading plan and a collection of unsupported assertions about the effectiveness of spending money on undefined research projects.

An interesting twist on the Martin plan is worth noting. The emissions trading plan for large final emitters included a "safety valve" provision that guaranteed that the price of an allowance to emit a tonne of carbon dioxide would not exceed fifteen dollars during the 2008-2012 period. This provision came under heavy criticism, especially from environmental organizations, for limiting the amount of incentive that emitters would face to reduce greenhouse gas emissions.

Such safety valves are not new to environmental economics. If the safety valve level is low enough, it sets the price of emissions and essentially creates a carbon tax ...

Provincial Experiences with Greenhouse Gas Regulation

While greenhouse gas policy has been a political football at the federal level, provinces have proceeded as if there were no prospect of federal-provincial conflicts at all. Provinces have largely gone their own disparate ways in developing or not developing their own greenhouse gas policies. In 1999, Alberta convened Climate Change Central (CCC), a climate change policy group composed of government and business interests to develop Alberta's policy response to Kyoto. In 2002, Alberta announced its plan to reduce carbon intensity by fifty percent below 1990 levels by 2020. Again, no actual emissions reduction was required, only an improvement in the rate of greenhouse gas emissions per unit of output. The non-profit Pembina Institute issued an analysis showing that the intensity targets were so lax that it would have allowed a 72% increase in emissions by 2020.

An updated plan was announced in 2007, which called for a new set of intensity targets to be met starting in 2010. The government of Alberta also announced that it would embark upon a program to fund carbon capture and storage, an end-of-pipe technology that captures carbon dioxide as it leaves the smokestack, and pipes it to underground caverns to be stored in perpetuity. Generally sticking with its 2002 plan, Alberta projected that Alberta emissions in 2050 would be 14% lower than in 2005. As did the federal government, the Alberta government more prominently announced that the 2050 emissions reductions would be 50% below business as usual levels, which certainly sounds better. But that compares the emissions reduction with a projected upward trajectory of future emissions growth, essentially congratulating itself for diverging from its current profligacy.

British Columbia and Quebec, which have implemented carbon taxes, have levied a carbon tax at the point of sale, in essence taxing the sale of a fossil fuel in the province. This approach has many administrative advantages, as the wholesale purchase of fossil fuel is an easily trackable transaction, and therefore a convenient enforcement point. In general, carbon taxes are administratively simpler to design and carry out than any emissions trading scheme, particularly an intensity-based scheme.

The Quebec carbon tax applies to the distribution within the province of "gasoline, diesel fuel, heating oil, propane, petroleum coke or coal, but not aviation fuel, marine bunker fuel, hydrocarbons used as raw material by industries that transform hydrocarbon molecules through chemical or petrochemical processes or renewable fuel content ..." The carbon tax is administered by the Regie de l'energie, the provincial energy regulatory agency, which determines the tax rate annually, taking into account "greenhouse gas emission reduction objectives ... and the overall financial investment to be made to meet greenhouse gas emission reduction objectives and to carry out measures arising from any government policy or strategy that is designed to fight [and adapt to] climate change. ..." The actual levy paid by distributors of fossil fuels is determined at the end of the year by dividing the desired amount of "overall financial investment" into a "Green Fund" by the total amount of carbon emissions, and calculating each distributor's share of those emissions, taking into account the carbon content of different fossil fuels. Fossil fuels sold in Quebec are presumed to be intended for consumption in Quebec unless otherwise shown by the distributor. Quebec's carbon tax took effect in November, 2007.

British Columbia announced a carbon tax in February, 2008, which would be levied against the sale of all fossil fuels within the province, at the rate of $10 per tonne of carbon emissions (as measured by the carbon content), starting July 1, 2008. The tax increases by $5 per year to $30 per tonne in 2012. For gasoline, the tax would amount to 2.41 cents per litre in 2008, increasing to 7.24 cents per litre by 2012. Diesel fuel and home heating oil would start at a tax of 2.76 cents per litre and rise to 8.27 cents by 2012. An important political piece of this plan was the stated intention to make the carbon tax revenue neutral, in that revenues from the tax would be returned somehow to B.C. individuals and firms. Forecasted tax revenues seem to allow the Ministry to announce specific cuts in corporate, small business, and personal income tax rates, and lump sum payments. Notably, the lump sum payments and the personal income tax reductions are tilted towards lower-income British Columbians, to address perceptions that consumption-based taxes such as carbon taxes and gasoline taxes are regressive.

In addition, the British Columbia government has introduced a bill providing for a cap-and-trade program that will apply to greenhouse gas emitters within the province. Almost all of the pertinent details have been left to regulations, but this is understandable since the Province has committed to participate in a California-led state-and-province greenhouse gas emissions trading reduction plan, the Western Climate Initiative, the details of which have not been finalized.

Manitoba, which also joined the Western Climate Initiative, announced that it intends to legislate a commitment to meeting its share of Canada's Kyoto targets, a six percent reduction in greenhouse gases below 1990 levels. Unfortunately, Manitoba's plan, "Kyoto and Beyond", seems predicated on some of the same creative accounting employed by the last two federal governments, one that measures emissions reduction in terms of its divergence from a "business as usual" baseline.

Also jumping on board with the Western Climate Initiative are the provinces of Ontario and Quebec, which penned their own bi-provincial memorandum of understanding earlier this year, agreeing to agree on a cap-and-trade scheme between the two provinces. While details are lacking, a joint initiative of the two most populous Canadian provinces is clearly a signal of widespread impatience with federal efforts. Ontario's initiative also defies federal politicians' expectations that greenhouse gas regulation would be a political hot potato in that greenhouse gas-intensive manufacturing region.

Curbing greenhouse gas emissions in Canada will obviously be challenging, as it will be for any industrialized country subject to Kyoto targets. But an overly cynical treatment of the greenhouse gas problem as a political football and the dubious use of "business as usual" baseline calculations are surely not helping matters. This, and the perception that constitutional barriers exist, are unnecessary obstacles to the formation of Canadian greenhouse gas regulation. British Columbia and Quebec have certainly taken a lead in greenhouse gas regulation, but the magnitude of greenhouse gas reductions required of Canada necessitates a federal response, and one that is considerably more serious than any proposed to date.

Notes and Questions

1. What factors, in your view, account for the wide range of approaches Canadian governments have taken to responding to climate change? Over time, would you expect policy convergence or continued policy diversity? What factors will determine which outcome is more likely?

2. In the next article, the authors consider whether a carbon tax or a cap and trade system would be the preferable major economic instrument for the US. In reviewing the article, consider how persuasive you find the arguments made, and how relevant the issues raised are for Canada. Which of the two instruments would you favour for Canada?

. . . . .

Reuven S. Avi-Yonah & David M. Uhlmann, "Combating Global Climate Change: Why a Carbon Tax is a Better Response to Global Warming than Cap and Trade"

(2009) 28 Stan. Envtl. L.J. 3.

Key Features of a Carbon Tax and Cap and Trade

An upstream carbon tax arguably is the most straightforward approach to the global climate change problem. A carbon tax would be imposed on all oil, coal, and natural gas production in the United States, as well as all imports. The tax rate would be based on the marginal cost of carbon dioxide emissions (also referred to as the "social cost of carbon") and would be increased annually to reflect the increase in the harmful effects of carbon dioxide emissions. A carbon tax thereby would provide a price signal that captures what is now an externality, namely the harmful effects of carbon dioxide emissions. Tax credits would be provided for carbon sequestration programs, which eliminate or reduce carbon dioxide emissions (and, in some circumstances, could be used to generate energy). Tax revenues would be used to expand tax credits for development of alternative energy and to address any regressive effects of the carbon tax.

If the carbon tax did not produce the desired reduction in carbon dioxide emissions, the tax would be increased; if the tax "overcorrected" and produced greater than anticipated reductions, it could be decreased. Implementation and enforcement of a carbon tax would occur through existing programs within the Internal Revenue Service and the Energy Department. Moreover, by establishing a carbon tax in advance of any international agreement on global carbon dioxide emissions, the United States would meet its obligation to begin reducing its carbon dioxide emissions and establish much-needed credibility in the ensuing international negotiations.

An upstream cap and trade system would establish a cap on the carbon content of fuels in much the same way that an upstream carbon tax would impose a tax on those fuels. The cap would decline over time to achieve the desired level of carbon dioxide emission reductions. Where a cap and trade system becomes more complicated and, as Part III discusses, potentially unwieldy, is in the setting of baselines for the distribution of allowances and in the monitoring and enforcement of a complex allowance system.

Under an upstream cap and trade system, all producers and importers of fossil fuels would be required to have allowances to "cover" the carbon content of the fuels they produce. The number of those allowances would be limited by the overall "cap" imposed by the system. Allowances could be distributed either for free, through an auction system, or some combination. The leading cap and trade proposal in Congress, the *Lieberman-Warner Climate Security Act of 2008*, would distribute the majority of allowances for free in the early years of the cap and trade system, with increasing percentages distributed by auction in subsequent years. Absent an auction, no revenue would be generated by cap and trade to support the development of alternative energy or carbon sequestration technologies. But, theoretically, market forces would provide a substitute for government subsidies: companies that developed alternative energy and otherwise found ways to limit their carbon dioxide emissions would have "surplus" allowances that they could sell to companies that needed more allowances.

The best example of a cap and trade system on a national level in the United States is the cap and trade program under Title IV of the *Clean Air Act*, which was implemented under the *Clean Air Act* Amendments of 1990 to curtail acid rain. The acid rain program is widely viewed as an overwhelming success, both in terms of the environmental protection it provided and the degree to which change occurred without significant economic dislocation. Because the acid rain problem focused on 111 facilities in the Midwest (the so called "Big Dirties"), however, we do not have experience in the United States — or the rest of the world — with an economy-wide cap and trade system.

In contrast to the limited experience in the U.S. with cap and trade, carbon taxes have been successfully implemented in a growing number of countries. Carbon taxes have been implemented in Quebec and British Columbia as part of Canadian efforts to meet the requirements of the Kyoto Protocol. In addition, Denmark, Finland, Italy, the Netherlands, Norway, and Sweden have introduced carbon taxes in combination with energy taxes. The existing carbon taxes are too new to draw meaningful conclusions about their long-term benefits, but many economists believe that a carbon tax would be the most effective method of reducing carbon dioxide emissions. Cap and trade systems for carbon dioxide emissions have been implemented by the European Union and on a regional basis in New England; in addition, seven Western states and four Canadian provinces have taken steps to develop a cap and trade system. As discussed in Part III, the European Union system has not been particularly successful to date, but that has not diminished enthusiasm in the United States and abroad for relying on cap and trade systems as the principal method of reducing carbon dioxide emissions.

The Case for a Carbon Tax

Given the urgency of the global climate change problem, and the increasing acceptance of a cap and trade system as a desirable alternative, the argument could be made that a cap and trade system should be implemented in the United States (and abroad) without further delay. This Part provides a comparison between a carbon tax and a cap and trade system and concludes that a carbon tax is preferable to cap and trade.

Advantages of a Carbon Tax

Simplicity

... A carbon tax is inherently simple: a tax is imposed at X dollars per ton of carbon content on the main sources of carbon dioxide emissions in the economy, namely coal, oil, and natural gas. (Other greenhouse gas sources, such as methane, are not included because energy accounts for nearly eighty-five percent of the 7147 million metric tons of greenhouse gases in the U.S. economy.) The tax is imposed "upstream", *i.e.*, at the point of extraction or importation, which means than it can be imposed on only about 2000 taxpayers (500 coal miners and importers, 750 oil producers and importers, and 750 natural gas producers and importers). Credits can be given to carbon sequestration projects and to other projects that reduce greenhouse gas emissions (although this would need to be addressed in a way that does not dilute the price signal or create undue complexity), and exports are exempted. Beyond that, the main question is what to do with the revenue, which will be discussed below.

Cap and trade, on the other hand, is inherently more complicated. While the cap can also be imposed "upstream", it has several features that require complexity. First, baselines need to be set for purposes of establishing the emissions cap. Second, the proposal needs to determine how allowances will be created and distributed, either for free or by auction. Free distribution requires deciding which industries receive allowances, while an auction requires a complex monitoring system to prevent cheating. Third, the trading in allowances needs to be set up and monitored: a system needs to be devised to prevent the same allowance from being used twice, and penalties need to be established for polluters who exceed their allowances. Fourth, if allowances are to be traded with other countries, the international trading of allowances would need to be monitored as well. Fifth, to prevent Cost Uncertainty, cap and trade proposals typically have complex provisions for banking and borrowing allowances, and some of them provide for safety valves. Sixth, offsets are needed for carbon sequestration and similar projects, and those are more complicated than credits against a carbon tax liability. Finally, most cap and trade proposals involve provisions for coordinating with the cap and trade policies of other countries, and for punishing countries that do not have a greenhouse gas emissions control policy.

It is important to note that this difference in complexity is inherent in the two policies as initially proposed, before any legislative amendments and before any implementation and enforcement issues. A pure cap and trade system is inevitably more complex than any carbon tax.

Cap and trade is also relatively untried: we have never had an economy-wide cap and trade system, while we have extensive experience with economy-wide excise taxes on a wide variety of products, including gasoline. This is why Congressman Larson's carbon tax bill can simply envisage adding three new relatively short sections to the existing excise tax part of the *Internal Revenue Code*. Cap and trade, on the other hand, is a major new and separate piece of legislation. A new administration determined to implement cap and trade would probably have to take at least two years to get the program passed in Congress and set up for implementation, even with swift Congressional action, because of the inherent delays in the rulemaking process. A carbon tax can be enacted and enforced practically tomorrow. Given that we have already delayed action for decades, and that every year that passes makes the climate change problem more difficult to solve, a carbon tax may be preferable to cap and trade — as well as traditional regulatory approaches — based on timing concerns alone.

In addition to its inherent complexity, cap and trade also is more difficult to enforce. Under cap and trade, an elaborate mechanism would need to be set up to distribute and collect allowances and to ensure that allowances are real (a difficult task, especially if allowances from non-United States programs are permitted) and that polluters are penalized if they emit greenhouses gases without an allowance. A new administrative body would need to be set up for this purpose, or at least a new office within EPA, and new employees with the relevant expertise would need to be hired. A carbon tax, on the other hand, could be enforced by the IRS with its existing staff, which has the relevant expertise in enforcing other excise taxes.

Cap and trade also raises collateral issues that are not present in a carbon tax, such as the need for the Securities and Exchange Commission to enforce rules regarding futures trading in allowances. A good example is the tax implications of both policies. A carbon tax, as a federal tax, has no tax implications: it is simply collected and is not deductible. Allowances under cap and trade, on the other hand, raise a multitude of tax issues: What are the tax implications of distributing allowances for free? What are the tax implications of trading in allowances? Should allowance exchanges be permitted to avoid the tax on selling allowances? What amount of the purchase price of a business should be allocated to its allowances? If borrowing and banking occur, what are the tax consequences? Can allowances be amortized? None of these issues arise under a carbon tax.

Revenue

A carbon tax by definition generates revenue. A relatively modest tax of $10 per ton of carbon content is estimated to generate $50 billion per year; the *America's Energy Security*

Trust Fund Act envisages a tax of $16.50 per ton and generates correspondingly more revenue. While the current federal budget deficit and even larger actuarial deficit may justify revenue raising measures in general, revenues from a carbon tax should be segregated and devoted to addressing any regressive effects of the tax and reducing greenhouse gas emissions. Some carbon tax proposals promise "revenue neutrality" and focus on eliminating regressive effects.

We agree that regressive effects must be addressed but otherwise would use revenues from the carbon tax to provide tax credits for alternative energy development and more energy-efficient motor vehicles, since the positive externalities that result from such research and development means that funding is likely to be undersupplied by the private sector even with a carbon tax in place. Revenues could also be used to support carbon sequestration projects and other projects that reduce greenhouse gas emissions, like mass transit and green building.

Segregating the revenue from a carbon tax and using the proceeds to support further greenhouse gas reductions is justified because it reduces Benefit Uncertainty, which is the most serious drawback of a carbon tax compared to cap and trade. In addition, segregating the revenue is likely to reduce some political opposition to raising taxes in general, at least to the extent that such opposition is based on the perception that government is wasteful.

In theory, cap and trade can be used to generate the same amount of revenue as a carbon tax, if all the allowances are auctioned. In practice, however, all cap and trade proposals introduced in Congress, as well as most academic proposals and existing cap and trade programs in the United States and abroad, include some free distribution of allowances. For example, the EU cap and trade regime distributed ninety-five percent of the allowances for free, and most Congressional proposals distribute over half of the allowances for free. The reason is obvious: for politicians, a significant attraction of cap and trade is that it creates from nothing a new, scarce resource that they can use to reward their constituents and donors. But if allowances are distributed for free, cap and trade generates less revenue than a carbon tax, and this means less potential to support research and development, carbon sequestration, and other greenhouse-gas-reducing efforts.

Moreover, it seems unlikely that free allocation of allowances would produce the optimal reduction in greenhouse gas emissions. Some polluting industries are likely to get too many allowances, and that would affect the trading price of allowances. At the extreme, the result would be what occurred in Europe, where politicians created so many free allowances that no reduction from business as usual was required at all, the price of allowances collapsed, and the EU failed to meet its goals under the Kyoto Protocol. A similar risk to free distribution of allowances under a carbon tax would be pressure from affected industries for tax exemptions. The process of enacting tax exemptions is more visible than the process of distributing free allowances, however, and any exemption to one of the three industries affected (coal, natural gas, and oil) would be met by resistance from the other two, hopefully resulting in no exemptions at all.

Cost certainty

A carbon tax ensures Cost Certainty: the cost is the amount of the tax, and whatever the incidence of the tax (i.e., whether it can be passed on to consumers or not), the cost cannot rise above the tax rate. This enables businesses to plan ahead, secure in the knowledge that raising the tax rate beyond any automatic adjustment, which can be planned for, requires another vote in Congress that they can hope to influence.

A cap and trade regime, on the other hand, suffers from inherent Cost Uncertainty. While allowances may be initially distributed for free, the key question for polluting businesses that need to acquire allowances to address a reduction in the cap is what would be the future price of allowances. Existing cap and trade programs like the Southern California RECLAIM system for nitrogen oxide emissions, in which the allowance prices spiked in 2000 to more than twenty times their historical level, and the EU Emission Trading Scheme (ETS), in which the price of allowances collapsed when it became clear that too many allowances had been distributed, illustrate the problem of Cost Uncertainty in cap and trade programs. Cost Uncertainty makes it inherently difficult for businesses to plan ahead. The fundamental problem is that the reduction in the cap that is built into cap and trade would necessarily make allowances more expensive. How much more expensive depends on the development of future technologies, which cannot be predicted with any accuracy over the longer time period (fifty years or more) required for a cap and trade program to achieve its environmental goals.

Cap and trade proponents argue that Cost Uncertainty can be mitigated by provisions for banking extra allowances for use in future years, and borrowing allowances from future years to use in the present. These provisions add complexity, and it is unclear whether they will be effective: in the early years of the program, there are few allowances to bank, while borrowing risks leaving the business with insufficient allowances in the future when the cap is lower.

Ultimately, the only sure way of preventing Cost Uncertainty in a cap and trade regime is to build in a "safety valve", which would permit businesses to receive or purchase at a fixed price additional allowances if the market price of allowances becomes too high. Several of the current proposals in Congress have such built-in safety valves. However, the problem with safety valves is that they sacrifice Benefit Certainty, which is the main advantage of cap and trade: by definition, providing extra allowances when the cap is lowered means raising the cap.

Even if a cap and trade program has no safety valve built into it from the start, the commitment to Benefit Certainty may be misleading. If the lowered cap begins to seriously hurt businesses and the price of allowances spikes, one should expect strong pressure on politicians to stop lowering the cap. Benefit Certainty under cap and trade as implemented may therefore be an illusion, while Cost Uncertainty is very real.

Signaling

A carbon tax sends a clear signal to polluters: pollution imposes a negative externality on others, and you should be forced to internalize that cost by paying the tax. There is no ambiguity about the message that is intended to be conveyed. Greenhouse gas emissions are costly, and even if people are willing to pay the price, they should be aware of the societal cost they are imposing.

A cap and trade system, however, sends a different and more ambiguous message. On the one hand, its goal is to reduce greenhouse gas emissions. On the other hand, it achieves that goal by either allowing polluters to purchase the right to pollute (from the government or from each other), or to receive permits to pollute for free. The underlying message is that the government permits you to pollute as long as you are willing to pay. Of course, the message (and the cost imposed) may be the same, regardless of whether a tax is paid or whether an allowance is purchased, although it is not the same if allowances are distributed for free. Labels are important, however, and calling the cost a tax sends a different signal than calling it the purchase price for a right to pollute.

Admittedly, most of the activities that give rise to greenhouse gases were until recently considered perfectly legitimate and even positive. Driving a car or riding an airplane has no inherent moral value, and operating an industrial plant creates jobs. But we now know that these activities involve an additional collective cost, and taxing them directly or indirectly forces us to acknowledge this cost in an unambiguous way. Permitting polluters to purchase the right to pollute does not send the same signal.

Disadvantages of a Carbon Tax

Political resistance

A primary reason that both presidential candidates supported cap and trade during the 2008 election, and that other political leaders and many academics support cap and trade, rather than a carbon tax, reflects concern that a carbon tax cannot get enacted because it is a tax. Politicians vividly remember the fate of the Clinton-Gore BTU tax proposal in 1993, and "to be BTU'd" has become the shorthand among Clinton Administration veterans for what happens to supporters of politically unpopular proposals.

However, 2009 is not 1993. The public has shown overwhelming support in the United States for decisive action to curb greenhouse gas emissions. When asked, Americans express just as much willingness to support a carbon tax as a cap and trade regime (which is more difficult to explain). If a new administration were to propose a carbon tax in 2009, the political consequences might be less than past experience suggests, especially if the revenue is segregated and used to reduce greenhouse gas emissions, although this clearly is the most significant practical challenge facing a carbon tax.

Moreover, opponents of cap and trade inevitably liken it to a carbon tax. If allowances are auctioned, or even if they have to be purchased from private parties, the resulting cost is likely to be passed on to consumers. Thus, cap and trade is not just more complicated, it is also subject to the same criticism as a carbon tax: it will "increase gas prices at the pump" — an argument every voter understands. If we are to mitigate greenhouse gas emissions, politicians will need to face down inevitable resistance whether they propose a carbon tax or cap and trade.

Much of the opposition to a carbon tax is likely to come from organized groups that stand to benefit from cap and trade. These include industry groups that can easily reduce their emissions and can therefore expect to derive income from selling excess allowances (which they envisage receiving for free), and Wall Street, which can imagine the hefty fees it will charge for arranging trades in allowances and futures trading to hedge against Cost Uncertainty. However, the carbon tax will also have its supporters, primarily industry groups that will suffer from Cost Uncertainty under cap and trade and would prefer the Cost Certainty provided under the carbon tax.

Benefit uncertainty

The main substantive disadvantage of a carbon tax compared to cap and trade is Benefit Uncertainty. There can be no assurance that any given tax level will result in the desired reduction in greenhouse gas emissions. If the desired benefit is not achieved, the tax may have to be raised, resulting in renewed political opposition, which could defeat the tax increase and thereby limit the environmental benefits of the tax.

However, there are several reasons not to reject the carbon tax because of Benefit Uncertainty. First, as pointed out above, cap and trade may in fact be subject to similar Benefit Uncertainty, because if costs rise too high one can expect pressure to adjust the cap, even if there is no built-in safety valve.

Second, the tax rate can in fact be adjusted. General experience with other taxes has shown that once a tax is in place, it is usually not as hard to raise its rate despite political opposition to tax hikes; this is why people say that "an old tax is a good tax". The United States income tax began in 1913 with a rate of one percent, and has been raised (and lowered) many times since then (although Americans have become increasingly unwilling to accept tax increases). The Value Added Tax (VAT), which is now the most important tax in the world, was typically introduced in over 100 countries at a much lower rate than the current one. If it becomes clear that the carbon tax rate needs to be raised to achieve the necessary reduction in emissions, and if voters remain convinced of the need to reduce emissions, historical experience suggests that the rate could be raised, notwithstanding the political challenges.

Finally, neither cap and trade (without a safety valve) nor a carbon tax can truly achieve Benefit Certainty, because the desired level of emissions (450 ppm) is based on *worldwide* emissions, not United States emissions. We can have the strictest cap and trade regime and suffer the full cost, but if China and India do nothing, we will not have Benefit Certainty.

From this perspective, in addition to reducing greenhouse gas emissions in the United States, both a carbon tax and a cap and trade system serve the essential function of persuading the rest of the world that we are serious, and therefore that they should cooperate in a global policy to curb greenhouse gas emissions. Both cap and trade and a carbon tax are equally useful from that perspective, but for the reasons explained above, a carbon tax can be implemented much faster than cap and trade and, therefore, is preferable from the standpoint of international leadership. Stated differently, Benefit Certainty requires bringing large developing countries to the bargaining table, and a carbon tax is better and faster in doing so than cap and trade.

Tax exemptions

Proponents of cap and trade argue that it is better than a carbon tax because the political bargain over which industries will get relief from its cost has to be reached up front as part of the decision of how to allocate allowances. They also argue that a carbon tax will be subject to pressure to enact permanent exemptions for affected industries, which will permanently weaken its effect and exacerbate its Benefit Uncertainty.

However, it is not clear that a carbon tax would necessarily be weakened by any exemptions. This Article supports a proposal that would apply the tax upstream to only three industries: coal, oil, and natural gas producers and importers. None of these three industries is in a particularly good position to argue for exemptions vis-à-vis the other two, and the ultimate incidence of the tax is too unclear for other industries to effectively argue for exemptions.

The choice between free allocation of allowances under cap and trade and exemptions under a carbon tax is similar to the familiar debate in the tax literature over whether direct subsidies or tax expenditures are superior. Tax expenditures are indirect subsidies delivered through tax reductions or exemptions. While the traditional view has favored direct subsidies because they are arguably more transparent and easier to administer, recently the consensus has shifted to view both types of programs as equally transparent, and so the choice between them comes down to administrative considerations, which generally favor tax expenditures that can be administered by the IRS.

In the cap and trade versus carbon tax debate, the choice between free allowances and tax exemptions is simpler. Tax exemptions are not necessary at all, but if they are enacted they will be quite transparent and subject to criticism as giveaways to unpopular industries. They will also be relatively easy to administer by the IRS. Free allowances, on the other hand, are inherently more complicated to distribute and monitor, for the reasons given above. This debate therefore favors the carbon tax.

Coordination

Another alleged advantage of cap and trade and disadvantage of the carbon tax is that it is easier to coordinate with the regimes implemented by other countries, and especially the EU ETS. Proponents of cap and trade envisage direct transfers of allowances between the

United States cap and trade and the EU ETS, as well as other potential cap and trade regimes in, for example, Canada.

Coordination issues may become more significant over time, if cap and trade emerges as the dominant global approach to climate change mitigation. However, this advantage is largely illusory at present. The initial EU ETS has not been successful because too many allowances were distributed, and it is unclear whether its replacement will be more successful. Canada is still debating between cap and trade and a carbon tax. As a result, there currently is no global cap and trade regime for the United States to join.

Moreover, exchanging allowances with foreign cap and trade regimes exponentially increases the enforcement difficulties inherent in cap and trade. Foreign allowances would have to be carefully monitored and verified to prevent widespread cheating. This problem is exacerbated under the EU ETS because allowances are distributed "downstream" to many different polluters. A carbon tax, on the other hand, can easily be collected on imports and rebated on exports, and as long as it is also imposed on domestic production, it does not pose significant World Trade Organization compliance issues.

If, as a result of enacting a United States carbon tax, the United States is able to participate in negotiating a worldwide accord on curbing greenhouse gases, and if that accord is built on a global cap and trade regime, then we can consider adopting a United States cap and trade system to match with that regime. In the absence of such a regime, it would be unwise to enact cap and trade just because the EU has adopted a flawed cap and trade system.

Conclusion

The global climate change crisis will not be resolved simply by implementing a carbon tax or a cap and trade system — or by any other legislative approach. Fundamental changes in energy production, development, and conservation, as well as changes in transportation, land use, and natural resource policies, must be pursued alongside efforts to reduce carbon dioxide emissions.

An effective carbon mitigation strategy, however, will be the centerpiece of any successful program to combat global climate change. While the widespread embrace of cap and trade is a positive development after decades of inaction, before we move forward we should pause to consider whether a cap and trade system is the best approach to combating global climate change. This Article demonstrates that a better response to global climate change would be a carbon tax that is adjusted over time to achieve the necessary reductions in carbon dioxide emissions, as well as the corresponding improvements in alternative energy sources and land and resource management practices that are essential to conserving our planet for future generations.

Notes and Questions

1. Compare and contrast the various approaches different Canadian jurisdictions have taken to dealing with climate change: what factors might explain why some have adopted carbon taxes while most have resisted this approach?

2. Consider the current federal approach to mitigating climate change. How does it compare to the approach in your province? Do you see any policy inconsistencies that may pose problems in the future?

3. The European Union was the first jurisdiction to implement a cap and trade system in 2005. For a detailed analysis of the EU experience, see M. Rodi, ed., *Emissions Trading in Europe: Initial Experiences and Lessons for the Future*, (Berlin: 2008, Lexxion). For a detailed discussion of subsidies and social norms, see Andrew Green, "You Can't Pay Them Enough: Subsidies, Environmental Law, And Social Norms" 30 Harv. Envtl. L. Rev. 407. In this article, the author considered the role of subsidies in mitigating climate change. He concludes that subsidies are

of limited use for a number of reasons, including the drain on government resources, and their limited potential to contribute to a shift in norm that considers the engagement in activities, that contribute to GHG emissions unnecessarily, inappropriate. Why do you think subsidies have nevertheless been a tool of choice in Canada with respect to climate change?

Part IV — Constitutional Issues in Climate Change Regulation

As indicated in the Introduction, jurisdictional issues have dominated public debates about the appropriate response to climate change in Canada since Canada signed the Kyoto Protocol in 1997. Canada went into the negotiations in Kyoto with a federal provincial agreement for a target of returning to 1990 levels of emissions for the first commitment period (2008–2012). Negotiators returned from Kyoto with a target of 6% below 1990 levels of emissions]. As the federal government sought to implement measures to reduce GHG emissions following the Kyoto negotiations, it became clear that it had lost the cooperation of a number of provinces, most notably Alberta and Ontario. Since then, the picture has shifted, with some provinces, such as Quebec, British Columbia, Manitoba and Ontario taking on a leadership role, while others have continued to resist taking meaningful action. Consider the following excerpt on the division of powers with respect to climate change:

Shi-Ling Hsu & Robin Elliot, "Regulating Greenhouse Gases in Canada: Constitutional and Policy Dimensions"

SSRN http://ssrn.com/abstract=1265365 (posted September 11, 2008)

The validity under sections 91 and 92 of the *Constitution Act, 1867* of legislation enacted by the federal and provincial orders of government to regulate greenhouse gas emissions will depend on a number of factors ... We begin with three general observations about the manner in which the Supreme Court of Canada has tended to approach the task of reviewing on federalism grounds legislation designed to protect the environment.

The first is that the Court has made it clear that the power to protect the environment does not reside exclusively with either Parliament or the provincial legislatures. [...] The jurisprudence makes it clear that this connection to heads of power on both sides of the federal-provincial divide is present even if the word "environment" is understood in more limited terms to mean the physical environment alone. Hence, the courts have upheld as valid both federal and provincial legislation designed to protect the physical environment. They have been able to do that in part because they have shown a willingness to permit Parliament and the provincial legislatures to rely in support of such legislation on their respective jurisdictions over both some of the causes and some of the effects of polluting activities.

The second observation is that the Supreme Court has been willing to permit Parliament to regulate certain kinds of polluting activities under its POGG and criminal law (s. 91(27)) powers even though it has had to push the doctrinal envelopes governing those two heads of power in order to do so: see *R. v. Crown Zellerbach*, and *R. v. Hydro-Quebec*. Taken together, these two decisions can be said to reflect a willingness on the part of the Supreme Court of Canada to use the room to maneuver that the doctrine in this area leaves them with to afford the federal order of government broad authority to protect the physical environment. They also reflect a high degree of sympathy on the Court's part for the goal of environmental protection.

Thirdly, the law is clear that the power to enact legislation in implementation of obligations undertaken by the Government of Canada in an international treaty or convention does not fall to Parliament simply because the legislation has been enacted for that purpose: see the *Labour Conventions* case ... Jurisdiction to enact legislation to implement treaty obligations rests with the order of government that has jurisdiction to legislate in relation to the subject matter of those obligations. The federal order cannot therefore claim jurisdiction to enact legislation regulating greenhouse gas emissions on the basis that such legislation is being enacted in fulfillment of Canada's obligations under the Kyoto Protocol ... That said, there is support in the jurisprudence for the notion that the fact that federal legislation has been enacted to implement treaty obligations might assist the federal government's cause if that legislation were to be subjected to attack on federalism grounds, at least if the subject matter of the treaty can be said to relate to a matter of "predominantly extra-provincial as well as international character and implications".

Provincial Jurisdiction

We consider here the question of whether or not the provincial legislatures have the requisite constitutional authority to regulate greenhouse gas emissions through the vehicles of (a) a carbon tax, (b) a cap-and-trade/intensity-based trading regime, and (c) a command-and-control regime.

Carbon Taxes

The power of the provincial legislatures to tax is prescribed by s. 92(2) of the *Constitution Act, 1867* in the following terms: "Direct Taxation within the Province in order to the raising of a Revenue for Provincial Purposes". Those terms suggest that, in order for provincial legislation to be sustained on the basis of s. 92(2), the legislation must (a) impose a "tax", which tax must (b) be "direct", (c) be imposed "within the province", and (d) be imposed "in order to the raising of a revenue for provincial purposes".

Given the manner in which requirements (a), (b) and (c) have come to be understood, there is little doubt that provincial legislation imposing a carbon tax of the kind that we have discussed above would be held to impose a "tax", and that that "tax" would be held to be both "direct" and imposed "within the province". [...]

This leaves us with requirement (d) — that the tax be levied "in order to the raising of a Revenue for Provincial Purposes". On the face of it, that language would appear to provide the basis for a challenge to a provincial carbon tax that is revenue neutral, like the tax imposed by the Legislature of British Columbia. Can it not be argued that a tax that is advertised as being, and is required by the legislation imposing it to be, revenue neutral has not been levied "in order to the raising of a revenue"? And if the tax has not been levied for that purpose, can it not be said that the legislation imposing it exceeds provincial jurisdiction under s. 92(2)?

In our view, while an argument that provincially imposed taxes that are designed to be, and are in fact, revenue neutral cannot be sustained by s. 92(2) is certainly plausible, it is likely that, if such an argument were to be advanced in a constitutional attack upon a carbon tax like that imposed by the Legislature of British Columbia, it would fail. We believe that the courts would find the weaknesses of that argument to outweigh its strengths, and moreover, that they would be right to do so. [...] In the result, then, it is our opinion that provincially created carbon taxes would be held to fall within the scope of s. 92(2) of the *Constitution Act, 1867*, and therefore be upheld as valid.

Cap-and-Trade/Intensity-Based Trading Regimes

The validity of a provincially created cap-and-trade or intensity-based trading regime would depend to a very considerable degree on the form it took, with the controlling factor being the entities to which the regime applied. If the regime were to be limited to business undertakings that the provincial legislatures have the authority to regulate qua businesses under any or all of s. 92(5), s. 92(10), s.92(13) and s. 92A, there is good reason to believe that it would be upheld as valid. If, however, it were not to be so limited, and were made applicable by its terms to business undertakings that fall within federal legislative jurisdiction, there is good reason to believe that it would be held to be invalid, at least insofar as its application to those undertakings is concerned.

The industries that fall within [squarely within] provincial jurisdiction ... are numerous, and include many of the industries that emit large amounts of carbon into the atmosphere and are therefore good candidates for a cap-and-trade/intensity-based trading regime — oil and gas, manufacturing, mining, forestry, construction, intraprovincial truck and bus lines, etc. Moreover, the power of the provincial legislatures to regulate the business activities of those industries has been understood broadly by the courts. In particular, it has been held to permit them to regulate those activities for a range of different purposes — to protect consumers from fraudulent dealings, to protect the health and safety of consumers, to establish quality standards, to ensure adequate supply and to protect the economic and other interests of employees. It has also been held to permit them to regulate those activities for the purpose of protecting the environment. There is every reason to believe, therefore, that provincial legislation establishing a cap-and-trade/intensity-based trading regime that is limited in its scope to such undertakings would be upheld as valid. [...]

Would it be open to a provincial legislature to extend the reach of a cap-and-trade/intensity-based trading regime to include industries that normally fall within federal legislative jurisdiction, such as aeronautics, international/interprovincial truck and bus lines and nuclear power generation? Given the nature of such regimes, extending their reach in this way could only be accomplished by specifically including such industries in the list of industries to which they apply. This means that companies doing business within one of the listed industries that objected to being included would have a target within the statute to attack — the specific reference to the industry in question. Such an attack would likely be analyzed by the courts on the basis of what is called the necessarily incidental doctrine. The current understanding of that doctrine requires consideration of three distinct questions within the following analytical framework: (1) to what extent does the impugned part of the statute — here the inclusion in the list of industries to which the cap-and-trade regime applies of the industry in question — encroach on the legislative jurisdiction of the federal order of government when that part is viewed in isolation? (2) is the rest of the statute valid? and (3) given the answer to (1), is the impugned part sufficiently integrated into the rest of the statute to profit from its validity and be considered valid itself?

... the answer to the first of these questions would likely be that provincial legislation that imposes legally enforceable constraints on the amount of carbon which companies within a federally regulated industry in question can emit in the course of conducting their normal business activities would be held to be a very serious encroachment on federal legislative jurisdiction over that industry.

... if the first question were to be answered in that manner, the courts would almost certainly hold that the inclusion of the federally regulated industry in the list of industries to which the regime is intended to apply is unconstitutional [...]

As noted above, the cap-and-trade regime proposed by the Legislature of British Columbia may be integrated into a regionally defined cap-and-trade system that will include at least one other Canadian province (Manitoba) and several of the states in the western United States. Would the fact that such a regime has that kind of regional character render it constitutionally suspect in the eyes of the courts? We do not believe that it would. While it is true, as noted above, that the regulation of international and interprovincial trade falls within exclusive federal legislative jurisdiction under s. 91(2) of the *Constitution Act, 1867*, a regime of this nature merely makes it possible for the undertakings governed by the British Columbia statute to engage in the interprovincial and international trading of emission allowances if they believe that it is in their interests to do so. It is not, as it would have to be in order to be vulnerable to attack on this ground, directed at the regulation of such trading.

Command-and-Control Regimes

The ability of provincial legislatures to regulate greenhouse gas emissions on the basis of a command-and-control approach turns on the same considerations as their ability to do so through the enactment of cap-and-trade/intensity-based trading regimes. If the legislation is limited in its reach to those industries that are considered to fall within provincial legislative jurisdiction, it will therefore likely be valid. If, by contrast, the legislation is also made applicable to industries that are considered to fall within federal jurisdiction, it will be vulnerable to attack, at least insofar as its application to those industries is concerned.

Federal Jurisdiction

We explore here the question of whether or not it is open to Parliament to regulate greenhouse gas emissions through the mechanisms of (a) a carbon tax; (b) a cap-and-trade/intensity-based trading regime; and a (c) a command-and-control regime

A Carbon Tax

Unlike the provincial legislatures, the Parliament of Canada has a very broad power to levy taxes. Section 91(3) of the *Constitution Act, 1867* authorizes it to legislate in relation to "The raising of Money by any Mode or System of Taxation". There is neither any limit on the kinds of taxes Parliament can create under this grant of authority, nor any territorial limit. The only requirements are (a) that the legislation entail "taxation" and (b) that the legislation "rais[e] ... money".

We are confident that federal legislation creating a carbon tax of the kind we describe above would be upheld as valid under s. 91(3). Such legislation would both entail "taxation" and "rais[e] money". While it would be open to opponents of the tax to challenge the validity of such a tax if it were made revenue neutral — as the tax proposed by the Liberals would be — on the ground that it did not "raise money", we do not think that such a challenge would succeed, and for the same reasons we do not believe that a provincially created revenue neutral carbon tax would be vulnerable to attack on such a ground

A Cap-and-Trade/Intensity-Based Trading Regime

In our analysis of the constitutionality of provincially created cap-and-trade/intensity-based trading regimes, we argued that, provided such regimes are limited in their scope to industries whose business activities fall within provincial legislative jurisdiction, such as oil and gas, mining, manufacturing and construction, they should pass constitutional muster. It therefore follows that it is our view that a federal cap-and-trade/intensity-based trading regime that is limited in scope to industries whose business activities fall within federal legislative jurisdiction, such as aeronautics, nuclear power generation and international/interprovincial truck and bus lines, would also pass constitutional muster. The more interesting and difficult question is whether a federal cap-and-trade/intensity-based trading regime that, like the plan announced by the Conservative government in 2007, reached beyond those industries, and brought into its regulatory fold provincially-regulated industries such as oil and gas, construction and manufacturing, would survive an attack on federalism grounds. It is to that question that the following analysis is devoted.

In our view, the federal government could reasonably seek to justify such legislation on the basis of one or more of the following bases: the criminal law power (s. 91(27)), the national concern branch of POGG and the national emergency branch of POGG. ... We will now consider in turn each of the three possible bases we have identified.

Criminal Law

On the face of it, the highly regulatory character of a cap-and-trade/intensity-based trading regime dealing with greenhouse gas emission allowances would appear to preclude such a regime being upheld as "criminal law". It is true that such a regime would have offence-creating provisions to ensure that the companies to which the regime applied took seriously the obligations imposed upon them. But ... mere fact that federal legislation contains offence-creating provisions is not enough to qualify it as "criminal law". ...

The reason for including s. 91(27) in this list of plausible sources of federal jurisdiction is the recent decision of the Supreme Court of Canada in *R. v. Hydro-Quebec*. As noted above, the Court in that case, by a narrow 5-4 margin, upheld the toxic substances provisions of *C.E.P.A.* on the basis of s. 91(27) in spite of the highly regulatory character of those provisions.

[Could the SCC's reasons in *Hydro Quebec*] be invoked in support of upholding a federal cap-and-trade/intensity-based trading regime under [the criminal law power]? That is far from clear. There are differences between a cap-and-trade/intensity-based trading regime regulating greenhouse gas emissions and the regulation of toxic substances that might deter the courts from upholding the former under s. 91(27). One is that, unlike the release of toxic substances into the environment, the emission of carbon into the atmosphere cannot be said to cause the kind of direct and immediate harm that we generally associate with the use of the criminal law. Another is that a cap-and-trade/intensity-based trading regime permits companies to buy and sell the right to cause the very environmental harm at which it is aimed, and judges might have difficulty characterizing legislation with that feature — one that *C.E.P.A.*'s toxic substances provisions lack — as criminal law. Moreover, it would be difficult as a matter of both logic and principle for the courts to label a federal cap-and-trade/intensity-based trading regime "prohibitory" — as they would have to do in order to uphold it on the basis of s. 91(27) — while at the same time labeling very similar provincial regimes "regulatory" — as they would have to do in order to uphold them on the basis of ss. 92(5), 92(10), 92(13 and 92A. Finally, there could well be a concern on the part of the courts that, if they were to uphold a federal cap-and-trade/intensity-based trading regime under s. 91(27), there would be little if any practical significance left in the requirement that federal legislation must be "prohibitory" in character in order to qualify as "criminal law", and, as a consequence, very little in the way of meaningful limits on the scope of federal jurisdiction under that head of power.

For the reasons just given, we think the courts would be unlikely to hold that a federal cap-and-trade/intensity-based trading regime satisfied the requirement of being "prohibitory" in nature, with the result that such a regime would be held to fall outside the scope of s. 91(27). However, we should add that, if we were to prove wrong about that, it is our view that the courts would have little difficulty holding that such a regime satisfied the other two requirements for "criminal law", and that it could therefore be sustained on the basis of that head of power. Companies subject to the regime would obviously face penalties for violating the terms of their permits, and the Supreme Court has made it clear that protecting the environment qualifies as "a public purpose ... sufficient to support a criminal prohibition".

National Concern Branch of POGG

[...] the national concern branch provides Parliament with the authority to legislate in relation to "matters" that do have a connection with one or more of the classes of subjects assigned to the provincial legislatures. They also make it clear that, in the view of the Privy Council, the courts should be loath to uphold legislation under POGG in the face of such a connection. Only in relation to "such matters as are unquestionably of Canadian interest and importance" should they be willing to do so; otherwise, the interest in protecting provincial autonomy should hold sway.

Would the federal government succeed in having a cap-and-trade/intensity-based trading regime of the kind we are considering — one that applied to all of the industries responsible for emitting large amounts of carbon into the atmosphere, not just those that, like aeronautics and international/interprovincial truck and bus lines, are understood to fall within federal legislative jurisdiction — upheld under POGG on the basis that it dealt with a matter of national concern? The answer to that question would depend at least in part on the manner in which the "matter" of such a regime was formulated. [...] we presume that it would be formulated in terms of something like "protecting against the harmful effects of global warming by reducing greenhouse gas emissions on the part of Canadian industry".

In our view, it is unlikely that the courts would find that such a matter qualified as a matter of national concern. The fact that the federal legislation would have been enacted in furtherance of Canada's obligations under the Kyoto Protocol, and deals with a matter of "predominantly extra-provincial character and implications", would likely count in favour of such a finding. So too would the fact that the failure of provincial governments to regulate greenhouse gas emissions effectively could be said to result in harmful extra-provincial effects. How much weight the latter factor would be assigned, however, is an open question. The challenger would certainly be in a position to argue that it should be given minimal weight. That argument would be grounded in the fact that, by any fair measure, those extra-provincial effects would be very indirect and of little overall significance, given that Canada as a whole is responsible for approximately two percent of the total greenhouse gas emissions in the world and, moreover, that greenhouse gas emissions are one of a number of human and other causes of global warming. On the other side of the ledger is the fact that the "matter" of the kind of regime we are contemplating could very plausibly be said to lack the required "singleness, distinctiveness and indivisibility that clearly distinguishes it from matters of provincial concern". It would be very easy for the courts to find that that "matter" is not a single or indivisible "matter" at all — it is simply a combination of a federal "matter" — "the regulation of greenhouse gas emissions by federally regulated undertakings" and a provincial "matter" — "the regulation of greenhouse gas emissions by provincially regulated undertakings". Also on the negative side of the ledger would be "the scale of impact on provincial jurisdiction" of allowing Parliament to enact a comprehensive cap-and-trade regime for the entire country. That impact would almost certainly be seen by the courts to be extremely high, particularly for provinces like Alberta. Finally, and perhaps most importantly, there is the fact that provincial legislatures would be precluded from regulating greenhouse gas emissions by industries such as oil and gas, manufacturing and construction if the courts were to uphold a comprehensive federal cap-and-trade regime on the basis of the national concern doctrine. That, we believe, is not a consequence upon which our courts would look at all favourably.

National Emergency Branch of POGG

... The jurisprudence relating to this branch of POGG [...] has generated a body of doctrine upon which the courts would be expected to rely if the federal government sought to invoke it in support of a comprehensive cap-and-trade/intensity-based trading regime. That body of doctrine can in our view be summarized as follows: (1) the federal government can rely on the emergency branch both to respond to existing emergencies and to prevent new emergencies from arising; (2) emergencies can include economic emergencies, such as a high rate of inflation; (3) the courts should be loath to second-guess a decision by the federal government that an emergency exists or is threatened, and need only be satisfied that the government had a "rational basis" for making such a decision; (4) the emergency branch can only be invoked to sustain legislation of temporary duration; (5) the legislation should indicate, in a preamble or otherwise, that it has been enacted for the purpose of dealing at least with "a serious national condition" if not a national emergency; and (6) unlike in the case of the national concern branch, upholding federal legislation on the basis of the national emergency branch does not preclude the provincial legislatures from legislating in their own ways to deal with the emergency in question (assuming they can do so in a manner that respects the limits on provincial legislative authority under s. 92).

In our view, there is good reason to believe that courts applying this body of doctrine could well uphold a comprehensive federal cap-and-trade regime under the emergency branch of POGG. The fact that the doctrine permits Parliament to act in anticipation of a new emergency arising would serve federal interests in a very direct way, and there seems little reason to doubt that an environmental disaster of the kind that global climate change portends would be held to qualify as an emergency for this purpose. The posture of judicial restraint that the doctrine calls for in evaluating the need for legislative action would also serve federal interests well. The requirement of temporary duration is one that can be met by careful drafting, as can the need for appropriate signaling. Finally, the fact that upholding such a regime on the basis of this branch would leave it open to the provincial legislatures to take whatever steps they consider advisable to reduce greenhouse gas emissions would make it a much more attractive option to the courts than the national concern branch.

It will have been noted that the previous paragraph referred only to a cap-and-trade regime, rather than, as in all of our preceding analyses, to both a cap-and-trade regime and an intensity-based trading regime. The omission of a reference to the latter was deliberate. Even with a posture of judicial restraint, we think it unlikely that the courts would consider a regime that, like an intensity-based trading regime, permitted greenhouse gas emissions to increase over time to constitute a genuine attempt by Parliament to respond to a pending national disaster. It is only the cap-and-trade option that in our view could plausibly be defended on the basis of the national emergency branch of POGG.

Any suggestion that the federal government was considering the use of the emergency branch would undoubtedly result in strong opposition from the provincial governments, who would portray such an initiative as a direct and profound assault on their ability to devise and implement policies that they consider to be appropriate to their respective economies and populations. However, the federal government could minimize the sting of that opposition by making it clear that the federal government would only pursue such an initiative if the provincial legislatures did not take what it considered to be strong enough action over the course of a prescribed time period. It could also draft its legislation in such a way as to make its implementation contingent on that condition being met.

A Command-and-Control Regime

The ability of Parliament under s. 91 to enact a command-and-control regime designed to reduce greenhouse gas emissions would in our view turn on the same considerations as its ability to enact a cap-and-trade regime. If a federal command-and-control regime were limited in its scope to industries whose business activities fall within federal legislative jurisdiction, it would almost certainly be valid. Only if its reach extended into what we consider to be the provincial sphere — oil and gas, manufacturing, construction and so on — would its validity be open to attack.

Such an extended command-and-control regime could plausibly be defended on the basis of the same sources of federal legislative jurisdiction as an extended cap-and-trade/intensity-based trading regime — s. 91(27), the national concern branch of POGG and the national emergency branch of POGG. In our view, the analysis we provided above of the viability of the latter two sources of jurisdiction in the context of a federal cap-and-trade/intensity-based trading regime would apply equally well in the context of a command-and-control regime. Hence, we believe that such a regime would likely not be upheld under the national concern branch of POGG, but that it could well be upheld under the national emergency branch. Insofar as s. 91(27) is concerned, our view remains that the courts would be unlikely to sustain such a regime on that basis. However, part of the analysis we provided above of the viability of this source of jurisdiction in the context of a cap-and-trade/intensity-based trading regime would have no relevance in this other context. Unlike a cap-and-trade/intensity-based trading regime, a command-and-control regime does not permit the companies governed by it to sell the right to cause the very environmental harm at which the regime is aimed. That difference would in our view reduce somewhat the strength of the arguments against permitting Parliament to rely on the criminal law power. It would not, however, reduce their strength enough to persuade the courts to uphold such a regime as criminal law.

Summary

In summary, then, it is our view that both orders of government have a relatively broad array of options available to them under the Constitution to deal with greenhouse gas emissions. The provincial legislatures can levy a carbon tax on consumers. They can also impose a range of different kinds of regulatory regimes on the main industrial emitters of greenhouse gases within their respective boundaries, provided only that the regimes are limited in their application to industries that are understood to fall within provincial legislative jurisdiction. Parliament, too, can levy a carbon tax. And it, too, can impose a range of different kinds of regulatory regimes on industrial emitters. Its authority to create such regimes is clearest if the regimes are limited in scope to those industries that are understood to fall within federal legislative jurisdiction. It is possible, given the extent and nature of the problem, that, using the national emergency branch of POGG, Parliament could impose such a regime on all industrial emitters. And, finally, it is open to the federal government to use the provisions of the C.E.A.A. to assist in its efforts to control climate change. [...] What that means is that the choices that our governments make in this area will — or at least should — be based primarily on considerations of policy. And it is to precisely those considerations that we now turn.

Notes and Questions

1. Do you agree with the authors' conclusions with respect to the federal government's jurisdiction to implement a comprehensive cap and trade system, an intensity-based cap and trade system and a carbon tax? In a forthcoming article, Stewart Elgie argues that federal action on climate change could be constitutionally justified on the basis of a legal analysis that 'combines' federal jurisdiction under its criminal law, and trade and commerce powers. Alternatively, he suggests that the federal government could validly rely on its power to implement international treaties: see "Carbon Emissions Trading and the Constitution" Queen's L.J. (forthcoming). See also Nathalie Chalifour, "Making Federalism Work for Climate Change: Canada's Division of Powers over Carbon Taxes" (2009) 22 N.J.C.L. 119. What constitutional arguments do you consider to be most compelling and plausible in relation to federal jurisdiction in this realm?

2. Which level(s) of government has jurisdiction to implement energy efficiency and conservation measures? What about measures to promote renewable energy? Can the federal government pass legislation to restrict the consumption of fossil fuels across Canada? What about production?

Part V — The Common Law and Liability for Climate Change Impacts

In Chapter 2, we discussed the many challenges in utilising the common law to address environmental issues. Climate change is showing signs of becoming the testing ground for many of the issues we explored. The efforts to make use of the common law to force governments and private entities to address climate change will likely intensify as governments continue to struggle to implement effective legislative and regulatory measures to deal with this global challenge. Consider the following overview of the challenges involved in bringing a common law action related to GHG emissions, followed by a brief overview of recent developments in climate change tort litigation in the United States.

Deborah Curran, "Climate Change Backgrounder" University of Victoria Environmental Law Centre

(unpublished, December, 2007)

Introduction

Increasingly, attention is being paid to the potential of tort actions as a means of responding to harms associated with climate change impacts. Academics estimate that lawyers have already filed upwards of 25 cases worldwide.

These cases can be classified in four categories:

- Actions against public agencies for acts or omissions that contribute to climate change;
- Actions against public agencies to require consideration of climate change impacts in decision-making;
- Civil lawsuits against private entities that emit greenhouse gases (primarily in nuisance, with some in negligence); and
- Actions against public agencies regulating greenhouse gas emissions by the regulated entities.

Arguably the third category of cases — civil actions — offers the greatest potential for setting a precedent that could ripple through the corporate sector, drastically changing industrial processes because of fear of findings of liability for impacts caused by GHG emissions. However, even assuming a strong plaintiff (such as the Inuit who suffer both private and public nuisances) and a weak defendant (such as the electricity generating industry in most of North America) there are significant legal and scientific hurdles to overcome in such mass tort litigation.

The purpose of this backgrounder is to set out the primary legal challenges facing a civil law suit in Canada or the Unites States that seeks to impose tort liability for the harms caused by climate change. Among the challenges associated with pursuing litigation of this kind include issues relating to jurisdiction, duty of care, causation, and apportionment of liability.

Duty of Care

The tort of negligence requires defendants to exercise a duty to take care to those who are foreseeably at risk from their behaviour. They owe this duty to a class or classes of people who are put at risk by negligent activity. This duty does not extend to those put at risk by secondary impacts from the negligent activity. The question in climate change litigation is how wide the duty of care net will be cast: how big is the zone of foreseeable risk. Arguably the defendants in global environmental tort cases owe a duty of care to all people in the world. The foreseeability of harm has increased dramatically in the past year as the scientific understanding of the impact of climate change has increased. At what point did it become foreseeable that emissions of GHGs would harm, for example, Northern peoples? Courts may also decline to impose a duty of care for public policy reasons, for example where the scale of liability is so large that it would destroy industry and thus is contrary to public policy.

The notion of duty of care also finds expression in both Canadian and U.S. laws of public nuisance. Here, the duty extends remedies to plaintiffs that receive special injury as the result of actions by a defendant that interfere with a right (health, safety, morality, comfort or convenience) common to the general public. Courts in both countries use a balancing test that includes weighing the utility or reasonableness of the defendant's activity and how the activity conforms to industry or sectoral norms. While U.S. courts are becoming more lenient about plaintiffs needing to show special damage, Canadian courts require strict adherence to showing injury that is different in both kind and degree. For example, the court dismissed a case brought in public nuisance by a fishers' group for a toxic spill that killed fish, finding that the group did not show their injury to be different in kind from that of the general public who enjoyed fishing as well. Indeed, plaintiff injuries must be a direct, and not a consequential, result of the defendant's action.

Finally, the defence of statutory authority or legislative authority in both Canada and the U.S. can impede claims in this area. Where legislatures are able to override common law doctrines by statute, defendants can use this defence of statutory authority to have courts sanction a range of activities that the government could have contemplated in passing a statute: see, for example, B.C.'s recent Bill 44 *Greenhouse Gas Reductions Targets Act* S.B.C 2007 c. 42.

Duty of care analysis also plays a role in private nuisance imposing liability where a defendant interferes unreasonably with the use and enjoyment of another's property. In assessing the reasonableness issue, courts typically assess the nature, severity, forseeability and reasonableness of the impugned interference. Emitting GHGs or the impact of those GHGs can be seen as a reasonable part of acceptable industrial action that generates economic activity. The question becomes at what level does the conduct become intentional and the interference unreasonable where the harm (environmental, economic and social) outweighs the benefit (economic and social)?

When considering duty of care, Hunter and Salzman conclude:

> Our analysis suggests that changes over time in our understanding of climate change impacts are increasing the foreseeable costs of GHG emissions. At the same time, alternatives to inefficient technologies or practices are increasingly well known, and the avoidance costs are declining. This suggests that the relative risk-utility balance of climate-changing activities is shifting, and with that shift comes an increased likelihood that a defendant's activities or products will be found to present an unreasonable risk of foreseeable injury. Whether under theories of negligence, nuisance, or products liability, such trends in the risk-utility ratio are moving toward a finding of liability.

The focus on duty also helps us to look beyond a sector-wide approach to defendants — for example, all utilities, oil and gas producers, or automobile manufacturers — to a focus on those companies within a sector that are lagging behind the industry leaders in responding to climate change. Although initial tort actions have been suits against broad groups of utilities or automobile manufacturers with little differentiation, the next generation of tort cases may take a more nuanced approach to naming defendants. In the future, those companies whose approach to climate change is behind that of others in their industry run the risk of being singled out in tort actions. Inquiries into the reasonableness of a company's operations or products turn into inquiries about how they compare to those of others. In this way, today's industry laggards may be tomorrow's climate defendants.

Causation

The traditional test requires the plaintiff to demonstrate on a balance of probabilities that, "but for" the defendant's conduct, the plaintiff would not have been harmed. With multiple actors emitting GHGs over a century it is difficult to attribute specific causation for harms thousands of kilometers away to any particular industrial sector let alone specific corporate defendant. This is because the contribution of any one facility or identifiable group of emitters is fairly insignificant (e.g. far below a 50 percent level) and thus will not be substantial enough for a court to find that "but for" its emissions the alleged harm would not have occurred. The impact of U.S. and Canadian industry on climate change is also relatively small and declining with the industrialization of China and India.

The Canadian test of "material contribution" is the only significant departure from the traditional approach in recognition that the "but for" test is unworkable in some circumstances. To date, courts have provided little guidance on what makes a contributing causal factor "material". In one of the few cases to address this question, the SCC has opined (unhelpfully) that a cause may qualify as material if it "falls outside the de minimus range". Once a factor has been identified as materially contributing to the harm, the defendant cannot escape full liability simply because other tortious and non-tortious factors also played a role in creating the harm that was suffered.

It is critical to bear in mind, however, that the Supreme Court of Canada has emphasized that the "but for" approach to causation should be presumptively applied in all but the most exceptional of cases. In this vein, in a 2007 negligence case, it has stipulated that the material contribution test should only be applied when two requirements are met:

First, it must be impossible for the plaintiff to prove that the defendant's negligence caused the plaintiff's injury using the "but for" test. The impossibility must be due to factors that are outside of the plaintiff's control; for example, current limits of scientific knowledge. Second, it must be clear that the defendant breached a duty of care owed to the plaintiff, thereby exposing the plaintiff to an unreasonable risk of injury, and the plaintiff must have suffered that form of injury. In other words, the plaintiff's injury must fall within the ambit of the risk created by the defendant's breach. In those exceptional cases where these two requirements are satisfied, liability may be imposed, even though the "but for" test is not satisfied, because it would offend basic notions of fairness and justice to deny liability by applying a "but for" approach.

As such, the suggestion that a material contribution approach to causation should apply on the present facts is likely to meet with significant judicial resistance given floodgates concerns and the presumptive applicability of the "but for" test. Moreover, even if a trial court was inclined to apply a material contribution test, it is unclear how substantial a causative factor would need to be (i.e. how much beyond the de minimus range) to satisfy the test.

The only remaining alternative basis for establishing causation would involve invocation of a "market share"-based theory of causation. This approach has found favour in the United States and has recently been approved by the English House of Lords in a tort claim against asbestos manufacturers. In Canada, however, while the doctrine has been statutorily adopted in BC legislation, enacted to seek compensation for health related impacts from tobacco companies, no court has adopted it. The SCC referred to *Sindell v. Abbott Labs* in *Snell v.*

Farrell as an example of a challenge to the traditional approach to causation, but gave it no further consideration. The doctrine has only been referred to in passing by the Ontario Superior Court of Justice, the British Columbia Supreme Court, and the Saskatchewan Court of Appeal.

In summary, for causation to be established on the current facts — assuming Canadian and not American law applies — it will be necessary either to establish causation on the basis of "material contribution" or "market share", both of which would appear to be difficult arguments.

Remedies: Apportionment of Liability

As noted above, some courts in the U.S. have allowed the apportionment of liability based on a doctrine of market share. The percentage of market share that a corporation holds in a particular industry will be the amount of damage for which it will be held liable. Each defendant is liable for his or her share of the contribution to the harm. In the climate change context this could mean that defendants are liable to the extent of their historic emissions of GHGs.

In B.C. defendants are held joint and severally liable under the *Negligence Act*. Plaintiffs may recover 100 percent of the damages from one or more tortfeasors as an indivisible harm, even if other tortfeasors are not joined in the suit. Defendants may then recover from each other in accordance with the proportion of harm for which they have been deemed responsible. Because all defendants in climate change litigation are likely to have deep pockets, this doctrine is less likely than usual to lead to a single defendant being responsible for the entire judgment. However, given this possibility, courts may be even more reluctant to find any particular emitter liable.

Discussion

In a recent article assessing the prospects of litigating what many would contend is the best case scenario for a tort-based climate change lawsuit (i.e. brought by the Inuit against the U.S. electrical generating industry), Professor Hsu offers a relatively gloomy assessment for establishing liability in Canadian courts:

> In short, Canadian courts can be expected to be considerably less friendly to an Inuit lawsuit against the U.S. electricity generating industry. Public interest litigation simply does not enjoy the storied tradition in Canada as it does in the U.S. Following the British system of fees, Canadian courts as a default rule require the loser to pay for the attorneys' fees of the winning party. This is a double-edged sword, of course, but for relatively underfunded environmental plaintiffs, it is a significant bar to the courthouse doors ... What I can safely conclude, however, is that Canadian courts offer no better, and probably offer a much worse venue for the Inuit hoping to obtain some redress for climate-change-related harms from the U.S. electricity generating industry: see Shi-Ling Hsu *"A Realistic Evaluation of Climate Change Litigation Through the Lens of a Hypothetical Lawsuit" (2008) 79 U. Colo. L. Rev. 701–766.*

While his assessment of the prospects for litigating this scenario in U.S. courts is less pessimistic ... and while there appears to be a strong appetite on the part of some experienced lawyers — both north and south of the border — to consider seriously the potential for bringing such litigation, to date only very preliminary analysis of broad range of other doctrinal, scientific and practical issues associating with mounting litigation of this kind has been undertaken.

Notes and Questions

1. Should those affected by climate change be able to recover from those responsible for GHG emissions?

2. Assuming that liability should be assigned, do you think the common law is the appropriate vehicle to allocate liability?

3. What principles should guide the allocation of liability? How well equipped are the torts of nuisance, negligence and strict liability to ensure a fair allocation of liability?

4. What alternatives to the use of the common law do you see to deal with liability for the harm caused by climate change?

Climate Change Tort Litigation in the United States: A Snapshot

American-based plaintiffs have led the way in pursuing tort actions seeking redress for the impacts of climate change. The lawsuits commenced to date have targeted large corporations in the energy and automotive sectors seeking damages and injunctive relief with respect to past and present GHG emissions. The lead plaintiffs in the two most notable cases brought to date are the states of Connecticut and California. The Connecticut case (excerpted below) was filed against a group of energy production companies operating in eight states. As set out below, this action was dismissed on a preliminary motion in 2005. The California case, filed against a group of major automobile manufacturers, is still before the courts: see *California v. General Motors et al.* (N.D. Cal. 2007). The most recent major new case of this kind is one that has been filed on behalf of the Alaskan Inuit community of Kivalina: discussed later, in Part VIII of this chapter. Like the Connecticut case, the Kivalina litigation targets major energy-producers in the continental United States. In the Kivalina litigation, in an attempt to circumvent the evidentiary problems associated with litigation of this kind, lawyers for the plaintiffs have argued that the defendants have conspired together to "cover up" the impacts of their activities on the global climate; a strategy employed with some success in analogous litigation against tobacco companies.

The following excerpt provides an intriguing glimpse into some of the judicial concerns that large-scale, climate change-related tort litigation are likely to trigger.

State of Connecticut v. American Electric Power Company
406 F. Supp. 2d 265, 2005 U.S. Dist. LEXIS 19964, 35 ELR 20186 (S.D. N.Y., 2005)

PRESKA District Judge:

The Framers based our Constitution on the idea that a separation of powers enables a system of checks and balances, allowing our Nation to thrive under a Legislature and Executive that are accountable to the People, subject to judicial review by an independent Judiciary ... While, at times, some judges have become involved with the most critical issues affecting America, political questions are not the proper domain of judges. Were judges to resolve political questions, there would be no check on their resolutions because the Judiciary is not accountable to any other branch or to the People. Thus, when cases present political questions, "judicial review would be inconsistent with the Framers' insistence that our system be one of checks and balances". Nixon, 506 U.S. at 234-35. As set out below, cases presenting political questions are consigned to the political branches that are accountable to the People, not to the Judiciary, and the Judiciary is without power to resolve them. This is one of those cases.

Background

The States of Connecticut, New York, California, Iowa, New Jersey, Rhode Island, Vermont, and Wisconsin and the City of New York (the "State Plaintiffs") and the Open Space Institute, Inc. ("OSI"), the Open Space Conservancy, Inc., and the Audubon Society of New Hampshire (the "Private Plaintiffs") (collectively, "Plaintiffs") bring the above-captioned actions against American Electric Power Company, Inc., American Electric Power Service Corporation (together, "AEP"), the Southern Company ("Southern"), Tennessee Valley Authority ("TVA"), Xcel Energy Inc. ("Xcel"), and Cinergy Corporation ("Cinergy") (collectively, "Defendants") under federal common law or, in the alternative, state law, to abate what Plaintiffs describe as the "public nuisance" of "global warming". State Compl. P1; OSI Compl. P1. Defendants now move to dismiss the complaints for, inter alia, lack of jurisdiction and failure to state a claim upon which relief can be granted. For the reasons set forth below, Defendants' motions are granted.

The State Plaintiffs, claiming to represent the interests of more than 77 million people and their related environments, natural resources, and economies, and the Private Plaintiffs, non-profit land trusts, bring these federal common law public nuisance actions to abate what they allege to be Defendants' contributions to the phenomenon commonly known as global warming. Plaintiffs assert that the Defendants collectively emit approximately 650 million tons of carbon dioxide annually, that carbon dioxide is the primary greenhouse gas, and that greenhouse gases trap atmospheric heat and cause global warming.

As part of their venue allegations, Plaintiffs maintain that global warming will cause irreparable harm to property in New York State and New York City and that it threatens the health, safety, and well-being of New York's citizens, residents, and environment. According to the complaints, Defendants "are the five largest emitters of carbon dioxide in the United States" and their emissions "constitute approximately one quarter of the U.S. electric power sector's carbon dioxide emissions". According to the complaints, U.S. electric power plants are responsible for "ten percent of worldwide carbon dioxide emissions from human activities". [...]

... [the] Plaintiffs "seek an order (i) holding each of the Defendants jointly and severally liable for contributing to an ongoing public nuisance, global warming, and (ii) enjoining each of the Defendants to abate its contribution to the nuisance by capping its emissions of carbon dioxide and then reducing those emissions by a specified percentage each year for at least a decade". According to Plaintiffs, the unspecified reductions they seek "will contribute to a reduction in the risk and threat of injury to the plaintiffs and their citizens and residents from global warming".

... [the] Defendants move to dismiss the complaints against them on several grounds. First, Defendants contend that Plaintiffs have failed to state a claim upon which relief can be granted because: (1) there is no recognized federal common law cause of action to abate greenhouse gas emissions that allegedly contribute to global warming; (2) separation of powers principles preclude this Court from adjudicating these actions; and (3) Congress has displaced any federal common law cause of action to address the issue of global warming. Second, Defendants contend that this Court lacks jurisdiction over Plaintiffs' claims because: (1) Plaintiffs do not have standing to sue on account of global warming and (2) Plaintiffs' failure to state a claim under federal law divests the Court of jurisdiction ...

Discussion

The threshold jurisdictional question in this case is whether the complaints raise non-justiciable political questions that are beyond the limits of this Court's jurisdiction. Defendants argue that "separation-of-powers principles foreclose recognition of the unprecedented 'nuisance' action plaintiffs assert", which I take to be an argument that Plaintiffs raise a non-justiciable political question ... Accordingly, this issue will be addressed first.

The extraordinary allegations and relief sought in this case render it one in which an analysis of Plaintiffs' standing would involve an analysis of the merits of Plaintiffs' claims. For example, determining causation and redressibility in the context of alleged global warming would require me to make judgments that could have an impact on the other branches' responses to what is plainly a political question. Accordingly, because the issue of Plaintiffs' standing is so intertwined with the merits and because the federal courts lack jurisdiction over this patently political question, I do not address the question of Plaintiffs' standing.

To determine if a case is justiciable in light of the separation of powers ordained by the Constitution, a court must decide "whether the duty asserted can be judicially identified and its breach judicially determined, and whether protection for the right asserted can be judicially molded".

Plaintiffs advance a number of arguments why theirs is a simple nuisance claim of the kind courts have adjudicated in the past, but none of the pollution-as-public-nuisance cases cited by Plaintiffs has touched on so many areas of national and international policy. The scope and magnitude of the relief Plaintiffs seek reveals the transcendently legislative nature of this litigation. Plaintiffs ask this Court to cap carbon dioxide emissions and mandate annual reductions of an as-yet-unspecified percentage. Such relief would, at a minimum, require this Court to: (1) determine the appropriate level at which to cap the carbon dioxide emissions of these Defendants; (2) determine the appropriate percentage reduction to impose upon Defendants; (3) create a schedule to implement those reductions; (4) determine and balance the implications of such relief on the United States' ongoing negotiations with other nations concerning global climate change; (5) assess and measure available alternative energy resources; and (6) determine and balance the implications of such relief on the United States' energy sufficiency and thus its national security — all without an "initial policy determination" having been made by the elected branches.

Defendants have set forth just a few of the difficult "initial policy determination[s]" that would have to be made by the elected branches before any court could address these issues:

- Given the numerous contributors of greenhouse gases, should the societal costs of reducing such emissions be borne by just a segment of the electricity-generating industry and their industrial and other consumers?
- Should those costs be spread across the entire electricity-generating industry (including utilities in the plaintiff States)? Other industries?
- What are the economic implications of these choices?
- What are the implications for the nation's energy independence and, by extension, its national security?

Because resolution of the issues presented here requires identification and balancing of economic, environmental, foreign policy, and national security interests, "an initial policy determination of a kind clearly for non-judicial discretion" is required. Indeed, the questions presented here "uniquely demand single-voiced statement of the Government's views". Thus, these actions present non-justiciable political questions that are consigned to the political branches, not the Judiciary.

Action dismissed.

Notes and Questions

1. Do you agree with the court in the preceding case that deciding whether power plants can continue to emit unlimited greenhouse gases that contribute to climate change is a political decision that has to be left to the legislative and executive branches of government? Should it matter whether the claim is brought by a state or provincial government, or by a private individual?

2. To what extent do you see parallels between the justiciability doctrine applied in this case and the approach applied in the KPIA decision excerpted in Part II?

3. American states have a long tradition of bringing public nuisance claims in the environmental protection context: Such suits have been especially common and successful in relation to contaminated sites and water pollution: see *State of California v. Albert Campbell*, 138 F.3d 772, 1998 U.S. App. LEXIS 4036, 40 Fed. R. Serv. 3d (Callaghan) 399, 46 ERC (BNA) 1362. In Canada, public nuisance is most frequently used by private individuals who suffer special damages as a result of a defendant's interference with a public resource. However, it should be noted, as discussed in Chapter 2, that in the recent *Canfor* decision, the Supreme Court of Canada does not rule out the spectre of public nuisance being invoked to protect public resources in a more robust way than in the past.

4. How is the emission of greenhouse gases different from the release of noise, smell, and air and the contamination of land and water that the common law of nuisance is very accustomed to dealing with? How would you define the duty of care owed by owners and operators of power plants? How would you deal with causation and apportionment of liability?

5. Assuming that you can overcome the challenges of duty of care, causation, and apportionment of liability explored in the article at the start of this section, should courts in Canada be open to public or private nuisance claims related to GHG emissions? Explain.

6. Do you see room for governments in Canada bringing similar court actions to force large industrial emitters to reduce their GHG emissions?

Part VI — Climate Change and Environmental Assessment

Experience with climate change in the federal EA process has been limited in Canada. Most early efforts to force project proponents to develop EAs that addressed the effects of climate change were unsuccessful: see, for example, the 1997 Joint Public Review Panel Report on the Sable Project (www.ceaa.gc.ca). The usual rationale for this approach was that the GHG emissions of any one project were too small to make a noticeable let alone a "significant" contribution to climate change.

It would appear, however, the tide is turning. A notable illustration is the decision of the Federal Court in the Kearl Oil Sands case discussed *infra* in Chapter 6. In this case, the Court remitted an EA to the panel on the basis that it had failed to offer adequate support for its conclusion that GGHs emitted as a result of the project did not constitute a significant adverse environmental effect. The decision in Kearl is consistent with what appears to be more rigourous judicial approach to reviewing major projects with potentially significant climate change implications in other jurisdictions: see, for example, *Australian Conservation Foundation v. Minister of Planning*, [2004] VCAT 2029.

It would also appear that climate change impacts are increasingly being taken into account by EA professionals in government and the private sector. For example, a federal, provincial and territorial committee on climate change and EA developed a guide on "Incorporating Climate Change Considerations in Environmental Assessment". However, to date, initiatives such as these remain voluntary; as a legal issue, to borrow terminology from Chapter 1, climate change in the EA context has still to traverse the divide from "soft to hard law".

Two of the key issues on the horizon in this area are: (1) whether, and to what extent, there are constitutional fetters on the jurisdiction of the federal government to consider climate change impacts under CEAA; and (2) whether, and to what extent, the current CEAA regime adequately facilitates a full consideration of climate change impacts. Bearing in mind material covered in Chapters 3 and 7 consider the following article, which provides some reflections on these two important issues.

. . . . .

Shi-Ling Hsu & Robin Elliot, "Regulating Greenhouse Gases in Canada: Constitutional and Policy Dimensions"

SSRN http://ssrn.com/abstract=1265365 (posted September 11, 2008)

[In what follows, we propose to consider] the use of the C.E.A.A. to require federal authorities to consider the greenhouse gas implications of new projects governed by that statute before approving them. It will be recalled that that statute calls for environmental assessments in respect of projects that a federal authority is itself proposing, that a federal authority intends to support financially, that involves the sale or lease of federal lands or that implicates an area of federal concern identified by regulation. It will also be recalled that, in making such assessments, review panels are required to consider "any change that the project may cause in the environment", with "environment" to be understood as encompassing "... air, including all layers of the atmosphere".

In our view, there is every reason to believe that this option would, if challenged, be upheld as constitutionally valid. The Supreme Court of Canada in *Friends of the Oldman River Society v. Canada* made it clear that it is open to Parliament to require that the environmental implications of projects that engage areas of federal concern be considered before they are approved. The Court also held that, in assessing those implications, the reviewing bodies are entitled to take into account all of the possible environmental effects of such projects. In the course of his majority reasons for judgment in that case, Justice La Forest considered the example of a project involving the construction of a new interprovincial railway. In his view, a panel asked to assess the environmental implications of such a project would be entitled to take into account the impact of the new line on "ecologically sensitive habitats such as wetlands and forests", potential hazards to "the health and safety of nearby communities if dangerous commodities are to be carried on the line", and the possible "economic benefit to those communities through job creation and the multiplier effect that will have on the local economy". In fact, he said, not to permit the panel to consider such matters "would lead to the most astonishing results, and it defies reason to assert that Parliament is constitutionally barred from weighing the broad environmental repercussions, including socio-economic concerns, when legislating with respect to decisions of this nature".

Was it important to Justice La Forest's reasoning in this regard that interprovincial railways are federal undertakings under s. 92(10(a) and therefore, qua undertakings, within exclusive federal jurisdiction? Would he have taken a more restrained view of the permissible scope of a federally-mandated environmental assessment if the project in question had been one that fell prima facie within provincial jurisdiction — like the dam in *Oldman River* itself — with the federal interest being limited to the impact of that project on an area of federal jurisdiction — like the navigability of the Oldman River? We believe not. Justice La Forest did not draw any such distinction himself, as he could well have done given the nature of the case he had before him. Moreover, he referred with approval to an Australian case, *Murphyores Incorporated Pty. Ltd. v. Commonwealth of Australia*, in which the High Court had upheld the constitutionality of an inquiry under Commonwealth legislation into the environmental impact of the mining of particular substances by a company seeking permission to export those substances, even though the mining activity was acknowledged to be "predominantly a state interest". The decision in that case was used to exemplify the proposition that, even in a federal state,

> ... [i]n legislating regarding a subject, it is sufficient that the legislative body legislate on that subject. The practical purpose that inspires the legislation and the implications that body must consider in making its decision are another thing. Absent a colourable purpose or a lack of bona fides, these considerations will not detract from the fundamental nature of the legislation.

We conclude, therefore, that it is open to the agencies of the federal government to include greenhouse gas emissions in the list of environmental concerns to be considered by panels constituted under the C.E.A.A.

Notes and Questions

1. Do you agree with the Hsu and Elliot's conclusions on this constitutional law question?

2. Having concluded that, as a matter of constitutional law, the federal government is jurisdictionally able to consider climate change impacts under CEAA, Professors Hsu and Elliot turn their attention to the adequacy of the CEAA to tackle this task. As you will see, they argue that CEAA fails to provide appropriate guidance to decision makers in terms of what climate change impacts should be deemed "significant" enough to trigger remedial action.

. . . . .

Shi-Ling Hsu & Robin Elliot, "Regulating Greenhouse Gases in Canada: Constitutional and Policy Dimensions"

SSRN http://ssrn.com/abstract=1265365 (posted September 11, 2008)

Canadian Environmental Assessment Act

If a federal government were to score political points by undertaking some climate change action, there is no lower-hanging fruit than the use of the *Canadian Environmental Assessment Act*. The use of the environmental assessment process, a common one throughout the world, is one that other countries have used to challenge greenhouse gas-emitting projects or policies. In the U.S., a number of cases have involved administrative decisions with greenhouse gas implications. For example, in *Los Angeles v. NHTSA*, the city of Los Angeles challenged a decision by the U.S. National Highway and Transportation Safety Agency to loosen vehicle fuel efficiency standards by as little as one mile per gallon, arguing that this would lead to greater gasoline consumption, more greenhouse gas emissions, and the attendant increased danger of global climate change. In each of the cases, the administrative agency did not prepare an "Environmental Impact Statement" under the *National Environmental Policy Act*, which is required unless the agency makes a preliminary "Environmental Assessment" that the project will have no significant impact. All of these cases challenged the agency findings that there would be no significant impact. While the results have been mixed, no court has questioned the appropriateness of a fairly detailed evaluation of the greenhouse gas impacts of the projects or administrative actions.

In Australia, a similar cluster of cases involving the development of coal mines has arisen, in which plaintiffs sought to use the environmental assessment process to force consideration of greenhouse gas emissions. The suits were against administrative review panels that had considered applications to develop coal mines to keep coal-fired power plants in operation, and all of which failed to consider the greenhouse gas emission impact of the proposed mines. Plaintiffs were successful in forcing an administrative consideration of greenhouse gas emissions in two of the three. In New Zealand, as well, a number of cases have arisen involving the failure to consider net greenhouse gas effects in refusing applications for wind farms. Also, in *Greenpeace New Zealand Incorporated v. Northland Regional*

Council and Mighty River Power Limited, the High Court of New Zealand held that an administrative agency was empowered to consider greenhouse gas emissions in considering whether to grant an application for a coal fired power plant.

The idea of using environmental assessment to consider greenhouse gas effects is not new to Canada, but the practice has been spotty. A 2000 report published by the Canadian Environmental Assessment Agency ("CEA Agency") concluded that "[t]he extent to which climate change was factored into each environmental assessment varies considerably", and that "a gap exists between climate change science and its application to the EA community".

As part two of this environmental assessment project, the CEA Agency published a guidance document for project reviewers, entitled Climate Change and Environmental Assessment, Part 2: Climate Change Guidance for Environmental Assessments, but it is a bit unclear how this could assist project reviewers. The report is a competent review of the literature for the time in which it was written — 2000 — but it seems to propose that environmental assessments utilize climate models used to assess global climate conditions. [...] The CEA Agency has also published, with provincial and territorial agencies, a general guidance document for incorporating climate change into all environmental assessments, not just the CEAA.

As a formal matter, then, there is little in the way of procedural or substantive requirements that the environmental assessment process include consideration of the greenhouse gas effects of a project. This does not mean that greenhouse gas considerations are never taken into account under the CEAA. In a Joint Panel Review involving the National Energy Board ("NEB") for construction of a gas pipeline in British Columbia, the Panel undertook a very brief discussion of the greenhouse gas effects of the pipeline — two pages out of 229 for the entire report. Construction of the gas pipeline would emit 11,526 tonnes of CO2-eq, less than 0.02% of British Columbia's total, and a tiny fraction of Canada's emissions. The Panel noted that the emissions were "minor in comparison to overall emissions on Vancouver Island", and that [on] a global scale, any change in climate or the environment caused by GHG emissions from the Project could not be defined, measured or described. The Panel also complained that "at the present time, there are no defined criteria to measure significance in relation to GHG when considered in an environmental assessment. ... Had there been detailed policies or regulations for targets in place, the Panel could have evaluated GHG emissions against these". So how is a panel to meet its mandate under sections 20 and 37 of the CEAA, to determine whether it is "likely that the project will result in significant adverse environmental effects"?

In the absence of any federal or provincial guidance on how to evaluate the environmental effects of greenhouse gas emissions, the Panel laid the project against the backdrop of federal and provincial initiatives to reduce greenhouse gases, and assessed whether the pipeline would prejudice the ability of Canada to meet its Kyoto commitments. It concluded that it would not:

[N]ew natural gas pipeline and energy generation projects have been factored into the outlook. Because such developments have been incorporated in the outlook, the GSX project should not compromise Canada's ability to reach our Kyoto target.

In other words, the Panel concluded that the pipeline was consistent with the then-Liberal federal government plan for how Canada would meet its Kyoto Protocol commitment. The Panel evaluated the significance of the environmental effects not by any empirical determination, but by evaluating whether the greenhouse gases were anticipated by governmental greenhouse gas reduction plans.

Concerning another project, in *Pembina Institute v. Canada (Attorney General)*, the court held that, in conducting a joint panel review under the CEAA, the panel failed to address adequately the environmental effects of the greenhouse gas emissions resulting from the proposed Kearl Oil Sands project, one that would emit an average of 3.7 Mt of CO2 every year over its 5-year life, accounting for about 0.5% of Canada's annual emissions and 1.6% of Alberta's annual emissions. The court held that the panel erred in not "explain[ing] in a general way why the potential environmental effects, either with or without the implementation of mitigation measures, will be insignificant", and failing to provide a "clear and cogent articulation of the reasons behind the Panel's conclusion". The court remitted the matter back to the Panel for the sole purpose of stating the bases for its conclusion that the environmental impacts would be insignificant.

The Panel responded, in an amendment:

> [T]here was very little evidence before the Joint Panel to suggest that this release will result in significant adverse environmental effect. To the contrary, it was the evidence of [Alberta Environment] that it may require Imperial to reach its stated GHG intensity target of 40 kg of CO2e per barrel in any EPEA approval granted for the Project. The Joint Panel finds that it must give [Alberta Environment]'s endorsement of the target significant weight in its consideration of the adverse environmental effects of the Project given [Alberta Environment]'s role as the provincial agency responsible for establishing, monitoring and enforcing emission standards.

Like the Joint Panel Review of the British Columbia gas pipeline, the Kearl Oil Sands Panel looked to regulatory programs in place and decided that the project was in keeping with or accounted for by existing regulatory programs. Lacking any guidance as to whether projected greenhouse gas emissions were "likely to result in a significant adverse environmental effect", the panel essentially deferred to governmental agencies that are apparently working on the problem.

One can be forgiven for struggling with the determination of the significance of a large, project-specific increase in greenhouse gas emissions in a legal void. Making that determination by reference to a regulatory backdrop seems like a reasonable alternative to throwing up one's hands and concluding that the greenhouse gas emissions of any single project will have no significant effect in the global context. The problem is that this approach has no basis in law. Under the CEAA, the critical determination is whether a project is "likely to have a significant adverse environmental effect" ("SAEE"). Such an inquiry must focus on the environmental effects themselves, not on whether the project is in keeping with a provincial or federal agency's grand plan for reducing greenhouse gas emissions. In fact, environmental assessment is in part meant to act as a check on agency discretion, bringing to light environmental information that would otherwise be embarrassing or unfavourable to project development. It would thus be ironic to use governmental policy as the reference point for determining what is a SAEE. Moreover, greenhouse gas reduction plans, including Canada's and Alberta's, do not and could not purport to have any measurable effect on the concentration of global greenhouse gases in the future. These initiatives only attempt, as they could only possibly attempt, to constitute Canada's and Alberta's part in reducing greenhouse gases globally.

Lurking in the background is the much more difficult question of whether the CEAA, as currently constituted, can address climate change at all. If, as we argue, the CEAA does not permit a determination of environmental impact on the basis of a project's consistency with legislation or with some governmental plan or policy, then can the CEAA do anything to address climate change? The obvious problem is one that pervades every effort to address climate change: viewed incrementally on an individual project-by-project basis, even large projects are tiny in the context of global greenhouse emissions. While the Kearl Oil Sands project is unusually large in terms of greenhouse gas emissions (an expected 3.7 Mt of CO2-eq, or 0.5% of Canada's emissions), it would still have been a mere 0.05% of the world's carbon dioxide emissions in 2004.

This is true even if the reviewers diligently consider "any cumulative environmental effects that are likely to result from the project in combination with other projects or activities that have been or will be carried out". Considering the cumulative impact of a large project such as the Kearl Oil Sands project would sensitize the reviewer to the fact that this contribution to greenhouse gases comes on top of a century of an anthropogenic build-up of greenhouse gases, and that each incremental increase makes it that much more likely that some catastrophic outcome will result. But with emissions from China and India growing by leaps and bounds, it is hard to resist the expedient conclusion that no project, not even the gargantuan Kearl Oil Sands project, would make any significant difference in terms of greenhouse gases.

It would be difficult to see, under a common sense reading of section 37 of the CEA Act, how one of many incremental additions — even a large one — of carbon dioxide from the Kearl Oil Sands project would be "likely" to cause SAEE within the meaning of the section. The responsible answer to the more difficult question is, of course, that work must commence immediately on curbing greenhouse gas emissions, even if that work is, by itself, ineffectual in making a difference on climate change. The CEAA, having been in place for over a decade, and having acquired a body of jurisprudence (albeit maddeningly inconsistent), is an obvious mechanism for inserting a level of review that ensures that federal projects take greenhouse gas considerations into account. The CEAA has certainly been invoked in the past to halt projects with extremely compelling economic justifications, such as the Mackenzie Valley Pipeline. There is no reason to think that this same mechanism cannot now be invoked for the cause of climate change.

But the terms of the CEAA need amendment to specifically incorporate climate change concerns. Because the current CEAA standard of SAEE is not useful in the climate change context, another must be developed. Either a legislative change must be made to adapt this phraseology to climate change, or by regulation, the phrase must be defined in terms of what is permitted in the way of greenhouse gas emissions. Guidance documents, because of their legal ineffectuality, are unlikely to be of help.

A legislative solution would appear to be the cleanest approach to adapting the CEAA to climate change concerns. The SAEE concept is ill-fitted to the complicated and global problem of greenhouse gases, and a different standard would take an existing and familiar procedural mechanism — the CEAA — and incorporate a new type of consideration. Companion sections paralleling sections 20 and 37 of the CEAA might provide for a separate decision process evaluating a project specifically for its greenhouse gas emissions. We do not argue for any specific threshold standard for greenhouse gases, but note that a panel might be reasonably called upon to ensure that any project subject to the CEAA be "carbon neutral", or "have undertaken reasonable efforts to mitigate greenhouse gas emissions", or some other standard reasonably susceptible of review by a panel. The most important move would be to require explicitly some greenhouse gas considerations for CEAA projects, and to provide some guidance for panels and agencies reviewing such projects.

The problem with a legislative solution has more to do with politics. In the five years since Canadian ratification of the Kyoto Protocol in 2002, the Canadian federal government has failed miserably to enact greenhouse gas legislation. As discussed above, federal politicians have had far more interest in tossing climate change around as a political football than in any genuine resolve to address the climate change problem.

The simpler solution would be, then, to define by regulation SAEE for a federal project that involves greenhouse gases. By regulatory fiat, Environment Canada could decree that any federal project that is not, say, carbon neutral, has a SAEE, and hence must not be approved or must be "justified under the circumstances" in order to proceed. The usual objection to such an administrative approach — that it can be easily undone — seems less weighty in light of the pressing need to address greenhouse gas emissions sooner rather than later. Moreover, given the inability of the Canadian federal government to enact greenhouse gas legislation, the expediency advantages of this administrative solution seem that much more important. The danger with such a regulatory approach is that it could be challenged and struck down on the grounds that it is *ultra vires*. An argument can be made that the CEAA was never meant to be a substantive policy tool. One can argue that the purpose of the CEAA was merely to ensure that a serious examination of environmental effects is undertaken, not that effective substantive policy results are achieved.

Although the CEAA is a logical place to start in terms of engaging the federal government in greenhouse gases, it is important to recognize the limitations of this approach. It can only address new projects, and does nothing to bring existing sources of greenhouse gas emissions under control. With Canada needing a 25% reduction from current emissions to meet its Kyoto targets, holding firm on the status quo is insufficient. Adapting the CEA Act to include project review of the greenhouse gas implications is an important part, but only a part, of a Canadian response to the climate change problem.

Notes and Questions

1. Do you agree with Professor Hsu and Elliot's approach to "significance" under CEAA?

2. Is a legislative or regulatory amendment essential or is this an issue courts can address through judicial interpretation?

Part VII — Climate Change and Endangered Species

It is impossible to do justice to the links between climate change and biodiversity in this section. Any mitigation strategy, other than the reduction or elimination of human activities responsible for GHG emissions, involves some risk to biodiversity. For example, the use of natural and human processes to increase the recapture of greenhouse gases out of the atmosphere is a use of natural systems that has at least the potential to compete with biodiversity. Another climate change mitigation strategy that has clear implications for biodiversity is the replacement of fossil fuels with biofuels. These issues are not covered here. Instead, we propose in this part to focus our attention on the interactions between a central dimension of biodiversity — endangered species — and climate change.

The focus of much of Chapter 9 was a comparison of the Canadian *Species at Risk Act* (SARA) and its US counterpart the *Endangered Species Act* (ESA). This comparison involved a consideration of four key features of the two laws: (1) the listing process: (2) critical habitat designation and recovery strategies; (3) prohibitions on species takings; and (4) compensation to private parties. This comparative analysis tended to underscore why ESA has and continues to be considered the pit-bull of American environmental law. While differences in species protection outcomes may not be so dramatic, in many key respects, ESA reflects a much more robust, science-based, "hard law" approach to species than its Canadian cousin.

With the emergence of climate change and a growing appreciation of its present and future impact on species, as noted ecologist Jane Lubchenko has put it, "we've entered a new territory" (cited in Ruhl article, *infra* this chapter). In the balance of this section, we embark on an initial consideration of what this means for species and for law and policy makers in both countries. The legal literature addressing this topic is in infancy; to provide a focal point for this discussion, we offer excerpts from two early attempts to grapple with the topic.

In the first piece, Kostyack and Rohlf conclude in large measure ESA provides a legal framework — in terms of listing, habitat protection, takes and so on — that is adequate: in their words, "no radical changes to the law are needed to ensure that the ESA addresses the effects of global warming". In their view, the real challenges lie elsewhere: including significant regulatory and economic policy reforms aiming at capping and reducing GHG emissions; ensuring that the agencies responsible for administering ESA are properly resourced; and the need for these agencies to revisit their approach to species protection to by adopting approaches that emphasize adaptive management and ecosystem integrity. This will necessitate, in their view, a departure from the prevailing "species by species" approach to listing and recovery.

The second article, authored by Professor J.B. Ruhl, comes to many of the same conclusions but, in the final analysis, advocates for even more sweeping changes in the way responsible federal agencies (most notably, the US Fish and Wildlife Service or "FWS") discharge their duties under the ESA.

Notes and Questions

As you read the excerpts, consider the applicability of their analysis and conclusions to the Canadian context: in our country, is the interaction between climate change and species protection more of an environmental *policy* than an environmental *law* challenge?

John Kostyack & Dan Rohlf, "Conserving Endangered Species in an Era of Global Warming" *Environmental Law Reporter* (April, 2008) 38 ELR 10203

Global warming is the single most urgent threat to the future of wildlife and wildlife habitat. The 2007 reports of the Intergovernmental Panel on Climate Change (IPCC) conclude that human activity is "very likely" causing the world to warm. These reports also note that the average surface temperature of the earth increased 0.76 degrees Celsius in the 20th century and predict that this temperature will likely increase by another 1.8 to 4.0 degrees C in the 21st century, depending on pollution levels. The IPCC also finds that 20–30% of species worldwide are likely to be at increased risk of extinction if increases in average global temperatures exceed 2 to 3 degrees C above pre-industrial levels

Unless governments and people around the world take action quickly to curtail global warming pollution, we will face rapid warming and other climatic and physical changes, including disappearing polar ice caps, large rises in sea levels, and extreme floods and droughts. If this scenario unfolds, society would increasingly turn its focus to providing for the countless climate refugees fleeing sea-level rise and drought, developing new supplies of food and drinking water, and otherwise rebuilding the infrastructure of civilization. The ESA, and most other traditional wildlife conservation programs would likely face drastic curtailments in the face of these competing priorities.

Even as work proceeds to reduce global warming pollution, we must recognize that reducing GHGs alone will not be enough to prevent widespread extinctions of species with which we share the planet. Even with significant reductions in global warming pollution from human sources, at least another 0.6 degree C increase will inevitably occur (over and above the increase of 0.76 degree C in the 20th century) in the coming decades due to GHGs already released into the atmosphere. Therefore, even if we immediately act to curb warming pollution, wildlife will still face threats from altered climates and major ecosystem disruptions. [...]

At the domestic level, the ESA can play a significant role in conserving U.S. wildlife threatened by global warming. When Congress enacted the ESA in 1973 and amended the statute in the 1970s and 1980s, lawmakers did not see global warming as a significant threat to wildlife. However, policymakers designed the ESA to address all threats to wildlife, no matter what their origin. Thus, no radical changes to the law are needed to ensure that the ESA addresses the effects of global warming. On the other hand, climate change greatly increases extinction risks of species already imperiled for other reasons and thereby greatly reduces the margin for error in implementing the ESA's protections and recovery programs. Policymakers therefore will need to consider significantly strengthening ESA programs — as well as increasing ESA funding — to help fulfill the nation's commitment to conserve abundant wildlife and healthy ecosystems for future generations.

Global warming is exactly that: global. No ecosystem on earth is immune to its effects. Herein, we review the impacts of global warming by major habitat types. But it is important to note that across all habitat types, two serious problems have surfaced at the species level: (1) changes in phenology (timing of seasonal events); and (2) changes in distribution of wildlife (most notably, the disappearance of northern hemisphere wildlife species from the southern portions of their ranges and from lower elevations). An example of the former phenomenon is the shift in the time of springtime peak insect abundance, which affects the reproductive success of songbirds that depend on high insect levels during the critical nestling phase. The 90% decline of the northwestern Minnesota moose population in the past 20 years, which biologists have attributed to excessive heat, provides an example of the latter. Another example is the decline of the American pika, a small rabbit-like mammal that inhabits talus fields in the mountains of the western United States. One study of Great Basin pikas finds that their range has shifted upslope by 900 feet and 36% of populations have been extirpated.

Just as climate change poses encompassing threats to the planet's ecosystems, it raises fundamental challenges to our government's ability to stem and ameliorate these threats. Though the U.S. Supreme Court labeled the ESA "the most comprehensive legislation for the preservation of endangered species ever enacted by any nation", the federal agencies charged with implementing the statute are only now beginning to consider how it can remain an effective conservation tool in light of global warming's tremendous threats to biodiversity. It is obvious that climate change will demand more of everything — more species listed as threatened or endangered, more resources devoted to assessing and reducing biological risks and to restoration efforts, and more agency personnel for implementation. In this section, we go beyond the obvious need to devote greater resources to saving threatened and endangered species in a warming world to explore the difficulties and questions that the central environmental threat of the 21st century will raise for a law enacted 35 years ago at the dawn of the modern environmental era.

[*Ed note*: Portions of the article where the authors address the implications of climate change for the application of ESA's listing, critical habitat, recovery and take provisions have been deleted.]

Conserving Wildlife in a Changing Climate: Policy Recommendations

We have already begun to see the initial effects of climate change, and we must now act quickly to put in place new legal mechanisms to deal with its pervasive threats to biodiversity. At a broad level, it is crucial that Congress include within any climate change legislation specific provisions — and specific funding — to conserve biodiversity in a warming world. At the same time, policymakers must reaffirm the ESA's role as a primary legal tool for protecting the nation's at-risk species and their habitats. As noted above, the statute's comprehensive provisions and inherent flexibility enable it to deal with climate-based threats without major modifications to the law itself. However, within the framework of the existing statute, we recommend new policies and implementation schemes to ensure that agencies meaningfully confront threats to biodiversity posed by climate change.

Addressing Endangered Species in Federal Climate Change Legislation

While lawmakers do not appear poised to make fundamental changes to the ESA itself anytime in the near future, it seems likely that Congress will soon enact legislation with consequences for endangered species that are much more far-reaching than any ESA overhaul. As of this writing, lawmakers in the 110th Congress have introduced nearly a dozen bills that would place caps on emissions of global warming pollution, allow trading of emissions credits, i.e., permits, and generate substantial public funds (tens of billions of dollars) through an auction of emissions credits. Most of these bills contemplate that a portion of the auction proceeds would be devoted to programs to conserve wildlife threatened by global warming. The U.S. Senate Committee on Environment and Public Works has passed a bill with strong emissions caps and substantial funding for conservation of wildlife and other natural resources threatened by global warming, and the leaders of both the U.S. House of Representatives and Senate have indicated a strong desire to enact this or a measure of similar breadth and strength into law.

This is encouraging news for wildlife. As noted above, Congress can take no more important step to help wildlife and ecosystems than to legislate substantial, economywide reductions in global warming pollution. It is also crucial that auctions of emissions credits be used to generate billions of dollars of dedicated funding annually to enable federal and state natural resource agencies to confront inevitable global warming. Although some may consider dedicating a substantial sum of such new annual funding for wildlife (say, $5 billion) a steep price to pay for biodiversity protection given the other urgent priorities for addressing global warming, it is in fact a necessary investment to maintain and restore the natural systems that serve as the foundation of our economy and quality of life.

Making Adaptive Management a Central Focus of the ESA

Although each year scientists are able to identify and project the ecosystem changes attributable to global warming with increasing degrees of precision, the exact consequences of global warming will always defy prediction. The average surface temperatures around the globe already exceed levels ever experienced since modern wildlife management began roughly a century ago, and they will soon exceed levels experienced since the beginning of human civilization approximately 13,000 years ago. This means that careful observation and the flexibility to change course in response to new information will be especially important components of ESA implementation in the coming years.

The concept of adaptive management is not new. In recent years, natural resource agencies have often touted the use of adaptive management in implementing the ESA and other wildlife programs. Unfortunately, however, agencies' use of this term has often proven to be more in the way of lip service than actual implementation. In order to practice adaptive management, the Services should enact regulations that insist upon a high degree of rigor in carrying out adaptive management programs. Key elements of any adaptive management program promulgated by the Services would be:

- Systematic observations of the impacts of global warming on wildlife and wildlife habitats;
- Projections and conservation planning based on these observations and on models of future climate conditions;
- Conservation actions pursuant to such projections and plans;
- Monitoring and evaluation; and

- Adjustments to projections, plans, and conservation actions based on monitoring and evaluation.

Ecosystem-Based Approaches

Given the overwhelming numbers of individual species likely to be put at risk due to climate change, it will be vital for the Services to develop methods of identifying species at risk and planning for the conservation of listed species that are more efficient than the current species-by-species approach to listing and recovery planning. Though largely ignored for the past few years, the FWS in 1994 adopted a policy statement calling for an ecosystem approach to implementing the ESA; the policy specifically mentions making listing decisions and developing recovery plans on an eco system basis when possible. The Services should update this policy statement to address how ecosystems will be defined and managed in light of changes in species distribution, disassembly of ecological communities, and other disruptions caused by global warming. Regardless of how these difficult definitional issues are resolved, it will remain essential to pursue ecosystem-based listing and recovery planning strategies. In places where climate change affects a large number of species — in Arctic and coral reef ecosystems, for example — such strategies would advance conservation with much less cost and much greater speed than carrying out listing and recovery planning actions on an individual species basis.

In places where climate change affects a large number of species — in Arctic and coral reef ecosystems, for example — such strategies would advance conservation with much less cost and much greater speed than carrying out listing and recovery planning actions on an individual species basis.

Applying the ESA to the Causes of Global Warming Pollution

As noted in the previous section, the ESA will increasingly intersect with a broad array of activities whose only connection to risks to listed species is emissions of GHGs. The trigger for application of section 7's substantive and procedural obligations is a federal action that may affect listed species. Rather than denying the impact of global warming pollution on listed species, the Services should construe any action that results in non-trivial net increases of GHGs as meeting this threshold. Similarly, the Services should interpret section 9's prohibition against take of protected species as covering the actions of non-federal GHG emitters.

Conclusion

Congress took a bold and decisive step in 1973 when it enacted the ESA in response to its recognition of the significant cant threats to biodiversity. Today, similarly bold and decisive action is imperative to reduce global warming pollution and to ensure that the impacts of inevitable global warming do not wipe out the conservation gains of the past 35 years. Although the United States must commit to significant additional research on global warming impacts and potential management responses, we already have substantial scientific information on steps needed to protect species and their habitat in a warming world. First and most urgently, Congress must put in place a national cap on global warming pollution, with aggressive annual reductions in pollution levels, and the United States must work at the international level to achieve similar commitments from other nations. Second, policymakers and natural resource managers must design and apply adaptive management strategies so that both projected and unanticipated changes on the landscape can be addressed. Ultimately, we must integrate biodiversity protection and necessary funding into a comprehensive federal regulatory response to climate change.

While the ESA in its present form will provide an effective tool for conserving species and habitats in the face of global warming, legislative and administrative changes will be needed to strengthen its ability to deal with the dangers and uncertainties of climate change. The most important variable in determining the success of species protection efforts, however, is both simple and enormously challenging: our continued resolve to ensure the secure future of all life on earth.

J. B. Ruhl, "Climate Change and the *Endangered Species Act*: Building Bridges to the No-Analog Future"

(2008) 88 Boston Univ. L.R. 1

The task ahead of the Fish and Wildlife Service (FWS) is daunting, and it must use the discretion outlined [above] to develop a plan soon, lest climate change sweep away its mission along with its charges. ... manifestations of climate change already are well underway and already have had adverse impacts on some species. More can be expected. Indeed, the FWS must assume that more climate change impacts will unfold even if the global community takes measures to mitigate greenhouse gas emissions .... this assumption poses complex policy questions for the FWS, though ... the agency has considerable flexibility in how it answers them. It has the discretion, within bounds, to adopt passive or aggressive policies for how to integrate climate change in ESA programs.

With that foundation established, what should define the agency's set of operating assumptions about how the global community responds generally to climate change — pessimism or optimism? A worst case scenario would have the global community utterly fail to contain greenhouse gas emissions and, as a result, climate change spiraling into chaos for centuries. In that scenario, the FWS might as well pack up its bags and close shop, as climate change will become an unassailable force in ecological reshuffling, overwhelming any management of ecosystems or species. Exercising the ESA, in other words, is pointless in this scenario.

On the other hand, the agency also cannot afford to assume a Pollyanna future in which the global community comes together tomorrow, drastically reduces emissions, somehow sucks carbon dioxide out of the troposphere, and reaches 1990 overall levels by the end of this decade. The message of *Massachusetts v. EPA* [*Ed note*: See *infra* this chapter] is that a regulatory agency can't assume someone else will address the climate change problem. Each agency must "whittle away" with whatever knife Congress has provided it.

The ESA will be best served if the FWS adopts a cautious optimism that recognizes the limits of the ESA but keeps the statute relevant. Conceding that some human-induced climate change is inevitable even in the best of circumstances does not concede that it will be perpetual and chaotic. Rather, the FWS can reasonably assume that the global community will eventually arrest greenhouse gas emissions to a benchmark level and that, as a consequence, climate regimes will eventually settle into a new "natural" pattern of variation. We have no analog for what that pattern will be, and the transition from the present to that future will be, by all appearances, a rocky ride, but in all probability we will get there. The job of the ESA is to help as many species as is reasonably possible get there with us — to serve as their bridge across the climate change transition into the no-analog future.

Ironically, to do this will take some humility and restraint. Going for the jugular by regulating greenhouse gas emissions is not where the ESA can be of most help to imperiled species. There is little to be gained for the FWS or for climate-threatened species by having the agency go down this road. The agency has no explicit authority to do so, does not have the expertise to do so, and would risk undermining the political viability of the ESA by doing so. Rather, the FWS can provide expert assistance to the agencies more appropriately charged with regulating greenhouse gas emissions, such as the EPA, by advising them about the effects of climate change on species.

As for its direct role in addressing climate change, the FWS can employ the ESA most effectively by identifying species threatened by climate change, identifying which of those can be helped through the ESA's habitat-based programs, and devising a management plan — one that uses regulatory action as well as recovery planning — to build each such species its bridge. Indeed, this strategy allows the FWS to dispense with the distinction between human — induced and natural climate variation. Climate change is climate change — it does not matter to the species what is causing it. What does matter to them is whether and in what shape they survive it.

This brings us to the six policy choice pressure points raised in Part II. To implement the proposed bridge policy, I suggest the FWS approach the policy choices as follows:

Identifying Climate-Threatened Species

The agency's objective should be to use the ESA to define and monitor the ecological reshuffling effects of climate change. The agency should aggressively identify species threatened by climate change. Early identification of species threatened by climate change and of the critical habitat they require for survival through climate change transition will help in defining the extent of ecological reshuffling and guide human adaptation programs. Early identification also will provide the basis for listing species as threatened, which provides more flexibility in terms of regulatory effects and recovery efforts.

Regulating Greenhouse Gas Emissions

The agency's objective should be to not squander agency resources in a futile effort for which the ESA is simply not equipped. The FWS should not attempt to use its Section 7 and Section 9 regulatory programs in an effort to regulate greenhouse gas emissions. As for the take prohibition, listing species as threatened early will allow the agency to remove greenhouse gas emissions from consideration under Section 9 while keeping the take prohibition active with respect to other contributing threats. If an animal species is in endangered status, meaning Section 9 necessarily applies in full force, difficulties in establishing the burden of proof would support the exercise of prosecutorial discretion not to attempt to regulate greenhouse gas emissions. Under the Section 7 consultation program, project-specific jeopardy analyses should promote other federal agencies to consider ways of reducing greenhouse gas emissions, but should not lead to jeopardy findings.

Regulating Non-Climate Effects To Protect Climate-Threatened Species

The agency's objective should be to support the bridge function of the ESA and to reduce the adverse impacts on species from human adaptation to climate change. Where a species weakened by climate change is also threatened by other anthropogenic sources, such as loss of habitat, and where the agency reasonably believes addressing the non-climate threats will help carry the species through the climate change transition, the agency should use [its] regulatory powers to the extent necessary. In particular, where human adaptation to climate change exacerbates threats to a species, the agency should aggressively employ its regulatory presence through Section 7 consultations and enforcement of the Section 9 take prohibition. The agency also must monitor the impacts of human adaptation on species that face no direct or secondary ecological threat from climate change and employ Section 7 and Section 9 powers accordingly. Clearly, however, innovative approaches will be needed, such as market-based incentives and regional planning efforts, to facilitate human adaptation measures as much as species can tolerate.

Designing Conservation and Recovery Initiatives

The agency's objective should be to get as many species with a long-term chance at survival and recovery through the transition to the other side of climate change as is realistically possible. The agency must initially differentiate between species that are unlikely to survive climate change under any circumstances and those that are likely to benefit from assistance in their home ecosystems. Agency resources should not be wasted in developing recovery plans or other conservation measures for non-recoverable species. For species that appear likely to withstand climate change under the ESA's protection, recovery plans should identify the expected intensity of assistance required to manage or respond to primary and secondary ecological effects. Conservation measures for species that require intensive assistance ... should be designed around adaptive management techniques that involve ample monitoring and considerable room for adjustment of management actions in order to account for the possibility that continuing climate change will alter the effectiveness of those actions.

Species Trade-Offs

The agency's objective should be to not contribute to ecological reshuffling through its species management efforts. Where the measures described above are complicated by species trade-offs — when helping one may harm another — the agency should adopt an ecosystem-based management approach modeled on promoting long-term species diversity and ecosystem multi-functionality. When ecological models do not point to a particular management action to serve those goals, general default priorities, such as assisting top-level predators and resisting induced invasions, may help mediate between species in conflict.

Dealing with the Doomed

The agency's objective should be to avoid accelerating the decline of species who stand no chance of surviving climate change, but not to take measures on their behalf which could pose threats to other species. Under this standard, assisted migration should be employed for such a species only if the FWS has assembled conclusive evidence of the extinction threat, a quantitative model showing the likely success of assisted migration for the species with de minimis anticipated effects on other species, and an assisted migration management plan including long term monitoring and active adaptive management. Human adaptation measures that could accelerate the extinction of the species, which could cascade to affect other species, should be regulated under Section 7 and Section 9 as for any other listed species.

Conclusion

The "pit-bull" has met its match, but sometimes old dogs can learn new tricks. It is sobering to find that ecological reshuffling is inevitable and to realize that the ESA can't do anything about it. Yet this is precisely what leads me to my proposal that the statute be employed in a more focused manner in the decades leading to our no-analog future. What the statute has done best is stop the decline of imperilled species brought under its protective wings, and it has done so in the face of problems as intractable as urbanization and invasive species. The ESA has not solved urban sprawl or invasive species — it has helped species deal with them. Likewise, we must find a way for the ESA to help species deal with the effects of climate change, not its causes. The statute provides this flexibility — the means to proactively identify the threat of climate change and focus on helping those species that can be helped.

My proposal is unlikely to satisfy strong supporters of the ESA or its strong critics. The former are likely to believe the "pit bull" has found its ultimate calling in climate change. If there is any statute that can wrestle greenhouse gas emissions to the ground (i.e., to 1990 levels), they might think it is the ESA and its unrelenting biocentric mission, whereas my proposal keeps the statute at bay. The latter will object to my proposal's aggressive call for species listings, which is based on wholesale adoption of the premise of human-induced climate change, and to its continued use of the statute as a regulatory weapon against habitat loss and other non-climate threats to climate-threatened species.

Both views doom the ESA. Of course, that may be the intent and hope of the statute's critics, with or without climate change. But adopting the strong version of the ESA in the climate change era, in which the FWS charges hard after greenhouse gas emissions, would play right into the critics' hands — the statute is neither designed to regulate something so ubiquitous as greenhouse gas emissions nor so sacrosanct as to survive the political battle attempting to do so would ignite. Support for the ESA, therefore, must be tempered by practical and political reality if the ESA itself is to survive climate change. The trade-off I propose — standing back from greenhouse gas emissions but staying fully engaged in regulating non-climate threats, particularly those stemming from human adaptation to climate change — is the plan the ESA needs in order to build the bridge for species into the no-analog future.

Notes and Questions

1. One indication that the FWS is beginning to appreciate the need to approach its role in a new way given climate change is its landmark 2008 decision to list as endangered the polar bear: see Federal Register Vol. 73, No. 95. Professor Ruhl takes this decision as a positive sign, though he notes that it also reflects growing external pressure on the agency around climate change issues. As he puts it:

> ... although clearly not enthusiastic about the prospect, the FWS appears ready to carry the ESA into the climate change era, having recently proposed to extend ESA protection to the polar bear because of the diminishing ice habitat that the species depends upon for survival. The agency is getting strong nudges from the outside as well, as members of Congress have urged the agency to evaluate the effects of climate change on species generally, environmental advocacy groups have petitioned the agency to promulgate rules to address climate change, and one court has admonished the agency for failing to take climate change into account in its regulatory programs.

2. Do the key differences between ESA and SARA described above, and in Chapter 9, dictate a Canadian approach to responding to the impacts of climate change on endangered species that is different from what is argued for in the articles above? In other words, can the federal government mount an effective response to this challenge without amending SARA? What suggestions, offered in the excerpts above, have the most relevance and importance in the Canadian context?

Part VIII — Climate Change and Indigenous Peoples

Indigenous peoples of the far North have, in many ways, suffered the greatest climate changes impacts to date. Legal strategies aimed at redressing these impacts remain in their infancy. The excerpt that follow chronicles domestic and international avenues that US-based legal organizations have pursued to seek redress: by way of a tort action seeking relief from the oil, coal, and electric companies that the plaintiffs claim are responsible for the climate change-related damages that Indigenous communities have suffered, and through international human rights channels by means of a submission to the Inter-American Commission on Human Rights.

Ursula Kazarian, "The Forgotten North: Peoples and Lands in Peril"
(2008) 8 Sustainable Dev. L. & Pol'y 46

Introduction

Arctic indigenous peoples are extremely susceptible to the immediate impacts of climate change. While many indigenous groups face serious battles over rights to land and resources, the Arctic groups face the impending, compounding factor of some of the most drastic impacts from climate change. Their dependence on the integrity of local ecosystems for their survival as autonomous groups makes them even more vulnerable to the melting of ice and permafrost and to the decline of local animal and fish species.

The preservation of indigenous culture and traditional knowledge in the Arctic is both directly and indirectly threatened by the rapid and dramatic environmental changes occurring in the region. According to the Intergovernmental Panel on Climate Change ("IPCC"), warmer temperatures and unpredictable weather patterns have already caused increased incidences of non-fatal heart attacks and respiratory diseases. In addition, the residual effect of climate change — such as a reduction in traditional sources of food — has led to a shift to western diets and, consequently, to an increase in diet-related diseases including diabetes and obesity. Therefore, beyond encouraging environmental protection in the Arctic solely for its own intrinsic value, it is important to recognize the distinct challenges that climate change and the warming Arctic have created, and will continue to create, for the indigenous peoples whose survival as such is so intricately tied to the environmental integrity and health of the region.

Defining Indigenous Environmental Rights in the Arctic in the Climate Change Context

Every Arctic country has a different legal and custodial relationship with its respective indigenous peoples. However, it is clear that defending indigenous rights in light of climate change will be directly linked either to past national precedent or else by international cooperation. Given the frequent and obvious conflict between protecting indigenous rights and the national right to development, it is no wonder that the greatest hope to preserve indigenous rights lies generally through international mechanisms.

Thus, a brief overview of each Arctic country's relevant legal systems and the historical development of opportunities for indigenous peoples on a national level is helpful. [...]

[*Ed note*: Portions of the article dealing with applicable domestic laws of Norway, Sweden, Finland, Greenland and Russia have been omitted.]

Canada

Canada is home to many indigenous groups, with the Inuit covering the most territory. A significant achievement for the Inuit was the creation in 1999 of the territory of Nunavut, which means "Our Land" in the Inuit language, Inuktitut. As land is considered a fundamental right to the preservation of culture and identity, it is important to note that aboriginal title in Canada can be extinguished in two ways: by constitutional amendment, and by agreement of the aboriginal people concerned. Although the creation of Nunavut appears to be a victory in self-government, the Inuit have in fact ceded their aboriginal rights and title in exchange for a grant of rights from the Canadian government — something that could, in theory, open the door to a future constitutional amendment that would revoke the viability of Nunavut's semi-autonomy. This is significant in that the Inuit must take great care as to how they proceed within Nunavut's internal structure as well as with regard to Nunavut's political relations with the Canadian federal government.

Finally, while the Inuit comprise the largest ethnic majority in the Canadian north, they are actually the smallest group of aboriginal people in Canada. Other northern indigenous peoples include the Tlingit, Innu, Cree, Gwich'in, and Metis, who inhabit and claim aboriginal titles to Northern Territories. There have been the usual conflicts over land rights, and the overlap between indigenous rights and environmental protection will surely be an increasingly pursued topic in Canadian courts.

United States

The United States has historically dealt with its Alaskan natives in a very different manner from the native tribes living in the continental United States. When the United States acquired the territory of Alaska from Russia in 1867, Alaskan natives had a functioning relationship with the Russian Empire. There were very few ethnic Russians living in Alaska at that time, and the few settlements they did inhabit were generally impermanent. When the United States took possession of the vast territory, Alaskan natives were clearly able to see the strife that had plagued the natives of the continental United States since its inception and sought to avoid similar problems concerning title and rights to land and resources. [...]

Fearing legal entanglement that would lead to termination and thus non-recognition of their special status, native groups joined together to push forward the *Alaska Native Claims Settlement Act* ("ANCSA") in 1971, through which Alaskan natives traded aboriginal claims to vast tracts of land for recognized title to smaller tracts of land and a total monetary compensation of $962.5 million. However, the passage of ANCSA caused ambiguity in the status of native hunting and fishing rights and was followed in 1980 by the 1980 *Alaska National Interest Lands Conservation Act* ("ANILCA"). ANILCA

[...] Although ANILCA helped to clarify some of the concerns left by ANCSA, the fight to clarify native subsistence rights continues. For instance, in *Amoco Production v. Village of Gambell* the U.S. Supreme Court held that the outer continental shelf was outside the boundary of Alaska as defined by ANILCA and therefore was not subject to the subsistence provisions of ANILCA. By this decision, the Court favored the interests of oil production over the competing indigenous hunting and fishing rights. This is a perhaps ominous indication of the difficulties the Alaskan natives will encounter in bringing climate change-related claims to U.S. federal court.

[...] Thus, no established precedent has yet been set in any of these countries to directly link climate change, environmental protection, and indigenous rights to self-determination in the Arctic. However, the tide may be turning, as creative new uses of established legal tools are being developed to address the direct causal link between climate change and rights to cultural preservation.

The Use of the Public Nuisance Doctrine to hold Multinational Corporations Accountable

[...] the Inupiat Eskimo tribe of Kivalina in northern Alaska recently filed a complaint under public and private nuisance law and conspiracy in District Court for the Northern District of California against several oil and gas companies: see *Complaint, Kivalina v. ExxonMobil Corp.* (N.D. Cal. Feb. 26, 2008), available at http://www.adn.com/static/adn/pdfs/Kivalina%20Complaint% 20-%20Final.pdf.

The village is suing the companies for their role in causing and denying global warming and thereby causing the massive ice melt that threatens their traditional existence and is forcing them to relocate their village. A positive result for Kivalina could signal the emergence of a devastating trend for oil and gas companies in the United States.

[...]

In 1997, the Ninth Circuit Court of Appeals denied damages to Alaska natives from the Exxon Valdez oil spill, finding that although the natives were more severely affected by the oil spill than non-natives, the actual injury to their cultural, spiritual, and psychological benefits was no different than that of non-native Alaskans.

Whether such reasoning is applied to Kivalina's complaint may signal the legal trend for climate change-related damages. However, the policy question of enforcing corporate responsibility may support Kivalina's position. For instance, the payment for the relocation of a tribe, as the Kivalina village requests, may not be enough to promote a change in the policies of oil companies that would actually halt the environmental degradation from business activities; it would simply compensate the tribe for the displacement. Punitive damage awards may offer one possible method to help promote the change of corporate business ethics that impact global warming and climate change; however, how courts will respond to complaints such as that of Kivalina remains to be seen.

Other Tools for National Remedies via International Courts

Aside from seeking a decision on the national level, [...] indigenous groups also have the option of utilizing more broadly based international mechanisms. The binding level of the decisions of international bodies, however, depends on whether a given country has agreed to supranational jurisdiction.

[One] example is the Inter-American Court of Human Rights ("IACHR"). Unlike the European human rights system, an individual cannot bring a claim directly into the system; he or she must first file the claim with the Commission, and upon its approval it may be forwarded to the Court. A substantial portion of the cases heard so far has been from indigenous groups, and the jurisprudence has leaned in favor of enforcing indigenous rights throughout the Americas. However, the decisions are only binding in countries that have ratified the Convention and submitted to the contentious jurisdiction of the Court either on a blanket or individual case basis. The two Arctic countries in the Americas, Canada and the United States, have ratified the Convention, but they have not submitted to the Court's jurisdiction. In 2005 the Inuit Circumpolar Conference submitted a petition to the Commission that called for an investigation into the United States' contributions to global warming and for action to be taken. It is an encouraging step forward in increasing awareness, but it is questionable whether it will encourage any change in U.S. activity. If the Court is to have any "teeth" in addressing Arctic indigenous claims regarding climate change, the jurisdiction of the Court over both of the Arctic countries presents a critical necessity.

In sum, securing jurisdiction over the countries of the Arctic, including Russia, the United States and Canada, remains a major hurdle for the two regional institutions. Until national level legislation opens itself to international influence, enforcement of any of the decisions of international courts is less likely. The same holds true for the International Court of Justice ("ICJ"): while it will not be able to hear a case unless a country submits to its jurisdiction, the Court can still give an Advisory Opinion which can serve the same purpose as the non-binding opinions of the regional human rights courts. It is thus up to the appropriate UN agencies to bring cases to the ICJ for such opinions.

The recently released IPCC report lists policies, instruments, and co-operative arrangements to mitigate the impacts of climate change worldwide. These recommendations are generally aimed at economic incentives and strategies at the nation-state level. While this is probably the most effective direction to take at the international legal level, the best national-level mitigation strategy for the peoples whose lives are effectively outside of the nation-state system, remains a question. The patchwork of different fora for discussion of these issues offers promise that at least the Arctic's ecosystems and its peoples will not be ignored; however, the need for a streamlined approach for the region — cutting across Russia, Scandinavia, Canada, and the United States — is arguably apparent. Petitions to the IACHR for one set of tribes and to the ECHR for another set, with little to no recourse for groups in Russia, results in a dispersed and weakened minority group that threatens to be forgotten in the maelstrom of increasing state economic activity in the region.

Conclusion

International law is developing more quickly than domestic law in addressing the needs of indigenous peoples, particularly with respect to climate change. International legal institutions recognize the overlap between environment and human rights as a critical factor to protecting cultural and traditional integrity, as indigenous peoples are viewed as particularly vulnerable to ecological degradation. The most dramatic effects of climate change are being seen in low-lying coastal areas in the tropics as well as in the polar regions, and especially in the Arctic. Not only are the ice melting and the ecosystem changing; countries are clamoring to stake their claims to exploration for oil and gas on the now navigable continental shelf. Such new industrial activity would bring even more change to the places Arctic indigenous peoples call home.

Though the dialogue on the international level may be more willing to acknowledge the moral responsibility to protect indigenous culture and tradition, the real implementation and enforcement of such principles must necessarily come from binding, national-level initiatives and legislation. International pressure to strengthen existing national laws or to create new ones that properly reflect the relationship between indigenous cultures and global warming induced environmental changes will certainly play an important role in the coming years; however, until national governments take the definitive step to expressly recognize and protect these rights, the future of these northernmost indigenous communities remains uncertain.

Notes and Questions

1. For a more detailed assessment of the Inuit petition and its implications, see Paul Crowley, "Inuit Defend their Human Rights against Climate Change" in S. Berger & D. Saxe, *Environmental Law: The Year in Review, 2007* (Aurora: Canada Law Book, 2008) at 39. What are the main advantages and disadvantages of pursuing relief through international human rights channels, as opposed to other avenues?

2. What role do you see for human rights in addressing climate change? When would human induced climate change constitute a violation of the right to life as recognized in the IAHR regime? What about other rights, such as the right to food, cultural rights, or the right to a healthy environment as recognized in the 1999 San Salvador Protocol? What impact would the proposed American Declaration on the Rights of Indigenous Peoples have on a human rights claim by the Inuit? For further elaboration on these issues, see Meinhard Doelle, From Hot Air to Action? Climate Change, Compliance and the Future of International Environmental Law (Toronto: Carswell, 2005) at 215–254.

3. In Canada, the *Charter of Rights and Freedoms* is generally regarded as reflective of our international commitment to human rights. Would the Inuit have a claim under the *Charter*? What factual conditions would have to exist for the Inuit to be able to establish a claim under section 7 of the *Charter*?

4. What sources of international law would you consider using in constructing an argument that Canada's approach to climate change to date constitutes a violation of section 7 of the *Charter* with respect to Canada's Inuit population?

5. The number of climate change related court cases, particularly in the US, is clearly on the rise. Some have compared the emerging legal battles over climate change to the tobacco law suits in the 1990's. Check media coverage over the past twelve months to see what climate change cases in the US have made the news. See, for example Stephan Faris, "Conspiracy Theory" The Atlantic.Com (June 2008), http://www.theatlantic.com/doc/200806/conspiracy.

References

We thank the copyright holders for their permission to reproduce their materials.

Randall S. Abate, "Climate Change, the United States, and the Impacts of Arctic Melting: A Case Study in the Need for Enforceable International Environmental Human Rights" (2007) 26 Stan. Envtl. L.J. 3

Ngo Anh-Thu et al., "Bio-fuels in Canada: *Normative Framework, Existing Regulations*, and Politics of Intervention" (2008) 4 JSDLP 19

Tracy Bach & Justin Brown, "Recent Developments in Australian Climate Change Litigation: Forward Momentum from Down Under" (2008) 8:2 Sustainable Development Law & Policy 39

Camelia Bauch & Michael Mehling, "Tracking down the Future Climate Regime" (2007) 1 CCLR 4

Steven Bernstein, Jutta Brunnée, David G. Duff & Andrew J. Green, eds., *A Globally Integrated Climate Policy for Canada* (Toronto: University of Toronto Press, 2007). © University of Toronto Press Incorporated 2008. Reprinted with permission of the publisher.

Neil J. Cabral, "The Role of Renewable Portfolio Standards in the Context of a National Cap-and-Trade Program" (2007) 8:1 Sustainable Development Law & Policy 13

Nathalie Chalifour, "Making Federalism Work for Climate Change: Canada's Division of Powers over Carbon Taxes" (2009) 22 N.J.C.L. 119

Paul Crowley, "Inuit Defend their Human Rights against Climate Change" in S. Berger & D. Saxe, *Environmental Law: The Year in Review, 2007* (Aurora: Canada Law Book, 2008) at 39

Ahmed Djoghlaf, "Climate Change and Biodiversity in Polar Regions" (2008) 8:3 Sustainable Development Law & Policy 14

Meinhard Doelle, "Linking the Kyoto Protocol and other Multilateral Environmental Agreements; From Fragmentation to Integration?" (2004) 14 J.E.L.P. 75

Meinhard Doelle, *From Hot Air to Action? Climate Change, Compliance and the Future of International Environmental Law* (Toronto: Carswell, 2005)

Meinhard Doelle & Dennis Mahony, "A Shift in the Legal Climate: The Emergence of Climate Change as a Dominant Legal Issue across Canada", in S. Berger & D. Saxe, *Environmental Law: The Year in Review* (Aurora: Canada Law Book, 2008) at 1

Meinhard Doelle, "Global Carbon Trading and Climate-Change Mitigation in Canada: Options for the Use of The Kyoto Mechanisms", in Steven Bernstein, Jutta Brunnée, David G. Duff & Andrew J. Green, eds., *A Globally Integrated Climate Policy for Canada.* © University of Toronto Press Incorporated 2008. Reprinted with permission of the publisher.

Stewart Elgie, "Kyoto, the Constitution and Carbon Trading: Waking a BNA Bear (or Two)" (2007) 13 Review of Constitutional Studies 67-129

Christine Elwell & Grant Boyle, "*Friends of the Earth v. the Minister of Environment*: Does CEPA 166 Require Canada to Meet its Kyoto Commitments?" (2008) 18 J.E.L.P. 254–277

Daniel Farber, "Basic Compensation for Victims of Climate Change" (2007) 155 U. Pa. L. Rev. 1605

Andrew Green, "You Can't Pay Them Enough: Subsidies, Environmental Law, And Social Norms" 30 Harv. Envtl. L. Rev. 407

Shi-Ling Hsu, "A Realistic Evaluation of Climate Change Litigation Through the Lens of a Hypothetical Lawsuit" (2008) 79 U. Colo. L. Rev. 701–766

Shi-Ling Hsu & Robin Elliot, "Regulating Greenhouse Gases in Canada: Constitutional and Policy Dimensions" (forthcoming)

John Kostyack & Dan Rohlf, "Conserving Endangered Species in an Era of Global Warming" (2008) 38 Environmental Law Reporter 10203

Rosemary Lyster, "Separating the Wheat from the Chaff: Regulating Greenhouse Gases in a Climate of Uncertainty" (2007) 2 CCLR 89

Laurie A. Ristino, "It's not easy being Green: Reflections on the American Carbon Offset Market" (2008) 8 Sustainable Development Law & Policy 34

M. Rodi, ed., Emissions Trading in Europe: Initial Experiences and Lessons for the Future (Berlin: 2008, Lexxion)

J. B. Ruhl, "Climate Change and the *Endangered Species Act*: Building Bridges to the No-Analog Future" (2008) 88 Boston Univ. L.R. 1

Imke Sagemuller, "Forest Sinks and the United Nations Framework Convention on Climate Change and the Kyoto Protocol: Opportunity or Risk for Biodiversity?" (2006) 31 Colum. J. Envtl. L. 189